MORE FIRST AID FOR THE AILING HOUSE

MONEY-SAVING WAYS TO IMPROVE YOUR HOUSE AND PROPERTY

McGRAW-HILL BOOK COMPANY

New York   St. Louis   San Francisco

Auckland   Bogotá   Düsseldorf   Johannesburg   London   Madrid
Mexico   Montreal   New Delhi   Panama   Paris   São Paulo
Singapore   Sydney   Tokyo   Toronto

MORE
FIRST AID
FOR THE
AILING
HOUSE

Roger C. Whitman

Edited by
Robert Scharff

Library of Congress Cataloging in Publication Data

Whitman, Roger C
    More first aid for the ailing house.
    Includes index.
    1. Dwellings—Maintenance and repair—Amateurs'
manuals.   I. Title.
TH4817.3.W47   643'.7   76-29718
ISBN 0-07-069985-2

1234567890   KPKP   786543210987

The editors for this book were Robert A. Rosenbaum and
Carolyn Nagy, the designer was Edward J. Fox, and
the production supervisor was Teresa F. Leaden.
It was set in Electra by University Graphics, Inc.

Printed and bound by The Kingsport Press.

CONTENTS

This book, like *First Aid for the Ailing House* which was first published in 1934, has just one purpose: to help homeowners protect their homes. To accomplish this we studied the thousands upon thousands of questions and answers that have appeared in Mr. Whitman's nationally syndicated newspaper column "First Aid for the Ailing House" in which he solves problems for homeowners. These problems—in the form of questions from readers and answers by Mr. Whitman—range from damp basements to problem attics . . . with many other household items discussed.

The first edition of *First Aid for the Ailing House*, written by Mr. Whitman's father, the late Roger C. Whitman, best expressed the idea behind our present book: "In this book will be found solutions to the problems every homeowner must meet; the remedies and methods to apply as the house wears and begins to run down, the materials and methods called for in repair work and in maintenance, and in general, what to do to keep the house staunch and fresh.

" . . . when things begin to happen to the heating, to the finish, to the roof, the owner has only his own judgment to tell him what to do. It is for him to decide whether something must be replaced or can be repaired, and in case of repair, how extensive it should be. Work cannot be left to a mechanic without risk of having a small job develop into a big one, or of being overcharged. The owner may be told that what seems to him to be a small repair is actually of major importance, with serious trouble ahead should it be neglected; whether or not he believes it depends on how much he knows."

In preparing this volume, we certainly want to thank Mr. Whitman and the syndicators of his newspaper column for their cooperation. In addition, we want to thank Janet Just, who did the typing of the manuscript and Mary Puschak, who coordinated all the questions and answers.

In *More First Aid for the Ailing House*, we have endeavored to keep the "do-it-yourself" tradition of Roger C. Whitman at its very best.

PREFACE

Robert Scharff
EDITOR

MORE
FIRST AID
FOR THE
AILING
HOUSE

Some people enjoy painting the house; for others it's a chore. But it must be done occasionally. One reason is for appearance. An even more important one is for protection of the wood or other surfaces. Delay, when repainting is needed, can mean extra work when you finally do paint. Old paint that blisters, cracks, and peels will have to be removed before the new paint can be applied. If you wait too long, costly damage can occur. Wood rots when not fully protected. It also allows moisture to reach the interior where it can cause damage. Some metals rust when not protected; others develop a corrosive wash that stains surrounding surfaces.

Always take time to do a good job when you paint:

First, buy the very best paint. Believe us, cheap paint is no bargain when compared to the very best. In fact, although cheap paint may save you a few bucks when you buy it, it will end up by costing you perhaps two, three, or four times as much if you do the painting, and maybe ten times as much if you have the painter do the work.

Second, prepare the surface properly for painting. Even the best paint won't last on a poorly prepared surface.

Third, apply the paint correctly. Improper application can be as damaging as a poorly prepared surface.

Selection of Exterior Paint

A number of different types of paint are available. Fortunately, however, selection need not be too much of a problem. First, you must consider the type of surface you are going to paint. Are you going to paint wood, metal, or masonry? Some paints are suitable for all three, while others may be used on two or only one. The condition of the surface may be important also. Old chalky surfaces, for instance, are not generally a sound base for latex- or water-base paints.

Next, consider any special requirements that your home may present. For example, nonchalking paint may be advisable where chalk rundown would discolor adjacent brick or stone surfaces. Or mildew may be a problem in your area; in this case, be sure to use mildew-resistant paint. Lead-free paints may be employed in areas where sulfur fumes may cause staining of paints containing lead pigments.

Color is a third consideration, but it is

CHAPTER 1

EXTERIOR PAINTING

mostly a matter of personal preference. Some colors are more durable than others, and some color combinations are more attractive than others. The suggested color schemes in Table 1 may be of help. Also remember that your paint dealer can be of great assistance on the matter of color durability and combinations.

While "house paints"—the commercial term given to most exterior paints—are mixed with many different formulations, most fall into either the oil- or alkyd-base paints and latex- or water-base paints. The vehicle of oil-base paint consists usually of lead, zinc, or titanium pigment, a vehicle of linseed oil, a drying agent, and a solvent. Oil- and alkyd-base paints are made with drying oils or drying oil combined with alkyd resin. The solvents for both are usually turpentine or mineral spirits. Both oil and alkyd paints have excellent brushing and penetrating properties. They provide good adhesion, elasticity, durability, and resistance to blistering on wood and other porous surfaces.

Latex paint contains water as the vehicle thinner—its vehicle consists of fine particles of resin emulsified or held in suspension in water. Another type of water-base paint has a vehicle consisting of a soluble linseed oil dissolved in water. This paint has the properties of both oil-base and water-base paints. Advantages of latex paints include easier application, faster drying, and usually better color retention than oil-base paints, and resistance to alkali and blistering. Also, they can be applied in humid weather and to damp surfaces. Brush and tool cleanup is simpler because it can be done with water.

Other Exterior "House" Paints. Among the other exterior paints that should be considered are the following more popular types:

Wood stains are a semitransparent type of finish available for exterior wood but are not as durable as house paints. They improve the appearance of wood by highlighting the grain and texture of the surface. Wood stains are available in many colors, the most popular being cedar, light redwood, and dark redwood. Incidentally, they are not recommended for frames, windows, and doors which need a high degree of protection against the weather.

The various *exterior clear finishes* are not as durable as pigmented paint. For instance, alkyd varnishes have good color and color retention but may crack and peel. Some synthetics such as polyurethane varnishes have good durability but may darken on exposure. Spar varnish (marine varnish) is quite durable but will also darken and yellow. In most applications, use thin pentrating coats on the bare wood, followed by the unreduced varnish.

Bituminous *roof coatings* are made of asphalt (chosen for good weather resistance) dissolved in a suitable solvent. Asbestos and other fillers are added to prevent sagging on sloping roofs and to permit application of relatively thick coatings. Basically they are made in gray and black; however, addition of aluminum powders provides for other colors. Asphalt-emulsion roof coatings can be applied over damp surfaces. Special application techniques are usually required, and the manufacturer's instructions must be followed carefully.

Water-repellent preservatives (silicone type) are transparent liquids that help repel water without changing the surface appearance. They must be applied strictly in accordance with instructions to ensure adequacy of film and water repellency. Silicone water repellents should not be topcoated with paint until the surface has weathered for at least two years.

Trim paints are usually made with oil-modified alkyds. They are made in high sheen and bright colors and have good retention of gloss and color. More expensive silicone-alkyd enamels are also available for trim painting, but they are substantially more durable than conventional oil-alkyd enamels.

Oil-base primers are used on both unpainted woodwork and surfaces previously coated with house paint. They provide good adhesion and sealing as well as resist cracking and flaking. But oil-base primers are suitable only as a basecoat and should be covered with finish paint within a week or two after application.

Antirust primers prevent corrosion on iron and steel surfaces. The slow-drying type provides protection through good penetration into cracks and crevices. Fast-drying types are used only on smooth, clean surfaces, and those which are water-resistant are effective where surfaces are subject to severe humidity conditions or freshwater immersion.

Porch and deck paints for wood surfaces are available in a variety of alkyd-base paints and other types. They are tough and flexible and have good abrasion resistance. For con-

Table 1. Suggested Color Schemes for Trim, Shutters, and Doors Based on the Color of the House

If the roof of your house is	You can paint the body	You can paint shutters, or trim and doors															
		Pink	Bright red	Red-orange	Tile red	Cream	Bright yellow	Light green	Dark green	Gray-green	Blue-green	Light blue	Dark blue	Blue-gray	Violet	Brown	White
Gray	White	X	X	X	X	X	X	X	X	X	X	X	X	X	X		
	Gray	X	X	X	X		X	X	X	X	X	X	X	X	X		X
	Cream-yellow		X		X		X		X	X							X
	Pale green				X		X		X	X							X
	Dark green	X				X	X	X									X
	Putty			X	X				X	X			X	X		X	
	Dull red	X				X		X						X			X
Green	White	X	X	X	X	X	X	X	X	X	X	X	X	X	X	X	
	Gray			X		X	X	X									X
	Cream-yellow		X		X			X	X	X						X	X
	Pale green		X	X		X		X									X
	Dark green	X		X		X	X	X									X
	Beige				X				X	X	X		X	X			
	Brown	X				X	X	X									X
	Dull red					X		X		X							X
Red	White		X		X				X		X			X			
	Light gray		X		X				X								X
	Cream-yellow		X		X						X		X	X			
	Pale green		X		X												X
	Dull red					X		X		X	X						X
Brown	White		X	X		X	X	X	X	X			X	X	X	X	
	Buff			X					X	X	X					X	
	Pink-beige			X					X	X						X	X
	Cream-yellow			X					X	X	X					X	
	Pale green								X	X						X	
	Brown			X		X	X										X
Blue	White		X	X			X					X	X				
	Gray		X		X							X	X				X
	Cream-yellow			X	X								X	X			
	Blue		X			X	X						X				X

crete and other masonry surfaces you can use one made with a natural rubber base (chlorinated rubber resin). The manufacturer's instructions must be followed carefully with this paint.

Aluminum paints are resistant to water and weather and provide excellent durability in marine environments. They can be applied on new metal or wood surfaces—in one direction for best results. Creosote-treated wood must age for about 6 months prior to application of aluminum paint.

Cement powder paint is made from white portland cement, pigments, and (usually) small amounts of water repellent. It is mixed with water just before application. Painted surfaces should be kept damp by sprinkling them with water until the paint film is well cured. This paint does not provide a good base for other types of finish. These paints are generally applied with either a brush or roller.

Use Table 2 as a guide in selecting exterior paint. Your paint dealer can help you also.

Tools and Accessories

Easy does it with exterior painting when you have the proper tools and accessories. A little preplanning helps you paint more easily and even improves the look of the final job.

After selecting the paint or other finish for your job, you should take care to select the best application tool, or tools. Actually, there are three basic application tools: paintbrushes, rollers, and paint sprayers.

Paintbrushes. Brushes, as any other tools, must be of first quality and maintained in perfect working condition at all times. Brushes are identified, first, by the type of bristle used. Brushes are made with either natural, synthetic, or mixed bristles. Chinese hog bristles represent the finest of the natural bristles because of their length, durability, and resiliency. Hog bristle has one unique characteristic in that the bristle end forks out like a tree branch. This "flagging" permits more paint to be carried on the brush and leaves fine brush marks on the applied coating which flow together more readily, resulting in a smoother finish. Horsehair bristles are used in cheap brushes and are a very unsatisfactory substitute. The ends do not flag, the bristles quickly become limp, they hold far less paint than the hog bristles, and they do not spread it as well. Brush marks left in the applied coating tend to be coarse and do not level out as

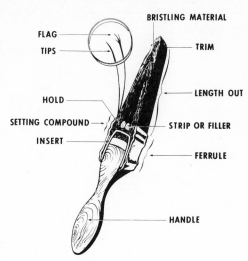

Figure 1-1. Typical paint brush.

smoothly. Some brushes contain a mixture of hog bristle and horsehair, and their quality depends upon the percentage of each type used. Animal hair is utilized in very fine brushes for special purposes. Badger hair, for example, produces a particularly good varnish brush. Squirrel and sable are ideal for striping, lining, lettering, and freehand art brushes. Of the synthetics, nylon is by far the most common. By artificially "exploding" the ends and kinking the fibers, manufacturers have increased the paint load nylon can carry and have reduced the coarseness of brush marks. Nylon is steadily replacing hog bristle because of the difficulties in importing the latter. Nylon is almost always superior to horsehair. The very fact that nylon is a synthetic makes it unsuitable for applying lacquer, shellac, many creosote products, and some other coatings that would soften or dissolve the bristles. Because water does not cause any appreciable swelling of nylon bristles, they are especially recommended for use with latex paints.

Brushes are further identified by types, that is, the variety of shapes and sizes as are required for specific painting jobs. The types can be classified as follows:

1. *Wall brushes.* Flat, square-edged brushes ranging in width from 3 to 6 inches and used for painting large, continuous surfaces.
2. *Sash and trim brushes.* Available in four shapes flat square-edged, flat angle-

edged, round, and oval. These brushes range in width from 1½ to 3 inches or diameters of ½ to 2 inches and are used for painting window frames, sash, narrow boards, and interior and exterior trim surfaces. For fine-line painting, the edge of the brush is often chisel-shaped to make precise edging easier to accomplish.

3. *Enameling and varnish brushes.* Flat square-edged or chisel-edged brushes available in widths ranging from 5 to 6 inches. Bristles can be of hog, other natural bristle, or nylon; the latter is preferred for rough surfaces because of its resistance to abrasion.

Use the right size brush for the job. Avoid a brush that is too small or too large. The latter is particularly important. A large-area job does not necessarily go faster with an over-

Table 2. Paint Selection Chart

	House paint oil or oil-alkyd	Cement powder paint	Exterior clear finish	Aluminum paint	Wood stain	Roof coating	Trim paint	Porch and deck paint	Primer or undercoater	Metal primer	House paint (latex)	Water-repellent preservative
Wood:												
Clapboard	X.			X					X		X.	
Natural wood siding and trim			X		X							
Shutters and other trim	X.			X			X.		X		X.	
Wood frame windows	X.			X			X.		X		X.	
Wood porch floor								X				
Wood shingle roof					X							
Metal:												
Aluminum windows	X.			X			X.			X	X.	
Steel windows	X.			X.			X.			X	X.	
Metal roof	X.									X	X.	
Metal siding	X.			X.			X.			X	X.	
Copper surfaces			X									
Galvanized surfaces	X.			X.			X.			X	X.	
Iron surfaces	X.			X.			X.			X	X.	
Masonry:												
Asbestos cement	X.									X		
Brick	X.	X		X						X		X
Cement and cinder block	X.	X		X						X		
Concrete/masonry porches and floors								X		X		
Coal tar felt roof					X							
Stucco	X.	X		X						X		

X.—Black dot indicates that a primer or sealer may be necessary before the finishing coat.

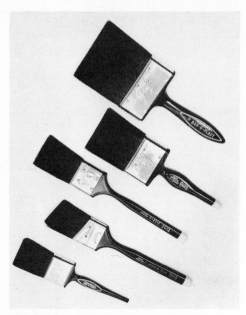

Figure 1-2. These brushes will cover almost every home painting task: (top to bottom) 4-inch wall brush, 3-inch enameling brush, 2-inch flat trim brush, 2-inch angular sash brush, and 2-inch "chiseled" varnish brush.

cial rollers are used for painting pipes, fences, and other hard-to-reach areas. The fabrics generally used are as follows:

1. *Lamb's-wool* (pelt). This is the most solvent-resistant type of material used and is available in nap lengths up to 1¼ inches. It is recommended for synthetic finishes for application on semismooth and rough surfaces. It mats badly in water and is not recommended for water paints.

2. *Mohair*. This is made primarily of angora hair. It also is solvent-resistant and is supplied in ³⁄₁₆ and ¼-inch nap lengths. It is recommended for synthetic enamels and for use on smooth surfaces. It can be used with water paints also.

3. *Dynel*. This is a modified acrylic fiber which has excellent resistance to water. It is best for application of conventional water paints and solvent paints, except those which contain strong solvents, such as ketones. It is available in all nap lengths from ¼ to 1¼ inches.

4. *Dacron*. This is a synthetic fiber which is somewhat softer than Dynel. It is best suited for exterior oil or latex paints. It is available in nap lengths from ⁵⁄₁₆ to ½ inch.

size brush. If the brush size is out of balance for the type of painting being done, the user tends to apply the coating at an uneven rate, general workmanship declines, and the applicator actually tires faster because of the extra output required per stroke. Synthetic fiber brushes are ready to use when received. The performance of natural bristle brushes is very much improved by a previous 48-hour soak in linseed oil followed by a thorough cleaning in mineral spirits. This process makes the bristles more flexible and serves to swell the bristles in the ferrule of the brush, resulting in a better grip, so that fewer bristles are apt to work loose when the brush is used.

Rollers. A paint roller consists of a cylindrical sleeve or cover which slips onto a rotatable cage to which a handle is attached. The cover may be 1½ to 2¼ inches inside diameter, and usually 3, 4, 7, or 9 inches in length. Special rollers are available in lengths from 1½ to 18 inches. Proper roller application depends on the selection of the specific fabric and the thickness of fabric (nap length) based on the type of paint used and the smoothness or roughness of the surface to be painted. Spe-

Figure 1-3. *How to use a roller.* Pour a little paint into the deep end of the tray. Work the paint into the roller by moving it back and forth in the tray until paint is evenly distributed around roller. Move the roller across the wall in slow, smooth strokes, working first in one direction, then in another. Quick strokes and heavy, uneven pressure may cause bubbles or spatters. Apply paint from top to bottom as recommended for brushing.

Table 3 can be used as a guide for choosing the proper roller cover.

Spray Equipment. Three main types of spray equipment are available to the homeowner. The most recent development, and one that costs the least, is the aerosol-type spray can. These sprays consist of a metal can with a trigger nozzle at the top protected by a removable cap. Pressing the trigger releases a fine mist of thinned paint which has been packed into the can under gas pressure. A marble is usually included in the bottom, which, when the can is shaken, aids in stirring up the paint (usually an alkyd resin). Like most spray equipment, the spray cans require practice in order to get a smooth finish without runs, sags, or pitted "orange peel" effects. Some cans have removable nozzles for cleaning, and so no enamel is imprisoned (and therefore wasted) in the can due to a clogged nozzle.

Electric, self-contained spray guns are available in most hardware stores. These

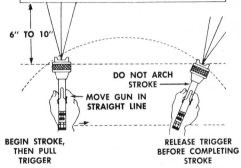

Figure 1-4. Proper spray-gun stroke.

usually have a vibrator pump mounted in the gun handle or cap and a glass jar to contain the paint. The paint used in these low-pressure guns must be thinned much more than for brushing in order to produce a proper spray without clogging the nozzle. Heavily

Table 3. Choosing a Roller Cover

Type of paint	Type of surface		
	Smooth*	Semismooth†	Rough ‡
Aluminum	C	A	A
Enamel or semigloss (alkyd)	A or B	A	
Enamel undercoat	A or B	A	
Epoxy coatings	B or D	D	D
Exterior house paint:			
Latex for wood	C	A	
Latex for masonry	A	A	A
Oil or alkyd—wood	C	A	
Oil or alkyd—masonry	A	A	A
Floor enamel—all types	A or B	A	
Interior wall paint:			
Alkyd or oil	A	A or D	A
Latex	A	A	A
Masonry sealer	B	A or D	A or D
Metal primers	A	A or D	
Varnish—all types	A or B		
Roller cover key	Nap length, in.		
A—Dynel (modified acrylic)	¼–⅜	⅜–¾	1–1¼
B—Mohair	³⁄₁₆–¼		
C—Dacron polyester	¼–⅜	½	
D—Lamb's-wool pelt	¼–⅜	½–¾	1–1¼

  *Smooth surface: hardboard, smooth metal, smooth plaster, dry wall, etc.
  †Semismooth surface: sand-finished plaster and dry wall, light stucco, blasted metal, semismooth masonry.
  ‡Rough surface: concrete or cinder block, brick, heavy stucco, wire fence.

pigmented paints are not successful in this type of gun.

Another low-pressure spray gun is the type provided with many tank-type vacuum cleaners. These guns frequently produce excellent results on small jobs, such as chairs or toys, if the homeowner takes time to practice and develop a proper spraying technique. A hand-pump insect sprayer may also be used for small jobs and touch-ups.

A standard production-type spray outfit is usually far too expensive to purchase for occasional home use, but most paint stores rent this type of equipment to the homeowner. The usual outfit consists of an electric motor which drives an air compressor. The compressed air is stored in a pressure tank, and a hose leads from it to the gun. The gun consists of a glass or metal jar to hold the paint and a metal cap with attached handle. This contains the spray nozzle and a release trigger. When this trigger is pulled, the air pressure forces the paint out in a fine spray that produces an even, smooth coating of paint.

Other Equipment. Shown here are the other materials and equipment you may need to do your painting easily and efficiently. Be certain there are plenty of drop cloths to protect shrubs and walks. Be sure your ladder is tall enough to reach the highest parts of the house easily. Finally, make sure you have the tools and materials necessary for preparatory work. Your paint job will last longer and look better if you start with a clean, sound, well-prepared surface.

Preparing for Painting

Before paint is applied, the surface should be properly prepared. Badly split or rotted boards or shingles should be replaced, and any loose ones should be carefully nailed down. Loose knots should be removed and the holes filled with wood filler, obtainable at paint or hardware stores. Windows and doors should be carefully checked for any needed caulking, and loose caulking should be replaced. Loose flashings should be carefully nailed down, and

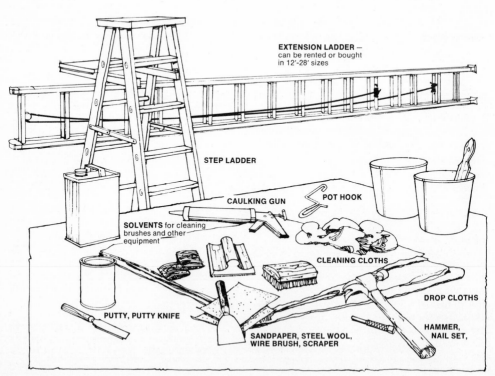

EXTENSION LADDER — can be rented or bought in 12'-28' sizes

STEP LADDER

CAULKING GUN   **POT HOOK**

SOLVENTS for cleaning brushes and other equipment

CLEANING CLOTHS

DROP CLOTHS

PUTTY, PUTTY KNIFE

SANDPAPER, STEEL WOOL, WIRE BRUSH, SCRAPER

HAMMER, NAIL SET,

Figure 1-5. Other items needed for exterior painting.

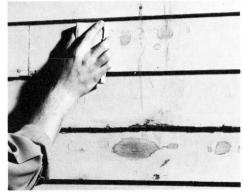

Figure 1-6. Scrape (left) and sand (right) down all loose and flaking paint.

edges sealed with roofing cement to make the openings watertight.

Corroded gutters and leaky downspouts should be repaired or replaced. If these are not attended to, they will cause staining and perhaps rotting. Window sashes should be checked for loose, missing, or cracked putty; this should be replaced before painting. Before applying new putty, prime the sash with boiled linseed oil to prevent the dry wood from drawing oil from the new putty. The guide areas of windows should not be painted. These should be brushed with two coats of boiled linseed oil.

Areas where the paint is locally damaged may be scraped or sanded to remove the failing finish and then primed with a coat of regular exterior primer before the finish coat is applied. The primer should be given 1 to 2 days to dry.

If nail holes or other spots are to be puttied, prime them first. Allow the prime coat to dry for at least 8 hours; then apply the putty. In new wood, preprime all knots and resinous-looking pores with aluminum paint before applying the primer.

When outside paint is firm and in fair condition and needs repainting only because it is chalky or discolored, two new coats of the same color should be sufficient. If one of the new "one-coat" house paints is being used, a single coat should suffice if the thinning, stirring, and application directions are carefully followed. Three coats of standard house paint and two coats of "one-coat" paint are needed when there is to be an extreme change of color. The first coat of a two- or three-coat job

should be thinned, depending upon the directions of the manufacturer for the particular type of surface condition.

The priming coat should be allowed to dry for 1 to 2 days, depending upon the weather and the label directions. Since it is the foundation for the later coats, it should be given ample drying time to become firmly attached.

For the outer coat of a two- or three-coat job or the single coat of a "one-coat" paint, the paint is used as it comes from the can. There is a tendency among nonprofessional painters to thin house paint "because it feels too tacky" and makes brushing difficult. Follow the manufacturer's directions carefully; a great amount of research and development went into the formulation of the paint, and its consistency is proper for the job. Unless thinning directions are given, use the paint as it comes from the can, stirring frequently. Latex or water-base paint should not be shaken—it foams.

On metal surfaces, prime both new metal and old metal from which the paint has been removed. Good primers usually contain zinc dust, red lead, zinc yellow, blue lead, iron oxide, or some rust-inhibiting pigment as one of the ingredients. After the primer has dried sufficiently, apply one or two finish coats.

Applying the Paint

Everything about a paint job should be kept clean; dust and dirt should not be allowed to get into the paint or onto the work. When working in a dusty area outdoors, it is a good idea to sprinkle water on the ground to settle the dust. Dust sills and crevices with a damp cloth before painting.

If mixing is required, it can be done at the paint store by placing the can in a mechanical agitator—or you can do it at home with a paddle or spatula. If you open the can and find that the pigment has settled, use a clean paddle or spatula and gradually work the pigment up from the bottom of the can, using a circular stirring motion. Continue until the pig-ment is thoroughly and evenly distributed, with no signs of color separation. If the settled layer should prove to be hard or rubbery and resists stirring, the paint is probably too old and should be discarded.

Between jobs, even if it is only overnight, cover the paint container tightly to prevent evaporation and thickening and to protect it from dust. Oil-base and alkyd paints may develop a skin from exposure to the air. When

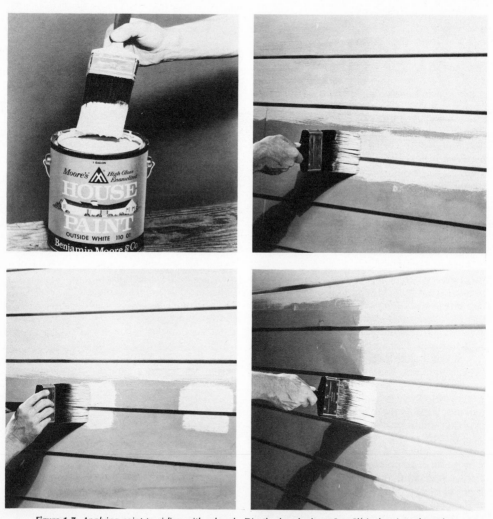

Figure 1-7. *Applying paint to siding with a brush.* Dip the brush about 2 to 2½ inches into the paint and tap excess off against the inside of the can (top left). Then apply the paint generously along the joint of the siding, distributing it evenly as you brush (top right). Brush the paint out well, taking care to coat the under edge of the clapboard (bottom left). Feather the ends of your brush strokes to assure smoothness where one painted stroke joins another (bottom right).

you finish painting, clean the rim of the paint can thoroughly and put the lid on tight. To ensure that the lid is airtight, cover the rim with a cloth or piece of plastic film (to prevent spattering) and then tap the lid firmly into place with a hammer.

If you are using a gallon of paint, transfer it to a larger container or pour about half into another container. It will be easier to handle and there will be room for the brush.

When using a brush, dip it half the length of the bristles into the paint. Tap the brush gently against the side of the can, but do not wipe it across the lip. Hold the brush comfortably near the handle base, applying light pressure with your fingertips. The bristles should flex slightly toward the tip as you begin the stroke, but you should not bear down on the brush. Use long sweeping arm strokes, keeping an even pressure on the brush. Apply both sides of each brushful. End each stroke with a light, lifting motion. Always apply the paint to an unpainted area and work into the wet edge of the previously painted portion. When you finish an area, go over it with light, quick strokes to smooth brush marks and to recoat any thin spots.

To prevent drips and spatters from spoiling previously painted areas, work from the top down, doing gutters and eaves first if they are to match the siding color. Complete one sidewall before starting another. In fact, finish an entire side, or at least complete the job to a door or window, before stopping for the day. But more important, do not start a new can of paint in the middle of a board or large wall area. If the remaining paint in a can will not finish an area, mix some of the new paint with the partially filled can before finishing the area. This will help blend the color.

If rollers are used to paint siding, two are usually required. A wide roller will coat the surface of the boards, and a doughnut-shaped one is used for the lap joints. Be sure that the paint is the proper consistency. It should be thick enough to go on without running, sagging, or dripping off the edges, but should be thin enough so that the roller does not stipple it on, leaving pimpled areas where the surface is not covered.

Paint must be thinned down for spray application. The surface must be free of dust and dirt, and all grease removed with a solvent. To spray heavily pigmented house paint, a high-pressure gun should be used. More

Figure 1-8. *Applying paint to siding with a roller.* Use the doughnut-shaped roller (in the pan) for the lap joints; the wide-roller can be employed on flat siding.

area can be covered at one time, and the heavy paint will be sprayed in a thin mist. Cover bushes and mask off glass areas and any trim that is not to be painted. Paint must be stirred frequently during spraying. The paint in the gun should be stirred if the gun is shut off for more than 5 minutes during painting. The supply container should be carefully checked for proper consistency each time the gun is filled from it.

Spraying should be done only from a scaffolding on which the painter can move from side to side. Ladders do not make a satisfactory platform for spraying because the reach is limited and it is clumsy to climb up and down with the unwieldy spray gun and hoses.

Trim, in a contrasting color or product, is usually painted last. If the shutters can be removed, paint them separately and replace them when the rest of the job is completed. Paint the window sash and recessed part of the window frame first, then the frame, and the window sill last.

Cleaning the Tools

It is most important that all equipment be cleaned immediately after use, especially brushes, rollers, and guns.

Figure 1-9. To clean brushes, work the solvent into the bristles with your fingers. Then squeeze out as much paint and solvent as possible. Repeat until paint disappears. Give them a final rinse in a clear solvent; then wash in soapy water, rinse, and let dry. To preserve their shape, brushes should be carefully wrapped in heavy paper.

To clean brushes used in oil-base paints, work the solvent (turpentine or mineral spirits) into the bristles with your fingers. Squeeze out as much paint and solvent as possible. Repeat this until the paint disappears. Give the brushes a final rinse in clear solvent; then wash them in soapy water, rinse, and let dry. To preserve their shape, brushes should be carefully wrapped in heavy paper.

To clean rollers, disassemble and submerge the cover in the solvent. When most of the paint has been worked out, you can wash the cover in a mild detergent solution and rinse in clear water. Remove the paint from the frame and hardware of the roller with the proper solvent.

After using an oil-based or alkyd paint, clean the sprayer with the same solvent used to thin the paint. If the fluid tip becomes clogged, it can be cleaned with a broom straw. Never use a wire or nail to clear clogged air holes in the sprayer tip.

When using water-thinned paints, follow the same procedure outlined above for cleaning brushes, rollers, and guns, substituting soapy water for paint solvent.

Drop cloths can be used again and again—indoors or out. If any paint did fall on the walks, scrub it out with the solvent and a stiff brush. Don't use solvents on shrubs; it may damage the plants. It's better to cut off

the spotted portions. Spatters from water-thinned paints can be scrubbed off with soapy water before the paint has been allowed to dry.

Questions and Answers

Here are some of the most frequently asked questions regarding exterior painting:

HOUSE PAINTING DURING HEAT

I plan to paint my house during my vacation at the end of the summer. Will hot weather affect the painting?

You can paint your house when the weather is clear and dry and the temperature is between 50 and 90°F. (Never paint when the temperature is below 40°F.) In hot weather, paint surfaces after they have been exposed to the sun and are in the shade. This will keep the top layers of paint from drying out too fast and causing wrinkling and cracking. Follow the sun around the house.

PAINTING TIME

What time of day can I safely start painting my house?

Start painting after the morning dew or frost has evaporated. Stop painting in late aft-

Figure 1-10. To clean rollers, disassemble and submerge the cover in solvent. When most of the paint has been worked out, you can wash the cover in a mild detergent solution and rinse in clear water. Remove paint from frame and hardware of roller with the proper solvent.

ernoon or early evening on cool fall days. (This is more important with oil-base paint than with latex paint.) Do not paint, of course, in windy or dusty weather or when insects may get caught in the paint. Insects are usually the biggest problem during fall evenings. Don't try to remove insects from wet paint; brush them off after the paint dries.

MILDEWING PAINT

For the past few years we have been troubled with mildew on our outside paint. In less than a month after we repaint, it is black again. What is the cause and the cure? We use a good-quality exterior paint. We have owned the house for 37 years and never had this trouble before.

The mildew spores may not have been killed after the original infection, so that new coatings are infected in turn. Is there an increase in dampness in the area, or in the house itself, to promote the growth of mildew? Check for leaks in the roof, around windows, flashings, etc. Before repainting again, scrub the mildewed surfaces with a strong detergent in warm water. Then kill any remaining spores by treating the surface with a household bleach solution (1 pint per gallon of water). Use a good-quality mildew-resistant paint, such as the latex type, or add a mildewcide to the house paint you use.

PAINT PEELED FOR 24 YEARS

Each time our house is painted, the paint starts to flake off within a year. The last time it was painted, the painter used latex paint. The results were the same: within 3 months, horrible flaking and peeling! A local carpenter thinks the trouble is moisture in the siding, which is not insulated. Could this be possible?

It certainly could be the cause. With no

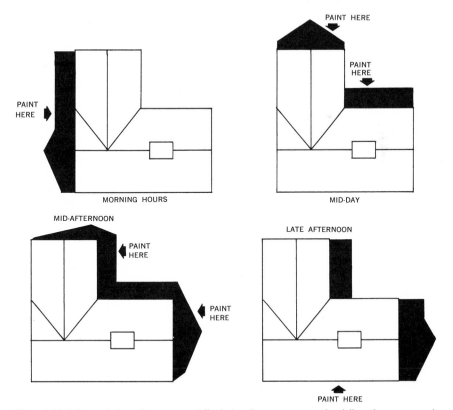

Figure 1-11. When painting a house, especially during the summer months, follow the sun around the house so that you will be painting in the shade.

insulation, the warm, damp house air can pass through the inside walls and condense on the outside walls and work through, eventually pushing paint off the surface. Insulating not only could stop this problem, but also could save you a great deal on heating bills too.

ALUMINUM PAINT STOP PEELING?

The outside oil-base paint is peeling again from our shingles. Under the shingles is insulating sheathing, the only insulation between the inside plastered walls and outside. Would aluminum paint on the inside surfaces of the outside walls make a good vapor barrier? Would this stop the exterior latex paint from peeling? Would venting the wall cavity be a good idea?

The aluminum paint will make a good vapor barrier; we assume you'd put some other paint over it. This would keep damp house air from working into the wall space and perhaps from promoting peeling. But it will also increase the chances of condensation problems indoors, by trapping the damp air. Venting the wall spaces certainly can't hurt.

PAINT PEELS

We purchased a new home two years ago and are having trouble painting it. Last summer we painted the siding, and shortly after it was done it started to peel. There is no basement, but the crawl space is pretty wet. How can we keep the crawl space dry? It seems to be the cause of our trouble. What can be done about the peeling?

Not only can dampness in the ground under the house cause paint to peel, but it is also likely to cause a damp condition in the house. You can cover the soil with polyethylene plastic sheets or a moistureproof and vaporproof paper. Building material yards sell them. The sheets should be overlapped at least 6 inches. If the paper is used, seal the laps with an asphalt roof cement. The crawl space should also be well ventilated.

WOOD TRIM ON BRICK HOUSE PEELING

We have an all-brick home. All that requires painting is the trim, but we have difficulty in keeping the paint from peeling in spite of using good-quality primer and paint. Is there something we can add to the paint or some way we can treat the wood to prevent this?

The usual cause of paint peeling is moisture working its way through from underneath and pushing the paint off. The trim may not be tightly joined to the brick; or the joints of the frames themselves may be loosened; or there may be faulty window flashings. All these points should be checked and any openings tightly caulked, using a caulking compound and caulking gun.

PAINT PEELS

The outside of my house is shingled. The paint on the windowsills peels off to the bare wood, which is spongy and full of cracks in places. Would you please tell me of some kind of paint that would not do this or something that would make the paint stay longer?

The spongy condition of the wood indicates that moisture has been in the wood for so long that rotting has set in. Both these conditions contribute to the peeling of paint. The only remedy is to replace the rotted wood. In the future, when cracks develop, always fill them with putty or a caulking compound before repainting. Cracks and crevices in exterior woodwork allow water to get into the wood.

PEELING AND BLISTERING PAINT

I have a paint problem. A few years ago I was asked to paint a 75-year-old house and suggested burning off the paint, as this had never been done through the years. This idea was rejected, and so I scraped and wirewooled all visible defects and applied paint. In about a year the new paint, in spots, caused blisters to appear, which extended to the bare wood. I am of the opinion that other reasons than moisture cause such conditions. I claim that paint upon paint for many years causes too heavy an accumulation of paint films and a new coat, like the "straw that broke the camel's back," can cause a complete breakdown. What is your opinion?

We agree that many layers of paint will eventually build up a thick film which becomes so heavy it will separate from the wall. However, this would not cause blisters to form unless the paint film cracks badly first and moisture finds its way into the wood. In most cases there is no blistering—just cracking and separation from the wood. As you know, blisters are generally caused by an accumulation of moisture under the paint.

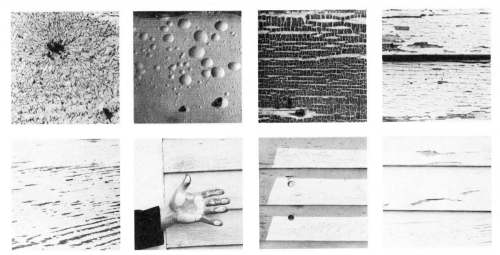

Figure 1-12. Common paint problems (left to right, top to bottom): Mold; blistering; alligatoring; scaling; checking; chalking; bleeding; and peeling.

PEELING PAINT REMOVAL

How can I remove the paint from bedroom walls? The paint blistered about a year after application. Is there any product on the market that can be used to help clean paint off walls? I have tried to sand the paint with a buffer and also tried scraping it.

If the paint adheres that tightly to the wall surface, don't worry about trying to remove any more. If it is smooth, apply the new coating over it, being sure the surface is free of wax, grease, grime, etc. Paste-type paint removers are available at most paint and hardware dealers; follow the manufacturer's directions carefully. The blistering of the paint may be due to moisture working its way through the wall from the outside, or from the wall space. Check for roof leaks, leaks around chimney and window flashings, etc.; and check for moisture from the ground working up through the wall space.

BURNING GARAGE BLISTERED SHINGLES

My neighbor's garage burned to the ground. In the process, my green-stained shingles became a mass of tiny blisters, and my yellow trim paint virtually disappeared. What has to be done?

Remove the blisters with a paint scraper or equivalent; or use a portable sander, either the oscillating or orbital type or a sanding-wheel attachment for your electric drill. Give the trim the same treatment. Then you can restain the shingles and repaint the trim. If the trim is down to bare wood, better start with a prime coat.

WHAT PRIMER FOR SIDING?

Bits of paint flake off the south side of my house siding almost every year. Each time before I repaint, I sand down to bare wood, and I always use a good grade of oil-base paint. Friends tell me I should prime the bare spots with shellac or exterior-grade varnish before I put on the paint. Is this a good idea?

We prefer another type of primer altogether: either a coat of linseed oil or your siding paint thinned 50 percent with linseed oil.

"OVERLAPPING" PAINT

I painted my home. When I finished, there were overlaps. To remedy this, I gave it a second coat, painting the opposite way of the first. But there still are overlaps. What went wrong?

It sounds, from your description, as though you tried to paint too large an area at one time, so that the paint at the edges of the area started to set up by the time you got back to do the adjoining section. This could be especially true if the surface was even slightly absorbent. (We are assuming you followed the label directions precisely and thinned the paint in the can as necessary. We are also assuming that the surface itself was smooth and completely free of ridges before you started to paint.)

PAINTED WITH BROOM?

The previous owner must have painted the trim with a broom. There are conspicuous brush marks and in some places heavy gobs of paint. How can I get the surface smooth for a proper repainting without risking damage to the siding paint?

Carefully brush on a paste-type paint remover, preferably the kind which needs no neutralizing afterward (to save an extra step as well as minimize chances of softened paint spreading onto the siding). When softening starts, you may be able to pry the gobs off with a putty knife. If any happen to be on the siding, better leave them alone or be prepared to spot-retouch.

SAP SHOWS THROUGH PAINT

The trim on the outside of our new house has sap coming through in some places. The wood has been painted with a primer and a finish coat. How shall we treat this trim when we repaint?

Scrape off the paint from the discolored areas; then wash off all traces of sap and resin with coarse steel wool and turpentine. The next step is to coat the trim with a knot sealer (sold by many paint dealers). If it's not available, a coat of pure, fresh shellac will give good results.

LOCK STAIN BEHIND PAINT

Last year a leak in the roof above our white-painted bedroom walls caused a stain on the outside wall from ceiling to floor. I would like to repaint, using more of the same type of white latex paint. But I have heard that if I paint over this, the stain will show through again in a short while. Is this true?

You can check the stain easily. First give the stained area a coat of aluminum paint. This is excellent at locking in the stain so that it can't bleed through. We assume you've already taken care of the roof leak. This treatment also works when painting over mahogany stain.

WHAT CAUSES WRINKLING?

The paint on my house has a rough, crinkled texture. What is the cause of this?

The main cause of this condition—which is known as wrinkling—is the application of too thick a coat. Never try to make one coat of paint do the work of two, since the top surface will dry first and leave the bottom still soft. As the bottom surface attempts to dry, it could absorb the binder of the top paint and make that paint wrinkle. Wrinkling can also occur if paint is applied to a cold surface. In this case, only the top surface dries while the colder bottom surface remains soft.

BLISTERING OF PAINT ON CEDAR SIDING

We recently painted our red cedar siding, and the paint blistered. Brown liquid runs out of the blisters. We used a coat of white shellac, then good yellow outside paint. What causes this, and how can we cure it?

Most likely the wood was moist when first sealed. The color in the burst blisters indicates that moisture passed through the wood, picking up the color. The other possibility is that water can penetrate behind the siding to be absorbed by the unprotected raw wood back. Unless every possible hole and crack is sealed, this happens. You'll have to remove the defective coat and then reseal and repaint the siding on a dry day with a temperature of about 55°.

"BLEEDING" GARAGE DOOR

I have an overhead garage door with four panels made of Masonite which has to be repainted every year. Please tell me what to do to keep these panels from "bleeding" through and loosening the paint. Before I repainted each time, I sanded off every bit of old paint.

First apply a coat of aluminum paint. This works excellently in keeping difficult wood stains from working through even white paint. It should work here. If the problem is greatest near the edges of the panels, it could be that water works in and gets the panels so damp the paint peels off. In such cases, caulking compound should close the joints between the panels and frame.

ORIGINAL COATING BLEEDING THROUGH

We have a dark-green shingle house. The shakes faded after a year or two, and so we painted them with a good grade of shake paint, the same color. Now the stain or paint that was on originally seems to be bleeding through, resulting in a blotchy

appearance. Would another coat cover the stain (we gave it only one coat), or is there something else we can do?

The bleeding effect may be due to the single coat having been applied over a mildewed surface. If the surface was free of mildew, and clean, the blotchy appearance may be due to uneven paint absorption. Another coat of paint might be effective; two additional coats would be better to remove the blotchy appearance. If mildew was present, wash the surface with strong detergent, rinsing well afterward with clear water before applying a new coating of mildew-proof paint.

SECOND COATS WON'T STICK

I have a 3-foot overhang. Where the gutter is attached, the first coat of paint is all right, but the next coat always peels. This has happened to me twice. I use expensive paints, and I have cleaned the surface smooth before applying paint. What is the trouble?

From your description, you have eliminated all the possible reasons for peeling except one. The wood must be dry underneath, because the first coat stays on. You say you clean the surface of the paint thoroughly before applying the second coat. That only leaves one possibility: Was the wood dry when you put on the second coat? If it was wet, not even good latex paint will stick. If only a little damp, latex paint would be okay (it lets wood "breathe"), but oil-base would come off. If the wood was thoroughly dry and clean, then we're as puzzled as you.

TRIM PAINT ONE STEADY PROBLEM

During our 17 years here, we have painted our house a number of times. We never had any trouble with paint staying on the cedar shake shingles. But the trim! We have tried every type of paint imaginable, with recommended undercoats, and have burned and scraped down to bare wood each time. But it has never ceased to peel off. Most irritating of all is that none of our neighbors have this problem, and they have not used the best paint the way we have. Can you suggest anything? This is really getting us down.

Regardless of what paint you use and how you put it on, the basic cause of peeling is dampness in the wood. You haven't mentioned this, but we do suggest your carefully examining the joint where the window frames fit into the siding. If the caulking is dried, old,

cracked, or shrunk, water can get in and then permeate the wood. A good recaulking with a caulking gun may close up all those leaks, and the wood may dry out and the paint stop peeling.

DOESN'T LIKE SCRAPING PAINT

I plan to paint the outside trim of my house with more oil-base paint. The present paint needs extensive scraping. I would like to remove all this paint, but to do as little scraping as possible. If I use paint remover, would it be risky for the rest of the paint on the siding when I used a neutralizing wash afterward?

To minimize the risk to paint below, we highly recommend your using a paste-type remover, which will stay put on a vertical surface. Further, if you get one which does not require a neutralizing wash afterward, your job will be considerably easier. These types of removers are widely sold. Check the label before you buy.

TORCH OR REMOVER?

Which would be better for removing cracked paint from an overhead garage door: a torch or paint remover? What paint should I use next?

If you're experienced enough in using a torch so that you won't burn the door or crack the glass panes, go ahead and use it. If not, use a good paste-type paint remover. Since the door is so frequently moved and flexed, we suggest thin coats of a top-quality exterior enamel over the recommended undercoater.

ESTIMATING AMOUNT OF PAINT

I know that the quantity of paint that will be needed for a job will depend on the character of the surface. More paint will be required for porous wood than for wood that is dense and less weathered. But is there any general formula for estimating the amount of paint needed to paint a house?

To estimate the quantity of paint needed for the outside of a house, measure in feet the distance around the house, that is, the length of the four walls, and then multiply by the height of the walls to the eaves. This will be the area of the outside walls in square feet. No deduction should be made for windows and doors. For a gable end, multiply the width at the bottom of the gable by one-half of the height from the bottom line to the peak. This area is added to the area of the outside walls. On the average, the cornices, trim, and similar parts will require one-sixth of the paint needed for the main part of the building. For an average roof, multiply the length by the width of the house and increase by one-third (multiply by 1.33).

PAINT SPATTERED ON SHINGLES

When we moved into our new split-level home, we decided to repaint the white trim on the windows. In doing this, some of the white trim paint splashed over the gray shake shingles. My father thought it would be a good idea to paint over the spots with a gray paint. We did this, but after the paint dried, the spots made the shingles look as if they were spattered with oil or water. Would advise repainting the whole house? If so, what kind of paint would cover up those dark spots? Should we go over the spots with paint remover?

We assume the shingles have been stained and the oils in the stain "bled" through the paint. Instead of going to the trouble and expense of painting the whole house, take off the paint with paint remover and steel wool. If the manufacturer directs, wash off all traces of the remover with turpentine. Sometimes this procedure takes out some of the shingle stain; if it does, touch up the areas with a matching shingle stain, which you can purchase from the dealer who supplied the original shingles. Or you can paint the walls with a special shingle paint.

MOISTURE SPOTS ON HARDBOARD SIDING

We have hardboard siding on our home, as do several others in the neighborhood. This spots badly from moisture (rain or snow). We have large water spots all over the house which do not disappear in warm weather. We first thought the original paint job inadequate, but after two coats of good-quality house paint, the spots remain. Is there a special treatment or a special paint we can use? No one seems to have an answer.

We recommend checking with the builder or the manufacturer of the hardboard; an untempered hardboard may have been used which is not water-resistant. In painting hardboard, a good primer or sealer is first applied, and then an undercoat and at least two coats of top-quality exterior paint. Be sure to seal and paint all edges carefully with each coating.

REPAINTING CEDAR SIDING

My house is six years old and has cedar siding that was given an undercoat and one coat of paint. A few years later, another coat of paint was put on. People who knew the previous owner (I'm the second) told me he considered himself an inventor and "souped up" the paint for the last coat. A year and a half ago the walls looked good, but now there is considerable chalking and some checking. A painter has advised a coat of aluminum paint and two of wall paint. The builder advises against it. Is aluminum paint more desirable as a vapor barrier inside rather than as an undercoater outside?

Aluminum as an undercoater on exterior siding does not perform miracles and is not a cure-all for a defective paint job. If there is no serious checking problem, brush off as much of the chalking as possible and apply the paint in the usual manner. Badly checked paint should be removed.

WHAT'S ON SIDING?

I have a ranch-style house 2½ years old with rough cedar siding. I cannot determine whether the original finish was stain or paint. Can I now use a latex paint on rough cedar siding, or is a stain recommended?

If you can see the natural wood grain all over, the finish (if any) was stain. Paint, even thinned down considerably, would hide this grain. While you can, of course, use a latex paint on this rough siding, if it were ours we would prefer a pigmented stain. Some excellent ones are on the market in a wide range of colors.

VARNISHED CEDAR SIDING

We coated cedar siding, when it was new, with oil and spar varnish. The varnish came off wherever rain and sun could reach it. Although we have applied new coats every fall and spring, the same thing occurs. We would now like to paint it and wish to know if it is necessary to remove the varnish, or can we just sandpaper it?

Just dull the varnish by rubbing it with sandpaper; then wipe off the dust and apply your paint.

RED CEDAR POST WALLS

I am interested in painting my red cedar split-post home. We have had it varnished several times, but the varnish seems to fade easily. The house always looks as though it has not been treated for years. We would appreciate knowing of a covering or coating that will help it keep its log-cabin effect.

One method is to remove the varnish down to the bare wood and then apply a couple of coats of a preparation known as redwood finish. It contains a color and preservative and is suitable for use on red cedar as well as redwood. Another method is to apply a couple of coats of a good-quality house paint in a reddish brown color that will approximate the color of the posts.

CLEANING ALUMINUM SIDING

I plan to repaint my white aluminum siding when the weather permits. Before painting, I would like to get it properly clean. Is there any special type of soap I should use?

No. Any moderate-strength soap or detergent will be okay.

REPAINTING ALUMINUM SIDING

Three years ago, our aluminum siding was painted. All the sides still look good, except the back. Facing south, this side gets most of the sun and the paint has begun to peel. I would like to repaint. How do I remove the peeling areas? What paint should I use?

Rub down the edges of the peeling areas with medium sandpaper wrapped around a block of wood. If you prefer, use the sanding-wheel attachment for your drill or a regular sander (which can get pretty heavy). Remove all edges down to where it's firm, solid paint. Then give it a good hosing, and when it's dry, put on your new paint. If you can get a good color match, we would suggest a good marine paint, made for exposure to sun and salt water.

GIVE IT A NEW ENGLAND LOOK

I wish to give my house that natural silvery gray appearance that I have seen on old shingled buildings which have been exposed to salt air along the New England seacoast. Can it be done?

There are a number of weathering and bleaching compounds on the market which speed the natural weathering process. Their final effect will depend upon the character of the product used. Bleaching oils are applied by either brush or spray.

OIL-TREATED SIDING

The front of our house has a redwood siding which the contractor treated with two coats of linseed oil. It has been 3 months since this was done, and the boards are still tacky and collect dust and dirt. What can be done to remedy this?

All surfaces that are treated with linseed oil should have all excess oil wiped off, not more than an hour or two after application. To remove the present semihardened oil, it will be necessary to wash the wood with steel wool and turpentine. If this procedure is not successful, use paint remover to take off the oil.

FADED REDWOOD

Two years ago we built our house, and it has a gable and two sides in a scalloped redwood trim. We did not finish the wood because it was late in the fall. In the spring the wood was given a coat of sealer and a coat of spar varnish. The original red color has now faded to a fawn color. We would like to restore it. Can you recommend a treatment we could use?

All redwood, when exposed to the weather, should be given a coat of redwood stain and spar varnish or a wood preservative preparation containing a redwood color. Remove the present finish down to the bare wood and finish with either material. The latter is preferred.

CHANGE COLOR OF REDWOOD SIDING?

Would it be possible to change the color of our redwood siding by applying a green stain? The present color is oil-base redwood stain.

You can change the color, but it may not come out the green you have in mind. First, consult your paint dealer and get a pigmented stain, either solid or semitransparent; the latter lets wood grain show through the color. Then brush out a sample on an obscure part to see if you like the results.

SHINGLE STAIN OVER PAINT?

The paint on our shingles has become so shabby and worn I must do something about it. Instead of repainting, I'd much like to have the shingles stained a cedar color. Is this a practical idea?

No, it's not the kind of thing you can do with stain. The only place you can use stain is on new shingles or over old stain; you never can use it over paint. As a matter of fact, if you insist on stain, it would be easier to put on new shingles than try to remove the present paint.

CRACKS IN GARAGE DOOR

I have a garage door that was varnished, and the veneer is cracked in spots. I would like to paint it. What would be the best way to go about it? What paint can be used on outdoor furniture?

The veneer may be cracked, but we assume it is not peeling. Fill all the cracks with wood putty. Directions for this will be found on containers of spackling compound. When the putty is hard and dry, smooth it by rubbing with sandpaper. If there is any gloss on the varnish, dull it by rubbing with "00" sandpaper and wipe off the dust. Finish with any good-quality house paint. Outdoor furniture should be painted with any well-known brand of enamel, recommended for outdoor use.

SUNNY SIDE ALSO CRACKING SIDE

In 18 years, my house has been painted four times—twice with oil-base, then twice with latex-type paint. The last time it was painted was three years ago. Now many fine-line cracks have developed, mostly on the south side. Why did this happen? Before repainting in the spring, what should I do to take care of these cracks?

The south side gets by far the most exposure to the sun, which is notoriously rough on paint. About all there is to do before repainting is to give those cracks a real good sanding. It's best if you sand them completely smooth. But if you can't manage this, at least wear them down enough so that you're sure they'll be filled with paint.

NAILHEADS SPECKLE SIDING

We had our house painted four years ago. Now it's time for another painting. But there are many nailheads which have turned rusty and speckle the siding. How should they be treated before the repainting?

If any are loose, pull them out and replace with rustproof nails. Sand down the others to get the really flaky rust off—not clear down to absolute bare, shiny metal (who can live so long?). Cover each with a dab of shellac or aluminum paint. Best of all, if you can, countersink each nailhead slightly; then smooth putty over it.

NORTH IS MOLDY SIDE

Why does the paint on our front porch always start turning moldy? This is on the north side, where it is always shady. We use good-quality porch and deck enamel.

There's nothing much you can do about the mold-producing conditions and the constant shade. However, next time you paint, have the dealer put some mildewcide in the paint, or buy a paint whose label claims it to be mildew-resistant. Painting the underside of the porch with aluminum paint will check rising ground dampness, which may contribute to the moldy conditions by saturating the floorboards.

FADED HOUSE NEEDS PAINT

My house is sided with asbestos siding, which has faded to a light gray and also looks dirty. I would like to paint it but do not know what type paint or what method to use. Could I use a roller, with a brush for the edges and corners the roller won't touch?

You can use either exterior latex paint or oil-base paint. Be sure to follow the label directions carefully. If your type siding is not mentioned on the paint you buy, be sure to ask the dealer for any special instructions. With latex paint, it may be just a case of one or two coats. With oil-base paint, it's wise to put on a coat of linseed oil, so that the dried-out material won't draw oil from the paint unevenly and give a blotchy look. This is not to say that oil-base exterior house paint won't make your house look very good; it certainly will. Using a roller and brush, as described, is okay.

SHINGLE STAIN

Can you tell me of a cheap method of staining wood shingles? All I want to do is to give them a dark-brown color. I do not care about the preserving part of it.

Coal-tar creosote is not expensive; but to obtain a better finishing stain, the following is advisable. Mix 4 gallons of raw linseed oil with 2 gallons of creosote oil and 1 gallon of japan drier. This will give a brown color. For a darker color add color-in-oil. Some buildings

Figure 1-13. Be sure that all nails are "set" (left) and puttied (right) before painting.

in rural areas have been coated with old crankcase oil, but this is sometimes unsatisfactory because the wood remains quite oily for a long time.

CREOSOTE STAIN THROUGH WHITE SHINGLES

Recently we moved into an old stone farmhouse. There is an addition at the back which is wood shingle. Originally the shingles were treated with creosote; now they are painted white. The brownish stain of the creosote is coming through the white and is unsightly. We would like to repaint, but have been told it would be useless because the same old thing would happen again. What do you suggest?

The Department of Agriculture recommends that shingles or other wood surfaces treated with creosote or creosote stains not be painted until they have weathered for several years. However, fairly good results have been obtained by coating the wood surface (first removing the present paint down to bare wood) with a good-quality exterior aluminum paint, allowing it to dry at least a week; then apply a second coat and allow this to dry for about a week. Finish with a topcoat of good exterior paint.

CHANGING COLOR OF SHINGLE

Can I spray an asbestos-shingled roof? I would like to change the color to white.

Can this be done? It is asbestos with small gravel on it.

The fact that the shingles are covered with "small gravel" makes them asphalt and not asbestos. Such shingles cannot be painted with ordinary paint, because the asphalt will bleed through the paint. You should use one of the bituminous roof coatings.

SHINGLES NEED PAINTING

Is it possible to paint the insulated-type shingles? They have become discolored on our cottage, but we do not want to go through all the work of taking them off. What type paint should we use?

It is perfectly possible to paint them. Use any top-quality paint for roofing, or use pigmented shingle stain. Don't skimp on paint quality, especially where it will have to take the roughest of all exposures up on the roof.

PAINTING A BRICK HOUSE

We are interested in painting our new brick house white. Could you give some information about it?

If the brick has never been painted before, you can coat it with a dampproof cement-base paint. It comes in powder form and is mixed with water. This might be desirable if the brick is comparatively soft and absorbs water. Absorption of water is not a problem with hard brick, and it can be painted with either the cement-base or rubber-base masonry paint. For good results, read the manufacturer's directions on the label, and follow them carefully.

PAINTING MORTAR

I recently bought a home which is part stone on the front. On the model home, the mortar between the stone was black, but on our home the lampblack wasn't put in the mortar. Is there anything we could put on the mortar to make it black?

Paint the mortar with an exterior masonry paint, following the manufacturer's instructions on the label carefully. Be sure to use a good-quality paint for good results.

POROUS BRICK WALLS

I have a ranch-type brick house with clapboard gables. These gables are painted with a self-cleaning paint. The brick is of a porous type. The absorbent brick contributes to a wet and damp basement. In wet weather water runs down the wall into the basement. The brick also absorbs the paint runoff and has become stained. What is the best way to clean and waterproof the brick?

To avoid or minimize further discoloration of the brick, discontinue the use of a self-cleaning paint. Such paint powders early, and the rain washes it down onto the brick surfaces. The clapboards will have to be painted more frequently, even when a good grade of ordinary house paint is used. Since the pigment has penetrated into the pores of the brick, it might be impossible to remove the stains, except by having the brickwork cleaned by sandblasting, done by a building-cleaning contractor. You might try the following methods: Wet the brick with clear water; then scrub it with a solution of trisodium phosphate or washing soda, using about 2 pounds to the gallon of hot water. After that, rinse with clear water. Wire-brushing might also help. Two coats of a liquid, transparent waterproofing can be applied on the brickwork. You should, however, make certain that the cause of leakage is not the mortar between the brick, Sandy mortar or breaks and cracks in the joints can cause water seepage.

PAINT STAINS BRICK SIDING

My home has brick siding with redwood siding on the second floor. The redwood is painted white. I have used excellent paints, but each one seems to run down and streak the brick. We tried acid to clean the brick but got no results. What can we do?

Brick is so porous that pulling out embedded paint is exceedingly tough. About all you can do is try the poultice method, which usually takes repeat performances, plus patience: Mix the poultice with liquid paint remover and powdered chalk or similar absorbent powder; cover the stains thickly. When the poultice is dry, brush it off and repeat the process. The idea is that the paint remover loosens the embedded paint and the powder blots it out. This is slow work. There's no reason, though, why you can't get an estimate from a sandblasting contractor. Sandblasting is fast.

REMOVING PAINT FROM BRICKS

We have an old brick home. Years ago, the owner painted part of the house with white paint. Is there anything we can do to get the paint off the red bricks?

Because of the porous nature of bricks, paint removal is very difficult. The best way is to have the paint sandblasted off (consult the classified telephone directory). Otherwise, a paste-type paint remover can be tried (which probably will not be completely and entirely successful), following the label directions as to use.

PAINTING BRICK WALL TO DEFLECT SUN'S RAYS

We own a brick-front ranch-type house and find that the bricks absorb the heat and hold it late into the night. We wondered if painting the front white would deflect the sun's rays and keep the wall cool? What kind of paint would we use for this job?

If the brick front faces west or south, painting the wall white (or any light color) will reflect the sun's rays and keep the house wall somewhat cooler. Insulation in these walls, especially the type combined with aluminum foil, will help even more. Use any good-quality latex paint, following the label directions carefully for application; be sure the surface is clean and free of soot, etc., before coating it with paint.

PAINTING GLAZED-TILE WALLS

Our foundation walls are of brown glazed tile. We would like to paint them to match the siding. What can we use that will stay on such tile?

The tile will have to be clean and the glaze scratched thoroughly with a very coarse sandpaper. Finish with a good brand of house paint. Success will depend on how dull you get the tile.

SPECIAL ROLLER FOR CONCRETE

I am having a new garage built with concrete block walls. I plan to paint it myself. A neighbor claims I must use a brush to work the paint thoroughly into the rough concrete surface. But isn't it possible to use a roller? It sure would be easier.

Rollers are made especially for concrete. They have a much longer nap, so that the paint will be forced into the crevices. You can use it perfectly well. To be on the safe side, keep an eye out for any missed spots.

PAINTING CONCRETE BLOCK GARAGE

Must I have my new concrete block garage painted with masonry paint? Or can I have it painted to match the latex paint on the house? Or could I put this latex paint on over a first coat of masonry paint?

Most "masonry" paint is the latex type anyway. So you could kill two birds with one stone by using masonry paint, providing you can get the color match. Otherwise, you can certainly put the latex house paint of the proper color right over as a second coat.

PAINTING STUCCO

My house is a combination concrete and portland cement stucco. Can I paint it with oil-base paint?

Oil-base paint can be used if the following precautions are observed: The concrete and stucco must be dry. After a rain, at least a week should pass before painting starts, and ample time should be allowed for the dampness of night to dry off. The free lime in new concrete will be destructive to paint oils and should be neutralized before painting or removed through at least one year of weathering. Lime in concrete is neutralized by soaking with a solution of zinc sulfate in water, 3 pounds to the gallon. The crystals are inexpensive and can be had at a paint store or from a dealer in mason's materials. The solution is applied liberally, allowed to soak in, and given several days for natural drying. The crystals that will then have formed on the surface should be brushed off.

CHIMNEY POSES PAINT PROBLEM

Our concrete block chimney has always been painted. We repainted it with latex-base paint and then found out the old paint was oil-base. Since then, big chunks of the rubber base have come off. Could we take off the rest with remover, then repaint with oil-base, to match the original paint? Or would we have to remove the old paint too?

The remover for the latex paint need not affect the oil-base paint at all. No problem there. Nor would you have to remove the original oil-base paint either.

PAINTING CONCRETE BLOCK FOUNDATION

Our unpainted concrete block foundation is an eyesore to us. Can this be painted to match the wood siding?

Latex paint can be applied to both wood and masonry surfaces, indoors and outdoors. Follow the manufacturer's instructions on the container.

LIMESTONE SIDEWALK

I would like some information about a limestone sidewalk which I laid from the rear of the house to the garage. I want to know if I could paint it with some kind of paint, something that I won't track into the house when it's dry.

Limestone is not an ideal stone for painting, particularly if it has been laid on the ground. The moisture in the ground may cause paint to peel. If you wish to take a chance, use a rubber-base floor paint.

PAINT SPOTS ON CONCRETE STEPS

While I was painting my white trim, some latex paint dripped down on the concrete steps. How can I get these spots out?

Scrub them with a strong solution of powerful cleanser—3 pounds to the gallon of hot water. Wear rubber gloves. If scrubbing isn't enough, make a thick poultice of this solution and powdered chalk, cornmeal, etc., and leave it on until dry. If needed, brush it off and repeat with another poltice. The idea is that the cleaning solution loosens the enbedded paint and the powder blots it out.

PAINT STAIN ON CEMENT

While painting a railing on the front steps, I spilled about half a can of green rust-inhibitive paint on the cement steps. I have gotten most of the paint off (using a liquid paint remover), but a green stain still remains. Is there any method of removing this stain?

Because of the porous nature of cement, complete removal of the stain may be impossi-

Figure 1-14. To remove splatter from concrete, scrub with solvent and stiff brush (left). Of course, the best way to prevent splatters is to use a drop cloth (right).

ble. We suggest trying a paste-type paint remover, or a thick paste made of dry trisodium phosphate mixed with twice as much whiting and moistened with water. The only other suggestion we can offer is to have a terrazzo-grinding machine grind off the surface.

SLATE WON'T WASH CLEAN

Our white slate siding now looks dirty and won't wash off clean. Before painting, is a base coat needed? Is any special treatment needed to keep nailheads from rusting?

Follow the label directions on the paint can for base coat recommendations. Some merely call for a thinned-down coat of the finish paint; others an individual undercoater. A dab of spar varnish over each nailhead will stop the rusting. If the nailheads are countersunk, smooth putty over them with a putty knife. With a little practice, this can go very quickly.

STEPS DON'T HOLD PAINT

The front steps of my house are of wood. They lead to an enclosed porch, with trellis sides at the foundation, giving plenty of air circulation under the steps. But they don't hold paint for any length of time. What do you suggest? I use top-quality deck enamel.

In spite of ample air circulation and venti-

lation under the steps, there may be ground moisture rising or cracks between the stair boards down which rain or snow drips and soaks into the wood. Remove all remaining paint down to bare wood. Fill any cracks between the boards with white lead or similar material to keep out water from above; run linseed oil into very narrow cracks. If possible, paint the underside of the steps with aluminum paint. Finish the upper surface with top-quality deck enamel, following the directions on the paint container carefully. Before refinishing the steps, cover the ground under the steps with overlapping sheets (about 6-inch overlap) of polyethylene plastic or roll roofing, to act as a vapor barrier to keep dampness from rising out of the earth.

CREOSOTE ON WOOD STEPS

I coated the underside of my new back steps with creosote, trying to combat ants and other insects. A considerable amount of creosote came through the top part of the steps. How am I going to cover the creosote so it won't show? I've already applied an undercoat and finish coat of paint, but the creosote comes through.

Hereafter, if you intend to paint or varnish a piece of outside woodwork and wish to preserve the wood, apply a chemical wood preservative—not creosote. However, remove the present paint; then apply a coat of stain sealer and finish with paint. Your paint dealer should be able to get the stain sealer for you.

NONSKID PORCH PAINT

What type paint should be used in repainting porch and steps to keep them from becoming slippery when wet?

Some paints are made for industrial plants to keep accident-prone sections of floor as nonskid as possible. But usually these are sold in large industrial quantities in big drums. You could ask your paint dealer about this. But a much simpler and very effective non-skidder is to add generous amounts of sand right into the paint can. Keep it stirred occasionally so it doesn't settle. You can also sprinkle sand over your wet paint, but it's much more apt to be tracked into the house.

VARNISHED PORCH FLOOR

I have an open porch that has a floor which was given two coats of varnish. After the rain and snow of the past winter, the floor is in very bad condition. How can it be refinished so that the floor can stand the weather this winter?

Varnish is not an ideal material for use on porch floors exposed to the weather all year round. Spar varnish may give you better results, but a more lasting finish can be obtained by coating the floorboards with a good brand of porch of deck paint.

PAINT PEELS OFF PORCH FLOOR

What is the reason for paint peeling or chipping from a porch floor, and how can I stop it from doing this? Just a year ago I had all the paint cleaned off down to the wood; then the floor was sized and repainted. The work was done during the best painting weather and with the best paint.

Ground moisture could be the cause of your difficulty, and there may be a lack of air circulation under the porch. Cover the ground with a moistureproof and vaporproof paper, overlapping the sheets at least 6 inches. Seal the laps with asphalt roof cement. Get plenty of air under the floor. If possible, coat the underside with aluminum paint.

PAINTING WINDOW FRAMES

Our outside window frames need painting. What is good for large cracks in the outside sills?

Fill the cracks with wood putty. Then sandpaper them level with the sill surface.

PAINTING WINDOWS

Our fairly old house has windows with many small panes, and I would appreciate any "tips" you might have in painting corners. I don't have a particularly steady hand, and I am afraid I might do an amateur-looking job.

We've run into this same problem ourselves and suggest using a liquid masking tape. You paint this generously where the glass and wood trim meet, getting it at least an inch or so on the glass. Then you simply paint over it, and when the paint has dried, you trim along the edge of the glass with a razor blade or sharp knife. The masking tape is then peeled off the glass, and you have a straight, professional-looking edge at the trim. Liquid masking tape is available at any paint or hardware store.

Figure 1-15. Another way to protect the window glass from paint is to stretch painters' masking tape along the edges of the window panes. When the paint is dry, tape can be pulled off, leaving a clean, sharp edge. Splatters on the glass can be wiped off when wet, or removed with a razor blade.

GLAZING COMPOUND CRACKS

Before having our house painted, the painter applied a good-quality glazing compound to our steel windows, where needed. This cracked and has been replaced, with the same results. Can you suggest a remedy?

A primer may not have been applied to the frames before putting on the glazing compound. Allow the compound to dry thoroughly before applying the primer.

RAIN-SPOTTED PAINT

Paint was put on our wood window trim quite heavily. On a couple of windows it rained right after painting, and the trim became terribly spotted. Can the trim be painted successfully without scraping it?

If the paint surface is pitted, it will be necessary to smooth it by going over the trim with "000" sandpaper; then wipe off the dust. All glossy surfaces should be made dull by rubbing with very fine sandpaper and steel wool. Wipe off the dust before painting. Paint supplied over glossy surfaces may develop hairline cracks and may even chip readily.

PAINTING WINDOW TRIM

We have a brick house at the seashore. We would like to paint the woodwork on the outside. The old paint is peeling like paper. I think it must be rubber-base paint. I would like to know the best paint I could use.

Peeling of paint from the window and door trims can be stopped by caulking all joints between the frames and brickwork. Use a caulking gun for the purpose. All paint should be removed down to the bare wood and the dry wood primed with a good brand of house paint, thinned according to the directions on the label.

SPRING BRINGS WINDOWSILL PROBLEM

We paint our picture windowsill every year. And every spring the paint peels. Last year I used a paint scraper on it and put two coats of paint, to no avail. Any ideas?

Most of the time, peeling is due to the wood getting damp under the paint. As the moisture works to the surface, it pushes paint off. Probably water is sneaking in the back way, through cracks or breaks in the caulking which is supposed to seal the joint where the window frame fits into the siding. Examine the caulking very carefully all around. If it isn't firm everywhere, especially if the caulking has been there for several years or so, then dig out the old stuff and replace the new.

WATER-DAMAGED WINDOWSILL

How can I repair an oak windowsill that has been badly damaged by water?

We're assuming the finish has been worn off and now there are dark water marks in the wood. Remove any remaining finish. If reasonable sanding doesn't remove the spots, use wood bleach (which can be obtained at a paint store). Restain the bleached spots to match. Sand them smooth, and wipe off sawdust with a turpentine-dampened cloth. Then apply a prime coat of fresh shellac, followed by finish coats of top-quality exterior (or marine) clear varnish.

PAINTING NEW GUTTERS

I have new gutters which are dirty, with all the paint off. Some advise putting iron paint inside, then a finish coat the same as the house. But I don't like using black iron paint; I'm afraid it will stain the light roof. What would be best?

We assume these are galvanized gutters. Apply a special primer made for galvanized metals, available at most paint dealers; follow the manufacturer's instructions, especially in regard to surface preparation. Then apply a good-quality finish coat to match the house. If there are wood gutters, give the inside surface a soaking coat of a chemical wood preservative. Then apply one or two coats of asphalt roof coating, being careful not to spatter it on painted surfaces because it is very difficult to remove.

PAINTING COPPER TROUGHS AND SPOUTS

I recently purchased a house more than 30 years old. The copper eave troughs and downspouts have never been painted; they look black. The rest of the house has been kept well painted. Will paint hurt the copper in any way?

Only a zinc paint will hurt the copper because of a chemical reaction between the two. Use a lead paint of good quality, applied in thin, even coats, allowing plenty of time between coats for thorough drying. And before painting, be sure to remove all surface dirt and soil with a wire brush or steel wool. Incidentally, the greater the tarnishing, the better the paint will adhere.

MOLDY-LOOKING COPPER SPOUTS

Is there anything I can do to copper spouting that is getting moldy-looking?

Dull and tarnished copper downspouts are in condition to be painted. First remove all surface grime, soot, dirt, etc., with a wire brush or clean steel wool. Then apply any good-quality house paint in a thin coat, allowing it to dry thoroughly, and then apply a second coat. If you wish to retain the natural copper color, apply two coats of spar varnish instead of paint.

BARBECUE COATED WITH RUST

The steel hood of our outdoor barbecue is really coated with rust. How can I get it off and then paint it properly?

Use any metal scraper, like a paint scraper, to get off the really loose flaky stuff. Then apply one of the rust-removing preparations now widely sold in hardware stores. Follow with a good metal primer and metal finish.

PORCH RAILING A MESS

My wide-board porch railing has been painted so many times it looks a mess—all cracks. How can I get the old paint off, and what can I do with the raw wood?

With so many coats, be prepared to use several applications of paint remover. Don't let any get on the floor or other places from where you don't want the paint accidentally removed. Paste-type remover will minimize this risk. We suggest a good exterior paint to complete the job.

PROTECTION OF ALUMINUM RAILINGS

Is there anything special I should do about my aluminum porch railings? A friend of mine, when he heard I'd bought a cottage near the ocean last fall, told me I'd have trouble with my aluminum railings in the salt air unless I protected them.

If they are made by a reputable manufacturer, the chances are that the aluminum has been either anodized or plated, and in either case, forget about it; you'll have no trouble. If the aluminum is of a cheap grade and not so treated, you should give the railings a coat of clear lacquer to keep the salt air from working on the metal. The only way to determine once and for all the quality of your aluminum is to ask the manufacturer or the dealer who sold those particular railings.

PAINT PEELS OFF METAL

Six months ago we purchased a five-year-old house. The redwood siding was painted with a good brand of brown house paint. The corners have galvanized metal covers, and now the paint is peeling off. Several boards are cracking. What can we do?

Scrape the paint off the metal and remove rust, if any, with steel wool and turpentine. Wash with vinegar; then apply a coat of rust-inhibitive paint, and when thoroughly dry, finish with house paint. The cracks in the boards should be filled with putty.

WIRE-LINK FENCE

Please advise me how to paint a wire-link fence. I have tried brush and roller and I had a hard time.

There is no simple and quick method of painting a fence. Spray painting would be fastest, but a fairly good amount of paint would be wasted. To keep any planting around the fence from becoming coated by the spray, hold a sheet of wallboard or plywood against the other side of the fence when painting. Hold the nozzle at an angle to get a wider spread.

PAINT ON CANVAS DECK

I have a canvas-deck porch which faces south. During the summer it is a target of intense heat. I have painted the canvas with regular porch and deck paint, but the paint cracks and chips off. Will a rubber-base floor paint remedy this condition?

We think that the condition is due to an accumulation of many coats of paint. Remove as much of it as possible; then use the same paint as in the past, putting it on in two thin coats. Use a light-colored paint, such as gray; it will not absorb as much heat. We do not think the rubber-base floor paint would prevent cracks and chipping.

Safety Precautions

The most dangerous phase of exterior house painting is when you are on the ladder. For safety's sake observe the following precautions:

1. Make sure that the ladder is not defective. Check the rungs and side rails carefully. Check any ropes and pulleys also to make sure that they are securely fastened and work properly.
2. Be sure that the ladder is positioned firmly—both on the ground and against the house. Set the foot of the ladder away from the wall one-forth of the distance to the point of support. If you use scaffolding, make sure that it is secure.
3. Always face the ladder when climbing up or down. Hold on with both hands. Carry tools and supplies in your pocket, or haul them up with a line.
4. Be sure that the paint bucket, tools, and other objects are secure when you are on a ladder or scaffolding. Falling objects can injure persons walking below.
5. Do not overreach when painting. Move the ladder frequently rather than risk a fall. A good rule is to keep your belt buckle between the rails.
6. Lean toward the ladder when working. Keep one hand free—ready to grab the ladder just in case.
7. Watch out for and avoid any electrical wiring within the area of work. This is especially important if you are using a metal ladder.
8. No matter where the job is, avoid setting

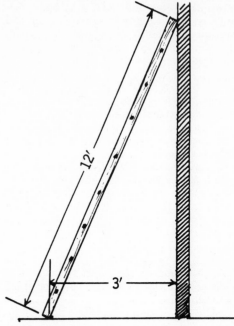

Figure 1-16. The safest angle for a ladder is to place its feet about a quarter of its length away from the wall.

the ladder up in front of a door, for if someone opens the door, down you go. If you must work in front of a door, then have a helper stand in front of the locked door.

Sooner or later, everybody gets bitten by the redecorating bug. Whatever the reason, there is a well-known, logical sequence you can follow which will present the least disruption to your normal living routine and will let you get the job done in minimum time. For example, once you get started with actual painting, you want to push right on without interruptions. This means that all the wall and ceiling areas not only must be clean and ready, but must be accessible; the more elbowroom you have to operate in, the better.

Start by dispossessing everything for which you can find temporary parking space in another part of the house. *Exception:* If your bookcases don't need repainting, you can leave the books; but tape newspapers or brown wrapping paper over the shelves to protect them against stray spatters.

Things which can't be moved out, because of size or lack of temporary storage space—such as heavy upholstered furniture, a grand piano, or a massive table—can be moved to the center of the room and covered with a drop cloth. Incidentally, an ample supply of drop cloths, or their equivalent, is absolutely vital if you have to protect wall-to-wall carpeting, and at least highly desirable in all other cases.

The other items needed for indoor painting are shown here. While brushes are shown, you may use a roller if desired. Indoor spray painting is not generally done by the homeowner, except for small jobs using pressurized cans of paint.

For speed and convenience, use a roller on the walls, ceilings, and other large surfaces, and then use a brush at corners, along edges, and in other places that you cannot reach with a roller. Woodwork is usually painted with a brush. Special-shaped rollers and other applicators are available for painting woodwork, corners, edges, and other close places. Some may work fine; others, not so well. You may find that a small brush is still best for such work.

Paint Selection

As with exterior paints, many different kinds and formulations of paints and other finishes are available for interior use. And new ones frequently appear on the market. Use Table 4 as a general guide in making your selection.

For a more specific selection consult your paint dealer. Reputable paint dealers keep

CHAPTER 2

INTERIOR PAINTING

abreast of the newest developments in the paint industry and stock the newest formulations. "Dripless" paint is an example of a fairly recent development. It has a jelled consistency in the can, but it loses that form when picked up on a brush or roller and spreads evenly and smoothly. It is particularly convenient when painting a ceiling.

The usual interior paint job consists of painting wallboard or plaster walls and ceilings, woodwork, and wood windows and doors. For these surfaces you need to choose first between solvent-thinned paint (commonly called oil-base paint) and water-thinned paint (commonly called latex paint, but not necessarily latex), and then between a gloss, semigloss, or flat finish. (Enamels, which are made with a varnish, or resin, base instead of the usual linseed oil vehicle, are included under the broad oil-paint grouping.) Oil-base paints are very durable, are highly resistant to staining and damage, can withstand frequent scrubbings, and give good one-coat coverage.

Many latex paints are advertised as having similar properties.

Both oil-base paint and latex paint are now available in gloss, semigloss, and flat finishes. Glossy finishes look shiny and clean easily. Flat finishes show dirt more readily but absorb light and thus reduce glare. Semigloss finishes have properties of both glossy and flat finishes. Because enamel is durable and easy to clean, semigloss or full-gloss enamel is recommended for woodwork and for the walls of kitchens, bathrooms, and laundry rooms. For the walls of nurseries and other playrooms, either oil-base or latex semigloss enamel paint is suggested. Flat paint is generally used for the walls of living rooms, dining rooms, and other nonwork or nonplay rooms.

Color Styling

As for the colors themselves, this is such a private matter we wouldn't think of making suggestions. But if you're in doubt, there's lots of free advice available. We're not referring to

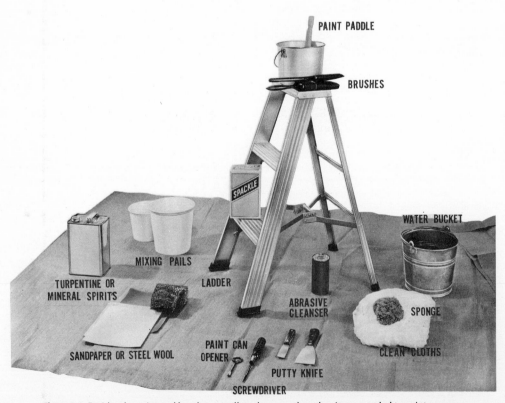

Figure 2-1. Besides the paint and brushes or rollers, here are the other items needed to paint a room.

Table 4. Guide for Selecting Interior Paint

	Flat enamel	Semigloss enamel	Gloss enamel	Interior varnish	Shellac-lacquer	Wax (liquid or paste)	Wax (emulsion)	Stain	Wood sealer	Floor varnish	Floor paint or enamel	Aluminum paint	Sealer or undercoater	Metal primer	Latex (wall) flat	Latex gloss and sealer
Masonry:																
Asphalt tile							X									
Concrete floors						X.	X.	X			X				X	
Kitchen and bathroom walls		X.	X.										X			X.
Linoleum							X									
New masonry	X.	X.											X		X	X.
Old masonry	X	X											X	X	X	X.
Plaster walls and ceiling	X.	X.											X		X	X.
Vinyl and rubber tile floors						X	X									
Wallboard	X.	X.											X		X	X.
Metal:																
Aluminum windows	X.	X.										X		X	X.	X.
Heating ducts	X.	X.										X		X	X.	X.
Radiators and heating pipes	X.	X.										X		X.	X.	X.
Steel cabinets	X.	X.												X		X.
Steel windows	X.	X.										X		X	X.	X.
Wood:																
Floors					X	X	X.	X.		X.	X.					
Paneling	X.	X.		X	X	X		X	X						X.	X.
Stair risers	X.	X.		X				X	X							X.
Stair treads					X			X	X	X	X					
Trim	X.	X.		X	X	X		X					X		X.	X.
Windowsills				X												

X. Black dot indicates that a primer or sealer may be necessary before the finishing coat.

the neighborly kind, but to books on decorating, folders you can get at the paint store, color styling books at the wallpaper and flooring dealers, as well as countless articles in the home and garden type of shelter magazines.

However, many color stylists suggest that a room facing south or west should be painted with cool colors, such as blue or green, and rooms facing north will look warmer if painted with members of the red, orange, or yellow families. Also light colors make a small room seem larger. Conversely, dark colors make an overly large room appear smaller. Bright walls in a large room detract from otherwise decorative furnishings. Furthermore, ceilings appear lower when darker than the walls and higher when lighter than the walls.

Another point: If the room you're painting is to be used mainly at night, then look at your samples in your night lighting—not by daylight. Remember that paint generally dries to a slightly different color or shade. For a fast preview of the final color, brush a sample swatch of the paint on a piece of clean, white blotting paper. The blotting paper will immediately absorb the wet gloss, and the color on the paper will be about the color of the paint when it dries on the wall.

Estimating the Amount of Paint Needed. Be sure to buy the right amount of paint by estimating the quantity needed for the job. Compute the number of square feet to be painted and compare it to the coverage given on the paint can label. Buy a little too much rather than too little. For the walls: add width and length of room, multiply by 2, and multiply by height. Then divide by paint coverage on the can label. For ceilings: multiply length by width, and divide by coverage. This will give you the number of gallons you'll need for the job.

Preparing the Surface

Don't just hide a bad surface—correct it. Repair, clean, and/or prime every surface before painting. Proper surface preparation is the secret of a good paint job. You can't hide a bad surface because sooner or later a bad surface will ruin a paint job. Inadequate surface preparation is the biggest single reason why paints sometimes fail to perform proper-

ly. Also be sure to read the label on the paint can before you start painting; it may contain additional or special instructions for preparing the surface.

New Surfaces. New plaster walls should not be painted with oil-base paint until they have thoroughly cured—usually after about 2 months. And then a primer coat should be applied first. If it is necessary to paint uncured plaster, apply one coat only of a latex paint or primer. Latex, or water-base, paint will not be affected by the alkali in new plaster and will allow water to escape while the plaster dries. Subsequent coats of paint—either oil-base or latex—can be added when the plaster is dry. Unpainted plaster readily picks up and absorbs dirt and is difficult to clean. The one coat of latex paint or primer will protect it.

For new dry wall, a latex primer or paint is recommended for the first coat. Solvent-thinned paints tend to cause a rough surface. After the first coat of latex paint, subsequent coats can be of either type. Clean or dust new surfaces before you apply the first coat of primer or paint.

Old Surfaces. The first step is to inspect the surface for cracks and mars. Fill small hairline cracks with spackle or spackling compound and larger cracks with special patching plaster. Follow the directions on the container label when using the patching material. When the patch is completely dry, sand it smooth and flush with the surrounding surface.

Nailheads tend to "pop out" in wallboard walls and ceilings. Countersink the projecting heads slightly and fill the holes with spackling compound. Sand the patch smooth when it is dry. It is desirable to prime newly spackled spots, particularly if you are applying only one coat.

Next, clean the surface of dirt and grease. A dry rag or mop will remove dust and some dirt. You may have to wash the surface with a household cleanser to remove stubborn dirt or grease.

Kitchen walls and ceilings are usually covered with a film of grease from cooking (which may extend to the walls and ceilings just outside the entrances to the kitchen), and bathroom walls and ceilings may have steamed-on dirt. The grease or dirt must be removed—the new paint will not adhere to it. To remove the grease or dirt, wash the surface with a strong household cleanser, turpentine, or mineral spirits.

Figure 2-2. *Start with a clean surface.* A thorough dusting of the surfaces to be painted is usually enough. But kitchen walls—or badly soiled or glossy surfaces—should be washed to remove dirt and grease and dull the surface. Wash from bottom up with an abrasive cleaner or a solution of trisodium phosphate. Rinse with clean, warm water.

The finish on kitchen and bathroom walls and ceiling is usually a gloss or semigloss. It must be "cut" so that the new paint can get a firm hold. Washing the surface with household cleanser or turpentine will dull the gloss, but for best results, rub the surface with fine sandpaper or steel wool. After using sandpaper or steel wool, wipe the surface to remove the dust.

Calcimine, whitewash, and cold-water paint formerly required complete removal by scrubbing with hot water before applying more lasting paint. There are now, however, special paints formulated to apply over calcimine and other chalk-based coatings. These paints are clearly labeled for the purpose.

Woodwork. Woodwork (windows, doors, and baseboards) usually has a glossy finish. First wash the surface to remove dirt and grease, and then sand it lightly to "cut" the finish so that the new paint can get a good hold. After sanding, wipe the surface to remove the dust.

You can buy liquid preparations that will soften hard, glossy finishes to provide good adhesion for the new paint. If there are any bare spots in the wood, touch them up with an undercoater or with pigmented shellac before you paint.

Painting the Room

With the room in order, equipment at hand, and surfaces prepared, you're ready for the actual painting. If you plan to paint both the walls and the ceiling, start with the ceiling. A single ladder will do, but two stepladders holding a long plank will allow you to cover more area quickly, comfortably, and safely. Use a strong plank and be sure the ladder legs are firmly placed on the floor.

Before starting any of the painting, read the label on the paint can most carefully. This

Figure 2-3. The use of plank and ladders for ceiling work.

is especially important today, when you can select from a wide variety of improved paint products that may call for specific methods of application. For best results always follow directions exactly. Also be sure to stir the paint thoroughly. Even if it has been mechanically shaken, paint or enamel should be well mixed just before using. Stir rapidly, working the pigment up from the bottom of the can. Remember that for an easier and better paint job, do the painting when the room temperature is comfortable for work—between 60 and 70°F. And provide good cross ventilation both to shorten the drying time and to remove fumes and odors.

While either a roller or a brush can be used to paint a ceiling, most people find a roller easier and faster. In either case, you'll need a small brush to get into the corners between the ceiling and wall. Paint in 2- or 3-foot strips across the shortest dimension of the ceiling. This will enable you to paint the next strip before the last edge is dry. Joining on a dry edge sometimes leaves a lap mark that will show later. Light strokes help to eliminate lap marks. Also, to avoid skips, always try to begin near the windows and work back into the darker part of the room. Reflections on the wet paint will make it easier to see if the surface is being uniformly covered.

When using a brush for wall work, be sure to dip the bristles only one-third their

Figure 2-5. When painting walls with a brush, dip the bristles only one-third their length into the paint and tap the brush gently against the inside edge of the can to release dripping paint. Starting at the ceiling line, paint down in 3-foot strips, brushing from the unpainted into the painted area. Flat paint should be applied in wide overlapping arcs. When a few square feet have been covered, "lay off" with parallel upward strokes.

length into paint and tap the brush gently against the inside edge of the can to release dripping paint. Starting at the ceiling line, paint down in 3-foot strips, brushing from the unpainted into the painted area. Flat paint should be applied in wide overlapping arcs. When a few square feet have been covered, "lay off" with parallel upward strokes.

When using a roller for wall work, pour a little paint into the deep end of the tray. Work the paint into the roller by moving it back and forth in the tray until the paint is evenly distributed around the roller. Move the roller across the wall in slow, smooth strokes, working first in one direction, then in another. Quick strokes and heavy, uneven pressure may cause bubbles or spatters. Apply paint from top to bottom as recommended for brushing. By the way, when using latex paint, wash your brush or roller occasionally with water. A buildup of the quick-drying paint in the nap of the roller or at the base of the bristles of the brush could cause excessive dripping. Wipe up spilled, splattered, or dripped paint as you go along. Paint is easier to clean up when wet.

It must be remembered that enamels and semigloss or gloss paints are flowed on more generously and with less pressure than flat

Figure 2-4. Painting the ceiling with a roller.

paints. Completing a small area at a time, brush on the paint with horizontal strokes; then level off with even, vertical strokes. Work quickly, and never try to go back and touch up a spot that has started to set.

Painting window sash calls for patience and a steady hand. Make the job easier by stretching painter's masking tape along the edges of the windowpanes before painting. When the paint is dry, the tape can be pulled off, leaving a clean, sharp edge. Spatters on glass can be wiped off when they are wet—or removed with a razor blade. When actually painting a window, first adjust it so you can paint the lower part of the upper sash. Then raise the upper sash almost to the top to finish painting it. The lower sash comes next. With the window open slightly at top and bottom, it can be finished easily. Paint the recessed part of the window frame next, then the frame, and the windowsill last.

When painting a door, do the frames first. Then paint the top, back, and front edges of the door itself. If the door is paneled, paint panels and panel molding first, starting at the top. Keep a clean cloth handy to wipe off any paint that gets on the area surrounding the panels. Paint the rest of the door last, starting at the top.

The baseboards are always painted last. A cardboard or plastic guard held flush against the bottom edge of the baseboard will protect the floor and prevent picking up dirt in the brush. Do not let paper or drop cloth touch the baseboard before the paint is dry.

Don't let the paint dry out in the can or in brushes or rollers between jobs or during long interruptions in a job. After each job, replace the can lid, making sure that it is on tightly, and clean brushes or rollers. During long interruptions in a job, also replace the can lid, and either clean brushes or rollers or suspend them in water or proper solvent.

Natural Finishes for Trim. Some doors are attractive in their natural finish. However, they will discolor and soil easily unless protected. Your paint dealer can offer suggestions on how to finish and protect your doors. Many kinds of finishing products are now on the market, and new ones often appear.

The first step in finishing doors is to obtain the proper color tone. This is usually

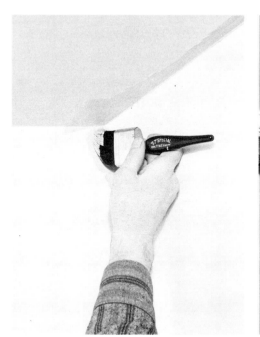

Figure 2-6. Before using a roller, paint the corner and the area next to the ceiling and baseboard with a brush (left) or a paint pad (right).

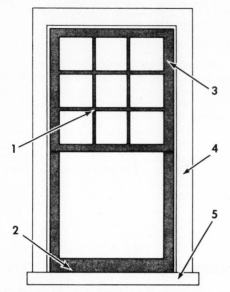

Figure 2-7. Paint windows in this order: (1) Mullions; (2) horizontal of the sash; (3) verticals of the sash; (4) verticals of the frame; and (5) horizontal frame and sill.

acquired by staining. However, sometimes no staining is required—the preservative finish is enough to bring out the desired color tone. With new doors, to help you make a decision, you can experiment on the trimmings or shavings.

The next step is sealing. One coat of shellac is usually adequate. When the shellac is dry, the surface should be sanded smooth, wiped free of dust, and varnished. Rubbing the surface with linseed oil, as is done in furniture finishing, provides a nice soft finish, but requires more work. Also, surfaces so finished collect dust more readily.

For a natural finish of other interior trim, you need to specify the desired kind and grade of wood at the time of construction. This can add substantially to the construction costs.

Questions and Answers

Let's take a look at some of the questions about interior painting that people often ask and some answers that may solve their problems.

PREPARING FOR PAINTING

We are planning to redecorate our kitchen and bathroom soon and would like your advice on how we should prepare the walls and wooden kitchen cabinets for new enamel. They now have a very heavy high-gloss enamel. In the past I have cleaned the cabinets with a preparation that is a cleaner and polish, leaving a protective wax film. What, if anything, is required to remove this film?

All surfaces should be washed down with a solution of trisodium phosphate or washing soda, using about a cupful of it in a pail of warm water. A fresh solution should be made up when the first becomes thoroughly discolored. A thorough rinsing with clear water should follow in order to remove all traces of the solution. After the walls have dried thoroughly, dull whatever gloss may remain on the walls and cupboards by rubbing with "000" sandpaper wrapped around a block of wood. Wipe off all dust before painting.

WHAT ORDER FOR ROOM PAINTING?

Is there any particular order to follow when painting a room?

Here's the order: Ceiling first, walls second, woodwork third, floors last. If the floor is to be varnished, protect it with drop cloths so that you don't have to be constantly on the alert to wipe up stray spots and splashes.

PAINT PEELING ON WALLS

I have painted plaster walls in my sewing room, and the paint is peeling and scaling off the walls, not the ceiling. I have always used top-grade paint. I would like to repaint this room. What do you suggest?

Peeling paint is usually due either to moisture working its way through the paint from the wall underneath or to poor adhesion on a glossy or improperly cleaned surface. Moisture in the wall spaces may be due to leaks from the roof, chimney flashings, window flashings, window joints, attic condensation, etc. Possible leak sources should be checked and repaired. Wipe the present painted surface with fine steel wool and turpentine to remove any trace of grease, wax, soot, etc., and to dull any gloss. Then apply top-quality paint, following the instructions on the container about thinning, etc.

PAINT PEELING ON OUTSIDE WALL OF ROOM

I wish to repaint a room painted some years ago with a water-base wall paint. Several places on one wall (outside) are peeling. I am sure there is no moisture in the wall. How can I treat the places that are peeling? Is it necessary to remove all the paint? Most of it is very tight. Can I use an oil-base paint over the water-base paint?

If there is no moisture in this wall, we suspect that this plaster may have been applied directly to an exterior masonry wall (brick, stucco, etc.), creating a condensation problem when warm house air touches a cooler masonry surface. If this is the case, and you do not wish to build a false wall (plasterboard on 1-inch furring strips), after scraping off all loose or flaking paint and cleaning the wall surfaces thoroughly (no trace of wax, grease, or soot should remain), spray shellac over the peeling areas. Oil-base paint can be applied over water-base; an important consideration, however, is that the surface be absolutely clean and free of any foreign matter and that the old paint adhere tightly and smoothly all over.

PAINT PEELS OFF WALLS

I live in a basement apartment. In several places the finish coat of paint has peeled off and the plaster beneath has effloresced. If I replace the plaster, what can I use to resist the dampness before putting on a new coat of finish paint? Is there a way of repairing this condition without replacing the plaster completely?

When plaster effloresces, there is moisture in it. In this case, it is evidently coming through the foundation walls from the damp ground outside. The only possible remedy is to dampproof the outside of the foundation walls. Patching is only a stopgap, and there is no way of waterproofing lime or gypsum plaster. You might, of course, remove all the old plaster; then replaster the walls with a waterproof portland cement mortar.

WATER STAINS ON WALLS AND CEILING

Our upstairs area has two finished rooms. One of them has walls and ceilings of pulpboard with 2-inch-wide molding strips about 26 inches apart. The pulpboard has a white finish, but there are stains from a roof leak which has been stopped. My problem is to cover the stains and paint the surfaces. What would you recommend?

Coat the surfaces with a primer sealer;

then finish with any good grade of latex or alkyd resin wall paint.

STREAKING WALLS

After we painted our living room, the walls appeared streaky. How can I cure this streaking effect?

Streaking walls are usually caused by spreading the paint over too large of an area. This results in skips in the paint film and allows the old color to show through. Streaking can also be caused by applying the paint in strips. Paints should *not* be stretched beyond the coverage stated on the label. Skips can be touched up if they are not too extensive. Streaking may also be due to inadequate mixing, which may leave an uneven concentration of color pigment in the can. The only solution to the problem is to repaint the entire surface, using a new can of paint which has been thoroughly mixed.

MUDDY STREAKS ON PAINT SURFACE

The walls of my newly painted kitchen have gray and muddy streaks on them. What caused this?

Gray or muddy streaks in the paint film are usually caused by a failure to wash very dirty or greasy surfaces. Grime and greasy surfaces must be thoroughly washed with a household cleaner and rinsed before painting.

PAINTING CEILING WITH RADIANT HEAT

I have radiant electric heating cables in my ceiling. Is it necessary to have a special paint for this ceiling or will an oil-base flat wall paint do?

Flat paint would be satisfactory, though an alkyd base might be better than oil since it is less apt to discolor. There is not sufficient surface heat developed to injure the paint itself. We assume you will use a light shade of paint, as it will reflect more heat into the room.

PAINTER'S CLOTH OR CANVAS

I have heard that a painter's cloth or canvas can be put on plaster walls that have a tendency to develop many small cracks, and that it is put up like wallpaper. What is painter's cloth or canvas? Where can it be obtained? Would muslin or unbleached sheeting do? What paste or glue should be used? What paints can be used over it?

The material is handled by wallpaper dealers. The cloth or canvas is a specially treated and "filled" fabric made for the purpose mentioned above. Ordinary cotton fabrics will not do. Wallpaper paste is generally used for the application of this material. Any type of paint can be used.

CLEANING UNPAINTED PLASTER WALLS

I have been using a small room with unpainted plaster walls as a sewing and "work" room. The walls have become quite dingy. Is there any way to clean them?

If the walls are dingy from an accumulation of dust, they could be cleaned with a wallpaper cleaner (after first vacuuming the surfaces). This is a doughlike substance available at paint and wallpaper dealers. It is rolled, not rubbed, over soiled surfaces. If the plaster is stained and badly sooted, cleaning is not possible. Painting or wallpapering is advisable.

UNPAINTED PLASTER WALLS

I have plastered walls that have never been painted. I would like to paint them soon, and would like to know the best way to patch the cracks. Do I have to put on any kind of base paint before I paint the walls?

Small cracks can be filled with a spackling compound, on sale at most paint stores. Large cracks should be cut open down to the lath and widened. After all loose particles are brushed out, the interior of the groove should be well dampened with water; then the cracks should be filled with patching plaster. Directions on mixing, etc., will be found on the box. If the plaster is to be painted with an oil-base wall paint, it should first be given a coat of primer sealer. When water-mixed paints are to be used, the primer sealer can be omitted.

TO SIZE OR NOT TO SIZE?

We have just had one of those shells put up as a start on our second home, and I plan to finish off the interior as time and funds permit. I am going to have painted dry wall, and my question is this: Will it be necessary to size these walls before I paint them?

It all depends on what type paint you use. If it is one of the oil-base variety, yes, you should definitely size the walls first, to avoid a possible blotchy appearance. If the paint is the latex type, sizing is not necessary.

PAINT IS CHECK-MARKED

Our kitchen walls and ceiling are all checked from previous coats of paint. What can be done without removing previous paint down to the plaster?

If the checking does not go through all the coats of paint, you might be able to get a smooth finish by rubbing down the walls with a piece of No. 1 sandpaper, wrapped around a block of wood; then finish rubbing with "000" snadpaper. Wipe off the dust and repaint.

CRACKING PAINT

The paint on my kitchen and dining room walls and ceilings has many cracks or lines in it. The rooms are separated from each other and were painted about four years ago, one with semigloss and one with flat paint, both of good quality. I want to repaint soon. What process do I follow to eliminate the cracks?

This condition is what is known as "alligatoring." It occurs when paint has been applied to a finished surface without first dulling the gloss or when a coat of paint has been applied on top of one that hasn't dried thoroughly. Rub down the present paint surfaces with fine steel wool and turpentine; if the cracks are a fine hairline type, the new paint coating will fill them. Be sure the surface is absolutely clean—completely free of any trace of wax, grease, etc.—before painting.

SMALL DENTS IN WALLS

We are converting an old storage room to a bedroom. The plaster walls have small dents all over. We want to paint the walls. How can these dents be filled?

Spackle, which is available ready-mixed or in powder form at paint and hardware dealers, can be used to fill the dents. Be sure the wall surface is thoroughly cleaned and free of all trace of soot and grime before applying the paint.

PAINT WASHES OFF

Six months ago we purchased a prefabricated house, about ten years old. All the interior is painted with what seems to be a water type of flat paint. After six months of wiping off bathroom and kitchen walls, this paint has almost all come off. There are some spill marks showing where the paint has worn thin. Do you know of any way these walls can be cleaned, short of sanding? My husband claims a good grade of semigloss paint will solve the problem.

If the paint adhered to the plaster without blisters or stickiness, your husband's idea should work out satisfactorily. But since you suspect the old paint was of the water-base variety, we suggest the application of a varnish size (not ordinary varnish) over the present surface first. Only a gloss or semigloss enamel or wall paint should be used in the kitchen and bathroom. Of course, a number of factors may cause paint to wash off on a cloth when washed or film removed completely when washed: (1) applying flat paints over a glossy surface without proper preparation; (2) washing with a very strong detergent or highly abrasive cleaners; (3) washing too soon after application; and (4) applying paint to a surface that is less than 50°F.

GLOSS DIFFERENCES

There is a difference in the sheen or gloss on my bathroom wall. What caused it?

Nonuniform gloss or sheen difference is usually caused by insufficient mixing of the paint before application, or application over a porous surface. Uneven application of paint can cause nonuniform gloss too.

ENAMEL ENAMEL?

The kitchen in the house we just moved into is enameled white. I would like to do it over. Can I put enamel over the present enamel?

If the present enamel is adhering tightly to the wall surface all over, and is smooth, a new enamel coating can be put over it. First, however, remove all grease, wax, soot, etc., from the wall using fine steel wool and turpentine; this should also dull the gloss; the gloss should be dulled to ensure tighter adhesion of the new paint. Be sure to use top-quality enamel for best results.

GREASE SPOTS ON WALL PAINT

Please tell me how I can remove grease spots from flat paint behind the kitchen stove. Several detergents have been tried, but to no avail.

In the first place, flat wall paint should never be used in the kitchen or bathroom. It holds moisture, grease, and dirt, which penetrate the surface. A gloss or semigloss enamel should be used in these two rooms. To take off

Figure 2-8. Enamels and semigloss or gloss paints can be spread on more generously and with less pressure than flat paints. Completing a small area at a time, brush on the paint with horizontal strokes, then level off with even vertical strokes. Work quickly and never try to go back and touch up a spot that has started to set.

the grease, apply a mixture of powdered whiting and a nonflammable liquid spot remover. The paste should be at least $\frac{1}{4}$ inch thick. When dry, brush off the powder and repeat the procedure if necessary. This treatment is not advisable on freshly painted walls.

HAIR OIL ON FLAT WALL PAINT

In attempting to remove a picture from the wall over the fireplace, I accidentally struck my head against the wall, and the hair oil on my head left a grease spot. The wall is coated with a flat wall paint. Is there anything we can do to remove the stain? We have tried various cleaners.

Try the following: Make a paste by mixing powdered whiting and a nonflammable liquid spot remover. Put this over the spot in a thick layer and allow it to remain until dry. Brush off the powder, and repeat the treatment if necessary.

PAINTING OVER WALLPAPER

Is it possible to paint over wallpaper? What type of paint, and with a brush or roller? Our paper was glue-sized when applied, and the seams are lapped.

If the wallpaper has lapped (ridged) seams, the paint job will have a rough, amateurish effect. Wallpaper with butted joints (no ridges) may be painted over. Only paper that is firmly attached can be painted over; there is always the chance that the paste will soften and the paper peel off. Use either a good-quality flat wall paint or a vinyl plastic latex paint, applied with either brush or roller; first be sure the surface is free of all grease, wax, grime, etc. Do the job when the air is dry, so that the liquid part of the paint will evaporate quickly.

PAINTED WALLPAPER

We painted our ceiling with a latex-base paint over wallpaper. The wallpaper has come off in places, and we would like to remove it all so that we could repaint. Water doesn't seem to penetrate at all. Can you advise what to do?

You will have to "scratch" the paint film to get the water to penetrate into the paper itself. Rubbing with a very coarse sandpaper wrapped around a block of wood will do the job. Soak the paper thoroughly with warm water, and keep it that way until the paste behind it has softened. Some wallpaper and paint dealers sell a wallpaper-removing preparation to be added to the water to give it better penetration. After removing the paper, wash the surface with warm water to remove paste and glue sizing from the plaster. A rented portable wallpaper steamer is very effective.

DRY OUT WALLS BEFORE PAINTING

The top-floor closet walls are damp (and cold in winter). I have removed the old painted-over wallpaper. But before I repaint, I would like to know if there is anything I should do to these walls. I don't want the paint to peel.

Since the rest of the walls are apparently dry, mainly because they are exposed to constant living-space heat and air circulation, you'll greatly help the situation by opening the closet doors and letting a lot more heat in. Leaving an electric light bulb turned on, located down low, near the baseboard, will help even more to dry out the walls. Or you can fasten stiff insulation board on the outside wall to check any possible leaks.

"SMALLPOX" WALLS AFTER PAPER REMOVED

We bought a four-room bungalow that has painted wallpaper on the walls. When we removed the paper, it took some of the finish plaster off, leaving an effect something like smallpox. I tried a sealer and a coat of paint on a section of wall, but can't get away from the hole effect. What can I use to cover these small holes? I wouldn't like to use sand paint.

Spackle can be used to get a smooth wall surface; this will easily fill small holes and depressions and cracks. This is available at paint and hardware dealers in powder form or ready-mixed paste.

PAINT CHIPS

We steamed all the wallpaper from our bedroom walls. We washed the walls but did not get all the glue off. We didn't put on a prime coat. Two coats of a base wall paint were put on, and we were told it would cover anything. You can see streaks of glue all over now, and the paint has started to chip. Can you tell me what to do?

Since the paint is comparatively new, it would be best to scrape off the glue spots and streaks with a putty knife or "000" sandpaper. After wiping off the dust, touch up the spots with the same type of paint.

CEILING DEVELOPED STREAKS

Our house is three years old. Last year, black streaks began showing up across the ceiling. I traced the course, and found that the streaks occurred in the area where water flows to the tank; the pipe is alongside a beam. Before I repaint, how can I hide this streaking?

A coat of aluminum paint is usually excellent at stopping other colors from working through paint. Fastening a strip of insulating tape over the pipe, to cover it completely, will help greatly to reduce any dampness caused by condensation (which could have caused the problem).

KNOTTY PINE PANELING CARE

Recently I purchased an 18-year-old house. The knotty pine paneling in the basement was badly soiled. How should this be cleaned? Can it be lightened in tone without too much work? After it is cleaned, how can it be beautified and protected against future soiling?

To clean, if the surface is waxed, try washing down an inconspicuous area with turpentine to learn if paste was used. If liquid self-polishing wax had been used, use a wax

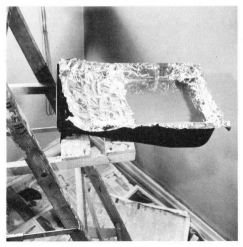

Figure 2-9. Line your roller tray with aluminum foil to save cleanup time (left). A section of screen helps avoid lumps in paint (right).

remover and "000" steel wool (available in housewares stores). Or one of the wax-base floor-cleaning preparations can be used. Cleaning cloths should be changed frequently to get good results. To lighten in tone, the present finish must be removed. Then bleach the wood with commercial wood bleach, following the label directions. After that use a stain of the desired shade. There are many ways to finish wood paneling. For a light, natural finish, use clear lacquer, semigloss varnish, or white shellac, thinned half-and-half with denatured alcohol. Or use one of the new wax stains for wood. Dealers in wood-finishing materials have these available.

FINISHING KNOTTY PINE WALLS

We are considering putting in knotty pine paneling in our living room. Does this wood darken? Is it difficult to finish the walls?

All wood, regardless of the type of finish, will darken with age; there is no way of preventing such a change. In order to obtain a good finish for the paneling, smooth the surfaces by rubbing with "00" sandpaper and then with "0000" or "00000" sandpaper and wipe off all dust. The wood can be finished with a clear lacquer-type coating or with a couple of thin coats of pure, fresh white shellac, thinned half-and-half with denatured alcohol.

PINE PANELING SMEARED

The builder who installed our pine paneling filled holes with putty and used his thumb for smearing it on. The result is smeared putty. Now I can't remove these gray stains. I've even tried staining them with varnish, but it didn't work out at all.

You can't stain the putty. About the only way we know of to take out the smears is to sand them down with very fine sandpaper. Then you can touch up the area with varnish or shellac, whichever was used as the finish. If the putty used to fill the nail holes is conspicuous, replace it with putty to which a light golden oak stain has been added to match the wood.

DULLED VARNISHED WALLS

Our knotty pine walls have a varnish finish which is becoming dulled. How can they be brightened?

Varnish dulling is frequently due to the presence of excess moisture in the air, plus a fair amount of surface dust. Gloss can often be restored by cleaning with a wax-base liquid floor-cleaning preparation.

KNOTTY CEDAR PANELING

Fifteen years ago, when our cottage was built, knotty cedar boards were put on the interior walls. The wood was given two coats of clear shellac. Nothing has been done since. The paneling looks dried out, and I know it is dirty and dusty. What can I use to clean the walls, and would you suggest a new finish?

We think a cleaning will restore the finish. Housewares sections of hardware and department stores, and also many paint dealers, sell a floor-cleaning preparation that contains wax. It can be used with very satisfactory results on wood paneling. The thin film of wax remaining on the boards should be rubbed to give the walls a lustrous finish. We don't think a new finish is necessary.

FINISH FOR CEDAR

We have cedar walls in the bedroom. What is the best way to finish such wood?

The usual treatment is to give the wood a couple of coats of clear lacquer or pure, fresh white shellac. If shellac is used, thin it half-and-half with denatured alcohol. The walls should then be given a coat of paste wax and should be rubbed well. A penetrating wax finish can be used in place of the above materials. It comes in a natural color and also other wood colors.

FINISHING MAHOGANY PANELING

I'm putting sheets of mahogany paneling (with grooves) on my basement walls. What kind of finish can I use to keep it as light as possible? I have checked the paneling, and it isn't necessary to use wood filler. Is there any disadvantage to leaving the wood unfinished?

The main disadvantage to leaving the wood unfinished is that dirt, soot, grease, etc., can easily penetrate below the surface of the

Figure 2-10. Wood paneling can be given "new" life by cleaning with a good paint and panel cleaner.

wood. Two coats of pure, fresh white shellac, thinned half-and-half with denatured alcohol, can be used to finish the panels; or a penetrating wax finish, available at wood-finishing materials dealers, can be used. We suggest you get the manufacturer's recommendations for finishing the particular paneling you have.

TWO SHADES OF MAHOGANY PANELING

We recently put up mahogany paneling in our basement. Now we find we have two different shades: one brownish, the other reddish. Is there any way to finish all of it in one shade and have it look alike? Worse than the wall is the encasing of a heat run that has odds and ends of both woods.

Other than coating the wood with an enamel or paint, which would not give a "natural" finish, we suggest bleaching the wood surfaces using prepared wood bleach, available at paint and wood-finishing dealers, following the label instructions carefully. Then sand the wood smooth, wipe off the dust, and stain in the desired shade; a penetrating wax stain gives an easy-to-care-for, long-lasting finish. Or finish with two coats of pure, fresh white shellac, mixed half-and-half with denatured alcohol.

DISLIKES DARK PANELING

We have dark mahogany wood paneling on a large wall in our living room, and we are thinking of painting it. Would it be necessary to sand this surface first? In the seven years we've been here, we haven't put a thing on it. It does have a little shine, though; perhaps it was prefinished at the factory.

First, ask the dealer if he knows whether it has a factory finish. This could be very important. Next be sure there is no trace of oil or wax; no finish will stick over it. Then apply a coat of knot and stain sealer (you could also use aluminum paint) to keep the mahogany from bleeding through the paint. Over this goes your finish coat(s).

HOMEMADE PAINT REMOVER

We have just purchased a very old house that we plan to repaint and redecorate gradually ourselves, cost being an important factor. Is there any kind of paint remover we could make ourselves that would be a lot less expensive than the ready-prepared?

The following is a good paste-type paint remover that can be easily mixed: 1 part trisodium phosphate, 2 parts powdered whiting, and enough water to make a thick paste. This should be applied about ½ inch thick over the paint, using a putty knife or trowel. The paint should be softened in 30 minutes or so, when it can be removed along with the paste. Be sure to rinse thoroughly with clear water afterward; otherwise new paint may not harden. Three pounds of trisodium phosphate in a gallon of hot water is also a good remover to use on horizontal surfaces.

PAINT REMOVER DOES BOTH

I am planning on repainting the walls and woodwork in our spare room. The walls are oil-base flat wall paint; the woodwork is varnish. What types of remover do I need?

Any good paint remover does both jobs. Some brands list both paint and varnish on the label. For vertical surfaces, such as walls and woodwork, a lot of people like to use a paste-type remover. It sticks instead of running and spreading, as liquids will do.

PAINT SPOTS ON GLASS

Last year, I had my house painted. The painters applied the paint just before a rainstorm. The rain spattered the fresh paint over the glass windows. What is the best method to remove the paint from the glass?

If there is some thickness to the paint spots, take them off with an old razor blade. To avoid scratching the glass, hold the blade almost flat against the glass before pushing the edge under the paint film. Paint smears can be taken off by wiping them with paint remover and then with turpentine. Paint dealers sell the remover in pint-size cans.

PAINTED WINDOWS STUCK

We have aluminum storm and screen combination windows. My husband painted the inside windows just before putting on the new aluminum ones last fall. Now we are unable to get the windows open. We put oil on the sills and between the frames, but they never budged. We almost pulled the handles off trying to pry them loose. Have you any suggestion on opening the windows, short of breaking them?

A small, heart-shaped, serrated-edge gadget is now available at most hardware, paint, and variety stores for just this problem.

It is run around the window and cuts the paint film. Frequently, tapping a small block of wood, held against the window frame, with a hammer loosens the window. Or tapping a putty knife, or small screwdriver, between the sash and frame, using a hammer, is also successful in breaking the paint film.

VARNISH ON GLASS

I varnished the kitchen window frames and didn't notice until too late that some varnish had been brushed onto the glass. How can I remove this?

Try scraping it off with a razor blade. If this doesn't work (and it usually does), use a paste-type paint remover, following the label directions and being careful not to get any of it on the window frame. When refinishing window frames, it's a good idea to use masking tape on the glass adjoining the surface to be painted; it is easy to remove, with any excess paint, after you've finished the job.

PAINTING GLASS

I wanted to make the lower half of my bathroom window opaque for privacy, and so I tried painting it. After a while the paint began to come off. How is it possible to make paint stick on glass?

The first step is to clean the glass thoroughly by wiping it with ammonia or turpentine. Then apply an undercoat of white (pigmented) shellac. This gives a nice flat surface for the finishing paint coat. This same shellac undercoat makes it possible to paint high-gloss ceramic tile and even polished metal.

PAINT ON GLASS BLOCKS

Is there any way to remove paint that has washed from white trim onto glass blocks? These are on the porch planter and on the lower half of one side of my house.

Try vigorous scrubbing of the stained areas with a strong detergent and a stiff brush, followed by rinsing with clear water. If this is not successful, use a paste-type paint remover, following the label directions.

REMOVING "STAINED-GLASS" PAPER

Some years ago it was the style to use a "stained-glass" type of paper on the side lights and transom around the front door. I am very anxious to remove this and have the glass clear. Someone suggested using a

detergent, but I am afraid it would hurt the white woodwork. What do you recommend?

The surrounding woodwork can be protected by covering it with masking tape (as for painting windows, etc.), available at paint, hardware, and variety stores. Scrape the paper off carefully with fine steel wool and a nonflammable liquid spot remover or naphtha.

BUBBLING VARNISH

Every time I put varnish on a door, or some woodwork, I always wind up with areas where there are bubbles in the varnish. I can't seem to get them out, and the results aren't what I'd like. Can you help me, or at least tell me if I'm doing something wrong?

There are several things to avoid. The first one is: don't stir the varnish in the can. This will almost always introduce air bubbles. Don't "slap" the varnish on the surface, or brush vigorously, because this, too, can cause bubbles. Instead, brush the varnish on gently; first brush in the direction of the grain of the wood, then cross-brush, and finally brush again following the grain. Don't worry about ridges made by the brush; these will flatten out by themselves. Another important point, although this doesn't have too much to do with bubbles: Varnishing should be done in a warm room—70° or more is the desirable temperature range. If the can of varnish is cool, let it stand in a warm room for several hours before using.

KNOTS THROUGH PAINT

I used a cheap grade of pine, with quite a few knots, for wall shelves, thinking that paint would cover the knots. But now some of the knots are beginning to show through. What can I do?

Scrape off the paint from the discolored areas or use paint remover. Then rub the areas with coarse steel wool and turpentine to remove any trace of sap or resin. Coat the unpainted areas with knot sealer, available at many paint stores; or use pure, fresh white shellac to seal the knots. Finish to match the rest of the shelf surface.

HIDING CHIPPED ENAMEL

I am in the process of redecorating our back room. This will include taking care of the present door and window trim, which is enamel. There are quite a few places where the enamel is chipped. How can I fix these spots before reenameling? Or must I remove all enamel and start completely from scratch?

If the rest of the enamel is okay, then simply featheredge the chipped spots with very fine sandpaper or steel wool. Carefully paint penetrating sealer on the exposed bare wood with a small artist's brush. If there's a noticeable difference in level between the surfaces of the chipped areas and the rest of the trim, build up the chipped spots with one or two coats of the same enamel as you'll use for the complete job.

FINISHING BIRCH PANELING

We have bought ¼-inch birch paneling to place halfway up on the kitchen wall. It is unfinished, but with a very smooth surface; it may not have to be sanded. What do I use to finish the paneling? The birch kitchen cabinets have a shiny, yellowish stain.

Some paneling comes ready for finishing; yours is probably that kind. Try finishing an inconspicuous corner (after wiping off any surface dust and removing any trace of grease, grime, wax, etc., which occurred from handling) with pure, fresh white shellac, or orange shellac (giving it a slightly darker finish), thinned half-and-half with denatured alcohol. This may be the finish on the cabinets. Or it may be a clear varnish. If none of these give the same effect, get a matching wood stain as close to the cabinet color as possible, applying it according to the label directions. Then apply two thin coats of the shellac.

PHILIPPINE MAHOGANY PLYWOOD PANELING

We are paneling our recreation room with Philippine mahogany plywood panels. What finishing steps are necessary for a durable, attractive appearance? We wish to maintain the light color of the wood.

Philippine mahogany, or lauan as it is commonly known, is not a true mahogany, and the grain tends to raise with a water stain even more than natural mahogany does. After applying natural filler, apply two thin coats of pure, fresh white shellac, thinned half-and-half with denatured alcohol, or coats of clear varnish.

CARE OF PLYWOOD WALLS

We have a den which is finished in a plywood with the hard grain in the wood in relief. There is a finish on it, and we were told we didn't have to do anything with it for a couple of years, but we are wondering what we will have to do after the couple of years have passed.

Wipe off the dust periodically to prevent it from accumulating. Since most walls do not get much wear and tear or abuse, go over the wood with one of the wax-base wood-floor cleaners; then buff the thin film of wax to bring out a light luster. If necessary, use a soft-bristle brush to buff the wax in the depressed areas.

"FLATTENING" FIR PLYWOOD

Is it true that plywood made of Douglas fir needs a special treatment before finishing to flatten the grain?

Yes. Fir has a "wild" grain which behaves something like a small boy's "crew cut," and if it isn't given a coating of a product made especially for flattening the grain, it will show through almost any number of finish coats. The coating, a very well-known product, is made by a nationally known plywood manufacturer and is sold at almost all paint and hardware stores.

PREPARING SOILED, DISCOLORED WOODWORK FOR FINISHING

We moved into a new house last fall and were not able to varnish the woodwork then. It has collected dust and fingerprints. How can I remove these before varnishing? Also, where moisture collected on the windows and ran down, there are discolored (black) spots. Is there any way to remove these so that they won't show when varnished?

The best way to remove the surface soil would be to sand the surface with an electric sander; or use turpentine and fine steel wool, followed by sanding the surface until it is satin-smooth. Be sure to wipe off all dust before varnishing. The black spots may be removed by sanding; if not, apply a wood bleach, available at paint and hardware stores, following the label directions. If the spots become lighter than the surrounding wood, apply matching wood stain. Then finish as desired.

VARNISH OVER WAX STAIN

The living room woodwork was finished with a penetrating wax stain and sealer.

Now we want to refinish it with varnish. Must the old stain be removed first?

It's not necessary to remove the old finish before applying the varnish. Just remove the wax on the surface, using a good wax remover, following the label directions, or turpentine and fine steel wool. Be sure the surface is thoroughly dry and clean and free of any trace of grease, dirt, or grime, as well as wax, before the varnish is applied.

SOILED UNFINISHED WOODWORK

I have a problem with unfinished mahogany woodwork. Somehow it acquired some grease spots, dirt, and soil smudges. I am planning to give it a light bleached finish and wonder if there is any way to remove the soil spots?

Most of the soiling will come off by going over the surfaces with "0" steel wool or "000" sandpaper. If the oil and grease spots are fairly deep, try wiping them with naphtha. Or apply a paste mixture of powdered whiting and a nonflammable liquid spot remover. When the paste is dry, brush it off and repeat the process if necessary.

FINISHING WHITE PINE

Would you advise me about how to finish door and window trim made of new white pine? I would like to have as light a finish as possible.

A light natural finish can be obtained by giving the wood a couple of coats of a clear lacquer; pure, fresh white shellac; or a semi-gloss varnish. If a lighter finish, such as a pickled pine or a blond tone, is desired, a wood stain of this type is first applied and then lacquer, varnish, or shellac is put on. Dealers specializing in wood-finishing materials could furnish the stains, etc.

UNFINISHED PINE WOODWORK

We bought a home and found that someone had painted the stained and varnished woodwork with a high-gloss enamel, with the result that it chipped easily. After removing all the finish, my husband wants to leave the wood as it is, because he likes the natural color, but I think it needs some protection. The woodwork is pine. We would like to have your advice.

Without some protective coating, the wood is apt to become soiled and spotted. It will also darken quickly because of atmospheric moisture and dust. You can have it coated with a clear, lacquerlike coating sold by paint dealers and many dealers in plywoods. If this is not available, give the wood a coat or two of pure, fresh white shellac, thinned half-and-half with denatured alcohol. A thin coat of paste wax can then be applied.

STAIN "BLEEDS" THROUGH PAINT

I painted the woodwork in my living room white several months ago. Now the dark mahogany stain is starting to come through in several places, and it looks blotchy. What can I do about it? I am planning to paint the woodwork in the hall, but before I do, I'd like to be sure this won't happen again.

Before attempting to paint over previously stained and varnished wood surfaces, first sand them thoroughly and wipe off all dust. Then apply a sealer; one good type is a coat of shellac. Allow this to dry. Then you can apply the paint or enamel. I'm sorry to say that you may wind up having to remove the paint in the living room. But you might get away with putting the sealer over the paint. Try it in one obscure section; it's worth the experiment. There's little to lose, but a lot to gain.

DENTS IN WOODWORK

The woodwork in the living room was painted white. Our landlord sanded the paint off with an electric sander, cutting large dents into the wood. We thought repainting in white would cover the dents, but it didn't. Is there anything we can cover the woodwork with, without replacing the wood?

Spackle is excellent for filling such dents, as well as splits and gaps (such as when woodwork baseboard becomes separated from the wall). When the dents are sanded smooth, put on a new finish of enamel. If the woodwork is very plain, it would be possible to do a fair job of covering it with adhesive-backed, plastic-coated paper, but it would not look as neat as enamel. This is particularly true if the woodwork is deeply grooved, fluted, or molded.

REMOVING MOLD FROM PAINTED WOODWORK

Due to the damp summer, the paint on the door, windows, and baseboard in my guest room has become moldy. Is there anything I can apply to this paint that will remove the mold?

Thoroughly scrub the painted surfaces with a stiff brush and a solution of household chlorine bleach, rinsing well afterward with clear water. Ventilate and air the room as much as possible on dry days.

FINISHING WOODWORK

We are building a new home, and we plan to do our own decorating and finishing. What kind of sealer do you suggest to use on woodwork? We plan to have clear woodwork in its natural color.

Clear lacquer or a lacquer-base coating will give you the lightest natural finish, not changing the tone of the wood to any great extent. If your local paint dealers do not carry it in stock or cannot get it for you, a pure, fresh white shellac can be used. The shellac should be thinned half-and-half with denatured alcohol.

WOOD GRAIN SHOW THROUGH PAINT?

I am redecorating my powder room. The cabinet, sliding doors, and window trim are birch wood. I would like to finish them in

Figure 2-11. Paint the baseboard last. A cardboard or plastic guard held flush against the bottom edge of the baseboard will protect the floor and prevent picking up dirt in the brush. Do not let paper or drop cloth touch baseboard before paint is dry.

white, so that the grain shows through. Is this possible?

If your paint or enamel is solid white, the grain will be completely hidden. However, you can experiment on some scrap wood as follows: Thin your paint down 50 percent or even more with linseed oil, and brush it on. Then, while it's still wet, wipe it off, across the wood, with a cloth. The idea is to take the paint off the surface, but leave it in the grain. It works best in really open-grained wood like oak, but it won't hurt to try this here. If the grain looks okay to you, let the paint dry, and then cover it with a couple of thin coats of clear enamel or polyurethane varnish. And if you don't like it, you can always go back to your solid white.

LIGHTEN WOODWORK WITHOUT REMOVING FINISH?

Is it at all possible to lighten dark woodwork by some other means than removing all the varnish? I mean some kind of bleach or similar preparation.

The only way to lighten the wood itself is by removing any finish, getting down to the bare wood surface, and then applying a bleach. The only other way to get a lighter effect would be to dull the varnish gloss and then apply a light-colored paint or enamel, after removing all trace of grease, wax, or grime from the surface.

DARK WOODWORK

Our woodwork is dark oak. How can we remove the varnish? It is quite marred, and of course if we varnish over it, it shows. How do you remove the dark spots? Can one paint over varnish, or must the varnish be removed?

One method is to soften the varnish by applying a paste type of paint remover; then scrape it off with a putty knife and steel wool. Another method is to hold a heat lamp about 12 inches from the surface; when the varnish becomes soft, take it off with a putty knife. If the wood is discolored, bleach it by applying a hot, saturated solution of oxalic acid (poison). The oxalic crystals can be purchased at paint stores. Leave it on overnight; then rinse well with clear water. When the wood is dry, smooth it by rubbing with "0000" sandpaper, wipe off the dust, and finish as desired. If the finish is not a mahogany or red color, you can

apply paint over the varnish. Dull the gloss by rubbing with "000" sandpaper; then wash the surfaces with turpentine and apply paint.

LIGHT SPOTS AROUND FILLED NAIL HOLES

There are light spots left by putty around each nail hole in our soft pine woodwork. We would like to remove them. Do we have to remove all of the finish and sand them, or is there an easier way?

We assume you have putty smears around the filled nail holes. To remove the smears, scrape away the finish around the smeared areas with fine sandpaper; then touch them up with the same finishing materials used originally on the woodwork.

FLECKS OF PAINT ON ENAMELED BASEBOARD

When my walls were painted, small flecks of paint fell on my baseboards, which had been sprayed with white enamel. How can I remove this paint without damaging the finish?

Since the flecks of paint have become dry, only paint remover will take them off, and naturally the enamel will also come off. Rubbing with "00" steel wool and a little turpentine may do the least damage. The dulled spots could be polished with paste wax.

FINGER MARKS UNDER VARNISH

We recently bought a new home. Whoever finished the woodwork did a poor job: in several places on doors and baseboards, there are dirty finger marks, which I found were under the varnish after trying to wash them off. Is there any way to correct this?

The only way is to remove the present finish down to bare wood; then clean off the finger marks from the wood and refinish the woodwork again.

MOLD ON WOODWORK FROM VAPORIZER

Because of sickness I had a vaporizer going in a small room. The wall, woodwork, curtains, and shades got mold on them. Should anything special be done to the walls and woodwork before we repaint?

Remove the mold from the walls and woodwork by scrubbing them with a stiff brush and a household bleach solution; then rinse with clear water to remove all trace of the bleach. Allow the room to air thoroughly for about a week. Then apply any top-quality mildew-resistant paint.

BLACKENED SILL

We want to refinish our windowsill in the kitchen. Because of moisture dripping down, there are black stains on the varnished sill. How can these stains be removed?

Remove the present varnish with varnish remover, following the label directions carefully. Then apply wood bleach or a hot, saturated solution of oxalic acid (poison) liberally over the stains and allow it to remain on overnight, rinsing thoroughly the next day with clear water. When the wood is completely dry, smooth it with "0000" sandpaper and wipe off the dust. Refinish as desired.

BURN LIKE BAD PENNY

On my painted windowsill a year or so ago, a cigarette left a deep burn about an inch long and $\frac{1}{8}$ inch deep. I scraped off the charred stuff, put on some filler to make it even again, and then painted it. But several times since, the burned mark has come back. I have to repeat the whole business, including more filler. Is there any way to stop this discoloration from constantly coming back?

Scrape it again; then sand the depression. Then dab on a couple of thin coats of aluminum paint, which makes an excellent barrier against this type of "bleeding." When the paint is dry, fill the depression again with wood putty, plastic wood, or whatever filler you've been using. Then repaint.

FINISH FOR OAK CUPBOARDS

We are having new cupboards made for our kitchen. They are of oak, and we want to finish them in a natural shade. How do we go about finishing them? What do we do to make them stay light?

After rubbing down the wood to a satin-like smoothness, wipe off the dust with naphtha. Be careful of fire. Don't rub hard, because friction will ignite it. Fill the open grain of the wood with a natural paste wood filler, thinned with turpentine to a thick creamy consistency. Brush it on with the grain, and when the gloss disappears, wipe off the filler across the grain with a coarse fabric or fine excelsior. Allow what remains to dry hard. Smooth the surface with "000000" sandpaper, and wipe off the dust. Finish with a couple of coats of a good-quality semigloss varnish.

BIRCH DOORS AND CUPBOARDS

I want to have natural-finished birch doors and cupboards in my new home. Would you please advise me how to finish these in a natural color. I want to keep the woodwork just as light as I possible can. I would also like a finish that is neither dull nor very glossy.

You can get a very light finish by first applying a pickled or limed oak stain; then finish with a water-clear, lacquer-type coating. If a light, whitish tone is not desired, apply two coats of lacquer coating. This will give you a flat finish, but waxing will give the woodwork a more lustrous finish. Finishing can be done with a semigloss varnish. This, however, will give the wood a more amber-colored tone.

REFINISHING BIRCH CABINETS

I have birch kitchen cabinets that are badly scarred. Will you tell me how to refinish them? I would like a natural finish.

Remove the old finish with paint remover, using it as directed on the label of the container. Try to get the nonflammable kind. If you can't get the nonflammable kind, be very careful of fire, and put out all pilot lights, shut off electric motors, and work in a well-ventilated room. If the wood is stained, apply a liberal quantity of a hot, saturated solution of oxalic acid (poison). Allow the solution to remain on overnight; then rinse with clear water. When the wood is dry, smooth it with "0000" sandpaper or garnet paper. Wipe off the dust, and finish with a semigloss varnish or a clear lacquer.

CLEANING PRESEALED SURFACES

Last spring we installed precut pantry cabinets, made of birch and presealed. We never finished them and now plan to put on a satin finish. However, we never anticipated our children's greasy finger marks and water stains splashed from the sink. Instructions said not to sand these presealed surfaces.

What can we use to clean the surface before applying finish?

Wash the surface with a household detergent solution or one of the liquid house cleaners, followed by a thorough rinsing with clear water and immediate drying. Or wipe it with fine steel wool and turpentine. Be sure the surface is thoroughly dry before applying finish.

CRACKS IN CABINET DOORS

The doors on my painted plywood cabinets have developed vertical cracks. What can they be filled with to make a smooth surface for painting?

You can fill the cracks with white lead paste thinned to the consistency of a thick cream. When the filler has become dry and hard, smooth it by rubbing it with "000" sandpaper and wipe off the dust.

MATCHING FINISH ON OLD AND NEW CABINETS

I have birch and pine cabinets in the kitchen, which we finished, five years ago, with one coat of shellac and two coats of varnish. We would like to install three more cabinets of the same wood and finish them with shellac and varnish. Will they all look the same in a few months, or should I add a little color to the shellac?

You will find it quite difficult to match the new finish with one that has been exposed to usage for five years. To obtain a truly uniform color and tone, it will be necessary to remove the old finish and finish all the cabinets at one time.

MATCHING CABINET FINISH

We bought several shopworn, unfinished kitchen cabinets in different woods of varying shades. Other than enameling, is there any way to finish these so they would look uniform? We prefer a "natural wood" finish if possible.

The grain and wood texture will vary, of course, but you can obtain a uniform color effect by first sanding the wood surface until it is as smooth as possible, wiping off any dust, and then applying a wood stain in the desired shade, following the label instructions carefully. Then apply a finish coat of pure, fresh white shellac, thinned half-and-half with denatured alcohol, or a clear varnish.

METAL CABINETS NOW "SCRAPED RAW"

Through the years, I have cleaned my metal undersink cabinets and drawers so many times they're scraped down to raw metal in some places. Is there any way to repaint them? I can't hope for a shiny finish like baked-on enamel, but I would like them to look neat and nice.

Most hardware and paint stores stock metal appliance enamels in various colors. Follow the label directions implicitly, paying particular attention to getting the surface clean, dry, and free from wax, grease, and soap film. While you may not get a real factory gleam, you can still do a beautiful job, and don't let anyone tell you differently.

WORN METAL CABINETS

My metal kitchen cabinets are about seven years old. I can't afford to have them refinished by the factory or professionally resprayed. They have yellowed very badly; the short ones over the stove are practically bare metal. Is there any way I could dull them down and reenamel?

The yellowing may be due to grease from cooking vapors; try scrubbing the surface with scratchless scouring power, rinsing well afterward with clear water. To dull the present glossy finish for reenameling, rub it with fine steel wool and turpentine, which will also

Figure 2-12. It is often possible to match colors by using tinting colors.

remove all trace of wax, grease, grime, etc. The surface should be absolutely clean before a new coating applied. Then apply top-quality enamel undercoater and enamel, following the label directions carefully. Enamel in aerosol form is slightly more expensive but is a time- and energy-saver.

REVARNISHING FRONT DOOR

The outside surface of my front door needs refinishing. When I revarnish it, how can I make the last coat go on smoothly? The door is not blistered.

Before revarnishing, be sure the surface is free of all traces of grime, soot, dust, wax, etc., and dull any gloss in order to obtain better adhesion of the new coating. Wipe the surface with fine steel wool and turpentine; then apply top quality spar varnish in several coats, being sure each coat has thoroughly dried before applying the next and dulling the gloss by light rubbing with fine steel wool. Be sure not to shake the can of varnish; air bubbles may form and be carried to the door surface, causing imperfections. Apply the varnish in straight strokes, along the grain, never across the grain. When the brush is empty, again brush over the same area to carry the varnish forward and spread it in an even coat.

WHITENING MAHOGANY

All the doors in our house are stained a dark mahogany, while the woodwork is white. We wish to paint the doors white. What preparation is necessary so that the mahogany stain will not bleed through?

Remove any present finish down to bare wood. Sand the wood smooth, and wipe off the dust. Then apply one or two coats of aluminum paint or pure, fresh white shellac, thinned half-and-half with denatured alcohol.

MATCHING ALUMINUM DOOR

We got an aluminum door for our front entrance; this can be used as a screen or a storm door. We would like it to match the trim on the house. Can it be painted?

If the door is relatively new, the oily film must first be removed. Weathering removes it; or wash it with a phosphoric acid wash, and then rinse thoroughly with clear water. Any good-quality house paint, not containing lead, should be used as a first coat.

PAINT AND PLASTER ON ALUMINUM

I have spent a great many hours trying to remove paint, putty, and plaster from our new aluminum windows, using steel wool and a razor blade. Is there an easier way to go about this job?

You should be able to remove the paint and putty with paint remover. Apply the remover, and when the paint or putty becomes soft, take it off with steel wool. The plaster will have to be scraped off. Try rubbing it with "00" sandpaper, being careful not to scratch the metal. The remaining thin coating will have to be rubbed off with steel wool.

PAINT FOR BASEBOARD

We have hydronic heat with baseboards. What kind of paint can be used on these units so that it won't discolor, peel or chip?

Any good-quality metal paint will serve. The trick for avoiding discoloration is to have the hot-water or hydronic heating units stone-cold from start until the final coat is thoroughly dry. Your best protection against peeling and chipping is, first, see that there's no trace of wax or grease before painting. Second, avoid banging into the units when moving furniture around. Remember: Keep the unit(s) stone-cold from start to final drying of the finish.

RADIATOR PAINT PEELS

Some of the paint on the radiators keeps peeling off. I scrape, sandpaper, and repaint, only to have it chip off somewhere else. What should I do for this?

If the surface was thoroughly cleaned of grease, soot, etc., before applying the paint, the peeling may be due to the fact that the radiators were allowed to heat up before the paint coating was thoroughly dry. The heat should be completely turned off in the radiator and the metal allowed to cool before putting on the paint. Don't turn on the heat until the paint has thoroughly dried.

PAINTING RADIATORS

At the present time our radiators are coated with aluminum paint, and we would like to paint them again. Is it advisable to put on a semigloss paint so that it will match the room's color scheme? Will such paint

prevent the heat from giving the room its proper temperature?

Colored paints on radiators will give you about 15 percent more heat than those coated with a metallic paint. The radiators must remain cold until the final coat of paint has dried hard.

RADIATOR PAINT QUALITY

The bathroom radiator needs repainting, and I plan to do it with radiator enamel. How do I calculate how much paint I'll need?

Multiply the front area of the radiator by 7. The result will be the total number of square feet to be painted. Divide this figure into the number of square feet that a gallon of your desired paint will cover [usually a gallon of enamel will cover about 600 square feet (1 coat)]. This will indicate the part of a gallon you'll need.

PAINTING RADIATOR COVERS

I would like to paint some radiator covers to blend with our walls. The present finish has a mahogany wood grain baked-on coating. I have been told it may be impossible to have the paint adhere properly to such surfaces. If it does adhere, would it last very long when the heat is turned on?

If the surfaces of the cover are well rubbed down with sandpaper or emery cloth to create a flat finish and one that might be slightly rough, there is no reason why a good grade of enamel undercoater and enamel would not adhere properly. Be sure all the dust is wiped off before painting is started, and do not subject the cover to heat until the final coat has become thoroughly dry and hard.

PAINTING PIPES

I hope you can advise me about the kind of paint to use in my bathroom. The pipes are an eyesore. I live in a basement apartment, and several of the pipes cross the bathroom ceiling. The paint peels off in little pieces. What kind of paint can I use?

In the first place, the pipes should be perfectly clean and free of all loose paint. Secondly, all surfaces must be cold while painting is done, and the heat should be kept out of the pipes until the final coat is hard and dry. Paint should also be applied in thin coats. For best results coat all surfaces in the bathroom with a good grade of enamel.

PAINTING CONCRETE FLOOR AND WALLS

Our house is being finished shortly, and we plan to move in as soon as we can. The basement has a concrete floor and concrete block walls. How long must we wait before painting?

Allow at least 4 to 6 months for thorough drying. The floor can then be coated with a rubber-base floor paint; a couple of coats of a cement-base paint, coming in powder form to be mixed with water, can be applied to the walls.

TAKING PAINT OFF BASEMENT FLOOR

Could you suggest something to use that will get paint off the basement concrete floor? I've tried different things, but they did not work.

The fastest method is to go over the floor with a floor-sanding machine, using a coarse-grained sandpaper. Another method is to hold an infrared heat lamp about 12 inches from the surface, and when the paint has softened, scrape it off with a wide-blade putty knife. We presume you have tried some of the well-known brands of prepared paint removers. They usually work, but it takes time and patience.

SAVE BIG JARS FOR PAINT LEFTOVERS

Each time I clean out my basement, I come across lots of paint cans with the tops firmly hammered on. But when opened, the paint

Figure 2-13. When painting concrete blocks, make sure you work the brush into the wall's pit marks. This is important to ensure that the paint covers the pit marks.

remainder is either hard as a rock or mostly a leathery film. How can you really keep paint so that it's usable again in a year or two?

You can hammer the top on tightly and then turn the can upside down. Then air can't get in so easily. Even better, in our opinion, is to pour the leftover paint into screw-top glass jars right to the top. Those jumbo-size peanut butter or mayonnaise jars are splendid. Glass also lets you see the color.

WHICH SOLVENTS FOR WHAT?

What solvent should I use to remove paint and clean brushes in?

Consult the paint can label for the proper cleaning solution. But as a rule, use turpentine or mineral spirits to remove oil-base or alkyd-base paints, enamels, or varnish; denatured alcohol to remove shellac; lacquer thinner or special solvents to remove lacquer; and water for latex paints.

A few years ago this chapter would have been entitled "Hanging Wallpaper," but today this is no longer the case. Why this sudden distinction between "wall*paper* and "wall *coverings*"? What it amounts to is this. All wallpapers are wall coverings, but not all wall coverings are made of paper. The main difference, however, is not in the cost of the materials. Wallpapers can be just as expensive as the most luxurious coverings for the wall printed on imported silk, while wall coverings, of a tough material like vinyl, may differ in cost according to whether they are produced by machine, automatic silkscreen, or entirely hand-printed silk screen, the difference to the eye being negligible. How a pattern is produced depends, of course, on whether it is styled to reach a large market or a limited one. It is rather reckless to generalize, what with popular taste changing so rapidly, but for the time being you might say that "wall covering," as a whole, conjures up a more conservative and durable product; "wallpaper"—with the possible exception of the mass market—suggests a more decorator-oriented approach to design.

Estimating Material

First, measure the length, width, and height of your room. When you know the distance around the room (length + width × 2), use Table 5 to determine how many rolls of covering you will need. If there are doors, windows, archways, or other such openings in the room, measure the size of each and ask your local wall coverings salesperson to help you figure how many rolls to subtract from the total indicated on the table. In general, deduct one single roll for every two ordinary-size doors or windows or every 30 square feet of opening.

Wall coverings are available in a number of widths. All rolls contain 36 square feet (the wider rolls are shorter). Thus, you can use Table 5 to determine how many rolls you will need to do a room, no matter what the roll width. Borders are sold by the yard. The distance around your room in feet, divided by 3, equals the yards of border needed.

Adhesives

The most common adhesive for hanging wallpaper is cold-water paste. This is available from paint or hardware stores in a powder, which is mixed with water in a clean, galvanized bucket. The day of preparing a paste of

CHAPTER 3

HANGING WALL COVERINGS

Table 5. Wall-Covering Estimating Chart

Distance around room in feet	Single rolls for wall areas			Number of yards for borders	Single rolls for ceilings
	8-ft ceiling	9-ft ceiling	10-ft ceiling		
28	8	8	10	11	2
30	8	8	10	11	2
32	8	10	10	12	2
34	10	10	12	13	4
36	10	10	12	13	4
38	10	12	12	14	4
40	10	12	12	15	4
42	12	12	14	15	4
44	12	12	14	16	4
46	12	14	14	17	6
48	14	14	16	17	6
50	14	14	16	18	6
52	14	14	16	19	6
54	14	16	18	19	6
56	14	16	18	20	8
58	16	16	18	21	8
60	16	18	20	21	8
62	16	18	20	22	8
64	16	18	20	23	8
66	18	20	20	23	10
68	18	20	22	24	10
70	18	20	22	25	10
72	18	20	22	25	12
74	20	22	22	26	12
76	20	22	24	27	12
78	20	22	24	27	14
80	20	22	26	28	14
82	22	24	26	29	14
84	22	24	26	30	16
86	22	24	26	30	16
88	24	26	28	31	16
90	24	26	28	32	18

boiled flour-and-water mixture has passed, thank goodness. The ready-to-mix pastes are far more efficient, much easier to prepare, and inexpensive.

In recent years, the prepasted wall coverings have become very popular. Actually, there are three methods for wetting prepasted wall coverings. One popular method is to fill a water tray (inexpensive and available at your wall-covering dealer) with cool-lukewarm water and place it on a towel or dropcloth at the baseboard where the first strip is to be hung. Set the ladder diagonally in front of the water tray. Loosely reroll the first strip from the bottom to the top with the pattern side in, the pasted side out. Submerge the rolled strip in the water for the length of time indicated by the manufacturer. Then pull the strip slowly out of the water tray, climb the ladder, and carry the top of the strip to the ceiling line.

An alternate method is to choose a convenient working surface (like a kitchen table) and apply cool-lukewarm water generously with a brush to the prepasted surface, working from the top of the strip to the bottom. Lay the pattern side down on the table, and fold the top of the strip toward the center, paste to paste. Do not crease. Fold the bottom of the

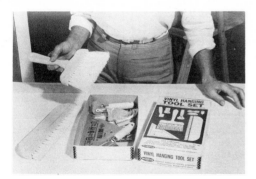

Figure 3-1. Complete sets of tools required for hanging wall coverings are available in any paint and wall-covering store.

If your wall covering has not been pre-trimmed, it is safer to trim it before pasting. Use a straight edge, and cut with a single-edge razor knife. To assure accuracy, make all measurements from the edge of the paper. It's the only true line you have to go by no matter where the trim marks may show. Generally the straight edge is placed on the pattern side of the trim marks; however, on very delicate wall covering such as flocks and foils the straight edge should be placed on the other side. Incidentally, kits containing tools needed for hanging wall coverings are available at wall-covering stores. Tables and steamers can be rented.

Hanging the Wall Covering

Wall covering can't cling to grease or dirt, and many householders are shocked to learn that the kitchen walls aren't the only ones that harbor grease. Bathroom walls, too, collect a film from soaps, bath oils, cosmetics, hair sprays, etc. Wash down the wall with water to which you've added soap powder and some household ammonia; then rinse thoroughly.

As a preparatory step, remove all switch plates, outlet plates, and light fixtures from the wall. If you're going to paint the ceiling or floor molding or any of the walls, paint those first and let them dry thoroughly before starting to hang the covering.

It's a good idea to reroll each roll of the wall covering to inspect for defects or possible

strip in the same way back to the center even with the top edge (this is called "booking"). Loosely roll the folded strip, and lay it aside for the length of time recommended by the manufacturer (usually at least 5 minutes).

Still another method is to use the water tray at a convenient table exactly as described when working at the baseboard. After pulling the strip slowly from the tray, you lay the pattern side down on the table, "book" it as described above, and carry it immediately to the wall. *Note:* Prepasted wall covering has been *fully* pasted at the factory with the proper type of paste, and we don't recommend any further pasting since the paste you use may not be compatible with the paste already on the wall covering.

When pasting unpasted wall covering, use cold water and mix the paste until it is absolutely lump-free and about the consistency of gravy—thin enough to brush smoothly, thick enough to permit sliding the covering on the wall. Turn the strip pattern side down on a clean work surface. Paste only one strip at a time. Use a large paste brush, and follow a figure 8 motion to apply the paste evenly. Be sure to cover the entire area (working in good lighting will help you accomplish this) because unpasted areas will show up as blisters on the wall. After applying the paste, "book" the strip as with prepasted wall covering edge to edge, paste to paste. Allow 3 to 5 minutes after pasting to permit the wall covering to "relax" before hanging it, so that the wall covering will expand or shrink on the work surface and not on the wall, preventing mismatching or parting of the seams when dry.

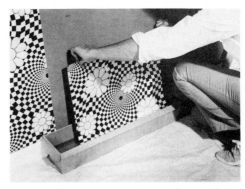

Figure 3-2. Use a water tray when you hang prepasted wall coverings. The water should be tepid. Check the manufacturer's instructions for the length of time the rolled strip should remain in water tray and how long it should relax after wetting. Place tray at the end of the cutting table or at baseboard. Hang as other wall coverings.

color deviations. This not only will prevent a disappointment when you're well into the job but will also help "uncurl" the wall covering and make it easier to work with when you start to hang it. Also if your wall covering is patterned, check the kind of pattern match you have. With a straight-across match, the point of match goes directly across the strips. A flower or plaid design, for example, continues in successive strips to form an overall design. The same part of the pattern in the first and following strips should be the same distance from the ceiling. A drop match design does not run in a straight line across the wall but runs diagonally. The design is staggered, so only every other strip is identical at the ceiling line.

To hang the first strip, the least conspicuous corner of the room is a good starting point. To make sure your first strip of wall covering is hung truly vertical, measure a distance from the corner that is ½ inch less than the width of the wall covering. Mark, with a pencil, three such measurements—near the ceiling, midway down the wall, and near the baseboard. Now tack a weighted string that has been chalked at the ceiling line or molding so that it drops to the mark that is nearest to the corner of the three measurements taken. Hold the string taut at the bottom and snap it against the wall. You will line up your first strip with the resulting chalk line. (If you don't have chalk handy, secure the string, after it is still, with another tack or tape at the baseboard. Then pencil a vertical line with your yardstick along the path of the string.) Now, before wetting the first strip, take the roll to the wall and measure and cut a strip at least 4 inches longer than the distance from the ceiling line to the baseboard.

Place the wetted or pasted strip high on the wall so that it overlaps at the ceiling joint approximately 2 inches. Line up one edge of the strip with a plumb line so that the other edge laps into the corner of the wall. Give the upper section of the strip a couple of horizontal strokes at the ceiling line to force it into the ceiling corner. Follow with down strokes. Then step down from the ladder and slide the lower section (open first if folded) carefully into position using the palms of the hands. Check for alignment with the plumb line; then smooth again using down strokes as illustrated. When the covering is positioned even with the plumb line, smooth again over

the entire strip. Remove any air bubbles, and be sure the ½-inch overlap is firmly secured into and around the corner of the wall.

To hang the second strip, take the roll to the wall, and after matching the pattern to the edge of the first strip, again measure and cut a length 2 inches above the ceiling line and 2 inches below the baseboard. After the new strip has been properly soaked or pasted, bring the two strips together so that the patterns match, and form a seam by butting the edges without overlapping. To avoid the possibility of stretching the wall covering, use the palms of the hands and work at the center of the strip as much as possible when positioning each strip.

When hanging nonpatterned or textured wall covering (grasscloth, burlap, etc.), it is desirable to reverse each strip as the wall covering is hung. When this type of wall covering is printed, color tends to be heavier at one

---

Figure 3-3. Steps in hanging wall coverings: (A) Measure the height of the wall from ceiling to baseboard, the distance around the room at the baseboard, and the height and width of each door, window, etc., which will not be covered to figure out how much wall covering is needed. Take these measurements along to the store. (B) Don't count on your eye to give you a completely straight first strip on the wall. Use a plumb line. Tack it near the ceiling where you want to start with the wall covering. Hold the weight tight at the end of the plumb line and snap the string. This leaves a vertical chalk mark on the wall. (C) Long, wet-paste-covered strips of wall covering are easy to handle when you use the professional's folding trick (called "booking"). After pasting the bottom section, fold it paste-to-paste toward center without creasing. Do the same with the top section. Get the edges even and just press gently so the material will separate easily. (D) To hang, unfold the top section and place on wall so it overlaps ceiling joint about 2 inches. Tap upper section of strip with the smoothing brush to hold it to the wall. Now open lower folded section, slide it into position, and brush. (E) Use a smoothing brush, not your hands. Using downward strokes with the brush in the center of the strip makes the seams look better. (F) Using a wall scraper as a guide, trim excess material at door casings, baseboard, and ceiling moldings with a sharp single-edge razor blade. (G) Use clean water and sponge to rinse all baseboards, casings, and ceiling moldings before paste dries. (H) Hanging the wall covering around windows and doors is done the same as on walls. Check for match, then paste. Position strip along the edge of the last strip hung. Using scissors, make a diagonal snip at the corners, fit the wall covering into place and trim.

edge than the other. By reversing each strip, dark edges will butt to dark edges and light to light, minimizing any mismatch of color shading. As you hang strips (and it's always best to finish with one roll before starting on the next), rinse each entire strip with a wet sponge to remove any paste on the surface. Be sure to thoroughly rinse ceilings, baseboard, moldings, etc., to remove any excess paste. Use clean water for rinsing. Change the rinse water after hanging two or three strips. After each wall is completed, use a seam roller and roll the seams with firm but not excessive pressure. Keep the seam roller clean and free of paste. *Reminder:* Do not roll the seams of flocked or embossed covering. They might crush.

When you come to a window or door, don't try to cut the wall covering to fit around doors and windows before you hang it. Put the covering on right over the edge when you come to a door or window. After cutting the excess away with scissors, make diagonal cuts at the corners as illustrated. Then use scraper and razor blade to trim around the window frame. Continue to match the pattern without interruption above and below the window by using matching sections from full-width strips. *Note:* Treat a fireplace in the same manner as a window or door.

When you come to an inside corner, measure a distance into the corner and onto the next wall that totals ½ inch less than the width of the new strip you will be wrapping around the corner. Mark a new plumb line at this point. Butt the first portion of the new strip to the last strip, press firmly into the corner, and smooth securely to the wall. With a few horizontal and vertical brush strokes secure the last portion of the strip at the ceiling line of the new wall. Before smoothing the entire strip to the wall, cut the full length of the strip with scraper and knife ½ inch from the corner. Now slide the strip into the corner so that the outer edge parallels the plumb line. Secure the overlap in the corner with vinyl-to-vinyl adhesive. By the way, the strip you have just hung on the new wall will overlap the last strip approximately ½ inch in the corner. Overlapping is necessary on all inside corners, on some outside corners, and on ceiling lines when the ceiling is papered.

Unless the adjoining walls to an outside corner are badly out of line, the most practical way to proceed when you come to the corner is to wrap the strip you're hanging around the corner (snip the 2-inch overhang at the ceiling and baseboard so that it will be easy to secure the strip around the new wall). Since no ceiling or corner is truly straight, you may have to tolerate a slight pattern drop or slant at the ceiling line when butting the next strip on the new wall. For this reason, when you know you'll be hanging covering around an outside corner, you should start on the longer wall. This way any pattern drop at the ceiling line caused by an imperfect corner will be on the shorter wall and will be inconspicuous. Incidentally, when you are not going to cover the wall adjoining the outside corner, be sure to cut back ¼ inch from the edge to eliminate fraying or peel from the edge. This ¼ inch will not be noticeable since it will be the same color as the paint on the adjoining wall.

How to Hang a Ceiling. Always hang the ceiling before the walls. Hang strips the sort way across the room. Shorter strips are easier to handle. Ask someone to help you. One person should hold the strips of wall covering while the other one positions the strips and smooths them into place. It's also easier if you make a scaffold by placing a plank between two ladders. Make a guideline for the ceiling in the same way you plumb walls. Deduct ½ inch from the width of the ceiling wall covering and measure from each side of the ceiling. Place tacks at each end, and attach a chalk line. Plan to end the ceiling wall covering on the less critical side of the room, perhaps just above the main entrance. Cut, paste, and fold the ceiling strips as for wall hanging, adding about 4 inches to the ceiling width to provide a 2-inch overlap on the end walls. Line up the first strip on the plumb line, which will give you a ½-inch overlap on the adjoining wall. Smooth as you position the wall covering along the plumb line. Continue with additional strips to complete the ceiling, butting the seams as on the walls. Rinse the strips as you go with a wet sponge. Change the rinse water frequently. After the strips have been hung 10 to 15 minutes, roll and press the seam with a seam roller. Trim the excess wall covering from the walls if you are going to cover the ceiling only. But when you are planning to hang the side walls, trim the ceiling wall covering so that there's ½ inch left on each wall.

If your ceiling wall covering has a pattern and you plan to use it on the walls as well, keep in mind that only one wall can be matched to the ceiling. You'll want this to be the wall most frequently looked at. For example, in a bathroom this wall would normally be the mirror or vanity wall. For this wall, trim the ceiling wall covering so that there is an excess of ¼ inch left for the wall. When you hang strips for this wall, start with a match on the ceiling, force the strip tightly into the corner, and smooth the strip to the wall. Then score the overlapped wall covering with a pencil at the corner of the ceiling, peel the strip back from the ceiling, and cut on the penciled line with a scissors.

Instructions for Hanging Special Wall Coverings

Here are some special instructions that must be kept in mind when hanging the following special wall covers:

Fabrics. They should be applied with a nonstaining paste. Trim, paste, and hang one strip at a time, and avoid excessive soaking. Fabrics must be preshrunk if they have no backing. After preshrinking, test a sample to determine how heavily paste should be applied and if paste can be washed away without leaving a stain. Generally, apply the paste to the wall. Lining paper is usually recommended. When fastening, a soft roller or clean hands are best for smoothing the fabric into place. In fact, seam rollers are generally taboo on fabrics, grasscloths, foils, flocks, and mylars. They can easily flatten or burnish the seams. Your fingers or the gentle tapping of a smoothing brush will keep seams down.

Flocks. They have raised fibers, usually nylon, applied in a design to simulate the look of velvet. To preserve the velvety look, avoid hard overbrushing in smoothing the flocked wall covering to the wall. Never use a seam roller to press down the seams. Gently tap the seams with the edge of a smoothing brush. If any paste gets on the face of the flock, remove it promptly by rinsing with a clean damp sponge. Cut and hang one strip at a time, rinsing as you go. After flocked wall covering is completely dry, set the direction of the flocked fiber by gently brushing the wall covering with a soft brush. Start at the ceiling line, and use long vertical strokes.

Foils and Mylars. They require a near-perfect surface. Read the manufacturer's directions carefully. Many recommend a lining paper and instruct you not to use a glue size. Foils conduct electricity if allowed to come in contact with exposed wires. Turn off the current, and cut the foil clean around electrical outlets for safe clearance. Because of the delicacy of some foils and mylars, the adhesive should be applied to the wall. Use a premixed type of vinyl adhesive. It is best applied with a short medium-nap roller, rolling paste on smoothly to an even texture. Roll no more than ½ inch beyond the area to be covered by each strip. Immediately after rolling, hang the strip, and before the paste dries, work out air bubles with a soft smoother or medium-nap paint roller to avoid scratching the surface. If an air bubble develops that cannot be smoothed to the wall, puncture it with a pin and press down. Reverse every other strip of a nonpatterned foil. Be sure to rinse off excess adhesive immediately.

Grasscloth and Cork. These imports are "nature's" products and generally have a paper backing. Use conventional wheat paste, but avoid excessive soaking that might cause the material to separate from the paper backing. Reversing each strip hung is recommended on no-match patterns. Lining paper is also generally recommended. Actually, lining paper is often recommended by manufacturers for hanging foils, mylar, and unbacked fabrics. It minimizes the possibility of mildew and staining and maximizes adhesion and in most cases gives a smoother surface. Whether the lining paper is strippable or regular, it is usually hung horizontally. This is not obligatory, but it's a safe way to be sure the seams of the lining paper and wall covering do not fall on the same vertical line. Cut inside corners the same as with wall covering. Use the same adhesive for lining paper as for the wall covering, and be sure it is thoroughly dry before hanging the wall covering over it (usually 36 hours).

Vinyls. They are wall coverings with a continuous flexible film applied to a fabric or paper backing. Many are prepasted. Paper-backed vinyls come strippable and nonstrippable. Fabric backs are strippable. All nonpasted vinyls require a vinyl adhesive. Since there are several kinds—powder, liquid, premixed—get your wall-covering dealer's recommendation.

"Wet-Look" Vinyls. Hang these as you would regular vinyl wall coverings—but take extra care in preparing the wall. It is critical to obtain a very smooth wall since the glossy look of a "wet-look" vinyl will highlight any defect on the wall. Also, care should be taken not to

touch or "finger" the wall covering while it is drying on the wall (in some cases the adhesives take 3 to 4 days to dry), or your imprint will show when it dries.

Questions and Answers

Let's take a look at questions most asked about wall coverings, and we hope that the answers will help you.

REMOVING WALL COVERING FROM PLASTER WALLS

Is there any such thing as an easy way to remove wallpaper from plaster walls? We recently bought a house about 30 years old, and the paper on the living room, dining room, and hall is very dingy. I'd like to take it off and paint, but I've heard that removing it is quite a project.

Portable steamers which can usually be rented from places that rent tools and appliances for homeowners, can do the job. The tank of the steamer holds about 5 gallons of water, which heats into steam. The steam goes through a hose, terminating in a rectangular plate, like an iron, which you hold close to the wall covering, and the steam penetrates into and loosens the paste. In warm weather, however, this is apt to be an operation which can only be described as hot. Another method we've seen operate very successfully is to use an ordinary compressed-air garden sprayer (after rinsing it thoroughly). Fill it with hot water, adjust the nozzle to a fine mist, and spray the paper. The mist is rapidly absorbed, and readily loosens the paper and paste. Of course, this will not work on washable wall covering.

REMOVING KITCHEN WALL COVERING

We are remodeling our kitchen. We want to paint our walls. The problem is we have to remove the old wall covering in the form of a felt-type sheeting with a lacquered finish. Is there something that will loosen this material from the wall without leaving the old wall covering stuck in various places? I find the paste loosens with soapy water, but even scraping won't pry some pieces off the wall.

There is no solvent or chemical that will penetrate through the full thickness of the wall covering and loosen the paste behind it. After pulling off as much of the covering as

possible, try to work some hot water with some washing soda in it around the edges of the pieces that are sticking. If this does not help, force a wide-blade putty knife under the sticking pieces and pry them off. Tapping the handle of the putty knife with a hammer will help.

REMOVING THIS WALL COVERING IS RISKY

The previous owner of our house apparently did not do his own work very well; he evidently was more interested in speed than care. Now some of the wallpaper is loosening, and we would like to remove it from the dry wall. We are told that if the dry wall was not sized before papering, the removal of wallpaper can also remove the paper surface of the dry wall. How can we tell? And how do we remove the wallpaper if the dry wall has not been sized?

In an inconspicuous area, lightly score the paper and apply hot cloths, in an attempt to soak the paper off. If it loosens and comes off by itself, while the dry wall is intact, chances are the sizing was put on. But if the dry-wall surface appears to come off too, quit right there. Your best bet, on this unsized wall, is to tear any loose paper in a featheredge from where it's still solid. Then put the new wall covering right over it.

SMOOTH WALLS BEFORE PAPERING

The walls of our rented house were patched and repaired many times. Each time a small ridge and some bumps were left. I would like to paper these walls. I thought if I used a heavy textured patterned paper, it would hide these imperfections. Could I do this?

Nice idea, but no. Regardless of the textured surface, the paper should be put on over a smooth surface. If the ridges and bumps aren't too numerous, you could smooth them off with a sander. You could also chip them off carefully. If you chip a little too deep, you can fill the dent with spackle compound.

WALL COVERING OFF DRY WALLS

What can we use to remove wallpaper on dry walls? The walls were all sized before papering; there are two layers of paper. We intend to paint the walls in the fall.

Removal of the wall covering from dry walls is more difficult than from plaster walls because of the paper covering that is part of plasterboard. If the paper adheres well all over and the surface is smooth, we suggest painting over the paper. To remove the wall cover, use only enough water on the surface to soften the paste; if it's soaked too deeply, the wallboard paper may separate from the board. Even so, the paper covering will doubtless be roughened and will require smoothing before repainting. When the wall has dried thoroughly, apply a coat of shellac to stiffen the paper fibers; then sandpaper it smooth. To get the wall covering off, soak it with warm water, beginning at one end of the wall and working in vertical strips, sopping water on with a large sponge. When the paper loosens, tear it off from the top; scrape the sticking places with a broad putty knife.

WALL COVERING OVER PAINTED WALLPAPER

Our dining rooms walls were papered, and after several years we painted over the paper. Now we want to put a chair molding around the room and paper the upper half. The old paper is still good and holds tightly on the wall. What will we have to do, and can we put the new wall covering over the present painted wallpaper?

The recommended procedure is to cut through the paint film by rubbing with coarse sandpaper, soak the wall covering with water or paper remover, and remove it. It is not advisable to accumulate several layers of wall cover. However, you evidently want to avoid this job. If you are certain the paper holds tightly in place, apply a glue sizing and put on the paper.

WALL COVERING ON NEWLY PLASTERED WALLS

We want to wallpaper new plaster walls. What preparation is necessary?

The plaster should be allowed to dry for at least 2 months. Since it is new plaster, it is advisable to neutralize the free lime by giving it a soaking coat of a zinc sulfate solution. Dissolve about 2 pounds of zinc sulfate in each gallon of water, and when the walls are dry, brush off any crystals that might have formed on the surface. The presence of free lime in plaster is apt to discolor or cause fading in the wall covering if the above treatment is not followed. The walls should be given a coat of glue sizing before applying the wall covering.

PAPERING WALLBOARD

We are using wallboard to partition off part of the attic. We want to decorate the walls with a paper rather than paint. Is any treatment necessary for the wallboard first?

In order to make the wallboard moisture-resistant, so that the paper can be removed at some future time, apply a coat of wallpaper sealer, available at most paint dealers and wallpaper dealers. If the sealer is not available, coat the wallboard with pure, fresh shellac or varnish size.

WALL COVERING OVER PAINTED CEMENT BLOCK WALLS?

We have a dry basement apartment with cement block walls that are now painted. Could we wallpaper these walls with good results?

You can do it, but it's a fairly big job. Wall cover (or plaster) cannot be applied directly to a masonry wall because condensation will develop later on and react badly. Before either step is possible, furring strips must be fastened to the masonry wall, using 1 by 1s, over which is applied dry wall or other type of wall paneling. This creates a dead-air space between the masonry and the wall in order to prevent condensation. Over this paneling, you can apply paper or plaster or paint. Another reason you shouldn't attempt papering over the concrete blocks is because the surface is far too rough; most wall covers must be applied over a smooth surface.

MILDEWED WALLS

There are various colored—yellow, black, green, and gray—fungi growing on my bathroom walls. Can I hang a wall covering over them?

Since these pesky fungus growths are most likely mildew, these discolored areas must be eliminated before applying the wall covering. Wash the walls thoroughly with this formula: to 3 quarts water add ⅔ cup strong liquid household cleaner, ⅓ cup powdered all-purpose laundry detergent, and 1 quart household bleach. Scrub the area with a medium-soft brush, keeping the surface wet till the stain is bleached out. Rinse with clear water, and let dry. To prevent mildew from forming under newly hung wall covering, use the paste or adhesive recommended by the manufacturer. Since adhesives used with nonbreathable wall covering sometimes take several days to dry, many manufacturers recommend adding a tablespoon of Lysol or Borax to their adhesives.

LOOSENED BATHROOM WALL COVERING

The plastic-coated wallpaper in our bathroom has loosened over the tub. We have been unable to make it stick with paste or glue. Is there anything you can suggest?

If you can get a knife blade or piece of sandpaper underneath the loosened wall covering, try scraping off some of the old paste and use a thick shellac as the adhesive. Spread this on the wall and some on the back of the paper. As soon as this becomes tacky, press it in place, and if possible, keep some pressure on it for an hour or so.

REMOVE UNWANTED CEMENT?

We installed ceramic tiles in our bathroom, and some of the tile adhesive got on the washable vinyl wall covering, leaving a yellowish line. Do you have any suggestions on how to remove this unsightly adhesive?

Any solvent strong enough to soften the cement would probably affect the vinyl too. You might try your luck with very fine steel wool. But be very careful; you might also rub off the surface of the vinyl. If you have some extra wall covering, you could put on a strip which would cover the line. If the pattern of the wall cover isn't too tricky, you could try painting out the line, using a small artist's brush and oil colors.

WALL COVER DOESN'T ADHERE

What steps should we take to ensure that our wallpaper adheres to plastered ceilings and walls? We live in an old farmhouse. After numerous paperings, the wall covers, immediately after drying, begin to snap, crack, and loosen. In cold weather, more of this occurs as soon as a little additional heat is forced. What will remedy this?

From your description, it sounds as though there are too many generations of wallpaper on the old ceilings and walls. The conditions you describe are often the result of this. The best remedy is to steam off all the layers of wall covering and start over.

PASTE SPOTS ON WALL COVER

What can I do to remove paste spots from dark-green wall covering?

Once wallpaper paste has dried, it is difficult and in some cases impossible to remove. Try sponging, not rubbing, with cloths dampened in lukewarm water. If the paper is washable, some light rubbing is possible. If the edge of the wall covering becomes loosened, you can repaste it by using a small amount of library paste under it.

INK SPOT ON WALL COVERING

How can I remove ink spots on wallpaper?

Ink and many other stains can be removed with a commercial ink remover, which is usually to be had inexpensively in two bottles; wet the spot with solution 1, blot excess, and then wet the spot with solution 2. You can also use Javelle water and then rinse with clear water. These solutions are most conveniently applied with a watercolor paintbrush only slightly wet; not enough of any liquid should be used to run down the wall. Another ink remover with less effect as a bleach is a half-and-half mixture of household ammonia and hydrogen peroxide.

GREASE SPOTS ON WALL COVERING

Some grease spattered on the wall cover in our living room. How can the spots be removed?

Cover the spots with a thick layer of a soft paste, made of fuller's earth or powdered chalk, moistened with trichloroethylene. Be sure the room is well ventilated while using the chemical. Allow the paste to remain on until dry; then remove it with a soft brush. Repeat the treatment if necessary.

WALL COVERING SPOTTED WITH CANDLE WAX

When a "helpful" dinner guest extinguished the candles, he did not hold his hand behind the flame when he blew. As a result, there are many spots on the wallpaper. I scraped off as much as I could with a dull knife, but the greasy spots are still there. How can I remove them?

Working on the principle of trying the easiest method first, hold a piece of clean white blotting paper over the spots and run a fairly warm iron over it. The heat from the iron will melt the hardened wax embedded in the paper, and the blotting paper will draw it out. Frequently this is quite successful. The other method is to cover the spots with a paste made of liquid spot remover or benzene, and powdered chalk, whiting, or other absorbent powder. When dry, brush the paste off and repeat the process until the spots disappear. One small word of caution: If the paper is several years old, the cleaned area may show up lighter than the rest of the surface.

PATCHING WALL COVER

Sun faded a small area of the wallpaper in our living room. I have more than enough of the paper on hand to recover this area. How should this be applied so that it won't look too "patched"?

Don't cut the paper for replacement with a razor blade or scissors, which will give it a sharp edge. Instead, tear the patch required from the back, so that the front surface will have a featheredge. Smear the back of the paper liberally with paste, and slide the paper into position so that it matches the pattern exactly. Wipe it firmly, working from the middle to the outer edges, quickly wiping off all excess paste. With care, a neat job can be done so that the patch will be unnoticed as such.

SHRINKING WALL COVERING

We have a gas heat unit in the wall. I have tried to hang wallpaper above this heater. The wall is painted plaster and gets hot when the heat is on. Twice I hung the paper and it shrank and came off. The third time, I removed the paper, washed the wall with a vinegar solution, rinsed with clear water, and then glue-sized it. The paper still shrank and came loose in spots. What can I do to keep the paper properly on the wall? The rest of the wall is perfect.

This particular area is probably very dry because of the heating unit. Shrinkage occasionally occurs when the wall covering is applied in a very dry atmosphere. When the heat is turned off, it is safe to go ahead and re-paper this section of the wall.

AIR POCKETS UNDER VINYL

Sometimes I can hang vinyl wall covering perfectly. Other times, being just as careful, air pockets form here and there under the vinyl. Why?

Perhaps your roller is a little too wide and occasionally bridges a slight depression instead of pressing the wall covering firmly. This could do it. So could inadequate sizing.

CHIMNEY WALL COVERING CRACKED

In a two-story frame house the wallpaper around the downstairs chimney is cracked and raised. The upstairs wall is painted, and the plaster falls off. What can I do to correct this when redecorating?

The wall covering on the chimney is probably cracking because the plaster underneath was applied directly to the bricks, causing a condition of condensation; when warm, humid house air touches a cooler masonry surface, it condenses. A false wall should be built on 1-inch furring strips, creating a dead-air insulating space; plasterboard can be used on the furring strips. This can be papered later, or painted, as desired. If the upstairs wall with the plaster problem is also on the chimney, the cause is the same and requires the same treatment.

CRACKING NOISE IN WALL COVERING

We finished the attic many years ago with a wallboard—I think it was an insulating wallboard. Four years ago we had our room insulated. In the past we have had some cracks in our wallpaper. Recently, we had new wallpaper applied. Two or three weeks after the job was done, we heard a noise in the attic, and on inspection, we found deep cracks in the walls and the wallboard in some places. Can you tell us what might be the matter with our home to make this happen? Someone suggested the vents at the eaves might be clogged.

If the wallboard is made of wood fibers and the work was done when the air was humid, it is possible that the cracking of the wall covering came about when the wallboard dried out. On drying, shrinkage took place, causing the paper to stretch and give way. If old wallpaper was not previously removed, several layers of it could cause trouble. We also wonder if the wallboard was properly varnished or shellacked or sized before the wall covering was applied. If not, it should have been in order to prevent the absorption of glue, sizing, and wall-covering paste.

PAPERING RADIATOR WALL

We are redecorating our bedrooms ourselves. We plan to apply wallpaper to the painted walls. However, we have high, old-fashioned radiators. How can we apply the paper to the wall behind the radiator?

If there isn't room to get behind the radiator with a smoothing brush, use a wooden yardstick or radiator brush to smooth the wall covering against the wall. Don't leave the wall covering hanging loose. Cut off the excess length before smoothing behind the radiator.

WATER STAIN ON WALL

Last fall, rain came in a slightly opened window and ran down on the wallpaper. Now there is a brownish edge along the bottom of the water stain. I have not been able to find any matching paper to make a patch. What can I do now?

Become an artist for the day. Borrow your youngster's watercolors and use the opaque white to hide the worst of the brown. No national academy diploma required. Try it. You'll be surprised how simple it is to soften the stain so that it's really unnoticeable.

RAIN-STAINED WALL COVERING

Is there anything that will blot out rain stains on wallpaper? They are on an area under one window which was accidentally left open during a storm.

Sorry, but we don't know any blotter or any disguiser for those troublesome spots— that is, unless you patiently touch them up with watercolors. Easiest of all, by far, is to patch the area, if you have a piece of leftover paper which has faded at about the same rate. If so, tear a piece slightly larger than the area of the spots. Tear it from the back so that it will give a featheredge. Don't cut with scissors; this will give a sharp, raised, noticeable edge. Generously spread paste on the patch; then slide it carefully into position to match the design. Smooth from the center outward, so that there will be no bubbles. Wipe off all excess paste. Step back and admire.

FABRIC WALL COVERING

At present I have a plastic-coated fabric covering on my kitchen walls. I would like to redo this with the same type of covering, but in a different color. I'm sure I ought to remove the present covering first, but it is on so firmly that removing it will be extremely difficult. Do you think I'd be safe in putting the new covering on over the present one?

We presume the reason the present coating is so firmly attached to the wall is because it was anchored firmly with several coats of paint; this is usually the case. Normally, we would recommend going through the effort of removing it, but we think you'll get away with not doing so this time, providing you clean the walls thoroughly of any grease and dirt. This is very important.

BRICK-TYPE WALL COVERING

I would like to install some type of brick alongside and behind my gas range. Something that can be installed easily. I have heard of a new type of three-dimensional-effect wallpaper with this brick effect. Where could this be purchased?

There are several kinds of this type of wall covering which can be easily applied over the present wall surface. There is a plastic-coated contact paper available in this pattern, a vinyl paneling, and a cork wall covering. These products are carried at wall-covering dealers, housewares dealers, department stores, and some variety and hardware stores. For any product, follow the specific manufacturer's instructions as to adhesive and installation method.

CLEANING VINYL "BRICK"

How do we go about cleaning this new vinyl brick which is cemented on individually? It looks and feels like the real thing, including the rough, dirt-catching surface.

Use the same treatment you'd use on the real thing: hot water, moderate-strength detergent solution, and a reasonably stiff brush.

COATING MUSIC ON THE WALL

I have used old sheet music to wall-cover a room. I need something to cover this paper. Shellac will turn yellow and so will lacquer. What should I use?

A clear plastic spray in aerosol form is available at many hardware, paint, and wallpaper dealers.

HANGING BURLAP ON WALLS

We plan to cover our entrance foyer walls with burlap. Is this hung like wallpaper?

No; the adhesive is applied to the walls instead of the covering material. But it isn't difficult. For tight-fitting seams, apply a 1-inch-wide strip of pure, fresh shellac along each edge of the underside of the burlap. When this is dry, trim ½ inch off, using a

Figure 3-4. Two types of plastic three-dimensional wall coverings.

straightedge and razor blade. This will give a clean edge that won't ravel and which can be butted neatly against the adjoining strip.

REMOVING WALL LINOLEUM

My bathroom walls are covered with standard wall linoleum. I would like to remove this linoleum. How do you recommend doing this?

Pry a corner of the linoleum loose with a blunt-edged tool like a putty knife or screwdriver. Then moisten the paste on the back of the wall covering. (If a waterproof adhesive was used, moisten with naphtha, being sure the windows are open and the room well ventilated; be careful of fire hazard.) As the paste softens, pry the covering loose from the wall.

Interior finish is the material used to cover the interior framed areas or structures of walls and ceilings. These finishes either are prefinished or serve as a base for paint or other finishes including wall coverings. The most common interior finishes used in modern homes include (1) lath and plaster; (2) gypsum wallboard; and (3) wood paneling, fiberboard, or plywood. Though lath-and-plaster finish is still found in many older homes, dry-wall materials [types (2) and (3)] are used in most modern house construction.

CHAPTER 4

INTERIOR WALLS AND CEILINGS

Lath and Plaster

In older frame construction, plaster was spread on lath nailed to the studding and other framework. If wood lath was used, as was the cases in most homes built before World War II, it was separated by ¼ to ⅜ inch between edges and ends. The first coat of plaster, mixed for strength and usually reinforced with hair or fiber, was applied with sufficient pressure for part of it to be forced between and behind the laths; it was through hardening there that the plaster was secured. Plaster doesn't adhere to lath or to other wood. Plaster binds itself to metal lath in the same way and is more firmly attached because of the greater number of openings through which it can pass. Because of this, metal lath is still sometimes used in bathrooms, where a rigid base is needed.

Today most of the lath used in home construction is either rock lath (the most commonly employed) or fiberboard lath. The plaster attaches itself to either by penetrating the open texture of the surface and hardening in the pores. Rock lath is made with ½-inch holes placed at intervals to hold the plaster more firmly. This type of lath material is nailed directly to the studs in sheets, with gaps of about ½ inch left between the edges in order to provide for expansion and to give an extra grip for the first plaster coat. The second coat of plaster, called the "brown coat," evens out the wall. The third coat gives a smooth surface and finish.

A dry plaster wall will last indefinitely. Plaster that is continuously wet for any long period, as would be the case from a leaking wall or a dripping pipe connection, will be so softened that its attachment to the lath will fail; under this condition a ceiling may fall. Plaster problems and their solutions are covered later in this chapter in the question-answer section.

Gypsum Board

Gypsum board is a sheet material composed of a gypsum filler faced with paper. Sheets are normally 4 feet wide and 8 feet in length, but can be obtained in lengths up to 16 feet. The edges along the length are usually tapered, although some types are tapered on all edges. This allows for a filled and taped joint. This material may also be obtained with a foil back, which serves as a vapor barrier on exterior walls. It is also available with vinyl or other prefinished surfaces. In new construction, ½-inch thickness is recommended for single-layer application. In laminated two-ply applications, two ⅜-inch-thick sheets are used. The ⅜-inch thickness, while considered minimum for 16-inch stud spacing in single-layer applications, is normally specified for repair and remodeling work.

When the single-layer system is used, the 4-foot-wide gypsum sheets are applied vertically or horizontally on the walls after the ceiling has been covered. Vertical application covers three stud spaces when the studs are spaced 16 inches on center, and two when the spacing is 24 inches. Edges should be centered on the studs, and only moderate contact should be made between the edges of the sheet.

Fivepenny cooler-type nails (1⅝ inches long) should be used with ½-inch gypsum, and fourpenny (1⅜ inches long) with the ⅜-inch-thick material. Ring-shank nails, about ⅛ inch shorter than the fourpenny nails, can also be used. Some manufacturers often recommend the use of special screws to reduce "bulging" of the surface ("nail pops" caused by drying out of the frame members). If the moisture content of the framing members is less than 15 percent when gypsum board is applied, "nail pops" will be greatly reduced. It's good practice, when framing members have a high moisture content, to allow them to approach moisture equilibrium before application of the gypsum board. Nails should be spaced 6 to 8 inches for sidewalls and 5 to 7 inches for ceiling application. The minimum edge distance is ⅜ inch.

The horizontal method of application is best adapted to rooms in which full-length sheets can be used, as it minimizes the number of vertical joints. Where joints are necessary, they should be made at windows or doors. Nail spacing is the same as that used in vertical application. When studs are spaced 16 inches on center, horizontal nailing blocks between studs are normally not required when the stud spacing is not greater than 16 inches on center and the gypsum board is ⅜ inch or thicker. However, when the spacing is greater, or an impact-resistant joint is required, nailing blocks may be used.

Nails in the finish gypsum wallboard should be driven with the heads slightly below the surface. The crowned head of the hammer will form a small dimple in the wallboard. A nail set should *not* be used, and care should be taken to avoid breaking the paper face.

Joint cement, "spackle," is used to apply the tape over the tapered edge joints and to smooth and level the surface. It comes in powder form and is mixed with water to a soft putty consistency so that it can be easily spread with a trowel or putty knife. It can also be obtained in premixed form. The general procedure for taping is as follows:

1. Use a wide spackling knife (5 inches), and spread the cement in the tapered edges, starting at the top of the wall.
2. Press the tape into the recess with the putty knife until the joint cement is forced through the perforations.
3. Cover the tape with additional cement, feathering the outer edges.
4. Allow the cement to dry, sand the joint lightly, and then apply the second coat, feathering the edges. A steel trowel is sometimes used in applying the second coat. For best results, a third coat may be applied, feathering beyond the second coat.
5. After the joint cement is dry, sand it smooth (an electric hand vibrating sander works well).
6. For hiding hammer indentations, fill them with the joint cement and sand them smooth when dry. Repeat with the second coat when necessary.

Interior corners may be treated with tape. Fold the tape down the center to a right angle and (1) apply cement at the corner, (2) press the tape in place, and (3) finish the corner with joint cement. Sand the cement smooth when dry, and apply a second coat.

The interior corners between walls and

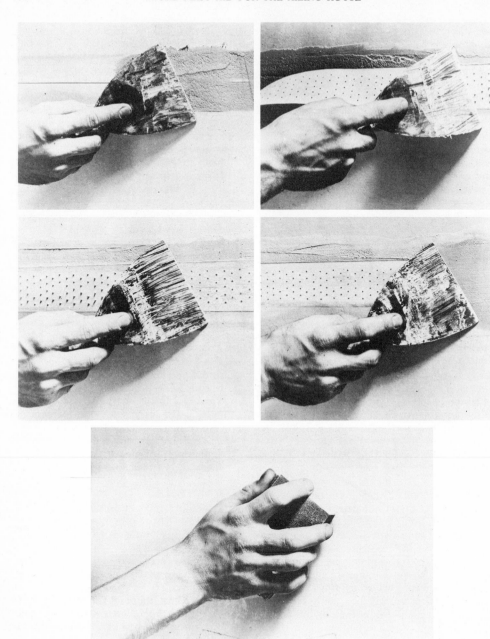

Figure 4-1. Steps in filling a gypsum-board seam.

ceilings may also be concealed with some type of molding. When moldings are used, taping this joint is not necessary. Wallboard corner beads at exterior corners will prevent damage to the gypsum board. They're fastened in place and covered with the joint cement.

Plywood

Prefinished plywood is available in a number of species, and its use shouldn't be overlooked for accent walls or to cover entire room wall areas. Plywood for interior covering may be used in 4- by 8-foot and longer sheets. The sheets may be applied vertically or horizontally, but with solid backing at all edges. For 16-inch frame-member spacing, ¼-inch thickness is considered minimum. For 20- or 24-inch spacing, ⅜-inch plywood is the minimum thickness. Casing or finishing nails 1¼ to 1½ inches long are used. Space them 8 inches apart on the walls and 6 inches apart on ceilings. Edge nailing distance should be not less than ⅜ inch. Allow ¹⁄₃₂-inch end and edge distance between sheets when installing. Most wood or wood-base panel materials should be exposed to the conditions of the room before installation. Place them around the heated room for at least 24 hours.

Adhesives may also be used to fasten prefinished plywood and other sheet materials to the wall studs. These panel adhesives usually eliminate the need for more than two guide nails for each sheet. Application usually conforms to the following procedure: (1) Position the sheet and fasten it with two nails for guides at the top or side; (2) remove the plywood and spread contact or similar adhesive on the framing members; (3) press the plywood in place for full contact, using the nails for positioning; (4) pull the plywood away from the studs and allow the adhesive to set; and (5) press the plywood against the framing members, and tap it lightly with a rubber mallet for full contact. Manufacturers of adhesives usually supply full instructions for application of sheet materials.

Wood Paneling

Various types and patterns of wood are available for application on walls to obtain desired decorative effects. For informal treatment, knotty pine, pecan, white-pocket Douglas fir, sound wormy chestnut, or pecky cypress, finished natural or stained and varnished, may be used to cover one or more sides of a room. Wood paneling should be thoroughly seasoned to a moisture content near the average it reaches in service, in most areas about 8 percent. Allow the material to reach this condition by placing it around the wall of the heated room. Boards may be applied horizontally or vertically, but the same general methods of application should pertain to each. The following may be used as a guide in the application of matched-wood paneling:

1. The paneling should be applied over a vapor barrier and insulation when appli-

Figure 4-2. Plywood and hardboard may be installed with nails on wall furring strips.

cation is on the exterior wall framing or blocking.
2. Boards shouldn't be wider than 8 inches except when a long tongue or matched edges are used.
3. Thickness should be at least ⅜ inch for 16-inch spacing of frame members, ½ inch for 20-inch spacing, and ⅝ inch for 24-inch spacing.
4. Maximum spacing of supports for nailing should be 24 inches on center (blocking for vertical applications).
5. Nails should be fivepenny or sixpenny casing or finishing nails.

Use two nails for boards 6 inches wide or less and three nails for 8-inch and wider boards. One nail can be blind-nailed in matched paneling.

Wood paneling in the form of small plywood squares can also be used for an interior wall covering. When the squares are used over framing and a vapor barrier, blocking should be so located that each edge has full bearing. Each edge should be fastened with casing or finish nails. When two sides are tongued and grooved, one edge (the tongued side) may be blind-nailed. When paneling (16 by 48 inches

Figure 4-3. Plywood and hardboard may also be installed with a contact type of adhesive as shown here.

or larger) crosses the studs, it should also be nailed at each intermediate bearing. Matched (tongued-and-grooved) sides should be used when no horizontal blocking is provided or paneling is not used over a solid backing.

Hardboard and Fiberboard

Hardboard and fiberboard are applied the same way as plywood. Hardboard must be at least ¼ inch thick when used over open framing spaced 16 inches on center. Rigid backing of some type is required for ⅛-inch hardboard.

Fiberboard in tongued-and-grooved plank sheet form must be ½ inch thick when frame members are spaced 16 inches on center and ¾ inch when 24-inch spacing is used, as previously outlined. The casing or finishing nails must be slightly longer than those used for plywood or hardboard; spacing is about the same. Fiberboard is also used in the ceiling as acoustic tile and may be nailed to strips fastened to ceiling joists. It is also installed in 12- by 12-inch or larger tile forms on wood or metal hangers which are hung from the ceiling joists. This system is called a "suspended ceiling."

Fiberboard comes prefinished in many surfaces—burlap, cork, vinyl, and cloth, to name a few. Hardboard also comes in many prefinished surfaces, but the most popular is the fused-on, glass-smooth plastic one. It's made in many wood-grain patterns as well as white and solid shades of various pastels. The surface is so hard and impervious to damage that it's almost impossible to dent, scratch, or roughen. Refinishing is something you can forget about. *Caution:* If you are trimming this type of paneling or planking yourself, always cut it with the finished side up. When fastening it, always screw the paneling to the wood, and not vice versa.

Any discussion about redecorating with wall paneling would never be complete without at least a reminder of that universally popular pegboard. This is the paneling of hardboard with regular rows of holes, about an inch apart, which has many uses in addition to its simple good looks. In the first place, pegboard's smooth surface can be painted in any manner desired. Secondly, the holes make this material just about the handiest saver of storage space imaginable. With all the many specialized hooks, brackets, and supports now available, you can hang just about anything on pegboard. At the same time, you can keep frequently used utensils or tools instantly at hand.

In the kitchen, you can use pegboard to support spice shelves, towel racks, cooking spoons, pots and pans. In the workshop you can hang all manner of tools—both power and hand types—on the wall behind the workbench where they're not in the way, but where you can grab them quickly. It makes this even easier if you draw an outline of each individual tool right on the pegboard. Then it can always be returned to its own parking place. In the garage, you can use a pegboard wall to hang all kinds of things that normally clutter the floor around the edges and in the corners. Garden tools, hoses, bicycles, even mowers can be hung on well-fastened pegboards.

A description of all the various types of panels and paneling available these days would take far more than the space available here. To get a better acquaintance and understanding of the tremendous variety available nowadays, visit a few lumberyards or building supply centers.

Questions and Answers

Here are some questions and answers that may aid in solving wall and ceiling problems:

CRACKS IN CEILING PAINT

I have been living in my house 17 years. The plaster walls have been painted several times; I don't know how much paint is on them, but when the colors were changed, I had to put on a couple of coats at a time. We always use a flat oil-base paint. Recently cracks appeared in the ceiling, leaving a gap of about ⅛ inch in some places; the paint has cracked, not the plaster, as the plaster is visible underneath. Are the cracks the result of something in the paint? How should we refinish the ceilings next time so that the cracks won't show?

We're afraid the cracking is due to too many coats of paint; the sheer weight of the paint is pulling down, separating it and causing cracks. As much of the present paint coating as possible will have to be removed before refinishing. Use a paste-type prepared paint remover, following the label instructions carefully. Spackle can be used to fill any remaining cracks and give a smooth surface for the paint coating. Or painter's muslin or cloth can be applied to cover the ceiling surface. This is a finely woven fabric, available at wall covering dealers, and applied like wall covering. It can be painted or "papered" as desired.

PEELING SPOTS ON CEILING

There are two spots on our bedroom ceiling, first floor, where paint keeps peeling off. We want to paint the room, but first we want to fix the spots. Ours is a story-and-a-half Cape Cod with two dormers. A carpenter checked for leaks from the dormers but found none. I suppose it's moisture from somewhere. How can we fix those spots up?

The spots may be due to moisture from the area under the roof, if there is insufficient ventilation and air circulation. Vents should be installed at the peak ends of the roof and at the eaves. If the ceiling plaster at the two spots has deteriorated from too long exposure to moisture, it must be replaced. Have you checked for leaks in the roof or around chimney flashings?

CRUMBLED PLASTER

We have a spot on the kitchen ceiling where paint is peeling. We removed the loose paint, and when we touched the plaster, it all crumbled down. The area involved is about 1½ feet from the outer south wall. The ceiling was insulated ten years ago, and siding was put on five years ago. During the cold months we kept one louver closed. Could the cooking in the kitchen cause enough moisture to do that? What do you think might have caused it?

Moisture disintegrated the plaster. Lack of thorough air circulation in the attic could cause condensation to form, which would form as frost in winter. Thawing would melt it and drip down on the ceiling. Keep the louvers open all year round. Snow and ice accumulation at the roof gutter may have caused water to back up under the shingles during a thaw. Resetting or eliminating the roof gutters will correct the latter condition.

BATHROOM CEILING MILDEW HAS THEM DESPERATE

We're desperate about mildew covering the ceiling above our tub-shower. We've repainted twice, this time using a sealer and enamel, after thoroughly scrubbing with Lysol. Still the mildew continues to spread. Can you help with a solution?

With all that steam and damp air trapped against the ceiling, it's a perfect place for mildew to form. If you'll open the bathroom window as soon as possible after showering, it will help draw the steam away. Best of all would be a ceiling fan, which could draw the steam up into the attic and over to a ventilating louver through a duct.

WATER-STAINED CEILING TILE

We had a leak from a room above, and our ceiling tile was badly water-stained. Could the tile be painted to hide the stains? Or is there any way to remove them?

Painting would be the only way we know of to hide the staining. Vacuum or brush off all dust. Apply a coat of shellac, thinned half-and-half with denatured alcohol. Finish with a latex base or resin-emulsion wall paint or vinyl plastic paint.

MOISTURE ON CEILINGS

Last March we bought a new home and moved into it the same month. We noticed when the temperature was raised to about 70 on the thermostat, the ceilings would have moisture on them. There are louvers in the attic and loose-fill insulation, but no vapor barrier. Instead of plaster, the ceilings and walls are plasterboard. What can be done to correct this situation before the cold weather sets in?

Not knowing more about the structure of your house—whether you have a basement or crawl space or neither, what type of siding you have, etc.—it is difficult to make any recommendations. In general, this may be due to too humid house air, to moisture rising up from uncovered ground under the house, to moisture from roof leaks or chimney leaks, or to attic louvers that are too small to let all the moisture out.

SOUVENIR OF SLOPPY PLASTERER

We had our bedroom ceiling plastered by a professional, if you'll excuse the expression. We have since found sloppy lumps of plaster on the white enameled woodwork in several places where he couldn't be bothered wiping it up when fresh. Now these lumps have hardened. Can I remove them without marring the nice woodwork finish?

Patience, care, and this method should do it okay: Scrape off what you can with a very dull blade. A small, square-ended piece of hardwood, tapped along with a hammer, will get quite a lot off, too; maybe all. Moisten the remainder with warm water and rub it lightly with fine steel wool.

NOISE COMES THROUGH CEILINGS

We have a two-story frame house with an apartment upstairs, and would like some advice on keeping sounds from being heard downstairs. Is there anything we can do?

It is difficult to obtain a large percentage of sound reduction unless such work is done by an acoustics engineer or contractor. You can, however, obtain a fair amount of soundproofing by constructing a false ceiling. The framing for it should be fastened to the walls and should not be in contact with the existing ceiling. A thick blanket or batt type of insulating material is then placed between the framing members, and the new ceiling is finished with a wallboard. Another method is to cover the floor above with a carpet cushion and then wall-to-wall carpeting (see page 107).

PUTTING UP CEILING TILES

I am interested in putting a soundproof ceiling of acoustic tiles in my basement playroom. At present, the ceiling consists of gypsum board nailed to the bottom of the beams. How would I fasten the tiles?

In this case, regular ceiling tile adhesive can be used. Put a dab near the underside of each corner, and press it into place. If the tiles have tongue-and-groove edges, you'll get a good snug fit with no trouble. Other methods are stapling and fastening with special clips that fit furring strips. For a dropped ceiling, you use acoustic panels which rest on a grid of aluminum or stainless steel strips hung from the original ceiling.

Figure 4-4. Ceiling tiles may be applied directly to the ceiling or to furring strips with cement or staples.

NEW BASEMENT BEDROOM MUST BE QUIET

I plan on adding a bedroom in the basement (it is very dry and comfortable). I would like to soundproof the ceiling from the overhead noises. What materials should I use?

For most soundproofing, we suggest a "dropped" ceiling of acoustic tiles or panels on a framework of aluminum strips, suspended a foot or so below the present ceiling. Into the space between, put in thick fiberglass wool or similar thick blanket insulation.

PAINT SMOKED-UP CEILINGS?

Our acoustic-tile ceilings, in both the living room and rec room, were stained by smoke due to downdrafts in the fireplaces. Is it possible to paint over this? Is there any special method we should use?

Go to it. Use whatever paint you'd normally use. But put it on in thin coats. If you press heavily with a roller or brush on a thick coat, you'll fill up most of the little holes that make the tiles acoustic.

GREASE ON CEILING TILE

Is it possible to remove grease spots from new ceiling tile? Quite by accident, some grease was spattered and reached the ceiling.

Make a paste of powdered whiting and a nonflammable liquid spot remover. Spread

Figure 4-5. Steps involved in installing a grid-type ceiling.

this in a thick layer over the spots, and allow it to remain until dry. Repeat the treatment if necessary. If the tile is on the kitchen ceiling, we strongly recommend enameling the surfaces, because vapors and other greases will soon discolor the tiles, making it difficult to get them clean. With an enamel finish, soap and water or one of the detergents could be used for cleaning.

WATER DAMAGED CEILING TILE

Not so long ago our insulating ceiling tiles got wet and spotted the ceiling. It is quite noticeable, and I wonder if it could be fixed without removing the ceiling.

Brush off all the dust; then apply a coat of shellac, thinned half-and-half with denatured alcohol, and finish with a latex-base or resin-emulsion wall paint.

CEILING ALREADY TOO LOW

Our basement has only a 7-foot ceiling, with wiring and pipes below the beams. We would like to refinish one area for a study, but without the expense of putting the pipes and wiring through the beams. It is now too low for a dropped ceiling, and we need access to the pipes. Can you suggest a portable yet attractive ceiling?

Even if it's impractical to move the pipes and wiring so that they're alongside the beams instead of underneath, you could still consider a dropped ceiling of translucent fiberglass panels, which are less than ¼ inch thick. They can be supported on a frame of thin steel strips. You'd scarcely notice the difference in height.

REMOVING PAINT FROM CEILING BEAMS

We recently purchased a home which has 6-by 6-inch ceiling beams. These have been painted. Is there any way to remove this paint without a lot of mess?

Sorry to say that any paint-removal job is messy. The easiest way would be to take the paint off with an electric sander, but that will scatter sawdust and paint powder.

FALSE BEAMS

I wish to make a beamed ceiling where no beams are. Can you tell me how to make false ones to fasten over plaster and how to hold them on?

You need an anchor board to fasten to the ceiling at each beam position, nailing through the plaster into the ceiling joists. The width of this must be exactly the same as the inside width of your false beams. Build the beam with one piece the full width for the bottom and two strips for the vertical sides. Glue and nail through the bottom piece into the two sides. Then nail through the sides into the anchor strips to fasten the beam in place. You may want to install a half-beam around the perimeter, which is easy enough, but you will need two strips or cleats inside the beam, one for the bottom and one for the side pieces to fasten to.

STAINS WON'T STAY PAINTED

Last winter I installed some beams of fake wood in our cathedral ceiling. They are plastic foam, hollow in the center. The beams meeting the outside walls began to leak, leaving large, brownish stains. What can I do to hide these stains? I have already tried painting, but that didn't help, since the stain "bled" through the paint.

Sand off any gloss. Then put on a coat of aluminum paint. This is an excellent shield against such stains bleeding through paint, even with mahogany stain, which is notorious in this regard. Then go ahead with your painting. Pure, fresh white shellac is also excellent for this job.

OIL STAINED CEILING AND WALL

The oil stove on our second floor leaked through the ceiling and wall on the first floor. What can be done to get rid of the stain. There is a mirror on the wall where the oil is. Will it be damaged?

The plaster or wallboard, whichever was used for the ceiling and walls, is saturated with the oil, and there is no way of removing it because the oil in the plaster or wallboard will continue to come through. Replacement of the oil-stained materials is the only remedy. To prevent the new material from becoming stained because of the oil in the wood, coat the stained-wood joists and studs with shellac. If the back of the mirror is well coated, it will not be discolored by the oil.

PLASTER PATCH FALLS OUT

I used a prepared plaster patch to fill deep cracks in two outside corners of my living room and along the baseboards. After a few months, it is all breaking loose and falling out. Can you advise as to the best solution?

To get plaster to stay in a crack, the crack should first be widened and opened down to the lath. After brushing out all loose particles, the inner surfaces must be made wet and the patching put into the groove. The crack should be wider at the lath than it is at the surface. If the above does not solve your problem, it may be necessary to install corner beads. This consists of sheet metal bent to fit a corner to which metal lath is attached. The old plaster is cut away from ceiling to baseboard, and the corner bead is fastened in place; then plaster is applied. Your local building material dealer should be able to furnish the bead.

HAIRLINE CRACKS IN PLASTER

Several years ago I used a spackling compound to fill light hairline cracks in plaster and then applied a rubber-base wall paint. Since then, the cracks have reappeared. I plan to sand down the walls lightly and apply enamel paint. I would appreciate any suggestion you might have for eliminating these hairline cracks.

Very fine hairline cracks are usually filled with a mixture of 3 parts of boiled linseed oil and 1 part of turpentine. Another method is to make a Swedish putty and place it in the cracks. This is a mixture of a spackling compound and paint or varnish. Instructions can be found on the spackling compound box. If your house is an old one, it would be best to cover the walls with a painter's cloth or canvas; then paint over it. It is put up like wallpaper.

NEW HOUSE WALLS CRACKED

We just moved into our newly finished house. Cracks have begun to develop in some of the plaster walls. How can this be corrected?

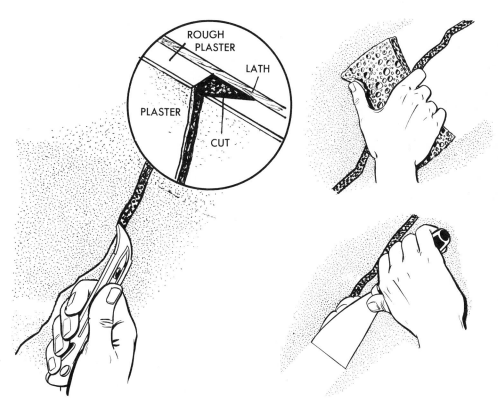

Figure 4-6. To repair a small crack in a plaster wall, first undercut it as shown, then wet it and fill with patching compound.

These cracks are probably due to settlement of the house structure itself; settlement of a new house may go on for several months. Repairs are a waste of time until settlement has ended. Mark the end of the crack with a light pencil. As the crack grows, make a new mark. When at least 2 months have elapsed since the last mark was made, you can be reasonably sure that settling has stopped and the cracks can be patched. Spackle can be used to fill the cracks, or patching plaster can be used. Instructions for use on the label should be followed.

CRACKED PLASTER

The plaster walls in my new house keep cracking in the corners. I have patched these cracks according to directions, but they still come back. What's the matter? I'd sure appreciate any help you can give me.

We're willing to make a small wager that the lath under the plaster was not brought around the corner to form a continuous piece. If you're willing to tackle the job yourself, cut away the plaster to its full depth, 6 inches on each side of the corners, and install what is known as metal corner lath. This is available at any building supply dealers. With this corner lath in place, you can replaster, and the cracking should not recur.

ROUGH-TEXTURED WALLS

The plaster walls of our living room are covered with a rough-textured coating that has large waves, or swirls, having a sequence every 2 or 3 inches. The walls are covered with an oil paint. What method of smoothing do you recommend?

Remove the roughest part of the texture

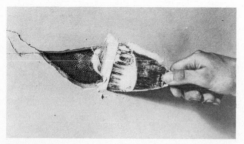

Figure 4-7. For a larger hole in a plaster wall, reinforce the hole with a strip of wire screen or lath and then apply plaster. Let dry and sand smooth.

with coarse sandpaper, wrapped around a block of wood; better yet, use a portable electric sander, if you can rent or borrow one. Wipe off the dust; then fill the light remaining indentations with a spackling compound applied with a trowel. Another method is to cut through the paint with coarse sandpaper; then wet down the walls thoroughly with hot water. After a few minutes of soaking, the rough material can be scraped off with a wide-blade putty knife, bringing up a finished plaster surface. Try this on a small area first.

WASHING PLASTER WALLS

What is good to wash new walls with, which have become very dirty? I am going to wallpaper but do not want to spoil the walls for possible future painting.

The walls are probably painted plaster. These can be washed with a solution of 1 or 2 tablespoonfuls of trisodium phosphate to a gallon of warm water. Begin at the bottom and work upward, using a circular motion. Working in this direction will prevent dirty water from trickling down on dry parts of the wall and making permanent stains. Wash a small area at a time, and rinse at once with clear water, not letting the wash water dry on the wall. There is a cereal paint-cleaning preparation in powder form, available at paint and hardware stores, which can also be used.

SWELLING PLASTER SPOTS

Recently we moved into an old brick house. The plaster walls developed swollen areas; when they were replastered, new swelling appeared. What do you suggest?

The plaster may not be adhering properly to the lath underneath, or the lath itself isn't firmly attached to the wall or furring strips. Excess moisture in the wall space, caused by leaks, may cause the loosening. It's recommended that you have a competent builder inspect and advise.

NEWLY PLASTERED WALLS

We have newly plastered walls. Is it all right to apply a sealer and paint to prevent loose particles of sand from dropping on the floor? It is said that these will be ground into the floor by walking, thereby ruining the floor. What do you advise?

After the moisture has evaporated, we also suggest painting the walls, but only to prevent the plaster from becoming badly soiled and sooted. If the walls were finished with a smooth, white finish plaster, do not worry about sand dropping on the floor; there is no sand in the finish coat. Plaster that has been properly mixed and applied will not sand or dust off.

CRACKS IN PLASTER

Last year we purchased a 20-year-old bungalow flat. Recently we noticed that slight cracks in our plaster had become deeper and longer. Also, patched cracks reappeared. Our wood beam in the basement is cracked and doesn't seem to be too sturdy. Could this be the cause? Is replacement by a steel beam advisable? Whom can we consult to get advice on the problem?

A weak girder could cause such difficulties, but if cracks reappear around doors and windows, there may be defects due to improper framing of such openings. Improper lathing could also be the cause. An architect or a competent builder could examine the home and recommend procedures for the correction of the difficulties.

WATER-DAMAGED PLASTER

The plastered ceiling in one corner of my living room was damaged by water leakage from the apartment above. The plaster is now loose and will have to be refinished. I had refinished this room with textured paint. Would it be possible and advisable to nail new gypsum lath over the old plaster and replaster, or should all old plaster be removed down to the lath?

It would be more practical to remove the plaster down to the lath, since the water-damaged plaster is becoming loose.

PAINTING MILDEW DOESN'T GET RID OF IT

Mildew forms about a foot up from the baseboard on a section of dry wall in one of our bedrooms. It has been painted several times. The mildew washes away, but forms again. Can this area be sprayed with anything to prevent mildew?

This part of the wall is damp, either from stagnant, humid house air or from a leak or condensation on the other side of the dry wall. Therefore, a spray won't stop this. (It would be nice if there were such a product which would!) If you have an electric heater, aim it at the wall and see if warming and moving the

air will dry the mildew. If this does not dry the mildew, the dampness is coming from the other side. Finding its cause could take some professional know-how. If the mildew were widespread, instead of concentrated in one small section, it would most likely be caused by very warm, damp house air that needs to be dried out and properly vented to the outdoors.

NAILS POPPING LOOSE

Apparently some of the wall studs are losing their grip, because nails through the sheetrock wallboard are beginning to back out. I drive them in at another place, but they come loose again. This is in a semi-finished attic. What should I do?

Use ringed or cement-covered nails. These will hold much better than the straight-shanked nails you've obviously been using. For a more finished appearance, you could then cover the nailheads with bridging tape.

NAIL BULGES ON WALLBOARD

We have occupied our new house only 6 months, and the ceilings across the center in both bedrooms have a line of what looks like nailhead markings, making a spotty, bulging appearance. How can we remedy this?

Evidently the nailheads were not driven below the surface of the board and the filler was merely applied on the surface instead of into the indentations. It is also possible that the person who applied this filler did not flush it off with the surface of the board. You will probably be able to improve the appearance by rubbing down the spots with "00" sandpaper.

OPEN JOINTS IN WALLBOARD

We have a finished attic in our bungalow-type home. The previous owner used a wall-cloth type of wall covering in one room and wallpaper in another. The walls were constructed of fiber wallboard, but I don't know what kind. Where the sheets join there is a slight space, causing the paper and the fabric wall covering to push and crack. We want to paint and wonder what could be done about these spaces.

If the walls are built of a fiber or composition wallboard, make a depression about $\frac{1}{16}$ of an inch deep and 4 inches wide, the full height of the wall. This can be done with a coarse sandpaper wrapped around a block of wood; a portable sanding machine is quicker, if you can rent or borrow one. Part of the space is then filled with a spackling compound of Swedish putty. While the filler is still soft, nail in place, over the joint, a 4-inch-wide strip or wire screening; then fill the rest of the depression with more spackling compound or Swedish putty. Swedish putty is made by mixing the compound with paint or varnish. Instructions will be found on the spackling compound box.

DRY WALL COMING LOOSE

The dry wall on the outside walls of our flat is starting to come loose. I have driven the same nails in again, but they pop loose. What can I do?

This is one place where batten strips can come in very handy. Using ringed or cement-shanked nails, nail these strips over the dry-wall joints and well into the studs. If you want the strips a different color than the dry wall, paint them before nailing them in place.

HOLE IN GYPSUM WALLBOARD

An accident has made a hole in our gypsum wallboard wall. How can I fix it?

First get a scrap of gypsum board. Then cut out the damaged area in the shape of an equilateral triangle, slanting the edges inward at 45 degrees. Enlarge the hole at least 1 inch on all three sides. Make a similar triangle from the gypsum wallboard scrap, and shape it with sandpaper to fit the hole, slanting the edges the same way. Butter the edges of the patch with compound. Set the patch in place, and scrape off excess compound evenly. You can apply joint tape and more compound the same as you did at any butt joints in paneling the room in the first place. Sand smooth when

dry. If the patch is large, back the opening with a slat of wallboard cemented to the back of the panel.

TIME FOR PAINTER'S CLOTH

We have many cracks in our dining and living room walls. We tried putting on tape and using dry-wall compound, and then went over the tape twice with more compound, letting it dry each time. After several days, lines appeared on each side of the tape, and the tape itself was loose. When we took the tape off, we saw it took off the latex paint down to the oil paint which we had put on many years ago. We sanded the oil-base paint, put on the tape, and even tried spackling compound. It did not hold either. What should we do?

Cover the walls with painter's cloth or muslin, and forget these problems (see page 37).

VISIBLE WALLBOARD SEAMS

We partitioned off our dining area from the kitchen, using plasterboard. The walls were finished with paint. Now the seams are beginning to become visible. Is there any way to remedy this?

Probably you didn't reinforce the joints; this prevents cracking of the joint. At least ⅛ inch should be allowed between the edges of the wallboards; the joints should be cleaned out and sized with thin varnish and shellac and then refilled with cement recommended by the manufacturer of the wallboard. The filled joint should be covered with special perforated tape, available at building supply dealers, and pressed into the cement. Finish to match the rest of the surface. If the wallboard

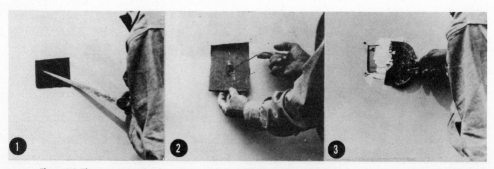

Figure 4-8. Three steps involved in repairing a large hole in a gypsum-board wall.

sheets were butted close together, cut out V-shaped joints. Nail strips of wood over the joints, ⅛ inch thick and about 2 inches wide; paint or stain them to match the wall.

SCRATCHES ON PREFINISHED WALLBOARD

A few weeks ago my husband remodeled our kitchen. He put a prefinished wallboard on the walls and ceiling. Since our home is quite old and the walls are not square, he had a difficult time with the ceiling. As a result it has quite a few bad scratches. The owner of a hardware store told him to use a white enamel to cover them. We tried one coat, but it did not cover them. Is there anything we could use?

What you should have done is to contact the maker of the wallboard to see if he could supply a small container of a touch-up enamel for the scratches. We think the reason the scratches show through is that they have not been filled in. Using a fine artist's brush, run some enamel undercoater into the scratches. When the undercoat is dry, smooth the areas with "0000" sandpaper and then apply the enamel.

SEALING JOINTS BETWEEN WALLBOARDS

We have a knotty pine room, and above the knotty pine we have an insulating wallboard. What can we use to seal the joints of the wallboard? We have used a spackling compound, but it cracks open.

Scrape off all paint and compound from the joints and sand down about a 4-inch-wide strip, the full height of the joint, to create a depression about ¹⁄₁₆ of an inch deep. Spread a spackling compound in the depression; then nail in place a strip of wire screening. Apply more spackling compound over the screening, and flush off level with the surface of the wallboard.

WATER STAIN ON PLASTERBOARD

We used plasterboard to finish an attic room. A leak in the roof caused a large water stain on one panel. We want to paint the walls, to hide the stain. Is any special treatment required?

Coat the surfaces with a primer sealer. Finish with any good-quality alkyd- or latex-base paint.

SOILED INSULATING PLANKS

Our walls are of insulating plank panels. Is there any method of cleaning unpainted plank-paneled walls? In painting such walls, what steps and methods should be used?

Dust can be removed by going over the surfaces with a wallpaper cleaner. This is a doughlike substance that is rolled (not rubbed) over the board. You should be able to get the cleaner from your local wallpaper or paint dealer. If painting is necessary, wipe off the dust and remove all grease stains by covering them with a thick layer of a paste mixture of powdered whiting and a nonflammable liquid spot remover. When the paste is dry, brush off the powder. The walls can then be coated with a rubber-base or resin-emulsion wall paint.

SMOKE AND FIRE DAMAGE

We had a fire, which resulted in considerable smoke and grease damage. What can we use to clean all articles and get rid of the smoke odor? Also what can we do about paper articles? Can paint be put on plaster walls after washing them? Except for smoke and grease, the walls are in good condition.

To get rid of the smoke odor, we suggest consulting a professional smoke odor removal service (check the classified telephone directory). All washable surfaces should be washed with a scratchless scouring powder containing chlorinol, followed by rinsing with clear water to remove all trace of the cleaner. Walls should be washed with a solution of trisodium phosphate, using about 1 tablespoon to the pail of warm water, followed by ample rinsing. Be sure to start at the bottom of the wall, working upward, to avoid impossible-to-remove streaking when dirty water runs down over dry-wall surfaces. Unwashable surfaces (such as paper) can be cleaned by applying a paste made of liquid nonflammable spot remover and powdered whiting or fuller's earth.

STRONG ODOR OF WOOD

We recently moved into a new house, the second floor of which is finished in knotty pine. The odor of the wood is very oppressive, and I would like to know if the wood could be treated with some kind of material which would subdue or eliminate the odor.

Evidently the contractor did not finish the pine. If the wood were given a couple of coats of a clear lacquer, shellac (thinned half-and-half with denatured alcohol), or semigloss varnish, the odor would be eliminated.

PANELING UNEVEN WALLS

Due to badly cracked plaster on the walls of our older frame house, the walls in two rooms are very uneven. I would like to resurface them with a smooth covering, such as paneling, and also insulate the outside walls with blanket insulation. How should I do this?

Cancel out the unevenness by putting up a frame of sturdy furring strips just out of contact with the plaster walls. Secure the strips at the floor and ceiling, and put the paneling over this "false wall." Place the blanket insulation in the space between the walls.

SEAMS BETWEEN SHEETS OF PLYWOOD

The walls in my prefabricated home are of ½-inch plywood (4 by 8) sheets. We have successfully taped the seams, but discovered that after 2 months there was a fine crack running along the seam. What should we have done to prevent the seams from cracking?

Wood shrinks and expands with changes in atmospheric moisture, and it is not possible to cover the joint with a flexible material without having the covering crack or wrinkle. It is best to cover the seams with a wood molding.

UNWARPING PLYWOOD SHEET

I have a piece of plywood 61 inches by 15 inches by ¾ inch. I plan to use this as a linen closet door in a bathroom. But first, how can I get rid of the bow in this piece?

Lay the sheet, concave side up, over a couple of chair backs or sawhorses, with a foot or so extending beyond the supports at each end. On these overhangs, place very heavy weights—pails of dirt, rocks, iron doorstops, piles of heavy books. In several days or a week, it should straighten out. Before hanging the door, be sure to seal every square millimeter of it with several coats of shellac, varnish, paint, or enamel, especially those vulnerable edges, so that all moisture will be firmly sealed out. If moisture gets in later on, the plywood will curl again.

PANELING CEMENT LOSING ITS GRIP

Several years ago, we had paneling put over the plaster walls of our den. Some sort of adhesive was used. Now a few of the panels are coming away from the walls. We have tried colored nails, but they do not help. Is there any way to remedy this situation without removing the panels?

Perhaps the colored nails weren't long enough, or you didn't drive them into the studs. You can get a "stud-finder" (very inexpensive) at any hardware store. The only other suggestion is to anchor the paneling top and bottom with quarter-round molding. This, of course, would mean going all the way around the panels.

PANELING CHICKEN-GREASY

How do you remove chicken grease that splattered and soaked into new wood paneling? Spot remover and lighter fluid didn't work.

Chicken fat is famous for being extra-greasy, so you'll need extra patience. Make a stiff poultice of powdered chalk or similar absorbent and benzene. Mix it outdoors, because of the extreme fire hazard benzene presents. Cover the stain thickly; then tape plastic sheeting over it to retard evaporation. When the poultice is dry, brush it off and repeat the treatment. The idea is that the benzene will work in and loosen the grease in the wood, and the powder will act like a blotter to draw it out, *Let us repeat:* Be very careful of the fire hazard; benzene is highly flammable.

WALL PANELING NEEDS CLEANING

Our oiled walnut paneling on the walls of our living room and dining room is showing signs of general wear. It isn't scratched or dented; just dull and fingerprinty. What is the best way to clean it? Or is there some special polish for this?

Recently some spray preparations have been developed for this particular job to make cleaning much easier. They are good at restoring a nice clean surface and getting rid of fingerprints and general shabbiness.

BARN LUMBER A TERMITE CARRIER?

I plan to use boards from an old barn as paneling for a basement playroom. Do I run the risk of bringing termites into the house?

Chances are overwhelming that if the wood has been termite-free this many years, it's still okay. Besides, when you saw across those long planks to fit them to your room height, you'd see any burrows that were there. You could also "spot-check" by jabbing an ice pick into various parts of the boards on the side you won't see. If you hit soft spots, investigate. If you don't, don't worry.

SOILED UNFINISHED PINE

We left the pine woodwork unfinished when our house was built, not wanting it to darken as it does when varnished, shellacked, etc. Now we have spots of soil to remove from doors, etc. What should be used as a cleaning agent?

Grease stains can be removed by sponging with benzene (being careful of fire hazard); heavy soil may require sandpapering. A seal should be applied to the surface to prevent penetration of soil into the wood. Even with no finish, wood has a tendency to naturally darken with time.

MARKS ON PINE PANELS

There are some dark marks on some knotty pine panels. How can I remove them before applying varnish? Some are pencil marks, and others are marks where something rubbed the boards and soiled them. Sandpaper does not seem to work.

Pencil marks should come off readily by rubbing with a pencil eraser. Other types of soiling are usually removed by washing with turpentine and "0" steel wool. Stains and mildew discoloration will have to be bleached out by applying a liberal amount of a hot, saturated solution of oxalic acid *(poison)*. Leave it on overnight, and then rinse with clear water. When the panels are dry, smooth them with "000" sandpaper, dust, and finish with varnish.

MARKS ON PLYWOOD PANELING

We have a recreation room paneled with mahogany plywood. What is the best type of cleaner to use for getting finger marks, crayon, etc., off? I have tried detergent cleaners, which leave white spots. The only finish on the paneling is wax.

Probably the white spots left by the detergent cleaners are due to the water used. We recommend using a cream cleanup wax, made by a nationally known manufacturer,

following the label directions; this leaves a coating on the wood surface which will protect against future soiling.

SOILED WALL OVER RADIATOR COVERS

We had a cover made to fit over two radiators in the living room, enclosing three sides and the top. Since then, the wall over the radiators seems to have become very soiled quickly. What is the trouble?

Since there is no back to the type of cover you had made, when the heat rises, it draws dust with it behind the radiator and deposits it on the wall above. Before the covers were installed, the dust was probably so diffused with the warm air rising from all parts of the radiator, it wasn't noticed. Fastening a sheet of aluminum foil as a back to the radiator cover will help prevent dust from rising from the back of the radiator and landing on the wall; the heat will also reflect out into the room, instead of being absorbed by the wall behind.

SCRUBBING PAINTED WALLS

A few months after we painted our frame house, the walls looked dusty. Is there any way to scrub them?

You can scrub down the walls with a solution of trisodium phosphate or one of the detergent powders. If trisodium phosphate is used, dissolve about ¼ cupful in a pailful of water; use about ½ cupful of detergent to the pail. To prevent streaking, wet down the walls with clear water before you start scrubbing, and always keep the surfaces damp so that when loosened dirt runs down the walls, it can be readily wiped off. All wall cleaning should be started at the bottom, and work should progress upward. The reason the new paint film picks up dust and dirt is because the paint contains a lot of oil, which slows down the drying process. A surface that is tacky for a long time will pick up particles of dust and dirt as well as soot. Do not add oil to the paint unless advised to do so by the manufacturer on the label of the paint can.

OIL SPOTS ON PAINTED WALLS

Can you tell us how to get some oil spots out of freshly painted plaster walls?

After the paint has been allowed to harden for several weeks, the oil can be taken out by covering the stain with a mixture of pow-

Figure 4-9. Often it is wise to prefinish wall panels such as knotty pine. To do so, apply the desired finish as follows: (top left) Sand boards most carefully; (top right) apply the finish and (bottom left) rub finish if desired; and (bottom right) smooth any installation marks with steel wool and retouch if necessary.

dered whiting and a nonflammable liquid spot remover. Apply this in a thick layer, and allow it to remain until dry; then brush off the powder. The oil spots appeared most likely after the paint had dried hard. If this is not the case, it is likely that the oil stained areas may not have hardened, and the treatment might also take off the paint. If so, touch up with new paint.

FINGER MARKS ON ROUGH FINISHED WALLS

How can I clean fingerprints from modern rough walls?

An oval paintbrush, with bristles at least 2 inches long, can be used to wash the walls. This type of brush penetrates and cleans out the roughness. Use thick suds of a pure, mild soap, and follow with ample rinsing with clear water. Be sure to start at the bottom of the wall, working upward. To clean a limited section of wall only, apply a paste made of powdered whiting and nonflammable liquid spot remover. When dry, brush off and replace with fresh paste if necessary. Be sure the room is well ventilated while working.

FILM ON WOODWORK

The woodwork and wood doors in our kitchen have a film which we cannot remove, no matter how thoroughly we wash, rinse, and dry them. Can you help us?

Try removing the film by wiping the wood with a mixture of 1 tablespoon of cider vinegar in a quart of lukewarm water. Rub it on with a soft, lintless cloth in the direction of the grain of the wood; then wipe with a dry cloth. If this does not help, the varnish is at fault, and a more moisture-resistant varnish should be used.

REMOVING PUTTY FROM PANELING

How can putty be removed from light paneling? I used it in the cracks, but it shows up like plaster. I tried several removers, but got no results.

Try careful removing with a sharp-pointed beer can opener or similar tool. Or soften the putty with a small pointed soldering gun, being careful not to scorch the paneling. A puttylike stick, in various popular wood colors, is now available for filling cracks; it is carried by plywood dealers and some hardware stores.

DISLIKES MOLDING COLOR

Around the base of the kitchen walls in our new house there is black rubber molding, the concave type. I don't like the color. How can I change it?

Pry it off, and stick on some new molding of the color you like. The molding dealer will also have the proper adhesive.

CRACK ABOVE BASEBOARD HEATERS

Somehow, over the years, our baseboard heating panels seem to have come loose at the top, leaving a crack between them and the walls up to ¼ inch wide. Someone had put plaster over the crack, but the plaster cracked due to the heat, and some plaster fell down behind the baseboard. What will fill this crack?

Shred three or four sheets of newspaper, and stir them into half a pail of hot water. When they become mushy, pick up a pinch and squeeze it so that most of the water is gone. Then, with a small screwdriver or similar tool, work this tightly into the crack slightly below the surface. Continue until the entire crack is packed. The smoother you can make the surface of this papier-mâché crack filler (that's what it actually is), the easier it will be to fill the remaining depth smoothly with built-up coats of paint.

NO-SCRATCH DECAL REMOVAL

How can I remove a decal from the closet door of my son's room? I don't want to scratch the paint by using any blade, even a dull one.

Hold wet toweling against the decal until it softens. This could really be done best if you remove the door so you can lay the wet cloth right on the decal. Then it's just a matter of gentle rubbing; not a scratch will appear! Note: If a decal is covered by varnish, such as on a child's chair, the varnish must be removed first.

STUBBORN TILE ADHESIVE

Some years ago, my husband put plastic tile on the wall behind my stove. Now some tiles directly behind the oven have fallen off. I would like to replace all these tiles with aluminum tiles. I can remove the tiles easily myself, but the mastic! I can't budge it. The wall is wallboard, not plaster, and chipping the mastic gouges the wallboard. I cannot afford a plasterer. I know I can put on the new tiles myself, but how do I remove the old, hardened mastic?

If you can manage a rental portable sander, give it a try. Use a drop cloth to protect the stove and stove area against dust. Slower, but perhaps easier on your shoulders, is the following method: Use a lady's hair dryer to soften up a few squares of mastic at a time; then scrape the mastic off with a wide-blade putty knife. Be careful that the corners don't gouge.

CERAMIC TILES OVER PAPERED WALLS

I wish to install ceramic tiles over a plastered wallpaper-covered wall. How do I go about it?

If the wall is sound and the plaster firm and unbroken, the easy way to put up tile is with adhesive. First remove the paper. Wash down the wall to remove any remaining paste that might come off later. Prime the surface, and spread the adhesive with a notched trowel according to the recommendations of the manufacturer of the organic tile adhesive you select. Set your tile, spacing evenly with toothpicks if yours are not self-aligning tiles. Wait at least 24 hours before using a latex-base grout to finish up the job.

REMOVING WALL TILE TRICKY

One wall of our house is covered with 12 by 12 mirror tiles. At each corner of the tiles is a small square of adhesive, which makes them stick securely to the wall. We are thinking of changing some things and would like to know how to remove the tiles without pulling off pieces of wall plaster too.

If these tiles are really individual mirrors, removal without damage to the plaster can be tricky. You can use either heat to soften the adhesive (using an iron set at "moderate") or dry ice to chill the adhesive so thoroughly it becomes brittle and loses its grip. The catch is that both the heat and the extreme cold could easily crack the glass. With a more tractable material than glass, the job would be much less risky to the tiles. However, even if some plaster does come off with the tiles, you can easily repair the damage by smoothing spackle over the holes.

TILE ON CINDER BLOCK WALLS

I have been contemplating installing some type of tile to cover cinder block walls and would like to know where to obtain information on how to install them, as my wall is very uneven. I am considering aluminum tile and wonder if it will be necessary to install some kind of furring strip.

It is not advisable to put tiles of any kind directly on cinder blocks or any other solid masonry, even if the walls are level. The walls should be furred out and gypsum wallboard put on over the furring strips. Aluminum or plastic tiles could be applied according to the manufacturer's directions.

DIVIDING LARGE BEDROOM

A growing family necessitates making two bedrooms out of one large room in this house. I can't afford the rates of a professional carpenter, and wonder if there is a simple way to do this which an amateur wouldn't mess up too badly.

Here's a method which is certainly simple in concept, even though it leaves out some of the usuals you'd expect from a pro. Your anchors are 2 by 4s fastened to ceiling beams and floor. They stretch from wall to wall where you want the divider. Toenail more 2 by 4s between, as vertical members of the framing; 16 inches apart is customary. For horizontal support, fasten short lengths tightly between the verticals, one-third and two-thirds of the height. Nail panels of dry wall or paneling over this, fill the joints, and put on wallpaper or latex paint (no sizing needed). Cover the top and bottom edges with quarter-round molding for a clean finishing touch.

CUTTING OFF VIEW, BUT NOT LIGHT

Could you suggest anything to fill in a space under a hanging china cabinet and a counter top? There is an opening of 17 inches. From the living room you can see the built-in stove top and part of the sink. Is there something decorative that allows light to pass through that could be put in that space?

Various plastic and fiberglass materials, in sheet form, are available at building supply dealers. These are available in colors or with a slightly "frosted" finish. Also the type of material used for shoji Japanese screens, in which butterflies, plants, etc., are embedded, or the undecorated, translucent variety, might be used. If you wish to use this space as a "pass through" for food, the material could be installed to slide on tracks.

PARTITIONING

I have purchased a rambler-type home that has an asphalt-tiled basement floor. I contemplate partitioning off the basement as a recreation room, spare room, and utility room. How is the studding fastened to a basement floor covered with asphalt tile? I've been told that I should fasten the studding to the floor with bolts or screws by driving lead plugs into the tile and cement. Is this correct?

The studding itself is not fastened to the floor, but you must put down what is known as a sill plate. It is a 2 by 4 laid flat. A hole is drilled through the tile into the concrete to receive a lead anchor or expansion shield (available at hardware stores). The sill plate is then fastened in place by bolts. The studs can then be nailed to the sill plate.

PARTITIONING ROOM

We want to convert our dining area, an alcove off the living room, into temporary sleeping quarters. Is there any way to put up an inexpensive type of partitioning?

The simplest method would be to install an accordionlike sliding wall on tracks. Another method would be to install sheets of wallboard or plasterboard on 1-inch furring strips nailed to the floor and ceiling. Consult larger building supply dealers or lumberyards. Manufacturer's instruction sheets for installing the materials are usually available at dealers, listing also the required accessories, etc.

DIVIDING TWO ROOMS

How can I go about dividing two rooms (living room and bedroom) without doing any plaster work? We have a large archway, but it is not squared off. I would like something in a shutter door or folding door. What would you suggest?

We have frequently seen large shutter-type doors used as attractive room dividers. Very often you can pick up just what you want along these lines at auctions. Lumberyards have acknowledged the popularity of shutters as folding doors by keeping them in stock. Of course, you could always make a very effective room divider simply by nailing wallboard to a framing of 2 by 4s.

IS IT A BEARING WALL?

We have just bought a tiny old farmhouse. Two bedrooms were too small for use, and so we began to tear down the common wall. Now all that remains are the studs. How can I tell if this is a bearing wall? There are no double 2 x 4s, and nothing continues up into the attic. Dare we go ahead and pull out the studs?

While you don't pinpoint the location and direction of the studs, we'd certainly agree this doesn't sound like a bearing wall. We'd also vote to pull down the studs. But to be on the safest side, subsidize an architect or builder to come and look. It wouldn't take him more than 2 minutes to tell you what kind of wall it is.

PREVENT SAGGING BEAM

We have lived in our older house for nearly 20 years. Recently, I noticed that one of the big beams across the basement ceiling has begun to split, and now I am worried that it may begin to sag. Can an amateur do something about this, or must I call in a professional basement engineer?

Judge for yourself: all that's really needed is an adjustable metal post, possibly two. This can be adjusted so that the post is the exact height needed. Such posts are also used to straighten beams which have already sagged. You can put it in position and leave it as long as you want.

FASTENING TOWEL BARS TO PLASTERBOARD

I have just purchased a winterized cottage and am in the process of installing a shower curtain rod and towel bar fixtures. The ceiling and walls are of wallboard. Is there any means of securing these fixtures other than putting a board on the wall extending from one stud to the next?

One of your local hardware dealers could supply you with a fastening gadget described as a toggle bolt. This is inserted through a hole drilled in the board, and as the screw tightens in place, the toggle spreads (spider fashion) in back of the wallboard, keeping the screw and fixture tightly in place.

BOOKSHELVES ON WALL

I am considering the installation of hardwood bookshelves that will cover an entire wall. I want to use the new metal standards that are screwed into the wall with brackets that fit into slots in the standards. Will this hardware support shelves 51 inches wide filled with books?

There are special wall fasteners now available to support heavy weights like this; your dealer for the shelves and metal strips doubtless will supply them. Three metal supporting strips may be advisable.

MAKE PLYWOOD EDGES LOOK LIKE WOOD

I am planning to build bookshelves of ⅝-inch plywood, with a birch finish. Is there any way to disguise the edges, so that the laminations don't show? Of course, this would be no problem if I were using paint.

Just about any hardware store or plywood outlet sells plywood edging tape. This is a roll of "tape" made of thin plywood, usually with its own adhesive backing. You merely stick it along the edges and that's all there is to it. This comes in various widths and all popular wood shades.

WHITE FILM ON BRICK

We have a brick planter in our living room, and found quite a bit of mortar on the brick. We were told to use muriatic acid to clean it off. This we did, not diluting the acid. We now have a white film on the brick. We put another coat of acid on the brick, diluting 10 parts of water to 1 part of acid. We still have the film. Can you help us?

Evidently you did not scrub the brickwork and probably never rinsed it with clear water. After the solution has been on the brick for about 3 minutes or so, scrub the surfaces with a fiber scrubbing brush; then rinse well with lots of clear water. Since the solution is highly corrosive, wear rubber gloves, protect your eyes and skin against splashing, and wear rubbers over your shoes. The proportion of 1 part of acid to 10 of water is satisfactory.

FASTENERS FOR PICTURE

I inherited a large, heavy painting in a deeply carved frame. Our living room wall is dry wall on furring strips over concrete block. Picture hooks in the dry wall would be useless. How should I hang it?

Use two expanding masonry fasteners; tell the hardware salesperson what you want to do. One excellent type works this way: You insert the outer cylinder (called an anchor) into a hole drilled into the masonry. When you drive in the accompanying screw, it forces the lead to expand tightly against the hole. Leave enough of the screwhead sticking out to accommodate the heavy picture wire.

HANGING PICTURES WITHOUT PLASTER CRACKING

Is there a foolproof method for nailing picture hanger hooks on a plaster wall without cracking the plaster? I have tried putting a piece of Scotch tape on the wall and then nailing through, but the plaster still cracks some.

If the pictures are relatively light (25 pounds or lighter), there are wall mounting fasteners which adhere to the wall with the new epoxy type of adhesive. Many hardware stores have these kits. If you wish to use a penetrating fastener, such as a nail or expansion bolt, first locate the joist. Then put an "X" of Scotch tape and drill through into the joist, using an electric drill. This method, properly done, will prevent the plaster from cracking.

NOISY WALL TOO THIN

I'm sure the wall between our bedroom and the next apartment must be unusually thin. We can hear the sound of voices so loudly at times it wakes us up. The super only shrugs his shoulders and says he didn't build the house. Is there any way to soften the sounds?

Put up a false wall of paneling or wallboard on furring strips, out of contact with the present wall. Staple blanket insulation in the space between. To deaden the sound even more, hang a heavy drape or equivalent on the wall.

INSULATION TO SOUNDPROOF WALL?

We have a duplex flat. The partitions are 2 by 4s, plastered on both sides. They are not

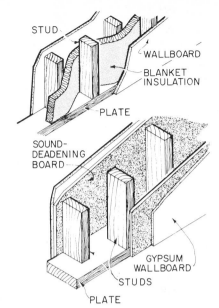

STUD

WALLBOARD

BLANKET INSULATION

PLATE

SOUND-DEADENING BOARD

GYPSUM WALLBOARD

STUDS

PLATE

Figure 4-10. Methods of soundproofing a wall.

soundproof. Would insulation blown in between the 2 by 4s help soundproof? Or what other suggestion do you have?

Blown-in insulation would help soundproof somewhat. More satisfactory, however, would be to install either acoustic tile on the plaster wall or a new synthetic material, available in rolls (like wallpaper) to be applied over the wall surface for soundproofing. We suggest consulting a tile or floor-covering dealer.

SOUNDPROOFING FLOOR

I live on the top floor and would like to shut off the noise from underneath, at least in one room. What is the best floor covering to deaden sound? I know it would help to put ceiling tiles up in the apartment underneath, but I don't want to bother the tenants.

Wall-to-wall carpeting over thick padding should help considerably in absorbing the

sound from the room below. Or putting down a new finish floor, on 1-inch furring strips, to allow an insulating air space between the two floor surfaces, will also help deaden the sound.

OVERHEAD NOISES

What can I do to soundproof my upper-flat floor against heavy walkers?

One method is to cover the floors of the apartment above with rug cushioning material; then cover that with a carpeting. The other is to construct a false ceiling out of contact with the existing one. The framing should be attached to the walls. Place an insulating blanket between the framing members, and finish with lath and plaster or wallboard.

SILENCE FOR POWDER ROOM

The combination of a toilet that does not flush quietly, ceramic tiles on walls and floor, a thin, hollow core door, plus proximity to the living room makes the powder room embarrassingly noisy. I really don't feel like buying a silent toilet when this one is perfectly good. Can you suggest any other steps for promoting more silence?

We assume you also don't wish to sacrifice perfectly good ceramic tiles, either. Weather-stripping felt around the door can help. So can wall-to-wall carpeting over the floor tiles. Not 100 percent silence, but a couple of good steps along the road.

INSULATING TO KEEP OUT NOISE

I would like to insulate an inside wall with insulating panels to keep noises from next door from penetrating. Is this practical, and how do I accomplish this?

Insulating wall panels, installed on 1-inch furring strips, out of contact with the wall, is very practical for cutting off the noises. Your building supply dealer will have detailed instruction sheets available for installing the panels.

The strength of a floor in a residence is in the beams, also called "joists," which support the flooring. In breadth and thickness these should be calculated amply to support the load that will be placed on the floor. In good construction the beams are placed not more than 16 inches apart from center to center. When the length of the beams is greater than 8 feet, each beam should be braced against those next to it by pieces of wood or of non-rusting metal in the form of the letter X. These braces, called "bridging," prevent the beams from swaying and will spread a weight or a shock, as of a piano or a falling trunk, over the entire floor instead of concentrating it only on the beams beneath.

The beams are covered with rough boards forming the subfloor, preferably running diagonally for greater stiffness. These boards should be solidly nailed to the beams, boards of 6 inches and less in width with two nails to each beam, and wider boards with three nails to each beam. Nails are driven through the surfaces of the boards, preferably at an angle for greater holding strength. The subfloor should be covered with a layer of building paper to prevent dust and dirt from sifting through.

The finish floor is nailed or glued to the subfloor. Finish floorboards in strips are usually tongued and grooved. The nails are finishing nails which have small heads; they are driven at an angle through the edges of the boards so that the heads are concealed by the board that follows. Parquet flooring made in blocks at the factory is either nailed or cemented to the subfloor. Resilient tile and sheet covering are cemented to the subfloor.

Squeaky Floors and Stairs

Squeaks are caused by friction. With stairs and floors, it's either wood rubbing against wood or nails moving up and down in the nail holes. Nails can become slightly loose in the nail holes either when the wood itself shrinks as it dries out (wasn't thoroughly seasoned) or if too-short nails were used. You can readily see how foot traffic's constant pounding can eventually make inadequate nailing work loose; the heavier and the more numerous the family members, the sooner the squeaks will begin.

There are several ways to cure a squeaky floor. The easiest situation is when the floor's underside is an unfinished basement ceiling.

CHAPTER 5

FLOORS
AND
STAIRS

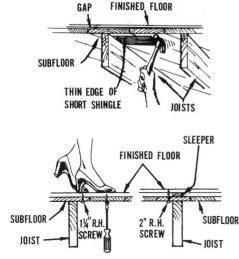

Figure 5-1. Two methods of curing a squeaky floor.

sinking the heads below the surface. Then you fill the dent over the screwhead with plastic wood or other crack filler, tinted to match the shade of the floor's finish. Sand it smooth and level, and dab on varnish or whatever finish is already on the floor. One favorite do-it-yourself crack filler of a "natural" wood shade is made by mixing sawdust and varnish, or sawdust and glue, to a fairly stiff paste consistency.

The other method is nailing the boards to the subflooring. Here you use nails which are amply long (certainly longer than those used originally!) and drive them in at an angle, rather than vertically. This will give much greater holding power. Drive them in pairs, at opposite angles. The best nails are finishing nails, or the spiral type with small "brad" heads. Use a nail set when within ¼ inch of the floor, and drive the heads slightly below the surface, the same as with the screws. Fill the dents the same way.

As a temporary way of promoting this golden silence, some people are successful at dusting talcum powder or powdered graphite so that it sifts down between boards which squeak against each other. This is strictly temporary, however—something to consider as a stopgap until you can really get down to doing the job right.

Stairs are silenced in the same manner. In better construction, the treads and side stringers are joined in a variation of tongue and groove, rather than the treads simply being nailed to the side supports and the risers. Regardless of the construction, by securing the treads solidly again to their supports,

You simply go downstairs and observe carefully while someone walks back and forth over the squeaky place. You'll see where there's motion, and right there you drive in a thin wooden wedge or two, jamming it between the subflooring and the large supporting beam. This will effectively stop any up-and-down motion of the floor, and so there'll be no more squeak. Shingles make good wedge material.

Some people prefer to handle this another way: While someone overhead stands on the squeaky board to press it down, several wood screws are run up through the subflooring into the floorboard itself, firmly drawing it down against the subflooring. There's absolutely nothing the matter with this method; just be sure not to use wood screws which are too long, and which could emerge through the top of the floorboard.

Unfortunately, lots of squeaky floors are over finished ceilings, and so it's impossible to use these underside corrections without cutting through the ceiling first. Quite understandably, everyone would avoid this like the plague. So the only other approach is topside. While there's considerably more work involved, none of it requires any real skill or experience.

Based on the theory that the nails have worked loose, you simply resecure the board solidly to the subflooring. You can do it two ways: Use long, thin wood screws, counter-

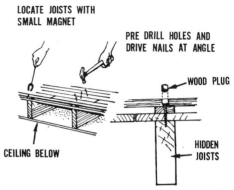

Figure 5-2. Curing a squeaky floor which is over a finished ceiling.

the motion that causes the squeaks will be stopped. Again, the job can be done with the long wood screws or the pairs of long finishing nails driven in at opposite angles.

If the stairs are covered by carpeting, we suggest your using the nails rather than screws. This is only in the interest of saving work. You can drive the nails down through the carpet and on into the tread, using the nail set, and the carpeting will close over the small hole so that you'd never know the nail had gone through. In fact, you won't even have to sink the nailheads and fill the dents; the only place you'll have to do this is in any areas outside the carpeting. But with the screws, the larger-diameter head would make it necessary to remove the carpet first and replace it afterward.

Speaking of stair carpeting, here's a method whereby you'll get twice the usual length of service. It works like this: When you buy the long strip of material, exceed the actual measured requirements by the height of one of the steps. This is usually in the neighborhood of 8 inches. This sounds like an insignificant amount of material, but it sure can mean a significant saving in dollars. Here's the trick: When you cover the riser of the lowest steps, make the carpeting double thickness; that is, double under that extra few inches. Then proceed with the rest of the job in the usual way. Now the place where stair carpeting wears the fastest is at the front edge of each tread. When these places begin to get worn-looking, it makes all the rest of the carpeting look shabby too. There isn't much you can do to disguise this, either. So the only real solution is to throw it all out and get a whole new stretch.

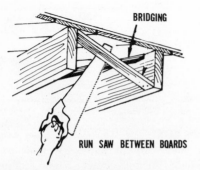

Figure 5-3. The rubbing of the floorboards can be cured by running a saw between them.

But see what happens with this little piece you've doubled under: When the inevitable wearing begins, you simply unfasten the carpeting and move the whole length upward by the amount of extra carpeting which was doubled under. What happens? A whole fresh untrodden area is exposed all the way upstairs. To all intents and purposes, you have a brand new carpet—and the money you save by this simple little maneuver is all your own!

Questions and Answers

Let's take a look at various problems floors and stairs can cause as well as some of the possible ways of solving them.

SPRAY WON'T SILENCE FLOOR

We are having trouble with creaking floors, which have plywood nailed to the beams for subflooring. The problem is general, under the rug, linoleum, and hardwood floor areas. Do you know of a noncombustible lubricating spray which could be used between the beams and plywood as a silencer?

You're on the right track, since you recognize that it's the up-and-down motion of the nails in the nail holes which causes the squeaks. But it takes immobilization, not lubrication. Drive very thin wood wedges (pieces from shingle tips are okay) between the beams and the subflooring to stop the motion of the boards.

FLOOR BOARDS LOOSE

Several boards in one of our upstairs bedroom floors are loose. How should they be fastened down?

Probably the finishing nails used were not long enough; or they were not driven at an angle into the subflooring to give them a better grip. The new spiral or ringed nails are excellent for this job; they have superior holding power. Use a nail set to drive the heads of the finishing nails slightly below the floor surface; then cover the nail holes with a matching putty available in various wood finishes at plywood dealers or many hardware stores; or cover the nail holes with wood putty, and touch them up to match the finish on the rest of the floor.

SQUEAKY PARQUET FLOOR

Can anything be done to silence a squeaky parquet floor?

Try to locate the nearest floor joist.

Usually (but not always) these run at right angles to the length of the room, 16 inches apart. Tap your way across, using the handle end of a hammer. When the sound turns firm and solid, that's the joist. With that point of reference, you can locate others. Drive amply long finishing nails (small heads) down into the joists. Do this in pairs, at slight angles, for better holding power. Use a nail set to sink the nailheads slightly. Cover the dents with wood putty or plastic wood, and retouch them to match the floor. Fastening the flooring firmly to the joist will stop the motion which causes the squeaks.

VIBRATING FLOOR

When someone walks across our living room, the floor vibrates. What can we do about it?

It sounds as though the floor needs more bracing, also called cross bridging. This is simply bracing between the floor joists, which is put in diagonally between each joist. At a good many hardware stores and building supply houses, you can get aluminum cross bridging all ready for "do-it-yourself" installing. Another cause of the vibrating might be that the joists or beams themselves are not large enough. We recommend asking a building contractor to inspect the floor construction. Request his opinion on how far apart the cross bridging should be installed, and whether or not the joists or beams themselves are undersized.

HOUSE SHAKES

What makes a house shake when buses pass by the house? One room, particularly, shakes when one walks across the floor or even when the dog runs across the room.

When heavy trucks and buses travel over a highway, the earth vibrates, and this is naturally transmitted into buildings close by. The condition is further aggravated if the floor joists of a building are not heavy enough or if the spans are too long for the floor weight they are supporting. There is nothing you can do, unless you wish to undergo some structural changes, which should be done by a competent builder.

SLANTING FLOORS

Can you give us some suggestions or reasons why the floors of all the rooms on the second floor of a 40-year-old house slant toward the center hall? The difference in level is perceptible and is about 1½ inches. The only other "defect" in the house is the bowing of three longitudinal wood beams on the first floor, but they are not in the center but near an outside wall. The house is well built— no cracks.

If there are no signs of termite infestation or rotting, the carpenter doing the timber framing probably placed a girder that was not of proper height, or possibly the joist hangers were not of the right length, thus giving you a lower level toward the center of the house. To correct this would be quite a task.

SAGGING FLOOR

My house is about 40 years old, and the floors are sagging in the center. Would it be wise to have supports in the cellar raised in order to level off the floors? There are two brick supports under the beam.

Before attempting to do any leveling, it would be wise to ascertain the cause of the condition. It might be due to rotting timbers, and replacement would be the only remedy. The two brick supports, we presume, are the columns supporting the girder across the floor joists. If the brick columns were built from the ground up instead of from the concrete floor, they might have sunk into the earth. In such cases, it should not be too difficult a job to raise the floor by using adjustable metal posts. Hardware and building material dealers sell them. Or you could rebuild the brick columns.

WARPED FLOORBOARDS

We have a very heavy rug in the living room. We employed a person to clean it with a machine that is brought to the house. The cleaner got the rug so wet that it took more than a week to dry. Now the edges of the floorboards are bowed up a little. Should I sand the floor?

Allow the wood to dry out thoroughly; then if the boards are still bowed, sand them down with a floor-sanding machine. Wipe off the dust, and finish with a floor sealer, a shellac, or a penetrating wax finish.

NOISY WOOD FLOOR

My floors are of hardwood laid over a subfloor. In the center of one bedroom, when one steps on the floor, it makes a resounding "bing-bong." It is not a squeak, and I can't find a loose board. There is a cold-air duct under this floor. I drove finishing nails through the finish and subfloors. Then I went to the basement and drove nails up through the subfloor—still I get the "bing-bong." What can be done?

We suspect that the sheet metal duct fits so tightly against the floor that the slightest pressure on the floor depresses the metal, causing the noise. Try to lower the duct a fraction of an inch. If you cannot do it, have a heating contractor do the job. It won't take long.

Figure 5-4. High boards in a floor should be planed smooth and all nails set before undertaking any refinishing job.

SHRINKING FLOOR BOARDS

About a year ago we moved into our newly built bungalow. The floors and doors are shrinking. My new floors were beautiful for about 3 months; now they are separating, and there is about ⅛ inch of space between some of the boards. Do you think they will ever go back in place? What would you suggest?

If the air in the house is very dry, it is only natural that the wood will shrink, and the use of a humidifier is advisable. However, if the flooring lumber and woodwork were kept outdoors for any length of time and then installed without allowing moisture to evaporate, there is nothing much you can do. Usually such materials are kept in the house for 10 days to 2 weeks before installation. The spaces between floorboards might be filled with a wood putty; otherwise they will have to be relaid. It might be possible to reset the frames and doors.

SPACES BETWEEN FLOORBOARDS

Do you know of any material to fill the spaces between the floorboards of hardwood flooring? We have used various kinds of wood crack filler, but with no success.

It is possible that you did not put the wood putty in deep enough. The procedure is to clean out the dust and dirt with a stiff piece of wire and a vacuum cleaner. The wood putty is then packed in the full depth of the open spaces. Work of this kind should be done during the winter when the heating system is in operation and the wood has dried out. If the spaces are more than ¼ inch wide, cut strips of matching wood to fit, and glue them in place.

DENT IN FLOOR

We have a wood floor in our living room. Recently we rearranged the furniture. There are two dents in the floor from the front legs of a heavy chest.

A puttylike material, in popular wood colors, is available at many plywood, hardware, and paint dealers. This can be used to fill the dents. Or fill the dents with wood filler or plastic wood, staining and finishing it to match the rest of the floor. Or use heat and dampness to penetrate the wood so that the wood fibers, which have been pushed down, may return to their original level. Hold a well-dampened cloth over the dent, and apply heat with an iron; or use a steam iron. Very often, this raises the compressed fibers in the dent enough so that the marring won't be easily visible. We suggest placing broad casters or furniture cups under the legs of the chest to distribute the weight over a larger area and prevent future denting at the new location.

GOUGES IN WOOD FLOOR

We moved into a small apartment and didn't like the painted living room floor. We removed the paint with a rented floor sander and refinished with good-quality varnish. The finish looks good, but there are gouges

Figure 5-5. When refinishing a floor, use a big machine for major portions, a small machine for close-up work and a scraper for corners.

Figure 5-6. Method of applying a penetrating finish.

all over, apparently from the sander. Is there any way to repair this?

Probably you used only a very coarse grade of sandpaper with the sanding machine. For good results, at least three sandings, with three different grades of sandpaper, are required: rough (about #2), to remove the paint and level off surface irregularities; then #1 or "0"; and last, a final buffing with "00" or even "000" sandpaper. We're afraid the only really satisfactory repair is redoing the present job. Patching by filling gouges with plastic wood and finishing to match is perfectly possible, but the results may look "patchy."

GAP UNDER BASEBOARD

I noticed that a gap has formed under the baseboard of one living room wall. When it first appeared I really can't say. But there's at least a ¼-inch space. How should I fix this?

It's possible that some slight movement caused the floor to settle down on the basement wall slightly. There is an easy method to keep such a crack hidden, even though it may widen a little more. Cover the joint between the floor and baseboard with quarter-round

molding, previously finished to match the baseboard. Secure it with amply long finishing nails, angled to go under the baseboard and into the floor, so that the quarter round is attached to the floor and not the baseboard. Thus, if the floor moves, the molding will move with it, keeping the gap closed.

GAP AT BASEBOARD

Our ranch is built on a concrete slab; we have no basement. We have slate on our foyer floor. Now the slate has separated from the baseboard. The gap is almost 1 inch. Can you suggest anything to close this?

You don't say if the gap is up and down or sideways. If the slate tiles have dropped, carefully pry the molding, if any, from the bottom of the baseboard and refasten it down so that it rests on the slates. If the gap is sideways, fill it in with white caulking compound or grout.

ATTIC FLOORING

We have a low attic which we use only for storage. However, we would like to put down flooring, to protect the ceiling and lath between the beams. Would plywood sheets be satisfactory?

If the attic is to be used only for storage, and there will be very little traffic, plywood sheets, at least ⅝ inch thick, should work out very well. They should be laid with the face grain across the joists. Plywood is not intended as a finish flooring, but is ideal as an underlayer and a subfloor.

FLOORS IN SAD SHAPE

We moved into a house whose hardwood floors are in sad shape, since they were uncared for during 12 years. I would like to get them in proper condition with sanding, varnishing, etc. But I have no idea how to do it. What finish would be most durable to protect the floors from young, rambunctious children?

The most efficient way to get the floors in shape for the new finish is to rent a floor sander from a tool rental agency. Don't be afraid to ask them questions, and by all means have them check you out on how the machine works. After you've sanded the floors glass-smooth and wiped up all sawdust, use a penetrating stain sealer for a prime coat. When dry, two or three thin coats of top-quality clear varnish, followed by a thorough waxing, will not only make those floors look handsome but give excellent protection. Contrary to what some people believe, properly applied floor wax will make the varnished surface less skiddy than no wax at all.

FINISH FOR A SOFTWOOD FLOOR

I have a problem with my pine floors. They have been sanded and varnished or shellacked—some of them twice. Whatever was put on them does not wear well. I want to avoid sanding them again and wonder if you could advise what I could use that would wear well. There seems to be a hard finish that wears well in public buildings.

Regardless of the kind of finish you apply on the floor, the old finish should be removed first. Liquid floor sealers are widely used on wood floors that receive considerable usage and wear. A good grade of pure, fresh white shellac, thinned half-and-half with denatured alcohol and applied in two coats, is also quite satisfactory. It is widely used in gymnasiums and on bowling alleys.

FINISHING PINE FLOOR

We put in what I was told was No. 2 pine flooring in the second-story spare rooms. What kind of floor filler is best to use, and what is the best finish to put on?

Number 2 flooring usually has large knots and surface imperfections. Cracks between boards can be filled with plastic wood or crack filler, available at hardware and paint dealers. Or fill the cracks in with a mixture of sawdust and varnish, after wiping or vacuuming all the construction dust from them. Have the floor sanded smooth and level, and wipe up all the dust. Because of imperfections in wood appearance, we recommend two or three thin coats of top-quality floor paint or floor enamel. Thin the coats according to the manufacturer's instructions on the label.

NATURAL FINISH FOR MAPLE FLOOR

We are building a new home and are going to put down maple floors. Is there any way to finish them so they will look natural? I do not want varnish or shellac.

Use a good-quality penetrating floor seal or penetrating floor wax, following the manufacturer's directions on the label carefully.

FINISHING FLOORS WITH SHELLAC

I anticipate refinishing my hardwood floors and would like to obtain a good finish with shellac. How is this done?

A good-quality, pure, fresh white shellac will give you a nice finish which is quite lasting. After sanding the floors, sweep off all traces of dust; then apply a thin, even coat of shellac, thinned as follows: add 1 part of clean denatured alcohol to 4 parts of shellac. When the floors are dry, sand the surface lightly with "00" sandpaper; then wipe off the dust and apply a second coat, thinned as above.

"TOUCHING UP" SHELLACKED FLOOR

We have shellacked hardwood floors in our living and dining rooms. There are worn spots, almost down to bare wood, in the finish at the thresholds. Is there are way to touch up these areas, or must the entire floors be refinished?

The worn areas alone can be touched up successfully. Get a floor cleaner made for this purpose, available at supermarkets and hardware and housewares dealers. Use this according to directions, rubbing with steel wool so that all wax and floor polish are removed. When the wood is dry, apply two coats of shellac. The touched-up areas will blend in with the rest of the floor finish.

WATER SPOTS ON SHELLACKED FLOOR

What is best to remove water spots with on a softwood floor which is shellacked and paste-waxed over the shellac?

Ordinarily, water spots on a shellac finish usually clear up as the water dries out. The wax may be retarding the moisture evaporation. Remove the wax with a wax remover made by a nationally known manufacturer, following the label directions carefully. Then wipe the spots with a cloth slightly dampened with alcohol (too much will remove the shellac). Then apply a thin coat of shellac, greatly thinned with alcohol.

REMOVER MESSED SHELLAC

In order to start from bare wood again before shellacking a worn area on the floor, I used paint remover to get the remaining shellac off. It turned out to be a mess. What went wrong?

Alcohol is the remover for shellac, not paint remover. The latter is for paint and varnish. And while we're on the subject, use lacquer thinner on lacquer.

WAXED HARDWOOD FLOORS

Our hardwood floors are unvarnished; just sealed and waxed. What is the best way to care for them?

Dust them with a dry brush or cloth, and polish them about every week. When signs of wear appear, rewax the worn places by applying a thin coat of wax and buffing well. Remove any dirt by wiping with a liquid wax (not self-polishing); this will soften the wax and permit it and dirt to be taken up with a clean cloth.

CLEANING PARQUET FLOOR

Recently we moved into an old house which has parquet flooring in the living and dining rooms. It's in good condition, except that years of dirt seem to be wedged immovably in between the floorboards. I've tried every way I can think of to get the dirt out, but with no luck. Do you have any suggestions?

Since the dirt apparently has worked its way deeply into the cracks, have the entire floor scraped with a floor-sanding machine. Then you can refinish the floor and have a really handsome one, sealing out dirt and dust at the same time. It's more work, of course, to refinish completely, but very satisfactory when you get through.

WOOD FLOOR HAS WHITE SPOTS, STREAKS

What is the cause of whitish spots or streaks in our strip-oak flooring? The floor lumber was marked A-1 when it was installed. The floors were finished with a plastic filler. The spots and streaks did not appear until a year later. Nothing else has been put on except an occasional coat of wax. There is a full basement.

We do not think the floorboards have developed the spots and streaks. We do suspect, however, that the disfigurement is in the finish. If there are such spots in an obscure corner of one of the floors, take off some of the finish with fine sandpaper, and if you find the finish is at fault, refinishing is advisable.

PURPLE STAIN ON FLOOR

I have just put down a new hardwood floor (oak). A leak occurred from the outside of the house, as it is not bricked in yet. The moisture turned the wood a purple color. How can I get this out of the raw, unfinished wood? I don't believe sanding will take out the discoloration.

If moisture was on the wood for a long period of time, the stain might be deep and sanding may not take out the discoloration. The stain can be taken out by applying a liberal quantity of a hot, saturated solution of oxalic acid (poison). Allow the acid to remain on the wood overnight; then rinse off all traces of the solution with water. Wipe off most of the water, and allow the wood to dry thoroughly. Finish as desired.

GREASE SPOTS ON NEW WOOD

Is there anything that can remove grease spots from new wood that has not been varnished?

If grease spots are on the surface, scrub them with mild soap suds and then rinse with clear water and wipe dry. Allow ample time for the wood to dry completely before applying any finish. If the grease has penetrated into the wood, cover the spots with a paste made of nonflammable liquid spot remover and powdered whiting or other absorbent powder, placing a sheet of plastic over the paste to retard evaporation. Be sure the room is well ventilated while working, and avoid inhaling fumes from the spot remover. When the paste is discolored or dry, replace it with fresh paste until the grease has been removed.

BLACK SPOTS ON VARNISHED HARDWOOD FLOOR

How can I remove black spots from a varnished hardwood floor? I want to revarnish the floor.

Remove the varnish from the discolored area. If the wood itself is still black, apply commercial wood bleach or a liberal amount of a hot, saturated solution of oxalic acid (poison) and allow it to remain overnight; then rinse the wood well with clear water to remove all trace of the bleach. When the wood is thoroughly dry, smooth it with "000" sandpaper. Apply a thin coat of good-quality varnish over the bare spots, and when dry, finish the whole floor with an overall coat of varnish, first being sure the surface is free of all trace of wax, grease etc. If the floor is in very bad condition, it would be best to have the floor scraped with a floor-sanding machine. This will take off all black spots and the old finish, so that the new coating will be uniform in color and luster.

INK STAIN ON HARDWOOD FLOOR

What will remove an ink stain from a hardwood floor? When I saw the ink puddle on the floor, I soaked it up and then tried to get the rest off with steel wool. But I still have a stain on the floor.

Ink stains that have penetrated wood are difficult to remove. Try applying ink eradicator, after removing the finish in the stained area down to bare wood. If the ink has penetrated deeply, it may require professional treatment for removal.

CHARCOAL ON WOOD FLOOR

Is there any way to remove charcoal from a varnished wood floor? I have tried cleanser, detergents, and ammonia, but to no avail.

Try using a cleanup wax. Or fine steel wool and a nonflammable liquid spot remover.

FUEL OIL ON WOODEN FLOOR

When the former owners occupied our house, a great deal of fuel oil was spilled on a wooden floor in the basement. We converted to gas, but the oil stains left a strong odor, which is especially evident when the basement is closed up. It is not possible to remove the boards. Is there anything we can do to get rid of the odor?

Old oil stains are difficult and sometimes impossible to remove because of the deep penetration. If only a little oil was spilled, you might be able to remove it by having the floor scraped with a floor-sanding machine. If not successful, try scrubbing the floor several times, using a solution of washing soda or trisodium phosphate. Dissolve 3 pounds of either chemical in each gallon of hot water; then rinse with clear water and wipe off as much moisture as possible with dry cloths. When the stain has become lighter, give it a couple of coats of shellac.

REDWOOD-STAINED APARTMENT FLOOR

We lined our new redwood planter so that it wouldn't leak when we watered the plants. But it leaked anyway and dripped down. The redwood stain has gone through the varnish into the wood. Please tell me how to remove this stain.

Use a no-wash paint remover to get the varnish off the stained area. Then apply wood bleach (available at paint stores). If you can control the bleaching action so that it stops when the stain has become as light-colored as the rest of the floor, you may save yourself the trouble of having to restain dead-white raw wood again. Of course, if the colors are too far apart, this shortcut won't work.

PALS SPATTERED PAINT

How can I get paint splatters off varnished floors, besides sanding? I have so very many splatters since my last paint job, which friends did for me.

First try your luck with a carefully worked putty knife. This often gets at least the blobby parts off, leaving a little ring. Next, try individually wiping each spatter, maybe 10 at a time, with a cloth dipped in paint remover (get the type which needs no neutralizing bath afterward). As soon as the paint softens, wipe it up. This is slow work, but still easier than wholesale paint remover, which would necessitate your revarnishing the areas.

DARKENED FLOORS

I have a new home with hardwood floors. One night the baby's wet pants were put on the floor and left a big black spot. I used some alcohol and took off most of the black discoloration, including the finish. But the wood is still dark. What can I use to remove the stain?

If all the finish has been removed down to the bare wood, apply a liberal quantity of a hot, saturated solution of oxalic acid *(poison)*. Allow it to remain overnight; then rinse well with clear water. When the wood is dry, smooth the surface with "000" sandpaper and wipe off the dust. Since the finish came off with alcohol, we assume shellac was originally used on the floors. Therefore, the cleaned-up area can be patched with shellac.

BLACK HEEL MARKS ON HARDWOOD FLOOR

What will remove scuffy black heel marks from a new hardwood floor?

A liquid floor wax, the type containing naphtha and that needs polishing, will do this job very well. It has good cleaning power for many other spots and stains too.

WALNUT STAIN ON FLOOR

Last fall we gathered some walnuts and placed them on some newspapers in an unheated room to dry. When we removed the nuts, we found dark stains on the pre-finished wood floor. We tried a wax floor cleaner with steel wool. The worst part of the stain was removed, but I would like to know how to remove the remainder.

You might be able to take off the discoloration by wiping the stains with denatured alcohol. Try it on an obscure spot to make certain the alcohol has no detrimental effect on the finish. If it has, the only solution is to remove the finish down to the bare wood. Then refinish, starting with a floor sealer made by the maker of the flooring used in your house.

VARNISHED WOOD FLOOR

Before we moved into our new house, we washed the wood floors with cold water and detergent to pick up the fine powder of plaster, dust, etc., which a dry mop would not pick up. There were also smudges from masking tape. I was told that varnished floors are never to be cleaned with soap and water. What might happen now that I washed them?

Many floor finishes, when wet, become discolored or turn white, and sometimes if the wood is not well protected by a water-resistant finish, the fibers in the wood are raised, giving the floor a "fuzzy" appearance. Wiping with turpentine would have been better. Turpentine also would act as a solvent on the gum of the masking tape.

SCRATCHES AND MARKS ON FLOOR

When we moved into our new home, I had my hardwood floors scraped and then finished with two coats of a plastic type of varnish. Now the floors have scratches and shoe marks. What do you suggest I use to clean my floors with?

Evidently the two coats of floor finish were too thick, leaving a film that could be easily scratched. There is nothing you can do to remove the scratches, except try to make them less obvious by using a "scratch remover," on sale at hardware and department stores. A couple of coats of paste wax, each coat well rubbed when dry, should help improve the surface.

LINOLEUM LOOSENED

We have inlaid linoleum on the kitchen floor, put down several years ago. Where two sections were jointed, one side is coming loose. We are afraid someone will trip over the loose piece and tear the linoleum. How can this be refastened to the floor?

Moisture may have worked into the seam, perhaps while the floor was being washed. Be sure the seam is thoroughly dry. Then work linoleum cement into the seam by lifting the loosened edge of the linoleum and pushing the paste underneath with a flat, thin stick or spatula. After the adhesive is spread, press down the linoleum, placing heavy weights (large books, rocks, pails of water) on top and allowing these to remain until the cement has thoroughly hardened. Wipe off any excessive adhesive on the surface immediately with a damp cloth.

TROUBLES WITH LINOLEUM BUBBLES

We put down vinyl linoleum, used the right adhesive, and followed instructions. But the first section has bubbles in places which do not look good. Before doing the rest, plus a hallway, we would like to know what went wrong. The firm which sold the linoleum has since gone out of business.

It sounds somewhat as though the adhesive was put on in dabs, rather than spread evenly. It is also possible that there were areas where grease on the floor or subflooring prevented the adhesive from sticking. Get an inexpensive, notched linoleum adhesive spreader at any hardware or floor-covering store.

PATCHING LINOLEUM

I would like to patch a section of the linoleum in the kitchen where it is worn. I have some extra pieces of the same color and design, but how can I make sure the patch will be exactly the same size? Even a very small error in cutting will make a gap which will be noticeable.

Place the piece of extra linoleum over the area to be patched. If there is a pattern, line it up exactly. Then, using a linoleum knife or other sharp blade, cut through both thicknesses at once. When you've pried up the piece on the floor, the patch should be found to fit perfectly.

DAMAGED LINOLEUM

We have several small holes in the inlaid linoleum on our kitchen floor which we would like to fill in, and we would appreciate any advice you could give us.

Get your floor-covering dealer to give you some scrap pieces of linoleum that he may have around the shop which will match the color of your floor covering. Pulverize it; then mix the powder with spar varnish. Fill the holes with the mixture, and allow it to harden. Of course, the surface will not be smooth, and some smoothing with "0000" sandpaper may be necessary. Polish with floor wax.

SHABBY LINOLEUM FLOOR

About a year and a half ago, my in-laws moved into an apartment and, of course, bought new linoleum. Now the kitchen floor looks terrible. It is worn in spots. We were wondering if there wasn't something they could use on the floor before putting down new linoleum. The landlord said that the new floor covering could be put down over the old. What do you advise?

Evidently the original floor is not smooth or level, and the floor covering wore down in the high spots. Don't put the new material over the old. Take up the old floor covering and level the floor with a floor-leveling compound; then put down the new linoleum. Leveling compounds are sold by floor-covering dealers.

LINOLEUM SEPARATED FROM BASEBOARD

The linoleum floor covering on a wooden floor has dried and separated from the baseboard about ⅛ of an inch. Is there any filler for the crack—plastic or other?

You could nail a quarter-round molding on the baseboard, large enough to cover the edge of the linoleum. The other method is to get some strips of odds and ends of linoleum of a matching color and pulverize them. Make a stiff paste by mixing the pulverized linoleum with spar varnish; then fill the space. When the paste is hard and dry, smooth the surface by rubbing it with "000" sandpaper and wipe off the dust. Polish with wax.

LINOLEUM HAS "BUMPED UP"

Last year I finished our attic, putting up plasterboard walls and putting linoleum on the floor. I did it all myself, and thought it looked satisfactory. But now there are three places where the linoleum has bulged away from the floor. Is there any way I can flatten these places where the linoleum has bumped up?

Slice across the "bumped-up" places with a linoleum knife or any other sharp blade. Then, using a long, thin blade, such as a screwdriver or kitchen spatula, insert some more linoleum cement under the loosened parts. Smear some on the floor too, but not too generously (too much will ooze up through the crack). Then press the linoleum back in place, and weight it with heavy weights, such as doorstops, stacks of books, or the like, and leave this weighting in place for several days. If any cement does ooze up through the crack during this time, wipe it up immediately, while it is still wet. Otherwise, if it's allowed to dry, it will be almost impossible to remove.

BUMPS IN LINOLEUM

The kitchen linoleum in our new home is less than a year old. In three separate spots are small round bumps, possibly nails. Is there anything we can do before they wear through?

They might be loosened nails, but they also could be small air pockets. You could cut into the linoleum, and if you find a loosened nail, pull it out. This may leave a hole. If so, pulverize some linoleum of the same color and mix it with some varnish. Fill the hole, and when the mixture is dry, smooth the area with very fine sandpaper. If they are air pockets, allow them to become larger; then slit them and place linoleum paste under each side of the slit. Press the linoleum down in place, and put weights on the spots until the cement has hardened.

LINOLEUM LOOSE AT SEAMS

We have vinyl linoleum in our five-year-old house. It is pulling up loose in certain places along the seams. How can I secure it again?

You have two choices: Pry or pull it back so that 4 or 5 inches are exposed in each side of the seam. Scrape the floor there as smooth as practical, spread more cement, and weight the linoleum down again until the cement has firmed. A much simpler way (and it may be enough) is to put more cement on a long, thin blade, like a spatula or skinny screwdriver, and work it under the raised edges. Then weight it firmly. In either case, keep a sharp, constant eye out for any cement oozing up. Wipe it up immediately before it can harden.

CIGARETTE BURN IN LINOLEUM

How can one remove a cigarette burn from linoleum, and also some purple print which may have come from a cake-mix box?

Rub the burn lightly with "0" steel wool and mild soapsuds; then rinse with clear water and wipe dry. Of course, there may be a slight indentation in the surface, but nothing can be done about it. The purple print will eventually come off by wear and traffic. However, you might be able to take off a good bit of it by rubbing as above.

SHINY FINISH FOR LINOLEUM

We have inlaid vinyl linoleum on our kitchen floor. It has a dull finish. We have tried various types of wax to obtain a shiny finish. The results were not satisfactory. Would a varnish job help?

Varnishing might appear to be fine for a few weeks, but in the kitchen it will soon become scuffed and scratched, and after several months the finish will be worn down to the floor covering. Revarnishing will build up a thick film in unworn areas, causing the linoleum to become discolored. A busy floor should never have a high-gloss finish. Keep on waxing the floor covering with any of the well-known brands of floor wax.

CAN'T PAINT LINOLEUM?

A neighbor who usually knows all the answers told me I will have to get new linoleum. While my linoleum is quite dull now, it is still in good condition. The subject came up because I wondered out loud to her if I couldn't get a few more years service by painting the linoleum. She said absolutely not. Why not?

Why not indeed? Sure, you can paint it. Use top-quality floor and deck enamel, and you should get several more years of service. (Clean off all traces of wax and grease first, however.)

PAINT SPOTS ON LINOLEUM

We repainted the window frame in the kitchen and didn't notice some paint spots on the linoleum until they had hardened. How can they be removed?

A new quick stain remover for floor tile is now available at large hardware and floor-covering dealers. It is easy to use, and is safe on linoleum, vinyl, and asphalt tile. If not obtainable, use fine steel wool and paste paint remover, allowing the remover to remain on only long enough to soften the paint for removal; if the remover is left too long, it may affect oils in the linoleum.

COATED LINOLEUM

Several years ago I applied a liquid on my kitchen inlaid linoleum. It was supposed to give it a permanent shine. However, it wore down in the walking areas and has left a yellowish discoloration where there is no heavy traffic. Is there any way I could remove this and restore the original color?

Please remember that there is no such thing as a permanent glossy finish for floors that will withstand concentrated traffic for a long time. You will have to use a paint remover to take off the present finish. Work in small sections, and as soon as the coating becomes soft, take it off with "0" steel wool; then wash off all traces of the remover as soon as possible. Do not allow the remover to remain on the linoleum longer than is necessary, because the linoleum itself may become damaged. Try to use a nonflammable kind of remover. If you can't get the nonflammable kind, be very careful of fire.

OLD FLOOR-WAX PROBLEM

What will remove old floor wax from linoleum? I have tried several commercial wax-removing preparations, but I still find the only way I really can take off the wax is with a dull knife. This would be a tremendous job for a whole floor, and I'd like to know if you have any better ideas.

It sounds as though there are so many coats of wax that one or two applications of the wax remover aren't enough. Have you tried using fine steel wool in combination with the wax remover? If not, you'll find it very effective. There is another remover you can use, which, however, is apt to be very harsh on the linoleum if it is allowed to remain in contact with it for any length of time. Dissolve 2 pounds of trisodium phosphate in a gallon of warm water, and apply the solution over a small floor area at a time. In this concentration, the chemical will act like a mild paint remover and should be treated accordingly. After giving the solution a few minutes to work on the hardened coats of wax, scour and rub the area with fine steel wool, promptly rinse the remover off, and wipe the floor dry. Do the floor by small sections in this manner.

CHIPPED-OFF LINOLEUM STRIP

We have beige-colored inlaid linoleum in our kitchen, and about 6 feet of it lines up with the hardwood floor in our hall. Due to expansion the linoleum buckled up, became brittle, and chipped off. There is about ¼ inch missing along this strip, which shows up black between the two floors and is very noticeable. Is there anything I can do to fix or repair this damage?

Edging strips are available in narrow widths for linoleum and other resilient floor coverings. Get a short piece in matching color and insert it between the two floors. Or the black strip could be covered with a thin layer of puttylike material, coming in stick form and available at plywood dealers in various wood colors.

REMOVING LINOLEUM

Our kitchen linoleum was put down years ago, with a felt underlayment. Now it is very worn, and we want to replace it. How can we remove the linoleum from the floor?

Pry up a corner of the linoleum with a wide-blade knife or narrow screwdriver. Then pull up as much of it as possible. Usually, it separates at the felt. To remove felt that sticks to the floor, wet it with hot water. After a few minutes, the paste will soften and both felt and paste can be easily removed. Another method is to scrape off as much of the felt as possible; then clean the floor with a floor-sanding machine.

TILING WORN WOOD FLOORS

We live in an old house with badly worn softwood floors. Can we apply asphalt tile directly to the floor after carefully sanding it? If the tiles are laid diagonally, will it eliminate cracks which appear as the wood floor expands or contracts?

If the old floor can be sanded smooth and any warped areas planed, so that the resulting floor surface is level and solid, the tile can be put down directly over the wood floor (using the recommended tile adhesive, of course). But it's best of all to put down plywood or hardboard subflooring. All cracks should be filled first, and the surface should be free of foreign matter such as oil, wax, grime, etc.

The floor can also be leveled with a cold mastic floor fill, made by tile manufacturers, following the manufacturer's installation directions. It makes no difference, for crack elimination, whether tiles are laid diagonally.

VINYL OVER INLAID FLOOR?

Is it okay to lay the easy-stick type vinyl tiles on an existing floor of inlaid vinyl? Or must the present flooring be taken up first?

It's perfectly okay to put the peel-and-stick-down vinyl tiles over the present floor, on two conditions: First, the floor must be solid and level all over. Second, you must remove every trace of grease and wax, so that the adhesive on the back of the vinyl tiles will be able to bond properly. Nothing spoils adhesion like wax, grease, soap film, and such.

ASPHALT-TILE ADHESIVE STAINS

We just put down an asphalt-tile floor in our kitchen. There are several stains from adhesive which were not removed immediately at the time. Is there anything we can use now to get the stains off?

A quick stain remover for floor tile is now available at some tile dealers and large housewares and hardware stores; this is particularly recommended for removing stains from flooring adhesives on linoleum, vinyl, and asphalt tile. Or rub the stains carefully with fine steel wool and turpentine.

REMOVING FELT AND ADHESIVE

Could you tell me how to remove the old felt and adhesive from used rubber tile, also asphalt tile, in order to relay them?

If the rubber tile was put down with an ordinary adhesive (not waterproof), it can be removed by scrubbing with a mild soap and hot water. Waterproof adhesives under rubber tiles and the asphalt mastic adhesives under asphalt tiles can only be removed with sandpaper. Solvents that have any effect on the adhesives will also damage the tiles.

DRY ICE FOR REMOVING ASPHALT TILE

I have heard that asphalt tile can be removed easily by using dry ice. If this is correct, how should I go about it? I want to remove the tile on my bathroom floor.

Yes, this is correct. Place about 10 pounds of dry ice on a small section of the floor, and allow it to remain 10 to 15 minutes. The intense cold of the dry ice makes the tile

Figure 5-7. To install a loose-laying floor, (top left) first remove the wood base or the shoe molding with a wrecking bar or a claw hammer. (top center) Measure and cut the sheet where it can be unrolled. Snap chalk lines 3 inches greater than the dimensions of the room. (top right) Line up the straight edge of the cut sheet with the longest and most regular wall. Let the material curve up the other three walls. (bottom left) Press the flooring firmly into place and trim waste with a knife or heavy scissors, allowing a $\frac{1}{32}$ inch clearance at the walls. (bottom center) At a doorway where the flooring meets hardwood, the edge of the sheet may be cemented or capped with a metal threshold. (bottom right) Replace the molding. Slip a piece of scrap sheet between the molding and the sheet. Nail the molding to the base, not to the floor. Then remove the scrap.

and adhesive underneath brittle enough so that the tile can easily be pried up with a putty knife. While prying up one section, brush the ice along to the next section. Be sure to wear heavy gloves while working with the dry ice.

TOO GENEROUS WITH CEMENT

In the kitchen of the apartment I moved into recently, something is squeezing up between the floor tiles. I suppose it is the paste used, but it seems like a black tar. What can I do to clean up this nuisance?

This problem is what happens when too much mastic (cement, linoleum paste, etc.) is put down under tiles. You have two tedious choices: Keep a small putty knife always handy, and scrape up every bit that oozes up as quickly as you can before it stains the tiles.

This oozing can go on for a year or more. The other choice is to take up the tiles and relay them, with the proper amount of mastic.

VINYL MOLDING WON'T STICK

I papered my kitchen with vinyl-covered, washable wallpaper and then put on vinyl cove molding. My problem is with the cove molding where the walls meet the floor. In spite of a special adhesive I was sold, the molding won't stick to the vinyl surface of the wallpaper. What can I try next?

After making sure the backs of the molding and the wallpaper are both clean, try an epoxy adhesive. This usually sticks things together with a grip of iron. But if not, then we don't see how you can avoid using nails with heads large enough so that they will hold. Get a metal finish the same color as the molding to touch up the nail heads.

DO-IT-YOURSELF WAX REMOVER?

Is there any type of wax remover I could make at home to use on rubber tile so that it will not affect the original sheen? Once the old wax is removed, what is the recommended wax I should use?

Wiping with the very finest, nonscratchiest steel wool and turpentine has always been a good method for removing wax; the steel wool is needed only when the accumulation is thick and stubborn. A water-base wax is always safe for rubber tile. However, some of the newer rubber tiles can also take a solvent-base wax. Check this point with your dealer.

CAN'T REMOVE OLD WAX

What may I use to remove old wax which has been splashed against the baseboard in the kitchen? Regular wax remover doesn't seem to budge it.

When wax is old, you sometimes need to repeat your treatment several times. If you really get nowhere with your wax remover, try these steps, in the following order: Use turpentine and finest steel wool. If you have no luck, try naphtha instead of turpentine. If you still have no luck, mix 1 cup of ammonia, ¼ cup of strong household cleaner, and ½ gallon of cold water (not hot; cold water locks in the ammonia fumes longer). Apply this solution, and let it remain 15 minutes. Then scrub with fine steel wool or nylon scouring pads. Wipe up the solution and softened wax immediately. Repeat the treatment if necessary.

RUBBER TILE LOOSENS ON CONCRETE

Our house is on a concrete slab. We installed rubber tile in the kitchen, but it keeps loosening. Is there any way to make it adhere permanently?

A special type of waterproof adhesive must be used to lay rubber tile on concrete that is in contact with the gournd. This material is available at large floor-covering and tile dealers.

WHITE FILM ON RUBBER TILE

The rubber tile on my kitchen floor has developed white film on the surface. I have been very careful about using only self-polishing wax on it. What do you suggest?

The wax may not have been applied properly. We suggest removing the wax coating with a floor-cleaning preparation made by a nationally known wax manufacturer; follow the label directions carefully. After rinsing the tile thoroughly with clear warm water, allow it to dry for at least an hour. Then apply a thin coat of the self-polishing wax.

DISCOLORED ASPHALT TILE

We have asphalt tile in our laundry, which is at the back entrance and gets very hard use. With what can I clean the tile? It is discolored and in some places is yellow with wax. What is a good cleaner for rubber tile?

Asphalt and rubber tile require the same kind of cleaner—one that has no volatile oil harmful to either product. Clean with a mild soap and rinse thoroughly with clear water to remove all trace of soap. Use only a nonrubbing (water-emulsion) wax. To remove the too thick accumulation of wax now on the asphalt tile, use a floor-cleaning and wax-removing preparation made by a nationally known wax manufacturer, following the label directions carefully. Then rinse the tile thoroughly with clear warm water, and allow it to dry for about an hour. Rewax.

MERCUROCHROME STAINS ON RUBBER TILE

There are Mercurochrome stains on the rubber tile in the bathroom. How can these be removed?

Try sponging them with a pad of cotton saturated with alcohol, not allowing the alcohol to remain on more than 2 to 3 minutes; then rinse with clear water and wipe dry. Or sponge them with warm liquid detergent, adding a few drops of ammonia; then rinse with clear water and wipe dry.

ASPHALT TILE

Some time ago, I saw some advice on the use of boiled linseed oil to put luster on kitchen linoleum. Is the same treatment used for brightening up asphalt tile on a basement floor? I scrubbed ours with a cleanser to remove tar and other soiling, but even with waxing and buffing, it does not come up to our expectations.

Never use any oil or petroleum derivatives on asphalt tile. The oil tends to soften the asphalt and make it tacky. You should try a brand of self-polishing wax, which might give better results.

BLACK TILED FLOOR

We have black tile on the bathroom floor, which I believe is either rubber or linoleum tile, and it shows water spots. Is there any way to get rid of the water spots completely, and also is there any treatment I can give the floor to prevent water from spotting?

A black color on a floor is difficult to maintain and keep clean. Water contains sediment, and where it is hard, also minerals. On evaporation, a deposit remains that is difficult to remove. Try rubbing the tile lightly with "00" steel wool and mild soapsuds. If this method is not successful, take off the present wax with wax remover; then try one of the well-known liquid waxes which the manufacturer claims that by buffing will make track marks and spots less obvious.

PLASTIC TILE DIFFICULT TO CLEAN

I have vinyl-asbestos tile on the kitchen floor. It gets badly scratched, probably by the children's leather shoes. It is impossible to remove the dirt, except by using a cleanser and lots of elbow grease. Occasionally, the tile is polished with paste wax and about every 2 weeks with a good liquid wax. Is cleanser harmful to the tile? I have been told by some not to wax this type of floor. Can you advise?

Vinyl-asbestos tile does not come with a glossy finish; therefore it is advisable to wax such a surface. You should be able to get better results by using one type of wax, and our preference would be for a good-quality self-polishing wax. It would also help to place a mat outside the kitchen door so that the youngsters can wipe off some of the grit and sand they pick up on the soles of their shoes while playing outdoors.

FLOORING FOR BATHROOM CARPET

We are planning to have carpeting in the bathrooms of our new house. What type of flooring will be most economical but also able to withstand any water seepage? We plan to have these carpets removable for washing.

Exterior-grade plywood should fill those specifications nicely. Even better, and for very little more money, will be a coat or two of floor and deck enamel, applied on the edges too.

PARTICLE BOARD AS SUBFLOORING

I am planning to build a home, and the builder has said he wants to use particle board as a subfloor for the wall-to-wall carpeting. It would be 5/8 inch thick. Do you think this material will be satisfactory?

Particle board will be very satisfactory as a material. But no matter what material is used, from plywood panels to flooring boards, a great deal depends on how carefully it is installed.

INSTALLING WALL-TO-WALL CARPETING

I want to install wall-to-wall carpeting in a bedroom. Is there any special equipment necessary to ensure its not wrinkling?

Professionals usually use a "knee-kicker" to stretch the carpet properly and prevent wrinkling later. You might be able to borrow this from the carpet dealer from whom you purchased the carpeting. He can also instruct you in how to use it.

ADHESIVE FOR OUTDOOR CARPET

What type adhesive should I use for laying outdoor carpeting on a deck which is covered with roll roofing?

Any type, as long as it's waterproof. There's no reason why you can't even use regular plastic roofing cement. But be very, very careful not to let any get on the carpet.

FUZZ FROM NEW CARPETING

I have recently purchased all-wool broadloom carpeting and have been vacuum cleaning it with a tank type of cleaner for

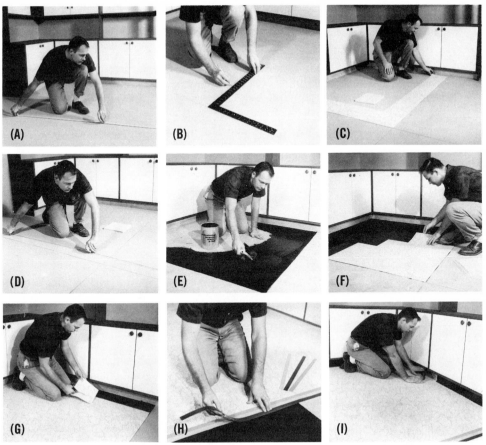

Figure 5-8. To lay resilient tiles, (A) Measure the two opposite walls and find the center of each wall. Snap a chalk line on the floor between these points. (B) Locate the center of the chalk line on the floor between these points. (B) Locate the center of the chalk line. Using a carpenter's square or a tile, draw a line at right angles to the chalk line. (C) Lay a row of uncemented tiles along the chalk lines from the center, where the lines cross, to one side wall and one end wall. (D) If the last tile in step C is less than 2 or more than 8 inches from the wall, snap a new line 4½ inches closer to the wall. (E) Spread the adhesive with a trowel or brush (depending on the adhesive) and cover one-fourth of the room. Do not cover the chalk lines. (F) Starting at the center, place tiles in the adhesive. The first tiles must be flush with the lines. Do not slide the tiles into place. (G) The border tiles are less than full size but can easily be cut to fit the space with a pair of ordinary household shears. (H) Solid-color strips can be used to create an unusual custom effect and enhance the decor of room. (I) The installation of a cove base completes the job. Lengths of the base are cut to fit, cemented on the back, and pressed against the wall.

about a month. There is always a bagful of fuzz when I'm finished. There seems to be a constant nap lying on the rug, and it is quite noticeable. Is this characteristic of new carpeting, and how long can I expect it to continue?

New rugs and carpets have a considerable amount of loose fibers, caused by cuttings in the process of manufacture. The amount of fuzz picked up should diminish in a couple of months' time. If there is no lessening of the quantity of the fuzz, I suggest that you consult the carpet dealer. However, we are sure you will find the quantity diminishing.

PROTECTION OF CARPETING

I keep several heavy-cotton shag rugs over heavily used areas on our carpeting, which is light-colored. Will the constant use of these rugs eventually press down the fibers in the carpet? Will steam ironing raise the nap if it becomes matted down? Will such areas remain light enough in color so that my original purpose of keeping the carpet clean and not too worn, in a heavy-traffic area, be defeated?

Eventually the pile in the carpeting may become matted down in areas covered with the rugs. However, this will depend on the height of the pile and the kind of fibers the rug is made of. Steaming and brushing should return the fibers to their original position. It is only natural that protected and covered areas will appear cleaner, after a time, than those exposed to the air, dust, and traffic. It would be wise to take up the covering periodically and expose it to some wear.

SHELLACKED CARPET TOO

I miscalculated a little when I was putting shellac on our dining room floor. I got too close to the carpet, and some shellac landed along its edge. I wiped it up immediately, but couldn't get it all off—too sticky. What will take the rest of the shellac off?

Wipe denatured alcohol on it generously. But lift the carpet so that you won't accidentally get some alcohol on your new floor. It will remove some of that shellac too, if it gets the chance.

PIANO'S LEGACY LINGERS

We finally sold our large old piano. What can I do about the deep dents it left in the wall-to-wall carpeting? Two are very conspicuous.

Try this, although we certainly don't guarantee 100 percent success: Set your iron to moderate, and run it over the dents; work on one dent at a time. As the steam drives down, it will tend to loosen some of the matted fibers. Help this along with a soft brush. Keep at it patiently. With medium-weight furniture, this often works fine. But with a ton or so of piano, we doubt it. If you're worried about heavy furniture dents, shop around for the types of furniture cups that prevent this.

RUG SKIDS ON SLICK FLOOR

Is there an easy way to keep a throw rug from skidding on a slippery floor? We will soon have a senior citizen living with us.

Some supermarkets sell antiskid sprays, which are also available in some housewares sections. A few strips of the no-slip safety tape widely used on the bottom of bathtubs will also serve very well. Another method that takes a little more effort: Brush on a coat of pure, fresh white shellac on the underside.

BURNED CARPET

I have a cigarette burn on my gray carpet. Is there anything I can do to make it less noticeable? I did not do anything to it yet in the hope that there may be a cleaner or stain remover that will take out the discoloration.

A burn is not a stain, and therefore there is no cleaner or stain remover that will do away with the discoloration. If the tips of the fibers were charred, carefully snip them off with nail scissors. But if the burn is rather deep, the damaged area will have to be cut out and a new piece of material inserted. Carpet and rug dealers could do a neat job, and we recommend having a professional do the job.

REPAIRING BURNS IN RUG

We have nylon rugs, easily damaged by cigarettes falling from ash trays. Is there a method for repairing the burnt spots myself? We have pieces of the same material; it's fuzzy.

This type of repair really requires professional attention. However, you might try patching the burnt spot by inserting a piece of the same material in the damaged area, using the "press-on" type of mending tape on the underside of the rug to hold it in place. Mending tape is available at notions counters of variety stores and sewing supply dealers.

EXCESS MORTAR ON TILE FLOOR

We have a mosaic-tile floor in our bathroom which was never cleaned thoroughly of excess mortar, etc., when laid. What can be used to clean this and give it a protective coating and shine?

We assume this is a cement mortar that was used. To remove the excess cement, moisten it with a solution of 1 part muriatic acid in 20 parts of water, and flush the solution off after 1 to 2 minutes with clear water. Then remove all trace of the acid by washing the

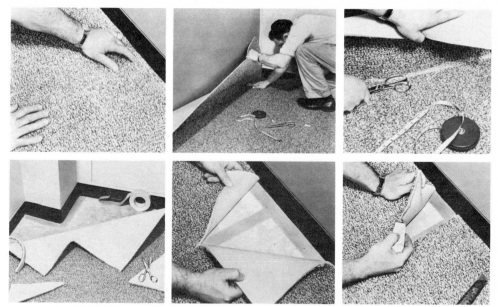

Figure 5-9. When using double-faced tape to install carpeting, be sure that the underflooring is clean so that no dirt or grease will impair the holding power of the tape at corners or seams. (top left) Start with the longest wall in the room, and butt the carpet carefully to the wall along its entire length. Trim the carpet with scissors to accommodate any irregularities at base of the wall. (top center) Bring the carpet carefully across the room to the facing wall. Keep it flat and smooth out any puckers. (top right) Where the carpet butts against the wall base, score heavily with the handle end of a pair of scissors. Mark lightly along this line with white blackboard or tailor's chalk (the chalk brushes off easily), and cut the carpet with the scissors. Trim where necessary to accommodate wall irregularities. Do not cut the carpet short; it is preferable to allow a slight overage, fit the carpet to the wall, and cut it again. The double-faced tape should be placed around the perimeter of the carpet in strategic or heavily trafficked areas. (bottom left) Where walls jut out, use the same procedure you would follow for a straight wall. Score, chalk, and cut, but cut only one wall edge at a time. Place the double-faced tape around all corners and juts, thus ensuring a tight bond of the foam backing with the floor. (bottom center) If the room is wider than the width of the carpet being used, take an additional strip of carpet and butt the seams together. (bottom right) To make a seam virtually invisible, use chalk to mark the seam line of the carpet on the floor. Lay the tape along this line (there should be about 1 inch of tape on either side of seam) and for a short distance along the wall across the seam to form a T. Then apply cement along both seam edges of the carpet. Replace the carpet on the floor and press down firmly.

floor with a solution of 1 pint of ammonia in 2 gallons of water, followed again by thorough rinsing. Because of the highly corrosive nature of the acid solution, be sure to wear heavy clothing, rubber gloves, and goggles while working. For cleaning the floor, use a cream cleanup wax; this will leave a protective coating on the surface.

WOOD FLOOR STAINING GROUT?

A year ago, we had our bathroom floor (dark wood) covered with white unglazed tile. Even though the installer applied a silicone coat, the grout has become steadily darker.

Could this be the floor stain working up into the grout?

Not too likely if the installer first put down the usual layer of waterproof mastic or cement. More likely the silicone began to wear off under foot traffic, and the resulting dirt became embedded in the somewhat porous grout. If you can't get it whiter with a cleaner, use bleach.

TILE FLOOR A PUZZLER

I think I have really goofed with my dining room floor. The dining area and the adjacent entry to the living room are tiled with small, white, rough ceramic tiles. These white tiles are so very hard to keep clean. The dirt penetrates to the pores, and it takes a tremendous amount of scrubbing to get them clean. Is there any way to paint the tiles a darker color, or will it be necessary to take all the tiles up and start over with something else?

The only trouble with painting or staining would be the difficulty of avoiding lap marks or blotches due to normal paint stroking. Once there, they'd be permanent. Try this: Get the tiles really clean. Then treat them with a transparent liquid masonry sealer containing silicones, to seal the surface. These sealers are widely sold in hardware stores and lumberyards. Then, as an easy cleanup later, try a good foam cleaner.

PROTECTION OF CARPET

Our living room door faces west and has three pieces of glass in it. The afternoon sun causes our carpeting and furniture to fade. Is there anything we can put on the glass so that the sun won't shine through? Would we have to take out the glass and put in something else?

The simplest solution would be to put on a window shade made with a heavy, opaque shade cloth. Coatings are made, but they are not distributed through retail channels and are sold only in large quantities.

ENDS OF RUG CURL

We have a new rug, viscose. Can anything be done to make the ends lie flat? They keep curling up.

New rugs are usually sized on the back to make them lie flat. The ends may flatten out by themselves, shortly. If not, turn the rug over and stretch it upside down where it can remain undisturbed for 24 hours. Then brush on a thin coat of pure, fresh white shellac. Or apply a solution of ½ pound of chip glue in 2 quarts of water. Allow the sizing material to dry thoroughly. Another anchor is the carpet tape that's sticky on both sides. Put it under the corners. Or if the entire edges tend to curl, use the tape all the way around. It's made for that.

RUG BACKING PEELS OFF

What can I do about throw rugs whose rubber backing is starting to peel off? These rugs have not been washed yet.

Get some rubber cement at an art or hardware store and stick the rubber back again. This may not hold through a rough session in the washing machine or commercial laundry, but rubber cement is so easy to use that repeating your repair is no big deal. You could also stitch a rubberized fabric over the entire underside of the rug, which will end the problem.

STICKY WASHABLE RUG

I have a washable throw rug with a rubber backing which has become too sticky to use. Otherwise the rug is in good condition. Is there anything I can do to eliminate the stickiness?

First, try sprinkling it liberally with plain talcum powder to see if it will absorb the stickiness. We recommend highly that you do this job outdoors. If this treatment isn't enough, wash off the powder and put on another coat of rubberized nonslip liquid, which is widely available in housewares sections of department stores and many good hardware stores.

RUG STUCK TO FLOOR

I have a small rubberized-back rug which has stuck to my bedroom hardwood floor. How can I remove this white rubberized material without damaging the finish of the floor?

Any solvent which would loosen this rubberized material would also soften (and possibly remove) some of the varnish. Try lightly rubbing one small spot with steel wool and turpentine. If this works, fine; if not, then you'd better resign yourself to refinishing this part of your floor, from the bare wood up.

CARPET WET FROM CONCRETE FLOOR

Is it possible for groundwater to seep up through a concrete slab floor and make the rubber-backed carpet so wet it develops a musty odor? If so, can it be stopped?

Yes, it's possible, all right, with a poor concrete mix and no drainage bed or waterproofing layer of sheet plastic under the slab. It's also possible that dampness is due to condensation on warm, humid days. If movable, get the carpeting outdoors into the sun to air out. On a clear day, close the house and run the heater up really high for a couple of hours, with minimum humidity. This will have a drying effect. Then ventilate it well. You can put a waterproofing layer of a thin coating of roofing cement on the floor covered with plastic sheeting.

CARPETING STOP CONDENSATION?

Our basement bedroom floor has linoleum-tile squares over the concrete slab. During hot, humid weather, the floor becomes extremely wet, due to condensation. Would indoor-outdoor carpeting cure this condition? If so, would it be a good idea to lay a sheet of plastic over the concrete first, as a vapor barrier?

The carpeting with a foam-rubber padding (the type that "breathes" so dampness won't be trapped underneath) should cure the condensation condition. If a plastic vapor barrier wasn't placed under the floor when it was originally poured, it would be a good "insurance" idea now. Stick it down with roofing cement.

CARPET TURNS ROOM MUSTY

We made the mistake of putting down a very nice carpet over a felt pad. Soon it gave the entire room a musty smell, like that of a very damp cellar. The room is over an open crawl space, but the ground area has been covered with plastic. What causes the odor, and what can we do about it? We'd like to keep the carpet.

Apparently, despite the plastic, a little dampness came up through the floor. But it was dissipated. Now it is trapped by the cushion and the carpet. Try covering the underside of the floor by stapling more plastic sheeting over the bottom edges of the joists, to keep dampness from striking the underside of the floor.

MUSTY ODOR IN CARPETING

Our house has a cement floor covered with wall-to-wall carpet. Under the concrete is 4 inches of gravel, and the concrete is waterproofed. But there is a musty odor in some of the rooms. Do you know of anything that will remove the odor?

Many department stores and boat supply dealers sell mildew-proofing preparations which can be sprayed or brushed on the carpeting to rid it of musty odors. The carpeting will have to be treated on both sides in order for the treatment to be effective. Evidently there is some moisture coming through the concrete. Covering the concrete with polyeth-ylene sheets (plastic) should help eliminate the condition.

CHANGE CARPET'S COLOR?

We have a gold-color nylon carpet in our living room. Can we change the color to green by using a spray or brushing on rug dye?

Middling to dark green, yes. Light green, no; it will turn out pretty muddy. When using fabric dyes, remember you can restore original brightness of the same color and you can change to a darker color. But you cannot change to a lighter color or a color of the same "lightness" as the present color.

NEW YOUTH FOR OLD CORK FLOOR

We have had cork tile on our living room floor for 18 years. I would like to give it a good cleaning and then wax it. Is there a simple way to do this job with good results? I don't have an electric polisher.

The simplest method is to use a product which cleans the floor and puts on a good-looking coat of wax at the same time. You can get this naphtha-base–type wax in two forms at almost any supermarket or housewares or variety store. One is a concentrated paste wax. The other is a self-shining liquid wax. Even though you may not have an electric polisher, you can easily and inexpensively rent one at any tool and appliance rental agency. It's well worth the modest fee.

REVIVING CORK TILE

The cork tile which has been in our bedroom for many years now is showing signs of old age. Is there any way to restore at least some of its original appearance? It has given exceedingly good wear and has been most satisfactory; I certainly don't wish to replace it.

The tile can be sanded with a very fine grade of sandpaper to take off the top layer of ground-in dust and dirt. This will uncover a fresh surface (as when you sand down the surface of the walls of a cedar closet to restore the odor of cedar by exposing fresh wood). Then wipe up all the dust with a cloth dampened with turpentine. After this, apply two coats of shellac, thinned half-and-half with denatured alcohol. When the second coat has completely dried, polish with paste wax. The results should be very pleasing.

SCUFF MARKS ON CORK TILE

How can I solve a scuff problem on my cork-tile floor? I use paste wax, but in 24 to 36 hours my floor is a mass of scuff marks. I have four children who use the room extensively.

Too thick a layer of wax will show scuff marks, and frequent waxing will cause a thick accumulation which will also disfigure the appearance when the floor is used. Wash off as much of the wax as possible with turpentine; then apply a very thin layer of wax. Allow it to dry for a half hour; then buff it well with a floor-polishing machine or soft cloths. Use a good standard brand of wax.

GREEN STAINS ON FLOOR TILE

How do I remove the greenish stains from bathroom floor tile around the water closet bowl? The stains were caused by condensation water dripping from the flush tank and pipe above.

If the discoloration is not too heavy, you should be able to remove the stains by wiping the tiles with household ammonia. Ventilate the bathroom when using this chemical, because the fumes can be overpowering. Old and heavy discoloration can be removed as follows: Mix 1 part sal ammoniac and 4 parts powdered whiting moistened with household ammonia. Spread this on in a thick layer, and allow it to remain on until dry. Repeat the treatment if necessary.

WHITE FILM ON TILE

A floor in our foyer has been laid with maroon 6-inch-square tile blocks, sometimes called "slaughterhouse" tile. In between is white cement. Instead of being the rich red-maroon color they should be, the tiles have a whitish film that can't be washed off. How do I restore the color and remove the film?

We are not familiar with "slaughterhouse" tile. However, if this is a quarry tile, as we suspect, try the following treatment: Wash with a solution of 1 part muriatic acid in 20 parts water, allowing it to remain on the surface about 5 minutes; then rinse with clear water to remove all trace of acid. Because of the corrosive nature of the acid, wear rubber gloves, heavy work clothing, and goggles.

CERAMIC TILE OVER OLD COVERINGS

Is it advisable in installing ceramic floor and wall tile to remove the old inlaid linoleum, which is in good shape, and to remove the paint (enamel) from the walls first?

Old floor covering should first be removed, for best results, before installing ceramic tile; and loose paint, which might hinder proper adhesion, should be removed from the walls before the mastic is applied. Detailed instructions for surface preparation, as well as tile installation, are usually available from your tile dealer.

TREATMENT OF CERAMIC TILE AND SLATE FLOORS

We are going to be the owners of a new ranch house. The bathrooms have light-cream ceramic-tile floors and the foyer a broken-slate floor. Should these floors be given any special treatment to make it easier for me to keep them clean and pleasing in appearance?

Scrub the floors with a strong solution of a detergent, and if necessary, use scouring powder; then rinse well with clear water. Allow plenty of time for thorough drying; then apply a couple of coats of paste floor wax. Each coat must be allowed to dry for a half hour or so; then rub well to bring up a polish. Self-polishing wax can be used instead, but you should use a type which the maker claims will not show water spots.

PROTECT NEW SLATE FOYER

Is there any special way to protect a slate foyer floor so that the slate will not be harmed by time and wear? This is a brand-new house.

First give it a thorough treatment with a transparent masonry sealer. Over this goes the protection of paste wax, well buffed. Depending on your popularity, as well as the climatic conditions, you should repeat the waxing two, perhaps three, times a year.

DIRTY MORTAR JOINTS

Our entrance hall has a floor of unpolished slate. The white mortar between the slate has become dirty, and nothing seems to whiten it. Is there some paint that could be used?

Try cleaning the mortar joints with a concrete and masonry cleaner and etcher, available from masonry supply dealers, following the label directions carefully; use one that does not contain muriatic acid. The joints can be painted with any good-quality floor paint. Be sure the surface is thoroughly free of any trace of grease, wax, soot, etc.

COLOR SMEARS ON FLAGSTONES

We have just completed a flagstone patio, and we put dry colored cement between the stones. A heavy rain splashed the cement onto the stones. I was able to remove much of it with a wire brush. But some of the colored cement still adheres to the surface. How can I remove it?

You should be able to remove the balance of the discoloration by scrubbing the spots with a solution of muriatic acid. Mix 1 part of muriatic acid in 10 parts of water. Pour the acid slowly to avoid splashing. Use a wooden pail to hold the solution. After wetting the stones with water, apply the solution liberally, and after 2 or 3 minutes scrub with more of the solution, using a fiber brush for the purpose. Rinse well with clear water. Muriatic acid is highly corrosive and should be handled with care. Use rubber gloves, rubbers over your shoes, old clothing, and goggles to protect your eyes. Avoid getting it on your skin.

PAINT-SOILED SLATE

Our slate floor in the entry hall and around the fireplace has white stripping which is badly soiled, and the paint used on the stripping has run into the crevices of the slate. How can I remove this soil and paint and make the slate colors come out bright again? I've tried paint remover and dry muriatic acid. This is a new home.

Scrub the slate with a strong solution of trisodium phosphate, using about 2 pounds in a gallon of hot water, allowing this to remain on long enough to soften the paint so that it can be scraped off. Then flush generously with clear water to remove all trace of the cleaner. Because of the porous nature of slate, complete removal of the paint may be impossible. A concrete sealer finish should be applied to the slate. The sealer finish is a transparent water emulsion that is water- and acid-resistant and dries to a good gloss. It is made by a nationally known wax manufactur-

er and is available at janitor supply dealers. Follow the manufacturer's directions for use.

STICKY LINSEED OIL ON SLATE FLOOR

I spread linseed oil on our new slate vestibule, and it was not drying. Then, illadvisedly, I applied some drier over it. I have been told that the drier should have been mixed with the oil. Can you help me?

Interior slate need not be treated with oil of any kind. Plain waxing would have been sufficient. Exterior slate flagging is coated with a mixture of 3 parts linseed oil and 1 part turpentine. After a half hour or so, all traces of oil are wiped off with a dry cloth. To clean the mess you now have, use a nonflammable paint remover. Or scrub the stone with a hot solution of washing soda or trisodium phosphate, using about 3 pounds in each gallon of water. Rinse well with clear water.

SHEDDING TILE FLOOR

We recently purchased an old Spanish-style house. The foyer, dining room, and breakfast room floors are made of some sort of brick tile, finished with some type of varnish and covered with a reddish wax which comes off on area rugs or anything touching it. How can we remove this wax and finish?

The fastest, easiest, but most expensive way is hiring a person experienced in cleaning terrazzo floors to clean it. The second fastest, very dusty, way is renting a floor sander. Cover everything you can't move out. Wear a dust mask. Dusty as this job is, it's nowhere near as messy and tedious as using wax remover and paint remover on that porous tile.

VERY DULL TERRAZZO FLOOR

I moved into a new office with a terrazzo floor. The building had been used for storage. The terrazzo floor is very dull and spotted, even after being wiped with a strong detergent. What can I clean it up with to bring back some of its original color? Can a new finish be put on?

For a perfect restoration job, the best method is to have the floor sanded with a terrazzo-floor machine before applying a sealer for marble and terrazzo floors. The sealer will restore the color and protect the surface from waterborne stains. This preparation can also be used for maintenance, or a good-quality polishing or self-polishing wax can be used.

The terrazzo sealer is available at janitor supply dealers.

INK ON TERRAZZO FLOOR

How can I remove ink from a terrazzo floor?

Different inks require different treatments. If this is ordinary writing ink, try the following method: Make a strong solution of sodium perborate (available at druggists) in hot water. Make a thick paste of this and powdered whiting. Cover the ink stain with a ¼-inch layer of the paste, and replace with fresh paste when the old paste is dry. If this is an indelible ink containing silver salts, apply a weak ammonia solution and then rinse with clear water.

BASEMENT STAIRS

The basement stairs of our new home are not too well lighted. Is there anyway I can make them easier to see without going to the expense of adding light?

While the added light is the best answer, try painting a 1-inch stripe of luminous paint along the edge of each step. The paint will show up in the light, and will glow for protection in the dark.

SAGGING STAIRWAY

Can you tell me what is causing the treads and risers of my stairway to pull away from the baseboard and plaster along the wall? The gaps are from ⅜ to ½ inch, and I'm worried.

The explanation is generally that a roomside stringer has bowed, shrunk, or rotted at the base, permitting that side to drop slightly, pulling treads and risers with it. In all probability the pulled-away portions are also attached to a stringer on the wall side that would prevent collapse of the stairs, but if not, then there does exist a future hazard.

COVERING FOR STAIR TREADS

I would like to know what could be used to cover a front stairway, other than a carpet or rubber stair treads, to make it attractive and yet easy to clean. The wood is now painted, but it chips easily. We cannot have a natural finish, because the grain is not attractive. I have heard of using tile on stairs but don't know what kind would be best.

You can cover the treads with linoleum, rubber, or vinyl tiles. The edges of the treads and the tiles are protected by an aluminum stair tread nosing which is usually carried in stock by floor-covering dealers. They can also show you a wide variety of colors in the various floor coverings.

USE STAIRS WHILE FINISHING

Our stairway to upstairs needs refinishing. But how can we do this and still use the bedrooms? We have a sizable family.

The best way, if every member of the family can manage it, is to do alternate steps and everyone takes them two at a time. When the finish dries, repeat with the other steps. If everybody can't make it, then finish one-half of each step at a time. However, this method is more apt to show lap marks in the center.

KNOTS IN CELLAR STEPS

I made new cellar steps, using a grade of lumber that was full of knots. I plan to paint the steps. Do the knots need any kind of treatment first?

Cover all the knots, and other dark areas, with a special knot-sealing preparation available at large paint and hardware dealers. Or use pure, fresh white shellac to cover the knots; then dull the gloss when dry. Finish with any good-quality floor or deck paint.

DRILL EXTRA LONG HOLE

I have an old sculptured banister post which stands 4½ feet high. I would like to make a lamp stand out of it, but in order to do this, I must somehow drill a hole through the core of the post. I do not have access to a lath. The post is too long for any normal-size drill bit. Any suggestions?

Simplest, quickest, and probably cheapest is to lug the post to a woodworking shop and let them drill the hole. A small drill or auger bit with one or two extensions will probably cost more, unless you already have them. You'll need a vise and some good precision drilling. Start at one end, go as far as the extension allows, and then start in again from the other end. Or buy enough extensions to go from one end to the other.

DUSTPROOF BACKING FOR OPEN CELLAR STEPS

I have a problem with basement steps. They have treads but no risers. Consequently, a lot of dirt and dust fall under the steps. How can my husband fix this condition?

Nail a panel of plywood underneath, against the back end of the treads, to close the gaps.

Every house needs a foundation. The function of a foundation is to provide a level and uniformly distributed support for the building. The foundation must be strong enough to support and distribute the load of the structure, and sufficiently level to prevent the wall from cracking and the doors and windows from sticking. The foundation also helps to prevent cold air and dampness from entering the house. The foundation forms the supporting walls of the basement and waterproofs the basement. It's the latter that causes homeowners most of their problems.

Causes of Wet or Damp Basements

There can be many causes of wet or damp basements. The trouble can be minor, readily apparent, and easily corrected. Or it can be a more serious condition, not readily detected from the surface, and hard to correct. Test borings to determine the subsurface or groundwater level should be taken during the wet season. Following are some of the more common causes of wet or damp basements:

1. The land is flat or slopes toward the house, permitting surface water (rain and melting snow) to drain down against the basement walls. Water leaks through cracks or other openings in the walls and causes wet spots on the walls or standing water on the floor.

2. There are no gutters and downspouts (or there are defective ones) to handle roof water from rain and snow. The free-falling water forms puddles or wet soil near or against the basement walls. Water leaks in or enters by capillarity.

3. The subsurface or groundwater level is close to the underside of the floor slab. Water rises through the slab by capillarity, producing dampness.

4. The subsurface or groundwater level is higher than the basement floor. Water leaks in or enters by capillarity, causing standing water in the basement and, in time, dampness in the rooms above.

5. Condensation ("sweating") of atmospheric moisture forms on cool surfaces—walls, floor, cold-water pipes—in the basement.

6. Leaky plumbing or other sources of moisture increase the humidity of the basement air. Dense shrubbery and other plantings around the basement walls prevent good ventilation.

CHAPTER 6

FOUNDATIONS AND BASEMENTS

Now let's take a further look at these possible causes and at possible ways to cure them.

Aboveground Precautions

A very big percentage of the expensive leaky basement problems start above ground. The principal problems grow from excess water being allowed to collect close to the foundation wall, instead of being properly drained away.

When water collects around a house, it doesn't obligingly evaporate or otherwise disappear. Most of it sinks down into the ground, right outside and against your basement wall, and sits there—forming an underground swamp. If the backfill contains many pieces of broken concrete and other building rubble, instead of firm-tamped earth, the spaces between pieces can catch and hold so much water that a little swamp can turn into an underground lake.

With constant exposure to this steady water pressure, many a basement wall finally succumbs. Water starts to work through mortar joints or through cracks in the concrete itself. And then the trouble begins. When the problem spots are caught in the early stages, repairing weak spots in concrete isn't difficult. But if neglected and allowed to grow, then repairs can become both extensive and expensive. So the point we would like to make is that many of these wet basement problems can be stopped before they get a chance to start. The method? Take steps which will prevent water from collecting by the side of the foundation. If any of these steps fit your circumstances, it's suggested that you consider taking them before the wet, cold months arrive (and make outdoor repair jobs much more of a chore).

One common source of standing water is the system of roof gutters and downspouts. When a gutter is clogged, for example, with an old bird's nest, or stray twigs and leaves, it can interfere so much with drainage that water overflows these sides, rather than being carried into the downspout, where it belongs. During the "falling leaf" season, gutters should be regularly cleaned out. More on the care of gutters can be found in Chapter 9.

Probably the best all-around way to get rid of roof drainage is to install a good system of roof gutters with downspouts connected to underground drain tiles. These tiles should lead to the city drains or to a dry well at least

15 feet from the house, preferably slightly downhill. Such a system will guarantee that all the water from your roof won't be added to all that has already been deposited on your lawn.

If you have no underground drain tiles, and haven't the inclination to do all the excavation necessary, at least make sure that water pouring through the downspout will be carried away from the house. You can get plastic hoses which are combined with a gentle spring. One end is fastened over the lower end of the downspout. The hose normally looks like a large coil. But while water is coursing through it, the water's weight uncoils the hose for its full length, and drains out from this extension of the downspout at least 15 feet from the house. Most garden supply centers and hardware stores carry these useful devices.

Another diversion technique is to use a concrete gutter or a splash block. The gutter or block should slope 1 inch per foot, and its edges should be flush with the grade.

In areas where there can be long stretches of dry weather and the soil contains a fairly high percentage of clay or adobe, many people are careful to have their flower beds and shrubbery at least 2 feet from the house. There is a good reason for this. The constant, necessary watering for the flowers works itself down into the soil. And when this type of soil becomes wet, it turns squashy.

If the flower beds are practically against the walls, this can soften the earth beside the house, and even underneath. This means that earth which has become even a little squashy no longer gives its former firm support. So the house may settle a little, which can cause cracked plaster walls, just as in the case of practically every brand-new house. But with the flower beds a safe distance away, there is no danger of the watering having any effect on the earth under the house.

Basement window wells should definitely have adequate drainage—at least a 4-inch bed of gravel, and preferably a drainpipe. This can either join up with the main drainpipe some distance away or proceed directly to the dry well. It can even end in its own small tile field, similar in pattern to that of a septic tank.

Some homeowners accomplish this in another way. Instead of the excavation for the drain tile, they simply cover the window well with a cover of clear, rigid plastic, hinged at the side touching the house. Being clear, it

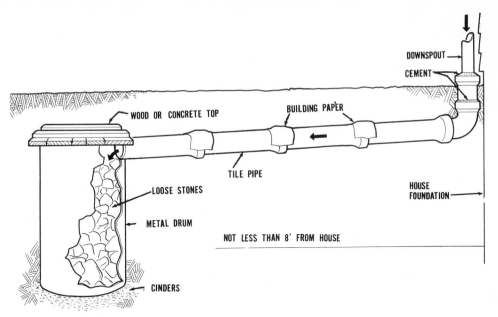

Figure 6-1. A simple dry-well arrangement.

admits light. In good weather, it is swung upward and hooked against the house siding, thus permitting free ventilation through the window. When it rains, it is flopped down to cover the window well. Very simple, very effective, quite inexpensive.

If your house is on a slant, the uphill part should have protection from water pouring down from above. This is best accomplished with a low retaining wall, built any convenient distance from your foundation, preferably a minimum of 15 feet away. This should extend down into the ground a couple of feet, if possible; actually, since it's best to go down a little below the frost line, this is automatically accomplished. The reason for the underground depth is because a considerable amount of downhill water seeps down through the ground, as well as flows down on the surface.

The wall should extend enough beyond each side of your house so that diverted water will flow past at a comfortable distance. The diversion will be even more positive if the wall has a slight slant from the center to the two ends.

The underground conditions vary mightily. In some localities, the soil is fairly loose, sandy, or loamy, and water drains down quickly. In such cases, there's rarely a serious problem with standing water. In other places, the soil has a high percentage of clay, which is so dense that drainage is very slow—especially if the water table in the ground is naturally high. In these cases, homeowners will do well to concern themselves with how well water drains away. If new to a neighborhood, asking builders or local engineers about drainage should pay dividends of helpful advice. Taking this advice, and some of the precautionary steps listed above, may well prevent future expensive problems with a leaky basement.

For houses where flooding is a fairly common problem, due to a high water table, land at the foot of a hill, or just plain near-swampy ground, one of the greatest friends in need is a sump pump. Located in a cavity below the basement-floor level, it starts to pump out any water that enters the cavity (called the sump). That is, the sump pump is equipped with a float, and when the water in the pit rises to a certain set level, the rising float automatically starts the pump, which carries the accumulated water to the outdoors through an iron or brass pipe connected to the discharge end of the pump. The cavity or sump is usually lined with a length of sewer pipe, 18 inches in diameter, to hold the earth in place.

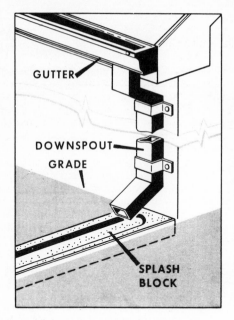

Figure 6-2. Two downspout arrangements.

Foundation Cracks and Waterproofing

Epoxy sealants have greatly simplified basement waterproofing problems. When mixed to brushing consistency, according to the manufacturer's directions, this paintlike coating is nothing short of wonderful in the way it can make damp or leaky basement floors and walls dry again. If the cracks are only the hairline variety or there are large damp patches, no work is actually done on the concrete itself. All that's necessary is to thoroughly brush the area clean. Loose dirt, flaky paint, or powdery mortar must be removed so that the epoxy sealant can make solid contact everywhere with the concrete. Give this type of material 8 hours or so to harden, and all worries are over. The epoxy element penetrates and becomes thoroughly bonded with the masonry itself, and the paintlike coating dries as smooth and hard as tile. In fact, the claim is that this shield will prove stronger than the concrete itself. Once treated, that masonry should never leak again.

If the crack, however, is somewhat wider, then it will require filling with patching concrete. Here again there is a modern improvement to thank for transforming what used to be a fairly tedious job into an easy one. This is the new type of latex patching concrete. Like the epoxy sealant, this is a dramatic shortcut. According to directions, all that's needed is to brush the crack thoroughly clean, then pack the patching concrete in thoroughly, and smooth the surface with a trowel. Thanks to the latex component, the repair should be completely waterproof.

However, standard patching concrete (considerably cheaper) can be used, as it has been for many years. It's a little more work, since more preparation is needed. And for absolute waterproofing, the epoxy sealant can be applied afterward. Here's the technique: Widen the crack, using hammer and cold chisel, to its full depth to permit packing in the patching concrete (mortar). Wear goggles, in case of flying particles. If the crack is in a wall or a ceiling, make the crack wider at the back

Figure 6-3. The right and wrong way to undercut a crack in a concrete wall.

than at the surface. In this way, when the patching concrete hardens, it will be wedged in. On a floor, of course, this wedge-shaped digging isn't needed; just make the crack's sides straight. Next, rake out all loose material. Then thoroughly soak the area with water. The idea of this is to prevent the surrounding concrete from drawing the water out of the new concrete, and thus permit the new patching concrete to cure slowly, the proper way. After troweling the patching concrete into the crack and smoothing the surface, sprinkle water over the entire area. In fact, the repair should be kept quite damp for a week or so. A tarpaulin, or some canvas awnings which aren't being employed at the moment, can be spread over the repair to retard evaporation. The reason for this protracted period of keeping the repair damp is that if the moisture is blotted out, the concrete may shrink a little. And that would mean another crack. But, actually, if this step is followed by treatment with the epoxy waterproof sealant, there'll be no problem about leaking. Before the development of epoxy, however, this slow curing was exceedingly important.

Even in the dire cases, where water is actually spurting through a hole, there are ready answers. There are modern products for plugging up these holes even as the water gushes through. These products have a consistency like heavy dough, which is kneaded and then forced into the hole. "Setting up" happens so fast that in a very short time after the dough is pushed into the hole, it's become thoroughly hard, with the leak thoroughly plugged.

Of course, contrast these simple repairs with what happens when a basement floor gets inches of water after a heavy rain or thaw. This can be caused by skimping on the proportion of cement in the mix, poor or no drainage bed or waterproofing layer under the floor, or much too thin masonry for the groundwater pressure. In terms of work, repairing is a huge job, whether it's approached from outside or inside. Inside, it's called membrane waterproofing: this consists of putting a layer of roofing cement over the floor and up a few inches on each wall; then a layer of overlapping strips of roofing paper, followed by another layer of roofing cement; and over this, another 2-inch-thick layer of concrete. If properly applied, the membrane is a very effective method of waterproofing.

However, it is one of the more expensive methods, and if leaks develop, they may be difficult to locate and costly to repair.

Outside, the same is done clear down to the footings (lots of digging). But the concrete parging layer need not be more than an inch thick. As a rule, two ¼- or ⅜-inch coats of portland cement mortar are applied to the exterior surface of the walls. The mortar should be mixed in the proportion of 1 part portland cement to 2½ parts sand.

The wall surface should be thoroughly cleaned to remove dirt and loose material. Just before the first mortar coat is applied, the wall should be moistened and given a brush coat of neat portland cement grout. The second mortar coat should be applied before the first one sets firmly, and the first one should be lightly scratched with a stiff brush to obtain good bond between coats. The surface of the second, or outside, coat should be steel-troweled to a smooth, impervious finish.

In very wet soils, the parged wall surfaces below grade may be given two coats of hot coal-tar pitch. The mortar must be dry when the coal-tar pitch is applied. *Caution:* Any movement or other disturbance to the walls can crack the walls and mortar coating. Don't backfill dirt against the walls until the first floor of the house is in place.

Condensation

Damp basement walls—even dripping wet walls—don't necessarily mean that water is

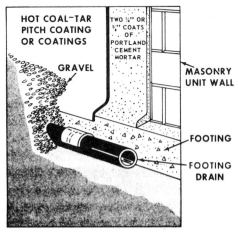

Figure 6-4. A footing drain prevents the accumulation of water around basement walls.

seeping through the masonry at all. This is especially true during damp, humid weather.

The cause of those damp walls, floors, and ceilings is frequently nothing but condensation. When warm, damp air strikes the always-cool masonry, it condenses and actually forms drops of water. The most effective and most inexpensive way to combat condensation is constant and thorough ventilation. On dry days, open the windows and doors and let the basement have every chance to air out. On damp days, keep the windows and doors closed; chances are good that the house air is quite a lot drier than what's outside—especially if fog is prevalent. Chemical dehumidifiers are very helpful, as long as someone remembers to empty the catch tray where the condensed water vapor is trapped; otherwise it will be dispersed into the air again.

Electric dehumidifiers, of course, do a most efficient job. If a basement room is habitually a bit damp in spite of frequent ventilation, one of these devices will make a tremendous difference. More information on how to fight condensation in a basement, as well as throughout the house, is given in Chapter 10.

In a new house, poured-concrete foundation walls, especially with outside waterproofing, are slow in drying. Water used in mixing the concrete can escape only through the basement, and pools may form on the floor. This is often mistaken for leakage. Drying may not be complete until some months after the heater has been started.

Questions and Answers

Foundation and basement questions have always been among the most frequently asked home repair questions. Following are some typical questions and their answers.

RAIN PENETRATES CELLAR WALLS

We recently purchased a fairly old house in excellent condition. The cellar walls are brick. We find that during heavy, windy rainfalls, water comes through the walls. Is there any preparation we can apply to the brick to overcome this condition which won't change the brick color?

A colorless, liquid masonry waterproofing preparation, containing silicones, is available at masonry material dealers. However, before applying it, examine the mortar joints and repoint any that are found to be cracked or defective.

BLOCK WATER FROM BASEMENT WALL

I am having a house built. The landscaping will be left to me, and I will be starting with bare ground. My question: Will it help keep water from collecting outside my basement wall if I spread roll roofing on the ground around the walls for about 3 feet, cover it with perhaps 6 inches of topsoil, and plant grass seed?

The idea is okay. You will make it much more effective if (1) the roll roofing is wider, say 6 feet, and (2) it is laid so that it slopes away from the house, thus preventing an underground lake from forming on the roll roofing. Since you'll be around, *be sure* when the back filling around the foundation begins that only good, clean earth is packed and tamped next to your walls—no collections of builder's litter such as sardine cans, beer cans, scraps of lumber, plastic cups, bunches of rusty wire, and such. These will cause little caverns where water will collect and press against your walls.

DRY WELLS COLLECT WATER

I want to build a dry well for drainage from rain gutters. How is this constructed?

Be sure to locate the well at least 10 feet from your house foundation. The hole for the dry well must be of ample capacity size, depending on the type of soil. We suggest inquiring from neighbors and local builders as to the general size necessary. Line the hole with any masonry material such as cinder blocks, stones, or bricks, without any mortar between them. Leave the earth bottom bare. Near the top bring the sides somewhat together to give the well the shape of a jug. The top must be well below the surface, so that 8 to 12 inches of soil can be placed over the reinforced-concrete cover. The intake is usually located near the top. Do not fill a dry well with stones or any other type of rubble that reduces the water storage capacity of the well.

WATER SEEPS INTO BASEMENT

After heavy rains, water seeps into my basement at the corner of the floor and wall. Could this be due to the drain tile or the storm sewer being plugged up? Would letting the downspout drain the roof water onto the ground, instead of down into the drainage tile, keep water away from my

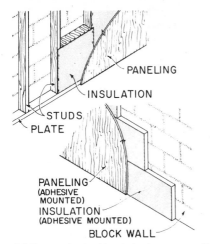

PANELING

INSULATION

STUDS

PLATE

PANELING
(ADHESIVE
MOUNTED)

INSULATION
(ADHESIVE MOUNTED)

BLOCK WALL

Figure 6-5. Two methods of insulating basement walls.

basement? Would putting in a sump pump be a good idea?

Without inspecting the tiles and the storm sewer, one can only speculate on the possibility of one or the other being plugged, and possibly both. Certainly you can let roof water come down the downspout onto a splash block, sloped so that water flows away from the house. You could also attach one of those roll-out plastic drains that fit over the end of the downspout. A sump pump is always a good idea in basements that get water. But wait until you see how this drainage works before investing in the time and expense.

WATER UNDER THE HOUSE

Last October I purchased a 10-year-old house. It has no cellar but was built on a 5-foot concrete foundation. In the past few weeks, during the warmer weather, I discovered 2 feet of water under the house. I checked the outside of the walls, and they appear to be in good condition. Could you tell me where the water came from? Also, what I can do to remedy this?

The house is probably located on sloping ground, so that in heavy rains water flowing downgrade would get under the house as the earth became saturated. It is also probable that roof gutters drain into the ground at the foundation walls instead of being carried away to a dry well at least 15 feet away. If there is a dry well, the connection may be broken at the leader pipe outlet and needs to be repaired.

Drain tile around the foundation walls should relieve the first possible condition.

WATER BACKS UP INTO CELLAR

We recently bought a home in town, and after several heavy rains our basement drain has been filled with water, apparently rain-water. It does not come from the walls, but right up from the drain itself. When it first happened, we ran a "snake" as far as it would go, without hitting an obstruction. Water drains away when the rain stops. Can you offer any advice or a solution?

It is quite probable that in your part of town the sewer lines are not adequate to handle storm water. To prevent the backing up of water, you can have a sewer backup valve installed. This acts as a check valve, permitting water to flow in one direction only. Plumbing contractors know about such equipment.

WINTER BULGES WALLS

Two years ago, we bought a house with a concrete block basement wall. Each winter, the wall bows inward all along the long wall and develops a crack. This gets worse toward spring. We even have a problem closing the door on that side. In summer, the wall straightens out again, the crack closes up, and everything returns to normal. The door, too. How can we strengthen this wall? I am afraid that one winter it may bow all the way in.

Your problem sounds like far too much water gathering outside your basement wall, instead of being drained away from the house. Perhaps your builder did a sloppy backfill of scraps of wood, plastic, and chips and bits of lumber, instead of solid earth. This would let water form a subterranean lake to press against the wall. If your roof gutter doesn't drain away from the house to a dry well or some type of storm sewer, it certainly should. Drain tile around the area of the bulging wall should be considered seriously. Surface water should run away from your house, not toward it.

WINDOW WELLS LEAK

We have found that the window wells of the older house we recently bought don't drain too well during heavy rains or thaws. Water almost pours into the basement at times. Any simple correction for this?

If you don't need the light, block them up. If you do need the light, make covers for the wells which will hinge up and hook against the siding. When necessary, unhook them and lower them over the wells. They can be made of painted exterior plywood, hardboard, or even heavy, clear, rigid plastic.

WINDOW WELL FILLS UP

We have a window well that fills up and runs into the basement during a hard rain only. What can we do to prevent this?

Drain tile should be installed from the bottom of the well leading to a dry well at least 15 feet from the foundation walls. When digging the dry well, make an ample-sized hole and line it with cinder blocks or stones, with no mortar between them. This will permit water to seep out of the dry well. Do not fill the dry well with stones or rubble.

BASEMENT WINDOWS

Are basement windows to be opened or closed in the summer during hot weather?

Basement windows, and the doors, should be closed when the weather is hot, humid, or rainy. But when the air is clear and dry, open the windows and ventilate the basement thoroughly. If necessary, place an oscillating fan on the floor to get air movement.

BASEMENT ALWAYS LEAKED

My problem is water seeping slowly through the basement walls and floor. This has happened ever since the house was built five years ago. I was told that drain tiles were not installed. Would digging up around the house, installing drain tiles, and asphalting the outside walls solve my problem? If so, how do I get rid of the water drained off by the drain tiles?

That treatment undoubtedly would do the job. You get rid of the water in the drain tiles through an underground drain pipe leading to a dry well or the municipal drainage system. However, before going to all this work and expense, try a much easier method: Treat your walls and floor to liquid waterproofing. If there are actively running leaks, use a quick-setting hydraulic cement. If this treatment works, you will have saved a good deal of money and lots of time. These waterproofers are sold in all building material supply centers.

WATER SEEPAGE THROUGH BLOCK JOINTS

Following a recent thaw and heavy rains, I had quite a seepage of water into my basement. It appeared to come through the joints between the cement blocks of the walls. What is the best way to deal with the problem?

Before replacing part of the present mortar, try the easier method of applying a liquid masonry waterproofing preparation, available at masonry supply dealers. If this doesn't work, rake out the present mortar between the blocks to a depth of a least ½ inch. Brush out all loose particles, and wet the inner surfaces. Then pack the joints with a fairly stiff, but workable, mixture of ready-mixed, waterproof concrete, available in 25-pound bags, or pack with a latex concrete, mixed according to the manufacturer's instructions. Keep the new mortar damp for several days to allow natural curing without shrinkage.

EVERGREENS CAUSE LEAKS?

When it rains hard or long, water comes through a block basement wall and runs down onto the floor. We have several such streams, but all on the front wall, where we have our hose situated and where our row of evergreens is planted. The other walls are okay. Could it be that the evergreens are causing these leaks? What can we do?

It is possible that the roots of the evergreens have done a little penetrating at those points, on the outside "walls" of the blocks, if not the inside. But before getting too drastic with nice trees, we would suggest your giving the problem wall a good treatment with liquid waterproofing, and the little streams some capping with thermosetting cement.

SPRING THAW BRINGS PROBLEM

Our older house has a full basement of poured concrete. Every spring thaw, when there's rain from the east, we get water in the basement from a spot about 3 feet long on the east side where the wall and floor meet. How can I fix this?

Being so seasonal, this has to be from added water pressure outside, where water collects next to the basement. You might check this simply with liquid waterproofing on that area of the basement. If the waterproofing is not enough, then you'll have to excavate. Cover the exposed section with roofing cement and then with asphalt-saturated roofing felt. Next, firmly tamp down the earth, using only good topsoil, so that there are no little coves and crevices where water can collect. (It's possible, of course, that a section of the drain tiles around your footings has collapsed or broken. If so, repairing it should cure the whole problem.)

YARD FLOODS PERIODICALLY

We have lived here 17 years. Once or twice we have been bothered with part of the backyard and garage flooding. But this past summer the rains killed a large area of grass as well as flooded the garage. What can be done about this problem?

Assuming that your land is flat (you don't mention runoff from nearby higher land), it sounds as though the soil is hardpacked, nondraining clay and the normal water table is very near the surface. A few shallow gravel-filled ditches, sloped toward a dry well or two, probably could help considerably, as well as a drain to draw water from the garage. Perhaps you should consider having the soil augmented with a sandy type, to promote better drainage. Best of all would be to call in a local engineer, who could make a survey of the problem. This is not a problem which can be accurately solved without knowing a lot more details.

WHAT CAUSES CRACKS?

What causes cracks in basement walls? How do you prevent and repair them?

Cracks can be caused by settlement, due to slight changes in the earth; improper or skimpy concrete mixing; and interruptions in a job before it is completed (such as quitting time arriving before the crew has finished pouring—the joint on which work is resumed the next day often becomes a crack). Pouring concrete in weather too cold and not keeping the concrete damp to allow slow, proper curing are other causes. Except for earth movement, prevention of other causes is pretty self-evident. Repair is done by chipping the crack at least ½ inch wide at the surface and slightly wider at the back, so that the patching mortar will wedge itself in place. Soak the crack, so that the dry concrete won't blot water from the new mortar. Then work in the new mixture (which should be fairly stiff) with a small pointed mason's trowel. Keep the repair

sprayed or damp for a week for slow curing (see page 117).

CRUMBLING MORTAR

What can we do about mortar between cement blocks in the basement which is crumbling in places, loosening the blocks? Is there anything we can put on to harden and stop the crumbling?

This may be due to an improperly mixed or improperly cured mortar. However, before replacement, try applying a liquid cement-hardening preparation, available at masonry supply dealers, according to the label instructions. Replace any missing mortar with latex patching concrete, after brushing out all loose particles.

KNOCK OUT THE TROUBLEMAKER

After a careful examination for the cause of a leak near the bottom of my basement wall, I found that the trouble comes from just one block—not a leak so much as a general sponginess of the block itself. Do you think I could safely knock out this block and put in another, without danger to the rest of the foundation wall?

With reasonable care, you should be able to chip out the block and its surrounding mortar without disturbing any neighboring blocks. To be on the supersafe side, soak the new block with liquid waterproofing before installing it. If you wish, you could also fill the gap with waterproof ready-mix concrete, but you'd need some forms (bracing) to hold it in place until it sets up. That's not difficult to do, however.

CEMENT SMEARS

We are in the process of building a house. When the mason laid the wall and poured the basement floor, some of the cement splashed on the wall in different places. Also, where the blocks were put together with mortar, some of the joints are quite messy. Is there something we can use to remove these smears?

Try wire-brushing some of the spots. If this is not successful, make a solution of 1 part muriatic acid in 10 parts clear water. (Add the chemical to the water very slowly to avoid splashing; a wood or glass container should be used to hold the solution.) Wet the smeared surfaces with clear water; then apply the acid solution. After 3 or 4 minutes, scrub with

Figure 6-6. Today's sump pumps, such as the one shown here, take up little space and require no maintenance to speak of.

more solution, using a fiber brush. Rinse thoroughly with clear water to remove all traces of the acid. Because muriatic acid is highly corrosive, wear rubber gloves, rubbers over your shoes, and old clothing. Avoid getting any of it on the skin. If working at eye level or above, wear goggles.

CRUMBLING BRICK BASEMENT WALLS

I am remodeling an old dwelling, about 50 years old. The basement walls are constructed out of semisoft brick. Water seeps through the walls, causing the brick to crumble or flake off in many places on the inside of the wall. Also, a lot of alkali and salts show on the inside. How can I prepare or treat these brick walls, so that moisture, etc., won't come through when the walls are painted? These walls have not been previously treated with anything.

Use cleaning and etching liquid for concrete and masonry, available at masonry supply dealers, to remove alkali and salts, following the label instructions. It is worth experimenting with a liquid cement-hardening preparation to see if it will stop the crumbling. Otherwise, badly disintegrated brick should be replaced with hard-burned brick and any cracked or loose mortar replaced with latex patching concrete. Then apply several coats of transparent masonry waterproofing, following the manufacturer's directions carefully.

OLD STONE FOUNDATIONS

I am interested in resurfacing an old rock foundation inside and out. What can I use with which to paint it?

We assume the stone has never been painted. If so, coat the walls with a dampproof cement-base paint. It comes in powder form and is mixed with water. Masonry and paint dealers sell it. The stone must be free of dust and dirt, which you can remove by wire-brushing. Broken mortar joints should be raked out to a depth of at least ½ inch and all loose particles brushed out of the grooves. Wet the inner surfaces; then pack the joints with a fairly stiff, but workable, mixture of 1 part portland cement and 3 parts clean, coarse sand. Keep the patches damp for several days.

MOISTURE MESSED UP HIS PAINT

About 15 years ago, I painted my concrete block basement walls with a cold-water white paint. To this day, any area not touched by moisture is still perfectly good. But in the laundry room and wherever rain got through windows, the paint flaked badly and is bare in many places. Can you recommend a way to remove all the paint and advise what type paint I could use?

You don't have to go to the huge amount of work involved in removing all the paint. Just wire-brush off any loose areas. Then put on a good brand of masonry paint. With vinyl or latex, you won't have to prime the bare areas, although they may need spot-painting first.

PAINTING PREVENTS WATERPROOFING

Although my basement walls have been painted with masonry paint, they are often damp at times, Would liquid waterproofing keep the walls dry?

No. Waterproofing must be applied before the concrete is painted. It must be able to work into the concrete, so that it can harden in there and form an antiwet shield. A coat of paint would prevent the waterproofing from working in. Try thorough ventilation on those days when the walls feel damp, since the dampness could be caused solely by condensation, particularly during warm and humid weather.

WHITEWASHED WALLS

The walls in my cellar are whitewashed. What do you advise me to do so that I can either put on another coat or paint them?

Whitewash is an inexpensive way of decorating and brightening cellar walls. If the walls are soiled, you can apply another coat of whitewash after first brushing off the excess powder from the present coat. A more permanent finish can be put on, such as a latex-base masonry paint or a dampproof cement-base paint that comes in powder form and is mixed with water. Before using either of these paints, all the whitewash will have to be removed. Wire-brush as much of it off the walls as possible; then wet down a small section of a wall with a hot solution of washing soda, using about a cupful in a gallon of water. After a few minutes, scrub with more of the solution; then rinse well with water, and repeat on another section.

TAR COATING ON FOUNDATION WALLS

When we built our house, my husband painted the concrete on our cottage foundation with tar, and he painted it too high. It shows above the soil around the front of the house. Will you tell me how it can be taken off?

Complete removal of tar is not possible, except if it is sandblasted off the walls by a building-cleaning contractor. Some amount of it can be taken off by covering it with a paste mixture of kerosene and powdered whiting. Apply a thick layer, and allow it to remain on until soft; then scrape off the thickest part of it. However, the discoloration will remain in the cement.

TARRED WALLS STILL DAMP AND DRIPPY

A year ago I bought a 24-year-old house. When built, the basement extended under the concrete front porch, and this room is a fruit cellar, 7 feet high but with 6 feet of it below ground level. Last winter, condensation formed inside the room from the frost outside. I tarred this room with asbestos roof cement, but the walls are still damp and drippy. What should I try now?

Weather-strip the door, so that the warm basement air can't constantly leak in and condense on that cold masonry. It would be even better if you could rig a double door.

BASEMENT ROOM TOO DAMP

Off the basement is a room which would be ideal for a root cellar, except that it's far too damp. We keep a 25-watt light bulb going, but it doesn't help enough. The floor is concrete, and the walls and ceiling are made of some porous type of masonry. Anything stored in there becomes moldy and rotten after a few months. How can we dry it out?

While some of the dampness probably is due to seepage through the walls and ceiling, we suspect most is due to condensation; the warm basement air is condensing on the cold masonry. You could cure a great deal of this by running weather-stripping felt tape around the door to block the warm air flow. Putting in an inside door, also weather-stripped, would really seal it. Painting the walls and ceiling with a waterproof masonry finish will help too.

DAMP SMELL IN BASEMENT

We have a problem of a damp smell in the basement in spite of two dehumidifiers going all day. The walls are paneled. What will help this situation?

Help the dehumidifiers by opening the basement door and windows on dry days and airing out the basement. You can further help this process by placing an electric fan in the doorway, facing outward. Although it's difficult to verify without some drastic inspection, there may be considerable dampness trapped between the paneling and the outside wall. A drain hole along the bottom of the paneling may help.

SEEPAGE THROUGH BASEMENT FLOOR CRACKS

Last year we purchased a new house. Since then some cracks developed in the basement floor, so that when there's a heavy rain, water comes through. I've applied two coats of concrete floor paint, and the sump pump works regularly. What can I do to seal the cracks?

The problem may be that the concrete floor is too thin. It should be at least 4 inches thick. Check with your builder, and if necessary, put down another layer of concrete. Seepage may also be due to loose fill around the foundation walls in which water collects as in a dry well, working its way under the floor and through cracks. A remedy for this is to excavate and lay drain tile at the footings of the wall, discharging at some lower point. The joints between the walls and floor, as well as any other cracks, should be properly sealed as recommended by the manufacturer of the sealing compound.

CRACKS IN BASEMENT FLOOR

There are cracks over the entire basement floor in our new house. Some of the cracks were filled by rubbing cement in, but have cracked again. The contractor suggests filling them in again. Is there any way to fix these cracks?

Very fine hairline cracks are not serious, and perhaps another filling with a neat cement over the dampened surfaces will stop their reappearance. If, however, the cracks have some width and are quite numerous, the floor is probably weak and not over 2 inches in thickness. Concrete cellar floors should be 4 to 6 inches thick. One or two cracks can be filled by cutting them wider and deeper, keeping perpendicular sides. After brushing out loose particles, wet the inner surfaces. Then pack the cracks with a fairly stiff but workable mixture of 1 part portland cement and 3 parts clean, coarse sand. Keep the patches damp for several days.

WATER RISE THROUGH FLOOR?

My problem is a leaking basement floor. It seems as though groundwater comes up through the floor and is now raising all the tiles. Is this possible? I do not feel any wet walls or see other signs. What can I do to stop this condition and keep the basement dry?

About as permanent a cure as we know is called membrane waterproofing (see page 117). This seepage could have been prevented during construction (with sheet plastic over a gravel drainage bed), but it's too late now. First, sorry to say, the remaining tiles will have to come up. Then the entire floor and about a foot up each wall get a coating of roofing cement as a waterproofer. Covering this are overlapping strips of polyethylene plastic or roll roofing, well pressed down. Next comes another layer of cement. Last is a topping layer of concrete. It's a pretty long, messy job, best done by a team of good pros. But it will surely result in a dry floor.

BASEMENT FLOOR PROBLEM

My basement floor is covered with vinyl tile. During the heavy rain and thawing last spring, there was about 1 foot of water on the floor, which left a film which looks like lime and rust. I've been unable to remove it. Could you suggest anything?

Experiment with different types of cleaners on small, separated areas, and complete the job with the product that works best. Try one containing trisodium phosphate; try kerosene on another; try one of the new liquid household cleaners, full strength. Be sure to follow directions carefully as regards thorough rinsing. After your experience with the flooding, it might well be worth your while to obtain one of the small brass draining attachments said to bail 300 gallons per hour. It is used with the garden hose, and works on the siphon principle. Most hardware stores now have these attachments in stock.

PAINTING DAMP CELLAR FLOOR

Our cellar floor becomes damp in spots on humid days. Could I remedy this without any great expense? We plan to paint the floor with porch and deck enamel, but only if the floor can be kept dry. Are there any products that could be applied as a sealer before applying paint, as the floor is quite porous?

The cellar should be ventilated and air circulated as much as possible, on cool, clear days. Are the present windows or louver openings of adequate size? They should be large enough to allow 1 square foot of opening to each 300 square feet of cellar floor area. Placing an electric fan directed toward the floor and toward an open window at the opposite wall will help air circulation. Excellent chemical air driers are available at many hardware and housewares dealers; follow the directions on the containers. Primers and sealers for concrete are available at masonry supply dealers; follow the manufacturer's instructions carefully. Be sure to use a top-quality rubber-base porch and deck enamel over a dry surface thoroughly cleaned of any trace of wax, grime, grease, dirt, etc.

SWEATING CONCRETE FLOOR

During hot, humid weather, like last summer, the water pipes under our concrete basement floor "sweat" a great deal and the moisture permeates the floor and the concrete block wall adjacent to it. What, if anything, can be done to keep a floor and wall dry during the humid season? Is there a chemical that will seal the floor? I'd like to do the job now so as to be ready for next spring.

A paint or sealer will not do. The condition arises because cold water travels through the pipe and chills the concrete. When warm, humid air comes in contact with the cold concrete, it deposits some of its moisture. Insulation of the pipe would solve the problem, but this would call for cutting out the concrete around the pipe, placing a vermiculite insulation around it, and recementing the area. It's not worth the effort. You could use an electric dehumidifier. It would help keep the basement drier and help minimize the sweating.

TRENCH OR NEW FLOOR?

There is a leaking crack diagonally across my entire concrete basement floor. Would you suggest putting a new floor on top of the old one? Or would you make a large trench out of the crack and fill it in with new concrete?

Instead of a trench, we suggest chipping the crack only wide enough for easy troweling in of waterproof concrete. There's no reason to do any more hard work than necessary, and a 1-inch-wide opening will be plenty. Clean out all loose stuff, and soak the surrounding concrete first, so that the old, dried concrete won't blot water from the new mortar. Keep the repair damp for at least a week to ensure slow, proper curing.

TAKING PAINT OFF A FLOOR

We would appreciate information on the removal of old paint on a concrete basement floor. We have tried a strong solution of lye and water, but find that the floor still is heavy with paint. We hope to lay asphalt tile.

The quickest and cleanest way is to scrape off the paint with a floor-sanding machine. Another method is to soften the paint with an infrared heat lamp, held about 12 inches from the surface, and then take it off with a wide-blade putty knife.

BONDING NEW CONCRETE TO OLD

I am trying to put down a new topping of concrete over the old. The present basement floor is irregular. How can I cement a layer of, say, 1 inch of concrete on top without having the dampness cause it to crack after a few weeks. I would also like to avoid roughening up the old concrete to get a bond. It has been brought to my attention that there is a compound that is brushed on which will bond the old and new concrete. Is this true?

Yes, such compounds are now available, and they seem to work out satisfactorily. Your dealer in masonry materials should be able to get it for you. Be sure to follow the manufacturer's instructions. For your information, dampness and damp conditions will not cause concrete to crack. Cracks in a basement floor, however, may develop if there is heavy groundwater pressure and the concrete is not thick enough to withstand it.

Figure 6-7. A simple method of concealing ugly drain pipes.

POCKMARKED CONCRETE FLOOR

A couple of months ago the contractor laid a concrete floor in the basement of my new house. The floor and walls were poured in one operation. Later a second coat was put down on the floor for the finish. The cement dust rubs off the floor easily, and where some workmen installed the furnace and plumbing, the floor has become pockmarked. What action can be taken at present to harden the surface of the concrete?

If the concrete is exceptionally soft, it might be of a poor mixture; frost might have damaged it when it was mixed or poured, or the sand and gravel were not clean. Such concrete cannot be hardened, and a new topping will be necessary. Ordinary plumbing and heating work should not cause deep gouges or marks in a hard concrete. Ordinary dusting can be eliminated by giving it a couple of liberal applications of a liquid cement hardener, sold by dealers in waterproofing and masonry materials.

WHITE POWDERY PATCHES IN CONCRETE FLOOR

I recently moved into a house that is about 16 to 18 years old. The previous owner recently painted the basement floor with a green rubber-base floor paint. There were two or three areas of a light powdery substance showing through the paint. Several weeks later, the entire floor became spotted with white, powdery patches. Can you tell me what might be the cause of this condition and what may be done to correct it? Do you think the painting caused this? Or do you think the condition existed previously and the floor was enameled to conceal it?

It is quite likely that the condition existed for some time and painting was done to conceal it. It is also possible that after the floor was painted, moisture from the ground under the concrete accumulated under the paint film, carrying with it mineral salts in the concrete. Evidently the moisture broke through the paint film, and as it evaporated, the mineral salts crystallized, leaving a white deposit. The remedy is to dampproof the old concrete with liquid asphalt dampproofing and asphalt-saturated felt and then put down a 2-inch layer of concrete on top. Of course, the paint would have to be removed with a floor-sanding machine in order to have the dampproofing adhere to the concrete.

ROUGH CONCRETE FLOOR

We recently had a home built and find that the contractor did not smooth off the concrete floor in the basement. There are trowel marks and small hills and valleys. Should we lay a new concrete floor on top, or try to smooth off the present surface? If a new floor is laid, what is the minimum thickness advisable and should it have any reinforcing?

You could have a terrazzo contractor grind down the surface of the concrete with a floor-grinding machine. Or you could put down a 1-inch thickness of concrete, but in order to get a good bond the present floor must be coated with a special bonding preparation, or it should be thoroughly roughened by chipping it with a hammer and cold chisel. No reinforcing is necessary.

BRUSH-ON CRACK FILLER?

My basement has deep cracks in the floor, some perhaps ¼ inch wide. Is there anything I could brush on the whole floor which would also fill the cracks and thus not look patched? The concrete is unfinished.

If hiding the cracks is the most important factor, then you have two choices: Repair the cracks individually (the conventional, economical method); then paint, carpet, or tile. Or cover the floor with another layer of concrete, making sure to work it down into the cracks. For proper results, the cracks should be soaked first to keep the dried-out old concrete from blotting water from the new.

NEW BASEMENT DUSTY

I recently moved into a new building and am having quite a bit of trouble with dirt from the basement floor. The new concrete is dusting excessively, and it is being tracked upstairs. Can you recommend something to stop this?

Was the floor given the usual new-floor concrete acid etching bath? If not, we suggest calling the builder; tell him he overlooked something and to get busy. Masonry sealer will stop the dusting and still make it possible to paint later on, if desired. Ordinary water glass (silicate of soda) is considerably cheaper

Figure 6-8. Laying of vinyl asbestos floor tiles is an easy way to have a beautiful basement floor. But when installing tile on a basement floor, be sure that it is one that is proper for below grade.

and does a good job. It's not always easy to find, though. Your best chance is a poultry supply wholesaler or farm supply store. It's sold in drugstores, but in such tiny, relatively expensive amounts it's not practical. Painting over a water-glass-sealed floor is rarely successful.

DRY BASEMENT FLOOR?

I know you don't go overboard for painting a concrete floor below grade, because of the possibility of dampness working up through the paint. But my basement floor really is dry; I mean bone-dry. What do you say?

Okay, try this: Put something large and flat on the floor, and leave it there for a week during a wet spell. A large black rubber mat will be fine, or a sheet of hardboard or metal; anything which will absolutely prevent evaporation from the floor underneath. If it's as bone-dry as the rest of the floor when you pick this up, then painting should be safe. *Remem-*

ber: Often the surface of a floor is dry, but the thickness of the concrete may easily be damp.

PAINTING CELLAR FLOOR

I would like to paint our concrete cellar floor. Nothing has ever been put on it. I may decide to lay some kind of tile later on, without having the paint removed. Can I paint over concrete, or must it be treated first? What kind of tile can I lay with good results?

Before applying paint to concrete, be sure it has thoroughly dried and cured; the surface must be absolutely clean—free of any trace of grease, grime, soot, wax, etc., before painting. Use a good-quality rubber-base concrete paint; it must be the type not affected by lime and alkali. Only a latex-base paint, which is adhering tightly to the concrete all over, can have tile put down over it; oil-base paints must be removed from concrete before laying tile. Vinyl-asphalt tile is suitable for use on concrete below ground; so is rubber or vinyl tile, using a special waterproof cement recommended by the tile manufacturer. Tile dealers usually supply the manufacturer's instruction sheets for putting down tile on all types of floors.

UNEVEN CONCRETE FLOOR

We want to cover our concrete floor in the basement with asphalt tile. It is quite uneven, but otherwise in good condition. Is there any material we can use to level the floor before applying the tile?

Floor-leveling compounds for this purpose are available at tile dealers and many building supply and hardware stores. Follow the manufacturer's directions carefully.

CELLAR FLOOR HAS WRONG-WAY SLOPE

One corner of our cellar floor slopes away from the center drain, causing any water to settle in this corner. Can anything be applied to the concrete to make it slope toward the drain?

Apply another layer of concrete to the desired slope of the floor. You can use a ready-mixed instant-pave asphalt product for this. It is easy to apply, needing no heavy rolling equipment, and is available in bags at garden supply centers. Sprinkling it with dry portland cement will make it lighter in color.

IT GOES ON NEW CONCRETE

We are building a new home and plan to seal the concrete basement floor so that it won't get dusty the way so many new concrete floors seem to do. Should I put anything on the concrete before the sealer? I recall having read somewhere that a presealing treatment is necessary.

The concrete should be etched with an acid bath. Usually the builder does this job automatically. The idea is to neutralize the lime so that it won't work out to the surface. Mix 1 part hydrochloric (muriatic) acid to 5 parts water. Let the concrete dry thoroughly before sealing it.

TILING NEW CONCRETE FLOOR

We had a concrete floor put down in our basement. We are planning a recreation room and want to have an asphalt-tile floor. How long is it advisable to wait before laying the tile floor down?

At least a month—depending on the temperature and moisture in the air. To be sure the floor is thoroughly dried and cured, make the following moisture test: Put putty in the form of a circle, about ½ inch high and 3 inches across, on the floor. In the center, place ¼ teaspoon of calcium chloride. Cover the area with a sheet of metal or glass or heavy plastic, to prevent outside air from coming in contact with the chemical. After 8 hours, if the calcium chloride is still dry and white, the tile can safely be put down.

WHICH CARPET FOR BASEMENT?

We asked three different stores what type carpet is best for a basement bedroom. We received three different answers. One said to use one that has a rubber backing. Another said not to use a rubber-backed carpet, but to use one with a fiber backing. The third said to put down tar paper and use anything. Who is right?

Unless your basement is bone-dry all year round (you didn't say), be ready for dampness. Rubber backing would trap dampness, unless it's the special foam-type which allows "breathing." Fiber would not keep dampness out of the carpet. So my vote is a slight variation of the third store: instead of a layer of tar paper, smooth a thin layer of waterproofing roofing cement on the concrete the size of the carpet. Press onto this a layer of heavy plastic

Figure 6-9. Proper way of installing sleepers for a wood floor.

sheeting. This will keep any dampness from working up through the concrete and into the carpet.

WOOD FLOORS ON CONCRETE

We are converting our summer home into year-round quarters. The bedroom wing has no basement, and the floors are concrete. We'd like to have wood floors installed. What is the procedure?

It is important to remember that no dampness should get at the wood. If it does, eventually it will cause the wood to rot. To protect the wood floor against this: First mop on a coat of liquid asphalt dampproofing, available at building supply dealers. Over this put down a layer of heavy asphalt-saturated felt, overlapping the sheets about a quarter of their width and sealing the seams with liquid asphalt. The wood floors are put down over this. If wood-block flooring is used, use mastic cement; if strip flooring is used, first put down wood sleepers in a mastic cement.

STAINED BASEMENT CEMENT FLOOR

During a heavy rainstorm, the water ran down my chimney and out my new basement cement floor. What can I use to remove the soot, water, and rust stains?

Rust-removing preparations are available at paint, hardware, and variety stores; follow the label directions carefully. To remove other stains, scrub with a stiff brush and a strong, hot solution of washing soda (using about 1 cupful to the gallon of water), followed by ample rinsing with clear water.

MILDEWED LINOLEUM IN BASEMENT

We have a two-story brick house with poured-concrete foundation walls. During heavy rains, water seeped in through a crack. This was repaired, and no other water was evident. The linoleum rug we had on the floor is mildewed, and so is the floor. We would like to know how the mildew can be removed from the floor. After the floor is cleaned, would it be advisable to paint the floor?

Remove the rug; then scrub the floor with a hot solution of washing soda or trisodium phosphate, using about 2 pounds to the gallon of water. Rinse the solution off with clear water. The mildew stains will not be removed, but the above scrubbing will kill off further growth. The floor can be coated with a rubber- or latex-base floor paint.

LIVING QUARTERS IN THE BASEMENT

Since the size of our family has outgrown our house, we are thinking of finishing off a couple of bedrooms in the basement, which is high and dry. Do you think it advisable? We now have 14-inch-high windows set in fieldstone. Would it be possible to install the conventional type?

If most of the foundation walls are above grade and there are no signs of dampness at any time of the year, it might be possible to satisfactorily convert the basement to living quarters. Conventional-type windows can be installed in stone walls if there is enough distance from the ground up. It is not advisable, however, to make the conversion when most of the foundation wall area is below grade and only small basement windows can be used. How about converting the attic?

FURRING STRIPS ON BRICK WALL

What's the best method to put furring strips for paneling on a brick basement wall?

Many different types of masonry fasteners, including masonry nails, are available at hardware stores.

DON'T PLASTER CONCRETE

In converting one area of our basement into a nice recreation room, I was thinking of putting a smooth plaster wall over the present concrete block. Is this a good idea?

You can put up the wall, but not directly on the concrete. This will cause condensa-

tion, followed by cracking and finally by the plaster falling off in chunks. The plaster would assume the same colder temperature of the concrete blocks, and when the warm house air landed on it, the plaster would sweat. That's the first step to the troubles. If you first build a false wall, on furring strips with paneling of wallboard, then you could plaster. This will provide the needed insulating space of dead air between both walls.

TREATING NEW PLAYROOM WALLS

We want to put a playroom in our basement this spring. Is it advisable to install batt or blanket insulation between wood paneling and the block walls? Should all the block walls be waterproofed?

A "yes" vote to the first question. Also, paint the back side of the paneling with aluminum paint to form a vapor barrier. If the insulation has aluminum on one side, this painting won't be needed. Before going to the expense of waterproofing, why not wait and see if it's necessary?

SEAL PLYWOOD BEFORE PANELING?

I understand that I should not put plywood paneling directly on the basement wall when putting up walls for my new playroom. If I put the plywood paneling on furring strips, so that they are at least an inch away from the masonry, is this okay? Or is there anything else I should do?

It would also be an excellent idea to put a coat of aluminum paint on the side facing the masonry walls. This will act as a vapor barrier and repel any possible dampness.

SMOOTH WALL FOR MURAL

I would like to paint a scenic mural on my basement playroom wall. This is regular concrete block, with about four coats of waterproof paint. Is there anything I could put on to make the wall smoother for painting?

By far the simplest way is to brush on a coat or two more of the paint. Plaster would be smoother, but you can't put it right on the wall because it's so apt to collect condensation and then crack. To use plaster safely you have to put up a false wall on furring strips and panel it before plastering. If you wish, you could sand down the mural area with an electric sander before applying the additional coats of paint.

BASEMENT CEILING

I have been thinking of sealing the basement ceiling of my house. Do you think it is a good idea or not? If you think it is all right, what material do you recommend and how is it supposed to be put on?

Nothing special is accomplished by covering the joists in the basement with a special material, other than improving the general appearance of the area and, by using a light-colored material, getting more daylight into the basement by reflection. An inexpensive material for the purpose is an insulating wallboard or gypsum wallboard. These are applied with staples. Dealers usually rent out the stapling machines. See your local building material or lumber dealer about these products. He can also furnish complete instruction sheets on the installation of the above.

REC ROOM VERY NOISY

When our teenage daughter and her friends turn up the record player in our basement recreation room, the house nearly rocks. Is there any way to soften those decibels? It's a bit rough on us old folks upstairs.

The best reliever (assuming you don't dare touch the volume control of the on-off switch) is a dropped ceiling. This can be of acoustic panels supported by a framework of metal strips. Filling the space between ceilings with fiberglass wool insulation will help a lot too. So will thick wall-to-wall indoor-outdoor carpeting.

SOUNDPROOF BASEMENT CEILING?

A few years ago I installed furring strips and a plaster-board ceiling in my basement. How can I install soundproofing over this?

Acoustic tile can be installed either with an adhesive or with staples. Consult your tile dealer or floor-covering dealer about the best method of installation for the tile you select; detailed manufacturer's instruction sheets for installation should be available at the dealers.

REPLACING WOOD BASEMENT POST

Is there any way to replace a wood post (in the basement) with a metal one? Is this a job an amateur can do, or must I get a professional?

Adjustable steel posts are available at building supply dealers. Installation isn't diffi-cult; just follow the manufacturer's instruction sheet carefully; be sure the bottom of the post rests on a firm surface.

PIANO IN THE BASEMENT

I am purchasing a split-level home and plan to put a piano in a recreation room at the lowest level. I know a humidifier might be used to keep the instrument from drying out, but what is to prevent warm, humid air during the summer from condensing on the strings, causing rust?

An electric dehumidifier would help reduce the humidity, provided that you keep the windows and doors closed during hot, humid spells. Of course, if the piano is to be located in a large room, more than one unit may be necessary to accomplish good results. We are assuming the walls and floors of this room will be dry and no ground moisture will penetrate.

BASEMENT CEDAR CLOSET

Would it be feasible to build a walk-in cedar closet in the basement? Our basement is always dry, and the closet would be located near the furnace. I like the idea of cedar, both for the pleasant odor and for making the closet safe against moths.

Dry or otherwise, when you close off a space like a closet, you immediately stop the air circulation that travels all around the basement. Trapped air becomes stagnant. If it also becomes even a trace damp, that's where troubles begin. So this is a calculated risk.

"DRY HEAT" FOR DAMP BASEMENT

Although my basement doesn't leak, and seems to be sound, there's a lot of dampness. It seems to me I read quite some time ago about a "dry heat." If I'm correct in my recollection, would this help me? And, also, what gives out "dry heat"?

If your basement is solidly built, as you say, we're fairly sure a dry type of heat will be all that's necessary, and probably only on damp days. You get dry heat from an electric heater, for example, although you'll probably find the expense a bit on the high side for keeping a whole basement dried out. Gas-fired or oil-fired space heaters can also be used, but they must be vented to the outdoors, because the afterproducts of their combustion are damp vapors.

MOLD ON BASEMENT WALLS

The outside walls of our basement recreation room are finished with knotty pine plasterboard. There is a 2-inch air space between the wallboard and the poured-concrete foundation. When the humidity is high, scattered mildew blotches form from the floor up, about 2 inches. Having the windows open does not help. Is there anything we can apply to the walls that will not ruin the surface?

Evidently the wallboard is in contact with the concrete floor, and in damp weather, regardless of the season, condensation has been forming often enough to bring about a growth of mildew. The first thing to do is to cut off the bottom of the wallboard to the extent of 2 inches or more. Then put in place a wood baseboard molding that has been coated with a chemical wood preservative (not creosote), and coat it with a good grade of enamel. Use an electric dehumidifier in humid weather; also keep the basement windows and doors closed until the weather is clear.

Figure 6-10. Using a plastic film to waterproof a plywood wall in a basement.

CHEMICAL FOR BASEMENT ODOR

Although our basement has waterproofed walls and appears to be dry, on damp days there is an odor of dampness that seems to remain even if it is not raining. We cannot afford an electric appliance that supposedly dries the air. We understand, however, there is a chemical that gives the same results. Can you tell us the name of the chemical, or suggest something else?

Chemical moisture absorbents are available at many large housewares and hardware dealers. Or calcium chloride (available at masonry supply dealers and some hardware stores)—using about 10 pounds per 1,000 cubic feet of cellar space—piled in wire baskets, with receptacles underneath to catch the drip from the chemical as it liquefies, can be used instead. Ventilating the basement on clear, dry days helps keep basement air dry; an electric fan, directed along the floor and toward an open window at the opposite end of the cellar, will help circulate the air. An electric dehumidifier will also help.

OIL ODOR FROM BASEMENT

Two weeks ago something went wrong with our furnace. Nobody was home at the time.

The furnace stopped, but the oil continued to run into the pot and ran over on the basement floor. We cleaned up the oil on the floor by throwing lime on the oily spots and where the fan is and cleaned up around the motor. But we still get a disagreeable oil odor all over the house. How can we remedy this? The smell is making us all sick.

Probably the best method would be to have a professional deodorizing company (consult the classified telephone directory under "Deodorants and Deodorizing Equipment") do the job to completely eliminate the odor. For home treatment, you might try the following: Cover all areas affected by the oil with a thick paste made of powdered whiting or other absorbing powder and a liquid nonflammable spot remover, being sure all windows are open and the basement and rest of the house are well ventilated. The spot remover will act as a solvent on the remaining oil and the absorbent powder like a blotter to draw it out. When the paste is dry, or discolored, replace it with fresh. Repeat the treatment until no more discoloration occurs.

ROOT CELLAR DRIPS

When we bought this place late last fall, I was very pleased to find an old-fashioned outdoor root cellar dug into a small slope. I don't know how the former owners made out, but this spring I have found that the concrete ceiling drips heavily, especially in warm, damp weather. Would it be possible to stop this?

There should be a double-door arrangement, like a storm door, to keep out warm air. If there is, you should tighten the fit by running weather-stripping felt around both doors. You could also insulate the ceiling by fastening sheets of ½-inch styrofoam, using masonry nails driven through furring strips.

MOLDY SMELL IN FRUIT CELLAR

I have a vegetable and fruit cellar built under my basement staircase. There is no window or vent in there. Is it advisable to have some sort of vent? I have found it to smell moldy at certain times during warm weather.

Proper ventilation and air circulation should be provided by installing vents in each wall; this will prevent condensation forming and mold developing.

FROST ON CEILING OF FRUIT CELLAR

Our fruit cellar has a concrete platform facing south, which forms a ceiling. A lot of ice forms on the ceiling and sides in cold weather. It starts melting when we open the door or the weather gets warmer. This condition makes the fruit cellar almost useless. The ceiling is about 2 feet above ground level. What can be done about it?

If in your part of the country you have to go down 5 to 6 feet below the frost line to prevent pipes from freezing, we wonder how a builder thinks 12 or 18 inches of concrete will keep frost out of a fruit cellar. The only suggestion we can make is to fur out the inside walls and ceiling and then place a thick insulation between the furring. In addition to this, in very cold weather, it may be necessary to use a small electric heater to stop frost.

CRAWL SPACE CONSTRUCTION

A house is going up in the neighborhood which has a part basement—a 4-foot crawl space under the bedrooms and family room. All of it is concrete. The basement has drain tile around the outside and is waterproofed; the crawl space has no drain tile and is not waterproofed, but has a concrete floor. Will the bedrooms and family room be damp

with this type of construction? I am planning to build soon and am interested in the problem.

Ample provision for ventilation and air circulation should be made in the crawl space (which you don't mention). Louvers should be installed in each wall; the size should allow 1 square foot of louver opening for each 300 square feet of crawl space floor. And providing a moistureproof and vaporproof barrier under the floor of the rooms above the crawl space is an added protection against dampness.

COVER FOR CRAWL SPACE

I am convinced I am losing heat because my crawl space is not covered with a concrete floor; this occupies most of the area under the house. Is there any other material I could use?

Heavy sheet plastic will do an excellent job. The wider you can buy it (the more awkward to handle, we admit), the fewer seams there will be for you to seal.

CLEANING CRAWL SPACE

We want to clean the crawl space under our house, but have no idea what to use as cleaning agents. There is a cement floor and cinder block walls. How can we rid the area of spiders? Is it a good idea to store clothes in this area?

We suggest using a vacuum cleaner to remove loose dust first. Trisodium phosphate, or washing soda, in warm, mild solution is a good cleaning agent, followed by ample rinsing with clear water to remove any trace of the cleaner. Clothes storage in a basement or crawl area is not recommended because of the presence of moisture from the ground; mildew is usually a constant problem on textiles, leather, etc. To get rid of the spiders, destroy any webs and insects. Then spray with an insecticide, especially in corners, cracks, and crevices.

SNAKEPROOF SCREEN FOR CRAWL SPACE

There is a crawl space 12 inches high under our porch. I would like to rig a cover of screening to keep snakes, skunks, and other small animals out of this area. Could a bottom frame be made of wood, such as 2 by 4s?

The 2 by 4s will be okay, but preferably of a decay-resistant wood such as locust, cypress, or even redwood. You'll get a great deal longer service if you'll also have them thoroughly treated with wood preservative.

WEEDS IN CRAWL SPACE

I have a house at the shore on a bulkhead of 100 feet. In the crawl space under the house, weeds are growing—the kind typical of the waterfront, about 3 feet high, with lots of seeds on top. The roots can't be pulled out; they break off. Is there something that will kill them?

Strong, effective weed killers are available at garden supply dealers; follow the label instructions for use. Or sprinkle a strong solution of calcium chloride or rock salt over the ground in the crawl space.

CHILLY CRAWL SPACE

We have no basement, but have a 36-inch-high crawl space, where our forced-air furnace is suspended from the floor joists. During cold weather, we felt cold air coming out of the heat registers in the living area. This happened when the thermostat was not calling for heat. There is a heating duct passing through the crawl space which has a vent to provide heat for the crawl space. The ground area is covered with plastic sheeting. Any suggestions on how to eliminate the cold air coming into the living area?

Start by closing the vent in the heating duct in the crawl space. Later, if necessary, you could consider covering any exposed heating ducts with insulation.

DON'T TRUST SPONGY BEAMS

I inherited an old farmhouse. It has no basement, but the beams the floor rests on over the shallow crawl space are getting spongy. I would like to fix up the house. But I am worried about those beams. What should I do about them?

Get estimates from several different builders on replacing the beams with new ones of seasoned lumber protected with wood preservative under pressure, or a few steel I beams (also primed and finished with rust-proof paint).

BIG DIP IN FOUNDATION

The top of our foundation has a big dip in it. This allows about four joists to sag below the level of all the others by nearly 1½ inches. Our refrigerator leans like the Leaning Tower of Pisa. Can this dip be filled in so that the floor is level again?

A good foundation company can jack up the sagged area (this is not a job for an amateur). If you have plaster walls, be prepared for repairing a few cracks when the lifting begins.

SAND DOESN'T STOP DAMPNESS

Like many other people, I have standing water in parts of the crawl space. To take care of this, I had sand blown in, as a thick covering. But this did not work out well. The sand also became damp and stayed damp. I am now thinking of covering the whole thing with heavy plastic sheeting. Should I leave a border at the edges for breathing? If so, how wide?

Leave no edge at all. That will allow dampness to work right up into your crawl space again. Don't you have screened ventilating louvers, at least one in each wall to permit cross ventilation? If not, you certainly should.

BEACH COTTAGE HAS DAMP SLAB FLOOR

Our beach vacation cottage has a slab floor which is almost always damp. Could I cover it with something to eliminate this condition?

We doubt if you could cure this 100 percent, as beaches are notoriously damp. But you could certainly eliminate any dampness rising up from underneath. First spread a waterproofing layer of heavy sheet plastic as a vapor barrier. Then lay 2 by 4s, well treated with wood preservative, as the supports for a raised floor. This can consist of plywood subflooring with finished wood flooring, linoleum, vinyl, tile, or any other covering you wish. This method isn't confined to beach homes; it works anywhere.

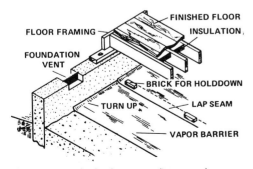

Figure 6-11. Methods of waterproofing a crawl space.

SLAB COLD AT EDGES

The edges of our concrete slab floor (no basement) seem somewhat colder and damper than the rest of the floor. What is the reason, and more importantly, how can I correct this?

It sounds as though the builder forgot to put in perimeter insulation. This merely consists of laying planks of styrofoam against the outside edges of the slab so that ground dampness can't work in from the sides. This is an excellent insulation and practically indestructible. When outdoor-working weather returns, you can dig down and do this job yourself or have it done professionally.

WOOD FLOOR ON A CONCRETE SLAB

My house is built on a concrete slab; asphalt tile covers the concrete floor. Could I lay 1-inch strips on the floor and then put ½-inch plywood on top of that, so that I could have a wooden floor? Would the floor then get damp? I don't notice any dampness on the floor now. Is a concrete floor healthy for people?

To be on the safe side, I suggest that you put down a coating of asphalt dampproofing; then apply a heavy asphalt-saturated felt, overlapping the sheets about 25 percent of their width. Seal the laps with the asphalt. This is advisable to prevent moisture from the ground from penetrating through the tile joints into the wood. For a good nailing base, use 2 by 4s, laid the flat way, instead of using the 1-inch strips. The plywood and flooring can then be put down. We have never heard of any detrimental effect to health, if a concrete floor stays dry.

Siding and the other types of coverings used for exterior walls have an important influence on the appearance as well as on the maintenance of the house. The present-day homeowner has a choice of many wood and wood-base materials which may be used to cover exterior walls. Masonry, veneers, metal or plastic (vinyl) siding, and other nonwood materials are additional choices. Wood siding can be obtained in many different patterns and can be finished naturally, stained, or painted. Wood shingles, plywood, wood siding or paneling, fiberboard, and hardboard are some of the types used as exterior coverings. Many prefinished sidings are available, and the coatings and films applied to several types of base materials presumably eliminate the need of refinishing for many years.

Questions and Answers

Because of the wide range of materials used on exterior walls, we have deviated from our normal format and will delve directly into the questions asked most about exterior walls and their "correct" answers.

WIDE CRACKS BETWEEN OLD BOARDS

My house is well over 100 years old. Many of the floorboards measure up to 12 inches wide. Some of the cracks are ½ inch wide. Before painting, what should be a good way to fill those cracks?

The best would be to use long, thin strips of wood, which you can shave to fit snugly and glue or nail in place. Do it during the heating season, when the cracks are at their widest (and the boards at their driest).

CHINKING FOR LOG WALLS

Is there any compound on the market that will harden like cement? The spaces between the logs of my cabin are crumbling. Is there any literature on the subject?

The following method is most frequently used: Drive lathing nails in a scattered fashion into the space that is to receive the chinking. Spacing the nails between 6 and 8 inches apart would be practical. Dampen the area with water, and fill the joints with a fairly stiff mixture of 1 part portland cement, 3 parts clean, coarse sand, and 1 part hydrated lime. A caulking compound applied with a caulking gun can be used in place of the above.

CHAPTER 7

EXTERIOR WALLS

CRACKING PRICE OF WEATHERED SIDING?

My house is three years old, with vertical cedar siding. A heavy vinyl sheeting was applied first, to protect the house from cracks, etc., which might develop. I have allowed the siding to weather; most of it has turned an attractive shade of gray. But several large cracks have developed; some ½ inch wide. Also some knotholes have been decaying. I have also been told to apply wood preservative, although this will stop or slow down the process of the house getting a more weathered look. What should I do?

Unless you've had some extra siding planks outdoors weathering too, any plank replacements would show up strongly. If you're dead set on a more weathered appearance, be prepared for more of the same. But if you want to prevent future damage, put on the wood preservative.

NAILS PULL OUT

I have asbestos shingles on the walls of the house, and several of the nails are coming out. Would a heavier nail do any good?

Replace such nails, making sure they will be at least ½ inch longer. Spiral or serrated ringed nails will hold better. If the shingles were nailed over an insulating sheathing board, all will eventually pull out, unless nailing strips were used. To have the nails hold in insulating sheathing without nailing strips, use self-clinching nails.

REPAIRING CLAPBOARD

Some of the clapboards on our house are warped or split. How can I replace them?

If the clapboard is warped, it may be sufficient to nail the area firmly with aluminum or galvanized rustproof nails. If this is not enough to flatten the wood, or if the nailing splits the board, the damaged section should be removed. A hacksaw blade or metal saw should be inserted under the lip of the clapboard, and the nails in the damaged area cut through. Then a vertical cut should be made through the face of the board at each end of the damaged area. When this is done, the larger part of the area may be split off, and a chisel will remove the small bit overlapped by the clapboard above. Once the damaged area is removed, another length of clapboard

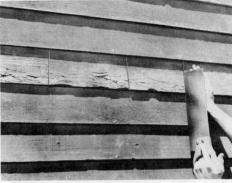

Figure 7-1. One method of removing a piece of broken siding.

of the same size and shape may be fitted into the space and nailed down.

RUSTY NAIL HEADS

What can be done to cover the nails in house siding? They have all rusted through and look bad. We want to repaint again and prevent this from showing again in a few years.

For the best possible results, countersink the nailheads slightly. Then touch them up with a rust-inhibitive paint or with shellac. Cover them with putty, smoothing the putty down to the siding. You can paint them when you repaint the rest of the house.

BROWN PATCHES ON SIDING

We built a new home three years ago and at the time put on a prime coat and finish coat of low luster. Brown patches keep appearing on the siding on the southwest where the sun hits it all afternoon. They come off

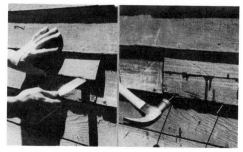

Figure 7-2. One method of replacing a piece of broken siding.

when scrubbed with a detergent and cleanser, but keep coming back, especially under the window areas. Could this be moisture, and what can I do to remedy this before painting again?

Since this appears under the window areas, I suspect the windows are not tightly caulked, which would permit moisture to work into the wall space and then out through the siding. Examine the frames closely, and fill any openings and spaces with caulking compound, using a caulking gun.

METAL SIDING

We have a lake cottage with outside metal walls over studs, 16-inch on center. There is no sheathing under the metal. Is it advisable to nail ⅝-inch new-style asphalt siding (the 4-foot lengths) over this metal? Or should I tear it off and then nail on the asphalt siding?

To reinforce the framing of the house and give more substance to the walls, we suggest the removal of the metal, then the installation of sheathing, and finally the application of siding. If you wish to avoid all this, the siding can be applied over the metal, but we would advise the application of wood nailing strips in order to provide sufficient surface for proper nailing of the panels.

CLEANING ASBESTOS SHINGLES

What can I use to clean asbestos shingles? They are only dirty from the weather.

Wash the shingles with a detergent solution or a solution of ½ cup of trisodium phosphate in a gallon of hot water. Then rinse with plenty of clear water to remove all trace of the cleaning solution. Be careful to keep the triso-

dium phosphate solution away from painted surfaces, as it will soften paint. Be sure to start the cleaning at the bottom of a wall, working upward in small sections and doing the rinsing immediately. Otherwise, dirty water dribbling down over dry, uncleaned surfaces leaves streaks almost impossible to remove later.

FITTING ASBESTOS SHINGLES

How are asbestos shingles cut to fit where necessary? We are building an extension at the side of our house and want to cover it to match the rest of the house siding.

Score the asbestos shingle along the line to be cut with a carbon-tipped blade. Then place it on a raised board, or step, so that the shingle can be snapped down to separate the excess part along the scored line. Asbestos shingle cutters are available at building supply dealers and can be rented. Inquire of your shingles dealer.

MOSS-COVERED BRICK

I have several thousand bricks which have been exposed to the weather for five years. Some of them have accumulated a thin coat of dirt and moss, which precludes mortar binding with them. I should be grateful to know of some practical way of removing enough moss to make them useful.

There is no simple chemical treatment that will remove the moss and dirt quickly. Wire-brushing will take off most of the dirt and moss. Another method would be to lay up the brick loosely, exposing the dirty surfaces, and then have them cleaned with a sandblasting machine.

PLAGUED BY MILDEW

Our 35-year-old, 5-bedroom house is our first. It is all on one floor. After last year's monsoon season, the north and west sides became black with mildew, right up to the roof edge. What caused this? The siding is varnished pine. Is there any other type of siding which would not be affected this way and could be put over the present siding?

The north side is the dampest because the sun usually can't reach it to dry it out. Perhaps your west side (as well as the north) is shaded by trees or high, thick bushes, which cut off air circulation. If so, thinning or transplanting could help a lot. Vinyl or aluminum siding would not be effective in this case.

SIDING SHOWING ITS AGE

Our aluminum siding is more than 20 years old and is showing its age very badly. What do we do with it?

With fine steel wool, clean off and featheredge any peeled areas. Scrub, if necessary, with a brush and a moderate detergent solution, to get the siding clean. One of those long-handled car-washing brushes will come in very handy. With the hose, rinse off any traces of detergent, and when dry, put on any top-quality house paint, either latex-type or oil-base.

CYPRESS SIDING PEELS

The former owner painted the cypress siding of my house. Now it is badly peeling. I was told that cypress does not need painting. What should I do? Repaint? Let the rest peel off? Remove the rest (but how)?

Until it's all peeled or repainted, your siding will look blotchy; how's your patience? To remove the paint, use a paste-type remover, which will be expensive because of the amounts you'll need. Or have someone experienced with blowtorch removal do the job, unless you can do it yourself. We know of the durability and resistance of cypress, but no wood is harmed by extra protection. You can keep the cypress color with clear stain. Or you can use pigmented stain or any top-quality house paint. It's your choice; all are good.

BLACK AREAS ON REDWOOD SIDING

Our year-old house has redwood siding to which a water-repellent type of approved preservative was applied. Several areas on the redwood surface are developing blackish stains. How can this be remedied?

The preservative used may have been stored too long before it was applied and may have become contaminated. When the treated redwood surfaces become wet, a bluish-black stain results. Apply a solution of oxalic acid (*poison*) of 4 ounces of acid per gallon of water. After an hour, rinse the acid off with plenty of water. Repeat the treatment if necessary. Or the blackish areas may be caused by mildew on the surface or in the finish film. To remove this, scrub the surface with a scouring-type cleanser. Rinse the cleanser off with a chlorine bleach solution, and then rinse the bleach off with clear water.

HAIL-PITTED SIDING

Our redwood siding was badly pitted by hail during a severe storm. It has been repainted since, but on the pitted area, the paint does not adhere. Before we paint again, what can we do?

The easiest way to smooth the surface again would be to have the job done by a sandblasting contractor. This will also put the surface in excellent condition for the new paint. Otherwise, you'll have to try wearing down the surface with a portable sander. That's okay if it's only a little area. Another approach would be to smear on a crack-filling preparation, using a putty knife, so that all the pit marks are filled. However, it is not as easy to get a smooth job as it might sound.

BLISTERED, STAINED SIDING UNDER KITCHEN WINDOWS

I rent out a cottage that has a new gas furnace; the kitchen ceiling is 1 foot lower than the other rooms. During winter, heavy cooking steam forms on the kitchen window; there is no ventilator fan, and the windows are never opened to let the steam out. An area on the outside of the house, wider than the windows and just below them (only under the kitchen windows), is rust-spotted and water-stained, with some blisters containing water. Is it possible that steam from the kitchen forces its way through the walls? In my own house, I always leave a kitchen window open to eliminate steam. Would plastic tubes, about 2 inches long, driven through the siding, take care of the dampness?

Steam will work its way through siding walls; in this case, it is probably working down on the windowsills into a loosened joint or an open space between the sill and siding. All such openings, or cracks, or separated joints, should be tightly sealed with a caulking compound. An outlet of some kind must be provided for the cooking moisture: either an exhaust fan vented to the outdoors, an open window (open at the top), or the miniature louvers you mention. These latter must be installed at the top and bottom of the wall, to permit air circulation in the wall space; they are easily installed and come in varying sizes from 1 to 4 inches in diameter.

RUST STAINS ON ASBESTOS SHINGLES

The walls of our cottage are green asbestos shingles of good quality. They have become rust-stained under the windows. How can we remove these unsightly marks?

To remove the rust stains: Dissolve 1 part of sodium citrate in 6 parts of commercial glycerin. Mix part of this with enough powdered whiting or other absorbing powder to form a paste. Cover the marks with a thick layer of the paste; when dry, replace with fresh paste or moisten with the remaining liquid. Complete removal of the stains may require a week or longer. If the staining is from screens, the screening should be cleaned with turpentine to remove all trace of grease, soot, etc. Then coat the screens with a good-quality spar varnish thinned with an equal amount of a half-and-half mixture of linseed oil and turpentine. This should be applied with a special screen applicator or a piece of carpeting tacked around a block of wood with the nap side exposed; a brush is likely to clog the mesh. Or apply pure fresh white shellac, thinned with one-half as much denatured alcohol.

INSECTICIDE STAIN ON SHINGLES

We used an insecticide spray on our asbestos-shingle siding for box elder bugs, and it has left black spots. Is there anything we could use to clean it? It would be quite a job to put on new shingles, as they are only a year old. The siding is gray in color.

Most insecticides are made with an odorless kerosene as the base. Such stains will eventually evaporate. If not, try washing the spots with a strong solution of one of the new detergent powders. Use about ¼ cupful in a pailful of water. First wet the shingles with water; then scrub with the solution. Before attempting to scrub, try cleaning with naphtha. Should these methods fail, the shingles can be painted with a rubber-base masonry paint.

IVY GONE, ROOTS REMAIN

I pulled off the heavy ivy growth from our asbestos-shingle siding and the concrete block foundation, but thousands of tiny roots remain embedded. Is there any easy and reasonably fast way to get these out? They look terrible.

We know of many cases where a small, cartridge-type blowtorch has been used very successfully on brick and stucco. Since your shingles are asbestos, experiment on an obscure section. We believe you can dry up and shrivel those rootlets without scorching the asbestos. Then they can be brushed off easily. Weed killer also works, but it's much messier and slower.

GET MOSS OFF SHINGLES

Please tell me how to eliminate moss growth from cedar roof shingles.

Apply a strong mixture of weed killer. Be careful not to let any drip down onto petunia beds. After a week or so, when the moss has turned brown and dry, you can brush it off. An application of bleach is often helpful to prevent future growth. We can't guarantee 100 percent effectiveness, so try it if you're inclined. Trying to eliminate the source of the moss growth will be better. Shade trees that are so close to the house that they cut off sunlight, resulting in constant dampness, are a common moss starter.

DINGY ALUMINUM SIDING

Our house, a two-flat building, was covered with white aluminum siding 12 years ago. It has turned a rather dingy white by now. Despite hosings, some parts remain stubbornly dingy, such as under windows and drains. How can we clean these parts?

Enlist the help of a detergent. Scrub with moderately stiff brush, which won't scratch the finish; then rinse. You'll make the job a whole lot easier if you have one of those long-handled car-washing brushes and a jar for the detergent solution, both of which can screw onto the garden hose.

POLLUTION "ORANGED" HIS HOUSE

I recently purchased a house with white aluminum siding. The siding has turned orange because of smoke coming from the nearby steel mill which uses oxides in its furnaces. What can I use to remove the orange film without ruining the siding paint?

Not knowing which "oxides," we can't suggest a chemical antidote. We can only suggest experimenting with various types of chemical household cleaners. Don't mix these more than double normal strength, and moderate pressure with fine steel wool or a stiff brush will help. Perhaps you could ask your EPA officer to find out which oxides are being used, which would give you the best clue. Haven't any neighbors coped with this same problem?

ALUMINUM CLAPBOARDS

Do you recommend removing the present clapboards before replacing them with aluminum clapboards? We are having trouble with the paint peeling off. Or is it to our advantage to just leave them on and place the new ones right over?

We do not advise the installation of aluminum clapboards until you have corrected the cause of the peeling paint. Paint usually peels because moisture gets under it, and by locking in this moisture with aluminum, rotting is quite likely to occur.

CONCRETE-SPATTERED SIDING

What will remove hardened spatters of concrete from aluminum siding without damage?

We can't guarantee 100 percent that anything will do this absolutely scratch-free. But try this: Use a small, square-ended piece of hardwood as the chisel, and tap it gently with a hammer. Often this will nudge such spatters loose. Sometimes you can break off several small pieces at a time, if it's a good-sized spatter.

PAINT-SPOTTED VINYL SIDING

Can you tell me how to remove paint spatters from vinyl siding? This happened when our window trim was being painted. Unfortunately, the paint has been dry for quite a while now.

To avoid dulling or otherwise harming the vinyl siding, lay off the harsh types of removers. Instead, mix up a batch of strong household cleaner, in the proportion of 3 pounds to the gallon of hot water. Daub this on the spots, give it a chance to soften the paint, and then begin scraping it off with a small, square-ended piece of hardwood. You can also use finest-grade steel wool. Be sure to rinse it all off afterward.

HAIRLINES IN STUCCO

We bought this stucco house two years ago. Now I notice some hairline cracks. Is this a sign of coming deterioration? Should I do something now?

The trouble with letting cracks in stucco become worse, or more plentiful, is that water will eventually be able to work in and get at the lath underneath. While it won't be an overnight process, eventually this could lead to decay of wood lath or rusting of metal lath. Either can loosen the stucco. The difficulty with filling the hairline cracks with a cement-base paint, which would be effective, is color match. We would suggest waiting to see if a lot more cracks develop. If not, great. If they do, then figure on a new coating of stucco.

PATCH STUCCO CORNER

A corner piece of stucco, not very large, has broken off the siding. Is it possible to patch this and keep the patch very white, so that I won't have to repaint? The stucco is very white; I had the painting done only a few months ago.

First of all, see if you can find out why the piece of corner broke off. If the metal lath is rusty, or the wood lath decayed, nail some new lath in place. You can mix your own patching mortar practically dazzling white with 1 part portland cement and 3 parts white marble dust. Only wet enough to be workable, and trowel and shape it into place. Keep the repair damp for a few days or a week, so that it cures slowly and properly. As with all masonry repairs, before you put in the patching stuff, soak the surrounding area to keep the old material from blotting water from the new patching mortar.

DISINTEGRATING STUCCO

We own a stucco house built about 1920, on which numerous cracks are beginning to appear. Some areas have loosened and fallen off. Most of the stucco areas are solid, even though they are cracked. Can such surfaces be preserved?

If the stucco has reached the stage where it is separating from the wall, we would think that it would be a waste of time and money to attempt to patch it. Undoubtedly, the reason for the condition is that the metal lath has disintegrated and there is nothing to hold the stucco in place. Restuccoing or the application of siding is advised.

FLOWERS SAFE WHEN WASHING WALLS?

Our siding is white Spanish-style stucco, which catches dirt, dust, and soot from the

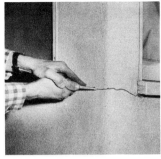 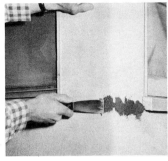 

Figure 7-3. Steps necessary to repair a crack in a stucco wall.

factory stacks. It really needs a good scrubbing with strong detergent. My worry is about the flower beds. Will this wash down and kill the flowers?

Probably not. You'll be rinsing with the hose a good deal, and this should dilute the cleaning solution so much that it won't bother the flowers.

RUST ON STUCCO

I have a white stucco house, and rust from the screens has disfigured the walls below the windowsills. What is the best method to remove the discoloration?

To remove such discoloration, dissolve 1 part of sodium citrate in 6 parts of water and add 6 parts of glycerin. Make a paste by mixing a portion of this liquid with powdered whiting; then spread it over the stain in a thick layer. When dry, either moisten the present layer with the remaining liquid or replace it with fresh paste. Ordinarily it takes about a week to remove a rust stain; but if it is an oil stain, it will take longer.

NEW SIDING

Our house is 28 years old, and the outside walls are covered with a magnesite stucco. It has been crumbling and cracking for months. There is an insulating sheathing board under this stucco. We know that all the stucco must be removed. Do you think this sheathing could stay on? Since we want to get away from painting, what is your opinion about aluminum siding? Is it a lifetime material that needs no paint or care? What other siding would you recommend?

If the insulating sheathing board is of the asphalt-treated variety, it is quite possible that it could remain in place if it has not been

affected by leaks through cracks in the stucco. Only through an examination of the sheathing, after the stucco has been removed, can you definitely ascertain the true condition. There is nothing wrong with aluminum siding, particularly the type that has interlocking edges and a baked-enamel finish. However, in time (after many years) the enamel finish may weather off, but it is not vitally essential to paint it because the metal will not corrode in most residential areas. You can cover the walls with an asbestos cement siding or a new type of brick siding. The latter is a clay product, and after it is nailed in place and cement mortar is put in the joints, the wall will have the weathering qualities of a full brick. Brick dealers will undoubtedly know about it.

BRICK

Please tell me the advantages, if any, of face brick or common brick.

Common brick does not come in a wide variety of colors, textures, and sizes, but does make a satisfactory wall. In some parts of the country, it may not be as hard-burned as face brick, but it usually runs much less expensive. Common brick will have some color variations in different parts of the country.

CHIPPED BRICK

Is there any way that face brick can be repaired? Pieces of our brick have broken off.

It would require the services of a color genius to match the color of brick, and if the brick has a surface texture, that also would require special treatment. If the brick has little or no texture, wet down the surfaces with water and fill in the chipped areas with a cement mortar consisting of 1 part portland cement and 3 parts clean, coarse sand. Make the mix fairly stiff but workable. Hold the mortar in place with varnished or shellacked cardboard. Masking tape will hold cardboard. The brickwork can then be painted with a cement-base or rubber-base paint,

BRICK COLOR TOO LIGHT

We recently purchased a 25-year-old house, which is all common brick. Is there any way to change or darken this brick other than painting it?

You can experiment with various shades of wood stains on sample bricks to see the results. (You'll never be sure just by looking at a color card.) Stain, whether pigmented or not, has the great advantage of never peeling or cracking. Consult your paint dealer.

WHITE-ENAMELED BRICK

Can you advise me? I have a brick building, about 40 years old. The brick is white. I would call it porcelain or white glaze. The surface is leaving the brick, and the brick under it is dark. This is taking place mostly on the upper story. I imagine it was caused by frost. Would it be advisable to touch up these bricks with white paint? I would like to make them look all the same.

Not all white paints are of the same shade, but if the affected bricks are high enough, it may not be necessary to attempt a close match. We would suggest that the brickwork be carefully examined to ascertain how moisture gets into the bricks to cause the scaling. Cracked mortar joints should be repointed. Or if the joints between the wall coping are broken, the coping should be reset. Parapet walls may need a couple of coats of an asphalt dampproofing on the roof side.

WATER SEEPS THROUGH BRICK-VENEER WALL

After a heavy rain, water appears in my basement. I have had the basement carefully checked, and it appears okay. Could my brick-veneer exterior wall be my problem?

Yes, a brick-veneer finish sometimes causes water to seep into the basement. This is due to a leak in the bricks and mortar joints by which water enters the space between the veneer and the sheathing of the house. As part of the job of veneering, sheathing is covered with waterproof building paper, starting at the sill. Water leaking through the brickwork col-

lects in this space (which may be an inch or more wide) and forms a pool at the bottom. It cannot escape through the bottom of the veneer, or through the building paper and sheathing, and is likely to find its way around the sill and between the sill and the top of the foundation wall. From here it runs into the cellar. This condition can be taken care of by drilling ¼- or ½-inch weep holes through the mortar joints of the lowest courses of the brickwork, which permits the water to drain away to the outside.

CRUMBLING BRICKWORK

We purchased a new brick house five years ago, and are troubled now by some of the brick crumbling, An invisible waterproofing solution was sprayed on. I am wondering if this will solve the problem, or is there something else that should be done?

Usually a condition of this kind can be remedied by the application of a couple of coats of a transparent waterproofing. If only one coat was applied, it will weather off too soon, and we would advise a second coat at an early and convenient time. Badly disintegrated brick should be replaced with hard-burned brick.

CLEANING BRICK WALLS

We have just purchased an older brick home. The outside walls look quite dirty and dingy. Can these walls be washed?

Yes. Wet the brick down with clear water (the garden hose is good for this). Then with a stiff brush scrub it thoroughly with a detergent powder, using about ¼ cupful to the pail of water. If the walls are really badly soiled, a gritty type of cleanser, such as the paste type of mechanic's hand soap that contains fine sand, may be necessary. Start working at the bottom of the walls, and keep the brick below constantly wet so that dirt streaks washing down from above will not penetrate deeply; this type of streak is almost impossible to remove. It is much easier to have the brick steam-cleaned by a building-cleaning contractor!

MUD ON BRICK

My house is of red brick, and the bricks near the ground are spattered with mud. It is useless to scrub them. Is there some way to remove the stain, or is there a paint of the proper color with which I could paint the discolored bricks?

There is very little you can do to correct the above condition. You might try scrubbing the brick with hot water and mechanic's hand soap, which comes in paste form and contains a fine sand. After scrubbing, rinse with water. Another solution is to plant shrubbery close to the house so that the bottom of the wall cannot be seen. Then, also, you might have the brick cleaned by sandblasting, and to prevent a repetition, you can put down a concrete walk around the house.

WHITE CHALKY SUBSTANCE ON BRICK

Our large brick chimney faces the front of the house and is coated with white chalky stuff. Someone told us that this is the result of not having enough lime in the mortar. How can we get rid of it?

The white substance on the brick is known as effloresence. It is caused by the presence of certain types of mineral salts in the mortar and sometimes in the brick. Rain and moisture bring these salts out to the surface, and when evaporation takes place, crystallization occurs. In many masonry surfaces the condition disappears after a few years. To remove the deposit use the following method: Mix 1 part of muriatic acid in 10 parts of water. Pour the acid slowly to avoid splashing, and use a wooden pail to hold the solution. After wetting the brick with water, apply the solution liberally on the brick, and after 2 or 3 minutes scrub with more of the solution, using a fiber brush for the purpose. Rinse well with clear water. Muriatic acid is highly corrosive and should be handled with extreme care. Use rubber gloves, old clothing, and rubbers over your shoes. Wear goggles to protect your eyes. Ordinarily, mason contractors do this type of work.

SPOTTED BRICK AFTER ACID WASH

We built a cream-color brick house last summer. When the mason washed it down with muriatic acid (as per contract), he ruined it; the color changed, and spots of brown have appeared. The mason said it would weather out, but it seems to be getting worse. Is there anything we can do to neutralize the stains?

The brown staining you mention is probably due to neglect to neutralize and remove all traces of the acid used in washing down the brick. The acid should be neutralized and removed by washing all surfaces with a solution of 1 pint of ammonia in 2 gallons of water, followed by ample rinsing with clear water to remove the ammonia solution.

SURFACE OF BRICKS NOW PEELING AWAY

The foundation of my home is made of soft, porous brick. In the basement, the face of these bricks is peeling and wearing off. I have tried to stop this with patching cement, but to no avail. Can you help?

We can't guarantee anything, but clear masonry sealer may halt this action or at least slow it up a great deal. These sealers are available at building supply dealers.

TUCK POINTING OR PAINTING

My brick building needs tuck pointing, and the porches and window frames need painting. Which should be done first?

Tuck-point first, and if some of the cement mortar gets on the trim or some part of the porch, it can be scraped off without the worry of damaging a new paint job.

SANDY MORTAR JOINTS

I have a two-story brick home which is about 40 years old. On the south and west sides of the house the mortar joints are becoming sort of sandy. The mortar, as yet, has not been washed out by the rain to any great extent, thanks to 3-foot cornice. I realize tuck pointing would be best, but this would involve more expense than I want to go to. Is there any preparation I can use to coat the mortar joints and make them waterproof?

It will be quite a tedious job to paint the mortar joints, but they can be coated with a dampproof cement-base paint. It comes in powder form and is mixed with water. Paint and masonry material dealers sell it. Of course, tuck pointing would be best.

GLASS BLOCK WALL

For greater privacy, we want to put up a glass block wall along one side of a covered patio area. Is a special cement needed for these blocks?

Yes; this is available at glass block dealers. There is also a type of joining technique involving thin wooden strips which eliminates the need for cement. Information about this should be available at your local dealer. Fiber-glass-reinforced paneling also gives excellent service for this type of wall and is easily installed.

HAIRLINE CRACKS IN ARTIFICIAL STONE

We purchased a house covered with an artificial stone made of cement that was put on in wet form with special molds. There are lots of hairline cracks and some that are slightly larger. What can we apply to close these cracks?

Hairline and slightly larger cracks can be filled by coating the walls with a dampproof cement-base paint. It comes in powder form and is mixed with water. Some paint dealers and dealers in masonry materials stock such paints.

LEAKY STONE WALLS

I bought an old house that has stone walls, and they leak. How can I repair them?

The usual problem with stone walls in an old house is leakage through weak or disintegrated mortar joints. If our supposition is correct, rake out the old mortar to a depth of at least ½ inch. Brush out all loose particles, and wet the inside surfaces of the joints with water. Pack the joints with a fairly stiff, but workable, mixture of 3 parts of clean, coarse sand and 1 part of portland cement. Keep the new mortar damp for several days in order to have the cement harden without shrinkage.

RUST SPOTS ON CINDER BLOCK

We have a cinder block building which has been painted. Rust spots keep coming through. How can this be prevented?

If the rust spots are due to pieces of metal within the blocks rusting, we are afraid there is nothing you can do. For surface rust stains, there are now excellent rust-removing preparations available at paint and hardware stores; follow the label instructions carefully. Or the following method can be used: Dissolve 1 part of sodium citrate in 6 parts water and 6 parts of commercial glycerin. Mix a portion of this with enough powdered whiting or other absorbing powder to make a thick paste, and spread a layer of this over the stains. When the paste is dry, brush it off and replace it with fresh paste. Repeat the treatment if necessary.

SAGGING GARAGE NEEDS HELP

The roof of our three-car garage has sagged so much the doors no longer operate. I have been advised to remove the layers of brick above the doors, install a steel beam, then replace the bricks. Is this a good idea? I plan to install new, automatic steel doors instead of the old wooden ones.

The steel beam should get the doorway square, without doubt. But you'd certainly be better off to have the builder examine the roof and supports, find the cause of the sagging, and fix that too. Your suggestions may be good but let the contractor be the final judge.

Doors and windows receive a great deal of usage in homes; yet most of us tend to take their service pretty much for granted. But because of this constant wear, doors and windows tend to deteriorate continually, will squeak and squeal when not lubricated, and will occasionally not close properly.

Door Problems

Doors don't suffer from very many ills that a comparatively few minutes' work won't cure.

Squeaky Doors. Practically always, any squeaking is in the hinges. The best cure is to knock out the hinge pin(s) (one at a time), after you have supported the lower outside corner of the door with a book or magazine. This makes it easy to wipe oil or a thin coating of grease on the pin—ever so much easier and better than trying to squirt oil around the top and hoping it will work down inside. If the hinge pin is rusty or stiff, a few squirts of penetrating oil spray can help loosen it. Be sure to shield surrounding paint and woodwork from the spray. And always keep a clean wiping cloth handy whenevery you're using oil.

Sticky Doors. Dampness from the outdoor air works into the wood and causes it to swell. As a result of the swelling, the door can no longer close in its frame. In most cases the best solution is to put a protective film on all wood, so that there is no place dampness can penetrate into the wood fibers.

To take this corrective action, remove the hinge pins, bottom pin first; lift the door out; and lay it flat across a couple of sawhorses or chair backs. (We'll explain a little later why removal is better than leaving the door in place.) Then shave down the area where the door catches; if necessary, you can use a plane, but sandpaper is better. But this isn't all; just because you have cut down the swollen section enough so it will clear the frame again is no guarantee this won't recur. So your next step is to apply the protective film to block the entry of more dampness.

In short, you give the door a couple of coats of paint or varnish. This means covering every square millimeter of the surface—both sides and all four edges, with particular emphasis on the top and bottom edges, because this is where the soft end grain of the wood most usually shows. The end grain is where wood is most susceptible to dampness penetration because it is softer and more

CHAPTER 8

DOORS, WINDOWS, AND SCREENS

porous. Now, with the door completely and thoroughly refinished, you can rehang it, with confidence that it will keep its shape.

While you are painting the door, you will realize why it is best to remove it from the hinges. If you left it in place, you would find it far more difficult to paint the bottom edge. Indeed, if the door has been painted several times already, it is more than likely that the top and bottom edges may have been overlooked. Yet these are the areas most likely to be victims of dampness penetration.

Should the front edge of a door strike the frame with space between the back edge and the frame, the hinges can be set deeper in the frame by cutting away the wood behind them; this is best done with a wood chisel. Should there be no space between the front and back edges and the frame, the back edge should be planed down to fit. This will require the resetting of the hinges, a job which is simpler than the resetting of the lock (which would be required should the front edge of the door be planed).

Should the door shrink so that the latch does not catch, shims of hard cardboard or thin wood can be inserted between the hinges and the frame. To permit this, the hinges are unscrewed; in refastening them, longer screws should be used to make up for the added thickness.

When a door sticks by striking the outer corners, as, for instance, when the outer bottom corner strikes the sill or the outer top corner strikes the top of the opening, the door can be tilted by setting a shim behind only one of the hinges. When the striking is at the sill, the cardboard should be placed behind the bottom hinge; when the striking is against the top of the opening, the cardboard should be placed behind the top hinge. The same effect can be obtained by setting one hinge deeper into the frame.

Sticking is often the result of loose hinge screws. Once or twice a year, an owner can well take the time to tighten these screws, for those of the top hinges will loosen under the continual strain.

When a door is properly fitted, the latch shouldn't slip into its hole in the metal strike plate on the frame until the door presses firmly against the moldings that form the stops. Should this not be the case, the door will rattle. To cure this rattle, the position of the plate should be changed by moving it closer to the stops. As the plate is usually set into the frame, this will require cutting, which can be done with a chisel; if no chisel is available, a pocketknife can be used. To permit the screws to hold in the new position, the old screw holes should be filled with wood pegs, glue, or wood putty.

A door may sag sufficiently for the latch to hit the center bar of the strike plate instead of entering its hole; to cure this, the bar can be cut away, which will be simpler and easier than resetting the strike plate.

Door Locks. With the exception of the locks of the front and back doors, the door locks inside a house are usually simple and give trouble only through clogging with dust, rust, and occasionally a broken spring. To remove a lock, one doorknob should be taken off, which is done by loosening the screw on its stem. The knob can then be pulled off or unscrewed, and the other knob, with the knob rod attached, drawn out. The lock is released by unscrewing two screws. One side of the lock is a loose plate secured by a single screw; withdrawing this exposes the mechanism for cleaning. Don't use oil to lubricate. It will collect dust and promote even more stiffness. Use powdered graphite.

Leaking Sill. In a driving rain, there may be leakage under the brass sill of a door fitted with metal weather strips. On removing the sill by withdrawing the screws, it will be found to have a lengthwise groove on its underside. This groove should be packed with either caulking compound or putty. Any excess will squeeze out when the sill is returned to position, and should be wiped away.

While on the subject of weather stripping, it should be pointed out that as far as doors—and even windows—are concerned, the greatest of leakproofers is metal weather stripping. These interlocking strips completely and positively seal up any gaps between windows and doors and their frames. Not only does weather stripping keep out every drop of water, but it completely eliminates cold drafts blowing in around these edges. In the areas where the soil is predominantly dusty or sandy, metal weather stripping is just about the only means of keeping dust and sand out of the house when there's a strong wind. Furthermore, this weather stripping is a great economizer for the air conditioner. It seals windows and doors tightly, so that cooled air can't escape wastefully to the outdoors.

While there is no denying that metal weather stripping, competently installed, can be expensive, its durability amortizes the cost over a good number of years. However, if the budget can't handle this installation cost, strips of foam plastic-backed felt make an effective substitute. Tacking or cementing these strips in position is not a tricky job. (But having the metal weather stripping put in is only a job for a professional.)

Window Problems

A window is made to do two things: let in light and let you see what's going on outside. It's not made·to steam up, frost over, let in drafts, waste good heat, leak, rattle, get stuck, or refuse to open and close easily. Yet lots of windows have a good many of these faults. All of them are annoying, and some are costly. Happily, every single one of them is a reasonably simple job for a homeowner to handle.

Steaming Up. This is a fault much more common now than before the days of good insulation—sort of a side effect of modern houses being built so well. In preinsulation days, damp house air could leak outdoors through all kinds of cracks through walls and around window and door frames. Of course, this made for constant ventilation, when drafty air leaked in to replace the damp air leaking out. It also meant colder floors and higher fuel costs. But, now, with good insulation on walls and under floors and roofs, and with well-fitting storm sash, the damp air is trapped in the house. The window glass, being so much colder than the walls, causes the trapped air to condense and fog on the glass. Often the condensation's so severe the water runs down onto the floor in puddles. If there's no storm sash, this condensation will actually freeze on the chilled glass.

As a matter of fact, if windows don't fit snugly, enough house air can leak around the sash into the space between the window and storm sash so that the moisture will freeze on the storm sash. That's the reason some storm sash is made with small weep holes in the bottom rail, so that damp air can pass through to the outdoors. With wooden storm sash, some homeowners have found that drilling a few small holes in the bottom rail is very effective—well worth trying if you have a problem with a fogging storm. The holes are easily plugged if it doesn't work.

At any rate, the answer to the whole problem is to make the house air so dry it won't condense on the windowpane. The methods range all the way from regular ventilation on dry days (if it doesn't chill the house so much your heater has to work at an uneconomic rate) to electric dehumidifiers.

The greatest producers of dampness in the air are devotees of long, hot showers, drying laundry (except in well-vented modern dryers), and cooking (which releases damp vapors, especially with a gas range). As soon as possible, the bathroom window should be opened after a shower to let out the steam. Ventilating wall fans should be installed near clothes-drying areas. An impressive statistic: Even after laundry has been spin-dried, every pound of laundry releases a gallon of water vapor into the air as it dries. Is there any wonder why the house air can become sodden? Hence, a fan to draw the damp air outdoors will help immensely.

Similarly, a fan placed high in the wall above the range will keep the damp cooking vapors from circulating through the house air. The ventilating hoods, especially the new electronic absorbing filter type, are extremely efficient.

Dehumidifiers, whether operating separately in individual rooms or hooked into the heating system (or a combination), are excellent at controlling dampness in the air. They're well worth considering.

Drafty, Leaky Windows. If cold air leaks in around the edges, it's a sign that either the windows weren't fitted well in the first place or the wood has dried out so much the sash has shrunk, so that the window's loose in the frame. In many cases, this kind of shrinkage can let in not only cold air, but wind-driven rain as well.

While it's true that corrective carpentry can do a great deal toward tightening the fit, it's even better to have metal weather stripping installed. This is best done by a professional, and believe us, it really makes an airtight closure. Second best is do-it-yourself weather stripping, using various types of foam stripping, available at many hardware stores.

Leaks in window frames themselves can be filled with caulking compound, run around the frames where they join the house siding. The caulking can also be used on the inside. So can spackle, or the do-it-yourself putty ropes, or carpentry.

Speaking of caulking, the compound can

Figure 8-1. Always make your windows weathertight by caulking around them.

be had in several colors or can be tinted to match the surroundings with color-in-oil. It is of the consistency of soft putty but never becomes quite hard. A skin will form on the surface, but the underpart will remain soft enough to take up the movement of the wood and other materials in expanding and contracting.

Caulking compound is best forced into a crack with a large syringe called a caulking gun having a nozzle of a size to match the width of the crack. Actually, there are two types of gun. One consists of a cylinder which is filled with the caulking compound. The compound is kept under pressure by a plunger extending from the rear of the cylinder. Squeezing a trigger on the pistol-type handle forces the compound from the nozzle. The other type of gun is more practical for the homeowner since it requires less cleaning after use and the compound will not dry up in the cylinder. This gun is a hollow frame with a handle, trigger, plunger or winding key, and nozzle. A special cartridge or tube of caulking compound is put into the hollow space with the tip inserted into the back of the nozzle, and pressure on the trigger compresses the

end of the tube to force out the compound. After use, the tube may be removed, and all that remains to be cleaned with solvent is the nozzle itself.

Before filling cracks, they must be inspected for moisture. Caulking will not adhere to a wet or damp surface. All dirt and dust must be cleaned out of the hole. Where wood or metal is being caulked, it is best to give a priming coat to the area before applying the compound. This will prevent metal surfaces from rusting and will keep the porous wood from pulling the oil from the compound. Any crack wider than a pencil should be filled with tow or oakum as described above.

Whether a gun is used or the compound is applied with a putty knife and the hands, it should be forced into the crack, not just laid over the top. The putty knife should be wiped with a light film of linseed oil so that the compound will not adhere to it. Too much oil will make the compound gummy. When the compound begins sticking to the knife, it should be cleaned and lightly oiled again. A ½-inch wooden paddle soaked in linseed oil may be used to force the compound applied with a gun into the cracks. Such a paddle is also handy for smoothing the surface and removing occasional excess. A small tuck-pointing trowel may be used for forcing the compound into masonry cracks.

Stuck Windows. One of the common causes of sticking is dried paint. If you can't wiggle the window enough to break the paint film holding the sash to the frame, get a putty knife and hammer. Very carefully tap the blade so that it cuts in between sash and frame. Even better is a tooth-bladed tool made specially for this job, which is widely available at hardware stores. We are referring now to the paint on the interior side of the window. If the window was painted shut on the outside during a house painting, the job is considerably more difficult.

Windows also stick when damp weather causes the sash to swell so tightly it jams in the frame. Usually this can be corrected by removing the front molding (do this delicately, so as not to mar the paint). Then you have a chance to pry the sash sideways enough to work the window up; you may have to wait for enough dry weather to shrink the wood. But when you can work the window open, rub paraffin along the grooves and the sash. This will be a good lubricant. You can also get some window-sliding preparations for these surfaces, which work effectively.

With the combination aluminum storms and screens, especially when exposed to city soot, the channels and catches often become so clogged the windows and screens won't move. We've found that the combination aluminum wax and lubricant spray, of which there are several types, works like magic at making the windows and catches operate easily again. These sprays are, happily, widely sold in hardware and variety stores.

Broken Sash Cord. The repair of a broken sash cord requires the removal of the sash. For a lower sash, the molding that forms the front of the groove is taken off, as has been explained. Should the window be fitted with the kind of metal weather strip that forms the bottom of the groove, this also must be taken off to expose a trap on the bottom of the groove through which the sash weight can be reached. This trap is held by a screw or nail at one end. By removing it, the weight is taken out and the broken piece of cord untied.

The new sash cord will be too curled to pass down to the weight box when pushed over the pulley. To get it in, a nail or other weight is tied to one end of a piece of string and dropped down; the sash cord is tied to the other end of the string and can then be pulled through. With the sash cord tied to it, the weight is replaced in the box, and the cord cut off a little longer than the required length. The proper length is adjusted by the knot at the other end. When correct, the weight will be clear of the bottom of its box when the sash is up and will not touch the pulley when the sash is down.

To remove an upper sash, the lower sash must first be removed. The next step is to take out the strip that separates the two grooves. This fits snugly in a groove, where it is held by hardened paint, and sometimes, in addition, by small-head nails. Hardened paint can be cut with a knife, to be run along the angles on both sides. If the strip will not come out with the fingers, it can be gripped with a large pair of pliers, the kind with parallel jaws. Pliers of this kind are necessary to avoid marring the wood and to secure a firm grip. A strip will usually start with a sudden pull on one end.

When metal weather strips are used, they cover the bottoms of the grooves and must be removed to disclose the cover of the weight box. The strips are of light metal and must be handled with care to avoid bending and kinking. Usually, they are not nailed, but are held in position by the strip between the grooves and by being nipped under the moldings that form the other sides of the grooves. They are released by taking off the moldings and can be lifted out by sliding them upward.

Sash chains are preferable to cords and, when possible, should be used in replacement.

Replacing a Broken Windowpane. Here are the steps, using an ordinary double-hung window as the typical example: Put on gloves, and start picking the broken pieces out of the frame. Use pliers if necessary. Use a small,

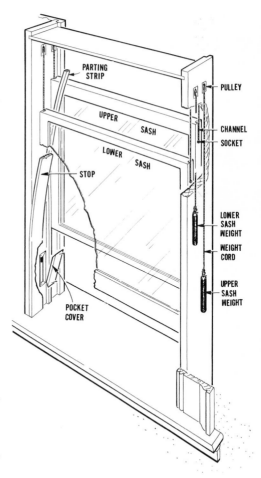

PARTING STRIP

PULLEY

UPPER SASH

CHANNEL

SOCKET

LOWER SASH

STOP

LOWER SASH WEIGHT

WEIGHT CORD

UPPER SASH WEIGHT

POCKET COVER

Figure 8-2. Parts of old-type double-hung window.

stiff scrubbing brush for any tiny bits. Next, get out the putty. If it's in good condition, not dried out or cracked, you may find it resistant. Try gentle prying with the corner of a putty knife. If it is slow going, switch to a chisel, but be very careful not to dig out the wood too. A few slivers, sure. But no real gouges. If it is still slow, switch to another team. Soften the putty with the tip of an electric soldering gun or slender soldering iron. Then scrape it out with the point of a beer can opener or screwdriver. Save the small, triangular bits of metal you'll find stuck in the frame. These are called glazier's points, used to hold the glass firmly under the seal of putty. You can use them again if they're not bent too much or if you can flatten them with pliers or a hammer.

Brush linseed oil on the wood where the new putty will go. This is to slake the thirst of the raw wood so that it won't draw oil from the new putty (which is what dries it out and makes it crack). You could also use oil-base house paint, thinned down 50 percent.

Now the frame is clean and ready for the new glass. Carefully measure the opening where the glass will rest. Take these dimen-sions to the glass man, and tell him to cut the new glass ⅛ inch smaller in each direction. You don't want an exact, tight fit in case the frame expands under excess humidity. Without this tiny bit of leeway, any frame expansion could crack the glass. When putting in the new glass, be sure that it is firm but comfortable. You achieve this by rolling and squeezing the putty between your palms until it's in the shape of a pencil. Press this onto the frame where the glass will rest. Form similar pieces until you've lined the frame clear around. Then you gently press the glass into this bed of putty, with the very slight curve toward the outside.(Window glass isn't flat; look along the edge and you'll see.) Be sure it's firm all around. To hold it in place, push the little glazier's points down into the frame so they're against the glass. Use the tip of a screwdriver to sink the point into the wood.

With the glass braced, you use more "pencils" of putty to cover the edges. Then run the putty knife along at a 45-degree angle, to change the putty into the smooth, flat-sur-faced bevel. Wait a few days for the putty to firm up a bit; then paint.

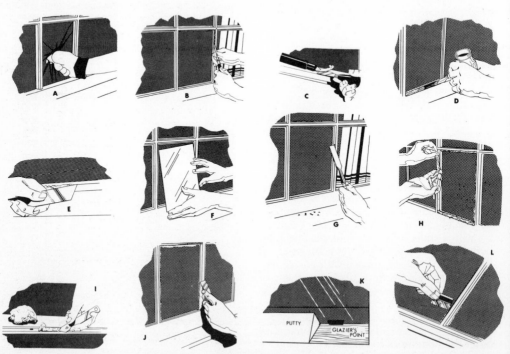

Figure 8-3. Steps in replacing a broken window pane.

Screens

While screens are beyond any doubt essential to living comfort, they can also become sizable items on the annual maintenance budget. That is, unless you know how to stretch their usefulness. The surest way to pay less for screens over the years is simple: make them last longer. Sounds a little oversimplified? Well, it isn't at all, because the use-stretching techniques are so completely simple in themselves.

Take the case of aluminum screens in your combination windows, doors, patio, Florida room, or lanai. Being aluminum, they won't rust. But they still need care—and most particularly if you live near the seashore. That's because the salt air has such a corrosive action. Exactly the same thing holds true for people who live where industrial plants and large apartment houses' smokestacks load the air with fumes and incinerator smoke. Such influences can weaken aluminum screening— and also roughen aluminum window and door frames with tiny pit holes. (If that can happen to aluminum, let's not think about what the same corrosive, polluted air can do to our poor old lungs.) But the perfect aluminum screen protection can't help appealing to even the most indolent homeowner. Just get a spray can of any good brand of aluminum cleaner and lubricant—available at any supermarket, housewares department, or hardware store. This type of spray puts on a thin coating which will definitely protect aluminum for at least several months. By applying some along the channels, the screens and windows will continue to operate easily, the way the ads say they will. If you don't enjoy broken thumbnails, spray around the catches too, so that they will not become stubborn.

If the screens have become pretty soiled from being up all year round, it's best to remove most of the dirt before spraying. There are two ways of doing this: If you wash them, take them out of the frames and bring them outdoors where you can hose them. If you leave them in place, for goodness sake avoid the hose; instead, use the vacuum cleaner. The reason is that if you blast the screens with the hose while they're still in place, you'll wash down a lot of grimy water onto the siding under the window. And that can be really messy. Besides, it gives you more to clean.

If you have copper screens, it's just as

Figure 8-4. Method of stapling a window screen.

important to keep a protective coating on them. Maybe even more so. Have you ever passed a nice white house and seen a green stain under the windows, spoiling the looks of the white paint? That's caused by rain washing down off the bare copper screens and leaving a copper oxide stain. It's very tough to remove, too. In fact, if there's zinc in the house paint, the stain won't come out at all.

Many hardware and paint stores carry colorless screen coatings, as well as special applicators, which prevent a finish from clogging the mesh; this is usually the case when you use a brush. There's also clear plastic in aerosol form. This type of coating gives perfectly adequate protection to the metal. And by shielding the metal, it prevents that green chemical reaction caused by rain washing down off bare copper.

A perfectly good homemade screen coating is a mixture of one-half spar varnish and the other half made of equal parts of linseed oil and turpentine. You can make your own applicator, too. Tack a small piece of carpeting, nap side out, around a block of wood. This will spread the coating very well, but not thick enough at any place so that it will fill up the screen mesh.

If you use a spray, there's a good shortcut. Stack three or four screens against a tree, and spray them all at once. The spray will go through the layers of mesh nicely. Then, to be sure the coating is sufficient, turn the stack around and spray from the other side.

Whatever application method you use, be

very careful to do the mesh where it joins the frame; that's one of the places where weakening is most apt to occur. The problem can be compounded if the tacks or staples fastening the screen to the frame aren't nonrusting copper. When rusted fasteners lose their grip, the adjoining area of screen can pull loose, bulge, and start a general loosening.

If there are a few very small holes—such as one or two wires worn through—you can make these bugproof again, and quite inconspicuously. Using a toothpick or kitchen match, put a little dab of clear household cement (or clear nail polish) at one edge of the hole. When this dries, add another dab. By working around the edges, and gradually closing the hole in this patient way, you can make a complete repair of a fair-sized hole. For larger holes, you can cut a patch of extra screening and weave the wire ends through the mesh, bending them tight. Or you can buy screen patches at the hardware store. However, these patches will be somewhat conspicuous, however effective they may be. Naturally, such patches should also have the protection of the clear screen coating.

Plastic screening is impervious to heat, moisture, salt, or other corrosive chemicals in the air. But because they lack the tensile strength of metal, sagging and bulging are naturally more common. The skill with which the plastic screen is mounted in the frames has a great deal to do with how long it keeps its initial tautness. And, of course, it does not require yearly refinishing to make it last.

Questions and Answers

Here are some questions and answers on doors, windows, and screens which we hope will be of some help to you.

DOOR RATTLE REMEDIES

Is there any way to stop a door from rattling? This happens when there are heavy gusts of wind.

Two cures: Move the strike plate so that the latch has no play (see page 146). Or close the "rattle space" by fastening felt weather stripping to the stops. This will also cut down materially on drafts.

OPENING DOORS

What could be the cause of doors not staying open? Friends say the house probably just settled; but I don't think so after 35 to 40 years.

The door frame may have shifted slightly, or one of the hinges has shifted; in either case, the door is no longer absolutely perpendicular. To correct the condition, either one of the hinge plates on the frame, depending which one is out of line, must be adjusted. A thin shim of wood placed under the hinge plate will move it out from the door frame; a more difficult adjustment is made by deepening the recess to move the plate in the other direction.

ADJUSTING DOOR HINGES

Is it possible to adjust the hinges on a bathroom door so that the door will swing at least partially closed?

The door's hang can be adjusted by placing a thin shim of wood or stiff cardboard under the upper hinge plate to move it out from the door frame. A more difficult adjustment is made by deepening the recess to move the plate a little deeper into the frame. With these two types of adjustment, you can experiment until the door hangs the way you want.

DOOR'S UPS AND DOWNS

A small addition to our house is on a foundation which apparently does not go below the frost line. With freezings and thawings, the outside door goes up and down, and now the lock and plate on the door frame don't meet. I have already had the plate lowered, but it changed again, so I cannot lock my door. Is there any solution?

Switch from a lock to a sturdy locking bolt, which would slide over a plate on the indoor surface of the door frame. The "loops" of brass or steel, into which the bolt slides, would have to be wider than normal to accommodate up-and-down motion; they could easily be tailored at a machine shop. Or you could do the job properly, though more expensively, by having a foundation mason put the proper support under the foundation.

INSTALLING A FOLDING DOOR

We would like to install an accordion-type folding door in a doorway now occupied by a swinging door. Is it a difficult job?

No, it is a fairly easy job just as long as the doorway is square. Just remove the old door, and pry off the doorstops. Cut the overhead track to ⅛ inch less than the inside measurement of the doorway. Align the overhead track, and then install it in place. Secure one edge of the folding door to the present door frame. Complete details are usually given on the installation instructions accompanying the folding door.

HANGING BIFOLD DOORS

We have a large bedroom closet which now has conventional swinging doors installed. To save space, could we hang bifold shutter doors in their place?

Bifold doors are easy to hang, but the instructions for installing the hardware must be followed explicitly. Generally, these instructions go as follows: The first step would be to hinge the two panel pairs together properly. Fasten the pivots at the top and bottom jamb-side corners of each pair and the pivot assembly that will ride in the overhead track in the top meeting corner. There is probably an aligning device to install at the bottom meeting corners too, eliminating the need for any floor track. When you have the opening prepared, align the track on the centerline and attach it to the head frame. Trim strips may be used to conceal the hardware if desired. Insert the doors in the track, and make necessary adjustments in pivot mountings and aligner.

FOLDING DOOR PAINTABLE?

Can one of those accordion-type folding plastic doors be painted? If so, is there any special way?

Painting can certainly be done. First make sure it is thoroughly clean, especially of wax or greasy fingerprints. Use top-quality enamel or latex-type paint, thinned at least 25 percent with its proper solvent. Then apply it in a series of thin coats, allowing each to dry thoroughly before the next goes on. Thin coats can stand the constant folding and unfolding a whole lot better than a few thick coats. Keep the door fully opened until the last coat has dried completely.

INSTALLING A SLIDING DOOR

I would like to replace the present conventional door to our living room with a sliding door, which will not take up so much space. Do I have to take down any part of the wall in order to do this?

Not at all. Install the sliding door so that it slides in front of the wall, as close as you can, so it will slide easily, but with as small a gap as possible between the door and the wall. The track can be camouflaged by a valance, if desired. But if you want the door to slide into a pocket, you will have to take down the wall itself as high as the door and as deep as the door must slide in, so that the studs can be replaced with two matching 1 by 4 or 1 by 6 verticals between which the door can slide. The lintel over the door is removed and replaced with a longer one which reaches to the back of the pocket to support the sliding door hardware and the door. It's best to install small rollers or tiny wheels along the bottom of the door to guide it away from the sides of the pocket. You also need special hardware for a handle to pull the door out.

REMOVING SWINGING DOOR

How can I remove a swinging door between my kitchen and dining room? We find it in the way. Before I start, is there anything tricky about it, or should I have a carpenter do the job?

Nothing tricky about it. Just remove the side plates covering the mechanical parts, and then remove these carefully. You can plug up any holes in the door frame with a round piece of doweling or simply fill them with plastic wood. Sand smooth, stain to match, and dab on the proper finish.

TAPE ON GLASS DOOR

How can I remove the sticky, papery residue of masking tape which has been on a sliding glass door for quite a long time?

The following method worked fine for us when we had the same problem with sliding doors to the porch; the residue was on the outside. We got the tape thoroughly wet with a small cloth soaked in high-test gasoline and then gently nudged it with a small putty knife. It didn't come off rapidly, but there's not a trace showing on the glass. Needless to say, be acutely aware and careful of the great fire hazard when using gasoline. If indoors, have all possible ventilation and make sure there are no open flames anywhere, including even your stove, your hot-water heater, and your furnace.

SOUNDPROOFING DIVIDING DOOR

How can I soundproof a door? I live in a divided house.

If this is an unused door, pack the joint around the door with felt (the weather stripping type is excellent for this purpose). In

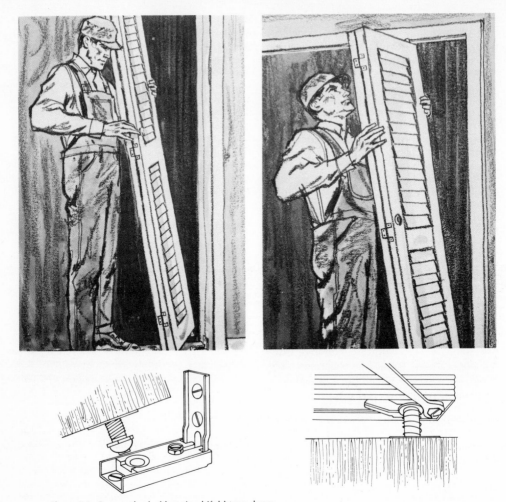

Figure 8-5. One method of hanging bifold-type doors.

addition, cut a sheet of stiff insulating board to fit in the doorway. It can be supported by 2 by 4s at the top and bottom, and at two places across the opening. Some acoustics contractors have special soundproof doors available.

CRACKS IN PLYWOOD DOORS

We have storage cupboards in our utility room. These have plywood doors which have developed cracks. What can I use to fill the cracks? I want to be sure the surface is smooth when I enamel the doors.

You can fill the cracks with white lead paste thinned to the consistency of a thick cream. When the filler has become dry and

hard, smooth it by rubbing it with "000" sandpaper and wipe off the dust.

NEW FACE FOR FRONT DOOR

The veneer facing of our front door is hopelessly weather beaten, cracked all over, and beginning to peel off. The rest of the door is good and solid. Could this covering be replaced? If so, with what?

Exterior-grade hardboard would serve very well. Let's hope the thickness is the same as the veneer. Then you won't have the tedious extra chore of moving the front stops to accommodate. If the hardboard is too thick, a competent carpenter could trim it so the new facing would fit exactly between the stops. You'd never notice this when the door is closed, but it would be apparent when the door is open. This procedure can be used to make modern interior flush doors. Quarter inch can be substituted for the hardboard if desired.

DENT IN HOLLOW DOOR

Is there any way to repair a dent in a new door? This is a walnut, stained and varnished, hollow-core inside door. The dent is about ¾ by ¼ inch, breaking through the wood at the top of the dent.

The best and most invisible repair would be to find a scrap of wood you could whittle, shape, stain, and varnish to match perfectly. Then glue it in position. This would take a lot more time and patience than most folks have. The second best would be to find or make enough walnut sawdust so that when you mix it into a paste with clear varnish it will fill the dent. Carefully smooth it into the dent. When the paste is dry, touch up the area with stain and varnish. If you can find wood plastic in the same shade as your door, that will be easiest of all.

WEATHER-BEATEN DOOR

Our outside door is very weather-beaten. It has a varnished finish. After the winter, when it becomes milder, how can we refinish it?

Remove the door, and lay it on a pair of sawhorses; it is easier to work on a raised horizontal surface! Remove the rest of the present varnish with paint remover, following the directions on the container carefully. If the wood has become discolored, bleach it by applying wood bleach or a liberal quantity of a hot, saturated solution of oxalic acid (*poison*) and allowing it to remain overnight. In the morning, rinse the door well with clear water. When the wood is completely dry, smooth it with "0000" sandpaper and wipe off the dust. For a light, natural finish, apply two coats of a good-quality spar varnish; for a darker color, first apply a wood stain of the desired shade, and then finish with the spar varnish. Be sure to finish all edges and surfaces of the door.

CRACKED, WARPED OUTSIDE DOORS

Our two outside doors are cracked and warped. What do you recommend?

The warping is due to moisture entering the wood and causing the fiber to swell. This may be due to an unsealed edge or to improper finishing. Remove the doors, and place them, concave side up, on wooden blocks or across chairs, in a area where they can remain undisturbed for several days. Place heavy weights, such as large rocks or books or pails of water, on the high ends, and allow them to stay until the doors straighten. The cracks should be filled with plastic wood when the doors are straightened. While the doors are being treated for the warping, remove all present finish down to bare wood. Sand the wood smooth, and wipe off all the dust. Then seal all four edges and both sides with two coats of either spar varnish or exterior paint, being sure to use a top-quality product. This will check absorption of moisture and prevent future warping.

DARK SPOT ON VARNISHED OUTSIDE DOORS

Both our outside doors are varnished, and right in the center they have turned very dark. The rain must have hit that part. How should we refinish the doors?

If the dark spot is due to rain penetration, this may be because a spar varnish was not used to finish the doors; an interior-type varnish may have been applied. Remove the doors, and remove the present finish down to bare wood, using varnish remover and following the label directions carefully. If the wood itself has been darkened, apply wood bleach according to the manufacturer's instructions. Sand all surfaces smooth, including all edges. Then apply two coats of good-quality spar varnish, being sure to coat all edges to prevent the entrance of moisture.

CRACKED DOOR PANEL

One of the front panels on my outside door has a longitudinal crack varying from ³⁄₃₂ to ¹⁄₃₂ of an inch wide and about 3 feet long. I have tried filling it with a fast-setting wood filler preparation and painting over this, but this chips out. Is there any other filler material that is available, or what can be done?

The best procedure is to remove the molding around the panel and put in a new one. If you wish, try the following: Coat the interior of the crack with linseed oil or thin paint. After a day or so, fill the crack with a good grade of putty. After a couple of days, coat the panel with a good grade of house paint.

STREAKED STAINLESS STEEL DOOR

Someone, when cleaning a large stainless steel door leading into our dairy cooler, polished it with either a wax or a sealer which has streaked it. We have used gasoline and turpentine, which tend to soften the wax somewhat, but it would be quite an expense to scrape off this softened mass. Can you suggest a solvent that would remove the wax without harming the stainless steel?

If turpentine softens the wax coating, take if off with stainless steel wool of a very fine fiber so that the metal will not be scratched. A sealer can only be removed with a prepared paint remover. Follow the directions on the label. We are afraid there is no inexpensive way of removing the coating.

FROST ON SLIDING DOOR

We have sliding doors in metal frames on the north and west sides of the house. In very cold weather, the metal frames become frosted on the inside, mostly on the fixed sections. What can we do to prevent this?

Actually, not much, if the trouble is with the metal frame. Such frames are supposed to have an insulating strip inside, so that cold won't be transmitted through to the inside surface. You could try lowering the humidity of the house air. On the chance there could be an air leak around the frame, you could also try a rope-shaped putty, available at hardware stores, around the outside edges of the frame.

STORM DOOR FREEZES SOLID

As soon as the temperature goes anywhere near freezing, our front storm door freezes solid. It faces east, and the ice usually melts away during the morning and early afternoon. What causes this, and what can be done to remedy it? Is there some connection with the fact that the foundation was originally built for a brick house, but a frame house was put up?

The foundation has nothing to do with the condition. The cause is usually excessive leakage of warm, damp house air through air spaces around the permanent door. Weather stripping of the permanent door should bring relief.

FRONT DOOR TRIMMED WITH CRUMBLING LIMESTONE

Our brick home has rough-cut limestone trimming the front door. Since the lime-stone is a many-layered sedimentary rock, rather than solid, every winter wears away another of the fine layers. How can this action be stopped?

This is a fine candidate for clear masonry sealer, available at most lumberyards and other dealers in building supplies. A treatment with this water-repellent shield will help a great deal.

ALUMINUM THRESHOLD A SAFETY HAZARD

On the thresholds of my front and back doors are strips of aluminum. In winter these become so slippery they are a serious safety hazard. What type of paint could I put on them?

Paint wouldn't last a week (or do any real good, either). Try a strip of that nonskid safety "tape" used to prevent spills in bathtubs.

WEATHER STRIPPING

The outside entrance from our cellar is a grade level. The door fits quite loosely, and I feel that weather stripping is the main solution to keeping out the cold air. Three sides of the door frame present no problem. But what should be done about the floor-door space?

Dealers in weather stripping materials sell brass and aluminum door saddles with a special type of "lip construction" so that the metal weather stripping on the bottom of the door will interlock into the saddle.

WEATHER STRIPPING UNEVEN DOOR BOTTOM

We have a door leading from the garage into a rear hallway. The opening between the door and flooring varies from ¾ to 1½ inches. Flies, mosquitoes, and even a mouse have entered the house through this opening. A concrete step leads to the door from the garage; the hallway side has asphalt tile laid over concrete. We have tried to obtain weather stripping to attach to the bottom of the door, but it isn't deep enough for the section where the floor and door are 1½ inches apart. Foam rubber tacked to the bottom wears off and is unsuccessful. Hardware and lumber dealers are unable to offer a solution. Do you have any suggestions?

A type of weather stripping is available which drops to cover the gap between the bottom of a door and the floor when the door is closed, and lifts up when the door opens; it can be purchased at some large building supply and hardware and lumber dealers. Or use a weather strip made for garage door bottoms or one having a pile fabric on a metal ferrule.

DRIPPY DOOR CLOSER

The automatic door closer on the storm door has, for several years, leaked oil down onto the sill. What will remove these stains?

Since this is an old stain by now, you'll find it stubborn. Make a paste of powdered chalk, cornmeal, or similar absorbent and dry-cleaning fluid. You could also use benzene, but it presents a great fire hazard. Cover the stain thickly; let the paste dry. Then brush it off, and repeat the process. The idea is that the cleaning fluid will work into the wood and loosen the embedded old oil, and the powder will blot it out.

DULL FRONT DOOR KNOBS

The front double-door brass knobs and fancy trimmings are very dull, almost dark brown. The inside knobs are bright. How can I restore the luster?

First you need a polish that will remove all that tarnish, and then a preserver so that you won't have to do it all over again tomorrow. Some people use clear lacquer over the polished brass. But when that begins to dull and flake off, you have to finish the job with lacquer thinner, which is extremely volatile.

KEYS DON'T FIT

Six years ago I was handed keys to my new home; some of them have not been used in all that time. Now, oddly, the keys don't fit, although I am sure they once did. What do you do for that?

If the keys originally really did fit the locks, and the locks also have been unused for this length of time, rust may have developed inside. Try blowing powdered graphite into the lock, and on the key also; if this doesn't work, try using a nonoily lubricant, available at hardware and paint dealers, for making locks and small metal parts move more easily. If unsuccessful, you'll probably have to replace the lock.

DON'T OIL STIFF LOCK

My front door lock is becoming so stiff I am afraid the key will snap off in it one of these days. The apartment superintendent tried a few drops of light oil some time ago. This helped, but now the lock is stiffer than ever. Can I try anything else?

That super should have his head examined; putting oil in a lock is disaster. All it does is collect more dust and dirt to make the lock stiffer. Lubricate only with powdered graphite, puffed in with a small snouted rubber bulb, or use one of the "dry" lubricant sprays widely sold in hardware and variety stores. If this treatment is too late to counteract the oil, you may have to get the locksmith over.

WANTS AIRIEST WINDOW

What kind of window will be best for a weekend cottage I am planning to build close to a lake up north near the border? Eventually I will have this cottage winterized for rental during the cold months, providing I don't use it myself. What window will give the best ventilation?

For the most air, either the casement-, louver-, or awning-type windows are best, as they all open the full window area. The double-hung window, while giving a better view when closed, perhaps, is never more than half open when it's "wide open," as one pane is in front of the other, and both cover half the area.

HOLDING UP PULLEYLESS WINDOWS

What can I buy to hold up some windows which do not have pulleys? We bought an old house. The first floor windows have pulleys, but the upstairs bedroom windows do not.

Many hardware dealers and some housewares stores stock small strips of clock-spring steel, slightly arched, about 3½ inches wide, with sharp teeth at each end. When forced between the front of the window frame and the back of the front stop, these exert enough pressure to hold the window where desired. No carpentry work is necessary.

REPLACING LEADED PANE

The doors in the upper part of the large storage units in our dining room have leaded glass inserts. One pane is broken and needs replacement. How can the broken glass be removed and replaced?

Work a pointed hook (an awl or very slender, pointed screwdriver) between the glass and the leading to scrape out the old cement and to open the space in order to remove the broken glass. Before replacing the pane, a fairly stiff paste made of a half-and-half mixture of linseed oil and spar varnish with a little japan drier and powdered whiting should be put in the grooves. Then embed the glass into the paste and add more if necessary for an absolutely tight fit. To force the leading back in place, place the handle of one screwdriver on the outside and the handle of another screwdriver inside, and press both together until the metal is forced back to its natural position. Wipe off all excess cement with turpentine.

REPLACE ROTTING WINDOW SILL

The outside of one of my basement windowsills is beginning to rot. No water leaks in, but yellow spots are appearing on the curtain. Is it possible to replace this sill, or is it a tricky professional job?

If the decay hasn't gone clear through, you could chisel out the bad part, cut a new piece, and fasten it to the solid remainder. You can also get prefabricated metal sills, made in several standard sizes. Check at your hardware store or lumberyard.

MOISTURE-STAINED WINDOWS

We are building a new home. Before we got our windows sealed, they got moisture-stained. They are Ponderosa pine. Is there any solution that will remove this stain?

Apply a hot, saturated oxalic acid solution (*poison*) or wood bleach to the stained areas of the bare wood; allow the bleaching agent to remain on overnight. In the morning, rinse off all trace of the bleach with clear water. Allow the wood to dry; then sand it smooth and finish as desired. It's a good idea to apply a thin coat of pure, fresh shellac to seal the surfaces before finishing.

SOILED CONCRETE WINDOWSILLS

We have concrete windowsills in a brick house. They are very soiled and grimy. How can they be cleaned?

Use a cleaning and etching preparation for masonry and concrete surfaces, available at masonry supply dealers, following the label directions. Or wet down the concrete surface with clear water. Then scrub with hot water and a mechanics' hand soap containing fine sand. Rinse with water. Be careful not to flood the sills; otherwise the brick underneath may become permanently streaked. This will work on stone sills, too.

BLACK STAINS IN WOOD WINDOWS

The woodwork around our windows is all varnished, and last winter the frost caused the woodwork to become very black in places. How can these spots be removed?

It will be necessary to remove the varnish from the wood. Then apply a liberal amount of a hot, saturated solution of oxalic acid (*poison*). Allow this to remain overnight; then rinse it off well with clear water. When the wood is dry, smooth the surface, if necessary, with "000" sandpaper; then wipe off the dust. To prevent a repetition of the stain, coat the wood with a chemical wood preservative. Then finish as desired.

RUSTED SCREWHEADS

As a rainy-day summer project, I have been doing some work on my very old wooden storm windows. Just now I can't afford new ones, and I'd like to make these I have a little tighter, so that they won't leak next winter. Nearly all of them have been braced with wood strips and screws, which now need adjusting. The trouble is that the screws are so rusted I can't turn them. Is there any way to do this, or must I drill them out?

Some time ago, someone suggested to us the following method, which we tried with complete success: Using a small electric soldering iron, heat the head of the screw. Apparently the heat causes an expansion just enough to loosen the screw so that it can be turned. This has worked whenever we tried it.

CAN'T GET WINDOWS CLEAN

Is there anything I can use on my windows which will get them really clean? I have used just about everything imaginable, including all kinds of soaps and detergents, both liquid and powder, and window and glass sprays. They helped somewhat, but that glass could still be made considerably cleaner.

With all those high-powered cleaners falling short, perhaps the trouble is with the glass. It may have become covered with tiny pittings from wind-driven sand, dust, and industrial soot. Anyway, here's a real powerhouse cleaner you can try: Wipe the glass vigorously with crumpled-up sheets of newspaper dipped in kerosene. For some reason, printer's ink is an excellent glass cleaner, especially when teamed with kerosene. Kill the odor of the kerosene by wiping afterward with vinegar.

PLASTER ON WINDOWS

During plastering, some of the moisture has run down the unfinished window frames, causing dark streaks. Can you tell me what I can do to lighten the wood before finishing?

Since the wood is unfinished, apply a hot, saturated solution of oxalic acid *(poison)* and leave it on the wood overnight. Thoroughly rinse the surfaces, and allow the wood to dry. Smooth with "0000" sandpaper, and wipe off the dust; then finish as desired.

MAKING WINDOW "FROSTED"

Since a house was built in a lot next door, I'd like to make my kitchen window facing it "frosted." I want the light, of course, but I don't want prying eyes.

There is a new aerosol-type product which was introduced recently. It gives a frosted appearance to glass when it is sprayed on. It should be available now in most good paint or hardware stores. Another way to do this job is to cut sheets of white tissue paper the exact size of the glass to be covered. Then the glass should be wiped clean with turpentine to remove any dirt and grease, and after it has dried, a coat of clear varnish is put on. While the varnish is still wet, the tissue paper is pressed and smoothed into position on the windowpane. The varnish will penetrate through the paper and bond it to the window glass, giving the desired "frosted" appearance.

WANTS TO ELIMINATE DRAFTS

Although we have aluminum combination storms in our older home, we get bad drafts from windows and doors. What would help eliminate them?

If the windows themselves seem tight, chances are the frames don't fit into the siding too well. Caulking around them will help a great deal; apply it with a caulking gun. Treat the frames similarly where they fit into the inside walls too, if needed. Strips of weather stripping felt where the door fits, perhaps a draftproof threshold too, will help make doors draft-free. These thresholds are made in many styles, in brass or cast aluminum, some with weather stripping. They are widely sold in hardware stores and lumberyards.

WINDOWSILL PEELS

The paint on several windowsills in an extension we recently added peels off in several spots soon after is is applied. What is the cause, and how can we remedy the condition?

The usual cause for peeling paint is moisture underneath working to the surface and pushing off the paint. Inspect the joint of the frame and sill, and fill all open spaces, no matter how small, with light-colored caulking compound or putty. The sill may be made of improperly seasoned wood, and resin is working to the surface (instead of moisture), forcing the paint off. Remove the present paint down to bare wood, using a prepared paint remover, following the label directions carefully. Sand smooth, and wipe off the dust. Then apply a coat of pure, fresh white shellac to seal the surface, or apply special knot sealer preparation, available at paint and hardware dealers, according the the manufacturer's instructions. Finish with a good-quality paint.

SO COLD, WINDOWS CRACKED

During one stretch of subzero weather last winter, 10 of my aluminum storm windows cracked. There are no inside windows; just the combination storms and screens. The porch is heated. What caused the cracking? What can we do about it?

Apparently the glass in your storms isn't of a quality which can stand up under such extremes of being warm on one side and extremely cold on the other. After all, storms aren't expected to be used alone. So understandably some of the less expensive types do not have glass with interior window quality. You could replace the old glass with better-quality glass. Or you could cut down on the porch heat during such extremely bitter weather.

SEA FROSTS WINDOWS

Two windows of our seaside vacation cottage face the sea. Over a few years, we have noticed a remarkable change. Apparently the combination of sea winds, flying sand, and salt air have covered the windows with so many small pits they look frosted. Is there anything we can do about this?

The only repair possible, as far as we know, is replacement of the glass. This would be many, many times cheaper than trying to have the present panes ground down enough to remove the pitting. We doubt if the glass is thick enough for this, anyhow.

LEAKS AROUND WINDOWS

I live in an old apartment house. Water has started to come in around several window casements when it rains. I examined them, and found that there's quite an air space between the frames and the brick siding, where the ancient wood has apparently warped. Is there an inexpensive way to fill these gaps?

You can make a very effective "mush" by shredding newspaper in a pail of hot water. Squeeze out most of the water, and force the paper into the cracks with a screwdriver. When dry, it will harden (becoming real papier-mâché), and it can be painted or shellacked.

FOG BETWEEN WINDOW PANES

We have a window with insulating glass which was installed about six years ago. It is now becoming cloudy between the two layers of glass. This window faces toward the east, and there are several trees. What could possibly have caused the cloudiness, and how can we remedy it?

Somewhere—somehow—the metallic seal between the two sheets of glass has broken, allowing moisture and atmospheric dust to get into the air space. We don't know of any remedy. We would suggest that you write to the manufacturer.

PUNCTURED INSULATING GLASS

We have an insulating glass in our picture window. One of the children on our block punctured the outer pane with his BB gun, so that the seal is broken and now the window steams up and is never clear. Can you suggest a way to get this window clear again?

There is no longer a dead-air space between the two sheets of glass, and as a result, heat and dust and moisture get into the air space. Your only solution is replacement of the glass sheet.

PICTURE WINDOW IS SCRATCHED

Somehow, the outer pane on our double picture window has been marred by a long, deep scratch. Since I know these double windows come as a sealed unit, I realize I can't replace only one pane; I'd have to put in a complete new unit, and this is an expense I'd certainly like to avoid. Is there any way to eradicate the scratch?

We are sorry to say that there's no homegrown way to eliminate the scratch. Grinding it down and polishing require heavy, specialized equipment, and we doubt if a glazier would want to undertake the job—at least not while the window is in place.

GLASS BLOCK TO REPLACE GLASS

Our 46-year-old upper duplex has two so-called upright-piano windows. I would like to substitute glass block in both, put a birch shadow box in the north opening, and close the east opening and plaster it like the rest of the wall. Would there be any condensation problems? Should a special kind of glass block be used? How can I be sure of a first-class job?

Installing glass block in place of the present glass shouldn't create any new condensation problem. Select the kind of glass block which will permit the type of light transmittal and transparency desired. To ensure a first-class job, have it done by a competent, reputable professional, or buy the block from an established, reputable dealer and follow the manufacturer's installation instructions carefully and exactly.

BLOCK CEMENT NOW BLACK

I have four glass block windows. My house is 18 years old, and the cement between the blocks and around the edges on the outside is now black. Some is falling out. I know I must scrape out all the black and loose material. But what do I put in to replace it?

You're exactly right about scraping out all that's loose. Fill the joints with glass block cement, available at any lumberyard. Tell the salesperson where you'll be using it. If you don't have a putty knife, get one at the same time.

SWEATING PICTURE WINDOW

I had a picture window put in my house last year. It is the stationary type. I don't want to have storm sash put on, but the window steams up all the time when the weather is cold. I wonder if you have a remedy for this? Would a dehumidifier help?

One treatment is to place an oscillating fan toward the window in order to keep the air circulating. Another method would be to place a dehumidifier in the room. But in order to have it function efficiently, the doors of the particular room would have to be closed; otherwise, humid air moving from an adjoining room would counteract the function. All large picture windows should be made with insulating glass, consisting of two sheets with a sealed air space.

STEAMING PORCH WINDOWS

Last summer I had a new porch built of concrete blocks, with four windows and a door. A storm door and windows were installed. The blocks were coated with tar before plaster was put on. The walls were plastered for about 6 to 8 weeks, but the plaster still seems to be damp. There is no heat in the porch. It is 5 feet from the ground to the floor of the porch, and it is all closed in at the bottom. How can I stop the windows from steaming?

When plaster is applied over an asphalt-coated surface, all the moisture in it must evaporate through the face of the wall. Therefore it will take two or three times as long for drying out, and since there is not heat, the evaporation process is naturally slow. Such a condition could contribute to the problem of steaming windows. Ground moisture under the porch may also aggravate the problem, but it could be minimized by covering the earth with moistureproof and vaporproof paper or polyethylene plastic sheeting. The sheets should overlap at least 6 inches. If the paper is used, seal the laps with asphalt roof cement. Nothing can be done about the moisture in the plaster, but time will probably have an effect.

ALUMINUM STORMS BRING STEAMY WINDOWS

Why do our windows steam up since we put in aluminum storm windows? Whenever I cook almost anything, the inside windows steam up so badly you can't see out. We even turned off the humidifier on the furnace, but it didn't help. This steaming never happened when we had wooden storms. I suppose we could put in a vent fan over the kitchen stove. But it was never needed before. What is the trouble?

Metal frames conduct heat and cold much better than wood. This frequently results in more steaming (condensation). It's also possible that the new aluminum storms fit more tightly, so that damp air, which formerly may have leaked outdoors, no longer escapes and settles on the cold glass and frames. I think you'd better reconsider and have the vent fan put in. It will make a great difference.

DAMPNESS BETWEEN WINDOWS

Between the storms and inside windows, on the south side of the house only, moisture accumulates on the inside surface of the storms both winter and summer. When this happens, it usually takes a few days to clear up. Why is this, and what can we do about it?

When the sun heats the space between those windows, it can really heat up. Now if damp air leaks around the inside window into that space, it will condense. The next time this happens this summer, open the inside window of one section and open the storm of another section and see what happens. If the storm stays damp and cloudy, then you know your house air is too damp and that it's leaking into the space. Come cold weather, put on weather stripping. Also experiment with one storm by drilling some small holes along the bottom rail for letting damp air escape. If the inside window of the other section remains clear, you'll confirm the theory outlined above.

ALUMINUM WINDOWS

We have recently moved into a new home. The casement windows—of aluminum— are coated with white paint, shellac, and other substances. What type of cleaner can I use, and can steel wool be used? Also, should I wax the frames after cleaning?

Shellac can be removed with denatured alcohol and "00" steel wool. To take off paint, use a prepared paint remover. Gummy substances can be taken off by wiping with naphtha. Be careful when using this; hard rubbing will ignite naphtha, and open flames will ignite the fumes. When the metal is clean, coat it with a clear lacquer. Wax can be used indoors, but it will not withstand the elements when used outdoors.

PUTTYING CASEMENT PANE

I have to replace a pane in a metal casement window. I understand this requires a special kind of putty. Where do I get it?

The "putty" for metal windows is known as glazing compound, not the putty used for wooden windows. It is available at stores selling metal windows, glass dealers, and some hardware stores.

BENT METAL CASEMENT

Somehow last winter, when forcing my metal casement window closed, I managed to bend the frame at the bottom. This sprung area left a gap where cold air came in. Can you advise me how to straighten the frame properly?

Any good metal shop will be able to do this job in short order, without even cracking the glass. However, be ready with tarpaulin or clear plastic sheeting, just in case rain comes along while the window is out being fixed.

RUSTED METAL WINDOWS

Our home has steel window frames, and they show rust spots and patches. Can you tell me if there is a paint or enamel that will stop the rusting?

Take off the rust by rubbing it with sandpaper or steel wool; then wipe the area with turpentine. Apply a coat of rust-inhibitive paint, and allow plenty of time for drying. Finish the job with any good brand of paint or enamel.

METAL FRAMES NEED STRIPPING

Due to excessive sweating in cold weather, the paint on our metal casement window frames has begun to wear off and show rust in spots. I should strip and repaint. But what kind of paint stripper can be used here? What type paint can be used to refinish?

Use a paste-type paint remover. It will cling to a vertical surface. For the refinishing, we would suggest a rust-resistant metal finish, such as Rust-oleum. This is well known to any paint store. You should take steps to lower the humidity of the house air during cold spells to cut down on the condensation.

REPAINT BAKED-ON ENAMEL?

We had the opportunity of buying storm windows for our new house at a very favorable price. The only problem, though, is that they are finished in white baked-on enamel. Our house is trimmed with black. I have heard that it isn't possible to paint over a baked-on enamel finish. Is this true?

You can paint okay, but first the finish should be deglossed. Use fine sandpaper, and the new paint will get a much better bond. If the fit is at all snug, be careful about how much paint you put on the sides to prevent sticking. Also, be sure to use a good exterior enamel.

CRACK CROSSES SKYLIGHT

Recently we bought a fairly new home (about six years old). At the time we inspected it, I did not notice a crack clear across the plastic skylight. Now it's all

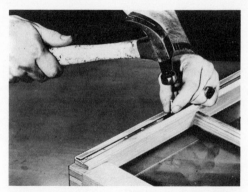

Figure 8-6. One method of weather stripping a window. The metal weather stripping goes on the side rails of window. The strips are "U" shaped.

mine, and I would like to know how this can be fixed.

You can buy a clear cement (butyl caulk) made especially for this type repair on this material. While we can't say that the repair will be as invisible as before the crack occurred, it will really seal the crack tightly. For best results, apply this on both sides of the crack (inside and outside).

WOBBLY SCREEN FRAMES

The frames on my screens seem to be quite rickety, and they wobble at the corners. Is there any relatively simple way to make them more rigid?

Probably the simplest way to strengthen the corners would be to reinforce them with small right-angle irons, which are available at any hardware store. These are nothing more than a right-angled strip of iron, each side 2 inches or so long, with screw holes already drilled. Fastened on the screen corners with screws, they will make the frames rigid again. Another way to do it is to drill a hole diagonally through the corner, starting at one edge about 1½ inches from the corner itself, and the other end of the hole an equal distance from the corner of the other edge. Fit a piece of dowel through this hole and glue it. This will also greatly increase the rigidity of the frame.

TIGHTENING WINDOW SCREENING

I have made a few window screens and wish to make more. When stretching the screen over the frame, I can't get it tight enough; it bulges. What is the correct way to fasten the screening?

After cutting the screening to the required width, tack it to the top of the frame, fastening it down every 3 inches. It is best to work on a horizontal surface, at a convenient height (a workbench top). Nail a strip of wood, the same depth as the screen frame, but slightly longer in width, about ½ inch from the bottom of frame. Roll the screening from the frame top down over the wood strip, nailing the second strip of wood over the first to temporarily anchor the mesh. Insert wood wedges, one on each side, between the frame and wood strip, and tap them in firmly. Tack screening across the bottom of the frame and along the sides. Trim the screening, and fasten the molding in place.

COPPER SCREENS TURN GREEN

A few months ago I saw a suggestion for cleaning copper screens, using a mixture of vinegar and salt. We did that, and our screens have turned greenish black in spots. We tried washing them with soap and water, but it did not help. Please advise.

Try scrubbing the mesh with household ammonia. Then rinse with clear water and wipe with dry cloths.

DISCOLORED COPPER SCREENS

My home is equipped with copper screens that have become dull and discolored. Is there some way to bring back the original color and then coat or treat the wire to preserve this shiny appearance?

To remove the discoloration, scrub the screening with a salt-saturated solution of household vinegar, followed by thorough rinsing with clear water to remove all trace of the vinegar solution. Or use one of the new copper-cleaning and -polishing preparations widely available at supermarkets and housewares and hardware dealers, following the label instructions carefully. Wipe the wire mesh with benzene to remove any trace of grease or oil. Apply a coat of good-quality spar varnish, thinned with an equal amount of a half-and-half mixture of linseed oil and turpentine; or apply pure, fresh white shellac, thinned with half as much denatured alcohol. Special applicators are available for use on screens at hardware and paint dealers. Or make your own by tacking a small piece of carpeting, nap side out, around a small block of wood. (A brush tends to clog screen mesh.) Treat the screens every spring.

CASTOR OIL ON SCREENS

Last year we followed someone's suggestion that castor oil be applied to screening in order to discourage mosquitoes, etc. While this was not 100 percent effective, we did find some relief. This year we discovered that the castor oil had dried to an ugly brown mass. Is there any way to clean the screens?

Try scrubbing the mesh with a strong solution of washing soda or trisodium phosphate, using about 2 pounds in a gallon of hot water. Then rinse with clear water. If the results are not entirely satisfactory, you may have to use a paint remover to dissolve the oil. Scrubbing with a fiber brush would be advisable, but do this work outdoors if the remover is flammable.

COPPER SCREEN STAINS ON BRICK

How can I remove the dark stains on brick from copper window screens?

Make a paste of 1 part sal ammoniac and 4 parts powdered whiting or other absorbent powder, moistened with household ammonia. Cover the stains with a thick layer of the paste; when it's dry, brush it off and replace it with fresh paste until the stains have disappeared. Special brick-cleaning preparations are available at some hardware stores and dealers in masonry supplies.

OIL ON PLASTIC SCREENING

Before closing our summer camp last year, we had plastic screens installed. In order to protect the porch floor from weather, I covered the screening with a cloth and coated the fabric with linseed oil. When we opened the camp this year, the screening was oily and dirty looking. What can be done to the screening?

You should be able to remove the oil by scrubbing the screening with a strong solution of trisodium phosphate, using about 2 pounds in each gallon of hot water. Protect all surrounding painted surfaces, because the solution will soften or remove paint. Rinse well with clear water. Trisodium phosphate is sold by paint dealers as a soapless cleaning powder.

AWNING FOILS FADING

Our new rental house has a picture window facing west. I find the sun here is very strong, and already I notice some fading of upholstery. If I pull the draperies, they will fade too. What do you suggest?

An awning of translucent fiberglass will filter out a great deal of the sun's rays. An aluminum awning will give full shade and also reflect heat away. If neither appeals to you, get an estimate on having the glass professionally tinted.

ALUMINUM AWNINGS LOSING PAINT

I have some aluminum awnings with the paint wearing off in patches. They need repainting. What steps should I take for a good job?

If the major area has peeled, complete the job with paint remover. If the worn-off areas are just here and there, use fine sandpaper or steel wool around the edges, removing all flaky paint to where it seems rock-solid. Spot-prime these areas with good metal primer. Also prime awnings where you have removed all the paint. When the primer is dry, repaint the awnings with exterior enamel or marine or house paint.

Figure 8-7. Lubricating the slides to make the window slide more easily.

PAINTING ROLL-UP AWNINGS

I have a problem with my aluminum roll-up type awnings. They are tan with two pink strips. I would like to have just plain tan. Is there any way I can spray the pink strips tan? If I cannot do this, can I remove the pink strips somehow and replace them with tan ones?

If you can find a perfect color match in outdoor spray enamel (or regular brushing enamel), your main problem will be solved. Chances are that the finish was baked on at the factory. Not only will the surface of the strips be very firm and sleek, but they will be in a shade of finish perhaps difficult for you to match. If you are successful, then you'll have to sand off the gloss on the pink strips to give the new enamel a good bond. If you insist on spray enamel, you'll have to mask the neighboring tan strips. Frankly, it would be easier to use brushing enamel. Of course, you could refinish the entire awnings, but you would have the much bigger job of sanding the gloss off all the strips. As for replacing, check with the awning dealer.

EYESORE AWNINGS NEED PAINT

Our fiberglass awnings, about 15 years old, have become so worn by exposure they're getting to be eyesores. Can this material be painted?

Yes, after a good cleaning. Use any high-quality exterior paint. Remember, however, that paint is opaque. If these awnings are translucent now, they won't be after you paint them. To keep the translucence, spray them with clear plastic or brush them with clear marine varnish.

AWNING CANVAS LEAKS

We have an awning over the front porch. It is about three years old and leaks very badly in heavy rains. The seams are not split, and the fabric seems to be in good condition. Is there anything we can do to waterproof it?

Boat supply shops and dealers in canvas products sell preparations which can be used on canvas and awning fabrics to waterproof them. If not available, follow these suggestions: Shave about a pound of paraffin into a gallon of turpentine or clear kerosene. Keep the mixture in a pan of hot water until the paraffin has dissolved. Do not—repeat—*do not* place it over an open flame. Stretch the awning fabric, and apply the mixture over a thoroughly dried surface.

PAINT BROWN AWNINGS?

I have old, dark-brown canvas awnings. They are still in perfectly good condition, but I would like to change the color. They stay up the year round. Can they be painted? If so, with what type paint?

If you were changing from a lighter color to dark brown, that would be a cinch. You would apply greatly thinned down (50 percent) regular house paint in thin coats, allowing plenty of drying time between coats and keeping the canvas stretched taut until the last coat is thoroughly dry. But the trouble with your dark brown is that it can't be made a lighter color. You can put on more brown to freshen it up, but that is all.

CANOPY NEEDS REPAINTING

We have a large aluminum canopy over our back door, now 15 years old. It was originally red, but that's all worn off. Can we paint it? We cannot take it down because it is firmly fastened, caulked, and fitted to the house.

Painting is the best thing you can do. First, however, give it a good going-over with detergent and scrubbing brush. One of those long-handled car-washing brushes will be very useful. Be sure to rinse off all traces of detergent, and be sure the aluminum is completely dry. Then apply any top-quality exterior enamel or house paint, either oil-base or latex.

CHAPTER 9

ROOFS, GUTTERS, AND LEADERS

Prowling your rooftop is not highly recommended if you're not used to heights. But if you're even reasonably goat-footed, inspecting your roof now can certainly pay off later on. The man who coined the phrase about "a stitch in time" may have had roofing in mind, because there are few other places around the house where early attention to inexpensive ailments can result in such truly impressive savings. For example, a stray shingle or two loosened by a few wind gusts can be firmly anchored with a few cents' worth of roofing cement. Yet if they are allowed to flap around, more and more rain will work in underneath; pretty soon this will affect neighboring shingles, not to mention the damage done inside. Let this contagion effect go on, and it won't be too long before you will be getting quotes from roofers, running into several hundred dollars, on putting on a new roof—or, at least, re-covering the present one. This is figured for a small house. Roofing a large house can easily move into the thousands bracket.

If working on your roof doesn't bother you, put on your sneakers and make your own inspection. Be sure the roof is dry before going out on it; this caution holds for all roofs, except flat ones. However, unless you are really quite competent at spotting leaks or incipient roof troubles, and if the roof is more than a few years old, it's a sound idea to have the inspection made by a professional roofer. Anyhow, if he isn't more expert than you at finding incipient weaknesses, he should be in another business.

Loose Shingles

Anchoring stray shingles is easy. Gently lift the lower edge enough to slide a dab of roofing cement underneath with a putty knife. Doing this on a warm day is best, so that the sun's heat can disperse the cement better. If the shingle is curled up at the edges, split it and nail the sections down flat with rustproof nails.

If there are torn asphalt shingles, replace them with new ones; and the closer to the original color you can get, the less patchy the replacements will look. In cases where you can't slide the new shingle up under the course (row) above, then all you can do is cut a piece to fit, and cement it firmly in place. Incidentally, there are some practically tear-proof asphalt shingles; they're made with a wide strip of adhesive on the underside, and when the sun warms the new roofing, the

Figure 9-1. All loose shingles should be nailed tightly in place.

adhesive is activated and it bonds firmly and practically forever. (There is a case where a hurricane that hit the Louisiana coast a few years back lifted a complete roof off a house, but none of the shingles came loose.)

Painting Shingles

In recent years, some paints have been developed which offer considerable savings on some types of roof maintenance. Two of these are the polyvinylacetate and the vinyl plastic latex (also typed as PVA) paints. These are excellent for asphalt shingles, because they firmly anchor that final finish of fine gravel-like granules, which rough-coats the shingles. If a roof is occasionally brushed by overhanging branches, the PVA-type paint will prevent the gravelly surface of the shingles from being scraped off.

Another type of paint is one containing aluminum flakes. Made in a variety of colors, this roofing paint is excellent at closing many small cracks and crevices. In addition, it gives the added heat-reflective qualities of aluminum: it keeps homes cooler in summer, warmer in winter. In summer, aluminum reflects the sun's rays away from the roof to such a degree that the space underneath may become as much as 15 percent cooler than before. (Let us add that this is also true with aluminum roofing. In the winter, aluminum reflects rising house heat back into the house, where it belongs, Thus you save on heating costs. This type of paint, therefore, offers definite advantages. Most of the leading paint

manufacturers, incidentally, now make this leak-sealing roofing paint containing the aluminum flakes.

Flashings

Naturally, any roof inspection includes a good, careful look at the flashings around the chimney, around the vent stack, in the valleys around dormers, and between gables. Often these are prime sources of leaks, simply because they aren't looked at for years on end. Yet unless they have become so weakened by rust and corrosion that there's no hope for them, very often cementing along loosened edges or seams will lengthen the metal's life tremendously, thus saving the considerable expense of replacement.

Even a pretty good temporary repair can work on actual holes in flashing the way it will work for gutters: First smear cement generously around the entire area, well back from the hole itself. Then smooth a doubled-over sheet of freezer-grade aluminum foil on the cement. To seal the edges of the foil into the cement, and give fullest protection, spread another layer of cement over the entire repair. Fiberglass cloth or thin polyurethane sheeting can be used just as well as foil. You'll be surprised at how long this do-it-yourself patch will last.

Figure 9-2. Asphalt shingles can easily be painted. But when working on a roof, be very careful.

When using nails to secure metal sheeting on a roof (or, in some cases, patching under siding), roofers have a very effective trick of assuring that there won't be any leaks developing where the nail punches through the metal. First, a generous dab of roofing cement is put on the metal where the nail will go. Then the nail is driven through the dab of cement. Not only will the cement form a watertight seal around the shank of the nail and under the head where it jams against the metal, but the cement will close over the nail-head's top surface, effectively shutting out the weather. Certainly, those waterproof neoprene washers are excellent for watertight nailing of metal sheeting, but this trick with the roofing cement works splendidly.

Figure 9-3. To get years of service from gutters, they should be kept painted.

Gutters and Leaders

By and large, roof gutters and downspouts require an absolute minimum of maintenance. Yet they perform jobs which are of the utmost importance in keeping things in good shape around the house. The function, as was described in Chapter 6, is simple: to catch the major part of the rain and melting snow running off the roof, and to conduct it to drains which will carry it well away from the house. In this way, water is kept from collecting in the ground next to the foundation wall. One of the biggest contributors to wet basements is surplus water pressuring against masonry walls until it finally seeps through. But if such standing water is minimized by an efficient roof drainage system, you can see how it helps minimize the wet basement problem. At the same time, flower beds won't become over-drenched quagmires (no good for most planting, unless you're trying to raise purple flag, marsh marigolds, or cattails). Obviously, in order to assure that all water will be promptly carried along the gutters to the downspout, the gutters must not be full of accumulated leaves, pine needles, twigs, stray rubber balls, birds' nests, or similar debris. In winter, neither ice nor packed snow should clog the troughs. Not only can this cause expensive ice dams, but if the supports can't bear the considerable added weight, the whole length of gutter may be torn loose.

Many homeowners, especially when their houses are located where lots of leaves are regularly blown onto the roofs, save themselves a great deal of this cleanout work. They simply cover the gutters with screening. The top rim fits under the roof edge, and the screen slants down so that the lower edge covers the outside of the gutter. The slope makes everything slide off, but the water drains down through into the gutter, where it belongs. Some hardware stores sell handy "snap-on" units of this type of screening.

If a gutter is rusted through in one spot, chances are the entire section may have become so weakened that more may give way fairly soon. So if you're going to do any mending, you can do the whole section with only a little more work than it takes for one or two spots. What you do, actually, is put in a waterproof lining. It consists of a sandwich of heavy (freezer-grade) aluminum foil between two layers of asphalt roofing cement. First you paint the inside of the gutter with the cement. Then you press the precut foil into the bed of cement, and finish by painting another layer of cement over the foil. That repair should last for a good long time, several years at least, unless some sharp branches happen to fall just right and tear through the foil. A word of caution about the asphalt roofing cement: Don't let it drip accidentally down on white siding; it's almost impossible to remove.

If the leak isn't due to rust, but to joints between sections, many times such gaps can be closed by roofing cement, or that handiest of handy new menders called plastic steel. This is actually pulverized steel in plastic form. When you use it to fill a hole, or build up a broken metal part, in a few hours it hardens into actual steel. It's available in any good hardware store.

Sometimes perfectly sound roof gutter sections will leak at the joints. In such cases, the usual answer is that somebody became absent-minded when assembling them. You know there's imperceptible slant downward of the lengths of gutter toward the basement. Each section of horizontal gutter should be placed so that the lower end of the upper section fits over the upper end of the section next below. However, if the sections are joined backward—that is, if the top end of the lower section is on top of the upper section's lower end—well, some of the water flowing down the line will be trapped at each joint, and a leak is inevitable. Simply reversing the way the sections are joined will prevent this.

While it should be checked year-round, spring is a good time of the year to thoroughly inspect your roof drainage system and make sure all's clear. Lots of water can fall during the storms of spring and summer, and there's no reason to let it pile up unnecessarily right next to your basement wall or floor slab. Let your properly working gutters prevent all possible problems; there are enough of them around as it is.

Ice Dams

An ice dam results when snow and ice so fill up a roof gutter that the resulting pileup along the edge of the roof often forces sun-melted snow water back up the roof and under several rows of shingles. A similar block can develop on the edge of a wide overhang, where the underside of the structure is wide open and exposed to freezing. Unless corrected quite promptly, an ice dam can cause expensive repair problems. That's because the backed-up water is forced between roof shingles for a considerable number of layers up the roof—maybe three or even four. There's no place for this water to go except to seep down through the layers of roofing, down through

interior ceilings, and along exterior walls. You should take measures to correct this situation as soon as you can. Not only can the steady drip-dripping of water so thoroughly saturate wall and ceiling material that it will need replacing, but it can cause bad staining on wallpapering and peeling of paint.

There are several types of preventive measures, one of which is a strip of roof-edge flashing wide enough to block any water dripping down. Thus even if the ice dam forms along the roof edge and water is forced up the roof again under the shingles, the flashing keeps the water from working down inside the house. As a matter of fact, we saw several communities in the snow belt with a large number of houses all equipped this way. A few years ago, we made a trip through upper New England for the purpose of spotting winter-protection measures which could be passed along to any readers who could put them to good use—and thereby have a snugger house during the cold weather, and possibly cut down fuel costs at the same time. For example, in White River Junction, Vermont, you can see bands of aluminum, about a foot wide, running along the lower edge of many a roof. What you don't see is the additional 3 or 4 feet extending up under the shingles. "When the flashing band is 3 or 4 feet wide," one such homeowner told us, "that's for certain more than enough to take care of snow-water back-up by any ice dam I ever saw. Yep, it costs a bit to have the sheet metal put in. But it's a much smaller amount than the water damage you can have without it." Enough said, as far as he was concerned! He didn't mention the fact that if this flashing job is done carefully, with reasonably heavy-grade aluminum or copper, this protection will last for quite a few years.

Another method of preventing the frozen pileup along the roof edge is to fasten electric heating wire in a 2-foot-wide zigzag along the roof overhang. The idea is to keep this edge area warm so that snow and ice will melt enough to slide off. In theory it's perfectly sound, and it has been used successfully in many cases. The only possible drawbacks are the steady drain on electricity, a complete failure if a storm knocks out the power for any appreciable time, and the possibility of the wire being torn loose from its moorings by any heavy accumulations sliding down the roof.

Still another method of ice-dam preven-

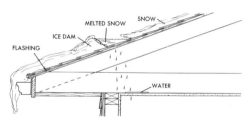

Figure 9-4. How an ice dam forms.

tion was described to us by a homeowner in Freeport, Maine. "I used to have ice dams because the roof gutter didn't drain fast enough, and pretty soon the gutters clear up to the edge of the roof would be frozen solid— I guess about 4 or 5 inches. This made a pretty firm foundation for the ice dam to build on. But I fixed it. I just moved the whole roof gutter down about 6 inches, and haven't had any trouble since." That extra distance was too much for the buildup to form over.

This brought up another question, however. The weight of heaping gutters full of frozen ice is often enough to pull them loose. In areas where this can happen, annual inspections should be made, and if any supports look weak and shaky, they should be reinforced firmly. In fact, the more supports, the better. This is also a pretty strong selling point for electric heating cable. The idea is that by laying this inside the gutters and turning on the heat whenever needed, most gutters can be kept open. No water can freeze in the gutter and cause blockage.

Chimney

An important part of the roof inspection is the condition of the chimney. Any signs of cracking mortar or crumbling brick should be fixed; this is a condition which should not spread. If rain or wind-driven snow works through cracks into masonry and then freezes, the powerful force of the expansion into ice makes cracks wider and opens up new ones. You should mark any doubtful areas or mortar or brick with chalk and have them fixed. Very often, one of the transparent liquid cement-hardening preparations will be enough to cure any crumbling in the brick; and often in mortar too, if it hasn't progressed too far. But don't take a chance; if the mortar really looks in sad shape, rake it out and repoint it.

TV antennas secured by metal straps to the chimney must be checked to see if all the joints are still firm and that no rust is developing. Sometimes, when these are installed, the installer neglects to use rustproof screws. This is acceptable provided he weatherproofs the screwheads with a dab of spar varnish. When this is forgotten, rusty streaks develop. If this condition exists, this is another place where a dab of roofing cement makes an excellent first-aid treatment. Of course, it is best to substitute the faulty screws with the rustproof type, but this can turn into a bigger production than there is time to spend.

More on chimney repairs is given in Chapter 12.

Underside Check

A leak in a roof can be sometimes located by examination of the underside during a rain. The point where water drips may not be at the leak, for water will often run for long distances along rafters and other parts before falling; the path of the water should be traced back to the leak. When the leak is found, a wire or thin sliver of wood should be run through it to locate it from the outside.

To locate a leak in dry weather, the garden hose can be played on the approximate location in such a manner that the water will strike the bottom edges of the shingles. An examination of the inside should follow.

When an attic cannot be entered, or finished rooms in it prevent the inspection of the underside of the roof, topside inspection, described earlier, is a must.

New Roof

If your roof inspection indicates a new roof is an excellent idea, there are many durable materials you can select. One of the newer developments is the heavyweight asphalt shingles, which have a life expectancy of 25 years. They come in a variety of colors, including white and black, and have a richer, more textured look than the lighter-weight ones. In addition, they bear the Underwriters' Laboratories label for fire-resistance.

Fire-resistance, we should add right here, is a superb quality for a roof to have. Do you remember that disastrous fire in the residential area outside Los Angeles some years ago? Photos published afterward showed that many of the homes whose roofs had fire-resistant covering did not immediately catch as the fire jumped from tree to tree, and quick action with the hoses was enough to save them. But those roofs which caught at the first lick of the flame generally meant another home burned to the ground.

Questions and Answers

Here are some of the more common roofing problems that have troubled people over the years and their solutions.

ASPHALT SHINGLES VERSUS CEDAR SHINGLES

I am going to have a new roof put on my house, which has had cedar shingles for the

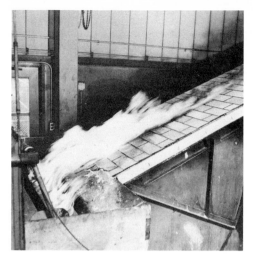

Figure 9-5. Fire testing of asphalt shingle deck is conducted by Underwriters' Laboratories, Inc. Here, fire at 1300°F is applied in the Class C spread-of-flame test.

past 15 years. They have stood up well, and I like their appearance. But I have been told that heavyweight asphalt shingles would be a better choice from the standpoint of protection. How do you feel?

We have to agree with your informant, especially with respect to those asphalt shingles which seal themselves to each other. All edges are solidly sealed down, so not even hurricane-force winds can get underneath to loosen them. Furthermore, heavyweight asphalt shingles are fire-resistant. However, although cedar shingles are not, they will give wonderful service.

LIGHT COLOR FOR ROOF?

Is it feasible to paint a roof a light color? If so, with what?

You can get light-colored paint containing aluminum flakes, which is excellent at reflecting heat away during the summer. Conversely, roof paint containing aluminum helps reflect house heat back into the house and thus saves a little on fuel during the winter.

AVOID WINTER ROOF WALKING

Will walking on a roof in winter, while removing snow, damage shingles or roofing? I have been told that this is a poor practice, as shingles are brittle and break in cold weather, causing leaks. Do you agree?

We agree. Asphalt shingles are certainly vulnerable to rough treatment in cold weather; but the heavyweight type with edges sealed to the rows below wouldn't be affected this way. Our main "no" vote is for personal safety. Roofs are good for amateurs to stay off, and most particularly in winter; even more particularly if they are slippery with snow.

REROOFING

I have some roofing questions: How many roofs are laid one atop the the other before some removal is made to lay another? When one roof is laid atop another, is there great deterioration in the lower (older) roofs? Would the number of roofs already on the building determine the weight of shingles used and the manner in which they are to be laid?

The answer to most of your questions is the load-carrying capacity of the roof rafters. If, for example, your rafters can carry a load of 55 pounds per square (100 square feet of roof area) and you now have two layers of 240-pound asphalt shingles on the roof, another layer of 240-pound asphalt shingles could give you trouble. Even if your rafters are large enough, we wouldn't advise having more than three layers of roofing. There is no deterioration of the underlayers if the top is in good condition.

COMPOSITION SHINGLES OVER CEDAR?

In the spring a new roof is to be put on our house. At present we have cedar shingles

Figure 9-6. Method of repairing large crack in a roof with roof cement.

which have been on about 25 years. Should the new composition shingles be put on over the present cedar shingles? Or should the cedar be removed first?

There are definite advantages in placing a new roof on top of the old: Stiffness and heat-resistance of the roof will be increased. Dirt inside and outside the house will be avoided. There will be a considerable saving in labor. In preparing the old roof, replace any missing shingles, split any curled shingles to flatten them, and nail down any loose shingles.

REPLACING ASPHALT SHINGLES

The asphalt shingles on my roof have been on for six or seven years, and in general they still look well. But there are several shingles which were loosened during some of last year's heavy storms, and I'm afraid they will cause leaks unless something is done about them. I have a few extra shingles stored away, which were left over. Can I use them now, and how do I do the job?

The extra shingles will do nicely as replacements. To do this, carefully lift up the edge of the shingle above, and pry up the nails holding the defective shingle so you can slide it out. Slide in the new shingle, and nail it in place with galvanized nails made for use with asphalt shingles. Seal the old nail holes with dabs of roofing cement.

WIND RAISES ASPHALT SHINGLES

We have had a number of strong wind-storms. The wind blows up the ends of the asphalt roof shingles and slaps them against the roof. How can we fasten the shingles down permanently and prevent damage?

Put a dab of asphalt roofing cement under each shingle to secure it more tightly. If this is done on a hot day, the heat of the sun will disperse the roofing cement better, giving the shingles better adhesion. Unless you are accustomed to working at heights, we strongly recommend having a professional roofer do the job.

ROOF NAILS DRIP WATER

When the weather was real cold, I found ice forming on all the roof nails which protrude through into the attic space. When the weather turned warmer, the ice melted and water dripped down all over everything stored up there. How can this be fixed before next winter?

Figure 9-7. Laying a wood shingle roof over an asphalt one.

Clip the nails off flush with the roof underside (much easier said than done, we'll freely admit!). The nails are excellent conductors of heat and cold. When a chill affects the nailhead outside on the roof, the cold travels the full length of the nail into the attic space, where warm house air condenses on it and freezes. By clipping off the nails, 99 percent of the trouble will stop.

ROOF PEAKS VERY WET

We bought a small house. In the attic we noticed both roof peaks were very wet, down to the flooring. We put in a dormer and insulated it, and then put up plasterboard, and it's just the place for visiting grandchildren to sleep. But what can I do about those wet roof peaks?

Sounds as though there are no roof peak vents at all. These should be installed to let all that damp, soggy air out of the house and to stop the condensation causing the problem.

LEAKY VALLEYS

I renewed our roof five years ago, using asphalt shingles over plywood sheathing and aluminum valleys. The aluminum was apparently excessively distorted when applied, or expansion and contraction caused cracks in the bottom of the valleys, allowing water to enter. Caulking has not proved entirely satisfactory, since it requires replacing. Would a more permanent solution be to repair each crack with aluminum cement or coat each valley with plastic or nonhardening material?

Any breaks in the aluminum can easily be fixed with plastic aluminum, available in any hardware store. It's very simple to apply. In our opinion, if you do a good job of plugging the leaky cracks, you won't need to put a total cover over all the valleys.

RAIN COMES THROUGH ROOF

My porch roof adjoins the house roof. I have laid tin, and then tarred the tin and applied shingles over that. I have caulked all flashings. Yet when it rains, the water comes through the porch ceiling at a point where the roof joins the house roof and halfway down the porch ceiling. Will you please advise what can be done?

We would suspect that the flashing was installed under shingles of the main roof and the nails holding the shingles punctured the flashing, causing the leaks. It would have been better if the flashing was installed under the siding. Of course, the upper end of the roof would be a bit lower, but results would have been better. Try cementing the first course of shingles of the main roof with roof cement. Cementing an 8-inch-wide strip of roof felt or roll roofing over the top course of shingles on the porch roof could also hold.

CAN'T ENCLOSE PORCH UNTIL LEAKING STOPS

Before we can finish enclosing our front porch, I must repair the joint where the porch roof meets the siding. When I look up, I can see daylight through the crack. How can I close this permanently?

It can be closed with copper, vinyl, or aluminum flashing. Use a foot-wide strip the length of the porch, bent so 6 inches can be firmly fastened to the siding and 6 inches to the porch roof. It would be best if it can be slipped under the siding and under the roofing and then thoroughly cemented in place with roofing cement. If this is not practical, then secure it with roofing nails and have the whole thing well plastered with roofing cement. This wide black strip will look pretty awful, though; it's really best to have job done professionally.

DORMER HAS LEAKS

Leaks have developed around one of our dormers. It is a shed-type dormer, and the leaks have occurred where the sides meet the roof. Do you think I could fill these leaks successfully with caulking, or should I have metal flashings put in?

We would prefer the metal flashings. While a good caulking job will undoubtedly stop the leaks, the metal flashings will be more permanent. The caulking might oxidize with age and require a "redo" of the job, in time.

TV ANTENNA STREAKS ROOF

I have a very light-colored roof, and now I notice there are streaks left on the roof by the TV antenna. What can I use to remove this streaking? Not being a steeplejack type, I don't relish making periodic trips to the roof to "destreak" it. Can I treat the antenna so that this won't occur in the future?

This streaking can be caused by using fittings and screws that are not rustproof; hence, rust streaks will eventually develop. (The antennas themselves are mostly aluminum, so it is not their fault.) Also, particularly in big cities, rain can wash down soot which has accumulated; since the soot washes down the antenna in a concentrated area, it can easily cause streaking. Liquid rust-removing preparations, available at many hardware stores, can take out all or most of the rust; that depends on the porosity of the roofing itself. Ordinary soot can be scrubbed away with detergent. To prevent future rust streaking, wipe the antenna fittings clean with turpentine or benzene, and then apply spar varnish. Better still, replace any rusty screws or fittings with those made of nonrusting metal.

ROOFING LOSES PEBBLES

We have an upstairs airing porch which is over our back entrance hall. This was covered by a carpenter with roll roofing. Everything is fine except that the pebbles keep coming off and I track them into the house. Is there any way to anchor these pebbles firmly?

Coat them with any good paint used for roofing; polyvinyl acetate, for example, is a good type. These paints are made by several paint manufacturers. Paint can work down between the pebbles and hold them firmly in the film, and the paint really lengthens the life of this type of roofing.

ROOFING NOW VERY DRY

Our house has a wood-shake roof, installed over an existing asphalt shingle roof. Now the wood shakes are very dry and brittle. Is there anything we can do to preserve these shakes so that they won't be so brittle?

Unfinished and dried-out shingles can be revived by a liberal brushing of linseed oil, although with no lasting effect. It's better to put on a good shingle stain, which usally contains a good preservative such as creosote. If the shakes are as thoroughly dry and brittle as you describe, perhaps a second coat would be a pretty good "make-sure" idea.

NAILS LEAK

I recently put some roll roofing on the roof of a prefabricated garage I put together. The roof leaked in the first heavy rainstorm. What did I do wrong?

Nails along the edges of strips of roll roofing will occasionally cause leaks by backing out, these being the nails that have entered the joints between the roofing boards. To secure these nails, tear lightweight cotton sheeting into strips 3 inches wide to be laid over the nailheads and the margins of the roofing and stuck down with liquid roofing cement. Follow by spreading plastic roofing cement on top, using a putty knife. This will not only close the leaks but will prevent the nails from backing out.

BLISTERS ON ROOF

Blisters have appeared on my roll-roofing garage. What causes them, and how can I correct the situation?

The blisters may be due to the separation of the layers of felt or of the entire thickness of the roofing from the sheathing beneath. A slit should be made in the center of the blister to permit plastic roofing cement to be introduced and spread heavily on the surface beneath; the blister can then be pressed back and for a few hours should be held by a weight. When exposed tar, cement, or similar material remains sticky, this can be remedied by a scattering of sand.

SPLIT WOOD SHINGLES

Some of my wood shingles have split, and they have started to leak. What can I do?

A leak from a shingle that is split or otherwise defective can be closed with a piece of single-ply tar paper, 3 or 4 inches wide and 6 inches or more long. The end of the defective shingle is raised slightly, with a putty knife if necessary, and the paper is slipped under and

secured with a dab of roofing cement. If a wood-shingle roof leaks all over, it can have its life extended for some years by brushing on a heavy compound of asphalt and asbestos fibers made for the purpose. This thick liquid will sink into holes and splits, and is prevented from dripping by the asbestos fibers. This liquid is available in black or very dark colors; the effect of this on the appearance of the house should be considered before application. Before applying, loose shingles should be nailed, and curled shingles should be made to lie flat by splitting and then nailing the parts.

MORE ROOF PROTECTION

What can I use, other than paint, to cover a slightly sloping tin roof over an extended kitchen? Painting it every year gets quite expensive. Also, what do you think of these plastic roofing sprays advertised to fill all cracks between asphalt roof shingles and protect against leaks?

You can cover the tin roof with asphalt-saturated roll roofing, in various weights, topped with roofing cement and marble chips. Or, better, visit a roofing dealer and let him show you what's called built-up roofing, in various thicknesses. If you have been using the right type metal primer and paint, on a well-cleaned dry roof, you shouldn't have to repaint every year. The plastic spraying will give some protection, but whether it will last for the 15- or 20-year guarantee is another question. These products aren't that old yet. And it's also possible that the dealer may be out of business by that time or in another town.

COATING FOR FLAT ROOF

The little pieces of stone (or whatever they are) on my roof are beginning to loosen and come off the tar paper. Is there any product I can put on the roof to prevent the pieces from coming off? I don't want to use the black roof-cement stuff because the roofing sheets are a sort of reddish color and the black stuff would be unsightly.

While a few manufacturers make asphalt roof coatings in some colors, very few, if any, local roofing supply dealers carry such material. You might inquire about this from some of your local dealers. Otherwise, we are afraid, in order to preserve the roof you'll have to use the black material. To do the job properly, all the gravel should be scraped off, and after applying the roof coating, the gravel must be replaced.

COVERING FLAT ROOF

We are building a carport, to be used also as a patio. This will have a flat roof, with very little tilt. What type of roofing should we put on? Roofing paper has been recommended.

If the roof tilts no more than an inch per foot, use built-up layers of double asphalt-impregnated roofing paper, which comes in various weight combinations. Then top with gravel. Durability depends on how many layers of paper are used and the weight of the paper.

WHITE GRAVEL ROOF GETTING MOSSY

We have loved the looks of our white-gravel roof for 15 years. But now, thanks to some growing-large oaks close by which cast heavy shade, a mossy growth is developing on the gravel roof. We don't want to cut down these beautiful trees. Is there any way to get rid of the moss?

The usual treatment is to put on a strong solution of weed killer. Then when the moss has dried up and turned brown, it is brushed off and bleach is applied to prevent future spore growth. With your gravel roof, we don't know how impervious the roofing under the gravel is to weed killer. It may be perfectly okay. But instead of the usual soaking, try a farily light spray on a test area and see how it works. This should certainly not work down through the gravel in any risky quantities. Brushing up any dried brown residue after, if it forms, would be wishful thinking. You'd either have to put up with it or sprinkle on a little more weed killer.

MOSS ON WOOD-SHINGLE ROOF

A few spots of moss are starting to appear on the wood-shingle roof of my garage. Could I touch this growth with anything that will destroy it? I realize it is caused by lack of sunshine and will have the neighbor thin out some of the branches on the trees.

Scrub the moss with a stiff brush and any alkali cleaner, such as household chlorine bleach or trisodium phosphate, followed by thorough rinsing with clear water. Be careful to keep the trisodium phosphate, if it is used,

off painted surfaces, as it will damage the paint.

PROTECTING A TIN ROOF

How do I protect a new tin roof against rusting?

To protect against rusting, a tin roof must be kept painted, and must be repainted at the first signs of peeling or other defect. A tin roof is usually painted with red lead, which will give better and longer protection than paint based on white lead. Red lead paint for this purpose can be bought ready-mixed. Before painting, a tin roof must be thoroughly cleaned of loose and scaling paint and of all rust or other deposit with a wire brush, steel wool, or sandpaper. It should then be wiped with turpentine or benzene as a final cleaning. If the tin is not properly cleaned, the new paint will not hold. Red lead paint should be applied in thin coats and given ample time for drying; a week at least should pass between coats, and a longer period is desirable.

PAINT PEELS OFF TIN ROOF

My porch roof is tin and needs painting badly. The paint peels off terribly every year. There must be a better paint on the market than what the roofer recommended. What kind should I use that will stay on longer?

On a properly prepared surface, any good-quality exterior house paint should do better than that. Which leads me to believe that you may have bypassed a vitally important step: giving the roof a metal primer before the paint goes on. Without the primer, to provide the needed grip, no paint is likely to stay on roof metal, whether it's copper, roofing tin, or galvanized steel. Tell the paint dealer the type of metal and your problem with peeling, and ask him to recommend the right primer and surface treatment for the paint you'll be using.

ROOFING PAPER LOOSENS

I have a small tool shack covered with asphalt-impregnated roofing paper. I have tried several times to fasten down one piece with roofing cement where it loosens, but without success. What can I use?

Some roofing papers require special adhesives, recommended by the roofing paper manufacturer. Check with your roofer or dealer. Or try the kind called lap cement, which is a liquid asphalt. Nailing the piece down with a batten should anchor it securely. Use rustproof nails.

REPAIRING BUILT-UP ROOF

How can I repair a flat roof that has built-up roofing? It has been tarred but shows wear. I would like to put new paper on it. How is this put down? How is it fastened to skylights?

Remove the worn areas, and sweep the surface free of dirt (if there is a slag or gravel surfacing, this should be scraped off). Before mopping on the new asphalt-saturated felt, put down one layer of dry felt over the old roof. Use flashing cement to fasten the roofing around the skylights; be sure the flashing around the skylight is in good condition before putting down new roofing.

VENTS FOR FLAT ROOF

We have a two-year-old brick-veneer ranch house, with a flat roof. There is too much moisture in the attic, which has no ventilation. There is insulation with a vapor barrier between all the overlays. What size vents are needed?

For a flat roof, the attic should have a vent area of one square foot for each 150 square feet of roof area. Mechanical ventilation may be necessary to provide proper air circulation.

LEAKY SLATE ROOF

My slate roof leaks only during heavy wind-blown rains and snows. What can I do?

Your problem can usually be prevented by raising the lower edge of each slate enough to put a dab of roofing cement underneath to secure it to the slate of the course below. This job is best done in warm weather when the roofing cement is plastic and spreads easily.

FLAKING SLATE

The slate roof on our house is beginning to flake away. It is about 30 years years old. What, if anything, can be done to prevent this condition from continuing? Would a coating of roof cement or tar work?

Nothing much can be done because the disintegration has set in. Tar or asphalt may prolong the life of the roof, but either coating is likely to become softened by the heat of the sun and "run" down off the shingles, creating a shabby appearance. Water glass (silicate of

Figure 9-8. Repairing a slate roof.

soda), 1 part in 4 parts of water, brushed on liberally might help if the disintegration has not gone too far. Try it on a couple of obscure shingles to see what effect it will have on the appearance.

SLATE ROOF REPAIR

A few tiles in my slate roof require replacement. Where can these be purchased? How do I do it?

To replace a broken slate, a piece of sheet copper is used, about 6 inches long and 3 inches or more wide. This is nailed at one end of the space left bare by the fallen slate and near the bottom. The new slate is slipped into position under the slates of the course above, and the free end of the copper strip is folded over its lower edge to hold it in place. Replacement slate tiles can be purchased at roofing material dealers.

CHEMICAL WEATHERING OF COPPER ROOF

Our new home is to have a portion of the roof made from copper. We would like this to turn to a mellow green color, but understand this does not happen by natural weathering in our climate. What chemical treatment may be used to effect this change?

The green tone of oxidized copper can be achieved by the following method: Remove any protective coating on the copper (usually lacquer; use lacquer thinner, being very careful of the fire hazard). To an absolutely clean metal surface, apply a solution of ½ pound of common salt to 2 gallons of water, allowing it to remain at least 24 hours. Then rinse it off with clear water.

ROOF FLASHING TOUCH-UP

I just made some repairs on my roof's flashings, and the patches are most noticeable. What can I do?

Such spots may be touched up with paint of the approximate color of the surrounding metal, and will thus blend in with the rest of the roof. On aluminum and galvanized, or tin-plate, roofs, this is done with aluminum house paint. On copper roofs, the paint should be blended on the job. Burnt umber and a green paint often combine to match weathered copper.

CHICKEN LADDER FOR ROOF WORK

I plan to do some roof repairs, but I have been told that I can make my lightly leaky roof into a sieve if I walk on it. Is this true? What can I do?

The answer to your first question is "yes." But since the roof must be walked upon to make repairs, the best method is to fasten a "chicken ladder" over the ridge of the roof, making sure the ladder is long enough to reach down to the eaves. By spreading weight out over this distance, the force is less likely to cause new leaks. A chicken ladder is merely a flat board which has cleats fastened every few inches to provide traction and which has some kind of crosspiece at one end to hang over the ridge of the roof and hold the ladder in place.

CLAY-TILE ROOF CHIPPING

Each spring, especially after a severe winter, we notice a little more chipping and deterioration of our clay-tile roof. This is a solid brick house, nearly 60 years old. Would you know of a way to retard this action, if not cure it completely?

In our opinion, about all you can do is start treating the tile with clear liquid masonry sealer containing silicones. It won't repair any cracks or anything like that, but it will retard any further action.

SKYLIGHT DRIPS ON CHEF

Last winter when the snow melted after a storm, ice seemed to form on the inside of the skylight at the corners. Then it melted and dripped down on me when I was standing in front of the range. Roofers who have come to examine the problem say it's no fault of the roof. What can we do about this before next winter? I don't appreciate cooking under such dripping.

Your skylight suffers from an acute case of condensation. Cold snow outside chills the glass, warm cooking vapors rise up and condense, and ice forms. This later melts. The solution is to insulate the skylight from the warm kitchen air by making it, in effect, a storm window. Fasten a sheet of clear acrylic plastic, or even sheet plastic, across the entire opening, including the frame. This makes a new inside "window," which should keep the kitchen air in and the chef's shoulders dry.

ROOF LETS IN LIGHT

We would like a carport by our side door for unloading shopping bags on rainy days. But the roof would cut off so much light from the kitchen windows, it would make it gloomy. Have you a suggestion that will work for all year round?

Instead of the conventional roofing which you obviously have in mind, try those panels of translucent plastic reinforced with fiberglass. They provide very good light transmission and are strong enough for rugged weather conditions. Overlap the panels by a ridge and a half, using the specially cut wood joiners, and they won't leak. Any lumberyard sells this type of material.

SUN DECK FLOORING

Our house is on a slope, with the garage at basement level. We are using the roof of the garage as a sun deck and have roofing paper on it. This isn't holding up. What should be put on to make a more presentable appearance and give better wear?

Roofing canvas should be applied, following the manufacturer's instructions for installation. This is a special, heavy grade of canvas, giving excellent wear. Two coats of top-quality floor paint or floor enamel should be applied as a finish coat. Roofing canvas is available at roofing supply or building supply dealers.

LEAKING SUN DECK

On a six-year-old house which we recently purchased, there is a porch with a flat sun deck as a roof. The deck has adequate pitch, but it leaks like a sieve. Inspection of the original installation reveals one ply of canvas with some type of sealer tacked to the decking. The tongue-and-groove planking

appears to be sound enough, not requiring replacement. How should this decking be finished properly? The deck overlooks the ocean, and we would like to use it as designed—as a sun deck.

Replace the present canvas topping with roofing canvas, according to the manufacturer's instructions. This is available at roofing and building supply dealers and is a special heavy-woven grade for use on sun decks and roofs. The canvas should be finished with at least two coats of top-quality floor paint or floor enamel.

SUN TOO HOT FOR BUILT-UP DECKING

We built a deck over our porch, to be entered from an upstairs door. It consists of three layers of felt, with mopped hot asphalt between the layers. The final top layer is hot asphalt. Facing south, this deck got soft in the afternoon sun last summer. Would covering this with buckshot-size stones prevent this, so we could then cover it with indoor-outdoor carpeting?

A coating of white marble chips, which reflect sun heat pretty well, would be better, if you can get them. In either case, it would then be okay for the carpeting.

WATERPROOFING PORCH DECK

Our porch is a deck 6 feet wide by 48 feet long. It has been covered with marine plywood, which is now showing signs of rot. I would like to put on a waterproof cover before the rotting gets worse. We have access to roofing canvas. Would this be satisfactory? This porch decking is completely exposed to weather.

The roofing canvas, well cemented down and painted with marine deck enamel, should do very well. Have you ever examined the underside of this porch? The rotting you notice on top may be the result of years of ground dampness penetrating the unprotected underside. While some rotting may have progressed seriously, you may easily rescue the rest by painting the underside with a protective shield of aluminum paint.

RAIN GUTTER SAGS

We have a wooden rain (and melting snow) gutter that is sagging badly. Can this be straightened?

Tighten the loosened hanger strips holding the gutter in place, or add new ones, to raise the sagging section.

REJOINING GUTTER SECTIONS

A leak has developed where two of the sections of my eaves' gutters have slid apart. How can I stop this permanently?

Slide them back so there's at least a ½-inch overlap, where the "uphill" section fits over the other. Drill down through both thicknesses, and secure them with a short aluminum or galvanized bolt, with neoprene washers on each side.

LEAKING ALUMINUM GUTTERS

We have aluminum gutters, and they leak at the joints. How can we repair them?

Apply plastic steel or plastic aluminum, available in tubes at hardware, variety, housewares, and paint stores, at the leaking joints. Or plastic-impregnated fabrics for covering leaks can be cemented over the joints. Another good method is to cover leaks with asphalt roofing cement; then apply freezer-grade aluminum foil over which is put more roofing cement. This sandwiching technique is especially effective when gutters (whether wood, copper, or aluminum) have sprung leaks along the bottoms of the sections.

LEAVES STAINED GUTTERS

Last June I had aluminum seamless gutters put on my house. They stayed clean until the fall, when they developed dirty streaks. Could these streaks possibly be from leaves? I also had gutter guards (units of screening), which were not put back. But if they were, would it solve the streaking problem?

It's certainly possible that the decaying leaves soaking in the gutters, probably causing some overflowing too, could cause the streaks. Replacing the gutter guards, to keep out more leaves and debris, would stop new streaking from the same cause. But it won't get rid of the present streaks. This will take scrubbing and elbow grease.

GUTTERS WITH LEAKY CORNERS

A contractor installed prepainted aluminum gutters around our house two years ago. We find that peeling and other paint problems have been eliminated. But the leaking at the corners has been a perpetual source of trouble. The contractor returned to caulk them, but to no avail. Any ideas?

If your hardware store carries the fairly new type of aluminum foil tape, this would be a little neater. But if not, you can close those leaks most effectively. Spread roofing cement over the inside surface of the corners. Smooth freezer-grade aluminum foil or heavy sheet plastic over this, and cover with more roofing cement. This will plug those leaks for a long, long time.

NEW GUTTERS OVERFLOW

We had new gutters and downspouts installed two years ago. Ever since, we have had a problem with overflow and seepage under the roof. How can this be corrected?

Your gutters and downspouts may be undersized; larger-capacity gutters should have been installed. Be sure the roof is well cemented all along the eaves. If you have a shingle roof, apply shingle-tab cement to each shingle in the first five to seven courses. Ice-dam leakage can be prevented by installing eaves flashings, at least 3 feet in width, from below the gutter edge, up under the roof shingle. To keep ice from freezing and piling up in the gutters, running electric heating cable along the gutters will help.

ROOF GUTTER LEAKS IN CRUCIAL AREA

Can you tell me how to repair a leaking roof gutter? I have tried soldering, and I have tried caulking with all sorts of materials. I have even attempted rivets and bolts, all to no avail. The leak is not large, but it is located in the crucial area directly over the entrance. I would appreciate any suggestions.

Cover the leaky area with roofing cement, spread generously but without big lumps. Smooth heavy freezer-grade foil on the cement, and then spread another layer of the cement. This will last for years. For easier smoothing in cold weather, warm the cement first, but never over an open flame. Heat a covered container with cement for the job in a pan of hot water, or stand the container next to the furnace for a day or so.

REPAINTING GUTTERS

I want to repaint my rain gutters. Someone told me to use white vinegar before I paint.

Is that necessary? I thought a rust-preventive-and-cure paint would be enough.

Since you mention the white vinegar, we assume these are galvanized gutters. With modern finishing of galvanized gutters, and since you are repainting, the vinegar treatment is no longer necessary. Special primers and paints for galvanized surfaces are now widely available at paint dealers. Use any top-quality paint for galvanized metal and the specific primer or treatment recommended by that manufacturer for his product. The important thing to remember is to have a clean metal surface, free of all trace of grime, soot, and grease. And all loose or flaking paint or rust should be removed before applying any new coating.

LEAKY RAIN TROUGHS

The rain troughs on our three-year-old home have been soldered this year to keep them from dripping at the seams. This does not seem to keep the water from dripping through. Before doing this, we had them tarred. Do you have a solution for this problem?

From the description, it sounds like: (1) a poor soldering and tarring job, or (2) the gutters are so clogged that some water is forced over the edge, rather than draining properly. If it's the former, give the entire inner surface a coating of asphalt roofing cement or asphaltum paint. Over this coating, apply another coating of the asphalt product. In effect, this makes a waterproof gutter-inside-gutter and should last for years. If clogging is the only cause, clear any obstructions. Many hardware stores now carry adjustable screen gutter guards, which come in 2- and 4-foot units and are simply snapped over the outer edge of the gutter and fit under the eaves. This effectively screens out most debris from the gutters.

ICE BACKUP

Last winter we had trouble with ice backing up on the north side of the house. What do you recommend?

An electric heating cable, placed in the rain gutter, will help prevent freezing and ice formation. Metal flashing installed so that it extends at least 2 feet up the roof, so that ice cannot back up under the roof shingles, will also help greatly.

Figure 9-9. The use of heat cables to reduce ice dams.

RAIN GUTTERS

I would like to put up rain gutters on my house. Is it advisable to run the drains directly to the catch basin with clay-tile pipe? Or do I have to run the pipe to the soil pipe which connects to the main sewer?

Do not connect to the main sewer. The gutter can be run out to the street curbing, if it is permitted in your community, or to the catch basin. Another method is to connect the downspouts to a dry well at least 15 feet from the foundation walls.

DRAIN TILE BELOW FROST LINE?

I have a serious drainage problem on two sides of our home. Our wooded lot with quite a few trees nearby makes it impossible to grade the soil with enough of a slope away from the house. I believe that drain tile, properly located, would be the only solution. Must such tile be buried below the frost line?

By all means, drain tile should be located below the frost line. Otherwise, it wouldn't take too long for it to freeze, clog up, and cancel out its purpose.

FROST CRACKS DRAIN TILE

We have a drain that comes from the house, and part of the tile is about 3 feet under the walk. Every winter the tile freezes and cracks. We have replaced it four or five times. Is there anything we can do about this?

Evidently the tile has not been laid below the frostline. Cast-iron pipe can be used and should resist the pressures of frost to a greater extent than tile. Or you might use a fiber drainpipe. Your local dealer in masonry materials could supply you with it.

Proper insulation and sufficient ventilation will go a long way toward making your home a great deal more comfortable.

Insulation

Most materials used in houses have some insulating value. Even air spaces between studs resist the passage of heat. However, when these stud spaces are filled or partially filled with a material high in resistance to heat transmission, namely thermal insulation, the stud space has many times the insulating value of the air alone.

The inflow of heat through outside walls and roofs in hot weather or its outflow during cold weather has important effects upon (1) the comfort of the occupants of a building and (2) the cost of providing either heating or cooling to maintain temperatures at acceptable limits for occupancy. During cold weather, high resistance to heat flow also means a saving in fuel. While the wood in the walls provides good insulation, commercial insulating materials are usually incorporated into exposed walls, ceilings, and floors to increase the resistance to heat passage. The use of insulation in warmer climates is justified with air conditioning, not only because operating costs are reduced but also because units of smaller capacity are required. Thus, whether from the standpoint of thermal insulation alone in cold climates or whether for the benefit of reducing cooling costs, the use of 2 inches or more of insulation in the walls can certainly be justified.

Commercial insulation is manufactured in a variety of forms and types, each with advantages for specific uses. Materials commonly used for insulation may be grouped in the following general classes: (1) flexible insulation (blanket and batt); (2) loose-fill or "blow-in" insulation; (3) reflective insulation; (4) rigid insulation (structural and nonstructural); and (5) plastic foam (either polystyrene or urethane) insulation. For most do-it-yourself jobs, the flexible and reflective insulations are the most popular.

Probably the roof, as an area, offers the most dramatic differences between good insulation and none. It's imperative to keep heated house air from rising up through the roof. Otherwise, such an enormous escape route means a huge and unnecessary extra burden on the furnance. This is where good insulation proves such a welcome cutter of heating

CHAPTER 10

INSULATION, CONDENSATION, AND VENTILATION

Figure 10-1. Methods of installing flexible insulation (top) and loose-fill insulation (bottom).

costs. Not only does it keep house air from leaking into the cold winter sky, but it has an equally welcome reverse effect in summer: it can reflect the blazing rays of the sun away from your roof, thus keeping the underroof space measurably cooler.

But walls, windows, and floors over open crawl spaces are trouble areas too. Take an unprotected floor, for example. The chill and dampness rising from the ground work right through the subflooring. They not only cause a stone-cold floor, but create chilly drafts ideal for giving young children a steady diet of sniffles.

Depending on the accessibility of the underside of the floor, insulating to make the floor warm and draft-free is well within range of do-it-yourselfers. We promptly admit that doing the underside of the roof is easier, because there's unlimited elbowroom. But unless the crawl space is around 3 feet high, stapling the strips of blanket insulation

between the floor beams becomes awkward. You have to do the job lying on your back or in uncomfortable contortions. *Tip:* Wear goggles to keep specks from falling down into your eyes.

If you don't use insulation which contains aluminum foil (to act as a vapor barrier), then you should first fasten foil or plastic sheeting under the subflooring. Over this goes the insulation. To keep the insulation in place, staple chicken wire over the bottom edges of the floor beams.

Please note the frequent reference to using a stapler. This greatly underpublicized handy helper is far better than a hammer and nails (or staples or tacks). Not only does it drive the staple home with one quick squeeze on the trigger, but it's a one-hander. You have your other hand free to hold the insulation in place.

When there is no floor in the attic space, instead of insulating under the roof, you simply lay the vapor barrier and the insulation down between the beams. It's perfectly practical to fill these spaces with the granular or flexible type of insulation.

One very important step to remember is to be sure to carry the full thickness of the insulation clear to the very edge of the floor. Even though the angle where the floor meets the roof is a tight squeeze, this precaution must be observed, because any gaps, where warmed air rising from the rooms underneath can work through, can prove troublesome. The reason is that since the attic space itself is unheated, and therefore cold, any warm air rising into this space will condense. This, in turn, will cause frosting on the underside of the roof. When this melts, the water will drip down, eventually working into the plaster ceiling below, or down into the wall space. This is something which absolutely nobody wants to have happen. But, as mentioned, it's easily prevented, just by being sure the insulation is not skimped on anywhere.

Condensation

Air always contains an amount of water in the form of an invisible vapor; it will continue to absorb water vapor until saturated. The quantity of water vapor that air can hold depends on the temperature; warm air can hold more water than cold air. For example, air at 50° can't hold as much water vapor as air at 70°. Thus, if air that is saturated at 70° is cooled to

50°, the part of the water vapor that can no longer be held will return to liquid form and collect in drops on the cold surfaces that have chilled the air. The appearance of this water in liquid form indoors is called "condensation," "sweating," and "steaming"; outdoors it is called "dew."

On a warm and damp day the air in a house will become saturated with water vapor. Should the outdoor temperature drop, the window glass will be cooled; indoor air in contact with the glass will also be cooled and no longer will be able to hold so much water vapor; the part that can't be held will collect as drops on the glass. With these facts in mind, here are some ways to reduce condensation in the home.

Drying Clothes. If you have clothes to dry indoors, or if you have a clothes dryer which isn't vented, then you're loading the house air with dampness. As an almost unbelievable statistic, even after spin-drying, every pound of laundry will release a pound of water vapor into the air before it's dry. And that's a tremendous amount of humidity to ask a cooling system to get rid of. What you can do is either dry the clothes outside or put in an exhaust fan, so that the soaking wet air is drawn directly outdoors (see page 184). As for the dryer, you should have a vent pipe connected, so that all the vapor will be forced out of the house.

Steamy Showers. If any members of the family luxuriate in long, steamy showers, take positive steps to ventilate the steam out of the window. This doesn't mean a poor soul must take the shower with the window wide open— although it would help greatly. But if the window is only open an inch or so, top and bottom, this will provide good in-and-out air movement. When finished, though, open the window wide, and keep the bathroom door closed so that the steam can't work into the rest of the house. Here's another place an exhaust fan will help get rid of the damp, soggy air. Right here is a good place to emphasize the point that constant condensation of steamy air on bathroom walls and ceiling is the principal cause of mildew and paint failure.

While on the subject of showers, there's the shower curtain. If it's of an absorbent material like cotton, it can contribute handsomely to the house humidity. It's like a big curtain of water hanging there and releasing the damp vapor. Instead, get a curtain made of fiberglass or plastic, materials which shed water like a duck's back. Or you can convert to a glass door.

Cooking. Cooking releases considerable dampness. This comes both from steamy pots and from the very damp vapors released when gas is burned. The range hood fan is the most efficient way of removing condensation from the kitchen. That is, a hood fan over your range traps and holds cooking odors, steam, and greasy smoke right where the exhaust fan can suck them out immediately. But be sure to select a hood that covers your entire range or cooking space. It's not necessary to consider room size since the hood, not the room, is the collection area. The bottom of the hood shouldn't be more than 30 inches from the range-burner level.

Fans are usually employed with range hoods in three ways:

1. The fan is built into the hood area and doesn't occupy any of the cabinet space above it.
2. The fan is mounted in the cabinet space directly above the hood. Usually the duct work goes up through the cabinets into the soffit and then to the outside.
3. An exhaust fan may be mounted in the wall above the range. The hood acts as a collector to catch the cooking vapors.

When the hood fan is located on an outside wall, air may be channeled through the back of the hood, directly through the wall to a wall cap. This short, direct route to the outside assures top performance and satisfaction. Also if the hood fan is situated on an inside wall, the duct work may go through the back of the hood and up through the inside wall. Then it may be exhausted out through a roof cap or, if necessary, ducted through the ceiling to a wall or eave cap.

Nonducted hood fans are available which use a system of filters to clean the air and return it to the room. They may be hung on the wall above the range, either with or without cabinets. They are less desirable than hood fans that duct to the outside because they do not remove heat and moisture.

Wet Basement. As was stated in Chapter 6, a basement which is perpetually damp can be a heavy contributor to house humidity. If the cause is leaks or dampness seeping through the masonry from outside, these faults should be corrected. All cracks and breaks should be patched, and a waterproofing treatment given to the walls and floor. If the dampness is only due to condensation, the very inexpensive correction, as previously stated, is adequate and regular ventilation. On clear, dry days, open all windows and doors to air the basement thoroughly. Close them tight when the weather's damp.

Closets. On dry days, clothing, draperies, linens, and similar things will evaporate out any absorbed dampness, provided they're in a well-ventilated place. But if they're in a closet where damp air is trapped, they will remain damp. They will become damper with the next entry of damp air from outside. Pretty soon, in that static dampness, mildew can start forming. This unfortunate result happens quickly in locations close to the sea, a river, or near fairly large lakes.

When dampness is inevitable, there is only one really good way to check the destructive results in storage spaces. And that is to keep the air circulating and keep it dry and warm. There are several ways to accomplish this. If you put in complete air conditioning, this will immediately help cure the dampness problem while it makes the house or apartment more comfortable. Hanging moisture-absorbing chemicals in closets and other damp spaces helps considerably in reducing dampness. We have also known homeowners who have kept closets dry and warm by placing a portable electric space heater on the floor and an electric fan located so that it circulated the heater's warmed, dried air—a good principle, too. In fact, that principle is the one behind the very best damp chaser devise we know of. This is, very simply, a rod-shaped electric heater—2 or 3 feet long—enclosed in a perforated aluminum cylinder. The unit is fastened, for example, along the baseboard at the back of a clothes closet. The cord is plugged into any outlet.

As the gentle heat warms the nearby air, it rises, permeating and drying clothes, shoes, luggage, or whatever is hanging or stored on shelves. The displaced, cold, damp air is forced to circulate down to the floor, where the damp chaser warms it up, dries it, and sends it circulating through the closet again. This dry, warm circulation completely forestalls dampness and mildew formation, even in seashore closets. The devices are widely available in electrical and hardware stores.

They are quite economical, and burn only the equivalent of a 25-watt bulb.

Ventilation

One of the very best methods of reducing condensation and humidity, of course, is ventilation. This keeps drier, outdoor air moving through the house, taking away the moisture caused by day-by-day activities. In addition, movement of the air speeds evaporation and makes the summer heat more bearable. If an air conditioner is used, it will remove the humidity during the process of cooling the air. In fact, many small air conditioners of the window type don't lower the interior temperature greatly, but their removal of the moisture in the air speeds up evaporation and makes the house seem cooler.

Attic fans, air conditioners, and other cooling devices are covered in the next chapter. But here let's take a look at exhaust fans.

Exhaust Fans. Every home needs proper ventilation to remove air contaminators such as odors, moisture, smoke, and heat. Exhaust fans in kitchens, bathrooms, utility rooms, basements, and recreation rooms do the job nicely.

When locating an exhaust fan, place it in relation to the work it has to do. For example, if you want to remove cooking odors and smoke, a hood fan directly over your range is most efficient. To take heat and moisture out of your laundry room, place the exhaust fan as near as possible to the washer and dryer. "Makeup" air should come from other rooms in the house and sweep through the entire room. In locating your fan, also consider the duct work which carries contaminated air outside. It should be as short and direct as possible. Proper fan performance also depends on choosing a fan of the correct power. Fans certified by the Home Ventilating Institute (HVI) are labeled with the square feet of room area a particular fan will ventilate.

In a bathroom, an exhaust fan pulls steamy, moisture-laden air out of your bathroom before it can loosen wall coverings or corrode fixtures. "Makeup" air is generally drawn from space under the door. Types of bathroom fans are:

1. *Ceiling fan.* This blower-type fan is flush-mounted between ceiling joists. It can be controlled with either a wall or a time switch. Discharge may go to the attic or outside.

2. *Wall or ceiling fan.* Mounted on a side wall, this fan discharges through vertical duct work. In the ceiling, the duct work is horizontal to a roof jack or eave cap.
3. *Fan and light combination.* These dual-purpose ceiling units provide an exhaust fan plus a light. Sometimes they are combined with an electric heater in the same unit.

In the other rooms needing exhaust fans, any of the following types may be employed:

1. *Ceiling fan.* This fan can be mounted in the ceiling between joists or in a cabinet as part of a range hood. It is controlled by a wall switch, either single- or multispeed.
2. *Sidewall fan.* A single- or multispeed wall switch controls a sidewall exhaust fan, which can also be used with a range hood. A similar fan, with pull chain, is useful for kitchen remodeling.
3. *Ceiling or wall fan.* This is a versatile fan, built in several sizes, which can discharge horizontally through a wall or vertically when mounted in the ceiling. It is often mounted in the wall under a range hood.
4. *Blower-type fan.* A blower fan will usually overcome greater resistance of duct work. It may be installed in the ceiling or wall and often is used with a range hood.

Because the duct work is concealed in the wall, it's often neglected. Unnecessary elbows should be eliminated during the early planning stage, as they drastically reduce the flow of air from the fan. Actually, ventilating fans will give many years of trouble-free service if you follow these recommendations for their care:

1. *Oil the fan motor periodically.* Most fan manufacturers recommend oiling the motor about every 6 months. Use a few drops of lightweight oil in the openings provided.
2. *Keep the filters clean.* Many fans are equipped with filters which collect grease and prevent it from clogging the motor and duct work. If a fan doesn't have a filter, it may usually be purchased separately. The mesh filters on your fans should be cleaned regularly to keep them free of the greasy film that reduces the pulling power of the fan. Filters are easily cleaned by swishing them up and down in hot, sudsy water. Then rinse under hot

water and let them drip dry before replacing. Do *not* immerse the fan and motor in water. Wipe off the blades and housing with a damp cloth.

Crawl-Space Ventilation. Crawl spaces under a basementless house also should be well ventilated. Moisture from the earth will otherwise be carried by vapor pressure up through the rooms above, and the passage of the vapor may warp floors and rot rugs and pads. To be sure that crawl spaces are adequately ventilated, louvers should be installed just below floor level (preferably between the floor joists) on all four sides of the building. A good ratio is 1 square inch of opening for every square foot of crawl space within the foundation. This may be measured by multiplying the length of the house by its width. If the house has an irregular outline (not square or rectangular), consider it a series of blocks placed together, and multiply each block's length by its width; then add all the results together. Openings into the crawl space should be louvered or vented to prevent rain from entering, and should be screened with at least ¼-inch-square mesh to prevent entry of small animals. Building paper, plastic sheeting, or other vaporproof material may be laid on top of the ground in the crawl space to cut vapor rise from the ground. Edges should lap at least 6 inches. If the ground is uneven, laps should be sealed; if the ground is level, this is unnecessary.

Questions and Answers

Here are some typical questions and answers concerning insulation, condensation, and ventilation.

INSULATION TO PEAK OF ROOF?

I have a story-and-a-half house, with an unfinished upstairs which I don't plan on completing for about five years, but would like to insulate now to keep out the heat in summer. Should the insulation be run right to the peak of the roof?

Insulation shouldn't be run up to the peak; an air space should be provided above the insulation, between this and the roof. The usual practice is to place the material between the rafters to a 6- or 7-foot height, and then carry it horizontally across to the other rafters, to form a ceiling. The blanket, or batt, should be fastened to the outer edge of the rafter.

Vents should be provided at the eaves, so that there will be air circulation from the eaves to the louvers up in the gable ends. A vapor barrier should be included, toward the interior of the house.

VENTILATION OF ATTIC

There are small air vents at the eaves of our roof, but a neighbor tells me that ventilation louvers should be installed near the top of the roof. The attic is insulated, and the adjoining garage is open all the way to the rafters; it's not shut off from the attic. Would a false ceiling in the garage, with insulation added make the space warm enough for winter wash days? It's also a utility room.

In order to prevent an accumulation of humid or damp air in the upper part of the attic, you should have ventilating louvers installed as high up in the gable ends as possible. The vents at the eaves would assure more complete air circulation for the full area of the attic. The construction of the ceiling in the garage is advisable to prevent the garage from becoming too cold. But even with insulation, if there is no heat, we doubt if anyone would be comfortable doing the laundry during the winter. We would suggest some type of space heater.

INSULATION THICKNESS FOR ATTIC FLOOR

I plan to install batt-type insulation (mineral wool) on my attic floor during my vacation. What is the recommended thickness to use?

Until recently, inches of thickness were used as an indication of insulation value. But because today's insulating materials vary widely in physical characteristics, mineral wool and fiberglass insulation now have an "R" (installed resistance) number printed on them, showing the total insulating value when put in place in the house. The greater the "R" number, the greater the insulating value. Use at least R-9 for your attic floor. And be sure to include a vapor barrier, installed toward the warmer area (underneath).

INSULATION IN WALLS

We are building a house. The outside walls are to be of stucco, and we are going to have the inside walls plastered. We have been told that if we put insulation in the walls, the plaster walls will sweat. We want to use the insulation, but would not do it if it will cause this condition. Should we put the blanket insulation next to the outside wall or inside wall?

Walls will sweat if they are cold and the house air contains enough humidity to cause condensation to form. With insulation in the walls this is not likely to happen, providing the rooms are heated uniformly and the temperature is even in all parts of the house. The vaporproof paper on the blanket insulation should face the back of the plaster and the flanges nailed on the inside surfaces of the studs.

ATTIC DAMPNESS

Our problem is condensation between the attic insulation and the roof. The attic is used for living quarters. To make it comfortable for living, batt-type insulation was stapled between the ceiling joists and pushed up tightly against the underside of the roof. Now there is heavy dampness due to condensation on the insulation. It even drips down on the attic floor. Would louvers correct this condition? Or should I cover the insulation with wallboard?

The difficulty is that the insulation touches the underside of the roof. Unless there was a vaporproof barrier of aluminum foil between the two surfaces, there should have been an insulating dead-air space between the insulation and roof. It definitely would help greatly if the insulation could be withdrawn out of contact with the roof. Louvers wouldn't help for the particular condition you describe. However, panels of wallboard, backed by aluminum foil or aluminum paint (to act as a vaporproof barrier), would greatly help to alleviate the condition.

INSULATION KEEP COOKING STEAM INDOORS?

My home is insulated. The outside paint has a tendency to peel in spots. The last time the house was painted, the peeling spots were thoroughly scraped and the paint was applied when the weather was dry. Two coats were given to the peeled areas. After two years, it has started to peel again. I have been told this is due to insulation keeping cooking steam, etc., inside and that the moisture finally seeps through and peels the paint. Is this possible? What can be done to stop this condition?

If you have the type of insulation with a vaporproof and moistureproof barrier on it, it would tend to retain moisture within the house or would prevent its entrance through the walls, since it doesn't allow moisture to pass through. Cooking vapors, as well as steam from hot showers and drying laundry, will cause paint to peel as the moisture escapes through the siding, pushing the paint off. Roof leaks, attic moisture, and chimney leaks can also cause paint to peel. We would suggest you have an exhaust fan installed in the kitchen to draw off cooking vapors; vent the fan directly outdoors. Any mechanical laundry dryer should also be vented to the outdoors.

COLD WINDOW BAY

A few weeks ago, during some really cold weather, we moved into a well-built older house. We like it very much, except for one big flaw: the floor under the bay window is like ice in the cold weather. This bay projects out beyond the basement wall, and there is a 2-foot gap between the floor and the ground outside. As soon as working conditions permit, I want to correct this. But what should be done? Should I extend the siding down to the ground or slightly below the surface?

Staple very thick blanket insulation on the underside, between the joists. Have the aluminum foil side toward the floor, as a vapor barrier. To be sure the insulation doesn't fall out, staple chicken wire or other mesh over the bottom edges of the joists. With this insulation, extending the siding to the ground won't be necessary.

NO WARMTH FROM VAPOR BARRIER

After experiencing a cold floor last winter, I covered the ground underneath, in the open crawl space, with heavy plastic sheeting. Will this keep the floor warmer next winter?

Not so you'll notice it. What this cover does, which is excellent, is to check rising ground dampness and keep the crawl space and underside of the floor from getting damp and musty. To make the floor warm, staple thick blanket insulation between the beams.

BLACK STAIN UNDER INSULATION

My concrete basement walls had an area of condensation near the ceiling and so I cov-

ered them with sheets of styrofoam plastic. Having occasion to remove this insulation, I found the wall slimy and black. Can you advise as to the cause and the removal of this discoloration?

Since styrofoam plastic is an excellent insulation, we're much more inclined to blame seepage through the wall at the wet points, rather than condensation. The stain is mildew and can be attacked with scrubbing brush, strong cleansers, hot water, and determination. Adding regular bleach will help, and also help prevent growth of future spores.

HOUSE INSULATION

I have a semi-ranch house of solid-brick construction. Can you tell me if it is necessary to insulate between the walls, or is the air space sufficient insulation? If it is necessary to insulate, what type of insulation do you suggest? The attic floor is insulated.

A 2-inch thickness of insulation between the furring strips would help make the walls warmer, particularly walls built of solid masonry. You can use any one of the blanket insulating materials (R-9 or higher), or you can put in vermiculite pellets.

INSULATED ATTIC

Our house is well insulated and seems warm enough. However, when going into the attic, I find along both roof lines you can see outside light. Should we attempt to close the spaces?

We presume you see streaks of daylight through boards at the eaves of the roof. Don't close them, particularly when insulation is in the floor of the attic. The greater the circulation of air above the insulation, the better. Screening the spaces, however, is recommended.

COLD ROOM

I have added a 6- by 9-foot room to my kitchen as a utility room. It has a double floor, 2-inch wall insulation, regular and combination windows, and a 10-inch crawl space. The room is erected on concrete blocks and has no heat as yet. It is very cold, particularly the floor. What did I do wrong? Can I rectify this?

In the first place, the ground should have been covered with a vaporproof or moistureproof paper, with the sheets overlapping at least 6 inches and the laps sealed with asphalt

Figure 10-2. One of the many spots in a house that should be insulated.

roof cement. Secondly, a blanket or batt insulation between the floor joists would make the floors comfortable. Of course, the lack of heat would naturally cause the room to be cold, regardless of the amount of insulation. At present there is no way to make the floor comfortable, except to take up the floor and install moistureproof paper and the insulation between the joists; then lay the floor again.

WHICH INSULATION FOR CEILING?

My split-level home is air-conditioned in summer and gas-heated in winter. Which would be the best insulation to use over the ceiling: fiberglass wool, with foil on one side (the bottom); pouring wool; or styrofoam?

Since they're all apparently going to lie above the ceiling between the open beams in an unfinished attic space, there's no ease-of-handling factor to consider. So each will do as good an insulating job as the other. Just be sure you have comparable thickness to give equal insulation. Dealers have charts for this. Then you can get meaningful estimates.

HEATER WON'T HELP COLD WALL

The stairway and hall of our two-story flat is unheated. In cold weather we have noticed a big accumulation of moisture on the outside wall, which is staining our fresh paint job. Will putting a heater in the hall help get rid of this water? There is so much dripping that the bottom half of the wall is completely wet.

Putting in a heater could make conditions even worse, unless you take one big step beforehand: insulate that outside wall. Even though the hallway is unheated now, enough warm house air leaks out so that it can condense on the very cold outside wall. With the heater warming the air, the condensation would be increased. We would suggest your forgetting the heater until you have that wall insulated so that it won't be so cold on the inside.

INSULATION BECAME WET

We have two ventilators in the block walls of our crawl space. We have found that our 6-inch insulation, which has a foil vapor barrier, is wet on the underside. Should we put a plastic sheet on the ground or under the insulation?

Put it on the ground. Seal any laps with roofing cement, or overlap them so widely you can weight the laps with rocks and there won't be any air leaks. Ventilators in the other two sides would help greatly to promote cross circulation and reduce dampness.

VAPOR BARRIER

I have heard that aluminum paint applied in several coats over plastered walls and ceilings of insulated rooms makes a very effective vapor barrier. We have some rooms which have had the ceilings lowered and plasterboard applied to the new framing. Mica-fill insulation was put in over the ceiling, and the walls have mineral wool blown in. No vapor barrier was installed. Would you recommend painting with aluminum paint or some other treatment?

A good vapor barrier consists of applying two coats of any good brand of aluminum paint and then a finishing coat of semigloss enamel. You can use a flat wall paint instead, but the enamel is preferred. Another treatment is to cover the plaster with an "vinyl" type of wall covering. It comes in a wide assortment of colors and patterns suitable for all rooms in the house. Either method will be satisfactory.

INSULATION FOR PANELING

What is the best type of insulation to use in connection with paneling a basement playroom?

If we were doing the job, we'd go for the blanket type, with the aluminum foil side toward the paneling. The foil will act as the vapor barrier. Styrofoam is also very good.

FREEZE-UP AT CEILING

When it is extremely cold outside, frost forms in the joints between the ceiling and walls and also in the lower corners of the upstairs rooms. I understand this is an insulation problem. How do you get insulation in nooks and crannies like these?

Use the blown-in type of "wool" or granules. Any other kind, such as blanket, batt, or insulating board, would call for extensive carpentry.

FROST FORMS IN ATTIC

A few years ago we built a one-story home. During the winter, and in cold weather at other times of the year, the roof boards become wet and frequently covered with frost. The attic floor is insulated. We have windows on the north and side ends of the attic. We installed small-diameter louvers on the west, placing them in the face boards, but in the morning there was a light frost on the boards. What is the solution?

The solution is more ventilation. Place large ventilating louvers as high up in the gable ends as possible. Allow at least 1 square foot of louver opening for each 300 square feet of attic floor space. And in order to obtain thorough air circulation, install the small-diameter louvers in the face boards on the opposite (east) side of the attic. This will ensure ventilation from top to bottom and across the attic.

CLOSED LOUVERS?

We have a storage attic with louvers at each end. The floor of the attic is insulated. Should the louvers be closed off in the winter? It gets bitter cold up there. Would it be worthwhile insulating the ceiling and walls of the attic?

Attic louvers should be left open all year around to provide adequate air circulation and ventilation, to prevent moisture problems. If the attic floor is properly insulated, and the attic is used only for storage, insulation of the walls and ceiling isn't necessary.

SNOW COMES THROUGH LOUVERS

During a windy storm, snow poured through the slats of our attic louver. The attic took in a lot of snow, much of which leaked down on the walls. How can I prevent this in the future? And should I keep the louvers closed during the winter to keep out cold air?

It appears, unfortunately, that the louvers face the direction of the high wind which blew in the snow. So we suggest that when another such snow storm blows up, you close the louvers. But when the storm is over, the louvers should be opened again. They should definitely be kept open, winter and summer, to provide the ventilation which will prevent condensation. This is particularly important in cold weather, because if moisture condenses on the inside of the attic and subsequently melts, the water can run down through the walls and ceilings and ruin the plaster.

MILDEW ON DIRT FLOOR

Under my kitchen is an L-shaped crawl space with a dirt floor. It is very uneven, and mildew down there is very heavy. The unevenness is such that I doubt if heavy plastic sheeting would be effective at sealing rising ground dampness. Is there any kind of product which could be sprayed on this floor to stop the mildew? There is very little ventilation.

Your problem is the ventilation. If you'll have screened and louvered vents cut in those walls, at least one to a wall, you'll do more to stop the formation of mildew than even spraying on a concrete covering (the only "spray" product we can think of for this). Then cover the floor with the plastic sheeting, cementing the laps with roofing cement, and your mildew problem should diminish.

BLACK SPOTS ON UNDERSIDE OF ROOF

The underside of our roof (unfinished attic) is developing black spots; on cold days a lot of moisture collects on protruding roof nails. We're afraid this moisture will drip down enough to affect the ceiling below. How can we eliminate this condition?

We suspect lack of ventilation and air circulation is the cause of the excessive moisture. Ventilating louvers, as high up in the gable ends as possible, should be installed, allowing at least 1 square foot of opening for each 300 square feet of attic floor area. Vents should also be installed at the roof eaves to provide better air circulation. Clipping the protruding nails will help eliminate the dripping moisture. To prevent further growth of mildew (which the black spots are), coat the roof board with a chemical wood preservative, available at lumberyards or marine supply dealers.

INSULATE GARAGE WALLS?

Would it help to make the room adjacent to the attached garage wall warmer if I insulated the garage? I mean insulating all four walls and putting weather stripping not only on the door leading to the garage from the house but on the garage doors too.

If the rooms on the other side of the common wall are cold, and the wall is cold, there's no reason to do all that insulating work. Just add to the insulation in (or on) the common wall. Since it's a finished wall, fastening insulating boards on the garage side would do this nicely. Weather-stripping the door from the house is an excellent idea. But doing all those other walls and doors is a waste of good time and money.

COLD AND DRAFTY FLOORS

We moved into our house last January, and the construction seems solid, but I am everlastingly feeling drafts on my feet or back. We have an oil-fired, hot-water heating system. The heating contractor installed additional radiators, but this season, I can still feel the cool air moving around. Thermometer readings on the floor and higher are the same. Can you recommend any procedure?

If there's no basement under the house and there is a crawl space, insulation placed under the floor, between the joists, might be a solution. You might also look for air leaks between the top of the foundation walls and the walls of the house. Such spaces could be closed by packing with oakum or a caulking compound. A builder could do this for you. Very dry air in the house will also give you the feeling of coolness despite high temperature. If the air is dry, install a humidifier.

GARAGE DOORS SWELL

Our garage door swells in damp weather. At times we can hardly close it. Water that drips off the car seems to stay on the floor a long while. Would putting louvers in the roof of the garage help dry out the moisture and keep the door from swelling?

Ventilating louvers should help dry up the moisture, but to prevent swelling of the wood, apply a coat of good-quality aluminum paint and then finish with a good grade of outside paint. Particular attention should be paid to the top and bottom edges.

PAINT PEELS FROM OVERHANG

The paint always peels off the underside of our roof overhang. This has happened three times already. Would it help any if we put ventilation openings along the overhang? This would allow air to circulate around the inside.

If, as you imply by your comment about air circulation, there is much condensation in the space above the overhang, then the strip of ventilating louvers is an excellent idea. Give the overhang a chance to dry out thoroughly before repainting.

VENTS FOR NORTH SIDE

The paint has always peeled off the north side of my house. It is a one-story house, and it gets very little sun on that side—only a little in the summer. I'm not surprised it's so damp the paint peels. I have heard that putting rows of small metal louvers in the siding will vent dampness out of the wall space. This would mean drilling holes ¾ inch in diameter. Would this help?

In many instances these miniature louvers have proved quite good at drying out damp wall spaces. But this is one of those treatments you can't prejudge accurately.

STORM DOORS NEED HELP

Our living room door opens directly to the outside. Although there is a storm door, the winds blow in even when both doors are closed. Is there any way to make a more complete seal to keep the wind out?

Put good weather stripping around the edges of both doors. This includes a door bottom strip with a vinyl flap to close any gap under the door. The old-time expensive metal weather stripping worked fine, as long as the stripping didn't get badly bent. But you can get excellent weather-stripping materials today, fully "do-it-yourself" and not expensive.

WHAT NEW SIDING?

The clapboard siding on our old farmhouse has been on a very long time, and there is no insulation. Although we have storm windows, the wind blows in around them. What new siding do you recommend?

Maybe you can blame some of the windy problem on the aged siding. But we would blame most of it on your lack of insulation. With good insulation, your house won't be so drafty and your heating bills will drop. If you want to duck painting costs, give serious consideration to vinyl siding.

PERCENTAGE OF HUMIDITY IN HOUSE?

I would like to know what the percentage of humidity should be in the home during the winter season. Our new house is heated by a gas furnace. Is there anything that can be installed in a furnace to maintain the correct percentage of humidity throughout the house?

When the outside temperature is at freezing or above, a humidity percentage of 35 to 40 is satisfactory. When the temperature gets down to 15°, a 30 percent air moisture content is desirable. At zero, the humidity should be dropped to about 20 percent. Various types of furnace humidifiers can be used, but the adjustment to the amount of moisture content isn't automatic.

MOISTURE PROBLEM IF DRAFTS ELIMINATED?

Our frame bungalow is covered with asbestos shingles. In windy weather, I notice cold air around window sashes and door frames, and also around light switches and electrical outlets. These points also show dark areas from the dust carried, where the plaster meets the window and door frames. I have aluminum storm doors and windows. The air comes from inside the walls, which are apparently open to cold air at the sills beneath the house. If I should block these openings, would it create a moisture problem? If so, can you suggest a solution?

Block the openings. Moisture that might be trapped in the wall space might come from excessively humid house air, from the roof or flashings or window joint leaks, or upward from ground moisture. All these sources can be checked and corrected. Miniature louvers can be installed in the siding to help eliminate moisture in the wall space.

STILL GETS CONDENSATION

My home is equipped with storm windows, but during the cold weather we still get condensation on the inside of the regular windows. Please advise.

Pulling some of the dampness out of the house air with frequent ventilation and kitchen and laundry wall fans will certainly help considerably. Your storms may not fit quite as tightly as they should, allowing cold air to leak in and chill the inside window glass.

STEAMING WINDOWS

During the cold weather, most of our windows were steaming up. This was our first winter in our newly built house, and we want to avoid this next year. We have a two-story house, finished basement, unfinished attic, wood siding, and oil-fired steam heat.

This condition is apt to be aggravated in new houses because of moisture evaporating from new concrete, plaster, and wet lumber. The second winter the condition is not so pronounced and sometimes disappears entirely. Storm sash on windows will help greatly. Venting automatic clothes dryers, cooking vapors, gas- and oil-burning appliances to the outdoors—to draw off excess moisture from these—is advisable. During dry, clear weather ventilate the house as much as possible.

COLD AIR FROM WINDOWS

I get a considerable amount of cold air through my casement windows. I have had storm windows installed, but this has not helped, because they were installed on the outside of each sash, and they open and close with the permanent sash. Is there some way of weather-stripping them? There seems to be a leakage of cold air, which causes my furnace to run most of the time.

It is possible that your casements do not close tightly, thus causing air leakage. Weather stripping is available for such windows, and firms specializing in this kind of equipment could install it. You will find their names listed in the advertising sections of your newspaper. If not listed there, check your classified phone book under weather stripping.

CONDENSATION ON STORM SASH

I had trouble with condensation from my weather-stripped windows. I then had storm windows put in, thinking it would eliminate the condensation. However, condensation still forms on the outside of the storm windows. If I bore holes in the bottoms of the storm sash, will that eliminate condensation?

Several ¼-inch-diameter holes drilled into the bottom rail of a storm sash generally eliminate condensation. You should also try to lower the percentage of humidity in the air of the house. Shut off the humidifier, if you're using one, and use an efficient exhaust fan in the kitchen and laundry. If an automatic clothes dryer is used, exhaust the vapors to the outdoors, and ventilate the bathroom after showers and baths are taken. We assume you have a basement.

FIVE STEPS TO NOWHERE: WINDOWS STILL SWEAT

The aluminum windows on the north side of my house sweat so much that water runs from the frames and glass onto the sills and walls. I have asked many people about it, but they tell me my house has been built too tight. I have taken these steps: (1) covered the basement walls with polyethylene sheet plastic; (2) put on aluminum storm windows; (3) drilled small holes on the bottom of the storm window frames, to allow air between; (4) threw out the polyethylene from the basement, and put tar roofing paper all around the four walls; (5) kept all the ventilation windows in the basement open, to get air in there. None of these steps gave results. Can you suggest anything?

We agree that your house is too tightly built for the humidity that's in your house air. It can't leak out through your good insulation and tight windows, and so it condenses on the coldest surfaces, which are the windows on the north side. You're on the right track when you keep your basement ventilation open; you should try to ventilate upstairs too. Open doors or windows on opposite sides for a couple of minutes every hour or two on dry days. Install a wall fan above your range to carry damp cooking vapors outdoors. Open the bathroom window after steamy showers. If all these methods don't help, invest in a good dehumidifier.

FOOD ODORS REMAIN

We have been living in this home two years, and I'm afraid I'll have to sell unless I can overcome the condition we have. After I cook, the house has a peculiar odor all evening long. If I peel an apple, or have cigarettes lying around, you can smell them through the whole house. Also, the air is very dry. How can I overcome this condition?

For the cooking odors, installing an exhaust fan, vented to the outdoors, in the kitchen should help; or installing a hood over the range with a grease-and-odor-absorbing filter. Your local utilities company can supply information about dealers that handle these items. Thoroughly ventilating the house at regular intervals by opening windows an inch or so at the top should help, as will a room deodorizer. An electric humidifier should be installed to increase the moisture in the air.

NEW ROOF, NEW TROUBLES

My Cape Cod house is 25 years old. I had a new, tightly sealed roof put on, including "windproof" shingles. All sides are sealed too. Now I have bad moisture problems. The walls are sweating, and I can't open the windows, which are swelled up. I bought a dehumidifier, which helps a lot. Should I put in larger louvers or roof vents? Any suggestions?

Recognizing the help of the dehumidifier, you know that the air is still too damp. The more ventilation, the less humidity, the better. By all means, put in larger vents. Also put in a wall fan in the kitchen to draw damp cooking vapors outdoors. Put in one in the laundry room too. A ceiling fan for bathroom steam also helps.

ALTERNATIVE FOR FAN

How can we prevent our kitchen ceiling from peeling and spotting because of steamy cooking vapors without going to the expense of installing an exhaust fan? The area that peels the most is over the stove.

Here's one way, but you'll find it very impractical: Whenever cooking is in progress, open at least two kitchen windows and the back door. Also have an electric fan aimed at the ceiling to keep warm, damp air from settling. This will blow most of the damp air outdoors and help stop the peeling. This is highly impractical, as mentioned. It would be much simpler to put in the fan.

EXCESSIVE DRYNESS IN HOUSE

What can we do to reduce the excessive dryness in our house? We have a gas furnace. As a result of the lack of moisture in the air, the house always seems to have a "chilly" feeling, even though the temperature is around 77° during the heating season.

Electric humidifiers are available at many hardware and plumbing supply and electric appliance dealers. Or humidifying pans (to hold water for evaporation into the heating air) can be attached to radiators. These can be obtained at hardware and housewares and variety stores.

SWEATING WALLS, MIRRORS, ETC.

Recently we moved into a one-floor-plan home, built about 15 years ago. Every time I cook something, the walls, ceilings, mirror, and windows get much moisture on them. The walls become streaked after water runs down on them. Can this be stopped?

The fact that mirrors and the upper parts of the rooms become coated with condensation leads us to suspect that there isn't enough heat in the house, or it is not uniformly distributed. You should maintain an even temperature in all rooms—about 68°. If an oil- or gas-fired room heater is used and it is not vented to the outdoors, this could contribute further to the condition. All afterproducts of combustion should be vented to the outdoors. A central heating system with hot-air registers or radiators in the various rooms would remedy the condition.

NEW HOUSE PROBLEMS ALREADY

We recently moved into a brand-new home. We have discovered a problem with condensation on most of the windows. It is especially troublesome on our oversized picture window, which is not Thermopane. This has an attached inside storm window. People have told us that if the problem is not corrected, the wood framing will be ruined by the moisture. Can you offer us any suggestions?

Mainly the trouble is too damp, warm house air coming in contact with the cold window glass; this is the same effect as when the dew forms on your glass of ice water. In a brand-new house this problem can be increased, as water keeps evaporating while plaster walls, concrete floors, and basement walls are busy drying out. You can test the airtightness of your picture window's inside storm by sealing the edges of the frame with Scotch tape or equivalent. If the frosting stops, you'll know that there's an air leak around the frame of the storm, which needs weather stripping. Take all possible steps to lower the humidity of your house air, plus ventilate frequently on dry days. This should help.

MOLD ON WINDOW FRAMES, SILLS, AND DOORS

Can you tell us the cause and remedy for a moldy appearance on the window frames, sills, and doors of a house? The house is a frame building, but has had siding put on it. The house is heated by a furnace.

Excessive humidity in the house and the low temperature during the cold months on the affected surfaces caused condensation (sweating) to form. The prolonged moisture on these surfaces would cause mold to form. To remove the discoloration, take off the finish and bleach the wood with a hot, saturated solution of oxalic acid (*poison*). Leave this on overnight; then rinse well with clear water. When the wood is dry, smooth with "000" sandpaper, wipe off the dust, and refinish as desired.

REASONS FOR VENTING A LAUNDRY DRYER

I have been given many reasons why a laundry dryer should be vented—each one being different. The makers' representatives never mention this when selling the machines. Can you enlighten me?

When clothes are washed, they absorb gallons of water, and when they are dried, all this water is driven out of the clothes. This moisture is absorbed by the air in the house, causing an excessively humid condition. Excessive humidity in the house air, during the winter, will cause windows to "sweat" and doors and woodwork to swell, and it creates an uncomfortable feeling. By all means vent your dryer.

VENT FAN INTO CHIMNEY?

Recently I installed a bathroom ceiling fan to draw steam from showers up into the attic; I was considering running it to a vent through the roof. Then I thought that since the fan is next to the chimney, perhaps I could knock a 4-inch hole in the chimney, used only by the gas furnace, and vent the steam there, and save putting a hole in the roof for a vent. Is this practical?

Technically, we should say no; no heat source should share its vent or flue. But in this case you may easily pull this off without trouble. Try it. If the furnace draft seems affected, then you can switch to the vent.

WALLS SWEAT

We have purchased a one-floor house, with a basement under all except one back bedroom. There is one ventilator in the foundation walls. Our trouble is water on the walls of the back bedroom and sweating windows, despite the storm sash. Somebody suggested that we insulate under the floor of this room. Would you have any suggestions?

We suspect that the room is much colder than the others, and the sweating on the walls occurs on the lower sections. The installation of a thick blanket or batt type of moistureproof insulation on the underside of the floor should help. In addition to this, to reduce the amount of moisture from the ground, cover it with a moistureproof and vaporproof paper. More wall vents are also advisable. The size of the radiator in the bedroom should also be checked; it may not be large enough.

SWEATING OUTSIDE WALLS

The outside plaster walls in our upstairs bedrooms sweat during the winter. We have a brick house. The moisture doesn't seem to have any connection with rain or snow. What do you suggest?

We suspect the plaster in the bedrooms was applied directly to the brick. This would make the walls cold enough to cause the warm house air to condense on the surface. We would suggest furring out these walls to create a dead-air space and placing insulation between the furring strips; then finish with lath and plaster or gypsum wallboard. The latter can be painted or papered, as desired. Lack of sufficient heat in the affected rooms could also cause condensation. Uniform distribution of heat into all parts of the house, and the maintenance of a uniform temperature, will help.

SWEATING CABINET WALLS

My house is 10 years old. I have a problem with kitchen cabinets sweating during the winter and food in them becoming moldy. Could this be caused by there being no insulation between the wall and the cabinet backs? The cabinets are made of plywood. They are on the north wall. Would removing the backs of the cabinets solve this problem?

The cabinets are sweating during the winter most likely because of damp kitchen air

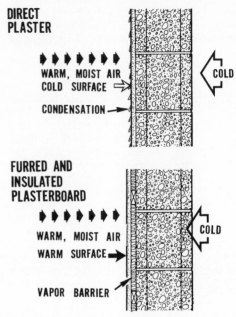

Figure 10-3. (top) Why condensation forms on direct plaster. (bottom) One way of preventing this problem.

which cannot escape due to closed windows during this season. When this damp air comes in contact with the cold (north) walls of the cabinets, it condenses, causing the sweating condition. Removing the backs of the cabinets wouldn't solve the problem; the moist air should be drawn out of the kitchen by installing an exhaust fan, vented to the outdoors, or keeping kitchen windows open at the top to allow the moisture to escape.

DAMP WALLS

As new owners of an old house, we would like to know what can be done with walls on which plaster was applied directly on the brick. They get damp whenever it rains, but water does not actually come into the room. Which of the following would be most economical and keep out dampness: to put 1 by 2 furring strips with plasterboard over it, or to use a dampproof cement coating and paint over that?

While the latter method would be more economical, it is not practical. For effective results, there must be an air space between the brick and the inside wall. The reason for this is to prevent the inner surfaces from becoming as cold as the brick and having condensation form on them. Insulation between the furring strips would help make the rooms more comfortable.

WALLS FROST UP INSIDE

Three of our basement walls are exposed to the weather. During the cold months they frost up inside, leaving the floors damp all winter long. Along the bottom and up the corners, the walls have a dark mildewlike stain. Would styrofoam insulation be the answer? Would it need an air space?

Styrofoam planks would indeed be an excellent way to solve this problem. While styrofoam needs no air space, you would have to cover it with dry wall, paneling, or another type of wall covering to protect the soft surface. To make the job even more thorough, first apply clear liquid waterproofing to the walls. This will stop dampness from working past the surface. Odors should disappear.

WALLS SWEAT IN HUMID WEATHER

Our cement back hall and stairway sweat in humid weather. The paint on them is wearing off. Can they be painted or covered to remedy this?

We suspect that the walls are of concrete block. Such walls remain cool despite the warmth in the air and the humidity. This coolness of surface causes the moisture in the air to condense. You should be able to overcome the condition by furring out the walls, placing a blanket or foam insulation between the furring, and then finishing with a gypsum wallboard or plywood.

UPSTAIRS WINDOWS FROST BUT DOWNSTAIRS CLEAR

I live on the upper floor of a duplex. My storm windows frost on the inside, but downstairs the windows are clear. Why is this?

The warm, damp house air rises up the stairwell. And if there were a floor above yours, those inhabitants would be getting the effect you're getting now. Your inside windows apparently don't fit too well, or all that warm air wouldn't leak out to condense on those cold storms. Generous ventilation on dry days will help the problem. Of even more help would be to install a kitchen fan in the apartment below to pull the damp cooking

vapors outdoors instead of letting them waft up to you.

HOW COME WALLS ARE WET?

We hardly ever get water in the sump pump from rains or spring thaws. But now there is enough moisture on the walls and on the sides of the sump pump enclosure to drip down. The walls were sealed and painted. Why are they wet now?

No leak, no seepage. Just heavy condensation from the humid weather. The masonry is cooler, and warm air condenses on it. A dehumidifier will help. So will all possible ventilation, with a fan blowing across the floor to an open doorway. Drier weather will help most of all.

PUDDLE OF WATER ALONG BASEBOARD

I bought a home a year ago last November. I noticed, last winter, small puddles of water along my outside walls by the baseboard. I thought this was moisture coming from the new plaster. But the walls were dry. This winter the condition is just as bad. The house is of frame construction with insulation, which has a vapor barrier. The floor is a concrete slab. Can you suggest a remedy?

When the outside temperatures are very low, the outer edges of the concrete slab become very cold. When the warm air in the house has a fair percentage of humidity, it comes in contact with the cold slab and condensation occurs. To overcome the condition it will be necessary to insulate the perimeter of the slab with a waterproof insulation, made especially for the purpose. Your dealer in insulating materials should know about it.

SLAB FLOOR DAMP

My house is built on a slab. During the hot, humid weather, the floors feel a little damp and have a slight musty odor. The living room carpet buckles in summer, which means dampness. How can I correct this condition?

Before taking on any major project, such as putting a new floor on sleepers over the slab, to provide insulating space, try some simple methods. Try to move that stagnant, soggy air off the floor and out of the house by placing a fan on the floor so that it blows across toward an open door. Try turning on the baseboard heating for a few hours; this should temporarily dry things up too.

TILE FLOOR GETS WET

Our summer home has a vinyl-tile covering on the below-grade concrete slab. This gets very wet due to condensation in damp, humid weather. Therefore we thought we would like to carpet the entire area. Is there some type of "dampness barrier" we can apply, so that we could use some other type carpet than indoor-outdoor?

No "barrier"-type application can block formation of condensation, but the carpet itself will become the insulation which will stop the problem for the most part. You can help things along a great deal on dry days by placing an electric fan so that it will blow across the floor toward an open door and keep the air moving. But for below-grade you're still safer with the indoor-outdoor type of carpeting.

EXCELLENT IDEA TO WATERPROOF SLAB

Should any waterproofing or vapor barrier be used when constructing a concrete slab floor? If so, when and where?

Definitely yes. This waterproof barrier consists of a layer of heavy polyethylene sheet plastic, laid on top of the gravel drainage bed before the slab is poured. Planks of styrofoam will make excellent insulation around the edges.

CARPET HEADING FOR TROUBLE

Would moisture always be present on a ground-level concrete floor covered by foam padding and wool carpeting? The concrete was initially painted in the room to keep down the dust. I have noticed the color of the rug change in different areas, and at times it seems a little moist in different places. Is there something I should do?

Since the wall-to-wall carpeting would probably prevent condensation, the cause of the moisture would be seepage through cracks or the slab itself. You can stop this simply by laying heavy plastic sheeting on the floor under the rug cushion. But very important: Do everything you can to get that carpeting dry again. Electric heaters or hair dryers will help a lot. Otherwise, the carpeting will be a

sure victim of mildew and the resultant musty odors. Do everything you can to lower the humidity in the house air.

GROUND-BORNE MILDEW

My house has mildew patches every 16 inches along all the outside walls, including the baseboard; the mildew runs 12 inches up the walls and the same distance out on the floor. The ground is wet under the house (the crawl space), but will dry up during long dry spells. I can clean the mildew off, but I can't find anything to prevent its returning. I don't dare put down wall-to-wall carpeting until I can cure this condition. What can I do?

The basic problem is that soggy ground. It keeps your foundation wall so wet that the framing on top (sill) is equally wet, and this soaks the joists and wall studs (which are 16 inches apart; hence the pattern). The most thorough job is digging down to waterproof the walls full depth. But try this first: Cover the ground with heavy sheet plastic; cement the overlapping seams. Then put liquid waterproofing on the basement walls from the ground level up. This may materially reduce the problem. If it doesn't reduce it enough, get a foundation firm to do the job right.

SUN PORCH WITH MUSTY SMELL

We have a seven-window sun porch off our living room. The windows are triple-track storm-screen combinations. The walls are paneled, and there is a concrete floor, tiled with asphalt tiles. Why does it have that awful damp smell? There is a vent at each end of the porch foundation. I use this porch for an extra bedroom, and the mattress and box spring smell terrible. Is there a solution?

Another vent (or two) in the long side of the foundation wall will greatly increase ventilation and reduce dampness and musty mildew odors. Cover the floor area inside the foundation walls, if accessible, with heavy plastic sheeting, to check rising ground dampness. Paint (also if accessible) the underside of the concrete floor with roofing cement, as a waterproofing shield, so that the concrete won't be constantly damp. If a week out in the sun doesn't take out the odor from the box spring and mattress, replace them.

ROOF NAILS FROZE IN ATTIC

In real cold weather last winter, the nails protruding through the roof shingles into the attic became coated with ice. Could this be because we do not have enough vents? There are vents in the front, and at the back there are vents where the roof meets the attic floor. There are windows at each end of the attic. I opened one, and the ice got worse on the nails and rafters. Should both of the windows be left open in the winter?

The ice on the nails is because they are freezing cold and damp air condenses on them. Clipping them off flush (often a monumental job) will stop this. The windows will provide good cross ventilation, true. But it would be better if you had louvered openings higher up, right in the roof peaks, for improved circulation.

COLD ATTIC NOW HOT

Last October, I completed finishing off two rooms in the attic space for living quarters. Under the roof, I put in blanket insulation, so that it would save heat and also keep it warm. This worked very well during winter. But now, with the hot sun baking down, it's like a fireless cooker. Is there any way to promote more coolness beside putting a fan in the window?

Cover the lower edges of the rafters with aluminum foil, under the insulation. This will help considerably at reflecting the heat upward. You'll also find in winter that the aluminum will reflect house heat down, and so you'll save on heating costs too. Ever notice how many barns and silos have aluminum shingle roofing? It keeps the inside cooler.

CRAWL SPACE

I have a small house, 24 by 28 feet, with no basement, just a crawl space. I have three windows for ventilation. I would like to know which is better: to leave the screens in the year round or to continue putting in the windows in the late autumn through the winter. Some people advised ventilation all year round. What is your advice?

It would be better to ventilate the area at all times of the year in order to prevent the timbers from becoming wet and rotting. This procedure, however, may make the floors

cold. To prevent this, place a vaporproof and moistureproof batt or blanket type of insulation between the floor joists. Place the vaporproof covering on the insulation facing the floor above.

MOISTURE RISING FROM CRAWL SPACE

We have a small home with a vented crawl space instead of a basement. We wish to use polyethylene sheeting to reduce the moisture coming up through the floor from the crawl space. Should the polyethylene be put directly on the ground, or should it be attached to the underside of the floor joists? We have heard arguments in favor of each method. Polyethylene placed directly on the ground should stop moisture from rising, but would not eliminate moisture coming in through the vents and going up through the floor. Polyethylene on the underside of the floor joists would stop all moisture from coming through the floor, but the crawl space would probably be very damp below the barrier. What do you suggest?

The usual procedure (see page 185) is to place the polyethylene directly on the ground, running it up at least 4 to 6 inches on the crawl space walls and being sure to overlap the seam edges at least 4 to 6 inches. Vents permit the escape of moisture and provide the necessary ventilation of dampness coming in. A ground vapor barrier, preventing the rise of ground moisture, results in only a minimum amount of ventilation being required: with ground cover, all that is required are vents in two walls, with openings the size of 1 square inch per each 1,500 square inches of ground area; without ground cover, 10 times as much ventilation is required.

PIPES FREEZE IF VENTS OPEN

The crawl space end of our basement has an earth floor. The entire basement has three air vents. We keep them open except in winter. Then they are closed, so that the water pipes won't freeze and we can also store vegetables safely down there. But it is very damp in winter. This made the floor above cold until I covered the underside with insulation. What can we do about the dampness?

To prevent the dampness, those vents should not be closed. You can protect the pipes from freezing by wrapping them with electric heating wires and insulation. But unless you can provide some type of nonfreezing storage for the vegetables, you'll have to choose between them and the dampness. (We're suprised you didn't report that the dampness caused some adverse effect on the vegetables; perhaps it's not too bad after all.)

CONDENSATION ON UNDERSIDE OF STOOP

We had a new house built several years ago. The front stoop to the house is of concrete and was poured so that it extends over the foundation and basement, making it a partial roof of the basement. We noted that during the winter months condensation and water droplets formed on the underside of the stoop area. We would like to remedy this situation. Would any of the waterproofing compounds prevent this?

It isn't a waterproofing compound that will solve this condition, but an insulating material will. If enough insulation is applied on the underside of the concrete, the warm air of the basement that evidently contains some percentage of humidity will not condense in that area. You should be able to find a contractor who does a spray-on insulation job. This type of material consists of a foam plastic and a binder. Another method is to fur out the concrete and install either a flexible or a plastic type of insulation.

LOCATING A DEHUMIDIFIER

Is it necessary to have a dehumidifier standing on the floor? Or could it be located 30 inches or more above the floor? I would like to mount it above and behind the laundry tubs so that it can drain into them.

Unless the dealer has specific, good reasons for floor mounting, we can see no reason at all why you can't mount it high enough to drain into those tubs.

HUMIDIFIER CAUSING DRIPS

I am having trouble with beads of moisture which form on the ceiling in an area 2 feet long and 1 foot wide, directly over the front door. I would like to know how to eliminate this problem, as it causes me to repaint this area every year. I use a portable humidifier near the front door, as this is the only out-of-the-way place we have for it.

From the relative positions of the dampness and drops and the humidifier, it certainly appears to be cause and effect. Move the humidifier somewhere else, and see if the drops and dampness don't disappear from that ceiling. We know this may cause a slight disruption, but what are you going to do? You say you need the humidifier, so locate it somewhere else.

DEHUMIDIFIER WATER DISTILLED?

Is the water from a dehumidifier the same as distilled water? Can it be used in a steam iron?

The water from a dehumidifier is the same as the "moisture" which solidifies around the ice compartment of a refrigerator. Either can be used in steam irons.

MILDEW ON NORTH SIDING

During the past two years, I have noticed an increasing amount of mildew forming on the lower edges of our siding on the north side. It doesn't occur on the other sides. Would small, thick evergreens have anything to do with this? They have grown noticeably since the house was new five years ago.

You've just about answered the question yourself. If the shrubbery has grown so dense that it retards air circulation, mildew often results. This is compounded by being on the side of the house where the sun rarely strikes, so that it cannot dry out collected dampness. Let's hope those evergreens are still small enough to transplant away from the house.

ATTACHED GARAGE NEEDS SOME CROSS VENTILATION

The walls of my attached garage get so frosted up in winter that the paint blisters. I have a rubber gasket at the bottom of the overhead door to keep out rain and snow and also a tight new roof. Why the frosting? Should I have cross ventilation?

It sounds as though quite a bit of the warm house air leaks out of the kitchen door and condenses on the colder walls. You should open that door and a window and air the place out frequently, to chase dampness. Weather stripping around the door will help a lot to prevent the escape of the warm house air, and it will save on your heating bills, too.

HOUSE SHAKES IN STRONG WIND

We bought a 60-year-old, three-story frame house, with stone foundation, about a year and a half ago. It seems in excellent condition. One thing troubles us, and it happens only when there is a *very* strong wind. We feel a slight vibration or shaking of the house as the wind hits it. Can you explain this?

This is a perfectly natural phenomenon, unless the vibrations are excessive. If this didn't occur, the house might be damaged by the force of the wind. In tall buildings, this swaying, or bending with the wind, is allowed for architecturally.

HOUSE EXPOSED TO HIGH WINDS

The northwest side of our house on a hill receives the brunt of all the storms, and the structure is a target for more than normal wind. There is no garage or porch on the northwest side. Is there any way of protecting the house from the full force of the wind?

If there were some good-size trees on that side of the house, the velocity of the wind would be cut down. Otherwise, we don't know of anything that would effectively reduce the force of wind. In short, in our opinion, you need a "windbreak" of trees, but that takes time.

CHAPTER 11

HOME HEATING AND COOLING

In most parts of our country, some type of heating system is necessary to warm our houses. Also to make our homes comfortable during the summer, it is necessary that we provide a method of cooling.

Heating

Heating a house means heating the air within it; heat passes from the air to the walls, ceilings, and floors; to the furniture; and to everything else in the house, until all has been brought to an even temperature. When the air outdoors is at the same temperature as the air in the house, heat will stay in the house indefinitely. When the air outdoors is colder than the air in the house, heat will pass from the house to outdoors.

Heat will be lost when there are leaks that permit heated indoor air to escape and cold air to enter, and as parts of exterior walls absorb heat from the inside air and pass it outdoors. Air when heated will expand; then, being lighter in weight, it will rise. If a house has a thin roof, open joints between the roof and the walls, or cracks around window frames and elsewhere, rising warm air will pass through to outdoors and be lost. Thus, the basic principle, obviously, is to do everything possible to minimize the escape of heat. Every bit of heat lost through walls or roof or carelessly left-open doors and windows must be replaced by an equal amount of warmed air. Otherwise, the house temperature will drop by the amount of heat lost.

With this principle in mind, here are some of the ways you can conserve heat:

Fireplace. Any fireplace worth its salt has a good draft, which is why your room doesn't fill up with smoke when there is a fire blazing away. That is just fine, except when you're not using the fireplace. Then that nice effective draft is equally good at drawing large quantities of the warm house air up the chimney. This alone can cause an immense loss of heat, which your heater must work overtime (and unnecessarily) to keep replacing. If you haven't a damper or similar device to block off the flue, then you should promptly arrange to have one installed. The amount of fuel saved by eliminating this one escape route for heat will pay for the damper many times over. It will also do handsomely at eliminating the usual drafts coursing along the floor between the nearest door and the fireplace.

Filters. These should be really clean, to make it as easy as possible for the warmed air to circulate out in the rooms. Dirty, clogged filters put up enough resistance to make the heater work harder to push the air through such obstructions.

Radiators. All heat-dispersing units— radiators, convectors, baseboards, etc.— should be uncovered, unobstructed. They shouldn't be covered by heavy draperies or crowded behind large, upholstered furniture (which can absorb a surprisingly large amount of heat). If these units are placed so that heat can radiate right out into the room, the governing thermostat will be satisfied just that much sooner. Radiator covers do, of course, absorb a certain amount of heat, which does detract somewhat from heating efficiency. However, you can increase the heating power of both the cover and radiator simply by fastening a sheet of reflective aluminum between the radiator and the wall. Heat that would normally be absorbed by the wall will be bounced back and into the room. This can cancel out some of the inefficiencies of a radiator cover. Of course, if there's no cover, the radiator itself will do an even more efficient job of heat radiation.

If you are planning to paint the radiators, absolutely do not use an aluminum paint or other type of metallic paint. Contrary to what you might think, a metallic paint can reduce the heating efficiency of a radiator or other such unit by as much as 15 percent. Use either radiator enamel or regular, normal wall paint. If there is already a coat of metallic paint on the radiator, it is not necessary to remove it before putting on the regular type of paint. However, there's one aspect about this which makes painting a job much better postponed until after the cold weather. The radiator must be stone cold during the entire operation and until the final coat of paint is thoroughly dry. If the metal is warm at any time, it won't be long before the nice new paint job will start to turn darker and eventually flake off. This, therefore, is a job much better done during the summer.

Thermostat. This should be carefully inspected to see that it still can operate with the required delicate balance to govern your heater's output with maximum efficiency. If you're at all doubtful about the location, by all means have a reliable heating engineer come over and check this vitally important point.

An improperly located thermostat can waste an enormous amount of heat. For example, if it's near a window or outside wall, or where a cold draft can strike it, this chill will cause it to demand heat, even though the rest of the house is perfectly comfortable.

Some of the split-level houses, and others which cover considerable ground area, achieve even greater heating economies by zone heating, with individual thermostats controlling the different amounts of heat desired in different parts of the house.

Windows, Doors. Normally, one of the great sources of heat loss is through and around windows and doors. So much heat can escape, in fact, that in only a couple of years, or three years at the most, the actual savings in fuel alone will pay for the weather stripping around windows and for well-fitting, high-quality storm sash and storm windows.

Insulation. Exactly the same kinds of savings are possible with well-installed insulation. For without insulation under the roof, in the walls, and under the floors over open crawl spaces, the house heat can readily work right through to the outdoors. The loss of heat can be so tremendous that by checking it effectively, the insulation will pay for itself in a relatively short time. See Chapter 10 for details on insulation.

"Instant" Hot Water. A hot-water circulating system can mean you get hot water just as soon as you turn on the faucet. This consists of a loop of pipe installed between the water heater and the individual fixtures, where hot water is kept circulating constantly. Thus, hot water is always ready; there's no waste of fuel as there is when water is heated and then allowed to grow cold again in the pipes waiting for the next time it's used.

Exposed Pipes. Any hot-water pipes which pass through an open crawl space or other unheated area must be thoroughly insulated. This is not only to prevent the pipe's freezing, but to prevent heat loss; the water which left the heater at the desired temperature should not be allowed to cool off in transit. Insulating tape is available at hardware stores; and insulating jacketing, made in various sizes to accommodate most pipe sizes, can be bought in plumbing supply houses. Another method of ensuring against a frozen pipe is to wrap it with electric heating wires. These are available where electrical supplies are sold.

Heater. In order to get the best from your

house heater, you should inspect it at least annually, preferably during the summer months. The longer you can keep your heating system in top operating condition, the longer it will run without repairs or replacements. Further, when it's running right, it will run on less fuel than when it is operating even a little bit below par. Both of these aspects can spell appreciable savings.

An inspection in the summer will usually cost less than if you wait until next fall's first cold snap. That is exactly the time when so many other people discover something's amiss with their heaters that the service crews are run ragged. And, being human, they can't take care of everybody at the same time. Even if you're quite willing to pay overtime labor rates for the sake of having a warm house, you may have to wait a day or two while the service crew takes care of people who called them up before you did. So there is a double bonus if you have your heater put in top shape during the summer shutdown. Many heating contractors offer enticingly low rates for this work during June, July, and August. In order for them to keep a solid, capable crew for the regular heating season, contractors have to pay their workers on a year-round basis. Rather than having them idle while drawing a salary, the contractors greatly prefer to have the workers busy, even though home-owners pay a lower hourly rate. True, there's no summer reduction on spare parts, but there certainly is on the labor. Your maintenance cost is thereby lessened on inspections and repairs you would need anyway—and you'll definitely not be inconvenienced or caught unprepared by the first cold snap.

It's also perfectly true that many heating service organizations operate on a contract basis. That is, for a certain amount, they will guarantee good performance all year round. This includes checkups and replacement of any needed spare parts. While this is the most foolproof way to assure yourself of complete heating comfort, there is also the possibility that you are paying for some of the others who also signed up. Mostly, families with heaters which are getting along in years and demand quite a bit of extra attention subscribe to this service. These costs must all be averaged out for the service company to operate efficiently. Therefore, if your heater has no problems at all, you pay, nevertheless, at a rate to bring in an overall business profit. But it will cost you nothing whatsoever to ask if the annual charge will be lessened if the annual inspection and tune-up jobs are done during the summer. It is very possible this inquiry could pay off handsomely.

Cooling Your Home

There are three common ways to cool your home: (1) with fans, (2) with air conditioners, and (3) with an evaporative cooler. The latter is generally used only in the southwest portion of the United States. In operation, water is sprayed on excelsior (or some other good water-absorptive material) at a rate of 5 to 10 gallons per hour for an average-size house. A fan then draws air through the excelsior. The water in the excelsior evaporates and cools the air; the cooled air, in turn, cools your home. In most sections of our country where evaporative coolers are used, 20 to 40 house-air changes per hour are necessary.

Cool with Fans. You can buy two types of cooling fans: (1) room fans and (2) attic fans. The former type stir up the air. The temperature inside your house can be several degrees cooler than outside, but it can seem warmer if the air doesn't move. Also, air movement increases moisture evaporation, and moisture evaporation cools the body, or skin surfaces. A good room fan has large blades, turns at about 1,000 rpm (it may have a speed adjustment), operates quietly, and has an oscillating mechanism.

Attic fans exchange inside air for outside air. You can use them for night cooling, or whenever the temperature inside your home is greater than the temperature outside. As was mentioned earlier, we know that since hot

Figure 11-1. Shaded portions of the country need evaporative cooler.

air rises, the upstairs and attic space are warmer than the ground floor. So if you can keep getting rid of the warmer air above, more of the cooler ground-floor air will come in to replace it. For example, here's what you do on a hot night: Set your fan facing outward on an upstairs windowsill or right by the roof vent. As it blows outward, it will pull the hot air in the upstairs outdoors. This will start an upward flow from below, and the cooler air from outside the ground floor will be drawn indoors. When it warms a little, it will float upstairs and be drawn out, in turn, by the action of the fan. A time switch can be installed in the electrical circuit to your fan to cut if off automatically at any time you desire. When you have cooled your house at night, keep the windows and doors closed during the next day as long as it is cooler inside than out.

For best results, you will need the help of an engineer in determining the size of the attic or window fan needed for your house (some retail firms provide the services of a trained technician). The air inlets and outlets, the horsepower of the fan motor, and the revolutions per minute of the fan blade all should be taken into consideration. However, you can determine the approximate size yourself and probably get satisfactory results. To determine the size fan you'll need:

1. Find the volume of the area you want to cool. Multiply the length of the rooms by the width. Then multiply that by the height.
2. If you live in the dotted area of the map, divide the volume by 1.5. This will give you a minimum cfm requirement. If you live in the undotted area, your minimum

Figure 11-2. Minimum air changes recommended for fan cooling.

cfm requirement will be the same as the volume you want cooled.
3. Pick a fan that has a cfm rating larger than your cfm requirement—a larger rating will allow for slight differences in test procedure and efficiency.

If you choose a fan that is driven with pulleys and a belt, rather than one that is driven directly by the motor, the size of the pulleys can be varied slightly to adjust the amount of air moved. Models with two- and three-speed motors are also available.

You can install the fan in three different ways. How it's put in is always as important as the size and power of the fan itself. So it's a good idea to give the dealer full details. It makes it easier for him to help you choose the best model. It's even better if he can come over and see your setup.

With unfinished attic space, the usual methods are either to locate the fan lying flat over a grilled opening cut in the attic floor or to cover the opening with a suction box with the fan mounted vertically at one end. In each case, the air is discharged through wall louvers in the gable ends of the walls.

If there is finished living space, the fan is put directly into the wall, either in part of the window opening or in a hole cut especially to accommodate it. There is a grilled opening cut in the attic floor, as close to the center as convenient. As the fan blows the overheated attic air out, it draws up more air from below through the opening in the floor.

With this wall installation, you have to remember there are other seasons in the year, meaning winter. So you must devise a way to close up the hole, or some of the polar air will be working into that attic living space and then on downstairs. One simple plug-up technique is to remove the fan and insert a piece of board or plywood cut to fit snugly. The edges where it fits into the opening can be sealed with reusable putty (the gray, ropy caulking which you can get in any hardware store). Comes the warm weather, you pull it off and put it away for next time. It's also practical to have this cover work like a small door to close the opening—either sliding or hinged. While the fan doesn't really have to be removed, it's better to give it protection from winter. You can, of course, protect it with a cover for the opening which works from the outside.

When cooling with a fan, you should

close off any portion of the house that you don't wish to cool; otherwise, the fan won't provide the proper number of air changes per unit time. You can also remove accumulated attic heat during the day with an attic fan. Often an attic is 25° or more hotter than outside; even if the ceiling of your house is insulated, this additional heat will warm your house. When you remove attic heat with an attic fan during the day, close the attic off from the rest of your house. Otherwise the fan will draw hot, outside air into your house.

Suppose you decide to cool your home with an evaporative cooler or air conditioning, but wish to ventilate the attic anyway. A fan—smaller than the usual-size attic fan—will do that; it should be capable of changing the air in the attic at least once per minute, and should operate continuously when the temperature in the attic exceeds 110°. It may be controlled by thermostat, time clock, or manual switch.

Cool with an Air Conditioner. There are two types of air conditioners: (1) room units and (2) central-system units. The cooling operation of both types of air conditioners is the same. Air passes through filters that remove large dust particles, and over a series of refrigeration coils where it is cooled and dehumidified. A fan then blows the cooled air into your home. Most air conditioners have either built-in thermostats or connections for wiring the conditioners to remote temperature controls. Some of the small units aren't equipped with thermostats, but you may find that a thermostat is available as optional equipment.

Room air conditioners cool one or more rooms. They range in output from about 5,000 to 32,000 Btu per hour. They operate on electricity only, and should have separate electrical circuits (this may require adding a circuit to your home). You can choose from many available models—models for conventional windows, models for casement windows, models for in-front-of-window consoles, and models that mount in special wall openings.

Central air conditioning systems are generally more efficient than room air conditioners. They also seem less noisy because they are located out of the living area. Central air-conditioning systems can be separate systems with their own ducts, or they can be combined with forced-air systems.

Cooling requires a greater amount of air flow than heating. If you choose an add-on system, it will probably be necessary to increase the fan capacity of your furnace, and it may be necessary to enlarge and even relocate the distribution ducts. Larger ducts also decrease the velocity of the cooled air and reduce the noise of air conditioning. For greatest uniformity in room comfort conditions, cold-air supply grilles should be high in the walls or in the ceiling and hot-air supply grilles should be near or in the floor. If economy dictates the use of only one grille for both heating and cooling, the near-floor location is preferred.

With either a room unit or a central air-conditioning system, the care you give it and how you operate it can mightily affect the total operating results. Here are some tips that will help you to get the best from your air conditioner:

1. Keep the windows closed, and don't let the doors stay open any more than absolutely necessary.
2. Don't wait until late afternoon (usually the hottest part of the day) before turning on the air conditioning. By starting it early in the day, it can operate at a steady, consistent pace to rid the house of solar heat.
3. Ventilate cooking areas so that heat and moisture will not remain in the air.
4. Keep the laundry area shut off from air-conditioned portions of the house.
5. Have your system installed and checked periodically by a qualified heating-cooling contractor.

As you can see, like the old saying about more than one way to skin a cat, there are several ways to keep your house cool in the summer.

Questions and Answers

Here are some of the more common questions and their answers about heating and cooling systems.

NOISY RADIATORS

What causes radiators to knock when heat starts to come up? My home is heated by gas and is a conversion from coal. I have emptied the radiators, put small disks under two of the legs, and treated the boiler with a compound. The noise subsided a little, but there is still some knocking.

In a one-pipe steam-heating system (we presume that is what you have), steam rises to the radiators under pressure, and as it cools, the water flows down to the boiler in the same pipe. If the branch pipe from the riser to the radiator sags, a pocket may form, holding back some of the water. As the steam reaches the pocket and meets up with the resistance of the water, a knocking noise will result. Raising the radiator ¼ to ½ inch may eliminate the pocket. Each radiator must stand perfectly level. Sometimes such noises are caused by building up excessive steam pressure in quick time. Your serviceman could adjust this.

UNCLOGGING RADIATOR VALVES

My radiator valves haven't been cleaned in a long time, so I'm not surprised that every now and then they clog. This interferes with the functioning of the radiators once in a while, so I thought I'd get busy and do a cleaning job on all of them. What is the best way to go about it?

Vinegar is an excellent cleaner. Boil the valves in it for 5 minutes or so. Let them cool off, and when they're cool enough to handle, slosh them around in the cooling-off vinegar, rinse them well in clear water, and shake off the excess water. This will do a good job of clearing the air hole and getting out any accumulated particles from the inside of the valve.

UNHEATING RADIATOR

One bedroom radiator isn't heating up. All the other radiators function satisfactorily. I tested the valve, and that is okay. We have steam heat, oil-fired. We moved into our newly built house a year ago, and the last heating season the radiator was fine. What do you suggest?

Since your house is new, the radiator may have tilted just a little away from level due to settling of the house, just enough so that the return flow of water to the house heater is impeded, and thus heat is prevented from entering. Try raising the valve end of the radiator a little bit by placing small blocks of wood, ¼ to ½ inch high, underneath the legs. Usually this will correct such a condition. If not, we suggest consulting a reliable heating contractor.

NOISY HEAT RISER

Our house is fairly old. A heat riser in the corner of our dining room is very noisy

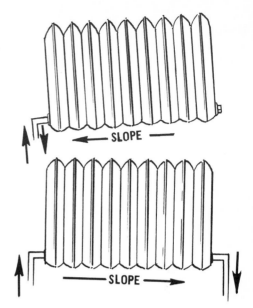

Figure 11-3. Slope of a radiator is most important.

when the heat is starting up and shortly after it dies down. It's very annoying. How can we correct this?

The noise is probably due to loosened supports, or to too few supports, for the pipe along its horizontal length. This will usually permit noisy vibration as the metal expands or contracts. Check the supports, and tighten any loose ones, or add more supports if necessary. Sometimes inserting small pads of foam rubber between the support and the pipe will absorb the vibration and make it less noisy.

RADIATORS KEEP BANGING

In one room I have a problem with banging steam radiators. I have installed a fast-bleed valve, pitched the radiators to drain properly, and had the expansions checked, but they still bang. Any suggestions?

Perhaps there's some partial clogging in the pipe, particularly if there's a sharp elbow or two. You've taken all the other usually effective steps to quiet noisy radiators like these.

HALF-AND-HALF RADIATORS

I have a hot-water heating furnace with old-type high radiators. I notice the radiators are hot on the top and cold on the bottom. I have removed all air from the radiators. How can I get the radiators hot all over?

You need to have the circulation speeded up. Consult a good heating man about putting in a circulating pump. This is neither complicated nor expensive.

LEAKY RADIATOR

The radiator in my bathroom leaks at the base, where the pieces are joined together. Can you tell me how to stop the leak?

If the radiator is a fairly new one (of cast iron), it is quite possible the leak can be stopped by tightening up the "tie rods" holding the sections together. To stop a leak in an old radiator, get some iron cement from your hardware or plumbing supply dealer and mix a small amount of it according to directions on the can. Place iron cement over the leaky spot in a thick layer; cover the cement with a strip of sheet metal, and tie it tightly in place with sturdy wire.

LEAK AT RADIATOR VALVE

What makes old-fashioned hot-water-heat radiators leak at the valve? What can be done to remedy the situation?

The packing may be loose or worn. If loose, it can be tightened by screwing down the six-sided nut under the handle. If this doesn't remedy the leak, the valve should be repacked. Free the handle by unscrewing the screw or nut securing it, and remove the nut beneath. If the packing washers on the valve stem are worn, they should be replaced. Or pack with cord impregnated with graphite, by wrapping it around the valve stem; this will be compressed when the packing nut is screwed down again.

SOME RADIATORS DON'T HEAT

Some of our radiators heat properly, but others don't, although their air valves are free.

One reason may be the location of the thermostat in a room that is quick in heating to temperature; as a result, the thermostat will shut down the heat before the rest of the house has warmed. The cure is to change the location of the thermostat to a position where the air temperature is more nearly average. Another reason for this condition will be the difference in resistance of different lines of piping. Some may be short and direct, offering so little resistance to the flow of steam that

their radiators heat with the first show of steam in the boiler. In others that are long and have many elbows, the resistance will be so much higher that steam will not be driven to their radiators by the low pressure sufficient for those on the low-resistance pipes. The remedy is to increase the boiler pressure until the distant radiators heat properly, the adjustment being left at that point.

WALL DARKENS NEAR RADIATOR

To improve the appearance of the living room, I bought a cover to go over the radiator. In a few weeks, the wall area above the radiator started to turn darker. What do you think can be the cause of this? I don't mind washing the wall once in a while, even though it is a big job, but I'd greatly prefer to know how to stop the trouble itself.

It sounds to us as though there's no back to the radiator cover. Therefore, when the heat rises, drawing up dust with it behind the radiator, the dust is deposited on the wall. Before the radiator cover was installed, the dust probably was so diffused with the warm air rising from all parts of the radiator, you didn't notice it. We would suggest fastening a sheet of aluminum foil as a back to the radiator cover. Not only will this help prevent dust rising from the back of the radiator and thus from landing on the wall, but it will also reflect heat out into the room, instead of the heat being absorbed by the wall behind.

HEATING BY CONVECTORS

We have been advised to have convector heating installed in a new house we are planning. What is the advantage of this method, and how does it work?

Convectors operate on the principle that warm air rises. As the convector is heated by the hot water from the boiler, the warmed air rises from the fins and out through the grille on top, creating a slight vacuum within the cabinet enclosure which draws cold air in at the bottom. All air in the room is warmed gradually by continuous passing through the convector, delivering warmth to all areas by natural circulation. This helps maintain a uniform temperature throughout the room.

LACK OF HOT WATER

I recently purchased a home which has hot-water baseboard radiators, and we like it, but we are having trouble with hot water for domestic use. I was told that I would get an abundance of hot water, both summer and winter. I seldom get water more than lukewarm and cannot get more than 10 or 12 gallons at one time. What can be done to have this corrected? I don't have a storage tank.

Evidently the heating system is equipped with an instantaneous hot-water heating coil. There are many reasons for the lack of hot water. The coil may be too small or the temperature of the water circulating through the heating system may not be high enough for the coil. The water temperature controls at the boiler may need adjustment. If there is a thermostatic mixing valve, which tempers the water flowing to the faucets, it might need adjustment or it might not function efficiently, thus allowing too much cold water to mix with the hot. Have a competent heating man check the installation.

REPLACING WATER IN BOILER

I have been told that the water in boilers of heating systems should be drained and the boiler refilled at the beginning of the season rather than at the end. Is this correct procedure?

Yes, draining and refilling of boilers should be done preferably at the beginning of the heating season. Water repeatedly heated is freed of air and has little corrosive effect on iron: fresh water, containing air, causes rust on iron. Water should be added as needed during the heating season. But water in the boiler should not be replaced. After the heating season, water should be added, if necessary, to what is already present. It is sometimes a good idea to drain several pailfuls of water from the boiler to remove rust that might have accumulated on the bottom. However, never completely drain the system at the end of the heating season.

HOT CLOTHES CLOSET

A heat riser pipe goes up through the clothes closet off our apartment foyer. It gets so hot at times that it can scorch anything hung within range. The super practically yawns. Is there any reasonably simple way I can cope with this myself?

Get a couple of boards, 1 inch thick by 8 inches or so wide, and a couple of sheets of asbestos to cover the hot side of each board. Then simply box in that pipe. Nail a couple of

pieces of quarter-round molding to the floor to anchor the boards. If you can't toenail into the plaster ceiling, fasten two more pieces of quarter round up there with epoxy adhesive. When it hardens, cement the top of the boards to the molding. Then cover the outer edges of the board tops with two more pieces of molding (mitred for neat appearance). This will cool that closet.

BASEBOARD HEATING

I am considering baseboard heating for a new home we are planning to build. But I'd like to be reassured about its advisability. What are the advantages of this type of heating?

There is excellent, even heat distribution through a room with this type of heating. As with radiant floor heating, baseboard heating usually keeps the floor heat within 2° of the ceiling temperature. Two or three conventional radiators around a room do not usually heat as evenly; there may be 10° difference between the floor and ceiling. Warmer floors means fewer drafts.

BROWN SPOTS ON BASEBOARD RADIATORS

When the bathroom tile was cleaned by the plumbers, in a new house, they evidently got some of the acid on the little baseboard radiators. I looked at the brown spots for two years, and then painted them. Two years later the spots are coming through again. How do I get rid of them?

If the brown spots are due to neglect to neutralize the acid, remove the present paint coating down to bare metal; then apply a solution of 1 pint of ammonia in 2 gallons of water, rinsing the solution off after several minutes with clear water and wiping the surface dry. However, the brown spots may be due to rust from moisture in the bathroom, a common problem. Steel-wool the rust spots off, and wipe the surfaces with turpentine to remove any trace of grease, wax, etc. Use a good-quality radiator enamel to coat the baseboard; this will resist both moisture and heat.

AIR PUTT-PUTTS THROUGH HEATING PIPES

For some reason, air is getting into the heating pipes of our hot-water system. It makes a putt-putting sound. How do we get rid of this?

This needs an on-the-spot inspection by a heating man. Your air vent could need adjustment or replacement.

PIPES LOSE HEAT UNDERGROUND?

We have a hydronic heating system with unwrapped pipes under the house. Is there much heat loss because of these unwrapped pipes?

If the pipes are in an open crawl space, you surely can lose heat by not having them wrapped with thick insulation. Heat loss is less in a heated basement, of course. If there are no heat registers or outlets in the basement, and it's still warm down there, it's these pipes which supply the heat (along with the furnace). If you don't want the basement so warm, wrapping the pipes will save heat for upstairs.

PIPE MAKES CLOSET WARM

In a corner of our foyer closet, a heating pipe rises up to bring heat to the apartments above. Not only is the closet uncomfortably warm, but the pipe is likely to scorch any fabrics which come in contact with it. What can I do?

The most effective cure is to box it in with a couple of boards, leaving a couple of inches air space between them and the pipe. Even better insulation will be given if you cover the "pipe" side of the boards with asbestos.

UNCOMFORTABLY DRY HOT AIR

During the heating season, the air in our home is so dry it affects our noses and throats uncomfortably. We have hot-air heat, oil-fired. How can we correct this dry-air condition?

Efficient humidifiers for hot-air furnaces are made by several manufacturers. Consult your heating contractor about the various makes and costs. Most of these humidifiers consist of a large water pan with ceramic or glass-fiber evaporator plates. The pan is connected to the water supply so that there is a constant amount of water in the pan for continuous evaporation.

DRY AIR

In our new house we have radiant heat, and there is no basement. We find the air is very dry. Is there anything we can do to solve this? The heat panels are in the ceiling.

Electric appliance dealers and some heat-

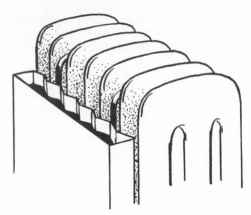

Figure 11-4. A pan attached to a radiator will put water into the air.

ing supply houses sell electric humidifier units, which should help increase the percentage of humidity.

RADIANT HEAT THROUGH TILE?

To settle an argument, will radiant heating pipes in the floor still work if the floor is covered with resilient tiles?

It certainly will, and very well. We can personally vouch that it works fine even when covered with a resilient flooring such as vinyl foam. Those warm floors feel great under socked feet, too.

FLOOR HAS HOT SPOTS

In our slab floor we have radiant heating pipes, where heated water circulates. There are several really hot spots, however. Now I would like to put carpeting over the asphalt tile, but am worried about possible fire risk. Is there some kind of fireproof padding I could put down over these hot spots, such as sheets of asbestos?

An excellent idea. But only put them over the hot-spot areas. The more extensive the asbestos, the more it will block the heat.

DUST IN HEATING SYSTEM

What would cause a forced-air oil furnace to throw off a white powderlike dust? We change the filters more often than is usually necessary, but the dust seems to be too fine to catch in the filters and it has saturated everything in the house despite constant cleaning.

The only thing we can suggest is that if your house is brand-new and the ducts were left open before you occupied the building, plaster or some other building material may have been dropped down; if the material has hardened, air passing over it may be dislodging particles. We highly recommend having the installation checked to see if any debris is present in the ducts and also to see whether the system is properly installed.

HOT-AIR DUCTS NOISY

The sheet aluminum ducts of our hot-air heating system make a lot of noise when the heat comes up and after it cools down. How can we quiet this?

Try placing more supports for the horizontal runs of the ducts, and tightening any that may have loosened. This should help absorb vibration of the metal as it expands or contracts. I've seen noisy ducts subdued by cutting out a foot-wide section and replacing this metal with leather or canvas. This "sleeve" breaks up the vibrations which formerly flowed without interruption from one end of the duct to the other. This idea might well work here.

HOT-AIR HEATING SYSTEM

I am having a house built, and I would like to have your opinion on a problem. I had a few heating bids from some dependable heating contractors, but they differ on the hot and cold register. Should the hot-air registers be on the outside or inside walls? Will either one way or the other have any effect on condensation on the windows or wall? If the register goes on the outside wall, does the register stick out from the finished wall? I understand it does so to keep the heat boot away from the cold outside wall.

The usual practice is to place the heat ducts and registers on the inside walls and the cold-air return ducts in the outside walls. The placement of heat ducts in outside walls is apt to cool the air entering the room. All register faces are mounted on the surface of the walls, and therefore the thickness of the plate will project from the plaster surface. Condensation on windows occurs with any heating system if the humidity is high.

SAVE HEAT NEXT WINTER

Our home has heating ducts running below the floor in a 4-foot crawl space. There was

great heat loss last winter. What can I cover the ducts with before the next cold weather?

Wrap them with blankets of thick insulation, the thicker the better. If the ducts are jammed so closely up against the underside of the floor that you can't completely encircle them with the insulation, run the insulation tightly up against the floor, with enough of a flange to each side so that you can secure them with batten strips or their equivalent.

HEAT DUCTS TOO WARM

Is there a simple way to insulate heat ducts in the basement? Even in cold weather, it gets uncomfortably warm down there. In milder weather, it seems like the tropics.

Stop in at a plumbing and heating supply house. Describe your problem, give them the dimensions of the ducts, and see if they can't fix you up with sheet asbestos insulation which you can fit around the ducts. Increasing the efficiency of your heating this way will cut down on your heating costs a little, perhaps enough to pay for the insulation in a fairly short time.

DON'T BLOCK COLD-AIR RETURNS

Our kitchen was designed with a lot of waste wall space. Along one blank wall are two cold-air returns. I would like to build a lot of storage cabinets on this wall, but I hear conflicting opinions about blocking the cold-air returns. One furnace man says don't, and the other says go ahead—it doesn't matter since there are two of them. What is your opinion?

We heartily agree with the person who says the cold-air returns should be kept open and unobstructed. You can still do this and have your cabinets too. They don't have to stand solidly on the floor. Put them on legs, so that they are above the level of the baseboards, where the cold-air returns are.

DRAFTY STAIRWAY

We have a Cape Cod home with an open stairway. There is a cold draft coming down the stairway. We have an upstairs bedroom and powder room, which are heated. There is no cold-air return upstairs. Would there be a difference if we had one?

There is no sure solution for such a problem. By trying to equalize the temperature of the rooms upstairs with the rooms downstairs, the movement of air could be slowed down. We don't think that a cold-air return upstairs would help.

COLD FLOOR IN SUN-ROOM

Early this year, I added a sun-room to my house with a cement-block foundation. The underside of the floor has blanket insulation; then a subfloor and finish floor. Plastic floor tiles were put on top. There is a space of 4½ feet under the house. We have a hot-air register about 12 inches from the ceiling. Registers in other rooms are at the baseboards. The lower part of the room and the floor, even in the spring, were cold, and heat seemed to stay at the ceiling. There is a cold-air register in the room. Is there some way of improving this so it will be comfortable in cold weather?

Perhaps the cold-air return is drawing off the heat from the room. Block off the return register with a piece of sheet metal or cardboard for a day or so to see if the results are satisfactory. If so, close off the return. Perhaps the hot-air register is not large enough to take care of the room. A louvered register, with the louvers directed downward, will also help.

MUSTY ODOR

We have a house with a concrete slab foundation and floors. There are registers in the floors of three rooms for ventilation. However, these rooms seem to have a musty odor in the summer months—caused, no doubt, by the moisture in the ground. Can you tell me something I can put in the registers to prevent this odor?

If the concrete slab and floor were on the ground, we see no reason for the registers. We suspect that the registers may be cold-air returns for a hot-air heating system, and condensation is forming in the ducts. There should be a damper under each register face, which could be closed during the time when the heating system is not in operation. If the first condition is a fact, we would be inclined to close the area completely. Or as a temporary expedient, pour some chloride of lime on the ground under the register. It will act as a deodorant.

STOVEPIPE FROM FLOOR BELOW

We have an upstairs bedroom that would make an ideal playroom for the children. But I have been afraid to let the children play up there because of a stovepipe that comes through the floor from the room below, which then goes into the chimney. I've been afraid that one of the children might fall against it and get burned or cause a fire. We can't afford to build a brick chimney from the ground up, and wonder if there was some way we could closet it to make it fireproof.

You could box in the lower part of the pipe with a cement-asbestos wallboard, but we would leave the upper part open to permit the heat of the stovepipe to escape into the room. It could, however, be enclosed with a perforated metal grille. Your building material dealer should be able to supply the wallboard, and the sheet metal shop furnish the perforated grille and moldings to hold the sheets in place. Leave several inches of air space between the pipe and the wallboard.

CLOSED ROOMS

We rent out a flat, and our tenants keep three rooms closed—two bedrooms and the pantry. They claim they cannot sleep in warm rooms. Those rooms get very cold in zero weather. I surmise the tenants think they are saving on fuel bills. We would like to know if this will do any damage to the plaster walls. We think it will, since they open the rooms occasionally. We are afraid that when the heat gets into the rooms, something will happen to the walls and perhaps crack them. Can you advise us?

Keeping the rooms very cold might cause excessive sweating on the walls when warm air containing a fair amount of humidity seeps from other rooms. A continued condition of this kind may cause paint to peel and plaster eventually to disintegrate. We don't think any serious cracking will develop. However, it's not wise to shut off heat from rooms, and we don't think much fuel saving would result, because some of the heat from the other rooms will be passing through the walls. Heat always penetrates through various parts of a structure to the cold side.

NOISY FURNACE TOO CLOSE

Our furnace in the utility room sits right against my bedroom wall. During the winter months, the fan running for so long a time is very annoying, especially at night when I'm trying to sleep. I keep my register closed, but can still hear the fan. The furnace people have slowed down the fan as far as they possibly can. Can something be done about this situation?

Building a false wall of furring strips and some type of wallboard or paneling, out of contact with the present wall, should help a great deal. Filling the space between with thick blanket insulation will help still more. If you can slip a panel or two of sound-deadening tile between the furnace and the wall, that will also help deaden the sounds.

SERVICING GAS FURNACE

Is it really necessary to have a professional furnace cleaner to clean a gas furnace? If so, how often should this be done? I thought that changing filters at proper intervals (two or three times during a heating season) was all that was necessary.

Regular inspection by a cleaning service is highly recommended. This should be done annually, before the start of the heating season. Gas furnaces require cleaning, occasional adjustment, and oiling to assure long, satisfactory service.

TOO HIGH GAS HEATING BILL

We have a conversion burner in our furnace, and our gas bills in the winter are very high. Would lining the furnace with firebrick cut down the gas bill any? It is a gravity furnace.

Have a heating serviceman check the installation and its adjustment. If the burner is correctly installed and adjusted, the heat loss may be due to insufficient wall insulation or inadequate weather stripping around the outside of the doors, windows, etc. We doubt if lining the furnace with firebrick would make any appreciable difference in your fuel consumption. Have you checked the size of your gas bills with neighbors having similar houses and heating requirements?

HIGH FUEL CONSUMPTION

We recently built a double flat, using two independent heating systems. Our heating bill upstairs is running almost double the amount of the one downstairs. The gas company has tested both units and advises that they are in good order. One-inch rock wool blanket was used in the walls, and one-and-one-half-inch insulation was used in the attic. Would closing the air vents in the attic lower the heat loss?

The reason for the greater fuel consump-

tion is that there is not enough insulation in the attic space. There should be between 3 and 4 inches of rock wool or fiberglass insulation. Closing the vents may cause trouble with condensation and frost on the underside of the roof during cold weather. Keep them open.

INSUFFICIENT HEAT

My small house is of brick veneer construction, and we heat it with a converted gas furnace. My bills are as high as $50 per month, higher than those of some larger homes of the same type. It is never warm enough. What could be the cause? The parlor and kitchen, and even the bathroom walls, are ice-cold. One can't sit near the windows, which face the wind, even with storm windows on. What do you advise?

If wind comes through the windows despite a storm sash, both outer and inner windows are not properly fitted. The permanent windows should be weather-stripped. We also suspect that the furnace or the burner is undersized and does not furnish enough heat for the rooms. The heat outlets in the various rooms may not be large enough. All these

Figure 11-5. When painting a radiator, use regular flat paint.

things should be checked by a competent heating contractor. Insulation in the attic will help reduce heat loss, resulting in more comfort and fuel savings.

HAMMERING GAS FURNACE

A new gas furnace was installed less than a year ago in our house. Whenever it is in use, it bangs most of the time, as though someone were down there hammering. We called the dealer who installed it, but he seems unable to repair this hammering. Do you have any suggestions?

The hammering may be due to expansion and contraction of the metal of the heating pipes, creating vibration in the lines. Check the supports of the lines, especially of the horizontal lengths, and tighten any loose supports or install additional ones if they are spaced too widely apart. If this isn't the cause of the hammering, I recommend your getting in touch with your local gas company or the furnace manufacturer.

VENTED GAS HEATER?

A room on the rear of my house is heated with an unvented gas heater; the thermostat is controlled for 70°. A door connects the room to the rest of the house. I am not bothered with fumes, or with oxygen being exhausted, but I am troubled with high humidity. Would it be worthwhile to exchange the space heater for a vented type to decrease the humidity in the room and prevent moisture from forming on the windows?

Certainly, a vented gas heater should be installed. For every 1,000 cubic feet of gas burned, as much as 2,000 cubic feet of water vapor may result; condensed, this is the equivalent of approximately 88 pounds of water.

WARM COLD WATER

We have a gas hot-water heater. Could this have any effect on our cold water? The cold water runs quite warm when it is first turned on. We have to run it quite a while before it becomes pleasant enought to drink.

The heater may be overheating the water so that it backs up into the water main. If so, closer control on the water heater, or a check valve, is advisable. Gas water heaters have thermostats, and the temperature can be lowered to prevent overheating. However, another cause might be the proximity of the hot- and cold-water pipes, so that when the cold water stands still it picks up heat from the nearby hot-water pipe. Insulation on the hot-water pipe would overcome this.

NOISY GAS HEATER

I was sold a larger gas heater than my brick bungalow needed. The gas man said this furnace is enough for a three- or four-flat building. It heats very well and fast, although it is expensive because it overruns the thermostat by several degrees before it shuts off. But the trouble is the vibration from the heat pipes attached to the joists above it. It makes my bedroom floor vibrate terribly. Can I do anything about this?

You can help tame the vibrations by surrounding the pipes at each support with firm cushioning material. Perhaps the gas company can do something to cushion the supports for the fan too, without affecting efficiency.

CLEANING GAS BURNERS

The burners on my gas range seem to be so grease-caked that they don't burn quite as well as before. Is it safe for me to try to clean them? If so, how?

If your burners are easily removable, dunk them in a solution of oven cleaner. If they are not removable, or it seems like too much of a production to remove them, shut off the pilot and wipe the burners with a cloth wrung out in oven cleaner. You can also clear holes and partially clogged supply lines with a hairpin, proving again that a hairpin is a remarkably handy tool.

LUBRICANT FOR STOVE VALVES

What should one use as a lubricant on the manual "on" and "off" valves on a gas stove? Some of ours have become a little hard to operate of late.

Penetrating "dripless" oil-type lubricants are now available at most hardware and paint dealers; use the thin, lightweight kind. These come in ready-to-use, spouted containers. Ordinary laundry soap will also serve as a lubricant in an emergency.

GAS-FIRED ROOM HEATERS

I recently purchased a summer cottage which is being converted for year-round use. It is built of concrete blocks with an enclosed porch of frame construction. The basement is 5 feet high. We have a gas range with a space heating unit. I want to install a wall-type heater run by gas. How does this compare in cost with electricity or oil? Must the gas units be vented?

All gas-fired, as well as oil-fired, space heaters should be vented to the outdoors in order to exhaust the vapors given off by the consumed fuel. We're sorry to say that to give fuel cost comparisons is not practical here, because these costs vary so much in different communities. The various dealers in the fuels involved can give you some help along these lines. You might consider the installation of a forced-air heating furnace that is suspended from the joists in your basement. Local heating contractors know about this and could give you further information. A furnace of this type would deliver heat by way of ducts into the various rooms, thus assuring uniform distribution.

BIRD'S NEST CAUSING ODOR?

Recently we have noticed an odor of gas in the house. Just a little at first, but it has been growing stronger. Can you suggest a cause? We have a gas range and a gas hot-water heater.

Our first instinct is that you should call the gas company. They don't like gas straying around the homes of customers and usually send an emergency crew in short order. We can suggest one possibility, especially in springtime: You might go up on the roof, or wherever the gas vent comes out, and see if a pair of sparrows or starlings are setting up housekeeping in there. This can clog a vent pipe in no time and cause odor backup.

SMOKING OIL BURNER

Our oil burner smokes quite a bit. What causes this, and what should I do about it?

Smoking usually indicates an undersupply of air and can be cured either by increasing the flow of air or by reducing the flow of oil. The adjustment should be made with a full knowledge of the burner and of the heating effect to be produced. An incorrect adjustment results in either a wastage of oil or insufficient heating. But remember that some smoking is inevitable. When a properly adjusted burner has been in operation for a few minutes, the interior of the firebox is hot enough to vaporize oil as it leaves the nozzle.

The mixture of oil vapor and air that forms is complete and burns without smoke. But when a burner starts up after a period of idleness—overnight, for example—the firebox is so cool that the first shots of oil remain liquid. Oil collects on the interior parts and, with later heating, turns to smoke and soot. The soot may eventually burn off from the burner parts, although in some designs it leads to clogging of the nozzle. In such cases, the burner is arranged for easy cleaning. Much of the smoke that forms is deposited as soot in the interior passages of the heater, often in such quantity as to interfere with the flow of heated gases. In steam and hot-water boilers the passages should be cleaned at frequent intervals.

OIL BURNER TURNS ON AND OFF

On occasion, our oil burner turns on and off at the start of intervals. Is this normal? If not, how can I stop this?

This is usually because of an interference with the flow of oil. One cause may be the clogging of the strainer through which the oil passes on its way to the nozzle. Another is that the tank is nearly empty; bubbles of air are entering the feed pipe, followed by small flows of oil. It's a matter of wisdom always to keep the tank at least one-quarter filled. A third reason may be the soiling of the contacts of the thermostat or other devices that control the burner. To clean the contacts, place a slip of paper with a hard surface (not newspaper) between them, press the contacts lightly against it, and pull the paper.

OIL BURNER BECAME NOISY

After a number of years of quiet service, our oil burner has become noisy. Can this be repaired, or do we need a new burner?

Noise in an oil burner that has previously been quiet is usually due to worn parts and can be stopped by replacements. A roar, apparently from the flame, may be caused by the construction of the burner, although in most modern designs this noise has been eliminated. Another cause of roar may be in the chimney flue; its size and height may put it "into tune" with the burner noise, and the resulting effect is that of an organ pipe. This can be avoided through reconstruction: raising the chimney or making other alterations to change the period of vibration of the column of air in the flue.

DRIPPY OIL BURNER

During the course of installation, some oil from the oil burner dripped onto the concrete floor. How can I get this stain out?

Pour dry portland cement on it, about 2 inches thick. Leave it on for a few days, so that it can blot up the oil. It usually does very well, especially with new stains. If it's not all out, repeat the process. You can also use dry hydrated lime, or the absorbent granules so many garages spread on their floors to absorb oil and grease spills.

FUMES FROM AN OIL HEATER

We have an oil heater in our house, and when the wind blows, the fumes come back into the rooms. Can you tell me what can be done to stop this? We put a chimney cap on one chimney which swings with the wind, but it did not help.

Frequently, the condition is caused by having the top of the chimney below the level of a peak rooftop. The top should be at least 2 feet above the highest point of a gable roof and 4 feet above a flat roof. A chimney that is blanketed by a nearby tree or tall building will also cause a back draft. It would be of help to install an automatic draft regulator. Your dealer in heating equipment can furnish it.

WHAT'S BEST LOCATION FOR OIL TANK?

We are building a house and are not sure where the fuel oil tank should be stored. Are there any restrictions about placement? Do you have any recommendations about whether it should be in the basement or buried outdoors?

In most communities, there are ordinances against tanks of larger capacity than 275 gallons located in the basement. Often two such tanks are okay. After making sure that you are conforming to local codes, give full consideration to the convenience of the oil delivery truck. If the tank is buried outdoors near the house, it's a good idea to protect the hose connection it would be better yet to put it in a small pit, with a cover. A "snow stake" saves searching time when it is buried under that white stuff.

OIL TANK LEAK?

There seems to be a very slight leak in our fuel oil tank. I don't notice any leakage now, but during the heating season there is a little oily moisture on the cellar floor.

Since the oily moisture occurs during the heating season, we would suspect that either the oil burner needs adjustment because of improper mixture of air and oil or some parts of the boiler or furnace have doors that don't close tightly, allowing oil particles to escape before being burned. We would recommend having your oil burner serviceman check the installation and the operating efficiency.

NOISY OIL TANK

A hum has developed inside our oil tank. What causes it?

This is because of the vibration set up by the burner mechanism. It can be stopped by wrapping the tank in a soft covering, such as felted hair. Another method is to brace the tank against the ceiling or nearby wall. If the hum is from a vibrating pipe, which is possible, the pipe can be stiffened by bracing. Another possible cure is to gradually close the valve in the supply pipe, or to install an anti-hum valve.

FULL OIL TANK

Should I leave an oil tank full or empty it in the spring?

The oil tank should be completely filled. If left partly or completely empty, moisture will condense on the uncovered inside surfaces; that moisture will drain into the oil and later may cause the oil burner to work sporadically or to shut down completely.

DON'T LEAVE TANK BURIED

Last fall I switched from oil heat to natural gas. Mechanically, this was no problem. But my 550-gallon empty fuel tank is still in the ground. I didn't think much about this until a friend said that with all the water in the ground after the snow melts, it's apt to pop the tank right out of the ground. Is this true?

Indeed it is. Quite a long time ago, we were inclined to consider this risk somewhat overrated. But when some very helpful and constructive friends sent us statistics and photographic evidence, we quickly became a believer in the immense power of underground water. It can easily float a tank like this clear out of the ground, and if any flowers, shrubbery, nice lawns, or paths are in the way, that's just too bad. The safest thing is have the tank removed as soon as possible. The second safest thing is to fill it with water until it can be moved out.

CONDITIONER NEEDS HELP

Last summer it seemed to me that my room air conditioner ran a great deal of the time. While it did a good job of cooling, I should think this nearly constant operation would shorten its effective life. If so, what could I do about this?

It's possible that the door(s) to this room may not be as tight in the frames as they should be. As a result, your expensively cooled air can leak out, thus raising the room's temperature and therefore making the conditioner work longer (for which you pay the power company). If so, we would suggest your fastening regular weather-stripping felt around the edges of the door(s) to keep the cooled air in. If the windows aren't shaded from the direct blast of the afternoon sun, this could also contribute to the conditioner's running overtime.

HARD-WORKING CONDITIONER

I purchased a room air conditioner second-hand, and it has been running very well. But lately it seems to be running quite a lot more than it did at first. Did I get stuck with a lemon?

Not necessarily, by any means. Maybe the filters only need cleaning. If they are getting clogged with dirt, dust, soot, and such, it really can block air passage into the room. And if the cooled air isn't coming in the way it should, the motor has to keep on trying to satisfy the demands of the thermostat. How is the airtightness around your door? Often you can keep a room a lot cooler and save running time on the conditioner if you run regular weather-stripping felt around the door.

LEAVE HOUSE UNHEATED?

We plan to go away for the winter this year. If we turn off all heat and drain everything, could this damage the house? Our house is new, and we have dry walls. Would the extreme cold crack the walls? We have considered draining all water pipes and traps, but leaving the heat on at a minimum, to keep the house temperature above freezing. What do you recommend?

I agree that there's a risk of cracking the walls with no heat for so long. We would go for your complete draining but keeping the minimum heat. If your insulation is tight, this shouldn't cause too high a heating bill.

CHAPTER 12

CHIMNEYS AND FIREPLACES

All fireplaces and fuel-burning equipment such as stoves and furnaces require some type of chimney. The chimney must be designed and built so that it produces sufficient draft to supply an adequate quantity of fresh air to the fire and to expel smoke and gases emitted by the fire or heating equipment.

Chimney Problems

To accomplish its mission, the chimney flue must have sufficient area to provide ample draft; for a small-house heater, the flue area shouldn't be less than 8 by 12 inches, or 100 square inches in another shape. The flue should be tight for its entire length, and preferably lined with a fireclay flue lining. That the draft may be free, the top of the chimney shouldn't be less than 4 feet above a flat roof or 2 feet above the highest point of a gable roof. The flue should be the same size to the very top; it's not unusual for a flue to be made smaller at the top or to be capped with a pipe extension that is smaller than the flue. Both of these will check the draft by choking it. There shouldn't be more than one opening into a flue. When two heat sources are connected to one flue, each will interfere with the draft of the other.

Following are conditions that will interfere with a free chimney draft and so prevent the proper operation of the fire:

1. Obstructions in the chimney.
2. A projection into the chimney, as, for instance, a masonry projection or the end of a beam supported on the chimney structure.
3. A break in the chimney lining, or a defect in the masonry that permits the leakage of air.
4. Projection of the smoke pipe part way across the flue.
5. An air leak around the cleanout door at the base.
6. The smoke pipe entering the chimney on a down slant.
7. Two or more pipe openings into one flue.
8. The size of the flue contracted at the top, or a small-size pipe extension.
9. The top of the chimney below the high point of the roof, or blanketed by a nearby tall tree or building.
10. The flue clogged with soot or dust, especially at a point where it makes a bend.

A straight flue can be examined from the cleanout door at the bottom or through the smoke-pipe opening by using a small mirror that's inserted into the flue at such an angle that the length of the flue will be reflected. A flashlight can be used to advantage.

A chimney can be tested for tightness by making a smoke test. A fire is built, and when it's burning briskly, a square yard or so of tar paper is placed on it. When the smoke from this appears, the flue opening is covered with a board or piece of wet carpet. The smoke in the flue will then seek another outlet and will disclose any leaks that may be in the masonry.

A fireclay or stainless steel flue lining is a protection to the masonry of the chimney and a safeguard against fire. Without a flue lining, the mortar in the masonry may eventually deteriorate and fall out. The openings thus made not only will allow air to leak into the chimney but may permit the escape of glowing soot particles and highly heated gases. The masonry of a chimney should be watched to note whether this condition is taking place. When the masonry becomes loose and can be displaced by jabbing it with a screwdriver or ice pick, the chimney should be taken down to a point at which hard mortar is found, and rebuilt. Not to take this precaution is to invite a fire risk.

Fireplace Problems

A fireplace in a closed room cannot be expected to carry a good fire because of the lack of a sufficient current of air to support combustion. A fireplace will smoke for any or all of the following reasons:

1. Chimney too low.
2. Flue clogged.
3. Wrong construction of throat and wind shelf.
4. Throat damper closed
5. Opening too high for the width, which can be corrected by setting a sheet of metal across the top of the opening. The proper width for this can be found by experiment with boards or even heavy paper.

The condition of a fireplace flue can often be examined from the fireplace by the use of a mirror, with or without a flashlight. A fireplace with square sides can be made more effective by a lining of brick or other masonry

to give the sides and the back a slope toward the front.

To prevent danger from flying embers, a spark box can be set on the top of the flue. This is made of heavy wire netting with meshes an inch or so square. The netting shouldn't be laid flat on the flue top, for the meshes would clog with ash and the draft would be choked. The netting should be formed into a five-sided box, long enough for the open end to go downward into the flue for a sufficient distance to give support. The rest of the box should extend at least 12 inches above the flue top. Wind blowing across the box will keep the meshes cleared of ashes.

Building a Wood Fire. For quick lighting and steady burning in a fireplace, andirons should be used. A large log is placed in the back, a slightly smaller log next to it in front, and a still smaller one on top of the two. Paper and kindlings are then put underneath for the full length of the logs. Sheets of newspaper, folded in quarters and then crumpled hard, make an excellent substitute for kindling wood.

Thick smoking on starting a fire is usually due to the air in the flue becoming too dense and heavy to be quickly started into movement. This smoking can be obviated by twisting newspaper into a long spill, lighting one end, and sticking it through the throat opening. The intense heat at the base of the flue will create a draft, and the fire can be started without difficulty.

Questions and Answers

In addition to the chimney and fireplace problems already discussed, the following are some questions, with their answers, that frequently concern homeowners about these two important items.

CLEANING A CHIMNEY

Before the heating season comes around again, I'd like to have everything in apple-pie order. One thing I'm sure needs attention, and that's my chimney. Is it a difficult job for a reasonably active homeowner to clean it?

Frankly, we do our best to discourage anyone but professionals from working around steep roofs, and especially chimneys; the risk is too great. Besides, the professional chimney cleaner will do a better job. But if you're determined to tackle the job yourself, you can do it by either of these ways: Fasten a tire chain to a light rope, and slowly lower it down the chimney. As you lower it, swing it with a circular motion, so that the chain scrapes off the soot as it goes down. Or you can stuff a burlap bag with straw, weight it with a couple of bricks, and lower it. It will loosen the soot as it goes down.

SMOKE STAINS ON CHIMNEY

Smoke from our oil burner has caused black stains on the chimney. How can we stop the smoking? Can the stains be removed?

The air and oil mixture used in the oil burner may require adjusting; have your serviceman check the burner. The smoke stains can be removed. Wet down the masonry with clear water; then scrub with a mechanic's hand soap that comes in paste form and contains fine sand. Rinse thoroughly afterward with clear water. If the top of the chimney isn't sloped from the opening to the outer edge, make this slope with cement mortar. Installing a piece of flue tile to extend 6 to 8 inches above the chimney top would also help reduce the possibility of smoke stains.

DIRTY STONE CHIMNEY

I bought an old frame house and had the exterior covered with an imitation stone and aluminum siding, but forgot to have the outside stone chimney cleaned or sandblasted. Stone men have advised me that lumberyards sell a cleaning preparation, but none of them seem to know about it. What can I use?

We have an idea that the stone workers had in mind a cement-base paint, which comes in powder form and is mixed with water. Some paint dealers also sell it. This coating, of course, will cover the stone completely. The other method would be to wet down the stone with water and scrub the chimney with a strong detergent. If the chimney is not a large one, a good cleaner is a paste type of mechanic's hand soap that contains a fine sand. Use plenty of hot water with the soap. Thorough rinsing should follow.

LEAKAGE AROUND CHIMNEY

Our house is not quite a year old, but there is leakage around the chimney. It has been caulked and recaulked several times, but there is still a leak. We figure it must come

through the chimney. Is there anything on the market for that?

If the masonry absorbs water, a couple of coats of a transparent waterproofing containing silicones may solve your problem. In some instances, however, it is necessary to coat the walls with a dampproof, cement-base paint. It comes in powder form and is mixed with water. Both these materials are usually handled by dealers in masonry materials. If you are located in or near a large city, you should be able to find dealers in waterproofing compounds that sell the above. We're assuming that you have checked the flashings between the roof and chimney, and also the condition of the mortar joints. If not, you should do so before coating the masonry.

CHIMNEY LEAKS MAPLE SYRUP

I am having trouble with the chimney of this old house. It looks like dark maple syrup running down the sides, on walls. Also the stain is starting on the ceilings.

That dark stuff is condensation, which heat is driving through the masonry. It could be assisted by rain working through cracks in the mortar around the chimney cap, as well as between the brick or stones of the masonry. Cracks and crumbling mortar should be repaired. Also ask a good chimney mason about improving the draft, too. If this can't be worked out well, then consider having a stainless steel flue liner put in. The improved results could make it well worthwhile.

KEEP PLASTER OFF CHIMNEY

We bought a development house recently, about eight years old. I saw that the chimney space above the mantel was covered with wallpaper which looked quite new. Recently, during a stretch of very warm weather, I noticed the wallpaper cracking — so much so, in fact, I could see the plaster underneath was also cracked. I cannot repaint until I repair the plaster, I'm sure. What should I do?

Repairing the plaster won't help at all. The basic trouble is that the plaster should not have been put in contact with the chimney at all. It should have been on furring strips, to allow a dead-air insulating space between. The reason for this is because masonry is always cooler. When plaster is applied, it also assumes the cooler temperature of the masonry. When warm house air strikes this cooler surface, it condenses. This dampness can work through, into the plaster, eventually causing it to crack. The only answers are: (1) Cover the area with painter's cloth, a lightweight type of canvas, which is applied like wallpaper. This can be painted or papered. It is sold in paint supply stores and some wall-covering stores. (2) Remove all the plaster, put up 1-inch furring strips, and then cover with panels of dry wall, wallboard, or paneling.

CHIMNEY MORTAR FALLING OUT

Recently I cemented some roof flashing, and noticed that the mortar of the chimney seems to be falling out in very small pieces. I don't know much about this, but it seems to me this condition should be corrected before it gets worse. How do I do this job?

You're quite right about attending to this before it gets worse. Buy some patching mortar and a small pointed mason's trowel, if you don't already own one. Using a sharp, pointed tool, like a beer can opener, rake out all the loose powdery stuff. Give the chimney a good soaking with the garden hose so that old mortar and brick won't blot water from the mortar. Mix the mortar pretty stiff, so you can just work it, and trowel it in along the cracks. If possible, try to keep your repair damp for a week, for slow, proper curing. A spray from the garden hose will do nicely.

CHIMNEY CAP CRACK

There is a small crack in the rain cap over the top of the chimney. What can I use to repair this? The cap is made of concrete.

Fill the crack with latex patching concrete, available at masonry supply dealers and large hardware stores.

SCREEN FOR CHIMNEY CAP

Last year we were bothered not only by squirrels getting into the attic, but by several pairs of chimney swifts nesting in our chimney. We finally got the squirrels out, and the swifts eventually moved away. But before the new season starts, I would like to fasten a wire screen, with ½-inch mesh, over the top of the chimney, to keep out the birds and the squirrels. My question is, how seriously will this interfere with the draft?

The interference will be practically zero. Go right ahead and have the screen installed. But make it so that it can be removed from time to time, in case it becomes obstructed with leaves, small twigs, etc.

DOWNHILL WIND MAKES CHIMNEY SMOKE

Our house is located at the bottom of a fair-sized slope, which is probably the cause for some trouble with our chimney. Whenever the wind blows down the hill, it blows smoke back down the chimney and out into the living room. Needless to say, this is very unpleasant. But a wind from any other direction is no problem at all. Can we do something about this?

You most certainly can. Have a chimney mason fix you some type of chimney cap to block the downhill wind; that's all. This can range from a flat piece of slate held a few inches above the chimney top to a complicated arch or dome.

CHIMNEY WAILS IN WIND

We moved into a new house with a fireplace on an inside wall backed to the kitchen. Even when there is only a slight wind, the chimney echoes the wails and eerie noises of the wind. The stronger the wind, the louder the wails. We have lived in houses with chimneys before, but this experience is new. What is the answer?

Through some quirk of location, construction, and size, the chimney acts like a pipe organ when air blows across the top. A chimney cap should cure this by breaking up the air flow.

FRANKLIN STOVE DOESN'T DRAW

How can I improve the draft of my Franklin stove? It is in the basement, located 3 feet from the chimney and attached 1 foot below my furnace flue. I have already increased the height of my chimney to 5 feet above the roof peak. I live in a ranch home between two larger homes and also have tall trees in the backyard. Could this be the problem? Unless we close the stove doors, the cellar gets extremely smoky.

It's certainly possible that the tall trees and neighboring houses can mess up the draft. But if we interpret you correctly, the stove and your furnace share the flue. This can result in real downdrafts and very inefficient heating. It's far better if each heat source has its own flue.

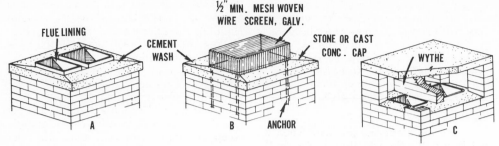

Figure 12-1. Top construction of chimneys. (A) Good method of finishing top of chimney; flue lining extends 4 inches above cap. (B) Spark arrester or bird screen. (C) Hood to keep out rain.

PREFABRICATED CHIMNEY

Our fireplace chimney must be replaced. Can I use one of the prefabricated types?

Prefabricated chimneys can be used for furnaces, heaters, and incinerators as well as for fireplaces. The chimneys are tested and approved by Underwriters' Laboratories, Inc., and other nationally recognized testing laboratories, and are rapidly being accepted for use by building codes in many communities. The actual installation instructions will depend on the model of chimney selected. Be sure to follow the instructions to the letter.

SMOKE DRIFTS BACK FROM FIREPLACE

Although our fireplace chimney is not clogged, we have a problem with smoke drifting back into the living room from the fire. How can we correct this?

Have you verified that the damper is fully open? Sometimes just opening a window in the room for an inch will improve the air circulation and prevent the smoking. If there are large trees around your house, they may be interfering with proper draft and air currents above the chimney opening. Or the chimney itself may not be high enough to provide proper draft; it should be at least 4 feet above a flat roof or 2 feet above the highest point of a gable roof. If the chimney flue is undersized, or smaller at the top, thereby checking the draft, this could contribute to the problem. Placing a metal hood across the top third of the fireplace opening sometimes eliminates the smoking. This increases the draft because of the reduced opening.

CHANGE FIREPLACE SIZE?

Our fireplace works quite well—we really have no complaints—but it is a very large opening in the room paneling. Would it be possible to make it lower? If so, what materials should be used?

A good fireplace is made on a predetermined proportion for most efficient operation. So any changes contemplated should be tested first. With the fire ready to be lit, hold a strip of cardboard or equivalent across the top part of the opening, extending down as far as you want the height lowered. Then see how the fire draws. If it draws satisfactorily, consult a good chimney mason about installing a permanent strip of metal, or (much more costly) rebricking this area.

REPLACING FIREBRICK

Some of the bricks in the rear of our fireplace opening are broken. How do I replace them?

Clip out the damaged bricks with a cold chisel, and replace them with firebricks (not common bricks, because they can't take the heat). Also, use fireclay mortar rather than standard brick mortar. Wet the surface thoroughly; apply the fireclay to the brick; then press the brick into place. Keep the surface moist as you work, and be sure not to start a fire in the fireplace for at least 48 hours.

95 PERCENT EFFECTIVE FIREPLACE

My fireplace is only 95 percent effective. It smokes just enough to make the living room uncomfortable. Is it possible to build a small hood at the top of the fireplace opening to force the escaping smoke up the chimney? I have a fireplace down in the cellar that is connected to the same flue. If the fireplace must be looked at by an expert, where do I find one?

The smoking of the fireplace may be due to draft interference because two units are connected to a single flue. A separate flue should be provided for each fireplace for this reason. We strongly recommend having a professional inspect your fireplace; consult your classified telephone directory under "Chimney Builders and Repairers."

SOOT ON FIREPLACE BRICK

We have been getting an offensive odor from our wood-burning fireplace when it's not in use. We thought it was ashes in the wall, but after cleaning them out, the odor is still there. Soot destroyer was used, but the black deposit is still on the brick. How can we take off the smoke stain from the brick?

There may be a deposit of a creosotelike substance in the upper section of the chimney that is causing the odor. Keep the fireplace damper closed, except when using it; then, to reduce the odor, use only dry, well-seasoned firewood. Green wood causes an accumulation of the above substance. To remove the soot from the brick, brush off as much of it as possible with a stiff, dry brush; then wet down the masonry with water. Scrub with a mechanic's hand soap that comes in paste form and contains fine sand, using lots of hot water. Rinse off the soap with water.

CHEAP FLUE CLEANER

I am being bothered by soot and other deposits on the lining of my chimney flue. I can't afford professional service right now, and I am frankly afraid of working on a sloping roof. I would appreciate any suggestions.

Try scattering several handfuls of ordinary table salt into the next fire. This is one of the principal chemicals used in chimney-cleaning compounds. If you notice an improvement, continue. If not, it may be that your draft isn't forceful enough to get the salty vapors where they can do the job. You could also get some cleaning compounds (more efficient than just salt) at plumbing supply houses.

IS A FIREPLACE DAMPER NECESSARY?

We have a summer cottage which we'd like to make into a year-round house so we can be comfortable if we come up on weekends when the weather is cold. One of the main things I want is a good, big, old-fashioned

fireplace. Now what about a damper? Do I need one or not? One of the stonemasons bidding on the job says I don't need one. Others tell me he's completely wrong. What's your opinion?

Put us down as agreeing that we're most emphatically on the side of having a damper; in fact, we wouldn't have a fireplace without one. Not only will it control the drafts over the fire, but in the winter you can close it down to keep out snow. Not only that, when it's closed, it will prevent cold drafts from coming in, and also reduce chances of smoke backing up into the room. Fortunately, if the fireplace is of "standard" construction with a smoke shelf at the back to constrict the opening just above the fire chamber, it's not difficult to install a damper. Measure the opening at the narrowest point, and purchase a ready-made damper to fit as closely as possible. Most damper units are held in place with metal pins or screws set into mortar joints on each side. To start the pins or screws, drill or cut the holes with a masonry bit or star drill and hammer. The joint, if any, between the flue and the damper should be sealed with fireclay.

PREFABRICATED FIREPLACE

We'd like to install a fireplace in our family room. Could you tell us how the prefabricated ones are installed?

The basic part of the prefabricated fireplace is a specially insulated metal fireplace shell. Since it's light in weight, it can be set directly on the floor without the heavy footing required for masonry fireplaces. A prefabricated fireplace is easy to install (exact installation procedures depend on the type and style selected) and can be installed freestanding or flush against a wall. Most units only require a hole in the wall or roof for the chimney, possibly fastening to the house structure, but seldom necessitate much building in.

FIREPLACE SLOW STARTER

Once the fire really gets going, our fireplace works just fine. But it's very slow to start—a real reluctant dragon. There doesn't seem to be any draft to speak of, and smoke comes back into the room. Is there something basically wrong with the design?

The trouble is in the chimney, most likely. It's full of a column of cold, soggy air. You have to get that mass of air moving upward so that the draft can start working. Do this: Get

Figure 12-2. A freestanding prefabricated fireplace will add to any room.

your fire all laid and ready. Then crumple a couple of sheets of newspaper, light them, and thrust them up the chimney as far as you can. This sudden heat will stir that stagnant air into action, so that when you light your fire, it will catch the way it should. Be sure to remember to open the damper before lighting a fire.

CRACKS REAPPEAR

Our living room wall, on both sides of the fireplace, has been repaired twice and repapered on account of cracking. Could you suggest anything we could do to eliminate the cracking?

We presume the cracking occurs in the corners. If, after proper cutting out and patching, cracks reappear, it is possible that the corners need reinforcing. Cut away about a 6-inch-wide strip of plaster on each side of the corner; then fasten in place what is known as corner lath, and replaster. If your local dealer does not carry it in stock, have him cut 12-inch-wide strips of metal lath; then bend them at right angles, and install them as above.

DRAFTY GAP BETWEEN FIREPLACE AND PANELING

In our family room, where the brick fireplace meets the wall paneling, there is a slight gap. A draft comes through here steadily and makes the room chilly. What can I do to fix this?

Stuff the gap with homemade papier-mâché, which you can poke in far enough so that it won't be conspicuous. It is made this way: Into half a pail of hot, soapy water, shred a couple of pages of newspaper. Swish them around until mushy. Squeeze a pinch of this when it is moderately dry, and poke it into the gap with a screwdriver. Use all you need to be sure the draft is blocked. When this dries, it will be rock-firm. If you've done your stuffing carefully, there'll be no place for drafts to work through.

SOOT ON FIREPLACE

We have a Butler rock wall with a fireplace. An occasional slipped log and resulting smoke caused a much darker gray area above the opening almost to the ceiling. I'm afraid to experiment with cleaning it, as we did this to my mother's wall in a similar circumstance, with disastrous results. Can you suggest a remedy?

Cleaning and etching preparations for stone and masonry surfaces are now available at most masonry supply and large paint and hardware dealers; follow the label directions carefully. Or scrub the surface with powdered pumice and water to remove the surface deposits; or use fine steel wool and a mechanic's hand paste containing sand, followed by ample rinsing with clear water to remove all trace of the cleaner. To remove deep stains, make a paste of powdered whiting and a nonflammable liquid spot remover and cover the discolored area with a thick layer; replace with fresh paste when dry; repeat until the staining is removed.

PROTECTING FIREPLACE BRICK

I have a fireplace of white roman brick. Due to the damper being closed, the front of it became smoked. Muriatic acid, in any strength, would not clean it. Therefore we took the face of the fireplace apart and refaced the brick, putting it back again. Is there anything to put on the brick to prevent its becoming smoked up in case of damper trouble again? Smoking grays the brick, which is quite porous.

Muriatic acid shouldn't be used to remove smoke. Use a stiff brush or steel wool and a scrubbing powder or mechanic's hand soap containing sand, followed by ample rinsing with clear water to remove all trace of the cleaner. If the soiling is too deep for this method of cleaning, rub the brickwork with a carborundum block, available at paint and hardware dealers; this will expose fresh, smooth surface. A chemical preparation is now available at some large masonry supply dealers for cleaning stone and stonelike surfaces; it leaves a protective coating. Follow the manufacturer's directions carefully, and use the preparation for rough, porous surfaces. Sealing the face of the brick with a transparent water emulsion sealer finish for concrete, made by a nationally known wax manufacturer and available at janitor supply outlets, may retard smoke staining.

CANDLE WAX ON STONE

We had a fire in our fireplace one evening, and it melted some candles which we had on the shelf over the opening. The fireplace is of Tennessee stone. The melted wax soaked into the stone. What would you suggest we try to use on this stone to remove the wax?

If the stone is smooth, you can take out the grease by covering the wax with blotting paper; then place a hot iron over the blotter. When stone surfaces are rough, it's more difficult to take off wax. Scrape off the thickest part of the smears with a knife blade; then cover the spots with a paste mixture of powdered whiting and naphtha. Apply this in a thick layer, and allow it to remain until it's dry. Be very careful of fire; ventilate the room thoroughly, and don't have an open flame or even a lighted cigarette anywhere near.

GREASE STAINS ON STONE SEAT

How can we remove grease stains from the crab orchard stone seat that is in front of our fireplace? The stone is beautiful, and we never thought about staining when we built the fireplace.

Make a thick paste of powdered whiting or fuller's earth and a nonflammable liquid spot remover. Put a layer at least ½ inch thick over the stains, and cover it with a sheet of plastic or glass to retard evaporation. The spot remover acts as a solvent on the grease and the powder like a blotter to draw it out. When the paste is discolored or dried, replace it with fresh. When as much of the stain as possible has been removed, scrub it with a strong solution of trisodium phosphate and hot water, followed by rinsing with clear water to remove all trace of the trisodium phosphate.

CLEANING NEW ROCK FIREPLACE

We have finished building a rock fireplace in our family room. We have been told to use acid to clean off the excess mortar and bring out the color of the rocks. Is there any finish that will bring out the color and give them a luster?

To remove the excess mortar: Moisten it with a solution of 1 part of muriatic acid in 20 parts of water (use a wooden vessel), and allow the solution to act for 2 to 3 minutes; then flush it off with plenty of water. This will soften the cement so that it can be scraped off. After cleaning the mortar off, be sure to neutralize the acid by washing the surface with a solution of 1 pint of ammonia in 2 gallons of water, followed by rinsing with clear water again. Be sure to wear old, heavy clothing, rubber gloves to protect your hands, and goggles to protect your eyes while working with the acid solution, which is highly corrosive. Put on a soaking coat of raw linseed oil, and remove the excess after a half hour; this will enhance the color of the stones.

DIRTY, SMOKY FIREPLACE STONES

Two years ago we purchased our 50-year-old house. We have a beautiful fireplace of large stones from different parts of the United States. With the years of smoke and dust, they are very dirty-looking. Is there any way these stones, and also the brick that lines the inside of the fireplace, could be cleaned?

First, remove as much as you can of the soot on both the stones and the brick with a vacuum or a brush. Then clean the stones and brick with a masonry-cleaning preparation, according to the label directions, available at masonry or building supply dealers. Or scrub them with a hot solution of 2 pounds of washing soda or trisodium phosphate dissolved in water. Or rub them with a paste of scratchless scouring powder and water, to which some household ammonia has been added. Or scrub them with a mechanic's hand soap containing sand. Whichever cleaner is used, rinse it off well afterward.

DARKENING BRICKS AROUND FIREPLACE

Our brand-new house has common brick around the fireplace. The color is that painfully new pink, which I don't like at all. Nor do I want to paint it. Is there a way to make the brick darker?

Yes. But try this on a test brick or two first: With a lavish hand, wipe linseed oil on the brick. Allow 2 hours for maximum absorption. Then vigorously wipe off all the excess. This step is vital; otherwise the brick will remain tacky. Let it dry for a week or 10 days; then repeat the entire process. This will darken the brick, giving it a richer shade. It's also an excellent antistain shield. It can keep foods, grease, etc., from staining your hearth.

WANTS TO STAIN FIREPLACE

Is it possible to use wood stain on a brick fireplace with a hearth that looks like concrete stone? Or is there some kind of finish other than paint to change the color? I want the different shadings of the used brick still to show through, and I know paint would hide this completely. But I would like a color other than gray for the hearth.

Use the process described in the preceding answer. It's a good way to darken and intensify the colors of the brick. And it may also change the hearth to a brownish tinge you'll like.

MAKING BRICKS STAINPROOF

We just moved into a house, about eight years old. It has a counter-top stove and oven set in a brick fireplace wall. I have finally scrubbed the bricks really clean, and would like to know how they can be sealed against food and greasy stains.

If a hardware store or lumberyard dealer can furnish you with a clear masonry stain which will do this, give it a try. To be sure, do a preview on an isolated brick or two. A good homemade method, which will also darken the brick a little, is to generously wipe on linseed oil. See p. 317 for instructions on how to apply it.

PAINT REMOVAL

We have a brick fireplace that has been painted. Is there any way to take the paint off the bricks successfully?

It's not possible to remove paint from the surfaces of rough-textured brick completely. If you could locate a building-cleaning contractor who has a sandblasting machine, he could remove the paint by the sandblast process. Oil-base paints can be removed from smooth surfaces with paint remover. After taking off the thickest part of the paint film, scrub with more of the paint remover, if you are using the nonflammable kind. Otherwise, you will have to take off the remainder by rubbing down the face of the brick with a coarse, abrasive stone, which, we may add, is not an easy job!

PAINT FOR FIREPLACE MORTAR

What kind of paint can we use for the mortar between the stones of our fireplace?

Paint the mortar with a cement paint, which comes in powder form to be mixed with water. Be sure all trace of grease, wax, soot, etc., is removed from the surface before applying the paint.

RUSTING FIREPLACE INTERIOR

The interior of my fireplace, which is made of iron, is rusting. What type of black paint should I use to remedy this condition?

Use a rust-removing preparation, available at most hardware and paint dealers, to remove all trace of the rust before applying any paint; follow the manufacturer's instructions. Or remove the rust with steel wool and turpentine. Be sure the surface of the iron is free of all trace of soot, grease, etc., before applying paint; then apply any good-quality black stove paint.

MOSAIC OVER FIREPLACE BRICKS?

Our rough fireplace bricks were painted over several times. To make them more attractive, we would like to cover them with mosaic tiles. Would it be safe to cover the bricks with wood, securely fastened, as a base for the mosaic tiles? If not, could I trowel cement mortar over the bricks and set the tiles in this?

Either method is okay in principle. However, if you have lots of small-to-tiny tiles which have to be set one at a time, you may find it a little easier with the wood foundation. With larger tiles or the types which have a backing of flexible mesh, either base will do fine. Remember, the more tile cement you can wipe off the face of the tiles while still damp will make final cleanup that much easier.

PLASTER ON BRICK

Could you give us the best method of removing plaster from a brick fireplace?

Scrape off as much of the plaster as possible with a dull knife; then use the following method: Mix 1 part of muriatic acid in 10 parts of water, pouring the acid slowly to avoid splashing. Use a glass or wood container to hold the solution. Wet the brick with water; then apply the acid solution. After 3 minutes or so, scrub the brick with more of the solution; then rinse it thoroughly with clear water. Use a fiber scrubbing brush.

REMOVING WAX FROM BRICK

We have a red brick fireplace. While polishing the glazed brick in front, I tried the wax on the rough brick. Instead of the shine

I expected, it has a dull, grayish look; evidently the wax has gone into the brick. I have tried removing it with a brush and soap and water without success. What can I use to take this wax off? It was a liquid wax.

Because of the porous nature of the rough brick, the wax did penetrate. Try making a thick paste of powdered whiting or other absorbent powder and a nonflammable liquid spot remover and cover the brick surface with a 1-inch layer of the paste; the remover may act as a solvent on the wax and the powder as a blotter to draw it out. When the paste dries, replace it with fresh. Although not always completely successful, the same treatment can be used to remove crayon from brick.

BRICK MANTEL

Our house is about 25 years old, and there is a large brick mantel in the living room, which I am told is of glazed brick (it is not shiny) and cannot be painted because the paint would flake off. It is an off-white color with pale-red mortar joints. The hearth in front is of a dull-red tile. I want to brighten it up and would like to know if there is any kind of paint that can be used. There is also a gray-colored imitation log of plaster-of-Paris.

There is no special paint for such purposes, and hard-burned or glazed-clay products don't "hold" paint too well. If you wish to take a chance, scrub the surfaces well with a strong solution of one of the detergent powders and rinse with clear water. When thoroughly dry, coat the brick with a good-grade of flat wall paint and the floor tile with a floor paint. Brush the dust off the log, apply a coat of primer, and finish with flat wall paint.

SLATE FLOOR AND HEARTH

We are going to lay slate in our entrance hall and in our hearth and would like to know how to give it a polish or lasting finish. The directions mentioned a coat of wax, but failed to name a special brand or type. Could you advise?

Any good brand of paste floor wax can be used. First scrub the floor with a detergent and rinse well with clear water. Allow plenty of time for the slate to dry; then apply two coats. Each coat should be allowed to dry and then should be buffed well. To get a uniform spread of wax, soften it by placing the open can in some hot water and apply it with a paintbrush.

REMOVING MASONRY PLATFORM

How can I remove a brick and concrete platform that is in front of a fireplace? It is about 4½ feet long, 2 feet wide, and 2 feet high. I want to remove the entire platform.

If you can borrow an electric power hammer, this should speed up the demolition considerably. Otherwise, the combination is a fairly heavy mallet, a cold chisel, and plenty of elbow grease. Be sure to wear goggles to guard against flying particles as you do the chipping. Painter's drop cloths will be of great help in keeping dust off any carpeting or furniture you can't remove while the job is being done.

BURNING PAINTED WOOD?

We have the opportunity of obtaining a quantity of painted scrap wood. Would this be okay to burn in the fireplace without danger of clogging the chimney?

We don't know how it could cause clogging or give any other problems, except possibly shoot a little more smoke up the chimney. Of course, if the scrap wood is still somewhat green, then you can naturally expect it to smoke. In short, we vote to go right ahead.

GAS LOGS NEED FIREBRICK?

I am in the process of building a recreation room. I would like to have a fireplace. But since there is no place for a flue, I thought of gas logs in a common brick fireplace. This, of course, would be vented. My question: Must I use firebricks for the interior, or will common bricks suffice? I doubt if gas logs are as hot as wood embers.

Use the firebricks. Those gas logs can get very toasty indeed. Common bricks couldn't take it.

COAL FOR FIREPLACE USE

Is there any special kind of coal recommended for fireplaces? We have been using cannel coal but we get fine soot from it all over the house. Do you have any recommendations in regard to burning coal in a fireplace?

Many people find burning chestnut-size anthracite coal in a fireplace highly satisfactory. This is available from anthracite dealers in 25-pound bags. If you have the basket-type grate, we suggest starting a good fire with paper and wood and then putting the whole bag of coal on this. Special grates are available with built-in ash receptacles underneath into which the ash sifts down, simplifying keeping the hearth clean. The fire can be kept going for several continuous weeks.

CHARCOAL BRIQUETS OKAY IN NATURAL FIREPLACE

We moved from a home with coal heat to a home with gas heat. We have charcoal briquets left over. Can these be burned in our natural fireplace without ill effects?

If you have a grate to hold them up for a reasonable draft, we see no reason why you can't use them.

A plumbing system can develop as many kinds of noises as a zoo at feeding time. Pipes can bang, thump, creak, and pound. Faucets can whistle, chatter, squeak, and groan. All of them are cries for help to fix ailments of one kind or another. And the reason why prompt remedial action is important is because there's so much weight and momentum in a heavy pipe full of moving water that a breakdown can occur in quite a short time.

One of the loudest noises is the well-named water hammer. This is a banging which sometimes occurs whenever a faucet is turned off. The reason is simple. Every time you turn on a faucet, you start a whole pipeful of water in motion. When you turn the faucet off, you abruptly stop the motion. But a column of water is heavy, and once you start it moving, it develops a powerful momentum. So when you suddenly stop it by turning off the faucet, the momentum slams the column of water's weight against the pipe and the parts of the faucet like a hammer. It not only makes a loud bang thereby, but can seriously weaken the parts of the faucet taking the brunt of this force, as well as jarring the pipe enough to shake the supports.

Quieting a water hammer is quite a simple plumbing operation. So simple, in fact, that if you've had any experience with making the most elementary pipe connections, you can handle this. The general principle is to provide a short length of sealed pipe beyond the last faucet in the line, where the forward motion of the column of water can be literally air-braked to a gentle stop. (The water continues beyond the faucet into the dead-end pipe, where it compresses the air in the pipe, which slows it to a silent, gentle halt.) Water-hammer absorbing units, embodying this air-brake principle, are sold in plumbing supply houses, and if you don't feel up to making this addition yourself, it's a simple matter for any plumber.

A good many times, you may not need even this simple addition; the built-up vibration of the pipe may be stopped just by tightly securing the supports. Or it may be that enough supports for the pipe weren't put in originally. Adding some more, along lengthy horizontal stretches and at elbows, not only may take care of the problem, but also may quiet some other characteristic noises.

A particular type of water hammer often happens with improperly hooked-up automatic washing machines, where water is so fre-

CHAPTER 13
PLUMBING

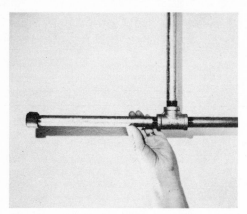

Figure 13-1. A length of pipe with an air cushion trapped inside will prevent banging noises by absorbing the shock wave created when a water faucet is closed suddenly.

quently turned on and off. This destructive pounding is readily stopped by having a special antihammer air chamber installed immediately adjacent to the washer's valves. In extensive plumbing systems, very often a single hammer-absorbing unit at the end of the line won't be sufficient. In such cases air-chamber units can be cut into any part of the water line.

While it's desirable to put the dead-end air chamber at the end of the plumbing line, this may mean breaking into a nice wall to get at the pipe. Well, as a matter of fact, you can get almost as good results by installing it at any exposed point where you can cut a T fitting. If you are planning to do this job yourself, remember that the cap must be screwed over the end exceedingly tight. And it's an excellent practice to seal around the lower edge of the cap and any remaining pipe threads with plastic steel. Be generous with it, too. The object is to make the cap fit on so tightly no air can escape. If any air leaks out, some water will seep in, and you'll lose your air-brake effect.

As for the chattering, squeaky (and dripping) faucets, try the easiest remedy first, in case it's all that's needed: tighten the fitting (usually a hexagonal nut) where the faucet emerges. If it's even a little loose, it may be enough to permit the stem to get out of plumb, and this can cause a noise; a good tightening may set things to rights. If the fitting seems tight, then you'd better see if the washer is worn; if it is, that's a sure cause for

squealing or chattering. To get at the washer, you loosen the fitting enough so you can draw out the entire works. At the very bottom, under the stem (spindle), you see the opening where the water comes in from the pipe. On the little platform (the seat) surrounding the hole is where you'll find the washer, held there by pressure from the bottom of the stem. Remove the washer, and feel the seat to see if it's still smooth. If it's become roughened, then it will start to roughen any new washer you put in. So the first step is to smooth the seat. Fortunately, there are complete faucet-repairing kits widely available. Fastened on a single card you'll find washers and a seat-dressing tool, and full printed instructions as well. With these inexpensive kits, you can tackle just about any problem faucet with complete confidence.

Once you've smoothed off the seat, a new washer should give long, silent service. However, if a new washer doesn't prove to be the complete answer, examine the spindle carefully to see if the threads are corroded or seem to be worn down. If hard usage has worn the threads so there's some play, probably you need a replacement faucet. This is a real possibility; few moving parts around the house are used under pressure so often as a faucet.

Sometimes there's a rumble when a hot-water faucet is turned on. This will happen if the hot-water supply is allowed to heat up to the boiling point, which is a whole lot hotter than you need for normal household use. When water is heated under pressure, it won't turn into steam until the pressure is relieved. This relief comes when the faucet is turned on, and the overheated water, flashing immediately into steam, is what causes the rumble. Proper temperature control is the answer here; don't let the water temperature reach the boiling point.

Before beginning *any* repair on water pipes or faucets, the water supply should be turned off. The main valve in the supply pipe is usually located just within the wall. In many houses no other valve is provided. In a high-quality plumbing system, there is, in addition, a shutoff valve in the cellar in each branch. There may also be a shutoff valve in each pipe at a fixture. Work can thus be done in one part of a house without interference with the others.

After a shutoff valve is closed, all faucets in its pipe should be opened; if only a low

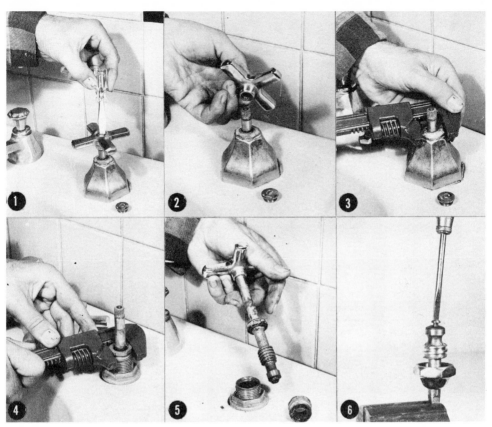

Figure 13-2. Steps in replacing a faucet washer.

faucet is opened, water may be retained in the pipe above by atmospheric pressure.

Questions and Answers

Following are some questions and answers about plumbing that may be of some help to you.

CLOGGED KITCHEN SINK

We sublet our apartment for a year. On our return, the drain in the kitchen sink worked very sluggishly and seemed clogged; pouring boiling water down hasn't helped much. What do you suggest?

The grease trap is probably quite clogged. Trying the easiest method first, use a rubber suction cup plunger called a "plumber's friend." Place the cup over the sink drain and work the handle vigorously up and down; very often this does the trick. If you have no luck with that, try pouring drain cleaner [potash lye or caustic potash (not caustic soda, which will be harmful)], dissolved in boiling water according to the label directions, down the outlet and allow it to remain overnight. Use these chemicals with great care to avoid spattering; they cause burns and are destructive to clothing. If drain cleaner is not successful, remove the plug under the trap (the lower part of the U-shaped pipe under the sink); first place a receptacle underneath to catch any drip or waste material. Remove the clogging material with a bent wire and stiff, bottle-type brush.

NOT PERFUME IN KITCHEN DRAIN

One of my sink drains gives off a strong, musty odor, which copious amounts of bleach and drain cleaner seem to mask only temporarily. Any solution?

First of all, we sincerely hope you never put the bleach and drain cleaner in at the same time. This can cause a lethal gas. Absolutely never mix the two. Clear out the U-shaped trap; something may be caught in there which will smell musty when wet. Next, put down a cup of baking soda the last thing at night. This makes a wonderful deodorizer.

THOUGH TRAP CLEAN, DRAIN STILL SLOW

My kitchen sink drain is still very sluggish, even though I removed the trap cover and cleaned out an accumulation of hardened grease and other stuff. Before that, I used drain-cleaning chemicals with no luck. I suspect the blockage is beyond the trap. But what can I do now?

We've had good luck with one of those flexible snake attachments for the electric drill. They come in 6- and 10-foot lengths and are made to help us amateurs with a problem like this. It's really a smaller model of the regular plumber's hand-operated snake, but spins around about 10 times as fast. You remove the trap cover and push in the business end of the snake as far as the obstruction. Switch on the drill, and keep pushing until the spinning snake pushes through the blockage. If this doesn't work, call the plumber.

SQUEAKING AND WHISTLING FAUCET

One of the kitchen sink faucets is very noisy whenever we turn it on; it squeaks and whistles annoyingly. Is there any way to eliminate the noise?

Unscrew the hexagonal nut under the handle. Then pack hard grease (the kind used by service stations for lubricating cars) inside the nut. Protect the nut from damage to the finish by the wrench's jaws by wrapping plastic tape around either the nut or the jaws.

KITCHEN FAUCET SLOWER, OTHER FAUCETS OKAY

What is causing the flow of water from the kitchen faucet to slow up while all the bathroom faucets are still going along as always? This is a one-control faucet for both hot and cold. The house is two years old.

The aerator sounds clogged, from your description. Unscrew it from the end of the faucet; place each little part down in the order it comes out, so that you can get it back

Figure 13-3. Methods of removing an obstruction.

together okay. You'll find the little screen clogged, so just rinse it out, reassemble the parts, and replace them, and all should be okay for another year or two.

BANGING WATER PIPES

My water pipes keep banging when I shut the faucets off. Plumbers have inspected and installed an air valve at the end of the line; the banging stopped for three days and then started again.

Check the supports of the horizontal lengths of pipe; they may be spaced too widely apart or may have loosened. Try adding supports and tightening loose ones; placing a pad of foam rubber between the pipe and each support may help absorb vibration, also.

HALF-OPEN FAUCET NOISY

When the cold-water faucet is opened only partway, it is very noisy; turned completely on, it is quieter. What is the remedy for this?

This is probably caused by a worn faucet washer. Replace the washer. Or, it is possible that an inside part of the faucet needs tightening.

NONSTOP TOILET

What causes water to keep leaking down from the tank after the toilet is flushed? It is a small but steady drip, and the tank takes quite a long time to fill up again.

The rubber tank ball which is supposed to drop down and cover the drain hole after the tank has emptied isn't behaving properly. There may be the slightest little bend in the copper rod which holds and guides the ball. This could get the ball off center and permit some water to seep around it. Or the rubber itself may be so old it's become spongy and can't close the hole properly. If so, replace it with a new ball.

LONG WIRE PREVENTS FLUSHING

Unless I keep holding the flushing handle down, the tank won't flush. Action stops the minute I release the pressure. What can I do?

The connecting-rod wire that lifts the ball which lets water out of the bottom of the tank is a little too long. Unhook it from the trip lever, snip off an inch or so, and replace it. Also the trip lever or lift wire may corrode and fail to work smoothly, or the lift wire may bind in the guides. Disassemble, and clean off corrosion or replace parts as necessary.

FLOAT BALL PROBLEM

It's impossible for the water in the tank to reach its proper level. What's the problem?

The float ball may have developed a leak, preventing the water to reach the proper level. (The correct water level is about 1 inch below the top of the overflow tube or enough to give a good flush.) If the ball fails to rise, the intake valve will remain open and water will continue to flow. Brass float balls can sometimes be drained and the leak soldered. Other types

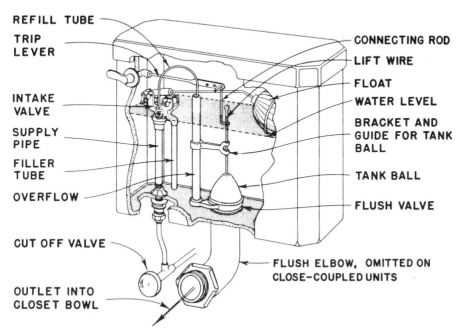

Figure 13-4. Parts of water closet.

must be replaced. When working on the float ball, be careful to keep the rod aligned so that the ball will float freely and close the valve properly.

LEAKY WASHER ON INTAKE VALVE

The plunger washer in our water closet is worn, which causes the valve to leak. How can I replace the washer?

To replace the plunger washer, shut off the water and drain the tank. Then unscrew the two thumbscrews that hold the levers, and push out the levers. Lift out the plunger, unscrew the cup on the bottom, and insert a new washer. The washer is made of material such as rubber or leather. Examine the washer seat. If it's nicked or rough, it may need refacing. If the float-valve assembly is badly corroded, replace it.

GURGLING, BACKUP IN SINK

I have a two-family house. There is a problem with the downstairs kitchen sink. Water, draining from the upstairs sink, backs up with a gurgling sound into the lower one. How can this condition be remedied?

The plumbing system may be improperly vented, causing the discharge from the upstairs sink to create suction as it passes the drain of the downstairs sink, destroying the trap seal. This permits the water to be drawn into the sink together with air, creating the gurgling sound. Or the drainpipe pitch from the downstairs sink may be incorrect. We would recommend having a competent plumber make a personal inspection and necessary correction.

CLICKING NOISE IN VENT PIPE

We recently moved into a house that is about five years old and has copper plumbing. Whenever water is used and drained out, there is a very disturbing clicking sound in the vent pipe, at least it seems to come from there. It makes the noise when either hot or cold water is drained out. Is there anything that can be done to eliminate this. Or can you tell us what causes it?

If the noise is in the vent pipe, it might be partially blocked with a bird's nest or some other object, and the suction created by water flowing down the soil pipe may cause a flutter, creating a click. It might also be possible that a sewer backup valve was installed, and the flap

may be striking the valve seat as the water flows through it to the sewer main. It will be necessary to change the pitch of the valve slightly to stop the flutter. It's also likely that some object like a boy's marble or a piece of metal is caught in the basement trap leading to the sewer. Open and examine it, or have a plumber do so.

NOISY RUNNING WATER

When the water is turned on in the kitchen sink, the running water seems very noisy. What causes this, and is there any way to correct it?

When a faucet is turned on and noise continues in the water line while the water is flowing, the cause is usually due to a loosened or worn washer or faucet part. Another possible cause of the noise may be due to the shutoff valve not being open sufficiently to permit the water to flow freely.

WATER PRESSURE LOW UPSTAIRS

The water to my upstairs bathroom has very little pressure now. The pipes are galvanized and are inside the walls. Is there any way to remove the rust in the pipes, or must I install new ones?

The only sure remedy for galvanized pipes clogged with rust is replacement. The cheapest method is with copper tubing, which can usually be pulled up through the walls, alongside the old pipes. Replacing with rigid pipe may require breaking into the walls and floors, also involving patching and refinishing. Tubing requires usually little more than taking up a board or two in the bathroom floor or making a small hole in the wall.

WATER TANK HALF-FILLED

Our commode does not function properly. It requires two to three flushings to get rid of the waste. The water tank has been examined, and there do not appear to be any leaks. However, the water level in the tank is a little below the halfway mark. Could the trouble be here? How can this condition be corrected?

You are right about the trouble being due to the water level in the tank. The water level should be about ¾ inch below the top of the overflow tube. This level will be reached if you carefully bend the metal tank-float rod upward so that the ball floats at the proper height.

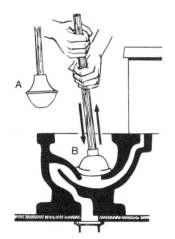

Figure 13-5. The proper use of a plumber's friend.

REPAIRING IRON PIPE

How can an iron sewerage pipe be repaired? It runs the full length of the cellar. There are two breaks, about 10 inches long; the breaks are not in the joints.

The breaks in the pipe can be easily mended with plastic steel, which is widely available in hardware and paint stores and is made for just such purposes. Follow the label directions for use.

MEASURING PIPE DIAMETER

Being faced with the problem of having to replace a piece of pipe section in a difficult-to-reach part of the basement ceiling, how can I determine the size of the pipe so that I can order the new length?

You can use calipers to measure the pipe. If you have no calipers, you can fit an ordinary wrench over the pipe, as close to right angles as you can make it, and measure the distance between the jaws. This will be the outside diameter.

FILLING HOLE IN SINK

Please tell me how I can repair a hole in a double-bottom sink. The sink is white cast iron with porcelain, and the hole is the size of a half dollar.

With patience, hack saw, and file, cut out a piece of metal scrap as close to the hole size and shape as you can. Secure it in place with Scotch tape or plastic tape across the top. Spread plastic steel over the bottom and the edge of the plug. Let it set up firmly for a couple of hours. Remove the tape, and spread the plastic steel as smoothly as you can over the edge of the plug so that it's all solid. Let it set up. When it's firm, file it down as smoothly as possible. Touch it up with white epoxy enamel to get as good a match as you can.

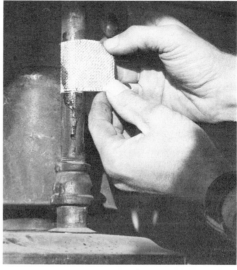

Figure 13-6. Most leaks in home plumbing occur at joints. An easy repair method is to use a liquid type of steel (left). A burst pipe can be mended with fiberglass and epoxy resin (right).

This enamel may need renewing as the years go by, but at least it won't leak any more.

RETURNED TO RUSTY TUB

When we returned from our winter away, we found a large brown stain on the sides and bottom of our bathtub in the drain area. What can we use to remove this?

Shop around hardware stores and plumbing supply houses for one of the new rust-removing preparations. Examine the label, and ask the dealer to make sure this particular one is safe for porcelain. Chances are pretty good, even so, that removing the stain will also remove considerable shine. Some elbow grease and white automotive rubbing compound will help. But don't expect restoration of showroom gleam.

LAUNDRY TUB LEAKS

My basement laundry tub has developed a leak from a crack near the bottom. How can this crack be filled?

Widen the crack with a screwdriver to make a groove into which patching material can be forced. Brush out all loose particles. Then fill the crack with a latex concrete, available at masonry supply dealers and some large hardware stores. Or fill the crack with powdered litharge and glycerin mixed to a paste (this hardens quickly, so mix only a very small amount at a time). Or pack the groove with soft cotton string smeared with white lead paste. Allow several days for thorough drying before using the laundry tub. In addition, there's a product, quite widely distributed, which is a liquid tile. When it is brushed or rolled on a masonry surface, it becomes an integral part of the masonry and dries with a finish as hard and smooth as tile. It will fill cracks at the same time. It has proved highly successful in many industrial installations.

LAUNDRY TUB SCUM

My stone laundry tubs in the cellar have been in use for a long time and have acquired a thick layer of soap scum that I haven't been able to remove. Is there any way to clean this off?

Try scrubbing it with hot, white vinegar; then rinse thoroughly with clear water. Or rub it with a paste made of kerosene and scratchless scouring powder (be very careful of fire hazard), also followed by thorough rinsing with clear water. If neither of these methods completely removes the scum, allow the stone surface to dry thoroughly; then rub it down with "00" sandpaper.

LAUNDRY TUBS TOO ROUGH

I washed a throw rug on which some battery acid had been spilled in my concrete laundry tub. The surface of the tub is now so rough it catches and snags. How can I smooth it again?

Not all paint, hardware, and specialty stores carry it, but try to find some so-called porcelainizing enamel or liquid porcelain, preferably the type made with epoxy. In the past we have seen ads for products of this type but have never tried them. They sound as though they could do just the job you want. If no luck, then you'll need a lot of elbow grease and a carborundum block to grind down at least the roughest parts.

PORCELAIN TUBS DISCOLORED

Our basement washtubs have become dark and discolored. Is there any way to remove the discoloration?

Clean them with a mild scouring powder, followed by rinsing with a solution of Javelle water, using about ½ cupful in each gallon of water (see page 339).

STOP SHOWER STALL MILDEW

How can I prevent mildew from forming in the shower stall?

Even though mildew forms where it's warm and wet, you obviously can't wave a heat lamp around the shower stall until the walls are dry. However, ventilate all you can. Open the window after showers to let the steamy air out. Frequently go over the stall walls with a cleaner containing bleach, which kills formation of mildew spores.

LEAKING METAL SHOWER STALL

I have a metal shower stall. After using it I notice a puddle of water beneath all sides, close to the base. Is there any home remedy to rectify this?

The seams may not be tightly sealed, the drain pan may be faulty, or the joint around the outlet may not be properly sealed. We recommend calling in a competent plumber to check the installation.

PAINT PEELS ON METAL SHOWER BASE

Is there anything that can be painted or cemented to a metal shower base? The paint peels, leaving rust. I have tried a rust-inhibitive paint, but that doesn't hold up either. We use very hot water.

Use the rust-inhibitive paint, as you have been doing, after first removing all trace of loose and scaling rust with steel wool and turpentine, or with one of the rust-removing preparations now available at most paint dealers. Then apply a coat of top-quality enamel or a ceramiclike liquid tile coating; this will resist water penetration, which is causing the paint to peel.

SINK GROUT NEEDS PROTECTION

Our sink has small tiles, and the grout has washed out after years of use. I have tried several recommended products, but they never stayed very long. Can you suggest something?

Get the sink as thoroughly dry and clean as you can; then regrout. To protect the grout, wipe on transparent liquid sealer. You can get this where tiles are sold (discount houses, hobby shops, etc.).

BRIGHT CHROME FIXTURES

The chrome plumbing fixtures seem to become easily water-spotted. What is the best way to keep them bright?

Any surface or material that has a glossy finish will usually show water spots; we know of nothing to prevent this. Keep a soft, dry cloth handy for wiping the fixtures when water is dropped on the surfaces. Avoid using scouring powders, because frequent use of abrasives eventually will scratch or dull the chrome finish.

CLEANING GOLD PLUMBING FIXTURES

A year ago we remodeled our powder room and had gold faucets installed. We're having a great deal of trouble with tarnishing and have found no successful way of polishing them, or the switch plate—even finger marks can't be removed. What is the proper way to clean them?

We suggest checking with the dealer from whom these were purchased or with the plumber who installed them as to the proper recommended care for these fixtures. No harsh abrasives or cleanser should be used; these will scratch the metal. Wash the metal surface with warm, soapy water, rinse thoroughly with clear water, and wipe dry. Or use a cream cleanup wax, made by a nationally known manufacturer, to remove finger marks, surface grease, etc. This also leaves a protective coating which will retard tarnishing. Follow the label directions.

STOPPERS DON'T FIT TUBS

My laundry tubs leak around the stoppers, and I can't get the water to remain in the tub. I have purchased new stoppers, but the holes are so worn these don't fit real tight. Otherwise the tubs are in good condition, and I don't want to replace them. Can you suggest anything?

There are stoppers available in various diameters that are like flat plates which fit over the outlets rather than in them, held down by the weight of the water. These would solve your problem. Variety, hardware, and paint dealers stock them. Or you might try lining the inside of the holes with a thin layer of one of the plastic-type metals, which come in tubes and are available at the same stores as the stoppers. Follow the label instructions carefully. However, the flat stoppers are a much easier solution.

HOT-WATER-TANK PROBLEM

During the winter our electric hot-water tank is seldom used. When used, we notice a very strong stagnant smell from the water. What can be done without dismantling the tank?

Drain and flush the tank several times. Then run in more water, adding a water-conditioning preparation widely available in supermarkets. Let this stand for several hours. Then drain and repeat. Several such treatments should clear up the odor.

IRON IN WELL WATER

We get our water from a well. It contains a lot of iron, which stains the sink and toilet if water stands in them. What can I use in the water when I wash clothes to keep them white and not get yellow from the iron?

The easiest solution would be to have a water-softening unit, or a filter, installed in the water supply system; consult a reliable plumbing contractor or water-conditioning dealer. A powdered water conditioner is available at most supermarkets; follow the label directions as to use. It will help prevent brown stains in laundering.

SWEATING WATER PIPES

Please tell me what to use to cover water pipes in the basement to keep them from sweating in summer. Is there any kind of paint I can apply? If not, what kind of covering will I have to get?

There is an asphalt-base coating that contains a corklike substance which can be brushed on in a thick layer. Plumbing supply houses and hardware dealers sell the product. If it's not available, you can purchase a pipe covering made of felt or fiberglass at plumbing supply shops. Ask for antisweat pipe covering.

HAD HIS SHARE OF FROZEN PIPES

The plumbing is in the crawl space of my winterized shore cottage. The cottage has concrete foundation walls and floor. During a very severe cold spell, the pipe froze. The plumber's bill for thawing was high, but he earned it. But how can I protect against any repeats?

Wrap the pipe in electric heating cable, equipped with a thermostat if you're not there to flip the "on" switch when needed. If the water supply is unlimited, leave the faucet open so that there's a very slight trickle. We have a friend who has a cottage up in the Pocono Mountains in Pennsylvania, who told us about this. She leaves the water trickling all winter and hasn't had a pipe freeze yet. Or you can wrap the pipes in thick insulation and hope it never gets cold enough to freeze water inside that (which would have to be extremely cold).

THAWING THE FREEZE

What is the best method of thawing frozen water pipes?

The use of an electric heating cable is a good method of thawing a frozen pipe, because the entire heated length of the pipe is thawed at one time. Thawing a pipe with a blowtorch can be dangerous. The water may get hot enough at the point where the torch is applied to generate sufficient steam under pressure to rupture the pipe. Steam from the break could severely scald you. Actually, thawing a pipe with hot water is safer than thawing it with a blowtorch. One method is to cover the pipe with rags and then pour the hot water over the rags. Whatever method you use—blowtorch, hot water, or other—open a faucet and start thawing at that point. The open faucet will permit the steam to escape, thus reducing the chance of the buildup of dangerous pressure. Don't allow the steam to condense and refreeze before it reaches the faucet.

REPAIRING LEAKS IN PIPES

How can a small leak be repaired in a pipe?

Small leaks in a pipe can often be repaired with a rubber patch and metal clamp or sleeve. This must be considered as an emergency repair job and should be followed by permanent repair of replacement of the pipe as soon as practicable. Large leaks in a pipe may require cutting out the damaged section and installing a new piece of pipe. At least one union will be required unless the leak is near the end of the pipe. You can make a temporary repair with plastic or rubber tubing. The tubing must be strong enough to withstand the normal water pressure in the pipe. It should be slipped over the open ends of the piping and fastened with pipe clamps or several turns of wire. A leak at a threaded connection can often be stopped by unscrewing the fitting and applying a pipe-joint compound that will seal the joint when the fitting is screwed back together.

BE VERY SUSPICIOUS OF PINHOLE LEAK

How can I repair two pinhole leaks which recently developed in my hot-water tank?

Drain the water below the leak level. Chew up a good wad of gum, jam it over the leak, and strap it tightly with electrician's tape. More permanent, by far, is forcing a lump of plastic steel over the leak, trying to poke some inside the hole with a pin. Let it dry before refilling the tank to normal level. Make frequent inspections of the tank. Some pinhole leaks can be forerunners of weakened seams or corroded areas, which can eventually result in bursting. A large leak can be temporarily repaired with a toggle bolt, rubber gasket, and brass washer, as shown here. You may have to drill or ream the hole larger to insert the toggle bolt. Draw the bolt up tight to compress the rubber gasket against the tank wall. Naturally a tank that is in this condition should be replaced.

CLEANING HOT-WATER HEATER

We were advised not to clean out our hot-water heating system at the end of the season. When should this be done?

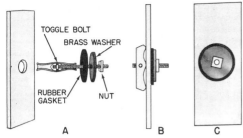

Figure13-7. Closing a hole in a tank: (A) The link of the toggle bolt is passed through the hole in the tank (hole is enlarged if necessary). (B) Side view of tank edge (nut is drawn up tightly to compress washer and gasket against tank). (C) Outside view of completed repair.

The beginning of the heating season is the best time to clean the hot-water heating system. Drain off several pailfuls of water to draw off sediment from the bottom of the boiler; after a few pailfuls, usually the water will run clean. Then refill the system to its proper level with clear water. Thorough cleaning with a boiler compound should be done about once every three to four years.

PLUMBING STAINS

What can I use to clean stubborn stains in my bathtub and sink? I've tried all kinds of scouring powders and detergents.

If the measures you've tried can't do the job, use the following method, which has been very successful many times: Saturate a cloth with hydrogen peroxide; then sprinkle on some scratchless scouring powder and then cream of tartar. When the powders are well dampened, rub this pastelike mixture on the spots and stains, and allow it to remain for half an hour. Rinse well, and repeat the treatment if necessary.

RUSTING WATER TANK

I would like to know if you can tell me of some method of protecting a galvanized steel tank from rusting. This is a storage tank for well water.

Remove all rust with steel wool or sandpaper, and wipe off all dust with turpentine. While the metal is clean, apply a coat of red lead or one of the rust-inhibitive paints. When thoroughly dry, finish with a couple of coats of a good grade of enamel or aluminum paint. The interior of the tank can never be painted.

RUST SEDIMENT IN HOT-WATER TANK

We recently purchased and moved into a house that is about 28 years old. The hot-water tank has an accumulation of rust sediment, causing the hot water to run rusty. How can I remove the rust sediment?

If the rusty water is due to rust sediment accumulated at the bottom of the tank, the sediment can be removed by closing the shut-off valve and leaving the drain cock open. The supply pressure will drive the water through the upper pipe and coil with sufficient force to flush out most loose sediment that may have collected. Sediment should be drawn from the bottom of the tank about once a month. Sometimes the installation of a device known as a magnesium rod may help. It's not a difficult job to put it in your tank, and we're quite sure this will be all you'll need to clear up the water and prevent the rusting from becoming more serious. Magnesium rods are available at any plumbing supply house. If the rusting is due to a badly coated inner tank surface, cleaning an old tank is not worth the cost. Replacement is the only practical remedy.

RUSTY HOT-WATER PIPES

We use an old house in the country for vacations. It is in good condition, but the hot-water pipes are rusty, and so the water runs rusty at first. Is there any method to remove the rust from the pipes? We want to avoid the expense of replacing the pipes if possible.

If you are sure the rusty water is due to the pipes, and not to sediment in the tank or water heater, pipe replacement is the only remedy. This need not be as expensive as you fear. Copper tubing can be used. This is flexible enough to be pulled up through the walls along the old pipes. Often only a board or two need be taken up, or a small hole broken in the wall. No extensive patching, redecorating, or refinishing is necessary. The copper tubing is available in lengths up to 60 feet.

DEPOSITS CLOG WATER PIPES

Lime deposits are apparently clogging the water supply pipes to our tub and shower. The water just barely trickles out. We have no trouble with water pressure anywhere else in the house. How can this be remedied?

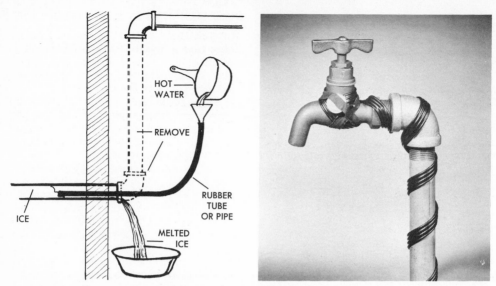

Figure 13-8. (left) One method of thawing a frozen pipe. Of course, this can be prevented by the use of an electric heating cable (right).

Sorry, but the only remedy is replacement of the faulty pipes. The cheapest replacement is with copper tubing, which is flexible enough to be pulled up through the walls, alongside the old pipes which can be left where they are. This eliminates the cost of breaking into walls and floors for replacement. We recommend having a water-softening unit installed.

FROSTPROOFING A WELL SYSTEM

My well is about 100 feet from the house, and I would like to install a deep-well pressure system. Due to solid rock, I would have trouble making a pit. Is it possible to build a pump house warm enough to keep the water from freezing? Also, the pipes to the house cannot be laid deep enough to keep them from freezing. Is there any way to overcome this?

A pump house can be built of frame construction and insulated, but despite the sturdiness of such construction, heat in the pump house will be necessary during prolonged spells of freezing weather. The only suggestion we can make to keep pipes from freezing is to wrap an electric heating cable around them, if you can't put them below the frost line.

ANOTHER LONESOME HOUSE

We plan to go south in January and spend 4 months away. Our house will be vacant, and obviously the heat must be turned off. How does one keep plumbing from freezing when there's no heat through a cold winter? How can we close the house completely and turn off all the facilities, so that when we return we can flick a switch and say "Ah, there's no place like home"?

You prevent freeze-ups by draining every pipe and trap. It would be best if you can have a plumber blow the pipes out. To any traps you can't drain, add some permanent anti-freeze solution. Drain any pipes, tanks, and radiators containing water in the heating system. As for the switch-flicking, that will start the furnace, refrigerator, freezer, and everything else run by electricity. But it won't refill the pipes, unless your valves are electrically controlled (not likely).

ROOTS IN SEWER PIPES

I have a problem with tree roots growing in my sewer pipes and have to clean them out about every 2½ years. I hope to solve this problem before the pipe is clogged with the roots. Is there anything on the market in

powder or crystal form that I could float
down to the roots to destroy them?

Have a plumber clear the pipe of roots,
using an electric root-removing machine.
Then use the chemical to prevent further
growth. Some plumbing supply and hardware
dealers have special preparations for destroying roots in sewers; follow the manufacturer's
instructions for use. Or, the last thing at night,
flush down a toilet fixture a solution of about a
pound of finely powdered copper sulfate in a
pail of warm water (use a wooden container
for mixing). During the growing season, the
chemical should be used every 6 weeks; at
other times, every few months.

PROTECT AGAINST TREE ROOTS?

We plan to put the septic tank and system
for our new house in a location that will
require the drain pipe to run within 30 feet
of a beautiful big willow. I have heard that
willows are notorious water seekers and can
clog drain pipes if given any chance. Is there
any way to guard against this?

Either see that the sections of tile are
sealed at the joints with uncompromising
security or use a single, unbroken length of
pipe. At least, come as close to this goal as
possible.

SEPTIC TANK

Can the water from a lavatory and bathtub
be run through a septic tank without harming the action in the tank?

You can drain all the plumbing fixtures
into the septic tank without interfering with

the bacterial action of the unit. The only time
a harmful condition might develop is if there
is a very large quantity of a strong solution of a
caustic cleaner or disinfectant poured into it.

WATER OVER SEPTIC TANK

We have a septic tank, and there is always
water on the ground above it. What causes
this, and how can it be remedied? We have
already put a can of septic tank cleaner into
it, but it didn't help.

The cover of the tank may not be properly closed, or there may be a crack in the tank,
causing the surrounding ground to be saturated. We strongly urge having the tank inspected by a cesspool builder and cleaner (consult
your local classified telephone directory).

DISCONTINUED SEPTIC TANK

I have discontinued using an old septic tank
at my summer cottage and had sand filling
put over it, but the water keeps coming up
to the top. Would it have been better to
have had the tank drained first and then
sand-filled?

Yes, indeed. In fact, we'd have the sand
covering moved to one side and the tank
drained and filled, just as you described.
Cleaned out and filled, the tank won't give you
any more problems.

DRAIN FIELD FOR AUTOMATIC
WASHER

Rather than have the water from my automatic washer drain into the septic tank,
would it be possible to dig a hole and have

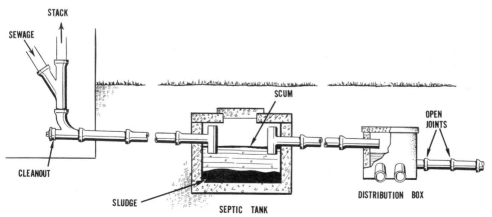

Figure 13-9. A typical septic tank system.

the water drain into the drainage field to serve this purpose?

Neither the water from the automatic washer nor the detergents will interfere with the action of the septic tank. However, a separate outlet can be installed to drain the water from the washer. Have the outlet pipe drain into a dry-well type of receptacle (see page 115), at least 15 feet from the house.

ODOR FROM SEPTIC TANK

We have a cement septic tank, and there are days when we can hardly stand to go outside the door because of the odor. We have had three before this one, and they were no problem. It was set up by a master plumber, so it should have been done properly. We have put in a chemical compound, but it does not seem to do any good. What do you advise?

Perhaps the septic tank is too small and doesn't retain sewage matter long enough for complete decomposition. The process would then be continued in the drainage field. There should also be about 12 inches of soil over the top of the tank. You might also see that the vent stack is clear. It also is possible that the inlet sewer line is below the water level in the tank, thus preventing the escape of sewer gas through the sewer line to the vent stack.

SEWER ODOR

Our bathtub drains into the septic tank. The vent from the tub through the roof is open and clear. However, whenever the tub is used, we get a disagreeable odor through the house and especially in the basement. The odor does not clear up from bath to bath.

It is likely that a trap was omitted at the point where the soil pipe leaves the building. We also suspect that the vent connections were not properly made. This would cause the condition you describe. Water from a fixture passing by another fixture would siphon the trap, allowing sewer odors to come through. Have a competent plumber check this.

SUMP-PUMP ODOR

Is there any way to cut down on the odor caused by a sump pump in the basement? The odor is noticeable especially after it empties. It empties into a leech bed. Even in driest weather the sump-pump well is wet.

There may be a problem with the backup valve in the drain pipe leading from the house; either it has run dry or it has a mechanical fault. We recommend calling a plumber promptly.

RUNNING SUMP PIPE BELOW GROUND

Will the discharge pipe from a sump pump freeze up in the winter if it is 4 to 6 inches underground? At present, the pipe is above ground and doesn't freeze up, but I would like to put it underground, as it is an eyesore and is in the lawn mower's way. Actually, when the water is discharged, all or most of it drains from the aboveground pipe anyhow.

Especially since the pipe presently drains clean, there should be no freezing problem underground. But you'll be a lot safer if you let the pipe discharge into a dry well. Four or six inches down isn't below frost line in your area, and so while the pipe could drain properly, the water could also freeze solid down there and cause a big backup problem. The dry well would take care of this.

SUMP PUMP TURNED NOISY

Before we bought this sump pump a month ago, we tried it out and it ran very quietly. However, when we set it in the concrete well, it developed a loud hum. I even covered all the pipes with foam rubber, but nothing seems to lessen the noise. I can't afford to pay $15 just to have a plumber look at it. The pump runs very well except for the loud hum. Can you suggest anything to make it quieter?

The hard sides of the concrete pit act like an amplifier, bouncing the sound waves back and forth. Lining the pit with sheets of styrofoam will deaden the sound. Covering the entire pit with this will be lots better. If the pump sticks up too high, make a box to cover it, lined with styrofoam.

SPRINKLER SYSTEM

We have a sprinkler system, and I would like to know how to blow the water out of the pipes for the winter.

Most installations of underground sprinkler systems have self-draining valves which protect the system during the winter. It's not advisable for the homeowner to attempt blowing out the water, because he lacks the necessary equipment. Plumbers, however, can do a proper job with compressed air.

FREE WATER ADVICE WIDELY AVAILABLE

We recently moved into a house where there seems to be quite a sulfury flavor in the well water. Would a water-softening serviceman be a help with this problem?

He might, but we doubt if he could supply all the information a general water-conditioning firm might give you. This kind of chemical flavor goes beyond just softening the water. Although many people are apparently unaware of this, in many states the installation of water systems in private homes can be supervised by licensed health officers for free. Check with your department of public health.

CHAPTER 14

ELECTRICITY IN THE HOME

A very simple test will tell you whether the wiring in your house is adequate. Just turn on every light and every fixture and other electrical device, so they're all operating at the same time. If you don't blow a fuse or flip a circuit breaker, the wiring's okay. We freely admit that for a few minutes of blaring cacophony of TV sets and radios, combined with dad's radial saw, drill press, and grinder, as well as the blender, dishwasher, and clothes dryer, the neighbors may wonder what's going on. If they ask, just tell them it's research they should be undertaking themselves.

It's a good idea to make this test periodically—and certainly every time you add something else which runs by electricity. The only difficulty is a human one: forgetting. It's certainly easy to forget to check if the third TV set or the new automatic coffee maker overloads any of the circuits. But this checkup should be a must, even though it may be inconvenient at the time. It's much better to make sure there won't be an overload, because most anybody, starting with the fire underwriters, will tell you a big percentage of house fires are started with faulty wiring.

The insidious thing about electrical fires getting started inside the wall space is that they don't flare up like spilled grease in the kitchen, for example. They sneak up into a smolder, often not breaking into a blaze until deep into the night, or even when there is nobody home. You never know, and one way to be sure you don't suffer the heartbreak of a home-destroying fire is to make sure your wiring is adequate.

Well, what happens if the turn-on-everything test starts blowing fuses right and left? You call the electrician and get an estimate for putting an adequate margin of safety in your wiring. Actually this margin of safety should be figured with a look into the future. If you think there is a reasonable chance of adding more appliances, either as the family grows larger or you grow richer, you should plan for ample electric power to handle them too.

As for how much power may be required, here are some averages: with a house of 1,000 square feet, for example, there should be capacity for 45,000 watts for interior lighting and plug-in appliances, plus capacity to handle any of the following permanently connected major appliances: automatic washer, 700 watts; built-in bathroom heater, 1,000 to 1,500 watts; dishwasher–waste disposer, 1,500 watts;

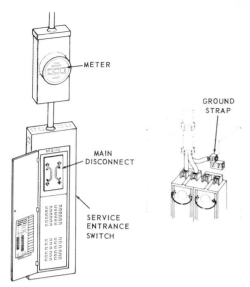

METER

GROUND STRAP

MAIN DISCONNECT

MAIN

SERVICE ENTRANCE SWITCH

Figure 14-1. A standard house service using circuit breakers.

electric clothes dryer, 4,500 to 9,000 watts; electric range, 8,000 to 16,000 watts; built-in cook top, 4,800 watts; built-in oven, 4,800 watts; home freezer, 350 watts; mechanism for house heater, 800 watts; room air conditioner (120 volts), 750 to 1,420 watts; room air conditioner (240 volts), 1,350 watts; fan, 250 to 750 watts; waste disposer (without dishwasher), 500 watts; water pump, 700 to 1,500 watts; workshop (wattage varies greatly).

The corrections needed to make adequate electrical capacity available may require replacing the main electrical entrance, which consists of the wires connecting your house to the power company's cable and the box containing your main switch and fuse box (or circuit breakers). This is usually needed when updating the wiring of most older homes, built before the advent of so many modern electrical work-savers. On the other hand, all that may be needed is the addition of some branch circuits, so that the load will be distributed evenly and lightly. One widely accepted practice is to put some major appliances like the freezer, range, dishwasher, and clothes washer on individual circuits.

Let us add right here that these electrical revisions should neither be skipped nor be postponed. It's also highly impractical to have the job done piecemeal. But one thing which

is immensely practical is to have extra wall and floor outlets put in at the same time. Or have single and double outlets converted to multi-outlets, so you can get rid of those many-wired octopus arrangements you often see, especially in older homes. It's also a great time to convert from chain pulls in overhead lights to wall switches. When one of those chains or cords finally breaks inside the switch housing, sometimes you have to take down the whole fixture from the ceiling and dismantle the switch (trying not to let the tiny spring and washers leap down to the floor and race into a dark, dusty corner), just to replace the chain. Let us suggest, in such cases, that a new switch is a time-saver, and a wall switch is best. In other words, don't take any chances with inadequate wiring. If it's needed, have the electrician come over and do what's needed, and you'll be done with a potentially serious danger.

Electrical Repairs You Can Do

Where additional wiring is needed or a major electrical problem arises, the homeowner should take the safest course and call in a licensed electrician. There are, however, some electrical repairs that you can undertake, and here they are:

Replacing Fuses. Replacing fuses is a simple and safe procedure, if certain safety precautions are taken. If the fuse box is in a basement, care should be taken not to stand on damp concrete when inserting or removing fuses. The main switch, if there's one, should be thrown, and the work done by flashlight if necessary. The burned fuse may be recognized by a burned spot on the mica "window" in the cap. Or it may show a broken or melted fuse strip inside the mica.

The new fuse should be of the same ampere rating as the one taken out. Simply replacing a fuse that continually burns out with one of higher rating throws the overload problem back on the wiring, which may over-

Figure 14-2. A good fuse (far left) and two blown fuses.

heat and start a fire in the walls. A penny, a nail, a twist of foil, or other metal object should *never* be placed under a fuse to keep the circuit operating. A box of the proper-value fuses should be kept on top of the fuse box or in a nearby handy place in order to have a ready supply in emergencies.

Circuit breakers are widely used today. These electrical overload switches replace fuses in a circuit and make it possible to do away with the annoyance of replacing burned-out fuses. On the surface, a circuit breaker looks much like an ordinary light switch of the wall variety. A switch lever protrudes from a slot, and it is usually marked "off" and "on." When a circuit becomes overloaded, the elements of the unit switch the lever to the off position. To reset, merely switch the lever to "on." If it snaps off again, this indicates that the circuit is still overloaded, and the cause must be found and corrected. Circuit breakers need not be replaced in ordinary service.

Whether circuit breakers or fuses are used to protect the various branch circuits, it is a good idea to list all the outlets and fixtures on each circuit. This list should be glued to the inside of the fuse box lid or tacked to the wall nearby. This enables the homeowner to locate quickly the fuse that controls the individual outlet which has shorted or is to be worked on.

Lamps and Cords. The most frequent causes of lamp failure are usually broken switches or shorted cords or plugs. These are the simplest of all fixtures to repair, and with the number of replacement parts that are on sale in hardware, variety, and even grocery stores, there should be no reason for the homeowner not placing a favorite lamp back in operation in a few minutes.

Many lamps profit by being converted to three-way operation. This is a simple matter of changing the socket to a three-way type which accepts bulbs that burn at 50-100-150 watts, depending on the position of the switch. This is accomplished by a special switch and base on the lamp. There are two filaments inside each bulb. The 50-watt filament or the 100-watt filament may be burned separately, or they may be burned together to give 150-watt illumination. All that is necessary for the conversion to the new socket is to remove the old socket by separating the brass shell where the two parts are crimp-fitted together. Be sure the lamp is unplugged first. The wires are then

disconnected by unscrewing the terminal screws, and the new socket is attached. If the new bulb won't fit in the wire loop, called a "harp," which supports the shade, a replacement for this may also be obtained at hardware or lamp stores.

When electrical cords are frayed, they should be repaired promptly lest the insulation underneath become broken and a short circuit result. Most of the time, cords fray at the end where the plug fits into the wall outlet or where the cord enters the lamp or appliance. (Right here, it should be urged that one should never unplug an extension cord from the outlet by pulling the cord; the plug itself should be grasped.)

Provided the insulation covering the wire isn't broken or cracked, the simplest way to protect a frayed area is to wrap it securely with friction tape or plastic tape. While effective as a temporary measure, this certainly isn't handsome, especially if a cord has several such patches. A coat of shellac will also serve.

It's much better to cut out the frayed end entirely and replace the plug, provided, of course, that this won't shorten the cord too much. If it does, the whole cord should be replaced.

To replace the cord in a conventional plug, simply strip the insulation about an inch from the end of the cord and twist the two newly exposed wires around the terminal screws in the plug in the same manner the old ends were fastened (you can note this when you remove them from the plug).

Several exceedingly handy plugs are available which require no stripping of the insulation whatsoever. These plugs are equipped with sharp prongs which, when closed on the cord, bite right through the covering and insulation and make a firm connection with the wires. The plugs are simplicity itself, and cutting off a frayed end of cord and putting on a new plug is literally a matter of seconds.

Replacing Switches and Convenience Outlets. There's nothing tricky about handling either of these projects. Just remember to always cut off the current first.

When removing a wall switch—either the push-button or toggle type—remove the cover plate on the wall, remove the screws which keep the switch in place, pull the switch out of the box as far as the connecting wires permit, and disconnect the wires. If it's a single-pole switch (only two connecting screws), connect the wires to either screw on the new switch. If it's a three-way switch (three connecting wires), the black wire is attached to the brass-colored screw (usually) at the top. The white and red wires are then connected to either of the lighter-colored screws at the bottom.

To replace a convenience outlet, remove the outlet cover and then remove the screws holding the outlet to the box. Disconnect the wires, and install the new convenience outlet, using the box already in place. Be sure you connect the white wire to the light-colored screw, the black wire to the brass-colored screw.

Don't attempt to install additional convenience outlets yourself. This is a job for a licensed electrician.

Questions and Answers

The questions and answers on electricity in the home are rather limited. And for a good reason—the amount of electrical work that a do-it-yourselfer can do is limited, both by local law and by common sense. That is, unless you're a licensed electrician, don't try to make major electrical repairs or improvements yourself. Even ordinary house voltage is highly dangerous. Further—and this is very important—in some communities you'll void your fire insurance policy unless a licensed electrician does the electrical work in your house. But here are questions and answers to electrical problems that you can do.

DRAFT FROM ELECTRIC OUTLETS

Our five-year-old home has blanket-type insulation in the ceiling and side walls. During colder weather, the walls near the electrical outlets on the outside walls are cold and cold air can be felt seeping in through the outlets themselves. How can this be remedied?

The cold-air seepage or draft is due to neglect to pack around the boxes inside the

Figure 14-3. How to use a wire nut.

wall when the insulation and wiring were installed. The builder should have been called to correct the oversight, or the dealer who installed the insulation. The switch plates and boxes in the walls must be removed. Be sure to first turn off the electric current. Then work small pieces of insulation or any thick padding (heavy felt from an old hat, etc.) around to surround each box on all sides when reinserted into its cavity.

FLUORESCENT LIGHT SLUGGISH

The fluorescent light over the kitchen sink has become very sluggish. It is very slow in lighting after being turned on. How can this be remedied?

The starter may be worn out or may be defective. A new starter is inexpensive. It plugs into a socket at an end of the fixture. However, test the bulb in another fixture to be sure it's the starter and not the bulb at fault.

REDUCING FLUORESCENT HUM

I have a fluorescent light over the kitchen sink which always has a hum when it is in use. What causes this? How can it be eliminated?

A certain amount of hum in the ballast is normal, and usually it is not very noticeable. There may be loose screws holding the ballast in your fixture. Try tightening the screws to correct the hum. Or place a piece of foam rubber under the ballast to act as a noise absorber. Be sure the current in the branch circuit is turned off before doing any kind of repair.

BLACK ENDS ON FLUORESCENT LAMP

What causes fluorescent tubes to turn black or brown near the ends?

This is a normal condition that indicates the life of the tube is near the end. It is caused by the filament burning the coating nearby. The tube may burn satisfactorily for some time after the ends blacken, but it is good practice to obtain a replacement tube when the condition is noticed.

BLINKING FLUORESCENT LAMP

How can I stop a fluorescent lamp from blinking?

The fluorescent lamp may blink because of loose fixture contacts. Check the condition of the contacts, and see if there is any vibration of the lamp when it is in position. It may be the plug, if the fluorescent fixture is a portable or plug-in type. If the blinking persists for a few times after the switch has been thrown and then the lamp burns normally, this usually indicates a defective starter, and a new one should be tried in its place. If the switch is turned on and the lamp does not blink but the ends remain lighted or reddish, this too is probably due to a defective starter. Sometimes this slow start may indicate that the temperature is too low. Fluorescent tubes are not efficient under 50°. Special low-temperature tubes are available for use outdoors, in refrigerated storage areas, or in basements or attics that become cold in winter.

"SOFTENING" LIGHT

We get a very harsh, glaring light from a clear globe over the electric bulb in a hallway. Is there any way to soften the light by coating the globe in any way?

Aerosol-form paint for frosting glass is available at most paint and hardware dealers. Or rub the glass surface with a lump of putty softened with a small amount of linseed oil; allow it to dry for 24 hours, and then repeat the application.

INSTALLING LIGHTING FIXTURES

We'd like to change the ceiling fixture in our dining room. Can I do the job?

Yes you can, and it involves two main steps: fastening the fixture wires to the house wires and fastening the fixture to the outlet box. That is, first cut the current to the fixture. Then unscrew the locknuts or cap nuts holding the fixture in place and pull the fixture away from the wall or down from the ceiling far enough to get at the connection wires inside the outlet box or junction that holds the fixture up. Then remove the old fixture by cutting the connections. When putting up the new unit, fasten the fixture's black wires to the black wire in the outlet box and the white fixture wires, or wires with colored strands, to the white wire in the box. Be sure to twist them together clockwise and then screw the solderless connectors on. There are various methods of fastening the lighting fixtures to the outlet box. However, except for recessed types, they usually consist of first fastening the metal strap (which is included with the new fixture) to the threaded stud in the outlet box, and then fastening the fixture to the metal strap by means of capnuts or locknuts. If the

threaded stud isn't long enough, use an extension nipple. The design of certain fixtures eliminates the metal strap, but in other respects, the principle is identical.

THE UL SEAL

Is the UL seal on appliances important? What does it mean?

The UL seal is most important. Electrical equipment, cords, and appliances should come with an Underwriters' Laboratory label fastened to them at some point. The labels are various sizes, colors, and shapes, depending upon the unit they are attached to. They indicate that the appliance or cord was manufactured to comply with the National Electrical Code, and doesn't present a hazard in operation. Before buying, insist on being shown the UL seal.

UNDERWRITERS' KNOT

What is meant by an Underwriters' knot? I read about it in a "do-it-yourself" electrical book, but the author didn't explain how to make it or what it was.

The Underwriters' knot is used when installing a plug to a cord and helps to protect the cord from strain. Actually, it is very easy to make. The first step is to remove the insulation by cutting at a slant—as you would in sharpening a pencil—about ½ inch from the ends of the wires. Remove all parts of the insulation so that the wires are bright and clean. After the wires are inserted into the plug, tie a knot as shown here. (The knot portion shouldn't have the insulation.) Then loop the wires by bending them so that they fit snugly around the terminal screws. Be sure you attach the loops in the same direction in which the screws turn when you tighten them. Usually this is clockwise. To complete the job, snip off the loose ends of wire and pull the cord until the knot and wires settle firmly inside the plug.

THREE-PRONG PLUG

We just purchased a new refrigerator, and it came with a three-prong plug. My wall receptacles, however, are of the two-prong type. Can I cut off the extra prong, which I understand is just a ground?

When installing a grounded appliance in a home that doesn't have a three-wire grounded receptacle, under *no* conditions is the grounding prong to be cut off or removed. It's

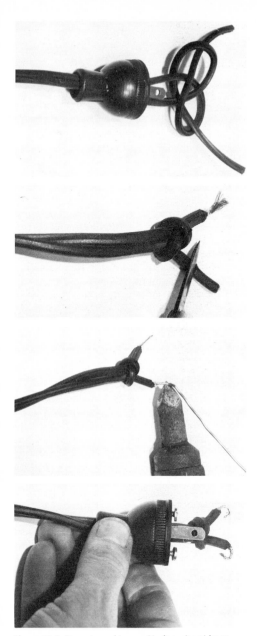

Figure 14-4. Steps in making an Underwriters' knot.

your responsibility to contact a qualified electrician and have a properly grounded three-prong wall receptacle installed in accordance with the appropriate electrical code. Should a two-prong adapter plug be required temporarily, it's your responsibility to have it replaced

with a properly grounded three-prong receptacle or the two-prong adapter properly grounded by a qualified electrician. Incidentally, the standard accepted color for ground wires is green or green with a yellow stripe.

DOORBELL DOESN'T WORK

About 6 months ago we moved into a 100-year-old house. The doorbell worked beautifully until just a few weeks ago, and then it stopped. What happened?

Doorbells in older houses are often battery-operated. A large, cylindrical, 1½-volt dry cell is usually hidden in a box somewhere near the bell itself. When such a doorbell goes dead, it is frequently the result of this battery having run down. A little searching will usually uncover the hiding place, and the battery may easily be changed. More modern doorbells have transformers which are connected with the 110-volt house circuits. These seldom require care or repair.

ONE FINGER PUSH RINGS TWO BELLS

I have a doorbell in my house, and I would also like one to ring in the basement. Could both bells be wired to the same circuit, or will I need two separate circuits to the door button? I would like to know before asking an electrician.

Both bells can be rigged for the same circuit. No complications at all. They will ring at the same time.

REMOVING OLD FIXTURES

We have some old-fashioned wall lights in our dining room. How can I remove them?

After turning off the current, remove the bulb and shade (if any) and remove the screws or knurled nut that holds the fixture to the wall box. Detach the fixture's wires from the wires entering the box from the house line. Tape the ends of the house line with electrician's tape, and cover with solderless connectors. Fold the wires back into the box. Cover the opening with a standard box cover. Then restore the electric current.

REPAIRING PULL CHAIN

Is it a difficult job to replace a pull chain?

It's an easy job. First cut off the current to the fixture and pull the socket apart. The chain is usually held by a small clamp. In some sockets, the clamp can be lifted out and the chain released by raising the little trigger sticking through it. In others, you pry the clamp apart to release the chain. Once the faulty chain is removed, insert the new chain and reassemble the socket.

WIRE SPLICE

What is the best way to join two wires?

Two pieces of wire can be joined together by splicing. To do it, remove the insulation for a length of about 3 inches from the end of each wire and scrape these portions bright. Then bend the ends at right angles to the wires, hook them together, and twist each end tightly around the other wire with pliers so that firm contact is made. To prevent corrosion and to obtain a good electrical contact, the joint should be soldered. It should then be wrapped securely with electrician's tape.

ELEMENT IN ELECTRIC RANGE

A short while ago, while sterilizing baby bottles on my electric range, the water in the pan evaporated and the enamel melted off the pot and onto the heating element. I have tried everything I know of to remove this dripping, unsuccessfully. Could you recommend a procedure to eliminate this baked-on enamel?

Try the following: Get the element as hot as possible, and after a few minutes, while it is still "red" hot, try wiping off the enamel with a thick wad of "00" steel wool. If the wool gets hot too fast, hold it with a pair of pliers. The

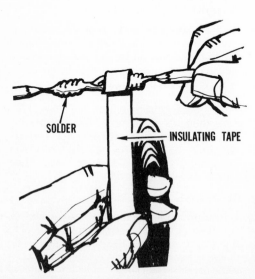

SOLDER

INSULATING TAPE

Figure 14-5. Proper method of taping a solder joint.

high temperature may melt the porcelain for easy removal.

LEAKY REFRIGERATOR DOOR

Our refrigerator seems to be "frosting up" more than it should. What could be the problem?

One fault may be the rubber seal around the inside of the door. If this isn't making a firm total closure, it will allow warm air to leak inside. Even though the rubber may appear in good condition, the closure may not be perfect. To test for this, hold a dollar bill half in and half out, and close the door on it. If the bill can be withdrawn with little effort, the closure at this point isn't tight enough. Work the dollar bill around the entire door. If there are many weak spots, it would be best to replace the entire rubber seal. If there are only two or three, a simple home repair is as follows: Mark each weak spot with chalk. Cover the seal at these places with several thicknesses of friction tape or black plastic tape, to increase the thickness of the seal. Do this until the dollar bill resists being withdrawn while the door is closed.

SHOP MOTORS

I have been using several power tools—a table saw, a router, a planer, and a drill press. What maintenance must I give the motors of these tools?

Household and shop motors require little maintenance and care outside of oiling properly, according to the manufacturer's directions. If the motor has an oil cup filled with felt at each bearing, see that the felt is kept moist, but not wet, with oil. A couple of drops every month or two should do the job. Universal motors require occasional brush changes, especially where they are run constantly. The brushes are usually accessible by removing small slotted plastic plugs at the sides of the motor case. Underneath these plugs will be found small springs with carbon pieces attached. If the carbon brushes are worn down almost to the spring, they should be replaced. Replacement brushes may be obtained by visiting an electrical supply shop with one of the old brushes as a model.

ELECTRIC IRON STICKS

My electric iron sticks to the fabric while ironing. Is there any way that I can prevent this from occurring?

Electric irons should be polished occasionally with waxed paper. Heat the iron on low; then slide it over the paper once or twice. This will melt a bit of the wax onto the base plate of the iron and make it easier to glide over the clothes. If stains occur on the bottom, they may be polished off with silver polish. Do not use harsh abrasives on iron-base plates; once scratched, they are harder to slide.

REPAIRING HEATING ELEMENT

The wire in the heating element of my toaster broke. Is there any way that I can fix it?

The coils of wire comprising the heating elements of toasters, hot plates, etc., are usually made of a combination of nickel and chrome wire. If the wire breaks, it can be repaired quite simply, if the element itself can be removed. The repair is made by looping the two ends of wire together and then covering the joint with a dab of nichrocite paste (available in electrical and hardware stores). This paste is made to fuse with the nickel and chrome wire. The current is turned on, and the heat will melt the paste, thus soldering the joint.

SETTLING TV ARGUMENT

To settle an argument: Does or does not a TV antenna, properly grounded, also protect the house from lightning?

It does *not* protect the house. It is put there solely for the protection of your TV set. However, we believe it's also mighty forehanded to disconnect the lead-in from the set when electrical storms begin banging around. Lightning is as unpredictable as it is potent.

CHAPTER 15

KITCHENS AND BATHROOMS

Two of the biggest problem areas in any house are the kitchens and bathrooms. We receive more questions on these two areas than any other portion of the house. Because of this, we are abandoning our normal format and, as we did in Chapter 7, are going directly to questions and answers.

Questions and Answers

We are dividing this portion of the chapter into two sections: kitchens and bathrooms. Let's first look at kitchens.

KITCHENS

PAINT KITCHEN-COUNTER LINOLEUM TOP?

I have a kitchen sink with a linoleum-covered custom-made top that was on when purchased. Now it is worn where the faucets are; water seems to remove the coloring. What can I do to refinish the top? It has metal all around, and so the linoleum can't be removed. Can it be painted?

The metal edging can probably be pried off, and a laminated plastic top put on the counter, if desired, after removing the linoleum. Or a ceramic-type coating can be applied (available in white or several pastel colors). Or apply several coats of enamel undercoater, finishing with top-quality enamel in the desired color. Before applying any finish, be sure the surface is absolutely free of any trace of grease, wax, grime, etc.

SOFTENED LINOLEUM COUNTER TOPS

The linoleum on our counter is soft and sticky to the touch, especially around the sink. There are no breaks, or cracks, although it has been on for four years. I stopped waxing it because of the stickiness. Is there anything I can do?

Splashes from caustic soap or scouring powder, from the sink, may have attacked the gum and oils in the linoleum and caused it to deteriorate. In this case, the only real remedy is to replace the linoleum. Or there may be too heavy a coating of wax on the linoleum; investigate this possibility before replacing it. Remove the wax with a wax remover made by a nationally known manufacturer, following the label instructions carefully. Then apply a cream cleanup wax made by the same manufacturer; this leaves a protective coating on the linoleum surface.

HIDING FORMICA SEAM

Apparently the plywood under the Formica on our kitchen-sink counter top has shrunk. As a result, a seam between two pieces of Formica has opened slightly. Is there any way to hide this?

Formica dealers also carry a preparation in tubes called "Seam-fill," made for this purpose. Let's hope (1) the plywood has stopped shrinking, and (2) you can get a perfect color match for the seam.

BURNED FORMICA

My counter top, which is made of a high-gloss plastic called Formica, became burned when a cigarette fell on it, leaving a brown spot. Is there any way I can patch this?

If the spot is deep, and you cannot remove the discoloration by steel wool and a strong detergent, we're afraid you are out of luck. It is difficult to patch this material, especially if there is a complicated design, because when separated from the wood or plywood underneath, it is quite brittle and difficult to trim, without some skill. It also requires a special cement. One suggestion is to keep the spot covered with a plate or the ashtray itself until you can have the counter top replaced.

COUNTER TOP COMING LOOSE

The blue Formica counter top is beginning to come loose. Mostly this is along the front edge and corner. It's not very far in yet, but I'd like to know how to fasten it back again permanently. This has been there for 17 years, so I guess I can't complain too loud about the adhesive.

It's quite possible that after all these years, water may have worked down the edge to soften the plywood under the Formica enough to loosen it. First, try to get the wood under the raised area dry. Don't use the counter top, or else cover it with sheet plastic to protect it from water. Turn your hair dryer or an electric heater on it. Then simply work clear epoxy adhesive under the Formica, as far in as a toothpick can poke it. Clamp it down firmly, but not so hard that you squeeze the epoxy out again. Protect the Formica by a piece of lath under the clamps.

FORMICA ON FORMICA?

Our Formica counter tops are now marred and scarred. No complaints, though. They have lasted for years. Could I now put new Formica on top, using contact cement?

An unhesitating "yes" if you are experienced with handling this type cement, where fairly large areas are involved. If you are a novice, be sure to get the Formica dealer (who will have the Formica cut the exact size for you) to give you detailed instructions. It isn't difficult to use contact cement, but you have to remember that once those two cemented surfaces come together, they had better be lined up exactly right. You don't get a second chance. An uninvited thought: For a neat job, you will probably need new edging to take care of the added thickness.

COUNTER TOPS DULL

Our 15-year-old home has Formica counter tops and tabletops—very durable and good-looking. But now the surfaces have become dull and look their age, although they are still very smooth. Could I put on varnish? Or is there anything else I could do?

Forget the varnish. You'd have to sand down all the gloss remaining on the surface for a good bond. Instead, use a good auto wax, well rubbed and buffed. This will restore shine and look very nice. It won't be permanent, however. You'll have to rewax once in a while, depending on wear and tear.

PLASTIC KITCHEN COUNTER TOP

The plastic on our kitchen counter top is only a year old and is showing scratches and dullness. Is there a protective finish that can be applied, like a wax?

Unfortunately there is nothing that you can use. To minimize further scratches, use a wood cutting board for all cutting and slicing.

FORMICA NOT TOO PAINTABLE

The Formica on our kitchen counter top must be at least 12 years old. Generally it's still in good enough condition, but now it's the wrong color for the new kitchen decorating plan. Can I paint it?

Painting is not really recommended. Formica has such a sleek, hard surface that even top-grade enamel will start peeling, especially when it's also exposed to soap, acids, etc. You'll have to sand the surface down to dull it in order to give the enamel a bond (which is one tough job!). It's really better to have another sheet of Formica installed over the present one.

ALUMINUM MOLDING

The plastic counter top in my kitchen is trimmed with aluminum molding. Recently, when anyone has come in contact with the aluminum, it has left a black streak on clothing. What can I do about this?

The difficulty is that the aluminum is of a cheap grade and therefore was not "anodized," a process which prevents this kind of problem. The only thing we can suggest doing about it, if you keep the present aluminum, is to coat it with clear lacquer. But you must realize this will be only a temporary measure; when the lacquer wears off, it will have to be renewed. Our recommendation would be to remove the molding and replace it with stainless steel or high-quality aluminum which has been properly treated.

KITCHEN COUNTER TOP BULGES

A year ago cabinets were installed in the kitchen. The counter top was of 12-inch pine boards. Adhesive was applied directly on the boards, and a good grade of vinyl plastic was put on. In a month's time the boards warped and the plastic bulged. This was replaced with a pine board, the full width of the counter, but the same trouble developed. For several months we ironed the counter and it was fair, but again we have the same difficulty and the iron no longer helps. What can we do? Was the wrong paste used?

The wrong base was used. A fir plywood not less than an inch thick should have been used. Such a base would be least likely to warp. Since we don't know just what type of vinyl and adhesive was used, we can't say if the right or wrong materials were involved in your problem. The manufacturer's directions should be followed as far as the adhesive is concerned.

TILED COUNTER TOPS

We bought a house, and the kitchen-sink counter is of black and white tile. At the edges of the border, around the sink, the joints are packed with a lot of dirt and there is a bad odor. I don't seem to be able to get it clean. Please advise.

Using a sharply pointed screwdriver or some other tool, scrape out the cement between the tiles and scrub the edges of the tiles with a solution of washing soda or triso-dium phosphate, using about 2 pounds to the gallon of hot water, and rinse with clear water. While the edges of the tiles are still damp, repack the joints with a white portland cement mixed with water to the consistency of thick cream. Wipe off all smears of cement, while still wet, with a damp cloth.

GRAYING GROUT

Recently we made a tile-top table for kitchen use. It is decorative and practical except for one annoying feature: the grout between the tiles becomes gray and dirty-looking. The only way to clean it is to use a scouring pad and scrub between the tiles—very slow and tedious. A tile dealer sold me a silicone sealer (invisible) which helped for a short time, but it is washing away and the grout is looking grubby again. Can you recommend a simple way to clean the grout without washing it out in the process? I used bleach at one point, but that didn't seem to do much good either.

Try using a cream cleanup wax. Or use a concrete and masonry cleaning and etching liquid (that does not contain muriatic acid), available at masonry supply dealers, following the label directions carefully. Or replace the present grout with a stain-resistant type, available at some large tile dealers and hardware and housewares stores.

GREASY WALL TILE

We have plastic tile on our kitchen walls. This has become very soiled and greasy and is covered with a yellow film. What is the best way to clean it?

Many efficient all-purpose household cleaners are now widely available at supermarkets, etc.; follow the label instructions for use on tile. Or use a cleanup wax made by a nationally known manufacturer; this leaves a protective coating, making future cleaning easier. Or wash with a solution of trisodium phosphate, using about 1 tablespoon to a gallon of warm water, followed by thorough rinsing with clear water.

TOUGHENING TABLETOP

How can I make a wood kitchen tabletop resistant to water, so that I could use it without a tablecloth and just wipe off the surface?

Sand the surface as clean and glass-smooth as you can make it. Then put on a couple of coats of polyurethane varnish, clear epoxy finish. Another good method is to cover the table with a plastic laminate such as Formica or Micarta.

REMOVING TILE CEMENT

I have plastic tile halfway up the wall of my kitchen and bathroom. I can remove the tile easily, but I can't get the hard cement underneath the tile off. I want to re-cover the whole wall with Wall-Tex. Is there any way to remove the cement?

If possible, find out what specific cement or adhesive was used in installing the plastic tile and the solvent recommended by the manufacturer for that adhesive. Solvents vary according to the particular cement. Otherwise try using steel wool with naphtha, or, easier, sand it off with an electric sander.

TILING AND PLASTERING PLASTERBOARD

We have remodeled our kitchen and have plasterboard walls now. Will we be able to put tile on the plaster to about a height of 6 feet? On the ceiling and upper walls, which will remain untiled, could plaster be put right on?

The tile can be applied to the plasterboard, using a special adhesive recommended by the tile manufacturer for the purpose. Consult your tile dealer for installation instructions, etc. Plaster can be applied directly to the plasterboard if the walls and ceiling are firmly and solidly installed. First fasten "self-furring" metal lath to the plasterboard; then apply the plaster.

BRICK WALL IN KITCHEN

We bought and are refinishing an old brick house. Much of it has to be plastered, and I wondered if we could leave one wall in the kitchen unplastered. How could we go about refinishing the inside brick wall, and would it be much colder in winter without the plaster?

Not only would the brick wall in the kitchen, during the winter, be very cold, but when cooking and baking are done, the brick would "sweat" so much it would be a mess. We suggest that you fur out the wall and finish it with gypsum wallboard (plasterboard) or lath and plaster. Then, to get the brick effect, cover the wall with one of the embossed plastic sheets simulating brick. Wallpaper dealers in the larger towns and cities sell it.

"BRICK" ON KITCHEN WALL

We are planning a knotty pine kitchen, and behind our stove we would like to put brick, halfway up the wall. What does one use for that? Is there an imitation brick, a real brick, or wood that looks like brick suitable for the purpose?

You can get an imitation brick made of plastic that comes in panels. This type of material is usually handled by wallpaper dealers. It is widely distributed, and you should have no difficulty in getting it locally. "Real" brick can be used, but this will require extra support in the floor because bricks are quite heavy.

REMOVING LINOLEUM-TYPE WALL COVERING

We are planning to remodel our kitchen this summer. We want to take the old wall covering (linoleum type) off the walls. Is there a quick and easy way to do this?

Yes. Pry one corner of the wall covering near the ceiling loose; then just pull the rest of it away from the wall, with a firm steady motion.

BLACK WALL ADHESIVE

What would be the best way to remove old black adhesive under a linoleumlike wall covering? We are doing our kitchen over and want to put birch hardboard to chair level.

The easiest way to remove the adhesive is with an electric hand sander. Or remove it with fine steel wool and naphtha, being sure the room is well ventilated and all pilot lights are turned off in the kitchen.

MARKS FROM METAL ON LINOLEUM

We have metal caps on the bottoms of our kitchen chairs and table. These have made ugly round marks on the linoleum, and regardless of how hard I rub, I can't remove them. I keep the floor waxed all the time. What do you suggest?

First, we would recommend replacing the metal caps with plastic ones, now widely available in an assortment of colors at many hardware, housewares, and variety stores. Try removing the marks with a liquid-wax floor cleaner, made by a nationally known manufacturer, following the label directions, using fine steel wool.

MOLD ON CABINET UNDER SINK

I recently moved into a new home and finished the oak woodwork myself, using two coats of sealer and two coats of heavy-duty seal, applied with a cloth as per instructions. Mold has formed on the outside of the doors of the cabinet underneath the kitchen sink. What can be done to correct this situation and prevent it from reoccurring?

Because of the cold-water line, there is always a possibility of dampness (and mold) under the sink. When cooking is done in the kitchen, the air becomes quite humid, causing the cold-water pipes to sweat. In addition, the drain pipe and trap also sweat as cold water flows through. The mold should be removed by scrubbing it with a stiff brush and detergent or household bleach solution, followed by rinsing with clear water. If possible, vents should be installed near the top and bottom of the doors for better ventilation and air circulation in the area.

KITCHEN SINK IS RUSTY

A section of the bottom of our porcelain kitchen sink is rusty, because the porcelain has chipped off. Since I am only subletting this apartment for a few months, I don't feel inclined to buy a new sink. Is there any way to get rid of the rust?

Frankly, except for a very temporary measure, you'll just have to "grin and bear it." The exposed metal can be cleaned with any of the rust-removing solutions now available in many hardware stores, and then touched up with a special enamel made for chipped porcelain. This is by no means guaranteed to last, due to the rough treatment of hot water and pots and pans.

STAINLESS STEEL SINK

We are planning to put in a new stainless steel sink, but friends have told us that they are not as stainless or as durable as cast iron. Can you please advise as to the good or bad qualities of both?

Stainless steel sinks can be easily cleaned and won't discolor when acid or alkaline liquids are used. A little mild scouring powder rubbed with the lines of the finish will make the sink look clean. In hard-water areas, drops of water on stainless steel or colored porcelain sinks will leave spots that are difficult to remove. To avoid this, both types of sinks should have drops of water wiped off as soon as possible. The porcelain on cast iron can be chipped by a hard accidental blow, but otherwise cast iron sinks are extremely satisfactory; handsome, too.

LIME DEPOSITS ON STAINLESS STEEL

Our home is four years old, but we are having increasing difficulty keeping that new look, particularly with the sinks and faucets. How can we remove lime deposits from crevices in sink fittings and faucet parts? There is a deposit of lime where the sink rim and sink meet (due to a leaky faucet spout gasket).

We strongly recommend having a water-softening unit installed to retain the new look more easily, and to make general laundering and cleaning and housekeeping much easier. The only suggestion we can make for removing the lime deposits is to use fine stainless steel wool and one of the deliming preparations now available at large housewares and some sewing notions dealers; these are used for removing the deposit inside steam irons. For the water-softening unit, consult a large plumbing supply house or a water-conditioning firm.

SINK FULL OF CRACKS

My kitchen sink is good, except that there are many, many hairline cracks in the enamel. These give a dirty look, even when the sink is really clean. How can I cover these cracks?

When you finally decide you can't stand it, get the sink as surgically clean as possible. Then apply a couple of coats of an epoxy-type enamel. Remember: This will not give the same showroom shine as a new sink, and it won't last forever, but it will look pretty good and hide those cracks.

SEALING CAP IN COUNTER TOP

Between the back of the vinyl Masonite sink counter top and the cabinet just installed is a gap about ¼ inch wide. How can I seal this so that it's watertight? I don't want water working down into the wood under the counter top and causing trouble.

Quarter-round molding will serve nicely. For greatest protection against water seepage, cut it to fit exactly and then seal all surfaces with paint before mounting it in place. To assure a tight, waterproof fit, in addition to securing it with nails or screws, coat the contact surfaces with epoxy adhesive or household cement. You could also do a very neat job with aluminum cove molding.

RUST SPOTS IN SINK

I have a kitchen sink where rust spots are coming through the finish. This is an iron sink with a porcelain finish. How can I refinish this?

You'll be much better off shopping around for a good secondhand sink. Even if you can find an epoxy-type ceramic-glaze finish in a big paint store, getting it on without ridges or brush marks is pretty tricky for the inexperienced. There's no law against giving it a good try, however.

BEST PLACE FOR KITCHEN WALL FAN

Where is the best location for a kitchen wall fan?

High on an outside wall, preferably above the range. However, if the range is on an inside wall, the damp cooking vapors can be brought over by means of a hood and ducting system so that the fan can push them outdoors. A ceiling fan is okay, but it's a second choice.

INSTALLING KITCHEN FAN

Will it be all right if I install a kitchen ventilating fan so that it feeds into the chimney?

We certainly don't recommend it. The fan very probably will interfere with the draft of the heating unit, which could cause serious problems. And if the wind should blow from the wrong direction, it could cause a downdraft, filling the kitchen with smoke and fumes. The fan should be vented directly to the outdoors.

ELECTRIC RANGE HOODS

There is no exhaust fan in our kitchen, and no way to install one. We have seen electronic range hoods advertised and recently investigated them at a department store. They seem to be very efficient. We should like to know more about them before investing in one.

These electronic (and ductless) hoods are efficient (see page 183). For descriptive information about any particular type, you can obtain literature from any dealer or from your local gas and electric company.

CLEANING RANGE HOOD

I have a metal hood over the kitchen range to absorb grease and odors. How is this cleaned?

The dealer from whom the hood was purchased, or your local utility company, probably has specific instructions available. Excellent metal-cleaning preparations and polishes are available at supermarkets and housewares and hardware stores. Or wash the hood with mild soap and water to remove all surface grease and grime, rinse with clear water, and wipe dry. If this is the type with an activated carbon filter, the filter should be removed, cleaned, and refreshed according to the manufacturer's instructions.

FINISH FOR RANGE HOOD

The enamel on the light hood of my kitchen range has worn off in some places. How should I remove the balance of the enamel so that I can put on new appliance enamel?

You needn't remove the rest of the enamel at all. Just give it a thorough sanding, both to roughen the surface and to clean off every trace of grease. Then put on your new enamel. Thin coats are much better than thick ones.

COOKING MOISTURE

The tenants in our upstairs apartment complain that when cooking is being done, the walls in the kitchen are quite damp and full of condensation. I have suggested opening the kitchen windows slightly to allow some ventilation. They insist this wouldn't help matters at all and asked for your opinion. Any suggestion you can offer?

We certainly heartily agree with you that opening the windows will allow for ventilation and the escape of the moisture from cooking. This would serve the same purpose as an exhaust fan vented to the outdoors. Cooking vapors are a frequent cause of excessive dampness in the kitchen.

CHIPPED PORCELAIN STOVE

A very heavy object dropped on the stove, chipping the stove's white porcelain in three different places and leaving the black steel showing through. What can I do to restore its original look?

Hardware dealers carry a special porcelain stove repair material which will withstand heat without discoloring. It's very easy to apply, following the manufacturer's directions. Be sure the surface is completely free of grease, wax, soot, etc., before applying it.

PAINT DISCOLORED ON BUILT-IN OVEN

Is it possible to repaint a built-in oven? Ours has discolored and peeled, indicating it was coated with a copper finish. The rest of the oven is in good condition. I would appreciate any suggestions to salvage it, as replacement is expensive.

If this is a fairly new oven, the finish should have given better service, and we suggest getting in touch with the dealer or manufacturer; sometimes a defective appliance gets by even the most rigid factory inspection. To refinish (we assume it is the exterior surface that is discolored and peeling), steel-wool off any flaking and peeling material and wipe with turpentine to remove any trace of grease, grime, wax, etc. Then apply any top-quality heat-resistant stove enamel, following the manufacturer's instructions on the container.

STREAKED OVEN DOOR

Streaks run lengthwise on the front of the oven door. The stove was bought second-hand and is in perfect condition except for the streaks. I tried cleanser to remove them, without success. Can you suggest anything to get these stains off?

Try removing the streaks with fine steel wool and a scratchless scouring powder; or use one of the excellent oven-cleaning preparations widely available in supermarkets and housewares, hardware, and paint stores, following the label directions carefully. This is probably baked-on grease from cooking spatters.

OVEN LOADED WITH RUST

I uncovered an old, very large, cast-iron Dutch oven when cleaning my mother's basement. The rust must be nearly $1/8$ inch thick. How can I get it off?

Put on goggles, gloves, and old clothes, and insert a wire-brush attachment in your electric drill and get the major stuff off. Then cover the rest with a rust-removing preparation.

FINISH ON REFRIGERATOR

I have an eight-year-old electric refrigerator which was in the kitchen when the room was partially burned out. The heat, smoke, and chemicals affected the finish of the refrigerator. Can this be finished with enamel by a good painter? If not, what would you suggest?

Appliance dealers selling refrigerators in most communities have a refinishing service, where their workers will spray on a lacquer-type finish similar to the original. Ask a dealer about it. If not, wash the box, rinse it, and allow it to dry; then finish it with a good brand of enamel.

YELLOW TINGE ON REFRIGERATOR

I have a refrigerator about 12 years old. The white enamel has begun to show a yellowish tinge. Is there any way of removing this?

It is difficult to say if the enamel has discolored with age or there is just a surface accumulation of a discoloration. Try the following on an obscure area: Saturate a piece of cloth with peroxide; then sprinkle it liberally with cream of tartar and a scratchless scouring powder. When the powders become well dampened, rub the surface with the mixture and allow it to remain for a half hour or so; then rinse it off with clear water. If there is no improvement, a new coating is necessary.

GASKET ON REFRIGERATOR DISCOLORED

Our refrigerator was in storage for about 3 months. The rubber on the inside of the door is discolored from mold. Can anything be done for this?

Replacement materials for gaskets around refrigerator doors are available at most hardware and electric appliance dealers; these are either rubber or plastic and are easy to install, following the instructions on the package. Before putting on the new gasket, be sure to wash the area with a household bleach, following that with thorough rinsing with clear water, to be sure all trace of the mold is removed; use a stiff brush for the scrubbing.

MUSTY ODOR IN REFRIGERATOR

We bought a good used refrigerator, five years old. We find there is a very unpleasant musty odor inside, including the freezer. I have cleaned the drain tube and the drip pan, but the refrigerator still smells. Is there anything we can put in to absorb this odor?

Sometimes the gasket around the door has absorbed odors. Wash this carefully with mild soapsuds, rinsing well and drying thoroughly. Then vacuum around underneath the gasket. Units of activated carbon, or charcoal, are available at many hardware and housewares dealers for deodorizing refrigerators, etc. We assume, of course, you have thoroughly washed all interior surfaces thoroughly with soda.

REFRIGERATOR SHELVES RUSTING

My refrigerator is getting along in years, yet still works perfectly. But some rust spots are beginning to form on the shelves and racks. How can I stop this?

Travel first-class, and let an electroplating shop plate them with chrome. Or travel tourist: wipe all grease off the shelves, rub the rust spots with the finest steel wool, and give them a well-buffed coat of paste wax. Renew the wax when needed.

REFRIGERATOR GOT TOO HOT

Due to very limited space in my apartment kitchen, the refrigerator is very close to the stove. After having this refrigerator a year or so, I noticed that there are places on the side next to the stove where the shiny white finish has begun to turn a little brownish. No doubt this is due to heat from cooking. Is there any way I can touch up these spots so that they won't be noticed, without having to refinish the whole refrigerator?

You would certainly have to do that entire side, and it would test your ability to feather-edge, to blend with the finish on the top or at one of the corners. After spraying it with appliance enamel, an auto rubbing wax will help. This won't prevent a repeat, unless you can slip a fairly thick sheet of asbestos between the stove and the refrigerator.

MOVING REFRIGERATOR

Our kitchen appliances are being rearranged, and we want to move the refrigerator to a different location. How can we do this to avoid denting or damaging the floor tile during the shift?

Work a piece of old carpeting (nap side down) under each leg of the refrigerator. By dragging the carpeting along the floor, the shift can be accomplished without damage to the floor tile. This should be a two-man job.

REMOVING "PHEW!" FROM FREEZER

Nobody noticed the electricity to the freezer had been accidentally turned off until all the meat had spoiled. I mean spoiled. Phew! How can the freezer be made usable again?

If at all possible, trundle it outdoors, where sun and breezes can get at it in between frequent scrubbings. Many remedies can help absorb odors. Activated charcoal is good. A dish of vanilla has been claimed great at chasing fish odors. Space deodorizers of the absorbent type can help. Unfortunately, if the rubber gasket has been thoroughly permeated, you'll do much better by having a new one put in; it would stay "stinky" long after the rest of the freezer is pure again.

REFINISHING WASHING MACHINE

During the summer, I kept my washing machine on a back porch where it was exposed to weather. Several rust spots have developed. Is there any way I can refinish this so that it won't rust so easily?

A fast-drying, rust-preventive enamel, available in aerosol form, can be applied; if your dealer doesn't stock it, he can probably get it for you. If the rust spots are widespread and deep, first apply a metal coat made by the same manufacturer. Remove any rust with fine steel wool and turpentine. Be sure the surface is clean and free of any trace of grease, soot, grime, wax, soap, etc., before refinishing.

WORRIED ABOUT RUST IN WASHER

How can I take out the rust in the top of my washing machine? It is blue-gray porcelain, and I could not remove the rust streaks with bleach and scouring powder. I am worried that the rust may discolor my wash.

Go to a good hardware store and look at the selection of rust-removing preparations. Many are made for particular surfaces and materials. Examine the labels to be sure porcelain is not adversely affected. If in doubt, check with the dealer. Be sure to follow the label directions to the letter.

SUCTION CUPS DISCOLORED WASHER

I attached a towel rack that has rubber suction cups to the side of my automatic washer. Upon removal I found brownish circles where the suction cups had been located. Is there any method of removal for these discolorations?

The discoloration may be due to a chemical action between the rubber and the finish on the washer, and thus impossible to remove. Try applying a household bleach to the discolored circles, followed by thorough rinsing to remove all trace of the bleach. If unsuccessful, you can try touching up the spots with enamel made for this type of repair, available at most hardware stores.

RUST WON'T STAY PAINTED

Our dishwasher has a small scratch inside, which is rusting. Regular appliance enamel does not adhere after a washing or two, and no hardware store seems to carry the high-temperature paint that they say is needed. Any suggestions?

Two suggestions: (1) Carefully sand the rusty scratch clean or apply one of the rust-removing preparations now widely sold in hardware stores. Wipe it with turpentine or another good cleaner to be positive not a trace of soap film remains. Brush on a couple of thin coats of epoxy enamel, allowing ample time for it to dry. Do the dishes the old-fashioned way for a couple of days to make sure the enamel is dry. (2) Write to the manufacturer, addressing your letter to the president. That's usually the surest way to get action.

BIRCH CABINETS NEED CLEANING

We have birch cabinets in our kitchen which need cleaning. Please advise if they could be washed with mild soap and water before waxing. They have a semigloss finish.

Chain and hardware stores sell a preparation that is a combination cleaner and polish which can be used satisfactorily on varnished or enameled woodwork. Or you can remove the grease and soiling by washing the surfaces with a thick suds of a mild soap, using as little water as possible. The suds are applied with a damp cloth over a small area, and when they become discolored, they are wiped off with another damp cloth. More suds are applied, and the process is repeated until no more dirt is picked up. After wiping with a damp cloth, the surface should be rubbed with dry cloths. Allow a couple of hours for thorough drying.

PAINT OVER VARNISH?

About five years ago, I antiqued my kitchen cupboards and put on a final coat of thin varnish. I now want to paint the cupboards. Must I first remove the varnish?

Not necessary. But you should sand down any gloss, and make sure to clean off all traces of grease, wax, soap film, etc. Then the new finish will stick properly. You'll find, we're sure, enamel better for this use than paint. It's more durable and very easy to clean.

KITCHEN CUPBOARDS

We are about to remodel our kitchen and plan on using birch plywood for cupboards. What is the best method for finishing them in a light, natural color?

For a light, natural finish, apply a couple of coats of a clear lacquer, but if it is not available in your community, a couple of coats of a semigloss varnish will do very well. Be sure the wood is clean and as smooth as satin, if you want a good finish. To obtain a light, modern finish such as a blond or pickled finish, there are stains made under these names which should be applied first before applying the clear finish.

CLOUDY LAMINATED-PLASTIC CUPBOARDS

The doors and sides of my kitchen cupboards are a gray wood-grain laminated plastic. They are always cloudy- and smeary-looking and seem to be getting a dirty yellow cast. I tried washing them with detergents, soaps, cleaning fluid, paint thinner, wax remover, silver polish, and window cleaner—to no avail. Any suggestions on getting these cupboards clean?

The best thing to do would be to consult the dealer or manufacturer of the specific laminated plastic you have as to treatment. Try cleaning it with a liquid cleaner for plastics, available at housewares dealers, following the label directions carefully; or use an auto-cleaning wax, in cream or paste form, not liquid, also according to the manufacturer's directions.

WARPED CUPBOARD DOORS

About 4 months ago we put birch cabinets in our kitchen. The upper ones have turned out to be an eyesore: they are all badly warped. What do you advise?

Unseasoned wood may have been used; or the top edges of the doors may not have been finished, so that they absorbed moisture (of which there is a lot in a kitchen!). Remove the doors, and lay them over blocks of wood or wooden horses, where they can remain undisturbed for several days; the concave side should be up. Then place heavy weights (large stones, books, pails of water) on the high ends of the warp. The doors will straighten after a few days and should be allowed to go slightly the other way. Before rehanging them, finish all the edges and surfaces to check moisture absorption (use paint, shellac, or varnish).

GREASE ON CABINETS

The kitchen cabinets near the stove have become, through the years, so greasy that paint will not stay on. The grease has penetrated into the wood, and will have to be cleaned out before new paint or enamel will hold. But how?

First take the rest of the old finish off, using paint remover. This will also take a lot of grease with it; probably all of it in some places. Then mix a stiff poultice of powdered chalk (or similar) and cleaning fluid. Hold this on the vertical surfaces and undersurfaces with heavy plastic sheeting and masking tape or thumbtacks. When the mixture is dry, replace it with a fresh batch until no more grease discolors it.

DOORS WARP ABOVE STOVE

I bought an older house five years ago. Before moving in, I had the kitchen redone in knotty pine—all the walls and cabinets. In time the two cabinet doors above the stove warped. I had new ones made; the same thing happened. What nonwarping material could I have the doors made from that will still go with my knotty pine?

Metal would be an obvious choice. But finding the contact-type covering to blend with the knotty pine could be very difficult. It's possible that the wood of the doors was not thoroughly seasoned. This, combined with stove heat, could cause warping. If you know of a good cabinetmaker, consult him about this. Also, covering the underside of the cabinet with sheet asbestos or insulating board, to keep heat out of the inside of the cabinet, might eliminate a major cause of warping.

UNWARPING CABINET DOORS

Is there any home method for straightening warped doors of a birch kitchen cabinet.

Remove and lay the doors, concave side up, over two chair backs. Leave 4 inches protruding at each end. On these overhangs place weights, such as heavy books, doorstops, bricks, etc. Leave them for a week, or until the doors straighten. Before replacing the doors, be sure to refinish them so that no moisture or dampness can penetrate into the wood, which is what caused the warping in the first place.

PROTECTING HARDWARE FROM PAINT

I plan to repaint our kitchen shortly. Is there any way I can protect the hardware, such as the hinges, catches, etc., against getting covered with paint? There is a lot of it, and I'd hate to have to remove it all.

Coat all such surfaces with petroleum jelly; then the paint can be easily wiped off. Or cover the hardware completely with masking tape, which is excellent for this purpose.

HOMEMADE CABINET DOORS

There are seven pairs of doors in our built-in kitchen cabinets, and every one needs replacement. No two pairs are the same size. Cabinet shops want too much money for making them. Also, I am not capable of doing a good finishing job on raw wood. Is there a sturdy prefinished paneling on the market? I'm sure I could work with that. A number of times I have recovered these doors with contact plastics, but the wood is too warped now to continue this process.

Wherever you find a dealer who carries hardboard, go right in and look over the samples and catalog of colors and wood grains.

EASY-TO-CLEAN CABINETS

When my husband finally finishes with paint remover and sandpaper, he would like to give my kitchen cabinets a finish that's as easy to clean as possible. What do you recommend? These are made of birch.

Several thin coats of top-quality enamel will be excellent. For a finish which shows the wood grain, either a clear marine varnish or (if you can buy it in less than gallon sizes) one of the special clear finishes used in gyms and bowling alleys. Check with your paint dealer.

"COPPER-TONING" WHITE CABINETS

I have white steel kitchen cabinets. The rest of my kitchen is copper-toned. Is there any way of making the cabinets copper-toned? Could an amateur do this?

This job is well within the range of amateurs. The main job isn't the refinishing, but rather the preparation. You have to get the white surfaces completely free of any trace of soap or grease, and you also have to roughen the gloss so that the new enamel will get a good bond. Sandpapering will do both jobs at once. A portable sander or sanding-wheel attachment for your electric drill will make it a lot simpler. You can get copper-toned metal enamel at any good paint or hardware store.

WORN SPOTS ON PAINTED CABINETS

I have baked-on white enamel metal kitchen cabinets. They are in excellent condition, except for worn spots (bare metal) under the drawer pulls and door knobs. It is impossible to send them to the factory for refinishing. What can I do?

Wash the bare areas with steel wool and turpentine to remove all grease, wax, grime, etc. Then touch them up with several thin coats of good-quality white enamel, feathering out the edges around the still-enameled surfaces.

REFINISHING RUSTED METAL KITCHEN SET

We have a kitchen set made of tube steel that has begun to rust. Is there any way to refinish this and make it look like new?

Remove all trace of the rust with steel wool and a rust-removing liquid, available at well-stocked hardware stores. Then touch up the spots with chrome or aluminum paint, after removing all trace of wax, grease, grime, etc., from the surface. Having a metal shop replate the steel will be best of all.

CELLULOSE TAPE MARKS

I cannot get off the cellulose tape marks left on my new varnished cabinets in the kitchen. I am afraid to try a cleaner for fear the varnish will come off.

You should be able to remove the tape marks from the surface by wiping them with trichloroethylene or one of the liquid non-flammable spot removers. Naphtha can be used too, but you should be careful about fire.

CUTTING BOARD TURNED RANCID

Before I knew better, I used salad oil instead of mineral oil to season a cutting board. Is there any way to get rid of the rancid odor and season it properly?

If it's thick enough so losing a little won't hurt, you can sand off the oil-soaked surfaces perhaps 1/8 inch per side. This should remove the major rancid areas. Then let a few days in the sun take care of the rest. Next time, as you say, do the seasoning with drugstore-grade mineral oil.

GLUE FOR CUTTING BOARD

Can you recommend a glue for a cutting board which has separated in the middle? Much food falls down in the crack, and I am leery of food poisoning. I'd like to fill this crack solid.

Clear epoxy adhesive is particularly good for a job like this, especially since the board will be washed frequently and also will be exposed to oils and acids like citrus fruits. First clean out the crack with a straightened-out paper clip or other stiff wire. Then carefully run the epoxy into the crack until it's full. Let it have 24 hours to harden.

BATHROOMS

PROMOTING BATHROOM SILENCE

What materials could be used inside bathroom walls in order to make them soundproof? The slightest sound in our bathroom can be heard outside.

Without major carpentry, all you can put in the wall space is the blown-in type of insulation. But there are many other silencers: wall-to-wall carpeting; insulating board fastened over the present wall (some are made with one side smooth enough for painting or papering); weather stripping around the door; or a heavier door, if the present one is a flimsy, light hollow-core type. The most elaborate (and effective) way is building a false wall on furring strips of 1- by 2-inch boards, out of contact with present wall, and then covering the new wall with acoustic sound-deadening panels. Filling the spaces in between with thick blanket insulation increases soundproofness. Shop around for prices and estimates.

VENTILATING A BATHROOM

Is it all right to exhaust a bathroom fan into the attic space if the attic is well ventilated? The large ceiling fan in the hall exhausts into the attic, and there are louvers at each end and in two wing gables.

If the attic is as thoroughly ventilated as you claim it to be, exhausting the vapors from the bathroom would do no harm. If, however, there is any doubt, it is best to run a duct through the roof or through the eaves. A considerable amount of moisture from a bathroom could cause trouble.

HIDE THAT BATHROOM DOOR

I have a lovely wood-paneled living room, with a graduated African gum ceiling, plus a handsome fireplace. But the whole effect is marred by an open archway which is directly in front of the bathroom door, which is directly across the hall. How can I block the sight of this door?

How about an arch-shaped door? Either a single door or two doors which meet in the middle. They could be of the same type paneling. This would be a less cumbersome solution than drapery, and a lot more convenient than having the opening blocked up and paneled.

SLIDING DOORS

Our bathroom door takes up a lot of needed space, and I want to replace it with one of those new folding-type doors, which are made of a heavy paperlike composition. My husband does not think it will hold up because of the steam in the bathroom. We only have a tub. What do you think?

We are inclined to agree with your husband, but for a little more money you can get an accordion type of folding door that has a plastic-coated fabric covering, which is more resistant to moisture and wear. It is on sale at some of the large department stores and some hardware stores.

DETERGENT FRECKLES CEILING?

My husband painted our bathroom ceiling a year ago. Since then it has peeled considerably, but what paint remains is all covered with brown spots, like freckles. My husband claims this is due to my using detergent to wash the wall but not rinsing it off. Is this true? What should he do before repainting?

Detergent has nothing to do with the spots. But rinsing after washing is a good idea. After sanding away all weak or "peely" edges, treat the remaining speckled paint with a sealer made for this. Then they won't bleed through the new paint.

PAPER OVER PAINT?

We wish to paper the upper half of our bathroom with vinyl wallpaper (the lower half is tiled). The present paint is glossy enamel. Would paper adhere to this? We will use the special paste for vinyl paper. Would moisture from bathing cause the paper to peel from the top? If so, how can I prevent this? There is no molding at the top to hold it.

Carefully sand off all the enamel gloss for better bond for the paste. This type of paste (enamel) should be waterproof to prevent any trouble with peeling from the top. Check with the dealer on this point. If you had any problem later on, you could always restick the paper with a waterproof household cement or epoxy-type adhesive.

PEELING BATHROOM CEILING PAINT

Almost one-third of the bathroom ceiling paint has dropped off, and it is loose around all the edge of the paint. The plaster underneath seems not to have been sized properly. I would like to get all this paint off before repainting or papering. Would a steamer be of any help? There is insulation above the ceiling, and the attic is vented all along the roof under the eaves.

The paint is probably peeling because a flat paint, instead of an enamel, was used; enamel is recommended for bathrooms and kitchens because of the moisture usually present. A steamer would be of no help; this is used only for loosening paper. Use a paste-type paint remover, following the label directions carefully. If you use a paper, use a moistureproof type.

REMOVING WALL DECALS

We have decals all around our bathroom. Is there any way of removing them without painting over them?

A specially treated blotting paper for removing decals is available at most dealers selling decals. Follow the instructions on the paper. Or apply moistened paper, sponge, or cloth to the decals until the edges loosen; then pry them off with a dull putty knife or kitchen knife. If the decals have been shellacked or varnished over, before applying moisture steel-wool or sandpaper the surface to remove the waterproof finish to permit moisture to soak through.

BROWN SPOTS ON BATHROOM WALLS

I have been noticing spots on our bathroom walls. They are small and brown and look like water splatters. However, they appear high on the walls where you ordinarily wouldn't splash water. They wipe off easily, but this has to be done frequently. Could this possibly be steam condensation from our tub-shower? Would a vent fan help?

A poor grade of paint or enamel will sometimes aggravate the condition of spotting, which is caused by condensation (sweating). Bathroom walls should always be painted with a good brand of enamel. To reduce sweating, try to keep the temperature in the room above 70°, if possible. Of course, an efficient exhaust fan in the room would help considerably.

DULLED FINISH ON WALLBOARD

Our bathroom walls are of wallboard with a white baked-enamel finish. Over the years the walls have lost their shine, and we would like to paint them. Is there a special way of preparing the walls before putting on a new coat of paint? Would you recommend a high gloss or a semigloss?

In order to have the new enamel adhere properly, dull the gloss of the present finish by rubbing with "000" sandpaper; then wash the surfaces with a mild detergent and rinse with clear water. When dry, apply an enamel undercoater; then finish with a semigloss or gloss enamel. The choice is entirely your own, but in the home, the semigloss finish is more desirable.

STEAM-COVERED BATHROOM MIRROR

Is there something that can be put on bathroom mirrors to prevent them from steaming up whenever a shower or bath is taken? When we take a shower or bath and later want to use the mirror, it takes a long time for the mirror to clear up.

Chemically treated antifog cloths, for use on automobile windshield and mirrors, etc.,

are available at many housewares, hardware, and auto accessory stores. Just rub the cloth on the mirror. Installing an exhaust fan, vented to the outdoors, will quickly draw off the excessive vapor and moisture in the room.

CHIPPED WASH BOWL

What can I do about a small chipped place on my wash bowl in the bathroom? I was told about a liquid porcelain, but it only comes in white, and my set is in color.

A waterproof liquid-porcelain glaze can be used. To color the glaze, use an aniline dye soluble in alcohol, or colors ground in oil, available at hardware and paint dealers.

CHROME FAUCETS

Is there any polish or wax that will keep the faucets shining all the time? It seems water spots them all the time, even when I polish them dry with a clean cloth after washing.

Any surface or material that has a glossy finish will show water spots, and we don't know of anything that will prevent it. Have a soft, dry cloth handy, and wipe the fixtures when water is dropped on the surfaces. Avoid using scouring powders on the faucets, because frequent use of this abrasive eventually will scratch or dull the faucets' finish.

YEAR-ROUND TANK TROUBLES

Our well water is so cold that our toilet tank sweats on the outside, no matter what month of the year it is. I have tried those tank covers made of chenille. They work pretty well for a while. Then they get quite wet, have to be removed, washed, dried, etc. Is there any really permanent cure for the tank?

Have a plumber install a small Y-shaped connection, arranged so that a little hot water will come in with the cold whenever the tank is flushed. The warmer water will keep the outside of the tank from getting so cold that it sweats.

WANTS SIMPLEST CURE FOR SWEATING TANK

When the weather turns real hot and sticky, the outside of my flush tank sweats like a glass of ice water. It drips down on the floor so much I always have to mop it up. Other times of the year, it's no problem at all. Is there any really simple way to take care of this problem just during those hot spells?

About the simplest solution we know is to wrap a bath towel around the tank, catching the upper edges under the tank top, but without letting the toweling touch the water inside (this would set up a blotting action). The towel will act as a good insulator between the cold tank and warm air. It will also catch and hold any drip. We're sure you know you can buy tank covers made especially for this purpose, in chenille of various shades. These covers are usually sold in sets, with matching seat cover and bath mat. You can also buy precut, install-it-yourself styrofoam liners for various-size tanks, which will provide an insulating liner, so that the outside of the tank won't get so cold it sweats in hot weather.

PAINTING TOILET SEAT

The upper part of our bathroom walls is painted. We are considering changing the present color. The toilet seat is an expensive one, and we wonder if there is any way to paint it?

Wash the seat thoroughly with a solution of trisodium phosphate or washing soda, using about a cup to each gallon of water. Then rinse thoroughly with clear water to remove all trace of the cleanser. If any gloss remains, dull it by rubbing with No. 1 steel wool and turpentine. Apply a coat of top-quality quick-drying enamel, according to the manufacturer's directions on the container.

SEEPAGE AROUND TOILET BASE

Around the base of my toilet the tile is coming up and turning brown. There's a leak somewhere. It's not from a sweating tank because I have a tray to catch the drip underneath. Could it be the disk between the toilet and the floor?

It may be that the packing (usually putty) around the heavy washer at the bottom of the toilet has hardened and cracked. The toilet will have to be removed and the old putty scraped out and replaced. Compounds which don't completely harden are now available at plumbing supply dealers.

STAINS IN TOILET BOWL

How can one remove the unsightly stains found in the bottom of a toilet bowl?

Leave weak household bleach solution in the bowl overnight. Or turn off the water to the tank, and empty the water from the bowl. Then apply a thick paste made of scratchless scouring powder, a little cream of tartar, and peroxide, rubbing this compound on the stains and allowing it to remain about 20 minutes. Rinse off the paste with clear water, and repeat the treatment if necessary.

TOILET KEEPS RUNNING

I cannot clean a gray cast at the bottom of the toilet bowl. I know I could probably do it with a bleach, but since the toilet runs continuously, the bleach gets too diluted. A brush does not do the cleaning. Can you suggest anything?

Whether you stop the continuous water flow or not, all you need to do is close the valve to the water supply pipe. Then flush the tank, and use a sponge to get out any water remaining down at the bottom. If you can't find this shutoff valve, you can even resort to closing the main supply valve to the house. Then use your bleach or other cleaners. Do *not* use them together; they can combine to form a deadly gas. The continuous flow can be due to a worn valve controlling the water entering the tank; replace it. Or it can be due to a waterlogged float which no longer floats up high enough so that the long rod can close the valve. Third, the rubber-ball closure of the drain may be so worn it allows water to escape; replace it. If it's a real old-timer, consider simply replacing the entire works. It's not expensive, nor is it a difficult job. But remember to shut off the water first (see page 228).

TOOK SHINE OFF LAVATORY

I made a really bad mistake when I used drain cleaner on my lavatory. As soon as I saw what I had done, I rinsed it immediately. But already the shine was somewhat dulled. I have tried other cleaners since, but nothing has helped restore the shine. Can you suggest anything?

Try white automotive rubbing compound and perhaps half an hour's worth of elbow grease. This will improve things a great deal. Let's hope none of the surface was eaten by the drain cleaner; rubbing won't bring that back.

TUB EMPTIES SLOWLY

Our bathtub empties very slowly. The usual drain cleaner doesn't seem to clear the pipe enough. Can you suggest anything?

Probably the trap is becoming clogged with an accumulation of hair strands, lint, soap film. Remove the plug from the drain, run a piece of "soft" wire with a roughened end toward the trap, give it a few twists, and pull it up slowly. An accumulation of strands of hair and soap scum will usually be found on the end. If so, repeat the process several times. Should this fail, have a plumber clean out the piping with a mechanical drain cleaner. Have you tried the universally known "plumber's friend"? It consists of rubber cup with a wooden handle. The cup is placed over the drain opening, and the handle is vigorously pumped up and down. This frequently "unplugs" pipes.

LEAK AROUND BATHTUB

Although I have tried to plug the joint where the edge of the bathtub meets the tile wall, there is still a leak. It shows up in the plaster ceiling of the kitchen below. I have used putty and other similar substances. What do you recommend that I should do?

Dig out the putty, which has probably dried out by now, thereby causing the leak, and use a white-colored tub-caulking compound. It comes in a tube, and with very little trouble you can seal the whole joint simply by running the tube along the edge, squeezing as you go. This type of compound gives a tight seal, but remains flexible enough so that it's not affected by changes in temperatures. It is available at most good hardware stores.

BLACKENED TUB CAULKING

Shortly after moving into our new house, we caulked around our bathtub with a tub caulking. Now we find areas on the caulking of black mildew or mold which are impossible to remove. We have tried steel wool, ammonia, nail polish remover, scouring powders, as well as bleach, with no success. Could you recommend a method for removing these black areas? The tile above the tub is plastic, but only the caulking has black areas.

The caulking should be replaced. Scrape out the present material with a beer can opener, or other sharp instrument, brushing out all loose particles. Use a stain-resistant grouting, available at some hardware and tile dealers; or use caulking compound, available in tubes for easy application between the tub and wall. Ventilate the bathroom as much as possible to permit the escape of warm, moist air; moisture helps the growth and development of mold.

BATHTUB IS COLD

What could we do to make taking a bath more comfortable? Our bathtub is so cold to sit in. Is there an insulation we could put under the tub that would keep the cold air out?

Keeping the air of the bathroom warm (around 70°) will also keep the tub warm. If there is no heat in the house, pour a couple of bucketfuls of hot water into the tub and allow it to remain for a few minutes; then temper it with cold water for your bath. A small electric room heater will also help.

DAMAGED FINISH IN BATHTUB

Five years ago I built a new house, and last summer I had a plumber put some root killer down the drain, which I believe he did by pouring the same into the bathtub. Now a considerable amount of the finish is off the tub, and the surface is rough and rusty-looking. The strong solution must have eaten off the finish. What can be done to refinish the inside of the tub?

There is no material that will give the tub a permanent finish. Plumbers and plumbing supply shops carry in stock touch-up enamels made especially for use on plumbing fixtures, which can be used to hide the imperfections. In time, it will be necessary to retouch the surfaces because of discoloration from soaps, detergents, and hot water.

DON'T PAINT BATHTUB

We would like to have our tub painted a different color, rather than replace it, and are wondering how dependable the paints are for this purpose. Would it be necessary for an expert to do the job?

Tubs are not painted; the colors are baked in. No paint would stand up under such constant exposure. New paint, if you thoroughly roughened the tub surface and used an epoxy-type finish, might last for a while before flaking. There are services which recondition tubs beautifully, such as when hotels or motels are being renovated. But don't be shocked at the estimate; it will be pretty high. A hotel maintenance manager in your neighborhood could probably tell you where such jobs are done.

GLAMORIZING OLD TUB

I would appreciate knowing if it is possible to glamorize, so to speak, an old bathtub, the kind that stands on iron feet. If it is possible, where could I get directions?

This type of modernization is done all the time. The main feature is enclosing the sides of the tub, up to the edge of the curved rim. The usual way is to enclose it with a sheet of plywood; then cover it with plastic or ceramic tiles, or any other waterproof covering which will match the rest of the decor. The joint along the floor can be waterproofed with caulking and then covered with quarter round or aluminum cove molding. Ditto for the side seams.

UNGLAMOROUS BATHTUB RING

We recently moved into an apartment where the previous tenants were none too clean. But we managed very well, except for a dark, not-pretty ring around the bathtub. Can this be removed?

Try this, which often works: Rub with a pasty combination of kerosene and scratchless scouring powder. Afterward, generously wipe with vinegar to kill the kerosene odor.

STAINED BATHTUB

My bathtub is stained from hard water. I have tried several things to get it off: bleach, scratchless scouring powders, ammonia, but with no success. How can I get this stain off?

Of course, the best, permanent remedy would be to have a water-softening unit installed by a competent plumber. To remove the hard-water stain, apply a solution of oxalic acid (*poison*) in water, using a dish mop; then rinse it off with plenty of clear water.

RUST STAIN ON BATHTUB

I would like to know how to get rust stains off the bathtub and wash basins.

Saturate a piece of cloth with peroxide; then sprinkle it liberally with cream of tartar and a scratchless scouring powder. When the powders become well dampened, rub the stains and allow the paste to remain for a half hour or so; then rinse it off thoroughly with clear water. Many department and chain stores now sell rust-removing preparations which are quite effective.

GREEN RING AROUND TUB

Every time we take a bath, a green ring remains around the tub. What causes this?

It is very difficult to remove; neither soap and water nor strong liquid household cleaners work. What can I use to remove the ring without damaging the tub? A few yellow marks are in the bottom of the tub also.

The staining may be due to hard water, although the ring that forms is usually yellowish. This can be removed with a solution of oxalic acid (*poison*), applied with a dish mop, followed by ample rinsing with clear water. A household bleach solution will also sometimes be effective. Green stain, sometimes resulting from new brass or copper piping, can be removed by wiping with a half-and-half mixture of household ammonia and water. Be sure to rinse well afterward with plenty of clear water to thoroughly flush the pipes and remove any trace of ammonia. The following home treatment is for removing rust stains from plumbing fixtures: Make a paste of scratchless scouring powder, a little cream of tartar, and peroxide. Rub it on the rust stain, and allow it to remain about half hour; then rinse it off with water. Repeat the treatment until the stain disappears.

CAULKING SMEARED ON TUB

When my bathroom was redone, caulking compound was smeared in the cracks around the top of the tub and the plastic imitation tile. I did not want to remove the excess until it had dried. Now I can't get it off. I have tried scraping it with a razor blade, gently. But I am afraid of scratching the tile with pressure. Is there anything which will soften the caulking compound?

If it were ceramic tile, we could suggest careful touching with the tip of a soldering gun, to let the heat soften enough for scraping with a putty knife. But with plastic tile, it would be too risky. Cut a small piece of hardwood, like maple or oak, so the end is squared. Helped with a gentle hammer, use this as a way to remove the excess; it won't scratch. Cross your fingers.

UNPROTECTED TUB PLASTERED

The workmen did not cover the tub when plastering our new home, and there is much hardened plaster in it. How can I remove this without harm to the shiny new finish?

Hold a small, square-ended piece of pine, birch, maple, or other middling soft-to-hard wood against a blob of plaster. Gently nudge it with taps from the heel of your hand. Use patience, not brute force, and it should all come off without trouble.

CEMENT SPOTS IN BATHTUB

I am building a house, and the bathroom tub has cement spots in it which I have not been able to remove. Could you tell me what to use to soften the cement or remove it? I've tried scraping it, but have only scratched the porcelain.

We're afraid there is nothing you can use on the cement. A solution of muriatic acid will soften cement, but will also damage the finish. This is why builders and plumbers cover tubs and other plumbing fixtures with a heavy layer of paper or other protective coating while plastering and other messy work is being done.

IODINE STAINS IN BATHTUB

How can I remove iodine stains from the bathtub?

Apply household ammonia or denatured alcohol to the stains. Photographic hypo (available in camera supply stores), using 1 tablespoonful dissolved in 1 pint of water, is also effective for removing iodine stains.

HAIR DYE STAINED LAVATORY

While applying some hair dye, I accidentally dropped the applicator in the lavatory. In the time it took me to wrap several layers of paper toweling on my hair, a stain formed in the lavatory. I tried to rinse it and then wash it, but it would not come out. No cleaner I have tried has worked. I notice that one of the listed ingredients is silver nitrate. How can I remove this stain?

Wipe the stain with iodine; this will change the color. Rinse the iodine off thoroughly with clear water. Then wipe the stain with photographic hypo, using a solution of any strength. That will do the rest of the job.

REMOVING TUB ADHESIVE RISKY

We have recently removed the shower doors from our bathtub, but we still have some remains of the adhesive on the tub. I have scoured and used grout cleaner, but they have not done anything. What else can I try?

Chances are, even if we knew the solvent for this particular adhesive, it would be so strong it might also affect the tub surface, causing dull streaks. You can try wrapping fine sandpaper around a very small piece of wood and see if this thins the adhesive down.

Or, using extreme care, you could try your luck with a narrow, sharp blade. The risk you run is permanently marring the porcelain finish. True, you can help things with white automotive rubbing compound, although it won't remove a scratch. Good luck!

SHOWER FOR OLD TUB

I am moving into a small apartment, desirable in every way but one: an old-fashioned, two-faucet bathtub with no shower. It's an open tub, standing on legs in a corner, about 4 inches from both walls. The plumbing comes up from the floor at the end of the tub away from the wall. I am a shower user. Is there a relatively simple way to add a shower at low cost?

"Add-a-shower" units are available at many plumbing supply dealers and large mail-order houses. Most have a rubber-tube connection (after installing the "mixing" unit for the present two-faucet arrangement) and an overhead shower head and rod arrangement for a curtain which can be attached to the ceiling or wall. Or some are available with a "roomier" arrangement for a curtain with separate rods overhead, approximately the size of the tub.

INSTALLING SHOWER STALL

I would like to take out our old-style bathtub and in its place put a shower stall. Our house is old and has wood floor and plaster walls. Could we build a stall in there?

"Packaged" shower cabinets, in knocked-down form, are available at large plumbing supply dealers. They are complete units, relatively easy to install; the manufacturers' instruction sheets should be followed carefully.

SHOWER CURTAIN BEAUTY BATH

What's a good way to get hardened soap film off vinyl shower curtains?

To a washer full of not too hot water, add 1½ cups of clear vinegar instead of any soap. Use the gentle cycle, but do not rinse. Hang over the wash line outside on a rather hot day. All the soap film will be gone, and the curtains will look like new.

NEEDS DOOR STRETCHER

When closed, my sliding glass shower doors do not completely fill the runner track. Therefore, at the back edge of each door there is a gap, from ⅛ to ¼ inch. Consequently, when we take showers, water splashes out onto the floor and causes damage to the plaster ceiling underneath. Can you suggest anything?

By far the simplest and least "mechanical" remedy would be to buy some plastic foam weather-stripping tape and cement up the walls between the door tracks. The idea is to build out this space so that the doors will butt against the tape, instead of leaving the gaps. Be sure the wall is absolutely dry and clean (no soap film), and use a waterproof, tenacious adhesive such as epoxy.

SHOWER ELIMINATES WINDOW

We are redoing our small bathroom—putting in a shower stall instead of the old tub and painting the plastic wall tiles. The shower will mean blocking up the window. What can we do for a window? What kind of paint should we use for the plastic tiles?

You could use glass block for the part of the shower wall which will block the present window. Get the plainest possible tiles, because bright light bouncing on thousands of little prisms can get bothersome. Top-quality enamel is excellent for the plastic tiles. The gloss should be sanded off for a better bond, and there should be absolutely no trace of soap film.

REMOVING SHOWER DOORS

We recently purchased a five-year-old house with aluminum-frame sliding doors in the tub-shower. I wish to remove them. Before I do, I would like to know if there will be any damage to the tub or wall, other than screw or bolt holes.

Only the holes will linger in memory, unless an adhesive was also used. If so, you'll have a very tedious, often unsatisfactory, job of scraping, fine-steel-wooling, or chipping. Very often, though, it's merely a matter of unscrewing the aluminum screws. Rock the track, and look carefully underneath to see if there's any adhesive.

SHOWER SOAKED PLASTER

The plastic tiling around my bathtub shows signs of coming loose here and there. By the time I noticed this, water from the shower had already worked behind the tile and ruined the plaster. So recementing would be no answer. If I have to pull off and replace all the tiles, what should I do to restore the soaked plaster? Would it be a more permanent job to replace all the tiles with ceramic?

The only answer to soaked plaster is replacement. If the lath is wood, examine it carefully; it should not be wet or warping. Metal lath should not be rusting. Ceramic tile, speaking only for installation, is no more permanent than its foundation. If the cement, especially along the top and other edges and corners, is good and tight, there's no reason any tile should come loose and the installation will be of a permanent nature.

SLIPPERY SHOWER FLOOR

The ceramic-tile floor in our stall shower seems especially slippery right after it is cleaned. How can I clean it and not get it slippery?

Use a concrete and masonry cleaner and etching preparation, diluted with water according to the label directions. This is available at large masonry supply dealers and hardware stores.

RUBBER MAT STAINS SHOWER FLOOR

We had a rubber mat on the tile floor of our shower stall. On removing it we found dark stains under it that ordinary scrubbing won't remove. What do you suggest using to remove the stains?

The stains are caused by chemicals used in manufacturing the rubber. Try rust-removing preparations, available at hardware and housewares dealers; follow the label instructions carefully. Or wipe the stains with chlorine household bleach, rinsing it off well afterward with clear water. Or make a thick paste of scratchless scouring powder, adding a little cream of tartar and peroxide; rub the stains with this paste, and allow it to remain about a half-hour; then rinse it off well with clear water; repeat the treatment if necessary.

SOAP SPOTS ON CERAMIC-TILE SHOWER

We have a ceramic-tile stall shower. There are a lot of soap spots that seem impossible to remove. Can you suggest anything?

Try cleaning the tile with a wax-base preparation generally used for cleaning glass. Or use a new quick stain remover for floor tile; this is also good for removing soap scum. Or make a thick paste of scratchless scouring powder and kerosene—being sure the bathroom is well ventilated and being careful of the fire hazard—and cover the tile surface; allow the paste to remain 2 to 3 minutes, rub the spots, and then rinse the paste off with clear, warm water.

CAN'T GET SHOWER CLEAN

We have a fiberglass shower and sauna. I cannot find anything to do a proper cleaning job. Could you give me any suggestions?

Hot water, very fine steel wool soap pads, and elbow grease are usually very effective. So is a scratchless scouring powder. It surely can get soap film off.

RUSTING SHOWER STALL

What can we do about a metal shower stall that has started to rust quite badly? It is only 2½ years old. At first the rust could be removed during regular cleanings with a detergent, but rusting has now progressed to the point where there is pitting. The worst spots are along the edges of the various metal sheets.

Evidently the joints between the sheets and at the base where the floor and walls meet are where moisture finds its way, causing corrosion. Clean as much of the rust off the surfaces as possible with steel wool, and apply a rust-inhibiting paint. Then fill the crevices and open joints with a caulking compound applied with a caulking gun. Finish with coats of a good brand of rust-inhibiting paint and a latex-base enamel.

MANY SHOWERS RUST CEILING

Rusty spots appear on my bathroom ceiling. I paint the ceiling, and they come right through. I admit the ceiling is usually wet; lots of showers are taken. What will stop this?

Open the window, when practical, after a shower to ventilate the soggy air. A wall fan will help a lot. Before repainting, get a stain and knot sealer from the paint store and cover the rust spots. Aluminum paint is also good at keeping rust and stains from bleeding through. Then repaint.

MARBLE SHOWER NOW A PROBLEM

My problem is a shower that has walls of beautiful marble slabs. It's only two years old, but I find the walls are getting yellowish and dull and are not as smooth as before.

This condition is mainly from the floor about halfway up. Any suggestion?

The yellowing is from accumulated soap film which has penetrated the porous surface. Before you can do anything else, you'll have to do your best to clean it all out, and even with an excellent cleaner, you'll find this a tedious job. Once you get the film out, then you should apply, at fairly regular intervals, clear liquid sealer, the type used to seal grouting. The sealer is available at discount houses where tile materials are sold.

BUTTERFLIES HAMPER REDECORATING

I cemented paper butterflies to the bathroom walls, using household cement. Now I would like to redecorate. But how can I remove the butterflies? They are applied to the wall paint, which is oil-base.

Instead of trying to soften that cement (provided you could find the solvent in the first place), sand and tear the paper to a featheredge. With no betraying hard outline, your new paint will hide the butterflies.

PUTTING DOWN BATHROOM TILES

Where can I get information for putting down small hexagonal-shape bathroom tiles? I tore out a chute in the bathroom, leaving a hole in the floor approximately 10 by 24 inches. I have a sheet of the tile, but don't know how to proceed. What kind of adhesive, etc.?

Dealers usually supply the manufacturer's instruction sheets for installation of their products; better go back to your dealer and get this. Be sure the "flooring" you have covered the hole with is straight, level, and smooth. Use waterproof adhesive, recommended by the dealer.

CERAMIC TILE FOR BATHROOM

I am removing old plaster from the walls in the bathroom and intend applying gypsum board first, then a ceramic tile. Is this advisable?

If the plaster is in good condition, we see no reason for removing it. Any loose paint should be removed and low spots filled. Spackle is good for the latter job. The high points should be sanded down. Installing ceramic tile with an adhesive instead of cement mortar makes it not too difficult a job. But we recommend consulting a tile dealer for detailed instructions. If you do apply the gypsum board first, be sure to seal all joints with the adhesive to prevent moisture penetration, and brush a coat of primer over the area to be tiled.

WARPED TILE WALLS

The bathrooms in our four-family apartment house are covered with ceramic tiles. The building is five years old, and in two of the units, the wall is warping. We were told that the walls are of plasterboard over which tiles have been installed and that the moisture caused the warping of the wallboard. What would you advise?

We would suspect that the affected walls are over the bathtubs and that water seeped through the joint between the tub and the wall. Plasterboard, when subjected to water for a long period of time, will disintegrate. You should be able to remove the affected part of the walls and put in new gypsum board (plasterboard); then apply the tile. To protect the new wall from warping, fill the space at the joint with a light-colored caulking compound or a caulking made especially for the purpose.

FILLER FOR CERAMIC FLOOR TILE

We have laid ceramic floor tile in the bathroom. The filler we used keeps falling out. What should be used?

The joints should be filled by wiping the surface of the tiles with a thick creamlike mixture of cement and water, called grout. When the mixture has settled into the joints, wipe off all the excess on the face of the tile while it is still wet; keep the grouting moist for several hours.

BATH OVERFLOW LOOSENED TILES

Too much water was in the bathtub, and it overflowed onto the floor. This loosened some of the caulking as well as the small ceramic floor tiles next to the tub. How can I repair this?

Pry up any loosened tiles, and scrape the cement residue, if any, from their undersides and the floor. Wait until the floor dries out thoroughly; then replace the tiles using fresh tile cement. Caulk between the tiles and the tub with grout (the lumberyard dealer will give you application details if you need them). Generously caulking the joint between the tub and floor and then covering with aluminum cove molding would probably have prevented this damage. It surely could prevent this in the future.

CUP DISPENSER STUCK ON TILE

Is there any way to remove a cup dispenser glued to ceramic wall tile? The dispenser is five years old, made of clear, solid plastic. We would like to replace it with a newer, smaller model.

Chances are that the "glue" is some kind of epoxy cement, which is both waterproof and exceedingly strong. We know of no solvents for softening the adhesive, and in our opinion it will be simplest (if you can get a matching tile) if you carefully chip out the whole tile and replace it with a new one. One of those thin, all-purpose abrasive wheels in your electric drill will make cutting around the edges much faster and will reduce the chance of accidental cracking of neighboring tiles.

TILE OVER POPPING TILES?

I have a ceramic-tile bathroom floor which I wish to retile. The small six-sided tiles are popping loose. Is there an adhesive that can be used over the existing floor for new tiles?

If the present tiles are popping loose, you're taking a somewhat calculated risk in putting new tiles over them. Sure, any good tile cement will stick to the present tiles, if they're thoroughly cleaned. Actually, chances are good that the tile-over-tile idea will work okay. But we did want to point out the risk if any areas of the original tiles began popping loose. It's a good gamble, though, with the odds in your favor.

EASIEST WAY TO REMOVE TILE CEMENT

Please tell me the easiest, quickest, and least messy way to remove plastic-tile adhesive from our bathroom walls. The tiles are all off, but it sure is a job trying to remove the rest of it.

Chip off what will come off reasonably with a putty knife and gentle hammer. For the rest, use coarse sandpaper and an electric sander. Sprinkle water on the working area occasionally to minimize dust.

PAINT BATHROOM TILE?

The lower half of the bathroom walls has white tile. I want to paint the upper, plastered part of the walls some other color. Do you advise painting the tile also?

Paint doesn't adhere well to a glossy surface, such as we assume the present tile has. In order to paint, it will be necessary to first dull this gloss by rubbing with sandpaper or steel wool—a tedious job. If the present tile is in good condition, we would recommend leaving it "as is."

PAINT ON CERAMIC TILE

Is there any safe method of removing hardened paint spots from ceramic tile?

Yes. Get a small can of paint remover, and apply some of it on each spot, and when the paint becomes softened, take it off with a cloth dampened with turpentine. Since most paint removers are flammable, be very careful of fire, and do not rub hard because friction may cause enough heat to ignite the remover. Another (and often easier) method is to scrape off the paint with an old razor blade, holding the blade almost flat against the tile.

STAINS ON CERAMIC TILE

We have moved into a new house and have found the ceramic-tile floor in the bathroom badly stained by paint, mastic glue, etc., which we can't account for. The small tiles are also dirty-looking. Washing with gasoline and turpentine has not helped. What would you suggest using?

Glue, paint, and spots of similar materials can be removed with paint remover. If possible, get the nonflammable kind. Apply it on the spots, and after a few minutes use more of the remover and fine steel wool to take them off. The tiles can then be scrubbed with a scouring powder and hot water, followed by a thorough rinsing. If the tile is still discolored, apply a hot, saturated solution of oxalic acid (*poison*), and after an hour or so, rinse off all traces of bleach with clear water. A low-quality tile might have that dirty appearance, and nothing can be done to lighten it.

SMEARY, SOILED TILE

The marble-tile floor in my bathroom always looks soiled, even immediately after I wash it; I wash it several times a day. In places, it looks as though something has been smeared on it; it is never clear-looking black and white, as it should be, except when it's still damp. Is there anything I can do about it?

The smeary appearance may be due to excess adhesive used in laying the tiles. Try using a quick floor-tile stain remover, now available at large tile dealers and housewares and hardware stores. Or scrub them with a strong solution of trisodium phosphate, using about 1 cup in a pail of hot water and rinsing immediately with clear water. Be careful to keep the cleaning solution from any painted surfaces, as it will damage the paint.

SPOTTED BATHROOM TILE

The tile in the shower appears to be discolored; spots on the tile stay after a thorough cleaning. What do you recommend?

These may be due to deposits from hard water; installing a water-softening unit would remedy this. To remove these, make a paste of powdered whiting or scratchless scouring powder and kerosene and rub it over spots; then rinse with warm water. If the discoloration is below the surface of the tile, it may be due to seepage from a pipe leak. A competent plumber should make an inspection.

DULL- AND DUSTY-LOOKING TILE

Recently we purchased a new house. The tile in the bathroom floor looked dusty and dull. We were told to apply muriatic acid. We did this, and it helped. I gave it another application, but it still is lifeless. Can you tell me what to do? Do you advise waxing the tile?

Evidently you did not scrub the tiles, nor did you rinse them. Mix 1 part of muriatic acid in 10 parts of water, adding the acid slowly into the water to avoid splashing. Use a glass or wood container to hold the solution. Apply it liberally on a small area of the tiles, and after 2 to 3 minutes, scrub with more of the solution, using a fiber brush. Thorough rinsing with plenty of clear water should follow. The solution is highly corrosive, so wear rubber gloves, old clothing, and rubbers over your shoes to avoid burns. It is possible you previously used too strong a solution and loosened some of the cement between the tiles, spreading it over the surface. If so, a thorough rinsing with clear water may take care of this satisfactorily. A paste floor wax can be used on the tile to improve the appearance.

DULLED PLASTIC TILE

Recently we painted our bathroom and spilled some paint on the yellow plastic tile. We removed the paint spots with a solvent, but got those tiles very dull. We also got some paste on the side of the tile which we could not get off. We tried soap and water but couldn't remove the brown paste. What can we do to restore the shiny surface on the tile? How can we remove the paste from the tile?

To restore the shiny surface of the plastic tile where it has become dulled from the paint remover: rub the area briskly with a paste of fine powdered pumice and water; then polish it with a thick paste of powdered chalk and water, and wipe it dry with a clean cloth. To remove the paste, which we assume is tile adhesive, use only the solvent recommended by the adhesive manufacturer.

RUSTING METAL TILE

Our bathroom has metal tile which is rusting near the bowl. We have sanded and enameled this section, but it has started to rust again. How can we correct this?

Rusting is due to the presence of moisture, probably seepage from the bowl. We suggest having a reputable plumber inspect the installation. Remove any loose or flaking rust down to bare metal, and be sure the surface is free of all trace of grease, wax, grime, etc. Then apply a rust-inhibiting primer that contains fish oil, available at most paint stores. When the primer is thoroughly dry, apply a coat of good-quality enamel.

ROUGH-LOOKING CEMENT BETWEEN GLASS BLOCK

What can we do to improve the appearance of the glass block windows in the bathroom? The cement used to put them together is rough-looking. What can this be covered with to make it look smooth and neat?

The only thing we can suggest is applying a smoothing coat of ready-mixed patching mortar over the present finish; keep it damp for several days.

HELP FOR OLD TILE

Our house was built during the Depression and still has the original dull-finished plastic tile in the children's bathroom. Is there any way to paint or to wallpaper over the tile? We are unable to go to the expense of replacing the old tile with ceramic tile.

Painting (with good enamel) is possible, but demands hard surface preparation: the tiles must be roughened by sandpapering to give the paint a good grip; if any gloss is left, the paint will peel. You can put up a self-sticking, plastic-coated, wallpaperlike covering, but if there are distinct "valleys" between the tiles, this will show up.

ELIMINATING "TILES" IN PLASTER

The lower half of the plaster bathroom walls have been scored to look like tile. Now I would like to smooth out the walls, either for a painted surface or for a washable cloth covering. Some grooves have been filled fairly well with paint over the years, but some are still real "dirt catchers!" Do you have any suggestions?

Spackle applied to the grooves would be much the easier way. This is used by professional painters for filling plaster cracks before painting. It is available at paint and hardware dealers.

COVER UP BATHROOM TILES?

My entire bathroom is covered with plastic tiles. I would like to cover all with a waterproof covering, particularly around the tub, which includes a shower. What could I put on without having to remove the tiles first?

There is quite a range of choices, beginning with professionally installed paneling of laminated plastic. Visit a lumberyard or two, as well as decorator departments of large department stores and discount houses, to see the various types of paneling available. Probably you'll find the simplest (and very effective) material to be the plastic-surfaced, adhesive-backed covering that you apply like wallpaper. A nearly endless variety of colors and patterns are available. Most important: Remove all traces of soap film and wax first.

PAINT WEARING OFF ON METAL TILE

Our bathroom walls have metal tiles. In the course of time, paint has disappeared in some places and the bare metal shows. How can the tiles be restored to their former state?

The metal tile can be repainted. If any rust is on the surface of the exposed tile, remove it with steel wool and turpentine or a rust-removing preparation. Then dull the gloss on the entire wall surface by rubbing with "0" sandpaper. Remove all traces of dirt, grease, wax, etc., by washing the walls with a good detergent, followed by thorough rinsing with clear water. When dry, apply an enamel undercoater; finish with any good-quality gloss or semigloss enamel.

MAKE GROUT WHITE AGAIN

Please let me know if there is a product to whiten grout around clay tiles. In time I find it yellows.

Wipe on a strong solution of general household bleach. That usually does an excellent job. If you're not satisfied, you can scrub off all traces of soap film with a stiff brush and detergent. After a good rinsing, you can paint. Use a very fine pointed artist's brush and a top-quality marine or exterior enamel, which can stand exposure to water. You'll also need a fairly steady hand, a lot of time, and patience.

FILMED GROUTING

We had a glazed-ceramic-tile floor installed in our bathroom. The grouting is black; the tile tan. It looked fine when laid, but the contractor then washed it with a muriatic acid solution, making a haze on the tile and leaving a white film on the grouting. It has been gone over three times, but the haze and film still come back after a day or two. How can we make the grouting stay black?

The acid wash may not have been neutralized to remove it completely. All traces of the acid should be removed by washing the grouting with a solution of 1 pint of ammonia in 2 gallons of water.

DARKENED TILE CEMENT

What can I use to clean the cement holding the bathroom tiles in place? It has turned a dark-brown color due to smoking, steam, and hot-air heat. I have already tried ammonia, various household cleaners and detergents, and bleaches. Nothing helps.

As cement doesn't respond to usual cleaning methods, the only other recourse is to replace it. Rake out the top ⅛ inch of the present cement with a beer can opener or sharply pointed screwdriver. Brush out all loose particles and powder. Wet the inside surfaces, and fill them with a special cementing preparation available at hardware and tile dealers; or fill them with white portland cement mixed with enough water to form a thick cream. Wipe off all cement smears from the surface of the tile with a damp cloth

immediately. A stain-resistant grout is now available at some hardware and department stores.

SHOWER LOSING TILES

Many of the tiles on the shower stall walls are coming loose. When I lift some off, plaster comes with them. What is the reason? What can I do?

Apparently the grouting between the tiles or the caulking around the top of the tiles has cracked, allowing water to soak through to soften the tile cement and plaster. It's also possible there's a leak in a pipe behind the tiles. If 75 percent of the tiles are this way, have the entire area retiled. Otherwise, remove any doubtful ones. Fill any plaster gouges with patching plaster. When the plaster is thoroughly dry, replace the tiles, grout, and caulking.

SHOWER TILE LOOSENS

I have a problem with the wall tile in my shower coming off. My house is three years old, and within a year after purchase the condition appeared and the builder gave me a new wall. My service guarantee on the house has expired. Three tiles have dropped off, and several more are coming loose. How can I get these tiles to stay up?

If there is no pipe leak behind the wall, we suspect a waterproof adhesive wasn't used to put up the tile. Waterproof cement for setting tile is available at large hardware stores and some tile dealers. Follow the label instructions for use.

REMOVING PLASTIC TILE

I want to remove the plastic tiles from my bathroom walls and put up ceramic tiles. I tried prying them off, but plaster comes off in chunks too. What can I do to make this job easier?

Consult the manufacturer or the tile dealer for the particular solvent recommended for the adhesive used. Then use the solvent to soften the adhesive before prying the tile loose. This will keep damage to the plaster underneath at a minimum.

REMOVING PORCELAIN TILE

We have porcelain-tile walls in the bathroom and want to remove the tiles on the upper part of the walls, to redecorate. How can the tiles be taken off?

Taking the porcelain tiles off the wall requires great care and patience, but isn't too difficult a job. We know of no solvent for the adhesive, but the tiles are not interlocked and can be pried up. Take one tile out of the wall, using a ½-inch cold chisel and light plumb hammer; chipping out between the tiles is easy. After a tile has been removed, chip carefully behind the other tiles and pry them loose.

CHAPTER 16

WALKS, DRIVEWAYS, AND OTHER EXTERIOR AREAS

When we talk of walks, driveways, porches, and patios, most of us think of concrete. This material is most useful to the homeowner.

Essentials for Good Concrete

There is a difference between "cement" and "concrete," even though the two names are often used for the same thing. That is, portland *cement* is an extremely fine powder manufactured in a cement plant. Portland cement when mixed with water forms a paste. This paste binds materials such as sand and gravel or crushed stone (aggregate) into *concrete*.

The quality of the paste determines the strength and durability of the finished concrete; too much mixing water makes the paste thin and weak. For example, concrete made with a mix containing 6 gallons of water per bag of cement will be about 40 percent stronger than the same concrete mix made with 8 gallons of water per bag of cement.

Water for mixing should be clean and free of oil, acid, and other injurious substances. Usually drinking water may be used for making concrete.

Fine aggregate consists of sand; coarse aggregate consists of gravel, crushed stone, or air-cooled slag. Good, sound aggregate is necessary for making quality concrete. Loam, clay, dirt, and vegetable matter are detrimental to concrete, and aggregate containing these materials should not be used.

Mortar is a mixture of mortar sand, masonry cement, and water. Mortar is used for laying concrete block, brick, and stone, and for plaster and stucco coats. Various types of cements are manufactured for every use. Normal portland cement is gray. If white concrete is needed or desired, as in flower pots, lawn ornaments, or other decorative work, use white portland cement.

Mixing Concrete. Table 6 gives the approximate amounts of materials needed for various-size batches of concrete. It may be necessary to vary the amounts of aggregates slightly, depending on their characteristics. The amount of concrete needed can be quickly found for any square or rectangular area by using this formula:

$$\frac{\text{width in ft} \times \text{length in ft} \times \text{thickness in ft}}{27} = \text{cubic yard;}$$

note that thickness is in feet, not inches.

Make a trial mix using the amounts of

Table 6. Materials Needed for Concrete

A 1:2¼:3 mix = 1 part cement to 2¼ parts sand to 3 parts 1-inch maximum aggregate

Concrete required, cu ft	Cement, lb*	Max. amount of water to use, gal		Sand, lb	Coarse aggregate, lb
		U.S.	Imperial		
1	24	1¼	1	52	78
3	71	3¾	3⅛	156	233
5	118	6¼	5¼	260	389
6¾ (¼ cu yd)	165	8	6¾	350	525
13½ (½ cu yd)	294	16	13½	700	1,050
27 (1 cu yd)	588	32	27	1,400	2,100

*A United States bag of cement weighs 94 lb. A Canadian bag of cement weighs 87.5 lb.

materials shown in Table 6. If this mix doesn't give satisfactory workability, vary the amount of aggregate used. Don't vary the amounts of cement and water.

All concrete should be mixed thoroughly until uniform in appearance. Add some of the mixing water, then the gravel and cement, and then sand and the balance of the mixing water. Each piece of aggregate should be completely coated with cement paste.

When hand-mixing small jobs, mix the dry materials (cement and aggregates) in a container or on a suitable hard surface. Make a depression in the pile, and add some of the mixing water. Continue mixing, and add the remainder of the measured amount of water. The mix should be workable. If the mix is too dry, reduce the amount of sand and gravel in the next batch; if too wet, add more aggregate. Never change the ratio of water and cement.

Premixed cement which has the correct amount of cement, sand, and aggregate mixed is available from lumberyards and hardware stores and all you have to do is add water as directed on the bag.

Ready-mixed Concrete. For larger jobs consider using ready-mixed concrete; this eliminates the work of mixing and proportioning. It's as easy to order as picking up the phone. When ordering ready-mixed concrete, remember the numbers 6-6-6. These stand for 6 bags of cement per cubic yard, 6 gallons of water per bag of cement, and 6 percent entrained air. You should be prepared when the concrete arrives. Be sure that all ground preparations have been completed, that forms are coated with light form oil, and that equipment and sufficient help are on hand.

Concrete shouldn't be placed on frozen earth, mud, or earth covered with standing water. If the supporting earth is extremely dry, it should be dampened to prevent absorption of the mixing water in the concrete. Chutes are recommended when the concrete is dropped more than 3 or 4 feet.

Striking Off Concrete. After the concrete is placed, it's struck off with a straightedge, usually a 2 by 4. The stakes holding the forms should be cut off even with the top of the forms to permit continuous movement of the strike-off board. One to three strike-off passes should be sufficient. A trowel or spade can be worked along the face of the forms to give a smooth side surface to the concrete.

Finishing Concrete. The type of finish depends upon the finishing tools used. A float gives a gritty texture. When a rougher texture is desired, the surface is floated and then broomed by dragging a stiff-bristle broom across the concrete. The stiffness of the bristles and the pressure applied determine the degree of roughness. Float and broomed finishes are recommended for sidewalks, driveways, and ramps. Steel-troweling gives a smooth finish that does not always provide sufficient footing. Floors, patios, and basement floors are a few places where a steel-trowel finish is often used.

After the concrete has been struck off, it is floated with a light metal float. A float with a long handle is excellent for finishing flat slabs. A final floating with a hand float is often given. Brooming is usually done after floating. Steel-troweling is also done after floating. The proper time to begin steel-troweling is critical. Premature troweling causes a mixture of water, cement, and fine sand to work to the surface, resulting in poorer wearability and surface crazing. Troweling should be done after the water sheen has disappeared. Don't sprinkle water or dry cement on the surface.

An edging tool used between the concrete and the form will produce a smooth, rounded edge that will resist breaking and chipping. The edging tool should be used early, while the concrete is still plastic.

Curing Concrete. After finishing, the concrete must be cured. Up to 50 percent more strength can be developed if fresh concrete is properly cured. Curing is one of the most inexpensive ways to ensure a long-lasting, satisfactory job.

Plastic sheeting or waterproof paper placed over the concrete soon after finishing is an economical method of curing. Sand, straw, burlap, and other materials that are kept continuously wet for an least 6 days may be used to cure the fresh concrete. Forms left in place for several days will also help cure concrete.

Colored Concrete. Attractive, long-lasting colors add to the beauty of many concrete improvements. Pleasing colors can be obtained for almost any color scheme. Bright spots of contrasting colors tastefully placed make the improvement more inviting.

Colors, textures, and patterns all contribute to the unlimited design possibilities of concrete around the home. Colored concrete is usually made in one of four ways: (1) mixing a mineral oxide pigment in the concrete, (2) working a mineral oxide pigment into the surface of the concrete after it is placed but while it is still workable, (3) using colored aggregate and leaving it exposed, or (4) applying commercial acid stains as a special surface finish. Table 7 is a useful color guide.

For true colors, white portland cement and white or light-colored aggregates should be used. Not more than 9 pounds of pigment should be used for each bag of cement. The directions of the pigment manufacturers should be followed.

Concrete Patterns and Finishes. Patios, walks, and other outdoor improvements may be made more decorative or rugged in appearance by exposing the surface aggregate of the concrete. Selection of the proper aggregate is the key to getting the color desired. Use ½- to ¾-inch aggregate such as marble chips, granite screenings, slag, garnet sand, or colored rock materials.

To obtain exposed-aggregate concrete, mix and place ordinary concrete in the usual manner. Immediately after the slab has been screeded and floated, scatter the special-colored aggregate evenly over the surface of the concrete. Pat the colored aggregate with a wood float to push it just below the surface of the concrete. After the concrete firms up, use a magnesium float to be sure that all the aggregate is embedded below the surface. After the concrete starts to harden, take a stiff brush and carefully work the cement-sand mortar away from the top portion of the colored aggregate. A fine water spray used in a limited amount will help.

Unique finishes may be imparted to concrete work from the inner surfaces of forms. For instance, a glassy smoothness is obtained by using polyethylene or plastic lines, while rough texture or pattern textures are obtained by use of paneling rough lumber or insert strips placed on the forms.

Geometric designs make decorative patterns in concrete surfaces. Random patterns may be made in concrete by the use of a bent

Table 7. Color Guide

Color desired	Materials to use
White	White portland cement, white sand
Brown	Burnt umber, or brown oxide of iron (yellow oxide of iron will modify color)
Buff	Yellow ocher, yellow oxide of iron
Gray	Normal portland cement
Green	Chromium oxide (yellow oxide of iron will shade)
Pink	Red oxide of iron (small amount)
Rose	Red oxide of iron
Cream	Yellow oxide of iron

piece of ¾-inch copper pipe about 18 inches long. Circles, squares, ovals, and other designs may be made with household cans of various sizes by impressing the can surface in the semihardened concrete.

Wavy broom finishes can be used to give variety to concrete surfaces. These textures also assure a nonslip surface.

Leaf impressions result in interesting and decorative patterns. Press the leaves stem side down into freshly troweled concrete. Embed the leaf completely, but don't allow the concrete to cover the top of the leaf. Carefully remove the leaf after the concrete sets.

For other types of patterns, there's the famous Graumann's Chinese Theatre in Hollywood, where the footprints of movie stars were embedded in wet concrete. Well, Graumann's has no exclusive on this principle. In Fort Myers, Florida, the beautiful Thomas Edison place has a Friendship Walk, where the concrete flagstones have scratched on them the names or initials of Mr. Edison's friends, including Henry Ford.

If you have a jigsaw and some plywood, you can cut out initials, or a pattern of stylized leaves, birds, fish or whatever strikes your fancy. Then, to make a raised design, you simply press this stencil into the wet concrete hard enough so that the concrete is forced up into the stencil. Keep a pointed mason's trowel handy for tucking in a little extra concrete to be sure the pattern is completely filled.

To reverse the process, and sink a pattern or initials or designs into the concrete, you fasten letters, numbers or the pattern on a board (remember to put them on the board backward) and press them into the wet concrete.

Another very simple but exceedingly attractive method of decorating concrete is to embed bits of colored stone, or sea-worn glass, or designs in metal, such as wrought iron.

For example, suppose you're planning a low wall around your patio or along one side of a garden. While the concrete's still malleable, press into it some square souvenir tiles, reminders of places you've visited. This immediately transforms the wall from a length of plain concrete into an individual and most attractive conversation piece! And, of course, one of the very handsomest outdoor tables you can imagine is one with a mosaic top. You can do this yourself, either with the small squares of tiles made for this purpose and available at any art supply store or with any material that you'd like to use, and set in the concrete in any pattern you wish.

Thin strips of copper or aluminum are excellent for putting a scroll-type pattern in concrete. They're simply pressed in until the top edge is flush with the surface.

Decorating and putting your own personal "stamp" in concrete work is just as simple as working with concrete itself. Many people find it highly enjoyable; others even work at it as a profitable and pleasant little sideline. There's such an endless variety of ways to make every project turn out handsomely that we do believe you'll enjoy at least giving it a try. What you can do with concrete and its decoration is limited only by your imagination.

Questions and Answers

Over the years, we have answered many questions on exterior area—patios, walks, porches, driveways, etc.—on care, repair, and improvement. In this chapter, we have selected and answered the questions most often asked.

PRIVACY FENCE FOR A PATIO

On one side of our patio we need a type of fence to provide privacy. Do you have any suggestions?

There are several so-called modern types of fencing which fit your needs very well. One very practical type has its bottom secured to the fence posts several inches off the ground. This adds greatly to air circulation, yet still shuts off the view most efficiently. One good design which carries this idea along is plank fencing in the shape of vertical louvers (like a vertical Venetian blind). It's surprising how completely this arrangement closes the view without impeding the breezes. Almost as effective is horizontal louvering, although this directs breezes downward. Another interesting modern effect is called "basket weave," which is secured in front of and behind the fence posts on an alternating basis (in the same pattern as basketing). This too permits good air circulation, though not as much as the vertical louver arrangement.

LEGAL ASPECT OF FENCING

Are there any limits to the heights of fencing?

We can't answer that question since limits vary from community to community. You should find out about any local ordinances that stipulate under what, if any, conditions fencing is permissible. Find out if there are any limitations on height, as well as proximity to public walks, thoroughfares, or other municipal land. While you're checking, you could ask about assessments, just to be sure you know. Next, make sure you know exactly where your property line runs. If the fence splits the line, your neighbor will share it, regardless of whether he chips in or not with expenses or labor. Put your fence an inch or two (some people make it more) inside your line. Remember, any land outside your fence you more or less abandon. If there's a usable strip, your neighbor can use it. Your lawyer can give you more good advice about locating your fence.

GATE-SWINGERS CAUSE SAGS

Our front gate sags pretty bad. While my children do swing on it occasionally, I don't believe that they are the full cause of the problem. Is there any other reasons for a sagging gate, and how can it be cured?

Very often the sag is the fault of the gatepost. It has to bear the full weight of the gate, as well as any swingers. So unless it was originally sunk well into a base of concrete or well-jammed rocks, this heavy pull can drag it down from the perpendicular. This tends to make the opposite top corner of the gate lean toward the other post, often touching it, and getting the latch out of alignment. You can work the post back to a perpendicular position, which will get the gate lined up again. But to hold the post there requires more bracing than simply tamping the ground around it. Ideally, you should dig down and surround the buried end in concrete, and be sure to keep this checked with a level when the concrete begins to set up. You can also brace the gatepost vertically with a turnbuckle and heavy wire, running from the top of the post diagonally down to the base of the next post farther along. Another common reason for a sagging gate is that the hinges are too small and the screws too short. The weight simply pulls them loose. Replacing them with larger hinges and longer screws is the solution. Actually, if a gate is over 4 feet high, a third hinge, slightly higher than halfway up, is an excellent idea. It's a must if the gate is higher than 5 feet. Still another generous contributor to sagging is exposure to year-round weather.

This is especially true of those gates made of unfinished, natural, "rustic" wood. Unless they're put together better than average, various degrees of warping, swelling, and shrinking can take place. This is one big reason why (when asked) we always recommend generous amounts of wood preservative, even on "weatherproof" woods, before hanging a gate.

WHAT COVERING FOR PORCH?

We have a screen-enclosed porch. The concrete floor is solid, about 16 inches above ground level. Would linoleum, tile squares, or indoor-outdoor carpeting be the best covering? In coldest weather, the porch is enclosed with framed heavy plastic sheeting, so that no snow lies on the floor.

Both the carpeting and the tile will be okay. But you must make sure that the tile is definitely made for on-grade, exterior surfaces; many are not. Linoleum won't work at all. It can't take the exposure or the concrete in contact with the ground.

COVERING WOOD PORCH FLOOR

We have a wooden porch over our bathroom, which is insulated. Recently some of the wood rotted away, and we replaced it with new boards. Which is better: covering with canvas or hardboard?

Exterior-type hardboard, while moisture-resistant, is not made to withstand constant traffic and is not suitable for this type of exposed floor covering. Roofing canvas, properly applied, would be excellent covering (see page 178). It gives years of excellent service. It can be painted.

WOOD OVER ASPHALT TILE

Our breezeway has a cement floor with asphalt tile on top. During humid days moisture seeps up from the cement, and the floor is quite wet. We want to lay a wood floor on top. Do we have to tear up the tile first and waterproof the cement?

Cover the tile with a layer of liquid asphalt dampproofing and then with overlapping layers of asphalt-saturated roll roofing (the overlap should be about one-quarter of the width). This should give a waterproof sandwich between the tile and wood flooring. The sleepers can be secured with mastic (in the case of flooring strips); wood-block flooring can be laid directly in the mastic. Of course it is safest of all if the wood has been thoroughly treated with liquid wood preservative.

TILING WOOD PORCH FLOOR

We recently enclosed a porch at the side of our house. This has a wood floor over which we want to put down vinyl-asphalt tile. Must anything be put over the wood before laying the tile?

If the porch floor, as is usual, is only a single thickness, it is necessary to put down plywood or a hard fiberboard underlay as the base for the tile. If there is a double flooring, and the surface is level, the underlayment is unnecessary. Complete installation instructions are available from the tile dealer; follow these carefully.

PORCH FLOOR

Our front porch has soft white pine flooring, which opens and closes during the year. We put "water putty crack filler" in last year, and it is cracking and falling out. Could you please advise what could be done to stop this?

Since wood fibers have an "affinity" for moisture, try sealing as much of the wood as possible by painting the underside of the floor-boards in addition to painting the surface. A couple of coats of aluminum paint on the underside should be sufficient. The space under the porch must be well ventilated to keep the wood from swelling because of ground moisture. Painting should be done when the greatest amount of shrinkage has taken place. After painting, refill the spaces with wood putty. Results would have been better if yellow pine flooring had been used.

COLD PORCH FLOOR

I have an enclosed porch with a hollow foundation. Even though there is a register for the heat, it is unusually cold in the winter. There is a hardwood floor. Will wall-to-wall carpeting help, with some kind of insulation under the carpet? Is there any other way of insulating?

Insulation against ground moisture from the hollow foundation should be provided. This can take the form of either batt-type, moistureproof and vaporproof insulation, attached to the underside of the floor, or over-lapping sheets of moistureproof and vapor-proof building paper or polyethylene plastic, the seams of which are sealed with roofing cement, placed on the ground itself. Insulation plus wall-to-wall carpeting will help greatly. Is the size of the register adequate for the size of the porch? Are the walls adequately insulated also?

BREEZEWAY FLOOR

The concrete floor in our breezeway has pulled away from the foundation, leaving quite a wide crack which allows water to drain into the basement when there is a hard, "blowing" rain. The floor is also very rough and full of deep cuts and scars. Is there any way we can resurface the floor without breaking up and removing it? The floor is now painted.

The open space between the concrete floor and the foundation wall should be filled with sand up to within ½ inch of the surface. The remainder of the space is then filled with a caulking compound or asphalt roof cement. Remove the paint from the concrete floor with a floor-sanding machine; then apply a concrete bonding preparation, and put down a 1-inch layer of concrete. If the additional thickness is not desirable, you can have the present concrete made smooth by a terrazzo-grinding machine. Terrazzo contractors could do this, but the paint will have to be removed first.

PROTECTING UNDERSIDE OF PORCH

After having heard some experiences of friends, I have become concerned about the underside of my wooden porch, which is over a dirt-surfaced crawl space. I am afraid that dampness from the ground may cause decaying. Is this right? If so, how can I protect the wood?

Your concern is well-founded. There are many cases where dampness rising from the ground has so seriously decayed the porch floors, and interior floors, too, that replacement of beams and flooring was necessary. If your wood is still sound, treating it with a chemical wood preservative is strongly recommended. There are several excellent such products, which are forced, under pressure, into the wood, and thus penetrate deeply. Also, they are odorless, which is a great advantage over creosote. Your lumberyard will probably be able to supply the preservative. To check dampness from the ground, cover the crawl space with asphalt-saturated felt or roll roofing, overlapping the strips about 6 inches. If the ground is perfectly flat, you

Figure 16-1. When replacing wood steps, be sure to apply wood preservative on the underside before installing.

won't need to seal the edges of the laps. But if there are any places where the edges gap open, they should be sealed with asphalt roofing cement.

RUSTING PORCH RAILING

The iron porch railing is painted with aluminum paint, but rust keeps coming through. How should it be treated before painting to correct this condition? Can it be sprayed?

Remove all loose and flaking rust with steel wood and turpentine. Apply either a dampproof red primer or a zinc chromate metal coat in aerosol form. Then apply finish coating in the same brand as the first coat, following the manufacturer's instructions.

SAVE THE LADY'S MOPPING

We have a screened-in porch over a garage (in a raised ranch). The porch floor is wood. I have wanted to put indoor-outdoor carpeting on the floor, but my husband feels that if the carpeting gets wet from the elements, over a period of time, the wooden floor will warp or rot. This sounds plausible to me; yet I really would like some kind of covering to save on the continual mopping up I have to do after rains. Would the carpeting work? Any other ideas?

If you don't have any "weep holes" in the bottom edges of the screen frames, that's probably why you have to mop so much. They will let collected water drain out. Surely the porch wasn't made absolutely level so that the

water won't drain. A top-quality floor and deck enamel will protect the wood from water. If you really want the carpeting, you certainly can have it. You put down a foam-rubber padding underneath, cemented to the floor, being especially careful to cement the edges, so that water can't sneak in underneath. This will protect the floor from rain.

CEMENTING CARPET BEST?

We plan to put indoor-outdoor carpeting, with foam-rubber padding, along our concrete breezeway. I have heard conflicting opinions about whether it is best to cement the padding down or simply place it there and the carpet on top. What is your opinion?

One loud vote for the cementing. No buckling, no bumping, and no chance of dampness working underneath via the edges.

MILDEW UNDERNEATH PORCH FLOOR

Our porch has been painted with deck and porch paint. Near the edge where it is most exposed to weather conditions, some of the boards are showing a slight shrinkage; dampness has gotten in between and caused the paint on top to peel as well as the underside, which was also painted; underneath, mildew has also formed. How can we get rid of the mildew and seal the cracks and separations in the floorboards?

To get rid of the mildew, scrub the underside with a stiff brush and a strong detergent or bleach solution, followed by rinsing with clear water. The ground under the porch should be covered with overlapping strips of polyethylene plastic of moistureproof and vaporproof building paper to prevent ground moisture from rising and striking the underside of porch. After several dry days, fill the cracks between floorboards with white lead thinned with linseed oil, a crack filler, or plastic wood; narrow cracks should be filled by running linseed oil into them. The floor should not be repainted until the filler has dried. Be sure the floor surface is free of grease, grime, and all peeling paint. Coat the underside with aluminum paint.

RUST MARKS ON CEMENT PORCH FLOOR

I have railings on my front porch, and they rusted. The rust stained the concrete. There also are rust marks on the floor from snow shovels left during winter months. How can these be removed?

Try making a paste of a rust-removing liquid, available at many hardware and paint dealers, and powdered whiting; cover the stains with a thick layer of the paste; when it is dry, replace it with fresh paste until the stains are removed. Or the following treatment is effective: dissolve 1 part of sodium citrate in 6 parts of water and 6 parts of commercial glycerin. Mix a portion of this with an absorbent powder, such as powdered whiting. Spread a thick layer over the stains, following the same procedure as with the preceding paste. There is an excellent cleaning preparation, widely used for cleaning buildings in large cities; it works well on rust. See if your hardware or masonry supply dealer can get it for you.

LEAKY ROOF

What can I do to waterproof the floor of an open, roofed-over porch on the side of the house? The 7/8th tongue-and-groove boards have shrunk or cracked and allow driving rains to seep through to the fruit room below. Porch paint by itself does not remedy the problem. The floorboards appear to be in good condition.

Floorboards and lumber of any kind never make a completely suitable roofing material. You should cover it with a roofing canvas. The fabric is specially woven and treated for use as a roofing. Don't use ordinary canvas or awning cloth. Dealers in canvas materials can get this roofing canvas for you, including the instructions on its application.

PORCH FLOOR LEAKS

My front porch floor leaks when it rains. It is over a part of the recreation room. I cannot cover the ceiling until I find a way of waterproofing the floor. I have painted it several times with floor and deck enamel, but this does not seal for long. Do you know of any way I can remedy this?

We assume this is a wood porch floor. Repaint the porch floor after a number of dry days so that the wood is thoroughly dry. Any cracks between floorboards will then be widest and should be filled with white lead thinned with linseed oil, crack filler, or some other similar material. Cracks too narrow to be filled should have linseed oil run into them. Allow

the filler to dry thoroughly before applying the paint.

WOOD STOOP SAGGING

We have a front stoop of four wood steps, which is beginning to sag. A space is developing at the top between the stoop and the house. Is there any way to brace the stoop, or what kind of repair do you recommend?

Bracing would only be a temporary measure. Probably, the wood structural supports have started to rot, causing the steps to sag. Complete reconstruction will be necessary. If you desire wood steps again, first put down a concrete slab footing of about 3 to 4 inches thick and treat all the wood with a chemical wood preservative. Keep the joints between the concrete and the wood well caulked at all times.

CANVAS FOR PATIO FLOOR

My roofless, rarely used, wood-floored patio has been somewhat damaged by exposure to weather. I was given a fairly large amount of flooring canvas, which I would like to put down as protection. My questions: How do I waterproof the canvas? How do I stick it to the floor?

To waterproof, paint with two or three thin coats of top-quality floor and deck enamel. To stick it to the concrete, use that handy all-around material—ordinary black plastic roofing cement. To assure tight adhesion, use a lawn roller.

CEMENT BED FOR PATIO

We are laying a patio and are in doubt about the type of cement to use. We have excavated the area a foot in depth and placed cinders 7 inches in depth for drainage. We plan to float the patio stone in cement. Should we use regular cement or mortar cement?

A regular 1-2-3 cement mix should be used (1 part portland cement, 2 parts sand, 3 parts pea gravel).

PREVENTING FROST DAMAGE TO PATIO

I plan to lay a concrete floor to be used as a patio. This will be completely exposed, adjoining the house. How can I prevent frost damage to the concrete?

Providing for adequate drainage under the concrete, so that water cannot collect and freeze (expansion of water when frozen is what causes heaving of concrete), will prevent frost damage. If the soil is clayey, a bed of well-tamped cinders, gravel, or sand, 8 to 10 inches deep, should be adequate.

PATCHING PATIO EDGE

We have a concrete patio-porch at the side of our house. It is badly chipped in several places around the edges. Is there any way to patch it?

Dig out the chipped places to at least a ½-inch depth, keeping the sides vertical; making them deeper would be even better. Use a hammer and cold chisel for the job, protecting your eyes with goggles against flying chips. Brush out all loose particles, and wet the area thoroughly with water. Pack with patching concrete, keeping the patches damp for at least a week to allow slow curing. Brace each patch with a greased board or piece of stiff sheet metal, while still wet, to prevent sagging.

COLORING PATIO STONES

I am planning to make a patio, using colored concrete for the stones. How is color added to the concrete mixture?

Usually the powdered coloring is added when the concrete is almost firm, and it is done by troweling over the surface. However, although this saves a great deal in the amount of coloring material needed, it does not penetrate too deeply. Therefore, in time, it will be worn off in high-traffic areas. The more permanent method is to mix the colors in when the concrete is mixed, so that the entire slab is colored throughout its thickness. All ingredients should be mixed thoroughly before the water is added. Add no more than 9 pounds of color for each bag of cement. For light shades, cut the amount to about half; for good light colors, white portland cement is preferable. Don't use any color pigment that isn't guaranteed by the manufacturer as being limeproof.

FLAGSTONE PATIO

Will you please tell us the best method for brightening the color of our flagstone patio? We tried linseed oil, but it came out tacky.

After using the linseed oil you evidently omitted one important operation—the removal of all excess oil after it had soaked into the stone for a half hour or so. To correct the present condition, try wiping the flagstones with turpentine. If they're still tacky, scrub

them with a solution of trisodium phosphate or washing soda, using about 3 pounds to the gallon of hot water. Then rinse them with clear water. The next application should be as suggested above.

FILLING HAIRLINE CRACK

Our concrete patio, 14 feet long, has developed a hairline crack. But over a 4-foot length, the crack is so thin I can see its location only after a shower, when the water shows it up. Is there something I could use to fill this—without having to chip the crack wider to put in patching mortar? This, I feel, will be an unnecessary piece of work, and the repair would look like a 14-foot-long repair.

If you have the patience, epoxy glue (clear), worked in with a toothpick, would be excellent. You could use grout, mixed very thin; this is portland cement and water. However, be sure to tint the grout the same shade gray as the rest of the concrete. Otherwise it will be a conspicuous white repair.

DON'T LET CRACK GET WORSE

Clear across our large concrete patio is a crack, and it's not a hairline. Will leaving this crack open create problems? If so, how can I seal it?

Leaving the crack as is can certainly cause problems, up to and including more cracking and actual breakup. If water were to work under the slab and then freeze solid, the expansion would really be destructive. Fix the crack with roofing cement, if you don't mind a black streak. Or else widen the crack full depth, rake out the loose stuff, soak the crack with water, and then trowel patching mortar into it. Keep the repair damp for a week to promote slow, proper curing.

PEELING PROBLEM WITH PATIO

We find it necessary to paint our concrete patio too frequently because the paint peels after a short time. Is there any special paint we should use?

If more such patios were built over a gravel drainage bed and over a waterproofing layer of heavy plastic sheeting, paint would stay on a lot better. But without this construction, we frankly don't recommend any paint, unless one is willing to repaint at regular intervals when peeling commences. By far the safest way of all to have a colored patio is to mix limeproof cement colors right into the concrete mix as it is being poured. Then the slab is the same color for its full depth.

TAR STICKS TO PATIO

We have a problem with a poured-concrete patio. When my father owned this home last year, he patched some cracks with roofing tar. Since this was very noticeable, he covered the entire patio with the tar, intending to paint over it. He did not, however, because the tar started coming off. After the hard winter, about half the tar has come off. How can we remove the other half? We have tried various acids, cleaners, sanders, and scrubbers.

Try the same dry ice treatment as for removing asphalt tile: Buy 15 or 20 pounds of dry ice at an ice cream store, and put the ice in a burlap bag. Let this sit on the area you'll start scraping first. After about 15 minutes, the intense cold should penetrate the tar, and make it so brittle you can start scraping it up with a wide-blade putty knife. While scraping, move the bag to the adjacent area to chill it. This may take more than one load of dry ice if the patio is of any size.

DIRT-RETARDANT FINISH FOR PATIO

I am building a concrete patio during my vacation this summer. Is there any kind of finish to put on to make it easier to keep clean-looking?

Apply a colorless, silicone-base water repellent, available at masonry supply and large paint dealers, following the label directions carefully. The coating acts as a moisture-proof surface, so that rain or water from a garden hose carries dirt away quickly.

RAIN CAUSED MOSSY PATIO

With all the rains last summer, the bricks in our patio are now partly covered with a mossy growth. Is there something I can do to combat this?

A reasonably strong solution of weed killer will take care of the moss very well. Apply it carefully, so that there's no chance of it slopping off the edges to wreck some planting. In fact, it would be better to use a small blowtorch on the moss along the edges. Don't hold the heat in one spot for any appreciable time, to avoid the risk of cracking the brick.

PORCH POST BASE

Porch posts supporting an overhanging roof get much damage during the winter from snow, etc., causing peeling paint. Is there any type of "cap" to use at the base?

Cast-iron ventilating column bases are available, permitting moisture to evaporate by allowing ventilation at this point and preventing peeling paint. Dealers in hardware should be able to get this item for you.

TWO SHADES OF CEMENT

Our concrete front porch has a rough surface, and there are a few cracks. We had the steps repaired, and now there are two shades of cement. Would it help the porch floor to put a paint on it, and what kind should we use? How often would we have to repaint?

A rubber-base floor paint should work out satisfactorily on the concrete surfaces. The frequency of repainting will depend on the amount of traffic. To smooth the rough surfaces, rub them with a coarse abrasive stone, but if the concrete is very rough and if the area is large, have a terrazzo contractor smooth it with a terrazzo-grinding machine.

CEMENT SMEARED ON BRICK

While making a new cement porch, we splashed some of the cement on our red brick wall. How can we get the cement off?

Mix 1 part of muriatic acid in 10 parts of water. Pour the acid slowly into the water to avoid splashing. A wood or glass container should be used to hold the solution. Apply the liquid liberally over the smeared cement, and allow it to remain for 2 or 3 minutes. Then scrub with a fiber brush and the acid solution. Rinse thoroughly with clear water. Because the acid is highly corrosive, protect yourself by wearing rubber gloves, old clothing, and rubbers over your shoes. If you're working above your head, wear goggles to protect your eyes. Avoid getting any of the liquid on your skin.

SLIPPERY BREEZEWAY FLOOR

For years we have been painting our breezeway with the same brand of rubberized paint. When the floor becomes damp on a rainy or humid day, it becomes very slippery and there is danger of someone falling. Can you suggest a remedy?

When next you repaint the floor, mix sand into the paint, or while the paint coating is still wet, sprinkle a little sand over the surface. This will roughen the surface of the floor just enough to prevent slipping.

ROUGHENING CONCRETE

We have a cement porch that is very smooth and dangerous when wet. How can I roughen the cement?

Sometimes scrubbing with a solution of muriatic acid will remove enough of the cement to roughen the surface. Mix 1 part of acid in 10 parts of water. Apply it over a small area, and after 10 minutes scrub with a fiber brush; then rinse with clear water. If this isn't effective, roughen the surface with a stone cutter's bushhammer. Or have a monument man do it for you.

DAMP CONCRETE PORCH FLOOR

We have an enclosed back porch with a concrete floor which is very damp most of the time. At times it appears as if water had been poured on it. What causes this dampness, and what can we do about it? We would like to put asphalt tile down.

The moisture may be from two causes: if the concrete is laid directly on the ground, with no moistureproof layer underneath, it may be ground moisture working up; or the concrete is enough cooler than the air above it to cause condensation to form.

SPOTS ON CONCRETE PORCH FLOOR

Our porch cement floor has various stains on it, such as rust, fruit juice, etc. Is there some cleaning mixture that can be applied and left on for a certain time?

All stains can't be treated in the same manner. Scrubbing them with a detergent solution, using about ¼ cupful in each pailful of hot water, could remove much of the soiling. Or try rinsing the stains with a hot, saturated solution of oxalic acid (*poison*), rinsing the acid off well with clear water after a half hour or so. Frequent use of this solution will disintegrate the cement floor. Cover the concrete floor with a coco matting to keep it from becoming stained.

PATCHES IN CONCRETE FLOOR

Five months ago my wife threw rock salt on patches of ice on a cement floor in a breezeway. Now the cement is all loose and bro-ken up. What can I do to stop this, and how would I go about pouring fresh cement over this to make it smooth?

Thoroughly roughen the concrete, or coat it with a liquid bonding preparation. If you roughen it, sweep it clean to remove dust and dampen it well with clean water. Then put down an inch-thick layer of concrete. This consists of 1 part of portland cement, 2 of sand, and 3 of gravel. The mixture should be fairly stiff.

GROUND TURNS BRICK WHITE

The back patio on our property has a large area made of red brick. Owing to the alkalinity in our ground, the bricks are a sorry mess. They look more white than red. Can anything be done to rectify this?

Scrub them with a solution of 1 part of muriatic (hydrochloric) acid in 5 parts of water. Leave this on for 10 minutes or so before rinsing off with clear water. How long this will cure the condition, it's hard to say. As more alkalinity subsequently works through the bricks from the ground, you'll need a repeat.

LEAKY FISH POOL

Each winter our backyard fish pool cracks in the same place. I plaster cement over it in the spring, but it still leaks. One winter I left it filled with water. There was no difference. What can I do?

Instead of merely plastering over the crack, repair it. Chip it wide enough for the waterproof ready-mix to be worked in. Keep the repair damp for a week to allow slow, proper curing. When dry, replaster, if you wish to hide the repair. Then coat the entire surface with a transparent liquid masonry sealer containing silicones. Sealers are sold in most outlets for building supplies.

PAINT KILLED FISH AND LILY

I built a little fishpond outside on my patio, about 4 feet across, five years ago. I've had water in it since then and also have a fountain pump. Last year someone gave me a water lily, and all summer it grew very nicely. It stayed in a container which I brought into the house last fall. Now this last spring I painted the pond with concrete enamel. When I put the lily into the pond again, it died. I also put some minnows into the pond, and they died overnight. What went

wrong? What can I do so that things won't die in the pond?

Something in the paint is the villain. Regular swimming pool paint would be safe. It's possible that a couple of coats would be sufficient insulation against the present paint. But it would be safer to remove all you can first. You should also ask a dealer in aquarium fish his opinion.

POCKETS IN CEMENT BLOCK WALL

How can pockets be made in bricks or cement blocks for plants? Could bricks or cement blocks be put on top of each other, without cement between? I wish to make a wall around a tree—about three or four blocks high—with a vine hanging down over the wall.

You can dent concrete blocks with a hammer and star drill—or you'll find it much quicker to drill irregularly shaped depressions with a carbide-tipped masonry bit in a quarter-inch electric drill. You can attack the concrete block with a mallet and cold chisel, but you'd probably shatter any bricks with this treatment. If the wall is brick, you should use mortar. However, with only three rows of concrete blocks, you might "get away" without using mortar—although it would be much safer and more rigid if you did use it.

CLOTHES POLE IN CONCRETE

I anchored a 4 by 4 wooden clothes post in concrete. It has now broken off at the top of the concrete, leaving 2 to 2½ feet of rotted post in the concrete. It will not come out in one piece or in large pieces, but only in small chips. Is there a simple way to remove this post without breaking up the concrete?

You should get good results by first drilling about a 2-inch-diameter hole with an auger; a larger hole if you can get a larger auger. Use a smaller-diameter auger for the corners, and the remainder of the wood you should be able to chisel or dig out.

HARDENED CEMENT ON WHEELBARROW

How can I remove hardened cement from a metal wheelbarrow? I have tried hammering it, but the thin layer of cement is still on.

Moisten the cement with a solution of 1 part muriatic acid in 20 parts water; allow it to act for a few minutes—only long enough to

soften the cement and not attack the metal underneath; then flush the acid off with plenty of water. Scrape off the cement with a dull tool to avoid scratching the barrow. Repeat the application if necessary. Because of the highly corrosive effect of the acid, be sure to wear heavy, old clothes, goggles to protect the eyes, rubber gloves on the hands, and rubbers over shoes while working.

KEEP FENCE AS IS

We recently installed a cedar stockade fence. How can I treat it so that it keeps its present yellow color, rather than turning gray through weathering?

Practically any paint or hardware store or lumberyard sells creosote stain in various shades. Consult the color chart.

ROTTING FENCE POSTS

My fence posts (five years old) show signs of rot at the ground level. I did not build the fence, having purchased the property a year ago. Can you suggest something to arrest further damage?

If only the grade level is affected, coat the wood with creosote or a chemical wood preservative. It should be coated well above the soil and several inches below. Check the condition of the remainder of the posts below the ground surface. They might become infested with termites unless they are also treated with a wood preservative.

CRUMBLED CONCRETE WALK

I have a short concrete walk where the top facing has crumbled, in some places an inch deep. Can I smooth it by using a premixed mortar or concrete that comes in bags? If so, what mixture should I use?

The spots can be filled with a cement mixture, but the depressions will have to be of a uniform depth. You will have to deepen the outer edges with a hammer and cold chisel, keeping the sides perpendicular. Patches of cement cannot be featheredged. Brush out all loose particles, and dampen the depressions with water; then fill them with a fairly stiff but workable mixture of 1 part of portland cement and 3 parts of clean coarse sand. If a depression is more than an inch deep, fill it with a mixture of 1 part of cement, 2 of sand, and 3 of stone or gravel, the gravel being not larger than 1 inch. Keep the patches damp for several days. Fast evaporation weakens the new mortar or concrete.

SIDEWALK FOUNDATION

What kind of foundation is advisable to provide drainage under a concrete sidewalk?

A cinder or gravel foundation is put down under a sidewalk when drainage is not good and there is danger that water may collect underneath. It should be at least 4 inches deep, if possible.

CRACKED WALK

The concrete walk leading to our front door developed a wide crack across it at the end of last winter. How can this be repaired so that it won't crack again?

The crack may be due to improper drainage under the walk or failure to fill and pack soft places underneath before the concrete was laid. Spaces must be allowed, also, between sections across the walk for expansion and contraction. If any of these faults is present, the only permanent repair is to relay the walk after correcting the basic fault. To fill the crack, undercut the sides to a depth of 1½ inches using a hammer and cold chisel. Brush out all loose particles and sand; then moisten the sides of the opening with clear water. Patch the crack with ready-mixed cement patching mortar, or latex cement, or a stiff but workable mixture of 3 parts sand and 1 part cement moistened with water. Keep the patch damp for about a week to allow slow, natural curing of the cement and to keep shrinkage at a minimum. Using latex patching concrete eliminates much of the preliminary chipping.

SETTLED CONCRETE SIDEWALK

Is there any way that our front walk could be fixed? It is of concrete, and after five years it must have settled. When it rains or snow melts, the water settles in one place near the stairs. Could I build up the concrete by putting more cement over the low spot? Or should we have to have a new walk put down? Will new cement stick to the old walk?

New concrete can be put down over the old by roughening the surface of the old, brushing off all dust, and wetting it down. But you cannot featheredge with concrete. A preparation is now on the market which,

when brushed on old concrete, provides a good bond for the new. The best procedure would be to cut away the settled sidewalk area and pour new concrete in its place.

FLAKING WALK

The concrete walk in front of my house is several years old and is flaking and in need of repair. Is there any way I can repair the walk, without replacement at this time, and prevent more flaking of the concrete?

Liquid cement-hardening preparations are widely available at masonry supply dealers; follow the label instructions. These are pretty effective at preventing further flaking of concrete. For small repair jobs, use a latex patching concrete, which is quick and easy to use.

FUNGUS ON SIDEWALK

Our sidewalk is slippery when wet because of a mold or fungus. We have large trees and little sunlight. Is there a way of removing this hazard by mechanical or chemical means without killing the grass?

Scrub the sidewalk surface with a stiff brush and a solution of household bleach, being careful to keep the solution from draining onto the grass section; rinse the bleach off with plenty of clear water. Then apply a liquid mildew-proofer, available at large marine supply and some department stores. Trimming the trees to permit more sunlight would also be a big help in avoiding fungus growth.

GRASS SPOILING SIDEWALK

What is the best way of disposing of grass growing in the cracks of a cement sidewalk? This happens every year and spoils the looks of our walk.

Put some of the weed killers that destroy all vegetation in a small-spouted can or bottle and carefully pour it into each crack. That will take care of the grass most definitely. If we may add, repairing those cracks would not only take care of the grass but make your sidewalk look a whole lot nicer.

DISCOLORED CONCRETE

About 8 weeks ago we had our concrete porch, walk, and stairs replaced. The concrete is discolored, dark, and spotty. How can we remedy this condition?

It is probable that in a few more weeks all the moisture may be out of the concrete and the color will be uniform. If after about 3 months' time, the discoloration remains, it seems evident that different brands of cement were used, thus giving variations in shade. There is no simple way of taking out the discoloration. Only a new topping of concrete, about 1 inch thick, or painting will give you a uniform color.

PEBBLES WON'T STAY PUT

I have recently relandscaped my backyard, making extensive use of bricks and small pebbles. The problem is that the pebbles have a tendency to move around under foot traffic. Can you suggest a way to anchor them?

There are two methods, each involving concrete. The first method is to remove the pebbles entirely. Cover the area with concrete. Before it hardens, place the pebbles in the concrete, each slightly below its "equator," which will keep them in place. The second method is to mix the pebbles with concrete and pour. While the concrete is still mushy, begin to brush the surface to expose the pebbles. Keep the hose handy for rinsing away any undesirable mush. Also be sure you will be able to reach each part easily before you start pouring. You might want to group a few of the bricks as stepping-stones.

CLEANING CEMENT PATIO

There are a few dark, dirty areas on our cement patio; it looks very disreputable. What is the best way to clean the surface so that it looks good for the new season?

Cleaning and etching preparations for concrete and masonry surfaces are available at masonry and large hardware dealers. Use the kind containing no muriatic acid, and follow the label directions carefully. Or scrub the concrete thoroughly with a stiff brush and a strong, hot solution of trisodium phosphate and water. Then rinse it off thoroughly with clear water. For any stubborn discolored spots or areas, try the following: Apply a thick paste of 1 part trisodium phosphate, 2 parts powdered whiting, moistened with water. Allow the paste to remain until dry; then brush it off. Repeat the treatment if necessary.

GRASS AND MOSS ON PATH

Last summer I dug a path across our lawn to the rose garden and lined it with bricks. By early fall, moss had started to form on the bricks and grass came up between. Is there anything I can do to prevent this?

You can use one of the soil-sterilizing weed killers or regular No. 2 fuel oil. But the trouble is, you don't know how far this will spread on either side. There's no problem, of course, about putting it down the middle of the path. Then, after you find out the spreading range, you can determine how much more you can put on. This is not a treatment where you can be hasty.

BRICK IT RIGHT FIRST TIME

I wish to set bricks into the ground for walks around flower beds. What do I put under and between the bricks? I will be bricking quite a few areas, so I might as well do it right the first time.

There are several choices. A very simple and solid base and "in between" is slightly damp sand. Once you get bricks solidly set in position, and the whole thing given several goings-over with a lawn roller, those bricks will stay remarkably put. For more solidity, fill up the top ½ inch of space between bricks with dry portland cement. Then set your lawn sprinkler to "mist," and let it play over the cement for a few hours. This will turn the cement to concrete, which will work down between the bricks. The ultimate method, of course, is setting the bricks in solid concrete. But we seriously doubt if you'll be needing this extreme.

LANNON STONE WALK

We were given a quantity of lannon stones in various sizes and shapes. We would like to make a walk. Can the lannon stones be split? Some are just 1 inch thick, some 6 to 7 inches thick. We would like to split them so that we have a sufficient quantity. Is sand a good medium to put them in, or can they be put just on the ground?

With a little practice using a mason's hammer, or even a hammer and cold chisel, you may do a pretty fair job of splitting the stones—although it is really not a very simple job (it might be better to ask a worker at the cemetery or monument yard to do it). Sand makes an excellent bed—even better than resting the stones in their own excavations on the ground (so the top surfaces are level with each other). All too often when the ground freezes, the stones will be heaved out of position unless there is a sand base.

PAINTING CONCRETE STEPS

Now my concrete front steps need repainting; the paint has flaked badly. Someone told me that paint makes concrete steps slippery, but in the 12 years these were painted, I never noticed any particular skiddiness. However, if there is some paint which makes steps less slippery I might as well use it. What type is it?

It's true that there are nonskid finishes made for industrial plants, but they're not packaged in retail sizes. However, you can get just as good results by mixing generous amounts of sand right into your regular paint.

CRACK IN CONCRETE STEP

How can I repair a concrete step which has a crack 2 inches from its base?

Make the crack wider and at least ½ inch deep, keeping the sides straight, so that the crack will be just as wide at the base as it is at the surface. After brushing out all loose particles of cement and sand, wet the inner surfaces and pack the crack with a fairly stiff, but workable, mixture of 1 part of portland cement and 3 parts of clean, coarse sand. The patch should be kept damp for several days to prevent shrinkage during the hardening process.

NEW CORNER FOR PORCH STEP

A big corner was knocked off one of our concrete porch steps. How can I fix this?

First drill a hole with a star drill or carbide-tipped bit in your electric drill into the place where the new corner will go. Insert a stub of reinforcing rod so that the new corner will be supported; let the stub stick out an inch or so. Make a form, of wood or a small sheet of aluminum greased on the inside, which will be braced tightly where you pour the new concrete. Thoroughly soak the old concrete; then pour your new "corner" into the form. When the concrete is well set up, remove the form and carefully smooth and shape the concrete. Keep the repair damp (using spray) for a week to promote slow, proper curing.

OPEN JOINT BETWEEN STEP AND FOUNDATION

We have a wide concrete step at our side door. The step and the foundation have an open space between them. How should this open joint be filled in?

If the open space is relatively small, ¼ to ⅜ inch, use a light-colored caulking compound to fill the joint. If the space is more than ½ inch deep, fill it with sand and then put in the caulking. For a larger open space, brush out loose particles, moisten the sides, and pack the space with patching cement, keeping the patch moist for about a week to allow slow curing.

CHIPPED CONCRETE STEPS

The concrete steps in my basement got chipped. What could I use to repair them?

Use a latex patching concrete, available at masonry supply dealers; follow the label directions for mixing. Be sure to brush away all loose particles before applying patching material; and set a form of sheet metal or wood as a support for the patch until it hardens.

ROUGH CONCRETE STEPS

We built a new home last summer, and the masons did a very poor job of the front and back stoops. How can we get the concrete steps and stoops smooth? Is there a sander that will do a decent job?

If there aren't too many steps and the surface isn't extremely rough, you can smooth it by rubbing it down with a coarse abrasive or grinding stone. A very rough surface will have to be ground down with a terrazzo-grinding machine. Terrazzo contractors can do such work. It cannot be done by an amateur.

FILLING THE GAP

A fairly large piece of brick was broken off the corner of one front step. One section was intact, and I got it back in place. I used clear epoxy adhesive instead of mortar, so that the repair would not show. But there is still a very noticeable V-shaped gap I would like to fill.

Break up another piece of brick into very small pieces. Do this on a piece of plywood or cardboard to save the brick dust. Mix the pieces with your clear epoxy to a fairly stiff paste and shape it into the gap. To cut the shine of the epoxy, sprinkle the brick dust over it.

CARPET MAKES STEPS ICY

I plan to carpet my enclosed front porch and would like to include the stoop and three steps outside. My problem is that all winter I have ice on the stoop and steps, due to water dripping down between the eaves trough and the roof (this cannot be corrected). Would the indoor-outdoor carpeting hold more ice and be more dangerous than leaving the concrete bare, where ice can be readily moved off?

With the present situation, we agree that leaving the outside stoop and steps bare would be safer. After all, you can keep them sprinkled with one of the harmless ice-melting granules sold for this purpose. However, if you could have a roofer run a strip of aluminum from the edge of the roof to the top of the eaves trough, to close the gap and stop the drip, then you could put the carpeting on the stoop and steps; it's best to make this strip at least 2 feet wider than the steps.

LEAKY RAILROAD TIES

Recently we remodeled our patio and put in a set of steps made of railroad ties. The problem: Creosote oozing from the ties makes it impossible to use the steps. Is there any way to remove the creosote so that the steps will be usable? We have tried loose cement and sand, scraping this off when the creosote oozes out, but this is a slow process.

From all indications, it will be a long time before the creosote works out of those ties. About all you can do (besides replacement) is to cover the top surfaces with something that will keep shoes from coming into contact with the creosote, yet still allow the weather to continue its slow action. Some of those old-time scroll-metal doormat foot scrapers would be perfect.

ADD RAILINGS TO CONCRETE STEPS

How do I go about putting iron railings in three concrete steps to my front door?

With a carbide-tipped masonry bit, drill holes at least 2 inches deep to accommodate the "feet" of the railings, leaving enough space around to pack in cement mortar. Pour in enough to fill the hole about two-thirds, insert the railings, and then trowel in enough mortar to fill the rest of the hole. Be sure the iron has been treated with metal primer and paint so it won't start making rust marks.

IRON RAILING POST BECOMES LOOSE

Embedded in my cement stairs, which lead to my front entrance, is an iron railing. At the bottom of the first step, where the rail-

ing begins, the post continues to remain loose in spite of my repeated attempts to secure it with patching cement. Is there some product on the market to secure this post once and for all?

After cleaning the bottom of the post and removing all rust, fasten it in place with an iron cement or pour melted lead around it in the hole. Iron cement would be easier to handle and could be purchased from your hardware dealer. If the post does not extend far enough into the step, it may come out again.

CRACKED CONCRETE DRIVEWAY

We have several large cracks in our concrete driveway, which are getting longer every spring. We can't affort to put in a new driveway. How can we repair these?

Chip each crack with a cold chisel and mallet at least ½ inch wide and full depth. Soak the inner surfaces with water, so that the old concrete won't blot water from the new patching mortar. Pack the crack full with fairly stiff mortar. Cover it, and keep it dampened for a week to promote slow, proper curing. You won't need a new driveway at all. However, don't do this until the nice weather returns.

POCKED CONCRETE DRIVEWAY

Our concrete driveway is beginning to be badly pitted with pockmarks all over. How can this be repaired?

The best thing would be to put down a new layer of concrete topping. If the "pocks" are very shallow, they might be ground down with a terrazzo-grinding machine, providing this won't make the concrete too thin.

PROTECT DRIVEWAY DRAIN

The back of my concrete driveway is about 25 feet square, sloping down to a drain in the center which leads to a clay sewer pipe with a 2-inch lip. Through the years, the concrete surrounding the pipe has sunk about 2 inches. This has caused the lip of the pipe to break off. What can I do to protect this end of the pipe before it might break or split and continue underground, where a repair would be extremely difficult and expensive?

Rebuild the center 3 feet or so with the drain at the middle. Rent a power hammer to cut out the present area so you can build it up with a full-depth concrete. Just pouring concrete on top of the present concrete would only cause cracks to form in short order.

CONCRETE CREEPING AWAY

Our concrete drive is creeping away from the house, forming deep, wide cracks. I want to caulk the cracks, but it seems to me that they should first be filled with something beforehand. But what?

You're right. At a marine hardware store, get some oakum and work this deeply into the cracks with a screwdriver. Over this you can do your caulking, or use patching mortar.

OIL LEAKED ON DRIVEWAY

A delivery truck leaked oil quite badly on my fairly new concrete driveway. Needless to say, the oil was neither new nor clean; it looks terrible. How can I get these spots out?

First, try a simple way that often works very well: sprinkle the spots with dry portland cement. This has good absorption powers and may draw the oil out. Give it time, and perhaps several repeats, before giving up. Second, cover the spots with a thick paste of powdered chalk, or a similar substance, and benzene or high-test gasoline. Cover the area with a sheet of plastic to retard evaporation. When the paste is dry, brush it off and repeat the process. If you get to the point where no more oil can be blotted up, scrub the stains with a strong solution of cleanser. Sun and time will then fade out the remainder, if any.

ASPHALT CEMENT STAINS CONCRETE

While repairing a leak on the roof over the back entrance, some of the asphalt roofing cement accidentally dropped on the concrete steps of the back porch, leaving several black spots. I scraped off as much as I could while it was still wet, but apparently some of it penetrated the concrete. Is there any way to remove these spots?

It is doubtful that you can get them 100 percent out. First make a paste of naphtha and an absorbent powder, such as powdered chalk or powdered whiting. Cover the stains thickly with this paste, and to prevent rapid evaporation, place a sheet of metal or glass on the paste. When the paste becomes discolored, through the blotting-up action, scrape off the paste and repeat with a fresh batch. After no more is drawn out of the concrete, scrub the remaining spot with a strong solu-

tion of trisodium phosphate, about 2 pounds to the pail of hot water. It may not remove every bit of the black cement, but there will certainly be an improvement.

GREASE STAINED CONCRETE

Last spring I cleaned my grease trap. There was snow on the ground and, not thinking, I dumped the contents of the trap on my concrete driveway. When the snow melted, there were ugly black stains on the concrete. What preparation would you advise using to remove such stains?

Make a paste mixture of powdered whiting and naphtha, and spread a thick layer over the stained area; then cover it with a piece of sheet metal or glass to prevent fast evaporation. This should take out the grease. Keep away all flame to avoid combustion. After two or three such treatments, it may be necessary to bleach out the stain. Make a hot, saturated solution of oxalic acid (poison), and apply it liberally. Allow it to remain for an hour or so; then rinse it off well with clear water. Frequent use of oxalic acid on concrete surfaces will cause disintegration.

WINTER RUINED DRIVEWAY

There were cracks in my concrete driveway last fall, which I did not fix. But last winter really messed it up. Ice got through the cracks, froze, and caused a lot more cracking; it even broke out some pieces. What would be the result if I simply had another 4-inch layer of concrete put right on over all this?

It would give you a good new driveway. If you wish, you could also use a 4-inch coat of blacktopping. But before the next spell of cold weather, be sure to give this a brush-on coat of top dressing to seal it. Get comparative estimates.

HEAT UNDER DRIVEWAY

This spring we plan to hard-top our driveway. I suggested to my husband to put some pipes under it to melt the snow, because no one wants to shovel it. He said we cannot have such a system because the house is heated by hot air. Is he right?

Hot water is circulated through the pipes under a driveway to melt snow. Since you have hot-air heat, this would mean that a separate water-heating system would have to be installed. If your electricity rate is comparatively low, a heating cable could be installed for the purpose. Ask your local utility company about this.

WIRE REINFORCEMENT FOR DRIVEWAY

We are going to put in a cement driveway, but don't know if it's best to put wire reinforcement in or not. We get conflicting advice. What do you suggest?

Putting wire reinforcement into the concrete doesn't add any structural strength, but it does help hold the sections together in case of cracking. It's not essential if there is a good subbase that provides proper drainage and support. But if cost isn't an important consideration, in our opinion the slight additional expense for the wire is well worth the extra protection it offers in keeping the driveway in good condition.

STEEL STUDS RUT DRIVE

For three years I have been using the steel-studded type of snow tires, and think they are splendid. But they seem to be hard on my concrete driveway. Is there any way to fill in these ruts? They really aren't deep; only noticeable.

Merely filling the ruts level again with concrete couldn't last a month or two. You really need another layer of concrete at least 2 inches thick. Or you could have it black-topped. Either way, it's a complete resurfacing that's needed.

WEEDS IN ROADWAY

We have a crushed-stone road, but there are weeds and grass growing in the center. Is there a product that will destroy both grass and weeds?

Calcium chloride or rock salt dissolved in water and sprinkled over the area will kill off the vegetation and prevent its regrowth for a long time. Use about a half cupful in each gallon of water. Garden supply houses sell weed killers which are also very effective for the purpose.

STAINED BLACK HARD-TOP DRIVEWAY

Our driveway, a black hard-top, has become badly stained with automobile grease. Is there anything I can do to remove it? I tried sal soda but haven't had much success with it.

Try grease-removing preparations widely sold in gas stations and auto supply houses. Or try the following method: Make a thick paste of powdered whiting or fuller's earth or other absorbing powder and gasoline (being careful of fire hazard), and spread a thick layer over the stain, covering the paste with a sheet of metal or plastic to retard evaporation. The gasoline acts as a solvent on the grease and the powder like a blotter to draw it up. When the paste is discolored, or dry, replace it with fresh until no more grease is being absorbed.

STAIN PROTECTION FOR ASPHALT

We have just had an asphalt driveway put down. Is there any way to treat the surface so that it won't develop oil and grease stains quickly?

To prevent this kind of staining, a liquid dressing for blacktop is available where asphalt products are sold; this is mopped on.

ASPHALT PATCH LIKE ICE

We have a 6-foot-wide patch of asphalt across the foot of our driveway, going up a small hill. My husband twice has put sealer on it. When the weather is wet or snowy, you can't stand on it; driving on it is worse, it's so slippery. How can we get rid of this icy slickness? Sanding it all winter is quite a chore.

Thoroughly roughen the surface by chipping it with a cold chisel; then reseal. Otherwise, keep sanding. In the spring, replace it with rough-surfaced concrete.

BLACKTOP EASY TO PATCH

A small section of my blacktop driveway has begun to crack and pull away from the rest. Is this something I can fix myself?

Yes, indeed. First cut out all the bad section, down to a depth of at least 2 inches. Rake out any loose pebbly stuff, and keep the sides of the cutout vertical. Pour ready-mixed asphalt blacktop so it fills the depression to about ¾ inch above the rest. If you have a regular tamper, that can certainly be used. So can the back of a shovel. It's best, though, to place a board over the repair and run your car over it a few times. That will really pack it down.

WATERY CRACKS IN GARAGE FLOOR

There are many cracks in my garage floor; some are ¼ inch wide. For the last two

springs, when the snow melted, water seeped through these cracks. I have asked people at the hardware store and in the concrete business how to fix them and they give me different answers. Can you help me?

It sounds like considerable water pressure under the floor at times. For the most permanent cure, a two-step repair is suggested, although it's a lot of work. First, fill the cracks with regular patching mortar. Widen the cracks if necessary to permit working the mortar in. Soak the concrete first to prevent the old concrete from blotting water from the patching mortar. Next, cover the area with a layer of heavy plastic sheeting. Then put down an entire new layer of concrete, at least 2 inches thick, over the whole floor. If you don't feel like all this work, just pour the floor.

CRACKING GARAGE FLOOR

The cement slab in our garage is cracking and separating quite badly. How was this caused? How can future cracking be prevented?

The cracking may be due to too large sections of concrete having been laid, or to insufficient allowance for expansion and shrinkage, or to poor drainage under the slab. These conditions must be corrected to prevent future cracking.

LOW SPOTS AND CRACKS IN GARAGE FLOOR

The garage floor has developed cracks in the concrete, and low spots have developed, restricting the flow of water out of the garage. How can this be remedied?

Apparently the concrete garage floor was improperly laid; the earth underneath may not have been firmly packed, or soft places not properly filled and packed. The concrete should be at least 4 inches thick and put down in sections no longer than about 10 feet square, with expansion joints between. If the low spots and cracks are due to wear, with a properly laid floor, repairs can be made with a concrete patching material containing latex, widely available at masonry supply dealers.

BUILD UP SUNKEN FLOOR

Part of our garage floor has cracked and sunk nearly 2 inches below the rest. Would it be possible and practical to build this part up level with ready-mixed blacktop?

Go to it; there's no reason why not. You could do this building up with ready-mix concrete too. This, of course, is no guarantee that the section may not drop some more in the future or that another part of the floor may not do this.

WORRIED ABOUT FLOOR

In damp, humid weather, the floor of my attached garage becomes very wet, and I am afraid of slipping and breaking bones. In warm, dry weather this does not happen. I cannot afford to have the garage heated or air-conditioned. What can I do?

You could scatter sand to make the floor nonskid, but you'd also put us on your blacklist every time you tracked the sand back into your house. We would suggest that you consider some good rubber runners to cover the places you walk most frequently. Another layer of rough concrete would also work, but it would cost more.

PREVENTING SALT EROSION OF CEMENT

What kind of solution can be used on a cement floor in the garage to prevent erosion due to salt from the car during the winter?

To protect a cement floor against salt damage, apply the following coating (almost colorless): a warm solution of equal parts of boiled linseed oil and turpentine. Because of the fire hazard, do not warm this over an open flame, but put the container with the solution in very hot water for about 20 minutes. A brush or pressure garden sprayer can be used to apply the mixture to the concrete. Allow the first coat to dry for about 8 hours; then apply a second coat. The temperature in the garage should be at least 50° when the work is being done.

LINSEED OIL STAINS ON CEMENT BLOCK

Linseed oil was splashed and dripped on the sills of our cement block garage. Is there any way to get off the ugly black stains?

Linseed oil stains are very difficult, almost impossible, to remove completely. Make a thick paste of hydrated lime or other absorbing powder and benzene (be very careful of fire hazard), and cover the stains with a layer at least 1½ inches thick. Over this place a plastic sheet or metal to retard evaporation. When the paste is dry, brush it off and replace with fresh paste until as much of the stain has been removed as possible. Then scrub the stains with a strong, hot solution of trisodium phosphate, using about 2 pounds to the gallon of water, followed by ample rinsing with clear water. It might be easier to disguise the stains with oil paint.

CHAPTER 17

PEST
CONTROL

We receive a great deal of mail each year regarding the best methods of controlling pests—animals, birds, and insects. Let's look at some of the questions regarding specific pests, and we'll try to answer them with present-day controls.

Questions and Answers

We have divided the questions and answers into three categories: animals, birds, and insects.

ANIMALS

SQUIRRELPROOFING WALNUT?

We have a very productive black walnut tree. The only trouble is the squirrels know this too, and so we get very few walnuts. I can have branches trimmed back enough on a neighboring maple so that squirrels can't jump from that tree to the walnut. But how do we keep them from running up the trunk?

Put a ring around the trunk with an upside-down funnel-shaped collar of aluminum or galvanized steel; this operates on the same principle as those collars they fasten around hawsers when ships are tied up at a dock to prevent rats from coming aboard. Make this so wide a squirrel can't swing himself over to catch the edge.

CHIPMUNKS AND SQUIRRELS

Chipmunks and squirrels are making their home in our attic. I have trimmed the overhanging tree branches away from the roof and closed or removed all direct paths of travel for them to attic. What else can I do?

A watch should be kept to discover the openings by which they can enter the house; these should be closed by pieces of sheet metal or insect screening. When established in a house, these animals will usually be out collecting food during the daylight hours; the entrance holes having been noted, they should be closed at that time. Burning a sulfur candle will drive them out, but be careful of fire. Mothballs copiously scattered about their nesting places will have the same effect, and be safer. Blowing moth flakes into the area with a vacuum cleaner is another method.

MANY MOLE TUNNELS

This spring I have found quite a few more mole tunnels than we ever had before. The moles run right under gravel paths and flower gardens. What can I do about them? I'm told they can really spoil a nice garden.

If a garden center doesn't have any of the various chemicals and other concoctions for mole control, visit a farm supply store. Here are a couple of old-fashioned tricks against moles: A few mothballs, or beans of the castor oil plant, placed in their tunnel runways at intervals of 5 to 6 feet, will deter moles from passing. An ounce or so of carbon disulfide injected into a runway with a long-spout oil can will also be effective; care must be taken in its use because of its flammability. Incidentally, more and more people are now believing that the real damage is done not by the moles, but by field mice using the tunnels.

NO SNAKE SPRAY

Is there any chemical spray available to keep snakes away from around a house?

No chemical spray or material can be depended on to keep them away. As snakes make no permanent nests, their presence in any particular place is temporary. Should they collect under a building, playing the hose on them will drive them out; spraying any bare ground, close to the foundation, with kerosene will discourage their return. (Don't spray this on any planting!) They can be driven from holes in the ground by pouring in a mixture of carbolic acid and kerosene in the proportion of 1 ounce of acid to the gallon of kerosene, but be careful of fire.

DOGS AWAY FROM POSTS

I have a problem of dogs soiling the fence posts of a white fence. How can I stop them?

To deter dogs from soiling fence posts, front steps, and similar places, spray the areas with water-white kerosene or pure and clear gasoline containing as much paradichlorobenzene or naphthalene as will dissolve. The liquid will be absorbed by stone, cement, or other porous material without harm, and to some extent by wood. On evaporation, the chemical will remain in the pores as fine crystals and give off an odor so greatly disliked by dogs that they will avoid it. This mixture should not be used on the trunks of trees or on foliage, especially of evergreens, for it will be destructive to them. Preparations having odors that dogs and cats dislike but that are otherwise harmless to them can be had at

garden and pet stores. These preparations are to be scattered about, to be renewed after rains.

TOMATOES FIX SKUNKED POOCH

Our German shepherd pup learned about skunks the hard way. In spite of scrubbings, it's still impossible to let him back into the house. What, if anything, will get rid of the awful odor?

Instead of soap, use large quantities of tomato juice. Or do the washing with tomato pulp.

DOGS AND CATS

Both dogs and cats seem to like to congregate under our two porches. Is there any way that we can stop them from doing so without harming them?

When dogs or cats frequent an outdoor sleeping place or congregate under a house or outbuilding, a scattering of mothballs will keep them away. If there's no fire risk to be considered, spraying with kerosene will also be effective, using a garden hose or a lawn sprinkler, turned on from inside the house or other place not visible to them. Thorough cleaning should follow before the gardening implements are again used for watering the garden.

KEEPING FIELD MICE OUT

How can we prevent field mice from taking possession of our attic when colder weather arrives? We live in the suburbs, and this is a problem with us during the winter.

Be careful to keep all doors, screen doors, cellar windows, etc., closed. Close any openings such as louvers, by which the mice might enter, using insect screens. Sprinkle mothballs or flakes around generously. As an added precaution, keep all food in tightly covered containers. If they do take the attic over, burn a sulfur candle there, being very careful of the fire hazard. Of course, a cat is one of the finest mouse deterrents ever invented!

GETTING RAT OUT OF HOUSE

I live in an older house. For the past few months we have been hearing a rat in the walls. How can I get it out of the house? I set traps in the cellar, but it just won't come out of the walls. If I make a hole in the wall, is there any kind of spray I can use to chase it out?

A handful of mothballs dropped into a rat hole will often cause rats to vacate; use plenty. Traps should not be placed in open areas, but against walls, behind boards and boxes, etc., with the trigger end placed against the wall. Excellent baits are rolled oats, peanut butter, bird seed, and whole wheat flour. Rat poison containing warfarin, fumarin, pival, or diphacinone usually causes rats to leave the house in search of water. But there is always the chance it might get stuck in the wall cavity, causing a highly unpleasant odor which might last for months.

BATS IN BUILDING ATTIC

Can you suggest something for getting rid of bats in the attic of a building?

To keep bats out of a building attic, or elsewhere, close all possible crevices through which they might enter. They can be driven out by burning a sulfur candle (be very careful of fire hazard). Bats are attracted by light. At night, open the attic windows at the top, and turn the automobile headlights up to draw the bats out of the building. A colorless gelatinous preparation used for discouraging unwanted birds from roosting, spread on the bats' roosting areas in the attic, will also discourage these animals. It is not harmful, but is unpleasant to their feet. The product is available at some large garden supply and hardware dealers.

BIRDS

DISCOURAGING SPARROWS

Do you know of any way to discourage sparrows from staying around buildings? They are just spoiling everything on the porch and sides of the building. I've tried filling in their nesting places on the porch, but they still stay around.

There is a gelatinous preparation available that can be spread around to discourage birds from roosting. An application is good for about a year; it's odorless and colorless. It's not harmful to the birds, but is unpleasant to their feet and claws. The preparation is available at large garden supply dealers and some housewares stores. It is very good in discouraging pigeons.

WOODPECKERS RUINING RED CEDAR SHINGLES

What can I do to stop woodpeckers from ruining my red cedar shingles on my lake cottage? We are not there most of the time. They peck holes through the shingles.

The birds are probably seeking insects under the shingles. Spraying an insecticide all over the shingles should eliminate this food pantry. To further encourage the woodpeckers to peck elsewhere, a practically colorless, gelatinous-type spray, (a treatment lasts a season,) is available at large garden supply centers and housewares dealers which discourages roosting wherever the preparation is applied. Also, if your garden hose has enough pressure to spray them when they arrive, a few showers might discourage long lunches at least. Garden centers sell long strings of jangly aluminum disks to scare birds from young seedlings. You might try tacking up a few of these strings over the area the woodpeckers favor.

STARLINGS MOVING INTO ATTIC

Our house is about 150 years old. Evidently, when it was built, people weren't so particular about little gaps. Our attic, for example, is quite open between the roof and siding, and through this space a good many starlings are bringing in considerable amounts of dried grass and weeds and so forth. Is there any simple way to get rid of them?

Headquartering an ill-tempered cat up there for a day or two might scare them all out. Be sure to watch the entry, so that you can block it up. If you can borrow a photographic floor light or two and leave them on, and make lots of noise up there, like shooting cap pistols and banging on pans and cymbals, they should get the message.

TOY SNAKE PIGEON CHASER

We have a double chimney on the south side of our house. The space behind it in winter gives pigeons a warm nook, and a nesting place in spring and summer. My bedroom is directly underneath. The pigeons wake me up every morning at daybreak with their cooing and scratching. Beside the nuisance, I am afraid of damage to the shingles. Can you suggest a remedy?

Get a couple of those many-jointed wooden toy snakes. Secure them so they will wiggle in the slightest breeze. Pigeons seem to be scared of these many times and may move elsewhere.

INSECTS

TERMITE PROBLEM

We're interested in buying a house and have learned that there are termites in the foundation sill plates. The house is of frame construction. Do you think that it would be a wise investment? It had been treated at one time, and termites have reappeared. If we put a new foundation in, would we be able to rid it of the termites? What do you advise?

Only a reliable termite exterminator contractor, after he makes an inspection, can give you the answer. There's no way of telling how extensive the damage might be. If the infestation has been going on for some time, not only will the sill plates be damaged, but the framing above the foundation sills and the joists may also be affected. A new foundation may not be a solution if the siding and timbers are less than 18 inches from the surface of the ground.

TERMITES IN SILL?

Inspection indicates several places where termites have eaten small areas in the foundation sill (wood). What can I do to prevent spreading of this condition? Is there anything I can spray on the wood to discourage termites? Carpentry repairs won't bother me; I am a professional.

The safest cure is to cut away all the areas affected, although this is admittedly a difficult project with the sill; it's practically an impossible project unless affected areas are widely enough spaced so that chipping out won't disturb the supports. New lumber should replace the sections that are removed (they should be thoroughly treated with wood preservative first). To be on the safest possible side, we recommend having a reliable exterminator examine the condition. It's also possible that your diagnosis of "termites" may be in error; it's worth verifying.

CHEMICAL SPRAY FOR TERMITES

What chemical is used for spraying to get rid of termites in a house?

For complete protection of wood, etc., the chemical should be applied under pressure in order to deeply impregnate the wood with the preservative. Various chemicals are used: 5 percent pentachlorophenol, copper nephthenate containing 2 percent copper, or sodium fluoride (5 ounces per gallon of water).

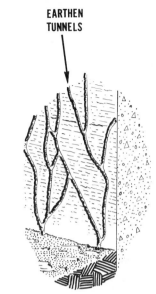

EARTHEN TUNNELS

Figure 17-1. Typical termite earthen tunnels.

Care is necessary in handling these, as they are poisons and either irritating to or absorbed by the skin.

CHEMICAL SOIL TREATMENT

What chemicals are used for soil treatment against termites? How effective are they?

Formulations of four materials—aldrin, dieldrin, chlordane, and heptachlor—are currently registered for use in treating soils to control subterranean termites. Directions for diluting with water the concentrated solutions to the strength of the finished emulsion recommended are usually given on the container. (Be sure to follow all mixing and application instructions to the letter.) In southern Mississippi tests (where termite infestation is about the highest in the United States), these chemicals, applied at the prescribed rates and methods, have provided complete protection for 17 to 21 years. To date, no alternative materials have been found that will provide comparable long-term, economical protection.

PROTECTING PLANTS AGAINST POISON

I am planning to treat the ground around my house against termites, using chemicals.

How can plants nearby be protected from the poison?

Roots of nearby plants can be protected from chemical contact with heavy aluminum- or copper-coated paper. Once you've dug the trench for the chemical, line the side of the trench nearest the plants with the paper.

CARPENTER ANTS A THREAT?

After having noticed medium-sized black ants in our home, I called an exterminator, who diagnosed "carpenter ants" with a fee for exterminating them. After mentioning the ants to various friends, I found that everyone had experienced their presence in his own home. Also, nobody had ever heard of "carpenter ants"—except a neighbor who had spent the same fee to get rid of them. Is there such a threat as carpenter ants? How much damage do they do? Is there an effective home defense?

Most decidedly there is a very real threat from the presence of carpenter ants in a house: they are destroyers of wood and may cause serious damage to beams, studs, rafters, etc. When carpenter ants are found emerging from cracks, a piece of the woodwork should be taken off to permit examination of the condition beneath and to locate the nest. The nest, if located, should be sprayed with a 5 percent chlordane powder or 2 percent spray, and the opening about it should be sprayed. If ants are getting into the house from the outside, spray porch landings, foundations, and

the sides of the house. Spray the surfaces around the opening from which the ants emerge. Liquid self-polishing floor wax containing insecticide is effective at killing many insects found crawling on the floor or windowsills.

BROWN POWDER FROM BEAMS

Under some of the beams in the ceiling of my basement, brown powder seems to fall. Can you give me an opinion about what this might be?

About the only thing which occurs to us is that the powder is caused by some wood-boring insect, such as a powder-post beetle. If by any chance there is bark on the beams, pull it off. Then coat all the beams with an odorless chemical wood preservative. We don't recommend creosote indoors because of the strong odor. Examine the beams for small pinholes, and thoroughly spray any with the preservative. If the infestation continues, consult promptly a reliable professional exterminator.

ANTS IN THE HOME

How can I get rid of common ants in my house?

If ants are in the house, find out whether they are coming in from outdoors or their nests are indoors. To prevent ants from entering the house, apply an emulsifiable chlordane in the form of a dilute drench. Apply it all around the foundation of the house. In preparing the drench, dilute the chlordane concentrate with water according to the directions on the label. Do not reuse the measuring devices for any other purpose. Do not use more chlordane per gallon of water than is specified on the label. Apply the drench with a sprinkling can to the soil, beginning at the foundation and extending out about a foot. Soak the soil thoroughly. A shallow trench next to the foundation is often useful in obtaining the desired penetration of the soil. The drench kills the ants as they attempt to cross the chlordane-treated strip, before they can enter the house. But if you decide that the ants have nests inside the house, use the same 2 percent oil-base chlordane spray mentioned above. Apply it as near as possible to where you believe the nests are located. Put it into any cracks or openings that ants can use to enter a room, and put it on nearby surfaces.

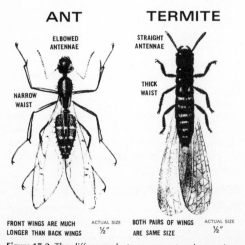

Figure 17-2. The difference between an ant and a termite.

ANTS IN THE LAWN

Our lawn is overrun with ants. How can we get rid of them?

To get rid of ants in the lawn, in a patio, and elsewhere near the house, apply chlordane to nests that you can find. Use 5 percent dust or granules; or use a spray made by mixing 2 tablespoonfuls of 50 percent wettable powder or 1 tablespoonful of 45 percent emulsifiable concentrate with 1 gallon of water. Put the insecticide into the nest openings. Apply it over the surrounding areas for several inches or feet, depending on the size of the nests; apply enough to cover the areas. Then soak the nest areas with water to wash the insecticide through the ground and into the nests. If the nests are so numerous that treating them one at a time is impracticable, apply chlordane to the entire infested area with a sprinkling can or a suitable sprayer. (*Note:* Some states have restrictions on the use of certain pesticides. Check your state and local regulations. For instance, where chlordane can't be used, several other insecticides—Baygon, Diazinon, lindone, and malathion—can be used for the control of ants in and around the home.)

SMALL-FLY ANNOYANCE

My son and his family have just moved into an old, but remodeled, 10-room house, unlived in for about two years. They have been annoyed by small flies, which don't get on people but which must be swept out every day; they seem to be dormant somewhere, but most die on the floor and around the windows. The house has no attic. Is there any insecticide that can be used?

Spray generously an insecticide containing malathion on all wall surfaces, baseboards, window frames, sills, and floors.

SLUG BARRIER FOR PATIO

What can we do to prevent slugs from crawling onto our concrete patio after a damp night or a rain? This was quite a problem for us last spring and summer.

Try ringing the patio with one of the slug baits sold in garden centers. These are usually in the form of pellets, which seem to attract all slugs within a radius of 1½ to 2 yards. They eat, and then sort of dissolve. We know that table salt sprinkled on a slug really does him in. There were times last September when

slugs irked us so much we took one of those big cylindrical cardboard containers of salt, with a spout, and sprinkled every slug on my tomatoes. That fixed them (for a while).

LADYBUGS

I'm not sure whether I have a serious problem or not. Lately I've noticed a number of ladybugs collecting on the inside of my windows. Is this just in the nuisance category?

Ladybugs do no harm to the house, and they are *beneficial* to gardens. Many insecticides, available in aerosol form, are effective in getting rid of these bugs if you find them becoming too numerous on your windows.

WORMS HAVE TAKEN OVER THE LAWN

Worms have taken over our lawn. What can we do?

To destroy worms in a lawn, dissolve ½ ounce of corrosive sublimate (bichloride of mercury) in 12 gallons of water and sprinkle the solution on the lawn after a shower or a wetting down with the hose; follow by spraying with a hose to carry the solution into the ground. The worms will at once come to the surface and die, and should be disposed of to prevent the poisoning of birds that might be attracted to them. Since corrosive sublimate is a deadly poison, every precaution should be taken in handling it; if used with a metal watering can, the can should be thoroughly rinsed afterward, for the chemical will attack metal.

WORMY CONCRETE PATIO

I have a concrete patio. After a rain, dozens of worms crawl out of the lawn on to the patio and die, creating a mess. Is there any way this can be remedied?

The only suggestion we can offer is to spray the patio several times with commercial weed killer, available at garden supply dealers. This may discourage the worms from coming on the patio. Using the weed killer to kill the insects on the lawn adjoining the patio might also work "agin' the critters," but might spoil the edge of the lawn.

SOWBUGS TOO MUCH IN EVIDENCE

We live in a two-year-old brick house and have a nice big basement. Last fall we were pestered for the first time by unbelievable numbers of sowbugs crawling all over the basement walls and floor and even coming up into the upstairs rooms. Insect sprays didn't help. During the winter they gradually disappeared, but in the spring they came again. I noticed them outside on the ground too. None of the neighbors, in older houses, has this problem. It is slowly getting me down. Any suggestions? The basement is very dry.

Sowbugs (or pillbugs) may be coming in from a garden area located in a damp, shaded place, where decaying vegetation is abundant. Clear out any spot of this description near the house. Then generously spray all surfaces in the cellar, especially around windows, and the outside foundation walls with insecticide containing chlordane.

TOO MANY SPIDERS AND CRICKETS

We recently moved into a fairly new house, a ranch type. We are bothered with many spiders and crickets. How can we get rid of these insects?

Spider eggs develop in crevices, under edges of wallpaper, etc. Destroy all webs as soon as they appear, and crush each insect. A vacuum cleaner is good for cleaning up the webs. Then spray all the surfaces with a special insecticide. For the crickets, pyrethrum powder is effective. Blow the powder with a powder puffer behind articles that give the insects shelter. Powder should be blown into the air, for its effect is smothering rather than poisonous. Repeat dusting at intervals of two or three days. Insecticides containing malathion are good for general use against insects.

WATER BUGS

We are being troubled by water bugs in the house we moved into several months ago. How can we get rid of them?

Wherever the insects are found, scatter sodium fluoride powder (poison) about. Or spray the areas with an insecticide containing 2 percent chlordane. A less toxic insecticide, containing combinations of pyrethrum, synergists, or rotenone, requires more frequent applications than chlordane sprays. With children or pets in the house, use the less toxic, naturally! If you feel it's risky, better put up with the bugs and take no chances.

SILVERFISH PROBLEM

Can you help me with my silverfish problem? There seems to be quite an infestation of the filthy things in the house.

Dust pyrethrum powder with a powder puffer in places where you see them. Since they are fond of starch, dust behind books on shelves, as well as in cracks in woodwork.

COCKROACHES

Which insecticide will kill roaches?

Use a household insecticide which contains one of the following: Diazinon, DDVP, ronnel, malathion, or Baygon. Spray as directed on the container in places where roaches run or hide.

PESTERED BY CARPET BEETLES

Can you help me with my carpet beetle problem? There seems to be quite an infestation of these in my house. I have tried different sprays; none have worked.

These pests lay their eggs in dark places. Beetle heaven is a dust-filled crack between floorboards under a carpet. Your sprays may not have gone into such cracks at all. The best cure and prevention is to clean out such cracks first; then dust with pyrethrum powder or a similar residual insecticide. Loosen dust first by running a straightened paper clip along the cracks and then vacuuming with the skinniest attachment. Scattering moth flakes under the carpet will help too.

RAID WASPS AT NIGHT

What is the safest way to get rid of a large wasp nest in a tree near the house, aside from calling in an expensive exterminator?

Unless the branches are small enough so that you can cut them with a long-handled pruner, leave this job to a pro. If you think you can clip the branches, get the pruner ready, plus a very large paper bag and kerosene. To be on the safest side, you and a helper (if any) should don heavy clothes, gloves, and one of those mosquito netting hats fishermen sport during the blackfly season. After dark, when the wasps are home, have your helper light the nest with a strong flashlight while you clip all necessary branches. Pop the nest into the paper bag, soak it with kerosene, and light it. The faster you work, and the less you jiggle the nest, the safer.

HORNETS IN WALL SPACE

Ours is an old house. Last year, hornets nested in between the walls and came into the house through the holes in the sashes, where the pulleys are. How can we get rid of these dangerous pests?

Because these are dangerous pests and the job of eliminating them is a dangerous one, it's best to call in an experienced, reputable exterminator, especially in such a difficult-to-get-at nesting location. For small nests in walls, a vacuum cleaner can be used, with its long tube supported in such a position that insects are sucked into the bag. This method does not excite or disturb the insects. When the bag is fairly well filled, a quantity of moth crystals is sucked into it to kill the insects. Remember that large nests may contain a swarm of wasps, which will make dangerous any attempt to destroy the nest. The swarm can be destroyed by spraying a liquid pesticide on the entrance of the nest with an aerosol spray or a hand sprayer. The liquid should contain pyrethrum and synergists for instant kill, and Ronnel or Malathion to be carried back into the nest by those which don't fly out. Insects will attempt to leave, but being stunned by the spray will fall to the ground. The liquid being sprayed into the opening will saturate the structure and destroy the insects or will at least render them incapable of flight. After a little time the nest can be taken down and burned.

CEDAR LETHAL TO MOTHS

One of the big sales features of the house we bought was the cedar-lined closet. There, the man said, we can hang out winter clothes and never worry about moths. I admit it's pretty. But is it really a moth killer?

The fumes of cedarwood oil, while actually refreshing to people, are lethal to moth larvae. It paralyzes the newly hatched insects so that they starve to death. Moth flakes, mothballs, or moth spray have very much the same action. But in any case, to keep the moth killer in, you should run weather stripping around the storage closet door.

ODORLESS CEDAR CLOSET

We had a cedar closet installed in our house when we moved in a number of years ago. Now the cedar odor seems to have disappeared. Is there any way to restore the odor to the wood?

All that's needed is to sand down the surface of the wood to expose the fresh new wood underneath, which should still contain plenty of the distinctive odor. If the wood is relatively new, sandpapering should be enough. If the wood is quite old, it may be necessary to plane it down. You can also obtain cedar-odor solutions to be applied to wall surfaces at many housewares and hardware dealers.

CHAPTER 18

REPAIRING
AND
REFINISHING
FURNITURE

A question frequently asked us is: "Is there any way I can keep a nice old rocking chair from squeaking?" The answer, fortunately, is a simple one: "Yes." The rocking chair (any chair or table, for that matter) can be unsqueaked, 99 percent of the time, by tightening any loose joints. Squeaks are caused when pressure (the sitter's weight) is enough to cause two or more pieces of wood to rub together. Most of the time such looseness is caused by wood drying out and shrinking, which allows some play in a formerly tight joint. Other causes are failure of glue, so that two parts are no longer gripped tightly together, or actual decay of the wood. Where metal furniture is concerned, the same principle exists. Even the slightest loosening of a nut or bolt, or rusting, can be enough to relax tightness between two parts. This will immediately permit them to be moved under pressure, and for sure a squeak will result.

With wood furniture, there are two principle ways to make joints solid and silent. The first method is to separate the parts, clean off the old glue, and refit the parts snugly together. This may even mean putting in a new rung, or at least increasing the diameter where the rung fits into the hole. The second method, often much quicker, is to force more liquid adhesive into the joint. The idea is that when it hardens, it will fill up enough space so that there won't be any room for the loose parts to move around. And if nothing moves, there won't be any noise.

Small metal angles or blocks of wood are often used to shore up weakened corner joints, such as are around the frame of a chair seat. Inserting small pieces of doweling diagonally into such corners is another excellent strengthener. So are those small corrugated metal strips, which are driven so they straddle the adjacent edges of two pieces of wood and bind them firmly together.

In the case of loosened rungs, which can become very squeaky, the usual cause, as mentioned before, is shrinkage of the wood by drying out. Often there's a double effect, accentuating the problem: the rung shrinks, making the diameter smaller. So does the leg where the rung hole is located; therefore the hole will actually shrink larger, odd as this sounds.

A most effective and simple cure for this is to make the end of the rung larger. And this is where squirreling away some of mama's discarded stockings pays off. First you clean out the rung hole as thoroughly as possible, soaking and scraping away the old glue. When the hole is dry, line it with more cement. For this job, one of the clear all-purpose cements, or the epoxy type, is at least the equivalent of the old-time glues. The next step is to hold a small piece of the stocking, doubled, over the hole and shove into the rung. The added thickness of the stocking is often sufficient to fill up the hole completely. If not, wedging in a few small shims of wood (even bits of wooden kitchen matches) and cementing will take up any slack. While the cement is setting, firm pressure should be applied to the repaired joint. This can be done with any arrangement of furniture clamps, C-clamps, or tourniquets of strong cord or clothesline.

In the case of squeaky metal furniture, very often the only silencer needed is a drop or two of oil or a puff of dry lubricant. Or giving a locknut a slight twist will tighten things up enough to stop the squeak-making motion between two parts. If age and dampness have corroded a nut or bolt so your wrench or pliers and screwdriver can't prevail, one of the new rust-busting sprays will loosen the corrosion in a surprisingly short time.

As mentioned before, there's another method to fill loosened joints so that there isn't any noisy play between parts. This is to force cementing in, hoping that you can get enough cement in so that when it sets up it will block any motion in the joint. While this sounds much simpler than the repairing methods, it isn't always possible to achieve the goal, because there might not be a wide enough crack or hole in the joint to permit working in the cement. It's almost hopeless to try and poke cement into a barely hairline crack around a rung or antique rabbet joint, even when assisted with a toothpick or piece of banjo string. The best luck we've had along these lines is with a "chair-lock" liquid made especially for tightening loose joints. The liquid is worked into the wood fibers, causing them to swell, and then hardens.

Another type of squeak in furniture is when the side rails of beds become a little loose in the grooves and sockets in the head and foot units. Working a little melted paraffin into these areas, which eventually penetrated the wood, was one of the ways the older generations solved this problem. It's still perfectly good, but the new dry lubricants are much simpler and less of a production.

Refinishing Furniture

There are so many ways to finish furniture that complete books have been devoted to this one subject. In this book, however, we're only going to concern ourselves with the basic principles.

When the finish of a piece of furniture is so marred that it cannot be patched, complete refinishing is required. For this, the first step is the removal of the old finish, either by scraping it off or by using a varnish remover. Scraping the finish down to the wood will not disturb color caused by staining; with a varnish remover the color will be taken out, and restaining will be required.

Scraping is not difficult; the knack can be quickly acquired. The common form of scraper is a steel plate, 3 by 5 inches in size or thereabouts, with square-cut edges. In use it is held nearly upright, with the fingers at the bottom, and pulled or pushed at an angle, so that a straight motion gives a slanting cut. Little pressure is needed to cut through and remove the finish. Pressure must be even to prevent a corner from gouging into the wood. A fine file is needed for sharpening, or a round steel tool, such as a nail set, to sharpen the scraper by burnishing. The hardware dealer who supplies the scraper will illustrate its use and the method of sharpening.

Another form of scraper which is easier to use has a slender, detachable blade in the form of a broad hook, set in a wood handle. When dull, the blade is turned over to offer another edge.

Scrapers of these forms can be used only on flat surfaces. For moldings and carvings, a contoured scraper can be obtained from most hardware stores. This scraper has an irregularly shaped head at the end of a round handle. The shapes have been chosen because they fit most molding curves and angles. A small electric sander will be found a tremendous time-saver on large flat surfaces.

Varnish removers are of several kinds. One is liquid or paste, consisting of solvents such as benzol and acetone. Another is an alkali, to be dissolved in water. Both can be bought at paint and hardware stores. A third type emulsifies the finish, making it water-soluble so that it can be washed off.

Most liquid removers are highly flammable, and their strong vapors are not healthful. They are safe to use, however, when there is

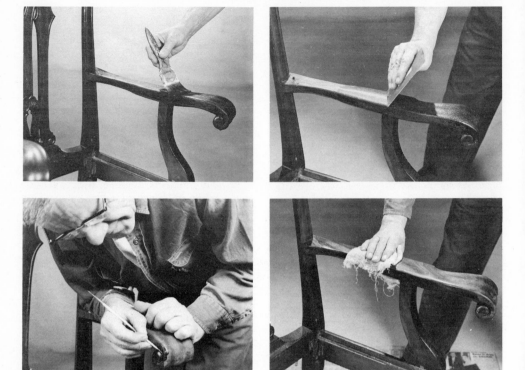

Figure 18-1. Steps in refinishing a chair.

plenty of ventilation and no open flames in the room. After cleaning, the bare wood should be washed with benzene or turpentine. Liquid removers don't raise the grain of wood.

When a remover is used, the floor and neighboring articles must be protected by plenty of newspaper or drop cloths. The remover is applied thick with a board brush and worked into carvings with a stiff-fiber brush. In 15 minutes or so, the varnish will have softened and can be taken off with a scraper, a stiff brush, a handful of fine steel wool, or cloths. Where there are several coats of old finish, two or more applications of remover may be needed. Here are a few other tips: To clean out cracks or deep carvings, an old toothbrush is a splendidly designed instrument. So is a wire-bristled suede brush or even a wooden toothpick. Don't use a straightened-out paper clip or similar wire, because of the risk of scratching or gouging the wood.

The final job will be a lot neater if you first remove any hardware, such as drawer pulls, handles, lock plates, etc., and clean them separately. If the metal has been painted, soak it in remover too. If you're working on an antique mirror frame, be extra careful to keep any paint remover away from the mirror backing. The chemicals are strong enough to soften the silvering.

Be sure removal of the finish is really needed in the first place. Before you put paint and varnish remover on a clear finish, give the piece a good hard scrubbing with soap and water; really scrub. Not infrequently it happens that once the coating of waxes, polishes, and dirt which has accumulated through the years is cleaned off, the finish may still be in such good condition that it only needs an additional coat. If so, you've saved yourself considerable time.

After the remover has done its stuff, there may still be a few deep stains left behind; this is often the case with end grain. Wiping with straight household bleach will take out most of the discoloration. In extreme cases, like end grain, you may need to remove the darkened spot with a file, rasp, or a handy sanding attachment on the electric drill. When the wood is dry, then you begin the sanding operation, which will leave it glass-smooth for the finishing steps.

For flat or fairly flat areas, like a tabletop or a chair seat, the sanding will be appreciably speeded up if you have an orbital sander in your workshop or a sanding attachment for the drill. For smoothing around rungs and spindles, reinforce strips of sandpaper with cellophane tape and go around shoeshine style. However, finish by sanding with the grain.

The final sanding, with the finest grade of paper available, will leave the wood as slick as it can possible be if you take the time for this extra step: Thoroughly dampen the entire surface, and let it dry naturally. This will raise any ends of loose wood fibers, or any depressed areas of grain. Then, when your finest-grade sandpaper is giving the final once-over-lightly, these stray ends will be cut down level with the rest of the surface.

The types of sandpaper to use? You'll get quite a few opinions on this. But one widely accepted method is to start the job with ordinary, inexpensive flint paper for the first cleanup stage. And when the paper becomes soiled, throw it out. In the later, finer steps, use aluminum oxide paper or garnet paper, which cuts better and lasts longer than flint. For the final smooth-as-possible sanding, the paper should be at least as fine as "000000," and even finer if it's available. The equivalent steel wool for this final step is "000" or even finer.

Staining. Most of the time, a stain is the first step of remodeling, even for some of the blond finishes; certainly for darker shades. Many stains used to take considerable practice, mainly in knowing when to wipe them off the wood. The longer the stain stays on, the darker it will make the wood. This is where the trick came in; and often's the time when a resigned sigh was followed by bleaching out the stain and starting over again. Happily, you can get stains which eliminate practically all of this annoying problem. You just brush them on with average smoothness, only making sure you don't miss any places. Then you wait until the wet appearance starts to dull, and wipe away all the stain that's left. You'll find the amount which has penetrated into the wood is the color you wanted.

While the major part of the final color is determined by the stain, the final finish counts too. To be sure you'll wind up with just the shade you want, there's no better preview than a couple of coats of the varnish, shellac, rubbed oil, or whatever put on over the stain, all done on an inconspicuous part of the furniture itself. On a chair, for instance, turn it upside down and do a patch on the underside of the seat.

For different colors, in addition to various standard stains, you can make your own shades by mixing different stains, or tinting stains with colors. Of course, the longer you leave a stain on the wood before wiping it off, the darker the wood will become, as mentioned before. But don't carry this too far and let the stain get so dry it won't wipe off cleanly. If you want a darker shade, it's much better to wipe off the first application of stain, let it dry, and then wipe on more stain. It's an excellent idea to practice on scrap lumber, preferably the same type as the furniture piece. But if you have had the misfortune to stain the item too dark, it's no catastrophe. You can remove the stain with wood bleach and start over again. When using bleach, be sure to follow the manufacturer's instructions most carefully.

Filler. After the staining, you have the question of whether to put on wood filler or skip it. Many devotees use filler for open-grained woods like oak, teak, mahogany, and walnut, so as to give an absolutely smooth surface for the finish. Tight-grained woods like maple don't need it. There are other purists who claim that filler detracts from the true beauty of the wood by partially concealing the grain. If you decide to use filler, follow the instructions that are printed on the container.

Final Coats. You have a wide choice among many good-looking finishes, ranging from a soft, dead-flat velvety look to glassy sleekness.

One quick and easy soft-luster type is done with two coats of a penetrating finish. This works into the wood, leaving a dull finish. A well-rubbed coat of paste wax over this gives a rich, soft luster.

A rubbed finish is considered by many to be the finest of all finishes, possibly because it's a lot more work and a bigger drain on the supply of patience than many people are willing to sacrifice. Starting with an absolutely smooth surface—which means wood filler for open-grained woods—you apply two or three thin coats of clear varnish, sanding each coat lightly when dry. For the third coat, and any others after it, you use waterproof sandpaper and keep the surface constantly wet; the paper should be at least as fine as "000000"; finer, if you can find it. When the rubbing coat of paste wax goes on over the final sanded coat of varnish, the result is a beautiful deep luster. However, you can approximate this luster quite simply and much faster. Apply two coats of varnish, sanding lightly between coats. The third coat is a satin-sheen varnish, one of the modern types of finish your paint dealer has been able to add to his stock. This gives a handsome soft-luster sheen.

If you're doing a simple, modern table and have a fondness for a smooth supergloss, this is another fairly simple proposition. With the wood utterly smooth, stain the desired shade and brush on a thin coat of pure, fresh white shellac. After this comes a series of thin coats of clear lacquer or clear plastic. If you prefer to brush on the lacquer, go right ahead. But you'll find spraying with aerosols quicker. As each coat dries, sand it lightly and put on the next. The principle here is that the more coats you apply, the deeper and more dramatically three-dimensional the finish will appear. Putting on as many as 15 coats is not too unusual, although most folks run out of patience after 8 or 10. And what a sleek, shiny finish this method produces!

If you are planning on varnish, get the best-quality water-clear varnish you can buy. Flow it on smoothly in thin coats. Do *not* stir it in the can, because air bubbles may form and spoil the job (you'll only have to sand off the bubbles later and start the varnishing over completely. After each coat dries out, and make sure it does, go over it lightly with fine sandpaper before putting on the next coat. Usually three coats are enough.

As mentioned before, the principles used here are basic. They'll apply, with only few variations, to almost any type of finish you select. For example, if you plan on paint or enamel, you substitute the recommended undercoater for the stain. Or if you want the soft, hand-rubbed oil finish, you start these treatments after applying the sealing coat of shellac (some people even start right on the wood, omitting the shellac). Remember when applying oil (or polish), go light on the oil and

heavy on the elbow grease. In fact, it's almost impossible to do too much rubbing.

In refinishing indoors, remember that one of the worst enemies to a smooth surface is dust. That is one reason why quick-drying finishes have an advantage over the older, slow driers; dust hasn't had so much time to collect. If you are working in the basement or garage, wet down the floor before you start. And use a vacuum cleaner on the firniture to get it clean. Don't use a cloth, because it will have lint.

Other Finishes. There are so many other finishes that it seems logical at least to mention them before leaving the subject. They can employ lacquer, shellac, paint, enamel, or just plain oil and polish. They can call for the use of decals, masking tape, or your innate skill with the striping brush. And for details, it's suggested that you consult any of the books written to help us amateurs turn out these intriguing projects.

"Antiquing," for example, takes some time but gives a very nice effect, especially for turn-of-the-century pieces with carvings and curlicues. On a base of flat paint, usually white, you add any decorations, or gold strips, or monograms, etc., and then a couple of thin protecting coats of flat varnish. When dry, you wipe on the "antique" brownish overtone, doing it with a saturated cloth. Almost immediately you wipe this off again, using a circular motion. The result is an interesting off-white effect, with most of the paint remaining in the corners and carved areas. The final step is protecting your work with two more thin coats of flat varnish.

There is another type of finish somewhat along these lines, most often used in open-grained woods. It is a two-toned effect, like a black tabletop with the grain showing up white, called "African" or "silver fox" by some people. It's easy to do. You stain the table black, being careful to apply a thin coat, so it won't fill up the pores. When dry, give it a sealing coat of thinned shellac. Then rub on white paste filler over the whole tabletop, and immediately wipe it off again across the grain, using a coarse cloth. This wipes all the white off, except what is caught in the grain.

For blond effects, running from honey color to silvery gray or other light tints, start by bleaching the bare wood. The color is achieved through wiping on the stain of the desired shade, sealing this when dry, and finishing with clear spraying lacquer.

Masking tape can be used to great advantage for putting designs on enameled furniture. For example, suppose you'd like the kitchen table legs striped like peppermint candy. First finish the table with white enamel. When it is dry, wrap masking tape in a continuous spiral around the legs, spacing the windings about equal to the width of the tape. Then paint the legs fire engine red. When the red has dried, unwind the masking tape, and where it covered the legs the original white will show up. The result: stripes like candy canes. This principle can be used for many designs; so can stencils.

One caution: When painting any furniture (or toys) apt to be chewed by the young fry, be meticulously careful to use paint containing absolutely *no* lead. Examine the label, and if in doubt, ask the dealer. Toy manufacturers long ago avoided the hazards of lead poisoning by never finishing their products with any paint containing lead. We should be equally careful.

The deep-gloss Oriental lacquer effect—another excellent finish—is so deep it looks almost three-dimensional. In brief, this is achieved by putting on 10 or more thin coats of clear lacquer over a base coat of colored lacquer. This takes a good deal of time, because you sand each coat lightly before putting on the next, but the handsome results are well worth the effort. And the more coats of the clear, the richer the luster.

Another "conversation piece" finish is "decoupage." This treatment, we believe, originated with some old-time Venetian cabinet makers. It consists of shellacking a table-top, or the top of a chest, and while the shellac is still wet, smoothing on sheets of old newspapers, or magazine covers, or sheet music, or any picture, for that matter. Then this novel covering is given another coat of shellac, followed by 10 thin coats of clear varnish. You can see, with some imagination, that this idea offers limitless possibilities.

While on the subject of finishes, let's not overlook the handsome and durable plastic laminates. For example, it is perfectly within the capabilities of any reasonably handy home handyman to recover a table with a sheet of the material. It will make an exceptionally good top for the bar in the rec room or the patio. And, of course, it's hard to beat as a kitchen counter top.

When laminating a surface, the adhesive used is contact cement. This has such enormous holding power that you get no second chance. You cannot make any position changes. You have to be dead right the first time. But there is a trick which is so easy that covering even a fairly large table with laminated plastic is well within amateur range. If you can borrow an assistant for a few critical minutes, fine. If not, a couple of ordinary C-clamps will do just as well. First, of course, you have the laminated plastic cut to the exact size and shape. Then you also cut a sheet of brown wrapping paper so that it's also the exact size and shape. If you can't find one piece big enough, tape a few together. Next, cut this sheet in half.

To make sure everything is exactly right, have a "dry run" before the cementing. Put the paper on the table, and push the edges of the halves together. Tack it in position with a few bits of tape. Then put down the sheet of plastic laminate. This and the paper underneath should come precisely to the edges. If this checks out, remove them. Next, spread the contact cement over the tabletop and the underside of the plastic laminate. Use a tooth-edged applicator made for this, so that you'll get it on evenly. Now you wait. You don't stick the two surfaces together until the cement is so set up it's no longer even tacky. This is what makes the job easy. As the cement sets up, keep testing its tackiness with small bits of paper. When finally you can touch it down and lift it off with no cement resistance, you're ready.

Lay the two pieces of brown wrapping paper on the cemented tabletop. (Don't worry; it won't stick.) Position it exactly. Over this, lay the sheet of laminated plastic and line it up. Now, while your assistant, or the C-clamps, holds the plastic material firmly along the edge opposite you, carefully lift up the laminate on your side and slide out your half of the brown wrapping paper. This immediately puts the two cemented surfaces together on your half of the table. You press down, and that's it.

The second half is easy, since your half is already anchored. You or the assistant merely pick up the other edge, slide out the other piece of wrapping paper, and press down.

Your sheet of plastic laminate is now cemented precisely in place. To assure maximum contact all over, run a photographic print roller or a rolling pin over the surface.

Questions and Answers

Here are a series of questions on furniture repair and refinishing that people have asked us over the years. Let's hope the answers will help you.

DENT IN MAPLE TABLE

I dropped an iron on my daughter's maple table. It made a definite little dent. How can I fix this so that it will not be noticeable?

Wash off the wax and furniture polish from the area with turpentine. Place a piece of wet cloth over the dented area. Keep dampening the cloth as the water evaporates. After several hours place a warm (not hot) iron on the damp cloth. The slight heat and moisture should swell the dented fibers back into place. The treatment may affect the finish, but wiping with camphorated oil may restore the color. If not, it might be necessary to refinish the top.

NICKED TABLETOP

I want to repaint a table used by the children for meals. They have managed to get a number of nicks and gouges in the top. Can these be repaired before painting?

Yes, easily. Spackle or plastic wood can be used to fill the nicks and gouges. When the filler is dry, sand it to the level of the surrounding area, wipe off the dust, and then refinish the table as desired. Of course, before applying paint, be sure that the surface is free of grease, wax, grime, etc., and that any gloss of the present coating is dulled for better adherence of the new paint.

CANNING MARKED TABLETOP

While canning, I placed hot-fill jars on layers of newspapers on my limed oak dining table. However, the newspapers did not afford the protection needed, and I now have white circles on the finish. How can the marks be eliminated?

If the marks have not penetrated too deeply, they may be removed by one of the following methods: gentle rubbing with fine pumice and light machine oil, using a piece of heavy felt; or gentle rubbing using very finely powdered rottenstone or scratchless scouring powder and light machine oil; or rubbing with your fingertip a drop of turpentine or camphorated oil. If none of these methods are successful, then the stains have penetrated too deeply and refinishing is required.

CIGARETTE BURN IN TABLETOP

A cigarette fell off an ashtray and caused a burn in a mahogany tabletop. How can this be repaired?

Remove the charred wood with "0" steel wool, or carefully scrape it off with a razor blade or sharp knife. Wipe off the dust; then touch up the spot with a couple of thin coats of varnish or fresh white shellac, thinned half-and-half with denatured alcohol, using a fine-pointed artist's brush. If the burn is down to bare wood, touch up the area with as closely matching stain as possible before building up the layers of varnish or shellac to the same level as the surrounding surface. This may not be a perfect repair, but will make the burn less conspicuous.

TRIVET SPOILED TABLETOP

Inadvertently, I left an electric trivet upside down in the middle of a nice mahogany dining table. There was a plastic-backed hush cover and a lace tablecloth under the trivet. Neither was scorched. But on the table is a mark the size of the trivet. It's full of tiny bubbles, and the surface is rough, but there's no discoloration. Is there any

Figure 18-2. Method of repairing dents.

method I can use at home to restore my lovely table?

First try gentle rubbing with the finest steel wool. The object is to see if you can melt down the roughness and bubbles. If this doesn't work, you'll just have to wipe paint remover on the area, following the label directions. The object is to get the bubbly finish off without working on the mahogany stain. So remove the remover as fast as practical. Then it's up to you to revarnish, featheredging to minimize the boundaries of your retouching.

SCRATCHED BLOND OAK

On a child's table and on our record player (both blond oak) are scratch marks made by metal, as deep as scratches can go. I first tried a polish, which didn't work, and then a special touch-up and blemish remover for blond wood, which did nothing either. Is there anything I can use to cover up the scratches, short of refinishing?

If this is a varnish finish, try running turpentine along the scratches, using a small watercolor brush. Build up a varnish finish with thin successive coats. If the scratch has really gone through the finish into the wood itself, try filling it with stick wax the color of the wood; these wax sticks are like crayons and are widely available at many hardware and housewares dealers.

GREASE STAINS ON REDWOOD

Our redwood picnic table has grease stains all over it. How can we remove the grease, and what can we do to prevent staining?

Cover the table surface with a layer of paste made of powdered whiting and non-flammable liquid spot remover; over this place a sheet of thick plastic to retard evaporation. When the paste is dry or discolored, replace it with fresh until all the grease has been removed. Applying a coating of spar varnish to the table will protect the surface against penetration of grease; food stains can be washed off.

REMOVING LONG-TERM TAPE

How can I get masking tape off a wood surface? It has been on for a long time and is very resistant. I want to repaint the article, and so it won't hurt if the finish is damaged.

Soften it up with nail polish remover so you can pull it off. If any remains, use a paint scraper; then smooth the spot with sandpaper if necessary.

WATER SPOTS ON TABLETOP

Could you tell me how to remove white water spots from a walnut tabletop? Too much water was used in watering plants, and the excess moisture developed the water spots.

If the discoloration has not penetrated deeply into the finish, you might be able to remove it by rubbing the spots with turpentine or camphorated oil. Should this fail, try rubbing them with very finely pulverized rottenstone and some light machine oil on the ball of the finger. Cigarette or cigar ash can be substituted for the above powder. Rubbing should be light and with the grain of the wood. Use no more than six to seven strokes in any area. Polish with a good grade of furniture polish.

VARNISHED TOP CLOUDY

The varnished top of a small bookcase (oak) has become quite cloudy-looking. How can the luster be renewed?

Try rubbing the surface with a cloth wrung out in a solution of 1 tablespoon of cider vinegar in a quart of water, following the grain of the wood. Then wipe with soft, dry cloths. If this isn't successful, the cloudiness has probably worked through the varnish. The only solution is to remove the present varnish finish with prepared paint remover, following the label instructions carefully, and refinishing from bare wood.

CRACKED VARNISH FINISH

We have a varnished chest that we used as a window seat in the living room. Fine hairline cracks are developing in the finish. What do you suggest to eliminate these?

Fine check lines in varnish are sometimes caused by exposure to sunlight and moisture; inferior-quality varnish also develops cracking. If the cracks are not very deep, rub them lightly with "000" sandpaper, following the wood grain. Wash off the dust with turpentine; then apply a coat of top-quality varnish. Deep cracks require complete removal down to bare wood and furniture refinishing.

DON'T SAND SCRATCH

An accident caused a very conspicuous scratch in our walnut dining table. Is there any way to remove it? Or must we sand down the area of the tabletop as deep as the scratch and then refinish? I'm sure this would also leave a noticeable depression.

There's a much, much easier approach. At almost any hardware or furniture store, you can get "scratch removers." These are made like a wax pencil you rub on the scratch; like a liquid, you paint into the scratch with it, and wipe off the excess afterward. There are still other types. All are made in a wide range of wood colors. After making the scratch visually disappear, give the table a good polish and be delighted.

TACKY SHELLAC FINISH

I have shellacked several book covers with newly opened, clear shellac. These covers are still tacky and refuse to dry. Why is this so, and what can be done with the book covers to make the books usable again?

Either the shellac was not a pure shellac or it was a very old mix. Another reason for tackiness is the application over waxed or oiled surfaces. You should be able to remove it by wiping it with liberal quantities of denatured alcohol.

LOOSE SLATS IN ROLLTOP DESK

My grandfather has given my son the old rolltop desk he had as a child. The slats in the rolltop are loose because the papers which apparently held them together have deteriorated. Is there any way I can repair this myself?

Remove all the old glue and paper with sandpaper. When the wood is completely clean, apply a piece of lightweight muslin, using a thick shellac as the adhesive. First give the slats a thin coat of shellac and allow it to dry thoroughly. Then apply a heavy coat of shellac and fasten the muslin in place. Do not move the top until the shellac has dried hard.

STICKY FINISH

We have had our mahogany dining room set for years and always polish it carefully. The wood is becoming very sticky. How can we remove this stickiness without damage to the furniture itself? We want to avoid refinishing, if possible.

There is probably too heavy a polish accumulation on the surface of the furniture. We suggest removing this with turpentine and fine steel wool, or with a good wax-removing and cleaning preparation (follow the label directions carefully). Then apply a thin coat of top-quality paste wax, buffing well. The thinner the wax and the more rubbing, the better the results.

PAINT SPOTS ON FURNITURE

How can I get a few spots of paint off a mahogany table and a wicker chair? I got the paint on them while painting the room and didn't see it until it dried.

Careful sanding might be the easiest way. Otherwise use a paste-type paint remover, being careful to avoid getting any on the area surrounding the paint spots and allowing it to remain on only long enough to soften the paint without affecting the finish on the furniture underneath; follow the label instructions.

VENEER BUBBLED UP

Recently, the veneer on my table loosened in a bubble near the middle, about 5 inches across. Is there any reasonably simple way to flatten this? I don't want to go to the expense of having the whole top reveneered.

Cut clear across the bubble with a very sharp blade; if you have one of those razor-bladed utility knives, that will be perfect. Keeping one side pressed down, butter the underside of the other half with epoxy adhesive, using a long, thin blade. Then reverse the process. After this, press both sides down heavily, and wipe up any excess that oozes out. Then cover the spot with wax paper and weight it with anything heavy and flat for 24 hours. Check during the first few hours to wipe up any more oozing.

STUBBORN VENEER

The veneer on our bed has separated in several places. The wood beneath is maple. I intend to remove the veneer and then stain and varnish the maple. The loose veneer came off with ease, but most of the rest is too difficult to remove without damage to the maple. I tried to chisel the veneer off, and also soaked it for about 4 hours. When neither of these worked, I tried applying heat, but still no luck. Could you suggest a method for removing the veneer?

Your soaking idea was all right, but it didn't last long enough; sometimes soaking jobs take several days of immersion. If the adhesive is waterproof glue, you have a much more difficult proposition, because soaking won't do any good. As an experiment, try holding a steam iron over one section near the edge and observe the result. If there is no loosening of the veneer, the only other way we can suggest is to tackle it with a power plane, followed by an electric sander. However, this is a good-sized job and takes some know-how.

REMOVING OLD VENEER

I have an old tea cart whose veneer is loose and broken in many places. I would like to remove all the veneer and replace it with new. How do I remove it?

Here's one of the widely accepted methods: Remove any finish and then sand the object to expose the wood. Using a constantly wet cloth, soak the wood for 12 hours. Then start trying to pry the veneer loose at the edges, using a sharp blade. If it won't come, resume the soaking. If you wish to keep the veneer for possible future use, scrape off any residue of glue with a sharp blade, doing the work on a flat surface. To prevent curling, store it between two flat surfaces heavy enough to keep it flat.

REMOVING CARVINGS

I am refinishing a chest of drawers. It has some glued-on trim. How can I remove these carvings without harming the surrounding wood?

If the chest is antique, the chances are the glue is water-soluble and only needs long exposure to water. If the carved trim is on a front area, lay the chest on the floor, with its back down, and cover the trim with thick, water-saturated toweling. Applying a steam iron to the toweling may help speed up softening of the glue. If the glue appears to soften, continue the process so that you may be able to pry the trim off with a carefully applied chisel. If the glue is unresponsive (a waterproof variety), the only removal method is to chip it off, removing the major portion with a chisel and sanding off the remainder (so as not to run the risk of gouging the basic wood).

WARPED TABLE LEAF

How can I straighten a dining table leaf that has become warped?

Place the leaf, concave side up, on a couple of chair backs or sawhorses, in an area where it can remain undisturbed for at least a week or 10 days. The leaf should project about a foot beyond the points of support at each end. On each end, beyond the supporting points, place heavy weights (large stones, heavy books, pails of water) and leave them on the leaf ends for several days. If the warp doesn't disappear in about a week, steaming may be necessary—preferably by a professional cabinetmaker—to straighten it. A home method is to clamp the leaf to a frame of 2 by 4s and slowly steam the concave surface with a steam iron, tightening the clamps slowly as the steaming continues, until the board is flattened (by "ironing").

DIFFICULT DRESSER DRAWERS

How do you treat dresser drawers that become difficult to move during humid summer weather? Until we moved into a damp house, they gave little trouble. It takes a couple of months of furnace heat to get them back to normal.

"Slide-easy" preparations are now widely available in housewares and hardware stores; follow the label instructions. To loosen a sticking drawer, place an electric bulb inside, out of contact with the contents of the drawer and wood, to help dry out (and shrink) swollen wood. Shave down the edges of the drawer with a plane, coarse file, or sandpaper. Rub paraffin or soap on the drawer edges and the parts against which the drawer slides. Unfinished surfaces should be coated with shellac.

MAKING DRAWERS SNAG-FREE

I bid on a nice old chest of drawers at an auction, and finished it up pretty well. However, I have a problem: once in a while a stocking or some other delicate fabric will snag on a rough spot or splinter. How can I fix this?

Here are two simple ways: (1) Use a self-adhering contact-type covering, or (2) sand the insides of the drawers smooth, and then brush them with three or four coats of enamel.

DRAWER MAKES SHELVES DUSTY

I have a problem drawer. I keep my silver in this drawer which is directly over two cupboard shelves. These shelves are continually dusty due to opening and closing the silver drawer so many times. What can I do about this?

Take out the troublesome drawer. Vacuum the insides of the cupboard where the drawer slides. Carefully wipe the sides and bottom of the drawer. Then coat all these surfaces with pure, fresh white shellac, thinned down 25 percent with alcohol. Make sure everything is totally dry before replacing the drawer. This should help keep the dust in check. It won't hurt a bit, at regular intervals, if you remove the drawer and wipe out the cupboard.

FURNITURE CHECKS AND SWELLS

What causes furniture to swell and check? Is it due to drying a wash all winter in the rooms, or to too much heat from a hot-air furnace? We always keep water in the water pan.

If the wood swells, it is certainly caused by excessive moisture in the air in the house. The drying of laundry indoors causes gallons of water to evaporate into the air, and wood fibers have a tendency to absorb this moisture. The shrinkage and swelling of the wood could cause the finish to check.

TERMITES IN FURNITURE

I bought an old table and two chairs at an auction. A friend examining the furniture carefully has discovered termites in the wood. Will these spread to other wood? Is there any way to get rid of them and still make use of the furniture?

These are probably nonsubterranean termites, as they are in furniture. Nonsubterranean termites fly directly to and bore into wood. Subterranean termites build tunnels from the ground to attack wood. To kill the termites, the table and chairs must be placed in a chamber heated to 150°F for 1½ hours, or at 140°F for 4 hours. Consult a woodworking company with equipment for bending and shaping wood about having this done. Conversely, if you can park the furniture in a community frozen food locker for a few days, the freezing will also kill the termites. These termites may damage other wood in the area. Insecticides, liquid or dust, can also be used to combat them. For this type of treatment, consult a reliable exterminator.

FIXING ROCKER ARM

The arm of my old platform rocker has come off. I tried gluing it, but it doesn't hold. What kind of glue should I buy, or where can I have it fixed?

Possibly you didn't scrape all the old glue off the end of the arm, or from the inside of the hole where it fitted. New glue doesn't stick very well over old, in the same way that paint won't stick over a greasy surface. The end piece must fit quite snugly into the hole. If there is a gap, a piece of discarded nylon stocking is wonderful as padding. The epoxy-type adhesives have tremendous holding power, and are now on sale at just about every hardware and housewares store.

LOOSE RUNGS

After a year in this dry climate, I've noticed that the rungs of several chairs have loosened. As a result, the chairs have become a little wobbly. How can I make them firm again?

There are various ways to go about it. One way is to use a kind of cement which, when applied to the end of the rung, swells the wood and then cements it into place. Many hardware stores carry it. If the rung isn't too loose, put a fair amount of almost any kind of glue in the hole and then jam in the rung. Wipe off all excess while the glue is still wet. For extremely loose rungs, saturate a small piece of cloth with glue, hold it over the rung hole, and then force the rung into the hole. When the glue has dried, trim off the excess cloth with a razor blade.

Figure 18-3. Method of clamping a leg after applying glue.

LEG WON'T STAY PUT

Weight and wear have worked on one of the metal legs of my kitchen table so that it won't stay screwed into the frame. I have to keep it propped and supported. In other words, the screw hole is now too large. I have tried epoxy glue, plastic wood, and everything in that line. The table wobbles, although propped, and I will appreciate any suggestions.

Try this: After cleaning out the screw hole, fill it with plastic steel. Coat the threads of the screw on top of the leg with grease. (The table is upside down on the floor.) When the plastic steel starts to set up, but is not yet hard, screw the leg down into the hole, using only gentle pressure; don't wash it down. Doing it this way, you can actually put threads into the hole, and the screw won't stick in the plastic steel because of the grease. So you could unscrew it, along with the other legs, if desired.

MATCHING TABLE LEG'S LENGTH WITHOUT SURGERY

It may be a slightly uneven floor in this old house. Or it may be the table itself. But the table does rock slightly; one leg has to be shorter. Is there any simple way to even it up? I don't want to begin sawing.

On a piece of aluminum foil, put a blob of plastic wood. Stand the table so that the short leg rests on this. Shape it a little around the foot, and cut off the major excess. When the plastic wood is dry, sand it to conform, and then touch it up to match the rest of the leg. The foil is just to keep the wet plastic wood from sticking to the floor. The plastic wood will automatically make the short leg the right length.

DUSTY CHAIR LEGS

I have kitchen chairs with plastic caps at the bottom of each leg. These caps leave what looks like a fine dust on the linoleum. It is easy to wipe off, but what will stop it from forming?

Wipe the caps thoroughly; then spray on a couple of coats of clear plastic. When this wears off, spray it on again.

FURNITURE MARS WALL

What can I do to keep the backs of chairs and a settee from marring the wall? I need the "domes of silence" on the legs, because I have to move the furniture to clean the floor, and without something like this, moving the furniture would be a problem. And yet somebody, usually the children when they're playing, bumps the back of the furniture against the wall.

Many furniture stores, department stores, and hardware stores sell very useful screws which have large, squashy plush heads. These are easily screwed into the chair backs and make effective cushions which will protect the wall from harm. Chunks of foam rubber, cemented in place, also are helpful.

OILCLOTH PRINT ON FURNITURE

I have a bedroom set that has a satinlike finish. Glass tops are on all the pieces. Oilcloth with a colored pattern was put on under the glass. I made the mistake of turning under about 2 inches of the edge with the print facing the varnish. The designs have all come off and adhered to the wood. How can I remove the oilcloth pattern without damaging the finish?

We are afraid you have already damaged the finish. The print has become bonded to the varnish. You might be able to remove the pattern by carefully running a dull knife blade under it. Do not use much pressure. After removing most of it, rubbing lightly and carefully with "000" steel wool may take off the rest. All rubbing should be with the grain of the wood.

DECALS WON'T BUDGE

What will remove some pretty dreadful decals from otherwise quite nice chairs I bid for at an auction recently? I don't want to resort to sanding except as a last resort.

First, are there any remains of varnish left on the chairs? If so, the varnish will protect the decals from any of the regular lift-off removing methods. If you're not sure, wipe the surface with paint remover, following the label directions, to expose the decal. Often decals will soften just by holding wet blotting paper over them for half an hour or so. You can buy special blotting paper for this job at fancy arts and craft shops, but it really isn't all that better to warrant the much higher price. Wet, hot toweling will also loosen decals, given enough time, so that they can be slid off. As you say, you always have one of the various sandpapers as a last resort. Sometimes it could be a lot quicker, too.

STICKY CEDAR CHEST

Two years ago, our son built us a cedar chest with sliding doors. We haven't been able to use it because the inside has a very sticky film. We have tried sanding it with glass and fine sandpaper, but there hasn't been too much improvement. How can we stop this stickiness, even at the expense of losing the cedar fragrance?

It's likely that the inside was finished with overage shellac, which often doesn't dry out and stays tacky. Try wiping the inside with fine steel wool and alcohol; the latter is the solvent for shellac. Then we recommend that you leave the inside unfinished; you'll get a lot more cedar aroma.

UNFINISHED PINE CHEST

Will you give me an idea of how to put a blond finish on an unfinished pine chest? The color I want is similar to the blond oak one sees on modern furniture. Should I bleach the wood first? Would varnish or shellac be the best bet? What would I use to rub it down for a shiny, smooth finish? Should I seal the knots first?

Bleach the wood by using one of the prepared wood bleaches sold by paint dealers specializing in wood-finishing materials. Use it according to the directions on the label. When the wood is dry, smooth it by rubbing with "0000" sandpaper; then make the wood smoother by rubbing with "00" steel wool and wipe off all dust with turpentine. Many paint manufacturers make several kinds of modern wood stains. Color cards are available through the dealers. You can finish with a clear lacquer or pure, fresh white shellac. Should you decide on shellac, thin half-and-half with denatured alcohol. The lacquer finish would be preferred, and if possible, apply it with a paint sprayer. Rubbing will not be necessary. Wash the knots with turpentine and steel wool; then apply the stain and finish.

BLOND TO BRUNETTE

What procedure would I follow in changing my blond organ to mahogany to match the rest of my furniture? That is, if this is feasible in the first place.

Remove the present finish (use paint remover for varnish, alcohol for shellac, lacquer thinner for lacquer; please be advised that lacquer thinner is one of the most volatile concoctions ever put together and the fire hazard is very high). On a small obscure area, apply a test treatment of mahogany stain. If it dries in the right shade, continue. But if it gives slightly yellowish results, you'll have to bleach off the present stain, using wood bleach. Then apply the mahogany, sand it as glass-smooth as you can make it, and refinish.

LIMED OAK FINISH

We have a round varnished oak table and six matching chairs which we want to refinish. We plan to remove the present varnish finish down to bare wood and want the new finish to be a limed oak. How do we continue?

After you have removed the present finish, bleach the bare wood with a prepared commercial bleach, available at paint stores, following the label directions carefully. Then brush on liberally, with the grain, a white or liquid gray paste filler, thinned with turpentine to the consistency of thick paint. When the filler begins to set (in about 20 minutes), wipe the surface across the grain with a coarse cloth. What remains in the grain, or pores, is allowed to dry hard and is then made smooth by rubbing with very fine sandpaper. Wipe off the dust, and finish with a light-colored varnish.

ANTIQUE GRAY FINISH

I have an enameled bedroom set which I would like to refinish in an antique gray. How can I do this?

Kits for refinishing furniture in various antique effects are available at many paint, hardware, and housewares dealers. Follow the manufacturer's instructions carefully. Or remove the present enamel with a paint remover, according to the label directions. Sand the wood smooth, and wipe off all dust. Then apply a coat of gray paint in the desired shade. Sandpaper it smooth, and wipe off all dust. Apply a coat of glaze (this is a thin varnish, with a tint of brown, black, or some other color). While the glaze is still wet, wipe it off across the wood grain, removing it from flat surfaces but leaving traces in the grain, carvings, etc. This results in an almost invisible tint on the flat surfaces which shades to deeper tones where most of the glaze remains. Glaze is available at paint dealers, or can be made by thinning varnish with one-fourth turpentine and tinting with color-in-oil.

REFINISHING FURNITURE OF VARIOUS WOODS

Our boys' bedroom furniture is of different woods and finishes. We would like to refinish them in a rustic finish, rather than a plain painted one. What would you suggest?

We suggest removing the present finish down to bare wood (use paint remover for paint or varnish, following the label directions carefully; use denatured alcohol for shellac). Bleach all the surfaces, using prepared bleach according to the manufacturer's instructions. Then, with wood stain, make any desired shade. Finish with a coat of pure, fresh white shellac, thinned half-and-half with denatured alcohol, or clear varnish.

MATCHING REFINISHING TO FURNITURE

I am refinishing an old drop-leaf extension table. All the old paint and original varnish have been removed and the wood sanded and made as smooth as I can. It is a dark oak. Is there any way I can give it a reddish finish to match an antique cherry china closet in our dining room?

If the finished shade you want is lighter than the present oak, bleach the wood with a prepared bleach available at paint and hardware stores, according to the label instructions. Sand the wood surface smooth again when the wood is dry, and apply wood stain of the desired shade (consult color charts available at paint dealers). Or a medium reddish brown cherry stain can be mixed as follows: 1 pint turpentine, 2 tablespoons raw umber, and 2 tablespoons burnt sienna (use oil colors). Vary the quantity of umber and burnt sienna to get the desired effect.

BAR-RESISTANT FINISH

I am planning to build a bar for our downstairs rec room. I have a very nice slab of red maple for the top. It is too nice to hide with some covering. But what type finish could I put on so it will be acidproof and alcoholproof and won't show stains or white rings?

There are some special finishes which will serve very well—notably the type made for gym floors, which can take just about anything. A well-rubbed oil finish will also do very well.

BLACK-LACQUER FINISH FOR TABLE

I have a small end table I want to finish in a black lacquer, to go with several Oriental pieces in the room. What is the best procedure?

Remove the present finish down to bare wood. Sand the surface satin smooth, and wipe off all dust. If you want a really beautiful finish, and don't mind extra work, after applying several smooth, even, thin coats of lacquer with an aerosol spray, apply 8 to 10 coats of thin clear lacquer. Be sure the black has thoroughly dried first, though.

WEATHERPROOFING OAK TABLE

We are replacing a large round oak table we had been using in the kitchen. Is there any way to make this weatherproof so that we could use it on an open terrace?

After removing all trace of grease, wax, grime, etc., and dulling any gloss of the present finish, applying two coats of good-quality spar varnish or deck enamel would make the table reasonably weatherproof. Be sure to coat all the surfaces and edges, including the bottoms of legs, to prevent moisture absorption. Refinishing may be necessary every two years or so.

FINISHING DRIFTWOOD

On our vacation we found a couple of interesting pieces of driftwood. What ways can the driftwood be finished?

Clean the surface of the driftwood thoroughly by wiping it with fine steel wool and turpentine to remove all trace of grime, soot, grease, etc. The wood is usually left in its natural color, but a wood stain can be applied if desired. Apply two thin coats of pure, fresh white shellac, thinned half-and-half with denatured alcohol; or use the shellac available in aerosol form, and spray it on the surface of the wood. If a wax finish is desired, apply a thin coat of good-quality paste wax and buff well.

BLEACHING DRIFTWOOD

How can driftwood be bleached?

Use prepared wood bleach, available at paint, hardware, and wood-finishing material dealers; follow the label instructions carefully. Or apply a hot, saturated solution of oxalic acid *(poison)*, allowing it to remain about 10 hours and then rinsing it off with clear water to remove all trace of the bleach. When the wood is completely dry, sand it smooth and wipe off the dust.

FRUITWOOD STAIN

I want to build some furniture to match some fruitwood-finish items. My intention is to use both solid wood and plywood. I understand that cherry wood is the basic lumber. What special finishing steps are necessary to give the fruitwood finish?

For a fruitwood oil stain, the following approximate proportions are necessary: 1 pint of turpentine, adding 3 teaspoons of raw umber, and 1 teaspoon of raw sienna, thoroughly mixing the ingredients; to lighten or darken the stain, use more or less turpentine.

PINE FINISH FOR VENEER

I have a bed table of either mahogany or walnut veneer. I would like to make it natural pine. How can this be done?

Remove the present finish down to the bare wood veneer. Then apply a commercial wood bleach, available at paint dealers, following the manufacturer's directions carefully. When the wood has thoroughly dried, apply wood stain in the desired color; then apply a coat of shellac, thinned half-and-half with denatured alcohol, or clear varnish. If this is a mahogany veneer, we don't recommend a lighter finish, because the mahogany may bleed through.

MAHOGANY FINISH FOR DRESSER

How can I refinish a mahogany dresser, which has been cleaned down to bare wood and has the red stain removed? It has been sanded down to a smooth finish. The top, sides, and drawers are mahogany, which I'd like with a natural finish, but the cabinet is not select wood, and I would like a uniform natural mahogany finish.

All wood surfaces can be stained to a uniform color with a mahogany wood stain, following the label directions carefully. Then apply a finish coat of pure, fresh white shellac or water-clear varnish.

CARE OF OIL-FINISH TEAK

We have a large dining table made of oil-finish teak. What care does this require?

Oil-finish teak requires only rubbing with a rough cloth, following the grain of the wood. If the surface becomes grimy, wash it with the following solution: Add 3 tablespoons of raw or boiled linseed oil and 2 tablespoons of turpentine to a quart of hot water. Stir thoroughly and cool. Then wash a small area of the table with a cloth dampened in the solution and well wrung out, wiping dry immediately with a clean cloth. Using any top-quality furniture polish or wax, polish sparingly according to the directions on the container.

OLD-TIME OIL FINISH

I have heard that one of the most beautiful furniture finishes in early colonial times was a combination of linseed oil and turpentine. True? If so, what are the ingredients and proportions?

True indeed. It gives a lovely glowing finish. Not shiny. The more you rub, the deeper and richer the appearance. The ingredients are mixed as follows: 4 parts linseed oil (boiled preferred here), 4 parts turpentine, 1 part japan drier. Use perhaps half a ton of elbow grease, plus cotton rags for rubbing.

REFINISHING A PIANO

We have an old upright piano, and we were wondering if it was possible for us to refinish it ourselves. We would like to paint it. Would this require a special kind of paint?

We assume the piano is of mahogany and has a dark-mahogany color. If the finish is in fairly good condition, dull the gloss by rubbing it lightly with "000" sandpaper; then wash the surfaces with turpentine to remove dust and furniture polish. Apply a stain sealer to prevent the mahogany stain from bleeding through the new paint, and finish with a good grade of enamel, gloss, or semigloss, according to your preference. To get a smooth finish, each coat, when hard and dry, should be rubbed carefully with "0000" sandpaper and all dust must be wiped off. If the varnish is in poor condition, remove it with paint remover, following the directions on the label. The stain is then bleached out by applying a liberal amount of a hot, saturated solution of oxalic acid *(poison)*. Leave this on overnight; then rinse it off well with clear water. When the wood is dry, smooth it with "000000" sandpaper, wipe off the dust, and finish as desired.

MODERNIZE PICTURE FRAME?

I have a fairly large wooden picture frame I wish to modernize. It has heavy plaster on wood, finished in gold paint. I tried cracking off the plaster, but it doesn't budge. How can I remove it?

As water is the only "solvent" for plaster and the gold paint acts as a moistureproof barrier, sandpaper the surface to allow entrance areas for water. Then cover the plaster with very moist cloths or sponges. When the plaster begins to soften, pry it off with a putty knife or screwdriver.

"GOLD ANTIQUE" FINISH

Last week I went into a furniture store, where I saw a handsome coffee table. It was black, with gold in the grain of the wood. I asked the salesperson how it was done (because I have an old table at home I'd like to do this same way), but he either didn't know or wouldn't tell me. Can you tell me how this effect is achieved?

From your description, we think it's done this way: First brush or spray on the black, in a thin coat. If one coat isn't sufficient (which it frequently isn't), give it another. Then, when that's dry, put on the gold paint, covering the entire surface, but don't let this coat dry out. Instead, while it's still wet, wipe it all off with a coarse cloth, such as burlap, and wipe across the grain of the wood. In this way, you'll take off all the gold paint except that which is in the grain, and which will give you the effect you like. Complete the job, we suggest, with a coat of clear lacquer.

GOLD GARLANDS ON MANTEL

We have a white mantel with garlands of roses across the top in gold. It now needs refreshening, and I don't know how the gold is put on. It looks as if the whole thing is painted in a flat finish first, then the gold on top of the garlands. How could I put that gold on the garlands?

We suggest you get good-quality gold paint and apply it with a fine artist's brush, after being sure the surface is free of all trace of grease, soot, wax, etc.

NEW LOOKS FOR OLD CLOCK

Is there any way to remove old, cracked varnish from antique pieces without removing the original color stain? We would like to revarnish an old clock but keep its lovely old color.

Ordinary paint removers don't take out the stain color, only the actual finish, and so your color would be safe. But as an extra precaution, test the remover on a small obscure area first.

GILT ON BRONZE CLOCK

I have a solid bronze clock, over 60 years old. Someone painted over the bronze with cheap gilt. I want to remove this and have a polished bronze again. How can I do this?

Remove the gilt with a prepared paint remover, available at paint and hardware stores, following the manufacturer's instructions carefully. Use the nonflammable kind if possible. For a highly ornamented surface, use a small brush or steel wool to get into the depressions. Then polish with a good metal polish, applying a thin coat of special lacquer.

SOILED GILT FRAME

The gilt frame of an old family portrait has become quite soiled. Is there any special way to clean it up? I'm hesitant about using soapsuds and water; I suspect this might damage the gilt.

You are quite right about not using suds and water, because it could easily affect the gilt, which is quite fragile. The safest way is to wipe on a half-and-half solution of household ammonia and denatured alcohol, using an artist's camel's hair brush. In a short while, this should loosen the dirt enough so it can be gently wiped up with clear, warm water. Drops of water which remain should be shaken off, not wiped. Let the frame stand on edge to dry.

SHELLAC ON OIL PICTURE

In an effort to give more depth to an oil reproduction, I applied two coats of fresh white shellac to the picture. Now it is very shiny and dark-looking. Is there any safe method by which I could remove this shellac coating and still retain the picture?

The usual solvent for removing shellac is denatured alcohol. As an experiment, you might try dabbing this on one small spot, using a little artist's brush. When the shellac is softened, wipe it off with a soft cloth. If the results are okay and the spot on the picture is apparently unaffected, then it should be safe to do the rest carefully. However, if the picture is valuable, it would be wise to take it to an art museum or a reliable dealer so that it can be personally examined, and you can get an expert's on-the-spot recommendation.

REMOVING CLEAR FINISH

I have put a so-called clear wood finish on my cabinet doors. Now it is wearing off in spots. I would like to put on a top grade of varnish, which I am sure will be better. But how do I take off this clear wood finish?

If regular paint remover, whether liquid or paste type, doesn't do the job, ask your dealer about some special solvent. Or write directly to the manufacturer of the finish.

YELLOWED FURNITURE

The dresser of my bedroom set is developing a yellow cast; the finish is a sprayed-on white, with black, for a gray effect. We had the furniture stored for a while. The set is only three years old. Is there any way to restore the original appearance?

The yellowing may be due to a surface film that formed while in storage, unless, of course, you wax the furniture too heavily. If you are waxing the furniture, try removing the accumulation with one of the wax-removing preparations made by a nationally known manufacturer, or with turpentine. For the surface film, try a cleanup wax made by the same manufacturer. If the yellowing is due to the deterioration of the white coating itself, refinishing is the only solution.

NATURAL FINISH FOR OUTDOOR FURNITURE

I want to use knotty pine for an outdoor picnic table and benches. Is there any kind of finish I could use to protect the wood but give it the natural wood-grain look?

Yes; use a top-quality spar or marine varnish. Thin the first coat, as recommended on the label; then apply two coats of the same material as it comes in the can. Another treatment is to apply two or three soaking coats of 3 parts of raw linseed oil thinned with 1 part of turpentine. After allowing each coat to soak for a half hour, rub with dry cloths to remove any excess oil. Otherwise a gummy deposit will form on the surface which is practically impossible to remove later on. Allow two days between applications. This will darken the wood, but not obscure the wood grain. Whichever treatment is used, be sure to coat all surfaces, including the bottoms of legs, etc., to prevent moisture penetration, which will cause the wood to deteriorate.

RED WAX STAIN ON LIGHT VENEER

How can I remove a red wax stain from a light wood veneer tabletop?

Scrape as much of the wax off as possible with a dull knife. Rub the area carefully with fine steel wool or sandpaper to remove any surface finish (get down to bare wood). If the stain is just in the finish, and has not penetrated into the veneer itself, this may be all that is necessary; then refinish the exposed spot, using a fine camel's-hair artist's brush, and apply either shellac or varnish to match the rest of surface. If the wood is stained, try bleaching the area with prepared wood bleach. Then refinish. Deep stains may be impossible to remove.

PAINT OVER PENETRATING WAX STAIN

Several years ago I used a penetrating wax stain for finishing a cabinet. I would like to apply a paint finish now. Can this be applied over the stain?

Just remove any surface wax, using a good wax remover, according to the label directions, or fine steel wool and turpentine. Be sure the surface is thoroughly dry and clean and free of any trace of foreign matter such as grime or grease, as well as wax, before painting. Then go ahead and paint. If the stain is mahogany, apply an undercoat of aluminum paint to prevent the mahogany color from bleeding through the finish coat.

SEAL MAHOGANY STAIN?

I am staining some unpainted bookcases mahogany and then plan to put on a finish coat of varnish. Must the mahogany coat be sealed first?

A sealing coat is advisable to prevent the varnish from being discolored from the stain ("bleeding"). An excellent seal is a coat of pure, fresh white shellac, thinned half-and-half with denatured alcohol.

APPLY STAIN OVER LACQUER?

I tried to finish a dark oak kitchen table in a natural color. After thorough sanding, I applied a filler, as advised. When dry, it turned white. A coat of lacquer was then applied. Can I put a stain of natural wood over this for the color I want?

The filler should be wiped off, across the grain of the wood, as soon as it turns dull. You apparently neglected to wipe the filler off. However, no stain will have any effect over a coat of lacquer (or varnish or shellac). Remove the present lacquer with lacquer thinner. Then remove the excess filler by wiping the surface with a rag moistened with naphtha (being careful of fire hazard). It may be necessary to use a sander. Sand satin-smooth; then apply the stain in the desired shade.

SEALING IN FURNITURE STAIN

I am finishing up a table in my shop, and I'd like to give it a mahogany stain. Is it necessary, or correct, to put a sealer coat over the stain, or can I put on the varnish as soon as the stain dries?

We recommend a sealing coat to prevent the varnish from picking up discoloration from the stain. An excellent seal is a coat of pure, fresh white shellac, thinned half-and-half with denatured alcohol.

REMOVAL OF WOOD STAIN

Can you advise me how a walnut stain can be removed? I have taken off all the paint, but a reddish walnut stain remains. How should the natural wood be finished?

Wood stains can be bleached by applying a liberal quantity of a hot, saturated solution of oxalic acid *(poison)*. Leave this on overnight; then rinse it off well with clear water. Allow sufficient time for the wood to dry; then smooth the surfaces by rubbing them with "0000" sandpaper. Wipe off the dust, and finish with two coats of a gloss or semigloss varnish. When the first coat is hard and dry, dull the gloss by rubbing it lightly with "0000" sandpaper. Wipe off the dust, and refinish as desired.

REMOVING SCRATCHES FROM MELAMINE

How can I remove scratches from a melamine tabletop?

Use the special preparations now available at large housewares and hardware dealers for cleaning plastic surfaces, following the label instructions carefully. Or use an auto-cleaning wax (either cream or paste, not the liquid), available at auto accessories dealers, also according to the label directions.

TRICK FINISH FOR CARD TABLE

I have a small card table. I would like to finish it in gold, with red showing through here and there. How can I do this?

First, brush or spray on the red enamel. Follow with a coat of gold or antique gold enamel. When putting on the latter, deliberately miss some spots so that the red will show through.

TENANTS LEFT CABINETS ON THE GUMMY SIDE

After renting our house for six years, we returned to it. We found the tenants left the birch kitchen cabinets rather gummy to the touch. In places, the original gloss is gone but the original tan color is still there. What do I do?

A good wiping with turpentine should remove the gummy film, as well as leave the surface in good condition for refinishing. Probably all you'll need will be a thin coat or two of top-quality clear varnish.

CLEANING CANE SEATS

We are refinishing a maple dining room set. The seats are cane, and we would like to know what cleaning solution to use to get the seats back in good condition.

Wash with soap and water, rinsing well afterward and drying quickly. If the cane has been varnished and this is worn, remove the varnish with paste varnish remover, following the label directions carefully. Rinse well afterward to remove all traces of varnish remover. Apply a coat of spar varnish after the cane has dried thoroughly; it's even easier to spray the cane with spraying shellac or a clear acrylic finish.

DUSTY RATTAN CHAIRS

I have several very dusty rattan chairs. What is the best way to clean them?

Remove as much dust as possible with a vacuum cleaner. Then wash them with cloths wrung out in mild soapsuds, followed by clean cloths moistened with clear water to remove the suds. Coating the rattan with pure, fresh white shellac, now available in aerosol form, will prevent dust and dirt from working into the rattan.

REFINISHING RATTAN FURNITURE

Would you please tell me if and with what type paint I can finish rattan furniture? Where can I get some more rattan for repairs?

Rattan furniture can certainly be refinished. If you want it natural, use clear acrylic or plastic. If you want white, black, or a color, use enamel. Use spray cans, rather than a brush-on finish. No matter how much you jab with a brush, you can never get the coverage in nooks and crannies that you'll get with a spray. This is also true for repainting wicker. Discount stores with large hobby departments usually stock rattan, plus instruction books for reweaving. *Note:* You could also use a shingle stain, if you like the color. It's water-thin, and so it would give excellent penetration and coverage.

READYING WICKER FOR PAINT

We now have use for some painted wicker furniture stored in our basement for many years. Is it necessary to recondition it before we repaint it? If so, what is the procedure?

At the very least, you will undoubtedly have to give it a good cleaning. Unless you had these pieces wrapped in plastic bags, there will be years of dust. Do this outdoors with the vacuum and a stiff brush; even reverse the vacuum to blow, too. Any loose joints should be firmed with epoxy or other good adhesive, working it into the joints. If the rungs or legs are really loose, work them out, scrape off all possible old glue, and replace them using epoxy. Brush off any flaky, powdery paint. If the paint is in terrible shape, have the furniture stripped at one of those places specializing in this. (An antique dealer can help you find one if they're not listed in the telephone book.) Do your painting with spray bombs of enamel in thin coats. This is the only way to work paint into all those nooks and crannies.

VINEGAR STAINED BLACK GLASS

I spilled vinegar and water on my beautiful black glass tabletop. I tried to wash it with soapsuds and also with Comet suds, but I could not get the stain off. I would appreciate any suggestions.

Try neutralizing this acid, which vinegar is, by wiping it with a tablespoon of baking soda to a cup of water. Or try ammonia in the same proportions. If the stain has been

there any length of time, expect to do this several times, especially if the edges of the stains are sharply defined.

SCRATCHED LEATHER TABLE

A leather-topped end table was accidentally scratched, not deeply, but enough to remove the color. How can this be repaired?

Paint the scratch with a leather dye the same color as the rest of the tabletop, using a finely pointed artist's brush. The dye is available at leather goods and housewares dealers. When the dye is dry, treat the scratch with leather dressing.

CRACKED LEATHER TABLETOP

What would make the leather on a nice tabletop crack? How can this be repaired? The table is about 50 years old.

Leather, like people, likes to be fed. Natural oils must be replenished with good saddle soap, leather dressings, etc. You can close the crack, but not hide it, by covering a small strip of matching brown imitation leather with household cement, epoxy, or a similar good adhesive, working it through the crack, drawing the edges of the crack together and pressing down until the adhesive hardens.

CLEANING LEATHER CHAIR

Recently I noticed that my leather chairs have become soiled. They're in perfectly good condition, except that they could stand cleaning. How do I go about this?

There are a good many preparations nowadays for cleaning leather, and you can get them in almost any housewares section of department or hardware stores. One foam type which we have found satisfactory cleans, dresses, and polishes leather, and is put out in an aerosol can. Or you can clean the leather with thick, firm suds of saddle soap or castile soap. Work in a small area at a time, wiping clean with a dry cloth before moving on to the next section. You'll notice the suds will become discolored. Don't worry about this; keep working at it until the discoloration has stopped.

STICKY LEATHER UPHOLSTERY

Our English oak dining room set has leather seats and backs. They stick to clothing in hot weather. What can I use to prevent this condition?

This condition is usually the result of

using polish on the leather. Wash the surfaces with mild soap, such as saddle soap, following the label directions. After the leather is thoroughly dry, restore the glaze by rubbing the leather with the beaten white of an egg. Only special leather dressings, available at paint and housewares stores, should be used on the upholstery.

TEAR IN LEATHER CHAIR

I have a modern leather recliner chair with an upholstered back and seat. Recently I noticed a small tear in the seat. Is there any way to patch it without it showing? Or will it require reupholstering? If so, how is this done?

You might try covering the tear with a strip of the clear, adhesive-backed, plastic tape available at variety, housewares, hardware, and stationery stores. For reupholstering, we suggest using one of the leather-type plastic fabrics available at upholstery dealers; the manufacturer's direction sheets are usually available on request giving information about recovering furniture.

BALLPOINT INK ON LEATHER HASSOCK

Our child marked a white leather hassock with a ballpoint pen. I have tried rubbing it off with saddle soap, scouring powder, and detergents, without success. Can you suggest anything else?

Ballpoint pen marks are difficult to remove. Try rubbing with alcohol or acetone.

WORN LEATHER CHAIR

We have an off-white real leather chair. The arms and seat are worn; there is no paint or covering over the hide. Is there any dye or paint that can be used successfully? Otherwise the chair is perfect; it only looks bad.

Leather can be painted with a good-quality enamel, applied as it comes in the can, with no undercoat. Be sure that all surface grease, wax, etc., is first removed. Leather cleaners and conditioners are available at many luggage shops, housewares dealers, and chain stores; follow the label directions carefully.

STREAKS ON A LEATHER TABLETOP

In removing the wax from my leather-top cocktail table, I possibly used too much soap and water, as the finish now is very streaked and, in spots, no longer shines. Despite repeated waxing, it still looks streaked. Is there anything I can do to make it look right again, outside of taking it to some professional?

If the color of the leather is brown, you might be able to improve it by applying some brown-colored shoe polish or a shade that might match the leather. When cleaning leather, use only a small amount of water and a thick suds of a mild soap, such as castile.

RESTORING LUSTER TO MARBLE

My husband has just completed a beautiful white marble-top coffee table. How can the shine and luster be restored to the piece of marble?

For a high polish, long and patient rubbing with water and putty powder (oxide of tin), applied with a damp, thick felt pad, is required. Putty powder is available at monument yards or marble dealers. For safe, regular cleaning of white marble, use a cream furniture wax or a cleanup wax, made by a nationally known manufacturer; this leaves a protective coating on the marble surface.

COFFEE STAINS ON MARBLE TABLE

I have a marble-top table that has become dull and stained. What can I use to remove coffee stains and bring back the luster?

Wash the stained area with clear water. Then soak white blotting paper or clean tissues in hair-bleach-strength hydrogen peroxide, adding a few drops of ammonia, and place this over the stains, covering with a sheet of plastic or glass or retard evaporation. This should draw the stain out of the marble, within 48 hours, depending on the depth and age of the stain. To restore the luster, polish the top with putty powder (oxide of tin).

CLEANING GRAY MARBLE

How can I clean a gray marble top of a table? It has stains and scars on it. Also, how is it polished after cleaning?

Marble-cleaning and -polishing preparations are available at some large housewares and hardware stores. Slight stains can be removed by applying hydrogen peroxide and ammonia, then rinsing with clear water and wiping dry. To remove slight scars, sand the surface lightly; repolish the entire surface by rubbing it with putty powder and a piece of damp felt.

YELLOWED MARBLE

I have several pieces of marble which have yellowed. I have tried a number of methods of cleaning, but have been unable to acquire their original whiteness. Can you suggest anything?

Probably you waxed the marble; this in time gives the marble a yellowish tone. You might try bleaching it with a weak solution of oxalic acid (poison): 1 ounce dissolved in 1 quart of water. Wipe this solution on, allowing it to remain only for a minute or two; then wipe it off with clear water. If necessary, repeat the treatment.

CRAYON STAINS MARBLE TOP

I bought a marble-top table at an auction, and noticed the price had been marked on the marble with red crayon. I didn't know what to do about this, after trying a pencil eraser. Finally I tried lighter fluid. This immediately made the crayon marks spread into a pink cloud, which more rubbing won't get out. What can I do?

The wax part of the crayon, at least, should come out by scrubbing with hot water and scouring powder. If the color remains in the marble, which we suspect it will, try bleaching the tabletop with a solution of oxalic acid (poison), using 3 ounces of acid to a quart of hot water. Apply it liberally, and let it stay on 5 minutes or so. Then rinse it off with clear water. Frequently, just one of these treatments will be enough.

CRACKED MARBLE-TOP TABLE

Our marble-top table has quite a crack. Is there anything that could be used to fill in the separation?

Thin slabs of marble (like tabletops) can be repaired permanently only when supported by a reinforcement. Plasterboard or a strip of wood can be used, cut to fit within the frame. Turn the marble upside down; cement the edges of the break with equal parts of litharge and powdered red lead mixed to a paste with glycerin, and press together. Then spread a thin mixture of plaster of Paris over the back of the slab and place the reinforcement in position. Allow several hours for hardening. If the crack has not caused the marble to separate, try filling the crack with white lead paste.

RED-STAINED PLASTIC CHAIR BACKS

The gray plastic backs on my kitchen chairs have become very discolored, yellowish, and even reddish, apparently from a red shirt. I have tried soap, bleach, liquid cleaners, powdered cleansers, and other cleansers, all to no avail. Can you suggest a way to remove the discoloration?

The dye from the shirt has probably penetrated into the plastic itself and permanently discolored it. You might try careful rubbing with fine steel wool and a nonflammable liquid spot remover; be sure the room is well ventilated while working, and avoid inhaling the fumes. If this doesn't work, we suggest your painting the backs with a good-quality latex paint, being sure the plastic surface is thoroughly clean and free of any trace of grease, wax, grime, etc. Plastic chair covers, in a variety of sizes and patterns, to fit most standard kitchen chairs, are available at many housewares and hardware dealers. Most department stores also carry these.

KITTY PINHOLED VINYL

Our cat, before being declawed, discovered that the shelf on top of our vinyl recliner made a great lookout. The way to get up there, of course, was to climb up the vinyl, thus leaving many tiny pinholes. Outside of reupholstering, the person I contacted couldn't help. Considering the price of the chair, this is out. Any suggestions from you would certainly be appreciated.

If these are actually holes, then outside of a slipcover, we're in the same boat as the upholsterer. However, if they are only nicks, and if you have the patience, you can dip a toothpick in fabric dye the same shade and camouflage each, so that any lighter-colored backing won't show.

PLASTIC STUCK TO TABLETOP

I placed a plastic tablecloth on my dining room table for protection. When I removed the tablecloth later, the plastic stuck to the tabletop. I am now faced with the problem of taking the plastic off without damaging the finish. Is there any way this can be done?

Usually, when plastic sticks to a finish, it is difficult to remove it, because it has become bonded to the top. Try lifting the plastic by forcing a dull knife blade under it.

PLASTIC SPOTS

I had a white plastic table cover on my dark maple table top, and it left spots that look like wax. Is there something that can be done to remove the spots, without damage to the tabletop?

Usually the discoloration is permanent, but you might try wiping the spots with turpentine. If there is no improvement, rub lightly, with the wood grain, using a scratchless scouring powder and a little light machine oil on the ball of the finger. Use no more than three or four strokes in any one spot. Wipe off the oil and powder with a soft, dry cloth. If this doesn't help, the spots have sunk in so deeply that complete refinishing is necessary.

CLEANING VELVET CHAIR CUSHIONS

My velvet-cushioned chairs are still fairly new, but the velvet is starting to look worn and in need of a cleaning. The material on the cushions is a print with a white background. Could I try this job myself?

Let us put it this way, for whatever it's worth: If the chairs were ours and we liked them very much, we would turn the job over to a competent professional. Velvet is one of the trickier materials. Besides, it would be very difficult to do the steaming technique; at least, you'd have to unfasten almost two sides of each cushion in order to let the teakettle's steamy spout deliver steam to the backside of the velvet. It has to go from the wrong side outward. It's easy to do this for a dress, but not for a chair.

REPAINTING METAL BED

I have an enameled metal bed that I would like to repaint a different color to match new draperies. What is the procedure?

First, remove any flaking paint and dull the gloss of the present enamel coating by rubbing it with steel wool or sandpaper. Wipe off the dust, and clean the surfaces with turpentine. Finish with an enamel undercoater and a good-quality metal enamel, either gloss or semigloss.

SILVER FINISH ON LAMP

How can I clean a floor lamp and two bridge lamps, which have a silver finish? The bases and fluted posts are badly stained. I have tried every kind of polish, but to no avail. If I could paint them, what kind of paint can I use? I'd like some paint that would make them look a little like they did when they were new.

We think the reason you were not able to clean the metal is that it still has some of the lacquer coating on it. You can take it off with lacquer thinner, but be careful of fire; the thinner is flammable. If, after polishing, the metal is still stained, you could have the lamp replated, or you could paint it with a finely powdered aluminum paint, but the latter will not have the appearance of the silver finish. Some of your local art materials shops may have a silver-colored paint which would give you a better effect.

RESTORING LUSTER ON METAL PORCH GLIDER

I have a porch glider made of aluminum or magnesium, which has become dull. Is there any way that I can restore its luster?

Magnesium does not usually corrode or tarnish. Try cleaning the glider with mild soap and water; if this is not effective, clean it with fine steel wool and a scratchless scouring powder, followed by ample rinsing with clear water, wiping dry with a clean cloth. If the glider is aluminum, excellent aluminum-cleaning and -polishing preparations are available at many hardware and department stores and some paint dealers; follow the manufacturer's directions carefully. These usually leave a protective coating to retard future tarnishing. Or clean it by careful rubbing with fine steel wool and kerosene (being careful of fire hazard), followed by applying a thin layer of kerosene which will evaporate, leaving a protective coating.

CLEANING BRASS HARDWARE

How can I polish brass window locks and handles? Also, other brass articles on furniture? I hope there is a solution for this rather than the polish-and-rub method.

Remove the hardware before cleaning and polishing. First remove the remainder of the lacquer from the brass by wiping it with lacquer thinner. The metal is then cleaned and polished with one of the fast-acting cleaning preparations, now on sale at most hardware and department stores and made especially for use on copper and brass. To prevent early tarnishing, wash off all traces of the polish with naphtha and coat the hardware with a clear lacquer. All the above materials, with the exception of the metal cleaner, are flammable, so be careful of fire.

RENEWING BRASS BEDSTEAD

Many years ago I painted a brass bed with white paint. Now that brass seems to be popular again, I am wondering if I can remove the paint with regular paint remover. What should I use to bring the luster back into the brass, or how can I polish it?

The paint can be removed with regular paint remover, following the label instructions carefully. To make the brass shine, you can use one of the many excellent brass-cleaning and -polishing preparations that are now available at most housewares and hardware dealers; follow the manufacturer's directions. Or you can clean the brass with a paste made of flour added to vinegar in which as much salt as possible has been dissolved; then rinse with clear water. To retard tarnishing, after cleaning and polishing, wipe the brass with benzene to remove any trace of grease or wax and apply a coat of spraying clear lacquer made especially for this purpose, available at paint stores.

CHROME DINETTE SET

What can I put on the chrome of a dinette set to keep it nice?

If you wish to keep the chrome in good condition, wipe it occasionally with a damp cloth and then with a dry one. If any part of the metal has a stubborn soil spot, use a little mild soap; then go over it with a cloth dampened with clear water and wipe dry.

FLAKY CHROME LEGS

Most of the chrome legs of our dinette table and chairs have begun to chip and flake. Is there any way I can replate them myself? My son suggested sanding them down and painting them with aluminum paint, but this would have a dull finish.

Many auto supply stores carry kits for do-it-yourself chrome plating, for rusted bumpers and such. This should work here too. We agree with you that the aluminum paint would look dull by comparison. You could also take one chair to a metal-plating shop and get an estimate for doing all. You may be pleasantly surprised.

PAINTING CHROME FURNITURE BLACK

We have eight kitchen chairs we would like to paint black and recover the plastic seats and backs on. The chromium on the legs is partly worn off. Is there any way to remove the rest of the chromium finish? What type of paint should we use?

It's not necessary to completely remove the chrome finish; just dull the metal surface thoroughly by rubbing it with steel wool and turpentine, which will remove all trace of wax, grease, grime, etc., at the same time. Chrome paint is now available at most paint dealers; two coats should be applied. If you prefer the black, first apply a metal primer according to the manufacturer's instructions, and then put on any top-quality black enamel.

CHAIR WEBBING COLLAPSED

When the seat of a favorite chair began to sag badly, I investigated. Carefully removing the black material covering the underside of the seat, I found that several of the broad, interlocking strips of webbing had come loose from their tacks in the frame. Is re-webbing such a chair only for professionals, or can an amateur have a reasonable chance to make this type repair?

We know that some professional upholsterers won't like us for this, but let us assure you that replacing ancient webbing with new requires no great talent or long experience. Of course, if there are complications, due to splitting or dry rotting in an antique frame, or broken springs, that's different. Perhaps you may not do the job as fast as a pro. But if you carefully note just how the old webbing was arranged, and if someone can hold it taut while you drive the tacks, there's no reason why you can't save yourself quite a few bucks with a good repair.

NEW WEBBING FOR METAL CHAIRS

I have several old outdoor metal (aluminum) chairs with woven seats and backs that are badly worn. Where can webbing for replacement be purchased?

Various colors and widths of plastic webbing, for replacing chair seats, etc., are available at large chain variety stores, upholstery departments of department stores, and housewares dealers. Dealers in outdoor and summer furniture may also have this item available.

To be prepared to remove all the different kinds of spots and stains, you'll need to keep four types of spot and stain removers on hand—absorbent materials, detergents, solvents, and chemical stain removers. Although some stains can be removed with only one type of remover, more often removers of two or more types are needed.

Absorbent Materials

Useful absorbent materials are absorbent powders, absorbent cotton, sponges, and white or colorfast paper towels, facial tissues, and soft cloths. Cornstarch, cornmeal, talc, or powdered chalk will also remove some fresh stains, such as grease spatters.

The absorbent powders are spread over the stain before it dries. Remove the powder as it absorbs the stain by shaking or brushing it off; or use the upholstery attachment of a vacuum cleaner. After the surface stain has been removed, work fresh powder into the stain; then remove it as previously mentioned. Repeat with fresh powder until as much stain as possible has been absorbed. Then you will generally use a solvent to remove the rest of the stain.

Absorbent materials like cotton, paper, soft cloths, blotters, and sponges are usually used to soak up staining liquids before they soak into a fabric. If much of the liquid can be absorbed quickly, the stain will be smaller and easier to remove than it would be otherwise. This technique will work only on fabrics that absorb the staining liquid slowly. It's often useful on such articles as rugs, upholstered furniture, and heavy coats.

Soaps and Detergents

Soap and detergents will remove many non-greasy stains and some greasy stains. They act as lubricants, coating insoluble particles of staining material (such as carbon and colored pigments) with a smooth, slippery film. The particles can then be rinsed out of the fabric.

For surface stains on washable articles, rub the soap or detergent lightly into the dampened spot or rub in a liquid detergent. Rinse the stained area or wash the article in the usual manner. If a stain is deeply embedded, work the soap or detergent thoroughly into the fabric. One way to do this is to rub soap or detergent lightly into the stained area; then, holding the fabric with both hands, work the stained area back and forth between

CHAPTER 19

SPOT
AND
STAIN
REMOVAL

your thumbs. Bend the yarns sharply so that the individual fibers in the yarn rub against one another. It's this bending of yarns, rather than rubbing the surface of the fabric, that is effective in removing the stain. Go over the entire stained area in this way. Then rinse thoroughly.

On articles such as rugs, on heavy fabrics that can't be bent easily, or on woolen fabrics that might be felted by too much bending of the yarn, work the soap or detergent into the fabric with the edge of the bowl of a spoon.

For stains on nonwashable articles, work the soap or detergent into the stained area in the same way as for washable articles. Dilute liquid detergents with an equal volume of water. Use as little soap or detergent as possible because it's difficult to remove the excess without wetting a large area of the fabric. Rinse thoroughly by sponging the spot with cool water or by forcing water through the stain with a syringe. If alcohol is used in place of water, the fabric will dry more quickly.

Solvents

Many common stains can be removed with the right solvent. Different kinds of solvents are needed for nongreasy and for greasy stains. Water is the most useful solvent for many common nongreasy stains, and it is the only solvent that is neither flammable nor poisonous.

Floor Stains

Of all stain problems, those, according to our mail, concerning the floor seem to trouble homeowners most. Table 8, compiled by the General Services Administration, is a fine guide for removing common floor stains. Some more specific procedures are given in the question and answer portion of this chapter.

Questions and Answers

We've selected some of the questions asked most regarding spot, dirt, and stain removal and have included their answers. Many of them expand further or give alternatives to the information just given in Table 8.

PUPPY-STAINED CARPETING

Now that we have finally housebroken our puppy, we'd like to remove the stains in the carpeting from the training period.

Make a solution of 1 pint warm water, 1 teaspoon detergent powder, and 1 teaspoon white vinegar. Apply this solution to the stains, allowing it to remain a few minutes; then mop the carpet dry. Repeat the treatment if necessary. When the carpet is dry, brush the pile gently. The chances of this working successfully are much better if the stain is tackled when it's fresh, rather than letting it dry.

STAIN ON CARPET

A dog vomited on our light-tan carpet. Though the carpet has been washed several times with soap and water, a dark stain still remains. Is there any way of getting rid of it?

If the rug is of wool or cotton and color-fast, try scrubbing the stain with a half-and-half mixture of household ammonia and water. It's also quite possible that the stain is caused by grease, in which case you should be able to take it out with the powder type of rug cleaner on sale at most hardware and department stores. If the carpet is valuable, we'd recommend turning it over to a professional cleaner.

CHEWING GUM ON RUG

We have a small rug on our foyer floor. Some chewing gum has become embedded in one spot. How can this be removed?

Harden the gum by placing an ice cube on it, to make it easier to scrape off. The remainder can be removed with trichlorethylene. Work from the outside toward the center, so as not to leave a ring. If the gum isn't deeply embedded, snipping off the tip ends of the fibers of the rug may be all that's necessary for removal; a manicure scissors is good for this job.

FUEL-OIL STAINS

My oil stove ran over, and the hardwood floor and fiber rug got soaked with the oil. Is there any way to remove the oil from the floor and the rug?

The following treatment will remove the fuel oil from the floor and the rug, but will require repeated treatment until all the oil is absorbed out. Make a thick paste of powdered whiting, or other absorbent powder, and a nonflammable liquid spot remover, being sure the room is well ventilated. Cover the oily areas with a layer about an inch thick, placing a sheet of glass or metal or plastic on top to retard evaporation. The spot remover acts as a

Table 8. Guide for Removing Common Stains

Stain	Procedure
Alcoholic Beverages	Rub with a cloth dampened in a solution of liquid detergent and warm water. If the stain remains, rub it with a different cloth dampened with denatured alcohol.
Blood	Mop or sponge with clear, cold water. If the stain remains, mop or sponge it with a solution of ammonia and cold water.
Candle Wax or Chewing Gum	Freeze the material to brittleness by using ice cubes. Then scrape the material off the floor with a plastic spatula.
Candy	Rub with a cloth dampened in liquid detergent and warm water. If you need friction, use steel wool instead of a cloth except on "no-wax," embossed vinyl asbestos, or hard-surface floors; on them use powdered detergent and a plastic scrubbing pad dampened with warm water.
Cigarette Burns	On resilient tile, rub the stain with a cloth dampened with a concentrated solution of detergent and water. For a heavier stain, rub with scouring powder and a piece of steel wool or plastic pad dipped in water. For wood or cork, rub with a cloth coated with a paste of cigar ash and water. For hard-surfaced floors, rub with a cloth dampened in a solution of lemon juice and water.
Coffee and Canned or Frozen Fruit Juice	Saturate a cloth with a solution of one part glycerine to three parts water and place it over the stain for several hours. If the spot remains, rub it gently with scouring powder and a cloth dampened in hot water.
Dyes	Rub with a cloth dampened in a solution of one part chlorine bleach and two parts water. If this is not effective, use scouring powder and a cloth dampened with hot water.
Fresh Fruit	Rub with a cloth dampened with a solution of powdered detergent and warm water. If this isn't effective and your floor is resilient tile, wood, or cork, rub the stain with a cloth dampened in a solution of 1 tablespoon of oxalic acid and 1 pint of water. If you have hard-surface flooring, rub the stain with powdered pumice.
Grease and Oil	Remove as much as possible with newspaper, paper towels, or a plastic spatula. On resilient tile, rub with a cloth dampened in liquid detergent and warm water. On wood and cork, put a cloth saturated with drycleaning fluid on the stain for 5 minutes. Then wipe the area dry and wash with liquid detergent and water. On

Table 8.   Guide for Removing Common Stains (cont'd)

Grease and Oil (cont'd)	stone, use Stoddard solvent and a soft, clean cloth.
Ink	Rub with a cloth dampened in warm water and liquid detergent. If the floor is not hard-surfaced, use a commercial ink remover and follow the instructions on the package.
Iodine	Rub with a cloth dampened in a solution of household ammonia and water. If this is not effective, saturate the cloth in the solution and place it over the stain until the stain is removed.
Lipstick	Rub with a cloth dampened in liquid detergent and warm water. If you do not get results, rub with steel wool dipped in water and detergent. If the floor is hard surfaced, "no-wax," or embossed vinyl asbestos, use a plastic scouring pad instead of steel wool.
Mustard	Place a cloth soaked in hydrogen peroxide over the stain. Over that place an ammonia-soaked cloth.
Paint or Varnish	On resilient tile, rub with a cloth or piece of steel wool dipped in warm water and liquid detergent. On wood and cork, rub with a cloth dampened in a solution of 1 tablespoon oxalic acid and 1 pint of water. On a hard-surfaced floor, scrub with a concentrated solution of powdered detergent and water.
Rust	Use a commercial rust remover made for your type of floor.
Shoe or Nail Polish	On resilient flooring, rub with a cloth dampened in a concentrated detergent solution, or use scouring powder, water, and a piece of steel wool. On wood and cork, rub gently with steel wool.
Tar	To remove the tar, freeze it to brittleness with ice cubes and then scrape it off with a plastic spatula. To remove the tar stain, apply a damp cloth wrapped around a paste made of powdered detergent, calcium carbonate, and water. Leave the paste on the stain for several hours.
Tobacco	Rub with a cloth dampened in a solution of lemon juice and water. If that isn't effective, place a cloth soaked in hydrogen peroxide over the stain, and over that place an ammonia-soaked cloth.
Urine	Rub with a hot, damp cloth and scouring powder. For greater effectiveness place a cloth soaked in hydrogen peroxide over the stain. Over that place a cloth soaked in ammonia.

solvent and the powder like a blotter to draw the oil up. Complete removal is frequently difficult.

CHOCOLATE STAIN

Some chocolate was spilled on my rug, and I've been unable to remove the stain. I've tried washing it with several kinds of detergents. Have you any suggestions?

First wash the stain with clear, lukewarm water. Then rub in a small quantity of pepsin powder, which you can get at any drugstore. Leave this on for half an hour or so, and then sponge it off with clear, warm water.

RUST SPOTS IN CARPETING

As a result of setting furniture back on carpeting that had been washed but not thoroughly dried, we have numerous rust spots in the carpeting. What will take off these rust spots?

You might try removing the discoloration by wiping the spots with lemon juice. After half an hour or so, rinse with clear water or a damp cloth. Should this fail, you might be able to lessen the discoloration by snipping off the discolored tips of the nap.

NAIL POLISH ON WOOL RUG

Some nail polish was accidently spilled, leaving a stain on a small wool rug in the bedroom. How can this be removed?

Soften the nail polish with amyl acetate (available at drug stores); then mop it up with a clean cloth or cotten. Wash the area with mild soapsuds, rinsing thoroughly afterward with clear water and sponging dry. Protect the floor underneath with several layers of newspapers or a sheet of plastic. Never use nail polish remover on the stain if your rug contains any synthetic fibers. While it will remove the nail polish, it may also eat a hole in the rug.

MILK SPILLED ON CARPET

Recently, I spilled some milk on my living room carpeting. I wiped it up, but it has left a white spot. Could you suggest some home treatment for this condition?

First sponge the surface thoroughly with cold or lukewarm water; then shampoo the area with one of the shampoo preparations on sale at houseware sections of department and hardware stores. Or you could use a thick suds of a mild soap. Another method is to allow the water to dry thoroughly, after sponging; then clean the carpet with one of the cleaning preparations that come in what looks like a wet powder. Follow the directions on the label.

WAX DRIPPED ON CARPET

While burning holiday candles, some wax dripped on my plush carpet. Do you know how to remove this hardened wax without having to tear up the carpet?

Scrape and pull off all you possibly can first. Use a very dull blade and your fingernails. Due to the thickness of the carpet, the usual wax-softening trick, running a warm iron over blotting paper, won't work here very well, although you can try it. Sponge the spot with a dry-cleaning fluid. Your hair dryer may help soften the wax for easier wiping.

COFFEE STAINS ON PATIO FLOOR

Our concrete patio floor has several coffee stains on it. We'd like to remove these before the winter weather sets in. What is the best way?

Coffee stains can be removed from concrete by applying a cloth saturated in a solution of ¼ cup of glycerin to 1 cup of water. Or apply Javelle water (see page 339) to the stains.

TOOLS LEFT RUST

We left some gardening tools on our concrete patio, which caused rust marks. Is there any way to remove these?

Some of the rust removers now being sold in hardware stores and mail-order catalogs specifically mention concrete as one of the surfaces they clean. Check the label carefully. An old reliable home-mixed method works more slowly: Dissolve 1 part sodium citrate in 6 parts water and 6 parts commercial glycerin. Mix some of this with enough powdered chalk to form a stiff poultice. Cover the stain thickly. When the paste is dry, scrape it up and repeat the treatment. The number of treatments depends on the age and condition of the rust.

NEEDS GOOD EGG REMOVER

I have fresh egg stains on my brick wall, and I can't get them off. What would be best to use to remove them?

Since the cleaners with enzymes aren't around so much any more, we don't know of any household cleaners effective on these stubborn stains. One of the great old-time mechanic's hand cleaners, which comes in a can and contains sand in the mixture, may do the trick, scrubbed on with a stiff brush and hot water.

STAINED PICNIC TABLE

We used our redwood picnic table a lot this past summer, and the top has become very stained and soiled. What is the best way to clean this?

Cover the tabletop with a 1-inch layer of dry portland cement, powdered whiting, or other absorbing material, mixed to a thick paste with benzene (be very careful of fire hazard) or nonflammable liquid spot remover; over this place a sheet of plastic or heavy canvas to retard evaporation. As the paste becomes discolored or dry, replace it with fresh paste. If the stains have penetrated very deeply, you may have to plane or sand off the surface.

YELLOWED PIANO KEYS

Our piano is about 10 years old. All the keys have turned yellow—not streaked, just all one nice shade of yellow. How can we make them white again?

Piano keys have a tendency to naturally yellow with age. This can be checked somewhat by exposing the keyboard to light for several hours a week. Try removing the yellowed surface by wiping the keys with alcohol and powdered chalk. Another effective method is to wipe the keys with a cloth dipped in fresh, pure lemon juice; then polish them with a clean, dry, soft cloth.

CLEANING MOTHER-OF-PEARL BOOK COVER

How can I clean and remove the discoloration of a prayer book cover of mother-of-pearl? This book is old, but my daughter plans to use it on her wedding day.

Try wiping it with mild soapsuds and rinsing immediately with a moist cloth or sponge; then dry it with a clean cloth. Or wipe it with a nonflammable liquid spot remover, being sure the room is well ventilated while working. If it's still discolored, apply a mild solution of chlorine household bleach; then rinse it off with clear water (use a moistened cloth or sponge in order to avoid getting too much water on the book cover).

BLEACHING ALABASTER

We have a very old alabaster clock on our mantelpiece. This has become very dark. Is there any kind of bleach we can apply or any treatment we can use to restore it to its lighter color?

Alabaster can be lightened or bleached by wiping or brushing on a weak solution of oxalic acid (poison), using 1 ounce to the quart of water. Allow the solution to remain only a minute; then rinse it off with clear water. If necessary, repeat the treatment. Before applying bleach, be sure the alabaster surface is absolutely clean and free of all trace of grease, wax, etc. When the alabaster has thoroughly dried, apply a thin coat of white beeswax dissolved in turpentine to prevent future darkening.

RESTORE WHITENESS TO CHINA

Can anything be done about a brownish stain that has worked into several of my antique white dinner plates?

Immerse the plates in a pan containing a moderately strong bleach solution. Bring the solution to a boil, let it boil 5 minutes, shut off the heat, and leave them overnight.

STAINS ON PORCELAIN

I read that turpentine or camphorated oil are good for removing stains from mahogany furniture. Would this work on porcelain? I have a clothes washer only two years old, and there are some light brownish stains on top.

The suggestion given was intended for varnished furniture. Many stains on porcelain can be removed as follows: Saturate a piece of cloth with peroxide; then sprinkle the cloth liberally with cream of tartar and a scratchless scouring powder. When the powder becomes well dampened, rub the stained area well and allow the paste to remain for a half hour or so. Rinsing with clear water should follow.

RUST RING FROM SKILLET

Recently I left an iron skillet in my sink for several hours, resulting in a rust ring. How can this be removed?

Housewares sections of department stores and many general chain stores sell rust-removing preparations which are quite effective. Or you can use the method given in the previous answer.

PREVENTING SILVER TARNISH

Is there any way to prevent, or retard, tarnish on silver serving pieces that are not used very frequently?

Keep air away from the surface of the silver when it is stored. Specially treated cloth is available for wrapping to prevent tarnishing; silver dealers and department and housewares stores carry this. Camphor placed in the storage place helps retard tarnishing.

STUBBORN STAINS ON STAINLESS STEEL COUNTER

There are several stubborn stains on my stainless steel counter. These don't come off with the usual washing with a hot, mild soap solution. What do you suggest using?

For stubborn stains, use fine stainless steel wool and whiting; then polish with a soft cloth. Special stainless steel cleaners are now available at supermarkets and hardware and housewares stores; follow the label directions. Occasionally, rubbing the stainless steel surface with a very light machine oil will remove marks and also retard staining. You are right to use only a hot, mild soap solution on stainless steel surfaces. This should be rinsed off thoroughly with clear water and then the surface wiped dry.

SILVER SPOONS TARNISH

I have a set of souvenir silver spoons hanging on a wall rack, but they tarnish very quickly. What can I do to prevent this? I have heard of using colorless nail polish. Would this harm the silver?

No, it won't harm the silver, but it would be quite an expensive operation if there are quite a few spoons to coat. A clear brushing lacquer or a spray-on plastic coating which comes in pressurized cans can be used. After cleaning the silver, wipe off all traces of the cleaner with naphtha. Handle the spoons with cotton gloves to prevent the oil from your skin from leaving marks on the metal. Be careful of fire because the above ingredients are flammable.

DULLED CAKE COVER OF COPPER

I have a metal cake cover that is copper-colored. I've been told it is anodized alumi-num. It has lost its original shine and is cloudy looking. Is there any way to restore the bright copper color?

Try cleaning the cover with a metal cleaner and polish, following the label directions. Or use a cream cleanup wax made by any of the nationally known manufacturers.

TARNISHED COPPER BOWL

I have a large copper bowl that is very tarnished. After I get it polished, is there any way to prevent future tarnishing?

After you polish the bowl, wipe the copper surface with benzene. Then apply a coat of clear brushing lacquer or clear spraying lacquer.

POLISHING AND LACQUERING COPPER

I have several pieces of antique copper and also a copper-lined dry sink. I would like to have these polished and lacquered to prevent tarnishing. Is there a method by which I can do both these steps at home? At present, the cost of having this done commercially is prohibitive.

You can use one of the excellent copper-cleaning and -polishing preparations that are available at supermarkets and housewares, hardware, and paint dealers; follow the manufacturer's directions carefully. Or wash the copper with a salt-saturated solution of household vinegar, followed by ample rinsing with clear water. Remove all trace of polishing material and grease by wiping the surfaces with benzene. Wear gloves while working to avoid depositing any trace of oil from bare fingers. Then apply a coat of clear lacquer made especially for this purpose, or a thin coat of a cream cleanup wax made by any of the nationally known manufacturers.

BRONZING COPPER

A new copper tray was given to me. It is too shiny and bright for my type of furnishings. Is there any way to give it a bronze or deeper-brown color?

Yes. Clean the surface of the metal thoroughly by washing it with a strong detergent; then rinse with clear water and wipe dry. If there is a lacquer protective coating, first remove this with lacquer thinner, being very careful of fire hazards and making sure that the room is well ventilated. Wipe the copper surface repeatedly with boiled linseed oil to give it a bronze color.

PREVENTING GOLD TARNISH

How can I keep candlesticks from getting tarnished when I paint them gold?

Apply a protective coating of special lacquer or plastic, available in aerosol form, usually used on brass surfaces to retard tarnish. Or wipe them with a cream cleanup wax made by any of the nationally known manufacturers; this also leaves a thin, protective coating on the surface to retard corrosion.

POLISHING PEWTER

How is pewter polished? I have a creamer and sugar bowl of pewter that are much duller than they should be after years of use.

Some housewares dealers carry special pewter polishes; follow the label directions carefully. Harsh, abrasive polishes shouldn't be used on this metal because pewter is a soft alloy. For a dull finish, make a paste of olive oil and rottenstone and rub this over the pewter surface with a soft cloth; rinse off the paste with clear water, and wipe dry with clean, soft cloths. For a bright finish, make a paste of powdered whiting and denatured alcohol, covering the entire surface with a thin layer; allow the paste to dry, and then rub the area with a soft cloth; rinse with clear water, and wipe dry with clean, soft cloths.

BROWN SCALE ON PEWTER MUG

I was given a very old mug for my pewter collection. This has a sort of brown scale on it that I have not seen before. Can this scale be safely removed?

Very old pewter sometimes develops a brown scale due to the weathering of the tin in its composition. The following method will remove the scale: Submerge the mug in a strong solution of lye (be very careful to follow the label precautions about handling lye), and allow it to remain about 15 minutes. With tongs, remove the mug, rinse it thoroughly with clear water, and scrub it with a stiff brush. For complete removal of the scale, repeated treatments may be required. Pewter articles with wooden knobs or handles, or japanned items, should not be given a lye treatment. Stubborn, bad spots should be rubbed with "00" steel wool and olive oil.

DISCOLORED LAMP BASE

We have a floor lamp that hasn't been used for years. Now I wish to use it again. Although the base is in good condition, it has become dark and discolored. How can I clean it so that I can use it again?

Not knowing the material of which the base is made, since you don't mention it, it's difficult to make any suggestion. If this is a metal base, effective cleaning and polishing preparations are available at supermarkets and housewares and hardware stores; get one for the specific metal, and follow the label directions for use carefully. If this is a wood base, use either a cream cleanup wax or a wood-floor-cleaning preparation made by any of the nationally known manufacturers. A general household cleaning solution might also be effective. Painting to match other room accessories is very popular.

STAINED COFFEE MAKER

I have a Silex-type chrome coffee maker. It has gotten very black inside; steel-wooling does no good. Can you suggest anything to remove this discoloration?

An almost magic stain remover for tea and coffee stains on plastic ware can be used, following the directions on the container. It's a white powder to be added to water in the coffee maker and boiled up. It's available at large housewares and hardware dealers.

CLOUDY CHROME COFFEEPOTS

I have two chrome coffeepots which I occasionally use. The chrome has become cloudy and even after washing doesn't clear up. What can I do to polish and clean them?

If the cloudiness is on the outside, excellent chrome-cleaning and -polishing preparations are widely available at supermarkets and housewares and hardware dealers; follow the label instructions carefully. If the interior of the pots has become cloudy, use a coffee stain remover for plastic dishes; this can also be used to clean coffee makers, following the manufacturer's directions. These are also available at supermarkets, housewares dealers, etc.

DEPOSIT IN TEAKETTLE

Please advise regarding accumulated lime in a teakettle. We have very hard water in our town. I have tried vinegar and marbles, but it is not very satisfactory in removing the deposit.

Many sewing notions and housewares dealers, as well as hardware stores, now have available a preparation for removing the deposit in steam irons. It comes in a plastic bottle. Try this for the teakettle, following the manufacturer's directions carefully. We're not familiar with the vinegar-and-marbles method, but the following is usually effective: Fill the kettle with water mixed with cider vinegar in the proportion of a cup to the quart of water. Bring the mixture to a boil, and allow it to remain in the kettle overnight. The best way of all, of course, is to have a water-softening unit installed in the water supply line.

SPOT ON BEADED SCREEN

What can I use to get a bug stain off a beaded screen? A big roach crawled in the middle of the screen. I tried to wash it with soap and water, but there's still an ugly yellow-looking spot.

Try sponging the stain with a piece of absorbent cotton and nonflammable liquid cleaning fluid or spot remover.

COLOR BLEEDING ON WHITE SWEATER

I washed a white wool sports sweater (the kind high schools buy for school sweaters) with red trim, rolling it in a towel and then throwing it over a line with the red trim hanging on the bottom. Still some of the red ran into the white. Is there anything I can use to restore the white wool?

Try wetting the stained area with color remover (available where textile dyes and tinting materials are sold), mixed according to the label instructions. This type of stain is difficult to remove because the wool itself has become dyed.

YELLOWED WHITE "WASH AND DRY" SHIRTS

I have been washing white cotton shirts, labeled "wash and dry," with other laundry in which I have added bleach. Some shirts have washed successfully; others have turned a very pale yellow. What is the cause of this?

Some special finish fabrics have a resin in the finish which absorbs and holds chlorine (you must have used a chlorine bleach); this sometimes yellows the material. Chlorine bleaches should never be used on this type of material unless the manufacturer's label or tag states it is safe to use. To remove the yellowing, rinse the garment thoroughly in clear water. Then use a textile color remover, available at notions dealers and variety stores, following the label directions carefully.

STAIN ON ANCIENT QUILT

I was given a quilt which is reported to be more than 100 years old, and judging by the state of the cotton and the type of needlework, I believe it. But in one corner there is a large brown stain, which I'd like to remove. Can you suggest a chemical which won't harm the old fabrics?

Not knowing the nature of the stain, we certainly would hesitate to guess. It could be caused by oils from the wood of the chest in which it may have been stored. But in no case, with an article as old and valuable as this, would we recommend trying any homegrown remedies; we'd most certainly turn it over to the very best dry-cleaning establishment. It might also be an excellent idea, if practical for you, to ask the opinion of a member of the staff of a museum.

TAR ON DRESS

My daughter got tar on a cotton dress. How can the stains be removed?

Rub crude creosote on the tar spots to dissolve the tar. A yellow smear will remain which can be frequently laundered out with soap and water. Lard or a vegetable shortening can be used instead of the creosote.

BLOOD-STAINED CLOTH

How can blood stains be removed from cotton cloth such as handkerchiefs or dental student's coats?

Blood stains should be removed as soon as possible for best results. Sponge the stain with cool water; if possible, soak it in cool water for about 30 minutes to remove as much of stain as possible. To remove the rest of the stain, work detergent into it; then rinse with clear water. If it's not affected by detergent, apply a few drops of ammonia to the discolored area; then repeat the detergent treatment, followed by rinsing. For stubborn stains, apply laundry bleach material, following the label instructions carefully.

RUSTED WIRE CLOTHES HANGERS

How can I prevent rust from accumulating on wire hangers, the type used by local cleaners? I make sure all articles are dry before hanging; yet after being in the closet for a while, rust accumulates and the clothes become spotted with rust.

There is probably dampness present in the closet. Installing a small, wand-shaped aluminum rod, which just plugs into an electric outlet and uses current equivalent to that of a 25-watt bulb, will help overcome this. It keeps the air circulating and dry. It's available at many housewares dealers. To prevent rust on the hangers: Wipe new hangers with fine steel wool and turpentine to remove any trace of grease, wax, grime, etc.; on older ones, steel-wool all the rust off with turpentine. Then apply a thin coat of pure, fresh white shellac, thinned half-and-half with denatured alcohol.

STAINS FROM IRON IN WATER

The water from our well is high in iron content. As a result, we are troubled with iron stains, particularly in the bathtub and commode. The usual commercial rust-removing remedies and lots of elbow grease have been tried. Is there a better way to get these clean and keep them clean?

The best way would be to have a filter installed by a water-conditioning firm to reduce the iron content. You may find the following "home" remover for stains on tubs, although also requiring elbow grease, easier: Make a paste of scratchless scouring powder and peroxide, adding a small amount of cream of tartar. Rub it on the stained areas, and allow it to remain about a half hour; then rinse it off with clear water. Repeat the treatment if necessary.

REMOVING FINGERNAIL POLISH

Recently, some nail polish spilled on one of my best bath towels. Is it possible to get this stain out?

Remember that for all intents and purposes, fingernail polish is lacquer. Whether it's on a towel or a tabletop, all you really need is nail polish remover, which, in turn, is lacquer thinner (with fragrance added). Acetone will also work. On the tabletop, work very fast, as

the remover may also start trying to remove the finish.

INK ON TABLECLOTH

I have spilled ink on my dining room tablecloth. Could you tell me what will remove the stain?

We presume it's ordinary fountain pen ink. If so, rinse out as much of the ink as possible in lukewarm water; then launder the cloth in the usual manner. Soaking the cloth in a mild solution of one of the liquid home bleaches will help take out the stain. Follow the directions on the bottle label.

REMOVING MILDEW FROM CLOTHING

How can mildew be removed from clothing?

Fresh mildew can be removed from washable materials with soap and water; or rub the areas with laundry soap, cover them with powdered starch and salt, and expose them to the sun; or soak the stains with sour milk and expose them to the sun. Weak solutions of oxalic acid (poison) and ammonia in water are also effective; but first test these on an inconspicuous part of the fabric. If the garments aren't washable, they should be dry-cleaned.

MILDEWED SCARVES

I have some dresser scarfs, hand-embroidered, that are badly mildewed. How can I get the mildew out of them without taking the color out of the handwork?

If the scarves are washable, launder them with soap and water and dry them in the sun if possible. If they're not washable, or the embroidery is not colorfast, the only solution is to have the runners dry-cleaned.

MILK STAINS ON BABY'S CLOTHES

My problem is as international as mothers, and so far not even an evaporated milk company has been able to help. How can I remove canned milk stains from my baby's clothes? I have tried soaking in: plain water, bleach, ammonia, Borax; and rubbing with plain water and laundry soap. Nothing removed the stains.

This type of stain (containing protein) needs immediate treatment. Try one of the following: Sponge the stain with nonflammable liquid spot remover to remove any grease, being sure the room is well ventilated. When the spot remover has evaporated, sponge the area with cold water to remove the water-soluble ingredients. Or, if the stain has dried, sponge it with lukewarm water and mild detergent. If the stain isn't completely removed, use a digesting enzyme, such as pepsin. (Moisten the stain with warm water, adding a little vinegar. Then sprinkle the stain with powdered pepsin, keeping the area moist and in a warm place to permit peptic action. In 15 minutes to 3 hours, the stain should rinse out with warm water.)

MILDEWED LUGGAGE

We had been storing our luggage in the basement, which is very dry and warm. Apparently some water seeped in through the wall, resulting in one of our pullman cases becoming quite mildewed inside and out. Is there any way to remove the mildew and its odor?

No matter how dry a basement appears to be, there is always the danger of ground moisture, and storage of items that are subject to mildew is never recommended. Scrub the pullman case, inside and out, with a stiff brush and a solution of detergent; rinse it with clear water and dry it immediately. Air it outdoors in the sun for a week or 10 days. Then apply a mildew-proofing liquid available at some large housewares dealers.

GREASE SPOT ON HANDBAG

I have a lovely handbag from which I would like to remove a grease spot. What can I use to clean it?

We assume the bag is of leather. Wiping it with a thick suds of a mild soap or saddle soap should remove the grease spot. To avoid a spotty appearance, it's advisable to wash the entire bag. When it's thoroughly clean, remove the suds with a damp cloth. After it's dry, polish it with a neutral shoe cream, or a leather conditioner, available at many variety stores, housewares dealers, and luggage shops.

SOILED SUEDE BAG

I have a light-colored suede bag I use for evening wear, and it has become quite soiled. How can I clean it?

Suede is sometimes very difficult to clean, and we would strongly recommend having a professional cleaner do the job. If you decide to do the job yourself, you can use one of the suede-cleaning preparations now available at some housewares and handbag dealers; follow the label directions carefully. Or you can brush the suede with a special suede wire brush, available at most housewares and variety dealers.

SOILED BUCKSKIN GLOVES

I have a good pair of white buckskin gloves that are quite soiled. What is a safe method of cleaning them?

The safest way is to have them professionally cleaned. If these are nonwashable gloves, use a cleaning-fluid spot remover, following the label directions carefully. If the gloves are washable, use mild, natural soapsuds (keeping the gloves on your hands while washing them). Don't rub, but press the suds through the buckskin. When they are clean, replace the suds with clear, fresh water and rinse several times. Roll them in a turkish towel to remove excess water. Then carefully shape them, and allow them to dry flat on a clean cloth or towel (away from heat). When they are dry, if they are stiff, fold them in a damp cloth and gently rub them until they are soft.

SCORCHED BLOUSE

My daughter helped with the ironing and scorched a white linen blouse slightly. How can I remove the stain?

Usually, slight scorch stains can be removed from linen or cotton material by laundering the item again and then exposing it to the sun.

CHAPTER 20

MISCELLANEOUS HOUSEHOLD TIPS

Over the number of years that we've been answering questions on home repairs subjects, it was inevitable that some of the problems had to be categorized as miscellaneous. But before delving into these, let's discuss, for a moment, one subject that we think is most important:

Home Safety

Safety certainly is no accident. It's planned. And the more planning you put into it, the safer your family is going to be—your home, too.

Unfortunately, accidents never announce their approach and thus give you the chance to duck them. The only way to minimize them is to reduce accident conditions and hope for the best. For example, a roller skate definitely doesn't belong on a stairway, an electric light shouldn't be within reach of the bath or shower, and a wooden ladder should never be painted. (For the benefit of brand-new homeowners, we'll list the reasons why; they're undoubtedly well known to all others. Stepping on an unsuspected roller skate while descending a stairway can be nothing less than catastrophic. Touching an electric switch when you're dripping wet is potentially tops as a method of self-electrocution. With paint covering the rungs of a ladder, you'll never be able to see if a crack or split develops. If a rung weakens while the unwary is perched on it high off the ground, the result can be a ride in an ambulance or even a hearse; both of these results have happened.)

Here are some more suggestions offered with the hope of helping make your castle as safe a haven as human ingenuity, horse sense, and reasonable care can make it:

Again Ladders. Avoid them when the wind is strong and gusty. If you're on a ladder painting the wall area above a doorway, be sure the door is locked (see page 28). If someone unsuspectingly came through, the suddenly opened door could cause the ladder and occupant some unpleasant moments.

Electricity. Never throw the main switch if you're standing where the floor is wet or damp. Stand on a dry board, or rubber mat, and wear rubber-soled shoes. Teach this to every responsible member of the family.

Clearly tag all principal switches. Instruct family members what circuit each controls. Even better, have a wiring diagram posted near the switches. Then if trouble develops while you're out of the house, there'll be someone at home who can cut off the juice. Prompt action like this has prevented many a fire due to faulty insulation on wires in the walls.

Instruct everybody, including yourself, unless you're a qualified repairman, to keep hands strictly away from the back of the TV set. Even when the switch is off, there's a tremendous amount of undrained voltage still lurking there which can be highly dangerous.

Floors. While glass-sleek floors are beautiful, they're also slippery. Especially with older folks in the house, consider toning down the gloss. Spray the undersides of throw rugs with a nonskid preparation (available at supermarkets and variety and hardware stores).

Hammer home any nailheads which have worked loose, and even up any joints which could cause someone to trip.

Stairs. All carpeting or other coverings should be firm. Any trim at the front edge of the treads should not be able to catch a toe; the top edge should be flat and even with the tread or its covering.

Any "low-bridge" sections, which are common with many basement stairways, should be either padded or striped with luminous paint (or both). This will prevent many a banged head. Painting the front edge of the top and bottom steps of the basement stairway with luminous paint will make navigation much safer in the dark.

Putting sand in the paint for the concrete porch steps (and floor) will make them much less slippery when wet or snowy. You can also get a ready-mixed gritty paint, used industrially, to prevent factory accidents in greasy areas; ask your paint dealer (see page 25).

Workshop. Even though you're probably quite fed up with reading endless safety rules for bench saws, drill presses, grinding wheels, and other electric-powered work-savers, those rules make a lot of sense. The manufacturer carefully spelled out the safe way to operate the tool, and the chances are it's also the best way. Besides, the manufacturers like to have their customers happy and in one piece. It's good for repeat business.

In other words, never lose your respect for that blade when it's whirring around at several thousand rpm's. Even though you've become so competent that it's a pleasure for spectators just to watch you in action, please

remember the reason why the safety fence or the blade guard was put on. Please continue to use a push stick instead of your fingers for guiding work through those whizzing teeth. Push sticks are easy to replace; thumbs aren't.

Please don't ever "graduate" from the necessity of wearing goggles whenever you're doing a grinding job or there are chips or shavings flying around your face. If you don't like goggles, you can get a comfortable, transparent plastic face guard which isn't expensive.

Whenever you're working with doweling or other round stock, don't let the stub ends stay where they fall on the floor. At least kick them out of range so that there's no chance you'll accidentally step on one, which could tumble you against the blade or some unpleasantly solid edge or corner. It goes without saying that you should never let the working area around power tools become slippery with grease. If you can't get it all cleaned out, then sprinkle sand on it so your footing will be firm. In other words, regardless of your skill and experience, don't take your safety for granted.

For you newcomers to the wonderfully satisfying world of power-tooling, please forgive our emphatic attention to two things: One is the really vital importance of carefully studying the operating instructions before you flip the "on" switch. Know what your new tool is made to do, and also its limitations—and don't try to exceed them. The other thing is the importance of what you wear; rather, what you don't wear. Avoid any loose clothing and long sleeves, and never wear a tie. The reasons will be immediately and painfully obvious when you consider the consequences of such items becoming caught in a whirling blade.

The National Safety Council has long been saying to car drivers that "alcohol and gasoline don't mix." This can be aptly paraphrased to "power tools run on electricity, not alcohol." None of the foregoing is intended to discourage anyone from the pleasure and satisfaction of making things with power tools. When your workshop has a clean, well-lighted working area and you know what you're doing, there's no reason to feel the slightest worry. It's when the safety rules are ignored that trouble can occur. Again, to paraphrase, "Work carefully; the fingers you save may be your own."

Safety Tour of Your Home. Before embarking on a tour of accident areas, let us start with the biggest all-inclusive safety device for the whole house. This is an adequate number of fire extinguishers, handily located for fast action, with every responsible member of the family able to operate them in time of need. Frankly, fire extinguishers or installed fire-extinguishing systems used to run into a fair amount of money. Therefore, many homeowners didn't do much about them. But today, with many different types of extinguishers easily available in aerosol cans, the expense is greatly lowered; price them yourself at the hardware store and you'll see.

How many? That depends on how many rooms you have. But one per floor plus one for the kitchen is a minimum. Be sure the extinguisher in the kitchen is the type which can smother a grease fire or an electrical fire. As an extra precaution (provided it can be kept where it won't constantly get in the way), a pail of sand will be immensely effective at putting out flaming grease. Never use water; it will only spread the flames.

An aerosol or another type of fire extinguisher may stand around for months or years without being needed (let's hope so!). But since all long-idle nozzles may become clogged when standing under constant pressure, you should periodically take extinguishers outdoors and give them a little test to be sure they're working. No extinguisher's any good if it doesn't instantly work when needed. Incidentally, many people keep a small extinguisher in the glove compartment of the car, just in case; it's a mighty good idea.

Similarly, there may be times when you'll be grateful for having a good burn remedy handy. One experience with my wife has won our permanent enthusiasm for an aerosol-type remedy; half an hour after spraying her arm when sizzling grease had spilled on it, she felt no pain, there was no sign of blistering, and the skin wasn't even red. We were certainly thankful that aerosol was handy on the kitchen shelf.

While discussing the kitchen, look out for any curtains which are close enough to the stove so that they could catch fire. Either have them flameproofed or put up fiberglass curtains instead. Test the handles of pots and pans, especially the larger ones. If any seems loose, tighten the screws, have the rivets renewed, or repair it with plastic steel. This is to be sure the handle won't loosen so that the pan will turn upside down under the weight of the hot contents, not only preventing a grease

burn or a scalding, but keeping your dinner from landing on the floor. Even if your children have outgrown the fascination of matches, keep matches stored in a tight container, preferably metal. Mice and squirrels have been known to nibble on the tips enough to ignite them.

Oily rags kept in a confined space, as everybody knows, can catch fire all by themselves. If you're really fond of some particular ones, keep them in a well-ventilated place. Better still, banish sentimentality and throw them out.

Luminous paint and luminous plastic are very fine preventers of tumbles, bumped heads, and barked shins. A glow-in-the-dark stripe painted along the front edge of a bottom step or at the "low-bridge" point of a stairwell makes a welcome beacon for safe navigating if the lights go out. Wall switches backed by luminous plastic eliminate fumbling and tumbling. There's a new type of night light made with a disk of dull-glowing plastic. This is plugged into any wall or baseboard outlet and costs about a nickel a year to run. The glow is never bright enough to be intrusive, but is ample to guide you along a dark hallway or to light a stair landing.

These luminous guides are especially good ideas if there are older people in the house. So are railings along all steps, indoors and out. In the same category are grab rails for the bathtub and shower. Countless thousands of bathroom falls could have been prevented by such supports.

Nonskid mats made of rubber or plastic make the tub or shower much safer. So will a nonskidding treatment of throw rugs, especially if you are justifiably vain about beautifully waxed and polished floors. There are several nonskid preparations available in aerosol form at supermarkets and hardware stores which really make small rugs stay put. Of course, there are homemade treatments, too, such as brushing a thin coat of shellac on the rug's underside or applying a solution of chip glue dissolved in hot water.

A rope or light chain ladder can be folded and securely placed next to a window of an upstairs room where a hallway fire would block any escape. If there's a radiator under the window, fasten the top of the ladder there.

Your garage is also a potentially big fire risk. True, it's primarily meant to shelter your car. But if you're like lots of other people, you also store things like paint, lumber, power tools, and even some gasoline and oil. In regard to these last two items, note that some fire insurance policies do not permit you to store gasoline and oil. You'd better check this on your policy, since, frequently, after a fire, an insurance company does not have to pay your claim if the company discovers you stored either product. Along the same line, if any basic electrical repairs or modifications are made by anyone other than a licensed electrician, this may also give the insurance company an "out" in case of fire. This too is well worth verifying in your policy's fine print.

A periodic inspection of all the cords for your appliances is another excellent safety precaution. Any frayed wrapping or broken insulation is a red flag; many's the fire that's been started by faulty wiring.

There are a great many other areas where paying attention to commonsense safety rules certainly pays off. For example, if there's some leaky flashing or faulty shingles on your steeply pitched roof, unless you're experienced in working at heights, why take a chance? Pay a little more for a professional repair.

If you're getting along in years, don't run the risk of trying to shovel your driveway clear of snow in time to make the 7:56. Miss the train, and miss having a heart attack too. (If you think this is farfetched, keep your eye on the papers next winter and see how regularly the headline pops up, "Man Collapses, Dies; Shoveling Snow Blamed.") If there's a young "George" around, by all means let him do it! Of course, all this problem is solved if you've installed those heating pipes with the antifreeze mixture right in the driveway pavement. This will keep the snow melted (and allow you to catch your train without lifting an extra finger).

A two-casual attitude toward some cleaners and solvents can spell trouble too. Just because a cleaning fluid won't burn doesn't necessarily mean its fumes can be safely inhaled. One of the former great cleaners, carbon tetrachloride, is about as noxious as anything you can breathe. Similarly, when you start dusting the garden for squash bugs or Japanese beetles and spray upward into the apple trees, or ladle cyanide powder down into woodchuck burrows, remember that you're not fooling around with any "kid stuff"; this is serious poison you're handling. If you're using it on a windy day, stand so that it's blown away

from you. Better yet, don't use it on a windy day unless it's absolutely necessary. Wear gloves, and really scrub your hands afterward.

Another splendid way to avoid rides in ambulances is not to try lifting or moving very heavy objects. If a furniture-rearranging mood strikes, get help instead of trying to juggle the piano, the overstuffed sofa, or the sideboard all by yourself. However, unless there's wall-to-wall carpeting on the living room–dining room floor, you can use the same easy method that we describe for moving a refrigerator. Even a self-styled weakling can slide a refrigerator across the kitchen. This is really simple. Work a piece of carpet, nap side down, under the legs. Leave 3 or 4 feet of the carpet sticking out in front, because this is what you actually pull. With a helper (who definitely does not have to be a strong-arm type!) to steady the refrigerator, you pull the carpet. Honestly, you'll be surprised at how easily you can slide that heavy refrigerator across the floor. No straining needed!

If you detect a general principle running through these last remarks, you're right: know exactly what you're doing, use tools and products whose characteristics you know, and work well within your strength. Maybe this philosophy doesn't exactly transcend heroic heights. But we'll guarantee one thing, friends: By following these principles you'll be mighty scarce around hospitals, unless you're visiting someone who let impulse override common sense.

These preventive measures, of course, don't cover the entire subject. But they will certainly help you reduce the chance of preventable mishaps. Possibly, too, they will bring to mind additional measures you can take, so that your home will be the safe haven your family deserves.

Questions and Answers

Now let's get started on those miscellaneous household tips that we promised at the beginning of the chapter.

MAKING JAVELLE WATER

Do you have a formula for making what is known as Javelle water? I hear it can be made at home.

Certainly it can be made at home. Here is the formula: Dissolve half a pound of washing soda in a quart of cold water; then add a quarter pound of chloride of lime, with the lumps crushed. Let the mixture stand until the sediment settles. Draw off the clear liquid, straining it through a fine cloth (not cheese-cloth). Put the clear liquid in brown or amber glass bottles, and keep it tightly stoppered.

PRESERVING MAP

My husband must frequently attend meetings in various parts of the country, and the children like to locate these on a large map we have. From frequent handling, the map is beginning to get worn around the edges and torn. Is there any way to preserve it?

Paste cheesecloth on the back, using shellac as a glue by applying a thin coat. Then apply a thin coat of pure, fresh white shellac to the face of the map. Be sure the surfaces are brushed free of dust and lint, etc., before coating; and thin the shellac half-and-half with denatured alcohol.

CLEANING A WATERCOLOR PICTURE

One of my favorite watercolors, which has been hanging on my living room wall for quite a number of years, has become quite soiled. Is there any way I can clean it without danger of making the colors run?

Here's a good, "safe" method which may sound odd, but which a skillful, experienced artist showed us, and worked much to our surprise. Take the center of the freshest baked loaf of white bread you can buy, and compress part of it into the size and shape of a golf ball. One ordinary loaf (don't get the already sliced kind) will make about three such "golf balls." Then rub this over the watercolor. Admittedly, you'll have crumbs all over the place, but the bread will pick up dirt very effectively.

BRIGHTENING OIL PAINTINGS

We have some old oil paintings which need cleaning up; we don't want to cast them away. How do we brighten them up?

If these are valuable, we strongly urge having the cleaning done by a professional. Before starting to clean the paints, wipe an obscure corner with a damp cloth to see whether it will resist water. If the color comes off, don't attempt the job yourself. Use a pure, neutral soap, applying it with a slightly moist cloth, and rub it gently on the painting in a circular motion. When the entire surface has been covered, take up the soap and dirt with a soft, clean cloth, wet with clear, tepid water.

When the painting is clean, shake off any remaining water; don't wipe it off. Then stand the painting at an angle in a warm, airy place to dry naturally.

MOISTUREPROOFING A STATUE

Please tell me what I can do to make a chalk statue moistureproof for all kinds of weather. I bought a statue and put it outdoors last fall. I was told that if I varnished it, the coating would preserve it. I find that the varnish is peeling off the statue. Could you tell me how I can fix it?

"Chalk" statues are actually plaster, and such material isn't suitable for exposure to weather, even with a protective coating. The plaster should have been given a coat of primer sealer. It will be necessary to take off the varnish, apply the primer sealer, and then apply a couple of coats of outside enamel. The bottom of the statue should also be painted.

OUTDOOR PROTECTION FOR PLASTER HEADS

I have two plaster-of-Paris statue heads from an old schoolhouse. Is there any kind of sealer I can use on them to leave them outdoors? They are starting to crack.

We don't recommend leaving this type of statue exposed to the weather continuously; the plaster will absorb moisture and deteriorate. Two coats of good-quality spar or synthetic varnish will give some protection, but will also yellow the statues somewhat. Be sure the surface is free of any trace of grease, wax, grime, etc., before applying the coating.

PAINTING VASES

I have two large pottery vases that are shiny blue, and I would like to make them shiny red. What can I do to make enamel stick to them? I painted them, and a few weeks later the enamel peeled off.

Pottery that is glazed cannot be satisfactorily painted or enameled. Such surfaces won't "hold" paint. Fair results might be obtained by scratching and dulling the glaze with coarse sandpaper. The surfaces then should be cleaned and wiped with turpentine. Apply enamel undercoater, and finish with a good-quality enamel, the kind the manufacturer recommends for outdoor use.

CLEANING ANTIQUE FRAMES

How would I clean some very old picture frames? I do not want to ruin the old gilt finish. Some of these frames have been used in the kitchen and have a greasy coating.

As you suspect, delicacy is needed, both in cleaning materials and in application. The greasy frames will take longer. Carefully, using an artist's brush, "paint" alcohol on the frames, a small section at a time. Neither wipe nor blot. Instead, holding the frame firmly, try to snap the remaining alcohol off. Although this slow job may try your patience, you won't harm the old finish, and you'll wind up with a lovely result.

REMOVING GOLD-LEAFED PLASTER FROM FRAME

Is there an easy way to remove the gold-leafed plaster of Paris from old picture frames? I was told that the plaster of Paris would soften and could easily be scraped off after soaking in water. This didn't work. The frame was soaked for two days.

The gold leaf probably acted as a moisture barrier for the plaster. Break the gold-leaf surface by rubbing it with steel wool; then try the water-soaking treatment. Water is the only softener for plaster. Judicious use of a chisel to chip away small areas of the plaster might also help, or an electric sander could be used.

RESTORED CHINTZ GLAZE

The chintz draperies in our living room have lost their glaze finish because of many launderings. Is there any way to restore the glossy finish?

The glossy finish can be restored professionally; the glaze is achieved by sizing the material and then rolling it between heated cylinders. For glazing at home, dip the material in a thin, hot clear starch solution to which a small amount of paraffin has been added, using a piece about 2 inches square for each pair of drapes. Or try a plastic starch, following the label directions. Be sure to iron the material on the right side with a warm iron to retain the luster.

CRACKED PIANO CASE

I recently acquired a small old upright piano. It was evidently kept in good condition because there are no nicks. But the wood is cracked on the sides. How can I get rid of the cracks? Should I use synthetic varnish for a shiny finish?

The cracks can be filled with plastic wood, available in several wood colors, or with a putty stick for plywood, also available in popular wood colors; hardware and paint dealers carry these items. For a shiny finish, wipe the surface with fine steel wood and turpentine to remove all trace of grease, grime, wax, etc. Then apply a coat of top-quality clear varnish.

CURING OLD FRYING PAN

When using motor oil to cure and restore an old cast-iron frying pan, do you put the oil in the pan before heating it over the embers? Or do you put on the oil after the pan is well heated?

Put the oil in first, when the pan is cold. It will save a great deal of sizzling spatters.

UNSIGHTLY IRON SKILLETS

How can I restore and dress up some of my unsightly cast-iron skillets which have begun to rust?

Work off the rust with soapy steel wool. If necessary, use a little kerosene to help. But you'll have more curing to do later, to get the odor out. Wipe on a very generous amount of cooking oil, and put the skillets in the oven or over an open fire or embers—the hotter, the better, so that the oil has the best chance to be absorbed. After two or three hours, let them cool naturally. Wipe the skillets carefully, and repeat the entire treatment. Clean the skillets by wiping, not washing.

FRYING PAN BOTTOM IS SOLIDLY CAKED

How can I remove a heavy accumulation of burned-on grease or whatever is caked on the bottom of a cast-iron frying pan?

Try this first: Get the pan good and hot. Then quickly plunge it into ice water or a snowbank. Try tapping the pan with the handle of a screwdriver, hoping to help break up the caking as the metal contracts. Or try this: Keep the bottom of the pan soaked with oven cleaner. Every few hours or so, try chipping the caked material with a putty knife. Or use the fastest way: Connect a wire-brush attachment to your electric drill. Do the work inside a box so that specks won't be flying all over. Wear goggles.

RESCUE FAVORITE PAN

Is there any inexpensive, simple way I can firm up the handle of a deep-fry pan? It is getting so shaky I feel it's risky to handle it.

Of course, I could break down and buy another, or take this to a machine shop. But I'd like to fix it myself if possible.

We're assuming the handle rivets are loosening. If so, the hardest part of the job is getting that part of the pan absolutely free of any trace of grease. The actual firming is easy. Work plastic steel all around the rivets. When it hardens, they'll be rock-firm. You can file the repair smooth after it hardens.

BAKED-ON GREASE ON ALUMINUM UTENSILS

Is there a commercial product that will easily remove baked-on grease from aluminum utensils? What is the best method of removing grease from aluminum?

We know of no commercial product to remove baked-on grease from aluminum; strong alkalies tend to discolor and dull the finish of aluminum; ordinary kitchen cleansers contain too harsh abrasives for this metal. Remove grease by using hot water and a mild soap or detergent; steel wool pads are good. For removing baked-on grease, soak the pan, if possible, in very hot water; then scrape off the grease with a wooden spoon or pot scraper. Finish with a steel wool pad with soap.

CLEANING FLATIRONS AND KETTLE

I have an old-fashioned iron teakettle and two flatirons that I would like to clean and finish to use in my living room. The kettle is dirty and dull, and the irons are a little rusty. Could you tell me what to do?

Iron kettles and flatirons can be cleaned by rubbing with steel wool and turpentine. After dirt and rust have been removed, wipe the surface with clean turpentine; then finish with a couple of coats of dull black paint or enamel.

HOLE IN ALUMINUM PAN

How can a tiny hole in an aluminum pan be fixed?

If this is a cooking pan, small repair kits are available for this kind of job at most hardware and variety stores; follow the instructions on the package. If it's not a cooking utensil, use the new plastic-type metals that come in tubes for repairs of this kind; these are also available at hardware, variety, and paint stores. Follow the manufacturer's directions.

CLEANING WAFFLE IRON

How can I clean my waffle iron?

Wipe the outside of the waffle iron with a damp cloth dipped in mild suds, and wipe it clean with dry cloth. Never wash the cooking surface with liquid because this removes fats or oils which keep waffles from sticking. Use a dry, stiff brush or crumpled paper toweling. Never allow water to touch the electrical connection or heating unit. Most manufacturers supply printed instructions for care of their products; we would suggest obtaining a copy from a dealer or the manufacturer of your appliance.

CLOGGED STEAM IRON

My steam iron has had hard use for quite a few years and is becoming clogged. Is there any way to remove the deposit inside?

Special preparations for removing the deposit inside steam irons are now available at most sewing notions and housewares dealers. Follow the label instructions on the plastic container carefully.

RAINWATER IN STEAM IRON?

Is it safe to use cistern or rainwater in a steam iron? I know ordinary tap water can be safely used in several makes of iron, but our water is hard and I do not want to take the chance of ruining my iron.

Rainwater is about the best water you can use in an iron; it is very soft and free of chemical impurities. Another good source for water to be used in an iron is the water that melts off the outside of the freezing compartment in most refrigerators after defrosting. You can always buy distilled water.

TOASTER GUMMED UP

Some well-buttered toast was left in the toaster until it turned black. It left the toaster so gummed up that any time we put in bread to toast, it starts to smoke. With even simple electrical repairs costing so much these days, I thought I would ask if you have any suggestions.

Take the toaster outdoors, hitch it to an outside outlet or extension cord, turn it on, and let it smoke. This will burn most of the residue off. Later, when it cools, you can help things with a careful, soft brush. Repeat if necessary.

TACKY SALAD BOWLS

My set of walnut salad bowls, which are composed of pieces of wood joined together, has become tacky on the inside. I washed them very quickly, without soaking, but this did not help. How can I remove the tackiness and care for them properly?

First get those inside surfaces smooth and dry by thoroughly wiping them with fine steel wool (not the soapy kind) or sandpaper. The object is to get back to clean, non-food-stained wood. This may take some time, so bring along your patience. When you finish the smoothing, carefully wipe out all sawdust. Then liberally soak the inside surfaces with drugstore-grade mineral oil. Give it 2 hours for maximum absorption, and wipe off all possible excess. Let it dry for a week, and then repeat the whole process. Then those bowls should be stainproof and smooth.

"BREAD TASTES LIKE WOOD"

I bought a beautiful early American bread box but can't use it. Bread and everything else placed in it smells and tastes of wood. I have tried putting baking soda and peeled raw potatoes inside. They have not taken away the horrible odor of the wood. Can you suggest something?

It may have been stored in a damp place before you bought it. At least, it won't hurt to try airing it in the sun and wind for a couple of weeks to be sure the wood is thoroughly dried out. Then brush on a couple of coats of pure, fresh shellac on the inside surfaces. This should seal in what odor (if any) remains. Activated charcoal is also an excellent absorber of odors. Keep some inside.

MILKY DISCOLORATION IN VASE

I have a very nice cut-glass vase that has a milky discoloration inside, due to a lime deposit from water. What can I use to remove the stain? I have used full-strength vinegar, a drain cleaner, and newspaper and soapy water, but have gotten no results.

Fill the vase with vinegar, and allow it to stand overnight; then pour off some of the vinegar and put in some coarse sand. Shake this vigorously for several minutes; then rinse with clear water. This has often been successful.

CLOUDY GLASS DECANTER

I purchased an antique glass decanter at a country auction, but I have not been able to get it clear; the glass stays cloudy, even though I have repeatedly filled it with hot water and soapsuds, with ammonia added. Please advise.

You were on the "right track," but didn't go far enough. Half fill the decanter with the same solution, and then shred up newspaper into very small bits and stuff it into the decanter. Use a generous amount, stirring it around with a stick or rod. The paper, in a short time, will become mushy in the soapy water. Then swish this around and around in the decanter, and the paper will work on the glass. A wadded piece of newspaper is excellent for wiping your car's windshield clean. Putting sand or BB shot in the decanter and whirling it around will also work, but it also might scratch the glass.

"BROWNED" GLASS OVERWARE

One of my clear glass ovenware platters turned brown under the broiler. I've tried all kinds of detergents and scouring powders, but the brown color remains. Is there any way I can make the glass clear again?

This discoloration is only on the surface, caused by baked-on food; it can't penetrate the glass itself. Many hardware stores and housewares sections of department stores have a paste-type cleaner for use on porcelain-enamel ovens which can be used very successfully on glass, too. It's well worth trying.

NYLON STUCK TO IRON

What can I use to clean the bottom of my iron? Some nylon stuck to it, and now the bottom is all black and rough.

If this is an iron with chromium plate, heat the iron and then rub the bottom with a mild abrasive such as powdered whiting, which usually removes melted nylon. Then rinse the bottom with a clean, slightly moistened cloth to remove the powder and wipe dry. If the sole plate is of aluminum, fine steel wool can be used, rubbing lengthwise of the iron.

BLEACH TASTE IN PLASTIC CUPS

I tried to bleach out coffee stains from plastic cups. The stain was removed, but now I can't get rid of the taste of bleach. What do you suggest?

We're afraid there is no way to eliminate the bleach taste. Chlorine bleaches should never be used on melamine; they remove gloss. When the gloss finish is removed, the plastic becomes absorbent to chlorine and stains. Only oxygen-based cleansers should be used; the special stain removers for plastic dishes are generally oxygen-based.

FLAKED-OFF COATING ON BRASS HARDWARE

The brass door knocker and door knob on our house have discolored, evidently due to the protective coating peeling or flaking off from exposure to the weather. How do we clean and polish this brass and prevent future discoloration?

Excellent brass-cleaning and -polishing preparations are available at hardware, housewares, and variety stores; follow the label directions carefully, after first removing the remainder of protective coating with acetone or lacquer thinner. After polishing, brush or spray on transparent metal lacquer made especially for this purpose; these lacquers are available at paint and hardware stores.

DULL, TARNISHED ALUMINUM GRILLE

The grille on our storm door has a cast-aluminum flamingo about 30 inches high which is very dull and tarnished. What do you recommend for cleaning it?

Aluminum-cleaning and -polishing preparations for use on exterior building aluminum are available at many hardware stores and department stores and some paint dealers; follow the manufacturer's directions for use carefully. These usually leave a protective coating to retard future tarnishing. You can also carefully rub the aluminum with fine steel wool and kerosene (being careful of fire hazard) and then apply a thin layer of kerosene which will evaporate, leaving a protective coating.

BROWN LEATHER BRIEFCASE

My son has a brown leather briefcase used for carrying books to school. It is badly worn. Is there any way to improve its appearance?

Leather goods shops and some housewares and hardware dealers stock leather dressings which will restore the general tone of leather and help preserve it. If these products are not available, polish the surfaces with a neutral shoe cream. Where the color has worn off, touch up the spots with a brown shoe stain. When the bag is dry, polish it with the shoe cream.

SHABBY TRUNKS

I am entering a home for the aged soon and in looking at their storerooms found the trunks there were neat-looking and not as shabby as mine. I have a brown wardrobe trunk, with brass fittings, and a black storage trunk. How can I dress them up? The brass is rusty on the bottom of the wardrobe.

To clean the brass fittings, use one of the brass-cleaning and -polishing preparations, available at supermarkets and housewares and hardware dealers, following the manufacturer's instructions carefully. Or wash the brass with a salt-saturated solution of household vinegar, following by rinsing with clear water. (The vinegar solution can be made into paste by adding sufficient flour.) Remove all trace of grease, soot, grime, etc., from all surfaces of both trunks by wiping them with fine steel wood and a nonflammable liquid spot remover, being sure the room is well ventilated while working. Then spray the trunks with shellac, which is now available at paint dealers in aerosol form.

STUBBORN OLD TIN TRUNK

I bought an antique tin-covered trunk, in fairly good condition. There is extensive rust, and much of the silver paint applied to the embossed tin is worn. I would like to remove all down to the plain tin. I have tried paint thinner, rust remover, and plain steel wool. These cleaned off the flat areas, but in the embossing it's still as bad as ever. I don't dare use a wire brush for fear I'd scratch the tin. What do you suggest?

Try paste-type paint remover, leaving it on until you notice the paint softening. Then try a small, stiff brush. With such ancient paint, you'll need repeats and patience.

PRESERVING LOOKS OF CHEST

While in Mexico I bought a solid-oak trunk-style chest which has a dark-oil-stain finish. Could I use good furniture wax to preserve the nice appearance? The hand carving is painted in gold leaf. Is there any way to clean this, or is it best to leave it alone?

Good wax over the present oil-stain finish will do very well. With gold leaf you have to be exceedingly delicate. Apply alcohol with a small, soft artist's brush. Keep repeating the process. But if the soiling is stubborn, leave it alone.

CHEST HAS LEAKY LINING

I made a pine chest about a year and a half ago. I lined it with cedar strips. Recently a sticky film has appeared next to where I cut the lock and also near several knots. It smells like cedar, not pine, so I know it's in the lining. How can I stop this leaking?

Clean off the sticky sap by wiping it with turpentine or mineral spirits. Then brush on a couple of coats of special knot sealer. If your paint stores don't stock knot sealer, use pure, fresh white shellac as the sealer.

MOLDY BOOKS

We recently acquired a lot of old books. A number of them are quite moldy and have a dank odor. Is there any way to treat them to make them more pleasant to handle?

Wipe the mold off the books with a clean, soft cloth, slightly dampened with alcohol. Pages can be cleaned the same way sometimes. If any of the bindings are of leather, to remove mildew, wipe them with a cloth dampened with a solution of equal parts of denatured alcohol and water; then dry them outdoors. Stained book pages can be dusted with French chalk or cornstarch, allowing the powder to remain in the closed book for several days and then brushing it off.

BROKEN CRYSTAL BOWL

A small crystal bowl was accidentally knocked off an end table and broken. I have all the pieces—not many—and there are no missing splinters. How can I repair this myself?

Use an epoxy-type adhesive, in transparent form, following the label directions carefully. Epoxy adhesives consist of two materials to be mixed together: the epoxy resin and the hardener. Or an all-purpose, clear household cement may work, following the manufacturer's instructions.

REPAIRING CANDELABRA

A candelabra was knocked off our dining room table, and two of the arms which hold candles broke. Is there anything I can use to repair this?

There are several types of cement for mending broken metal, and you can get them at hardware stores. We personally prefer the kind which is pulverized steel in plastic form and hardens with the strength of steel. Although on the market only a few years, it now is widely distributed.

BROKEN GARDEN STATUE

A statue of a duck that we kept in the garden was knocked over and the head broken off. Is there any way to repair this?

If this is a concrete figure, use either latex patching concrete, available at masonry supply dealers and some hardware stores, or epoxy resin mixed with sand to make a patching compound; for either material, follow the label directions carefully. If the statue is of metal, use an epoxy adhesive, which usually comes in a kit containing the resin and an activator; it's available at hardware, paint, and variety stores. Follow the manufacturer's instructions carefully.

BOTTLES INTO LAMPS

I have two beautiful bottles that I want to make into lamps, but am afraid of breaking them. I tried to drill a hole in an old bottle, but broke a drill and finally the bottle itself.

Inexpensive kits for converting bottles, vases, jugs, etc., into lamps are now available at many hardware, electric, and variety stores. No drilling of holes is required. The unit fits into the neck of the bottle, like a cork. We would suggest filling the lower part of the bottles with sand or pebbles to reduce the possibility of tipping them over.

"PERSONALIZING" GLASS TUMBLERS

Is it possible to write or draw a picture on glass? I would like to write my daughter's name on some glass tumblers as a birthday present.

It's not difficult to do at least a passable job, and even though it may not be professionally perfect, it will be interesting and certainly individual. First spread a thin coat of beeswax over the area to be inscribed. Then, using a stylus or a sharp-pointed nail, write the name or draw the design. Next, saturate the cotton of one of those little surgical "swabs" on a stick with hydrochloric acid, and wipe it gently over where you've inscribed, and the acid will etch into the glass where the beeswax has been removed. Wear heavy gloves, because this acid is corrosive. Rinse off the acid thoroughly; do this outdoors, and don't pour the acid down the plumbing drains. Scrape off the wax, as the final step.

PENCIL SCRATCH ON PLASTIC

My young niece drew a pencil line on a plastic counter top. I tried removing it with an eraser. Now there is a dulled area the length of the line, which I can't remove with furniture polish or mild soap. What do you suggest?

Pencil erasers usually have very fine grit which dulls gloss. Since the gloss has been rubbed off, it will be impossible to restore it. Try using a paste floor wax on the area; it might help.

REMOVING LABELS FROM PLASTIC ARTICLES

The makers of plastics are putting labels and stickers on that are nearly impossible to remove. Alcohol, acetate, and nail polish remover will remove some, but at the same time deface the article by leaving a cloudy, dull spot. Is there any way to overcome this?

Try removing the labels with warm water. Then remove the remaining glue with grease (lard, face cream, etc.) or lighter fluid. To restore cloudy spots, wipe them with a one-step auto cleaner-polish, following the manufacturer's directions.

FOAM-RUBBER ADHESIVE

What adhesive is used for cementing foam-rubber pieces together?

Rubber cement is used. The adhesive is applied to each of the surfaces to be brought together and is allowed to remain until tacky (usually, about 5 minutes); then the pieces to be joined are carefully brought together. Rubber cement is available at foam-rubber dealers, stationery stores, and art supply stores.

BENT CANDLES

My mother lives with us, and because of her age we necessarily keep our home very warm. Because of the heat, the candles on the console table begin to bend a little. Can anything be done to them to keep them straight up?

Try spraying the candles with shellac from an aerosol container. The shellac, when dry, will hold the candles erect.

CLOTHESLINE PROBLEM

Because I became weary of having to string up my clothesline every time I hang the wash, I tried an aluminum line. For a while it was fine. I simply wiped off the dust with a cloth, which I couldn't do with a regular clothesline. But after a while, the aluminum left black marks where the clothespins held the wash. Is there any way I can avoid this?

You can wipe on a coat of clear lacquer, after cleaning the aluminum thoroughly with turpentine. This will prevent the black marks, but when the lacquer wears off, it will have to be renewed. There are several types of non-corroding, nonmarking lines now available in many stores. One of them is a plastic-covered steel line, which is a twisted double line, with a sliding device which eliminates the need for clothespins.

NOISY LAWN SPRINKLER

When I sprinkle the lawn, the constant loud "sh-sh" noise of the running water makes it very irritating. I can't do a great deal of sprinkling because the noise in the house just bothers us all. One of the bathroom faucets also has the same "sh-sh" noise when the water is turned on. What can be done?

The supply pipe may be too small, the valve may be partially closed, or the diameter of the pipe might be diminished by the presence of a burr where a pipe had been cut. In the case of the bathroom faucet, a new washer might help. The other possible causes should be investigated, and a competent plumbing contractor should be consulted.

HANGING DOOR MIRROR

I want to hang a full-length mirror on a hollow-core door. What type of fastener is necessary?

Special hollow-wall anchors are now available at most hardware, paint, and variety stores for this type of project. Instructions for use come with the package of fasteners.

SCRATCHED MIRROR BACK

In shifting furniture about, the silvering on an old mirror got scratched. It's not a very good one, and I don't want to spend much on repair. Is there any way to touch up the scratches?

The only "touch-up" we can suggest is to use aluminum paint on the scratches; or scotch tape small pieces of aluminum foil over the scratched areas. Complete mirror refinishing can only be done professionally because of the elaborate machinery necessary. However, it's not a very expensive job.

FINGERPRINTS ON MIRROR

My husband moved my dressing table and a large, beautiful mirror on it. He put fingerprints on the mirror. I haven't been able to get these off with a window-cleaning preparation, scratchless scouring powder, or vinegar water. How can I get the fingerprints off without making the marks worse? I'm afraid to scrub.

Try making a thick paste of powdered whiting and a nonflammable liquid spot remover. Cover the fingerprints with a thick layer of the paste; when the paste is dry, brush it off and replace it with fresh paste until the prints disappear.

REMOVING SILVERING FROM A MIRROR

Can you tell me how to remove the silver backing from a mirror? We want to use the glass for a desk top.

One method is to take off the silver and protective coat with a razor blade, but if it is not done carefully, the glass might be scratched. Another method is to remove first the protective coating with paint remover. The exposed silvering should then be covered with a layer of salt, moistened with a solution of 1 part water and 3 parts vinegar. After several hours the silvering will be so softened, it can usually be wiped off clean. The work should be done in a well-ventilated room.

NEW LADDERS

Is it advisable to oil the stiles of a new set of ladders, or is any other treatment recommended?

We don't advise oiling, as all surfaces should be kept as unslippery as possible. To retard rot, we recommend applying wood preservative to all surfaces, but especially the area where the ladder rungs fit into the side rails. A paint coating should never be applied because this may hide cracks or decay.

WOOD LADDERS LEFT IN THE RAIN

My extension ladders have been left out in the rain a few times, and now that they have dried out, the wood is beginning to crack. What can be done to the ladders to get them back in good shape?

Further cracking can be stopped, but nothing can be done to eliminate the damage done to the wood. A couple of good soaking coats of a chemical wood preservative would protect the wood from swelling, shrinking, and cracking. If you can't get the preservative locally, coat the ladders with two soaking applications of boiled linseed oil, thinned with one-fourth as much turpentine. When the wood begins to show signs of weathering, repeat the treatment.

MOTH CLOSET HAS LOST ODOR

Our cedar-lined moth closet seems to have lost its odor of cedar in the last few months, and now I'm worried that it will be vulnerable to moths. Is there any way to restore the odor?

One way is to sand down the entire surface of the cedar, exposing a new surface. If you can lay your hands on a portable electric sander, it will save hours of work and many pounds of "elbow grease." If the cedar is quite old, it may even be necessary to use a plane before getting down to where the cedar is still aromatic. You can also treat the walls with a preparation—available at stores selling housewares—which imparts an odor of cedar.

MUSTY ODORS IN CLOTHES CLOSET

I am moving into a basement apartment. The present tenant told me there is a musty odor in the bedroom closet which even adheres to the clothes stored there. Is there anything that can be done about this before cleaning and painting the closet? Or is there something which can be put in the closet to counteract it?

Before painting the walls, clean them with a mildew-proofing compound to counteract and kill off the fungus. Dealers in boat supplies and equipment sell it, and also household sections of department stores. In addition, we think it would be wise to hang up a couple bags containing a moisture-absorbing chemical. Follow the manufacturer's directions. If the walls of the closet become cold so that condensation forms, a small electric heater, out of contact with flammable materials, should help reduce the possible formation of condensation and resultant mildew.

MUSTY ODOR IN BEDROOM

We are residing in a four-year-old prefabricated house with a crawl space under it. A musty odor which seems to come up into the bedroom has developed. The odor is now in the mattress and box spring. Since all the small windows have been open for quite a long while, I think the odor is slowly leaving from under the house. What can I do to correct the condition and deodorize the mattress and springs?

Try washing down the mattress and

spring with a mildew-proofing solution which you may be able to purchase through your hardware dealer. If not, try to locate a boat supply house which would have the same type of preparation. The small windows in the foundation should be kept open all year round in order to ventilate the crawl space. As a further precaution, cover the ground with a moistureproof and vaporproof paper, overlapping the sheets about 6 inches. Seal the laps with asphalt roof cement.

REMOVING MILDEW

A large beach umbrella was carelessly stored in the basement and has become mildewed. How can this be removed?

Fresh mildew can be removed with a stiff brush and a solution of laundry soap and water or a mild household bleach, followed by rinsing with clear water.

ECHO IN LIVING ROOM

We have just furnished a new home and are having difficulty with an echo in the living room. One complete wall has drapes from ceiling to floor; it doesn't seem to make any difference if the drapes are extended or drawn back. The floor has wall-to-wall carpeting. The wall opposite the window draperies has a large stone fireplace and an opening into the hall. There are no other wall openings. Can you offer any suggestions?

The echo may be due to sound bouncing back from the ceiling; we suggest soundproofing this surface by covering it with acoustical tile or a new multicellular plastic wall covering available in roll and tile form. These are both available at many tile and floor-covering dealers.

SQUEAKING BED SPRINGS

We have coil bed springs that squeak and are very annoying. Is there any way to correct this?

Squirt a nonoily lubricant, available at most hardware and paint dealers, at every point where one piece of metal touches another; or use a few drops of oil from an oilcan at these points. Wipe off any excess to prevent staining of the mattress. "Jounce" the springs several times to work the lubricant or oil into the joints.

RESTORING FADED SISAL RUG

I have a large sisal porch rug, badly faded by the sun. Local carpet cleaners say you can't dye sisal rugs successfully. One of them suggested painting it with latex floor paint. Do you think this is a good idea?

Frankly, no. Even if the paint is thinned down, it's likely to chip. After all, there's a great deal of flexibility in a sisal rug. Thinned-down shingle stain, clear or tinted, would be more satisfactory. Be sure to protect the porch floor first. Put down layers of building paper or many thicknesses of newspaper.

BRIGHTENING ANTIQUE CHESS SET

I was given a handsome old ivory chess set by my grandfather. The white chessmen, however, have turned quite yellow, due to having been stored so long in a box. (At least, that's what grandfather said.) Do you know of any way to at least lighten the color?

Alcohol is an excellent, gentle cleaner for ivory. First try wiping it on the chessmen with a soft cloth. If this doesn't work fast enough, make a paste of alcohol and powdered chalk. Mix it fairly stiff, and wipe it on the chessmen. Instead of wiping it off immediately, leave it there until it dries. Repeat as necessary. We can't guarantee 100 percent results. If the yellowing has worked clear through, nothing will help much. Leaving the pieces in the sunlight will help whiten them, the same as for ivory piano keys. It's confinement in darkness which produces the yellowing.

LAMPSHADES LOOK TERRIBLE

I bought two planter lamps about 10 years ago, and the parchment shades look terrible. I have looked everywhere for replacement shades, without success. So I wondered if perhaps I could paint these.

Painting will certainly solve your problem. We suggest spraying, in thin coats. Perhaps you may not want a solid-color effect, so see how you like the looks after each coat. You can use enamel, either gloss, semigloss, or eggshell. Of course, you can apply the paint with a brush, too, if you want.

WANTS HOME FORMULA FOR FLAMEPROOFING

Can you give me a formula for making a solution to flameproof clothing?

The following has been used for quite a number of years: 8 ounces of borax powder, 4 ounches of boric acid powder, and 2 tablespoons of any detergent, all stirred into a gallon of warm water. Dip in clothing or other fabrics and hang them up to dry. This keeps fabrics from bursting into flame, although they may smolder. This is good only until the next washing. After that, you'll need a repeat.

GLASS DRAPES

The previous tenant of our apartment, a bachelor, left some fiberglass draperies in the living room. They seem in quite nice condition, but could stand a good cleaning. However, I was told they cannot be dry-cleaned. Is this true?

True indeed. The solvent will work adversely. Washing them with soap and water and then hanging them up to dry in the shower is the best way. Since the material is, after all, glass, it's a lot easier to clean than an absorbent fabric.

PAINTING MATCHSTICK DRAW DRAPES

I have white matchstick draw drapes in my kitchen and dining area. They are getting drab-looking. How can I paint them?

The easiest way to paint these is to use good-quality enamel, in the desired color, in aerosol form. Be sure to protect the area in back of the drapes and adjacent to them with heavy wrapping paper or plastic sheets. Wipe the surface with fine steel wool and turpentine to remove any trace of grease or wax before applying the paint. Best of all, take down the drapes and spray them outdoors.

CURTAINS IN SUNNY WINDOWS

What would you recommend to protect matchstick curtains hung in sunny windows? I am afraid of their fading, even though they are new and have a natural appearance.

Mere humans can't do much against the fading power of the sun, especially if there's no paint on the surface. However, you can protect against their drying out and becoming brittle, possibly splitting, by spraying them with a clear lacquer or brushing on pure, fresh white shellac, thinned 40 percent or so with alcohol. Renew the treatment whenever you believe it necessary. Painting the curtains (or tinting the glass) is the only way to check fading.

MILDEWED BAMBOO SHADE

We have bamboo drop shades for the porch. Last year they mildewed. Can they be painted?

Yes, they can be painted. But first the mildew (fungus) must be removed. Scrub the shades with a stiff brush and a detergent solution or a household bleach. Then apply a top-quality, mildew-resistant exterior paint.

CLEANING LINEN ROLLER SHADES

Is it possible to clean linen roller-type window shades at home?

Yes, and it's not too difficult a job, but it requires care. Remove the shade from the window and stretch it over a flat surface. Sponge it with mild soap and water; then rinse it with clear water and allow it to dry, being careful not to wet the metal parts of the roller. First test a corner of the cloth to be sure the material is washable. If it's not washable, try cleaning it with wallpaper cleaner—a dough-like material which is rolled, not rubbed, over the surface and kneaded to expose clean material; it's available at wallpaper dealers and hardware stores.

BRIGHTENING UP ROLL-UPS

What will brighten up wood or vinyl roll-up porch shades? These are the shades made up of many thin strips. At present they are dull, although in perfectly good condition.

Wipe both types nice and clean with a damp cloth. Use a little ammonia if necessary. If this isn't enough for the vinyl, use any moderate detergent, the same as with Venetian blinds. When the shades are thoroughly dry, brush on pure, fresh white shellac, thinned 40 percent (about) with alcohol. Or spray them with clear plastic or lacquer.

PAINTING VENETIAN BLINDS

I have Venetian blinds that need painting. Is there any special paint or way of doing them over, as the tape and parts are in good condition?

Take the blind apart, to prevent the tapes from becoming smeared with paint and to apply enamel more evenly on each slat. Wash all the slats with thick suds of a mild soap, wipe them well with a damp cloth, and then rub them with a dry cloth. Dull the gloss of the old finish by rubbing it with "0000" sandpaper, and wipe with benzene (be careful of fire hazard). Then refinish the slats with any good-quality, quick-drying enamel. A thin coat of paste wax on the new finish will prevent quick soiling and give some protection against rain; it makes cleaning easier, too.

VENETIAN BLIND TAPES NEED STRONGER ADHESIVE

Several of the narrow tapes that hold our Venetian blind slats in place (which are attached to the long, vertical tapes) have come loose. We have tried a glue and a plastic, but they did not hold. What will hold?

First roughen the spots where the tape should be, using fine sandpaper. Then try one of the adhesives containing epoxy, following the directions on the label. Put no pressure against the adhesive until it has completely dried. Then it should hold.

SOILED METAL LADDER

We have a magnesium ladder, kitchen size, which has become soiled. What could be used to clean it? We've tried several things, but without success.

You should be able to clean the metal with one of the coarser scouring powders on a well-dampened cloth. If this is too mild, clean the metal with "0" steel wool and some mild soap and water. Rinse the metal well with clear water, and wipe it dry.

PROTECTING SCAFFOLDING PLANK

What do you recommend putting on a new scaffolding plank to keep it from warping and twisting?

Using well-seasoned, dry lumber, free of knots and splits, and keeping the plank in a dry, well-ventilated place should keep it from warping and twisting. Moisture absorption by wood causes warping. No finish is necessary for the plank.

STUBBORN IVY ROOTLETS

We bought a pre-World War II stucco-and-wood-trim house recently, heavily overgrown with ivy on two sides. We want to repaint the wood and are removing the ivy. Some of the rootlets have penetrated the stucco and are difficult to remove completely. Is there any method you can recommend?

Many garden stores have "ivy bombs" with which you can spray the embedded rootlets. This will cause them to wither, and there should be no problem when the new finish is applied. Weed killer can also be used for this purpose.

MOTHPROOF CLOSET

Is it necessary to line all four walls and ceiling and floor with cedar to build a mothproof clothes closet? Should all joints be tightly sealed?

The important points in having a mothproof clothes closet are to have it as tightly sealed as possible and to store only cleaned, moth-free clothes in it. While lining all interior surfaces with aromatic cedar makes a most permanent installation, this could also be done less expensively using smooth-surfaced wallboard or plywood paneling. The cedar aroma can be sprayed on; many such preparations are widely available where housewares are sold. As additional precaution, liberal quantities of camphor flakes or crystals should be sprinkled about. All joints should be tightly sealed, and the door should fit tightly (weather stripping around the door frame is a good idea). Your lumber dealer may have detailed instruction sheets available.

WATERPROOFING INSIDE OF WOOD PLANTER

I have a window box, made of wood, for flowers and plants to be used outdoors. How can I line the inside to make it waterproof and keep it from rotting? Should I drill a hole in the bottom of the box to let excess water drain out?

The inside of the planter can be painted with several coats of good-quality spar varnish, after being sure the surface is free of any trace of wax, grease, grime, etc. Or make a do-it-yourself lining box of aluminum, being sure the corners are sealed to prevent water seepage. The aluminum or varnish should be applied at least 1 inch higher than the planned earth line. It's a good idea to drill several "weep" holes through the bottom to drain off excess moisture; if aluminum is used, drill holes through this, too.

COMPOUND HARDENED IN CAULKING GUN

The compound in my caulking gun has dried and is so hard I am unable to squeeze it out. Is there any way in which I may soften it?

Caulking compound should not be left in a caulking gun (as you have found out!). To soften the compound, soak it in a mixture of half benzene and half turpentine (be very careful of fire hazard); this may require up to three weeks. The only other method is to try chipping and picking out the compound.

RUSTY FILES

I have heard you can clean rusty files with muriatic acid. Is this a practical idea?

It will work all right, diluted 1 to 10 parts of water and thoroughly neutralized with ammonia. However, there are excellent rust-removing preparations available in hardware stores, and their use won't run the risk of eating away the metal.

TIGHTENING HAMMERHEAD

The head on one of our hammers is coming loose. Is there any way to tighten it?

Small metal wedges can be driven into the head end of the hammer handle, expanding and tightening the head into place. These are available at hardware dealers. Another method is to soak the hammerhead and handle in linseed oil for about 24 hours.

REMOVING RUSTED SCREW

In my plans for modernizing my house, I have to remove some metal scrollwork on the trim of my front door. However, the screwheads are so old and rusted that a screwdriver only chews up the groove. Have you any suggestions?

Some time ago a solution was sent in to us, which we tried and found successful. Heat the head of the screw with a soldering iron, getting it quite hot. This loosens the screw so that it can be readily turned. Be careful not to scorch the surrounding wood when applying the heat. We have also found this helps loosen screws which are particularly stubborn, although not rusted. We can't say we know just why this works, but we've certainly found it effective in getting results.

WING NUT WORKS LOOSE

Even a lockwasher doesn't seem able to keep a wing nut on my power mower from working loose, due to vibration. Is there any other simple way to keep the nut from loosening?

Put on a dab of shellac. It will block the threads very well. Unscrewing it doesn't require appreciable pressure. But, if necessary, a little alcohol will loosen the shellac.

DOESN'T DARE BURN STUMP

How do you get rid of a wild cherry stump which is near a fuel tank? I don't dare try the method of boring deep holes, filling with kerosene, and burning.

You can bore deep holes and fill them with chemical stump killer, sold in most garden centers and many hardware stores and listed in almost every big mail-order catalog. Progress will be faster if you saw off the stump as close to ground level as possible.

CLOSING A HOUSE

Since we will be away this winter, we would like to close our house here. What has to be done?

Since the house will, obviously, be completely closed, we heartily recommend having a plumbing contractor take over the job of draining all pipes and fixtures. An amateur can do this, of course, but if any low-slung pipes or traps are overlooked, it can cause trouble from freezing. Besides, a professional has the equipment and "know-how" to do a worry-free job. Good rugs should be stored, so that dampness can't work in and cause mildew. While it isn't a "must," it's a good idea to close off all electricity at the main switch. It's also a good idea to notify the local police, so that they can keep an eye on the place. Close the chimney damper, too, to keep out ice and snow. If you have a friendly neighbor, ask him to come in every now and then on nice days to open the windows and give the house a good ventilating. There are a good many other obvious things to do, but these main ones will be found very useful in keeping the house in good shape until you return.

INDEX